DATE DUE

GAYLORD		PRINTED IN U.S.A.

The Experimental Analysis of Behavior

A BIOLOGICAL PERSPECTIVE

A Series of Books in Psychology

Editors: Richard C. Atkinson
Jonathan Freedman
Gardner Lindzey
Richard F. Thompson

The Experimental Analysis of Behavior

A BIOLOGICAL PERSPECTIVE

Edmund Fantino
University of California, San Diego

Cheryl A. Logan
University of North Carolina, Greensboro

W. H. Freeman and Company
San Francisco

Sponsoring Editor: W. Hayward Rogers
Project Editor: Pearl C. Vapnek
Manuscript Editor: Joan Westcott
Designer: Perry Smith
Production Coordinator: Chuck Pendergast
Illustration Coordinator: Batyah Janowski
Artist: Donna Salmon
Compositor: Graphic Typesetting Service
Printer and Binder: The Maple-Vail Book Manufacturing Group

Cataloging in Publication Data

Fantino, Edmund
    The experimental analysis of behavior : a biological
perspective.

    (A Series of books in psychology)
    Bibliography: p.
    Includes index.
    1.   Conditioned response.   2.   Psychology,
Experimental.   3.   Psychology, Comparative.
4.   Psychobiology.   I.   Logan, Cheryl A., joint author.
II.   Title.
BF319.F35   150'.7'24   78-31685
ISBN 0-7167-1036-6

Printed in the United States of America

9   8   7   6   5   4   3   2   1

To Claudio and Mary Fantino and
Glenn and Myrtle Morton with
love and gratitude

Contents

Preface   xi

I   Introduction and Overview

1   Introduction   3

PHYLOGENY   5
ONTOGENY   6

2   A History of the Experimental Approach to Learning   9

EMPIRICISM AND ASSOCIATIONISM   9
A Physical Account of Association / Early Scientific Studies
THORNDIKE'S CONNECTIONISM   13
THE GREAT AGE OF LEARNING THEORIES   18
GUTHRIE'S CONTIGUOUS CONDITIONING   20
HULL'S BEHAVIOR THEORY   24
TOLMAN'S PURPOSIVE BEHAVIORISM   28
SKINNER'S OPERANT CONDITIONING   33
RETROSPECTIVE: THE PROBLEM OF PURPOSE   37

3   Habituation, Sensitization, Classical Conditioning   40

HABITUATION   41
Stimulus-Specificity of Habituation / Rate of Habituation / The
Interstimulus Interval / Generalization / Recovery and Dishabituation

SENSITIZATION   52
Dual-Process Theory / Interactions Between Habituation
and Sensitization
CLASSICAL CONDITIONING   60
Basic Principles / Temporal Relations Between Stimuli
RESPONSE PARAMETERS IN CONDITIONING   68
The Conditional Response
STIMULUS PARAMETERS IN CONDITIONING   73
Contingency Versus Contiguity / The Correlational View /
The Rescorla–Wagner Model

4   **Operant Conditioning   81**

BASIC CONCEPTS   82
MEASURING OPERANT BEHAVIOR   84
Apparatus / Subjects
BASIC PHENOMENA   91
Acquisition and Shaping / Modeling, Imitation, and Behavior Chains /
Autoshaping / Schedules of Reinforcement / Extinction
APPLICATIONS IN BEHAVIOR THERAPY   101
Systematic Desensitization
THE NATURE OF REINFORCEMENT   107
Autoshaping Studies / The Premack Principle / Responding for Food
with Food Already Present / Economical Distribution of Activities

II   Research and Theory in Operant Behavior

5   **Stimulus Control   119**

BASIC PRINCIPLES   120
Generalization Gradients / Postdiscrimination Gradients / Behavioral
Contrast / The Peak Shift and Gradients of Not-Responding /
Interactions of Stimulus Control Gradients
THE SHARPENING OF STIMULUS CONTROL   143
The Hull–Spence and Lashley Theories / Assessment of Stimulus
Control Theories
ATTENTION   155
General Principles and Phenomena / An Overview of Attention
CONCEPTUAL BEHAVIOR   165

6   **Conditioned Reinforcement   168**

BEHAVIOR CHAINS   168
EXPERIMENTAL TECHNIQUES   173
STRENGTH OF CONDITIONED REINFORCERS   177
Magnitude of Primary Reinforcement / Number of Pairings
with Primary Reinforcement / Schedule of Primary Reinforcement /
The Interreinforcement Interval
CHAINED SCHEDULES   182
Chain Versus Tandem Schedules / Paired Brief Stimuli
BEHAVIOR MODIFICATION: THE TOKEN ECONOMY   186
Psychiatric Patients / Classrooms / Correctional Institutions / Problems

THEORY OF CONDITIONED REINFORCEMENT   193
Traditional Theories / Contemporary Theories
OBSERVING RESPONSES   198

7   **Choice Behavior**   **208**

METHODS FOR STUDYING CHOICE   209
CHOICE AS A TECHNIQUE   212
CHOICE AND REINFORCER MAGNITUDE   214
Concurrent-Interval and Concurrent-Ratio Schedules
CHOICE AND RATE OF REINFORCEMENT   217
SUPERSTITION AND THE CHANGEOVER DELAY (COD)   218
THE QUANTITATIVE LAW OF EFFECT   221
Strengths and Limitations / Alternative Formulations
CHOICE FOR SCHEDULES OF REINFORCEMENT   227
Molecular Characteristics of Choice
SELF-CONTROL   237

8   **Aversive Control**   **242**

PUNISHMENT: AN EMPIRICAL OVERVIEW   243
Maintenance of Punished Behavior / Parameters of Punishment /
Punishment as a Discriminative Stimulus / Conditioned Suppression
CURRENT THEORIES OF PUNISHMENT   251
AVERSION THERAPY   257
NEGATIVE REINFORCEMENT   258
ESCAPE   259
AVOIDANCE   262
Discrete-Trial Avoidance / Free-Operant Avoidance / The Reinforcer
in Avoidance / Shock-Frequency Reduction Theory / The Role of
Pavlovian Processes in Avoidance / Extinction of Avoidance and
Self-Punitive Behavior / Learned Helplessness

III   The Biological Perspective

9   **Species-Specific Behavior Patterns**   **295**

THE CONCEPT OF INSTINCT   297
The Anti-Instinct Revolt / Interaction of Heredity and Environment
EVOLUTION   306
THE GENETICS OF BEHAVIOR   308
THE ETHOLOGICAL APPROACH   310
Techniques
ETHOLOGICAL THEORY   314
Sign Stimuli / Fixed Action Patterns / The Hydraulic Model /
Alternatives to the Hydraulic Model
THE DEVELOPMENT OF SPECIES-SPECIFIC BEHAVIOR   329
The Lehrman Experiments / Specific Hungers / The Rozin Experiments

10   **The Natural History of Learning**   **340**

THE NATURAL ENVIRONMENT   341

GUSTATORY LEARNING, FORAGING, AND PREDATION   343
Taste Aversion Learning / Taste Aversion Learning in the Wild /
Learning to Locate Food
HOMING AND MIGRATION   356
The Ontogeny of Pigeon Homing
IMPRINTING   363
Sexual Imprinting / The Sensitive Period / The Function of Imprinting /
Nonvisual Imprinting / Naturalistic Studies of Imprinting
SONG LEARNING IN BIRDS   376
Developmental Stages in Singing / Biological Constraints on Song
Development / Theories of Song Learning
THE NATURAL HISTORY APPROACH   386

11   **Invertebrate Learning I: Protozoa, Coelenterates,
Platyhelminthes   387**

PHYLOGENETIC DIVERSITY IN LEARNING   390
PROTOZOA   391
Associative Conditioning / Habituation
COELENTERATES   403
Associative Conditioning / Habituation
PLATYHELMINTHES   412
Classical Conditioning / Instrumental Conditioning / Reactive
Inhibition / Habituation

12   **Invertebrate Learning II: Annelids, Molluscs, Arthropods   423**

ANNELIDS   424
Habituation / Classical Conditioning / Instrumental Conditioning
MOLLUSCS   433
Gastropods / Cephalopods
ARTHROPODS   453
Insects / Laboratory Research / Field-Oriented Research

IV   Integration

13   **Toward an Integrated Approach to Behavior   473**

THE NATURE–NURTURE QUESTION   475
LABORATORY AND FIELD   476
The Problem of Validity / Methods for Increasing Validity
LABORATORY ANALOGUES TO NATURAL PHENOMENA   481
Multiple Response Environments / Foraging
THE CHALLENGE TO REINFORCEMENT THEORY   494
EPILOG   498

References   501

Index of Names   545

Index of Topics   552

Preface

Within the past decade the experimental analysis of behavior has been profoundly affected by major developments in behavioral biology. The growing emphasis on evolutionary principles in the explanation of behavior, as well as the increased recognition that behavior must be considered in its natural context, has shaken the very foundations of the experimental analysis of behavior. Ethological and sociobiological approaches to behavior have flourished, and even those categories of behavior that have traditionally been the province of psychologists—learning and behavioral change—are now being viewed within an evolutionary framework. Hence the theoretical and empirical structure of experimental psychology, which has given rise to a powerful applied technology used extensively in both clinical and educational settings, must now itself be reassessed in light of recent developments. Over the past decade, therefore, it has become increasingly necessary to teach and discuss the experimental analysis of behavior within the context of developments in behavioral biology. Unfortunately, no book presenting an integrative approach has existed. The present book is intended to fill this void, which we have each felt acutely in our own teaching of courses in learning and motivation. Although such a book should have been written sooner, our efforts have profited by procrastination: The molar psychobiological approach to learning and animal behavior has made great strides in the past five years; hence our task has become at once more difficult and more rewarding.

It has, moreover, become evident that the biological perspective represents *not* an alternative, as others have suggested, but a complement to the bases of operant psychology. New complementary principles may be generated by a combined approach, and the existing principles of each discipline may be augmented and restructured in accord with those of the other. This complementary view provides the premise on which our book is based.

The book is divided into four sections. The first reviews the historical background of the experimental approach to learning and the critical question of how apparently purposive, goal-directed behavior may be understood within the framework of a deterministic science. It then deals with the traditionally recognized basic learning paradigms of habituation, classical conditioning, and operant conditioning. The second section constitutes a contemporary review of research and theory in operant psychology. Whenever relevant, we discuss the application of principles generated in operant psychology to the modification of human behavior in clinical, educational, and other applied settings where the power of the experimental analysis of behavior has been amply demonstrated. This section therefore familiarizes the reader with the ontogenetic principles critical for a complete understanding of behavior change as a function of experience. The third section shows how the principles of conditioning must themselves be understood against a background of the phylogenetic principles provided by the theory of evolution by natural selection. Here we discuss the importance of ecological diversity in generating a diversity of learning mechanisms. We then review the learning capacities evident in various animal phyla, and, where possible, discuss how these capacities serve the adaptive advantage of the species. The final section consists of an integrative chapter synthesizing the ontogenetic and phylogenetic approaches to behavior change.

Although a course in introductory psychology would be helpful, no prior knowledge of either psychology or biology is assumed in this book. We have tried to provide the necessary background for even the most complex issues. In those few instances in which complexity has been sacrificed for clarity, we have noted references providing missing details, which may reflect conflicting data or alternative interpretations. Teachers of courses in the experimental analysis of behavior may wish to omit the two chapters on invertebrate behavior to de-emphasize the material on phylogeny. Similarly, teachers of courses in animal behavior may wish to omit the chapters on conditioned reinforcement and choice to de-emphasize the material on operant conditioning. In addition, it is our hope that the book may be valuable for researchers in both areas who wish to familiarize themselves with the other view.

We thank Drs. Alan Neuringer and Richard Shull for their extensive and invaluable help in reviewing the entire manuscript. In addition, Drs. Peter Balsam, Anthony DeCasper, James Dyal, Phillip Hineline, Richard Hussian, Richard McClintock, Sara Shettleworth, William Timberlake, and Ben Williams provided numerous constructive comments on specific chapters. Thanks are also due to Ms. Marty Smith. Finally, we wish to express our profound gratitude to Ms. Karen Fiegener for generously assisting in the preparation of the entire manuscript.

January 1979   EDMUND FANTINO
                                                                CHERYL A. LOGAN

The Experimental Analysis of Behavior

A BIOLOGICAL PERSPECTIVE

I Introduction and Overview

1   Introduction

The process of evolution has given rise to an extreme diversity of animal societies. One creature that has been said to rival *Homo sapiens* in the complexity of its social organization is, surprisingly enough, the honeybee. Honeybee societies are composed of morphologically distinct social castes, each elegantly adapted to contribute in a unique way to the efficient functioning of the society. The queen, for example, is ideally suited to reproduction. With a lifelong supply of sperm stored in her abdomen she may fertilize and lay as many as 2,000 eggs per day. Workers, the queen's daughters, and the most populous group in the hive, perform the essential tasks of maintaining the hive—tending the nursery of developing bees, serving the queen, repairing the structure of the hive and regulating its temperature, defending and cleaning the hive, and foraging. The male drones, the third caste of the honeybee society, are produced only as needed and function largely in the service of reproduction. An amazingly complex system of communication, which makes use of chemical, visual, auditory, and tactile modalities, serves to coordinate social activities among these three groups of individuals.

One of the most extensively studied tasks of the workers is their foraging behavior—the means by which they locate and retrieve food for the sustenance of the hive. Foraging workers called "scouts" travel extensive distances from the hive to locate rich sources of nectar and pollen. After identifying the location of a field of flowers by both sight and scent, the scouts return to the hive and communicate the location of the food to other workers (see discussion in Chapter 12). Recent research has demonstrated that honeybee foraging involves heretofore unrecognized sensory abilities (such as sensitivity to the earth's magnetic field), intricate communication systems very likely representative of true language, and learning abilities perhaps unparalleled in the rest of the insect world. Though honeybees may seem unlikely subjects in an investigation of the psychology of animal learning, it is the involvement of learning in an adaptive response complex that is of interest to us here. Martin Lindauer and his colleagues, working in Germany, have reported that foragers *learn* to locate a field of flowers on the basis of a precise olfactory discrimination. Their work also indicates, however, that the bee's learning abilities have been rigidly structured by the requirements of the foraging environment. Worker bees can easily be trained to choose one scent over another as a consequence of the presentation of a sugar reward. However, certain odor cues can sustain conditioning far more readily than others. After only one rewarded trial, bees will choose the correct (rewarded) odor over an alternative in as many as 90 percent of the tests if the odor is related to that of a flowering plant. Odors not normally emitted by flowering plants require as many as twenty rewarded trials; tests with such odors indicate that, in these cases, choice of the correct odor never exceeds 75 percent (Menzel and Erber, 1978).

Koltermann (1973) has extended these findings to show that the bee's predisposition to associate certain odors with food is *species-specific*. That is, different species of honeybee consistently exhibit different odor preferences. Naive bees of different species were trained with seventeen different odors, which included jasmine, rosemary, lavender, thyme, orange, eucalyptus, and anise. The Italian species, *Apis mellifera ligustica*, was able to discriminate lavender and rosemary far more readily (with fewer rewarded trials) than the Indian species, *Apis cerana*. This species learned equally well, but only in response to a different set of odors—oil of rosewood and orange. In most species tested, the bees were most readily able to discriminate odors representative of the flora of their native regions.

In some species odor preferences can be modified by altering the amount of reward associated with each odor. Mid-European bees of the species *Apis mellifera carnica* will learn to choose an originally less preferred odor if the presence of that odor is associated with a 2 percent sugar solution and the presence of an alternative (originally preferred) odor only brings a 0.5 percent sugar reward. The ease with which preferences can be altered as a function of the amount of reward, however, differs among species. The Indian species, *Apis cerana*, is much less flexible in its behavior. Koltermann has speculated that these species-specific variations in degree of behavioral flexibility represent evolutionary adaptations to the character of the natural nectar supply in the bees' native areas. Indian bees inhabit tropical regions where nectar is abundant in most flowers throughout the year. The nectar supply provided by one type of flower is not likely to change substantially; behavioral flexibility will therefore be of little use. In seasonally fluctuating climates, such as that inhabited by the mid-European species, the seasonal availability of one particular nectar source will vary. At a certain time of year one odor may occur together with a particularly high sugar concentration; at a different time, however, another odor may signal a particularly rich source of food. Under these conditions flexibility becomes important for the continued sustenance of the colony.

In the process of forming an olfactory discrimination, the bee's behavior has undergone adaptive change. The organism can more readily discriminate those flowers that provide greater nutritive output. Hence the altered behavior enables the individual to more efficiently satisfy one of the major mandates of life: the need for food. Konrad Lorenz (1965) has stated that adaptive change in behavior can be brought about through the action of two and only two processes: ontogeny and phylogeny. Both processes are represented in the example of the bees' foraging behavior. In each, adaptive behavior change occurs through the acquisition and storage of environmental information. Behavior is thus altered in ways that directly reflect changes in the organism's environment. The two processes differ in both their time course—phylogeny acts over generations, ontogeny, over the individual's lifetime—and in the mechanisms by which change is realized. It is, however, only through the integration of both processes that either may exert its effect on behavior.

PHYLOGENY

The process of *phylogeny* is governed by the principles of evolution by natural selection; phylogenetic change represents evolutionary change. As such, phylogenetic change must take place across generations within a *species*, resulting in the adaptation of that species to the characteristics of its environment. In the process of evolution a species acquires information about its environment through the differential reproduction of individuals. Changes in the characteristics of the species that result represent a modification of the information contained in the genes. Because genetic change normally occurs only during the process of reproduction, the mechanism of phylogenetic change depends on the production of new individuals. Evolution, however, cannot occur in an individual; the time course of phylogenetic change requires the succession of generations.

Any change in the genetic constitution of a species, however, also requires the development of functional characteristics within the individuals of that species. The differential reproductive success of *individuals* constitutes the mechanism of evolution. That is, while evolutionary change is manifest in changes in the species as a whole, the mechanism for producing change operates at the level of the individual. Individuals carry the genes that define the species, and if an individual fails to reproduce, for any reason, that individual's genes are lost to the species. Phylogenetic change therefore depends on a second type of change: that which occurs within the lifetime of an individual.

ONTOGENY

The individual, too, may undergo adaptive change. Of necessity, such change is nongenetic and therefore does not require the generational time course typical of phylogeny. Changes in behavior that take place during the lifetime of an individual in response to alterations in that individual's environment are termed *ontogenetic* change. Traditionally, the study of ontogeny has centered on certain categories of change, each of which represents the acquisition and storage of environmental events by an individual. The prenatal development of the structures of an unborn infant, growth, and the age-dependent postnatal changes of maturation are ontogenetic changes, as are the relatively age-independent changes in behavior that occur in response to variations in experience. The latter category represents the type of ontogenetic change illustrated in our example of the bees: learning. As in the other categories of ontogeny, in learning change occurs in response to variations in the environment incorporated by the individual. The effect of the change adapts the individual to some aspect of its environment, and the change manifests itself during the lifetime of the individual.

Both ontogenetic and phylogenetic change are evident in the formation of olfactory discriminations in the various species of honeybees. Species-specific genetic information defines the ease with which particular odors can be associated with various nutritive substances. The European species, for example, learned to choose odors of oil of rosewood and orange only with great difficulty. These differences, as well as the species-specific differences in the effectiveness of amount of reward in reversing preferences, represent species change due to phylogeny. Within each species, however, behavioral change was produced by ontogenetic factors that allowed individuals to form discriminations. Environmental change —the presence or absence of the sugar reward—enabled the individual to learn which flowers (which scents) were most nutritive. In essence, both types of processes, ontogenetic and phylogenetic, worked together to adapt the organism to its environment. Moreover, ontogenetic flexibility is specifically manifest in ways that require particular species to respond differently from others as a function of differing ecological demands.

In the chapters to follow we will present an analysis of the factors involved in that category of ontogenetic change termed learning. No attempt will be made to address other areas of ontogeny. Following a review of the ontogenetic principles that account for experientially induced modifications in the behavior of individuals, we will consider how the occurrence of ontogenetic change interacts with the genetic information acquired in phylogeny. We have chosen the flexibility of the honeybee's foraging behavior to illustrate many of the questions that will face us in subsequent chapters. There we will become aware of the diversity of learning abilities characteristic of various species in various situations. In each, however, we may ask: What general principles characterize the nature of the learning process? How does behavioral flexibility enable the organism to meet the demands of its natural environment? And how do the ecological demands that differentiate even closely related species dictate that learning will occur differently in each?

We will first review the history of the experimental approach to learning, since the psychology of learning is best understood in its historical context. The major problem confronting early learning theorists was the apparently purposive, goal-directed behavior of organisms. How could such behavior be brought within the realm of a deterministic science? The answer lay in seeing behavior as a function of the organism's history. The principles of conditioning that were developed in the first half of this century provided the mechanism for explaining purposive behavior in a deterministic fashion. In this sense the principles of conditioning serve the same function for explaining ontogenetic change as do the principles of evolution for explaining phylogenetic change. The difference, of course, is that the consequences of behavior operate directly on the individual in ontogeny and indirectly on the species in phylogeny.

Two primary types of conditioning—classical (or Pavlovian) conditioning and operant (or instrumental) conditioning—came to be studied extensively (see Chapters 3 and 4, respectively). Classical conditioning deals with reflexive responding—that is, responding that invariably follows a specific stimulus—and the process by which reflexive responding comes to occur to a previously neutral stimulus. Operant conditioning, on the other hand, deals with nonreflexive responding that is strengthened or weakened by its consequences. Since much vertebrate behavior is operant in nature, principles of operant behavior are of profound importance to the study of behavior. Thus we devote five chapters (Chapters 4–8) to a contemporary review of research and theory in operant behavior. Special attention is focused on four topics, each of which represents a particularly active area of research in operant conditioning: (1) stimulus control, (2) conditioned reinforcement, (3) choice, and (4) aversive control.

These chapters will familiarize the reader with the ontogenetic principles critical for a complete understanding of behavioral change as a function of experience. The reader will then be in a position to learn how the principles of conditioning must themselves be understood against a background of phylogenetic principles. The interaction of ontogeny and phylogeny will be emphasized in Chapters 9 and 10. This review leads to the fascinating world of invertebrate behavior (Chapters 11 and 12), where phylogenetic influence is particularly pervasive.

The final chapter attempts to synthesize the ontogenetic and phylogenetic approaches to behavioral change. Until recently, experimental and theoretical analyses within each domain have proceeded largely independently of work in the other. Thus the two approaches have remained conceptually distinct. The reasons for this separation of approaches are discussed and the importance of combining the two stressed. The complexity and diversity of behavior require that both ontogenetic and phylogenetic principles be included in any general explanation of behavior. An important challenge will be to achieve the balance of ontogenetic and phylogenetic principles that best explains the behavior of an individual member of a distinct species in a given situation. This book explores the theoretical and empirical bases required to meet that challenge.

2 A History of the Experimental Approach to Learning

Speculation on the nature of learning originated, as did all psychological questions, within philosophy. *Epistemology* is the branch of philosophy that addresses problems of the source, nature, and content of human knowledge, and it is within epistemology that we find the early philosophical heritage of the experimental psychology of learning. Virtually all of the great philosophical systems of antiquity addressed epistemological questions, but it was not until the latter part of the seventeenth century that such questions became the cornerstones of entire philosophical systems. The *British empiricist/associationist movement*, because of its emphasis of learning—or the acquisition of knowledge, as it would have been called at the time—is regarded as a primary force in the development of the experimental psychology of learning.

EMPIRICISM AND ASSOCIATIONISM

British empiricism, the most prominent psychology of its day, was placed on firm footing by John Locke (1632–1704). In challenging the Cartesian epistemology of innate ideas, Locke revived the Aristotelian doctrine of the *tabula rasa:* The human mind is at birth a blank tablet, empty of knowledge, and dependent for its functioning on the acquisition of knowledge through experience. Locke crystallized his epistemology and clarified the source of knowledge in his famous *doctrine of psychological empiricism.* In so doing, he established learning as a perennial topic for speculation in psychology. Locke's doctrine states simply that all knowledge is based on experience. That is, all knowledge is learned. Before Locke, Descartes had postulated that certain very basic concepts, universal truths such as the concepts of self, God, infinity, and certain geometric axioms, arise from within the mind and are not dependent on the experiencing of external objects. Locke asserted that there are no innate ideas. Rather, experience alone gives rise to *simple ideas,* which can be compounded into *complex ideas.* For Locke, simple and complex ideas, derived either directly or indirectly from experience, constitute the totality of knowledge. On the details of this process of compounding, which he termed "association," he remained quite vague. Locke nonetheless became the founder of an empirical psychology of mind. The task of specifying the precise nature of the all-important process of association became Locke's legacy, to not only his philosophical successors but ultimately to experimental psychology as well.

These early speculations in learning, association, knowledge, and related questions focused entirely on human beings. Psychology *qua* philosophy was an exclusively human-oriented endeavor. Acquired knowledge and its attendant ideas were reserved only for those beings possessed of minds. And, as Descartes had so pointedly indicated, only humans had minds. In time, the work of Charles Darwin would change all this; but during the seventeenth and eighteenth centuries the phrase "animal learning" remained a contradiction in terms.

Each of the major British philosophers who followed in the Lockean tradition treated the question of the nature of association. The mentalistic philosophy of George Berkeley, for example, placed an even more exclusive emphasis on the primacy of conscious experience. Berkeley, moreover, agreed that associations among ideas are formed when those ideas occur together in experience. Similarly, in the work of David Hume laws of association were offered as a precise explanation of mind. Nowhere, however, was the treatment of association more complete than in the associationist philosophy of David Hartley.

A Physical Account of Association

David Hartley (1705–1757) began his account of association by offering a detailed definition of what was assumed to take place in the associative process:

> Any sensations *A, B, C,* etc., by being associated with one another a sufficient number of times, get such a power over the corresponding ideas *a, b, c,* etc. that any one of the sensations, *A,* when impressed alone, shall be able to excite in the mind *b, c,* etc., the ideas of the rest [Hartley, 1749, p. 65].

Experience (as Locke has said) gives rise to simple *sensations*. Each sensation, in turn, generates a corresponding *idea*. If two or more sensations occur at the same time or in rapid succession, they will, by virtue of contiguity, be associated. Similarly, their corresponding ideas, also necessarily contiguous, become associated. Following numerous sensory associations, eventualy the corresponding ideas are fused such that the occurrence of a single sensation, *A*, is now by itself sufficient to generate the compound, fused idea *a, b, c,* and so on. Suppose you see an apple. According to Hartley, your visual experience constitutes a sensation. Later when you remember or imagine an apple, you are having an idea that was generated by the original sensation. If when you saw the apple it was being eaten by a horse, you will simultaneously experience sensations of both the horse and the apple. Simultaneous ideas of horse and apple will be generated by these sensations, and, if the two sensations occur together frequently, eventually the sight of either alone will generate the compound idea of a horse eating an apple.

Hartley, however, went beyond mere definition in his analysis of the process of association. As a physician, he was determined as well to explain the physical mechanism by which the process of association occurs. Hartley wrote during the time of the great physicist Isaac Newton (1642–1727). The Newtonian philosophy of *mechanism* had defined the seventeenth-century intellectual climate, and Hartley was committed to devising his physical account of association in terms of the prevailing Newtonian model of the universe—tiny particles of physical matter in constant motion. Here, however, Hartley faced a problem. The brain, the presumed seat of ideas, and therefore of the process of association, did not move about overtly when associations took place. How, then, to arrive at a physical account of association based on matter in motion in an apparently stationary brain?

Newton himself had faced a similar problem in explaining the phenomenon of action at a distance. Here, too, objects could influence one another in the apparent absence of direct contact. To explain action at a distance Newton postulated that the entire universe was filled with a light, fluid-like medium, which he termed the ether. All spaces between objects were filled with the ether, and any effect one object exerted on another at a distance was in reality the result of *vibrations* generated by the motion of the first and transmitted to the second through the ethereal medium.

In Newton's ethereal vibrations, Hartley, too, found a solution. True, the brain does not actively move about. Elastic brain tissue could, however, like Newton's ether, sustain vibrations. Overt motion was not required; motive effects could be transmitted subtly, by means of vibrations. Hartley reasoned that brain tissue, too, could sustain vibratory action without actually moving about. The *vibration* became, therefore, the basis of Hartley's mechanism of association.

According to Hartley, the receipt of sensations generates "sensory" vibrations, localized at specific points in the brain tissue. By necessity, vibratory motion diffuses outward from the point of impact. Vibratory diffusions accompanying contiguously occurring sensations can therefore mingle with one another, becoming one and allowing for the physical interaction of sensations. But what of ideas? Hartley assumed that if a sensory vibration occurred frequently enough it would generate a faint miniaturized copy of itself, which he termed a *vibratiuncle*. When contiguous sensory vibrations repeatedly fuse in the brain, their miniaturized fused trace—a vibratiuncle—represents the physical basis for the association of ideas. Each individual sensation generates a corresponding idea. The fusing of sensory vibrations causes the fusion (association) of the corresponding ideas. Thus the physical foundation for the natural inhabitants of the human mind, complex ideas.

Early Scientific Studies

Following Charles Darwin's addition of humans to the animal kingdom, questions such as those posed by the philosophers regarding man's mental abilities could be asked about other animals as well. The impact of the associationist tradition on the development of animal psychology can be seen as early as the late nineteenth century. For example, Georges Romanes, in his search for objective evidence of the existence of mind in other organisms, appeals to association:

> The criterion of mind, therefore, which I propose . . . is as follows: Does the organism learn to make new adjustments, or to modify old ones, in accordance with the results of its own individual experience? [Romanes, 1884, p. 4]

If so, it could learn, and therefore it had mind. But Romanes was a biologist, and philosophy remained an exclusively human-oriented discipline. Where, then, were such questions to be addressed?

The answers came from within the newly formed science of psychology. Here traditional epistemological questions—questions that had formed the basis of the eighteenth- and nineteenth-century philosophies of mind—were inoculated with the scientific method to become the disciplines of a scientific psychology. The *psychophysical movement*, initiated by Gustav Fechner (1801–1887), addressed the nature of sensation in an effort to quantify the relationships between changes in the physical environment (stimulation) and the occurrence of mental events (sensations). Wilhelm Wundt's (1832–1920) *structuralism* was devoted to the scientific analysis of the structure of consciousness. Sensations and feelings were assumed to represent the basic elements of consciousness, and out of these were constructed all other contents of consciousness. This discipline quickly spawned efforts by the newer American *functionalist movement* to explain the function of consciousness. Charles Darwin had convincingly argued that those characteristics of an organism that function to its benefit persist; hence the organism is adapted to function in particular ways. Under Darwin's influence the functionalists were to address scientific psychology's attention to the explanation of the mind in use—as it functions to adapt the individual to the flux of environmental events.

The focal philosophical question of association had received little attention from either the psychophysicists or the structuralists. In the 1870s, however, a German intellectual by the name of Hermann Ebbinghaus (1850–1909) purchased a copy of Fechner's classic *Elements of Psychophysics* in a used bookstore in Paris. Impressed by Fechner's work, and presumably realizing that Wundt's psychology had underrepresented the important process of association, Ebbinghaus set out to do for the study of memory—or association—what Fechner had done for the study of sensation. Association, too, could be the object of scientific analysis. Repetition, or the frequency with which an event occurred, became the central factor in Ebbinghaus' analysis of memory. With the concept of repetition in hand, he attempted to formulate quantitative laws describing the formation of associations. He himself was the subject of his experiments. Measuring such factors as the effect of time on the retention of verbal material, Ebbinghaus made the first concerted attempt to bring the concept of association into the new science. E. G. Boring (1950) notes, however, that while Ebbinghaus' work was quite influential at the time, "he left no deep imprint on the psychological world" (p. 392). It was, instead, in the hands of American psychologists intent on a complete objectification of the science of psychology that concepts of learning came to assume their central role in scientific psychology. In America, under the rubric of the Theory of Evolution by Natural Selection, the study of association was extended to nonhuman as well as human organisms to become the experimental psychology of animal learning.

THORNDIKE'S CONNECTIONISM

> The careful, minute, and solid knowledge of sense organs of animals finds no counterpart in the realm of associations and habits. We do not know how delicate or how complex or how permanent are the possible associations of any given group of animals [Thorndike, 1898, p. 1].

Just prior to the turn of this century Edward L. Thorndike (1874–1949) set out to remedy this lack of knowledge and, in doing so, initiated the experimental psychology of learning in America. Generally regarded as the first psychologist to study animal behavior, certainly the first to focus on the phenomena of animal learning, Thorndike was, however, far more than just an initiator. Early on, he clarified and formulated a number of important concepts that have, for most of this century, provided the basis for the experimental investigation of animal learning. By virtue of his far-

Figure 2.1
Edward L. Thorndike (1874–1949).
[Historical Pictures Service, Chicago.]

reaching influence he can unhesitatingly be included in a survey of the more contemporary learning theorists. Many a new insight in the psychology of learning is, with some inspection, revealed to be a reassertion of a forgotten point recognized long ago by Thorndike.

Thorndike's theoretical approach may seem unusually familiar to the modern reader. That is as it should be, for many of Thorndike's ideas are still very much with us. Recall, however, that at the time Thorndike initially aired his views on learning most of experimental psychology was focused on the workings of consciousness. Both Wundt's structuralism and the American functionalist movement viewed psychology as the science of consciousness. Subjective introspective methodologies prevailed in the new science, and the topic of learning was still of relatively minor importance in experimental psychology. Like Ebbinghaus, Thorndike in fact took as his point of departure the traditional philosophical view of experientially based association occurring among mental elements. He diverged, however, from this associationist foundation and constructed a behaviorally-based theory of learning guided by objective experimentation. In working with animals, of course, Thorndike did not have the techniques of introspection at his disposal. Moreover, Thorndike's interpretations of objectively indexed accounts of animal intelligence thoughtfully avoided any reference to mediation by ideas as essential to behavioral change. Thorndike's contemporaries treated intelligent behavior as evidence of the occurrence of reasoned thought or ideation. Thorndike, however, regarded this influence as largely unnecessary. While the associationists dealt exclusively with associations between mental elements (Locke's "ideas") that mediate between sensation and act,

Thorndike focused on connections between the situations (stimuli) and the acts (responses) themselves. Hilgard (1956) writes:

> Thorndike . . . became convinced, contrary to the then popular beliefs, that animal behavior was little mediated by ideas. Responses were said to be made directly to the situation as sensed. . . . [H]e was convinced that the great bulk of learning could be explained by the direct binding of acts to situations, unmediated by ideas. A comparison of the learning curves of humans with those of animals led him to believe that the same essentially mechanical phenomena disclosed by animal learning are the fundamentals of human learning as well [Hilgard, 1956, p. 17].

With the first modern *stimulus–response (S–R) theory of learning*, the work of E. L. Thorndike became the forerunner of the objectivist *behaviorist movement*, which was to dominate investigations of animal learning for fifty years.

Thorndike's theory arose from the results of a series of experiments now counted among the classics of experimental psychology. Hungry cats confined in what Thorndike called *problem boxes* were required to unlatch the box to gain access to food located outside the box but visible to the cat inside. Thorndike observed that when the cats were initially placed in the boxes they engaged in large numbers of "chaotic" behaviors, seemingly unrelated to the solution of the problem at hand. Rather than quietly reasoning the problem through (via the mediation of ideas), the cats would at first "try" anything, no matter how unrelated the response might be to the effective solution. Responses apparently occurred automatically. Eventually, by chance, one response would occur that effectively unlatched the problem box door, leading to the food. When, on the next trial, the cat was again placed in the box, fewer of the unrelated chaotic behaviors occurred. Moreover, the previously effective response (or one very similar to it) occurred much more quickly. Across successive trials virtually all inappropriate behaviors ceased to occur, the latency to perform the correct response decreased substantially, and, when the animal was replaced in the problem box on subsequent days, fewer and fewer trials were required to produce the correct response. At this point learning was said to be complete.

Thorndike characterized the learning process as an automatic *selecting* of the correct (that is, successful) response from among the many initially occurring, and a *connecting* of that response to the problem at hand. The theory focuses on an explanation of the circumstances that bring about the formation and strengthening of connections based on initial trial and error. The central core of Thorndike's *connectionism* (as the theory came to be called) consisted of three primary laws of learning. The most important of these is the *law of effect*. One response is selected out from the *initially equally likely* set on the basis of the *consequences* associated with that response. That is, the correct response has the effect of unlatching the problem box door and gaining the cat access to the food. Successful responses yield "satisfying" consequences and, therefore, strengthen connections, while unsuccessful responses yield "annoying" consequences and, therefore, weaken connections. Future occurrences of the response in a given situation depend on the strength of the connections. Perhaps because of the normally subjective connotations of terms like "satisfaction" and "annoyance," Thorndike was careful to assign them what might now be regarded as operational definitions. Satisfaction was said to be characteristic of situations that "the animal does nothing to avoid" and may even approach. Annoyance, by contrast, referred to any situation that "the animal does nothing to preserve" (Thorndike, 1913) and may actively avoid. In the early statement of the law of effect, satisfiers and annoyers were equally potent in producing their respective effects. In later versions of the theory, however, Thorndike postulated the asymmetrical or *truncated law of effect*. The data suggested that satisfiers (rewards) were actually much more effective at strengthening connections than annoyers were at weakening them. Rather than being equally effective (in opposite directions), reward and punishment differed in effectiveness, with rewarding consequences being far more powerful than punishing consequences in altering behavior.

The second of the three primary laws, the *law of readiness*, describes in general physiological terms the circumstances responsible for the occurrence of either satisfaction or annoyance. Though Thorndike spoke in terms of "conduction units" (presumably neurons), his points are easily phrased in the language of behavior. If the organism is prepared to respond, completion of the appropriate response brings about satisfaction. Such preparation may be either physiological—as hunger might physiologically prepare the organism to eat—or more psychological, perhaps equivalent to the modern notion of set. On the other hand, if the animal is prepared to respond but the response is prevented, annoyance results. Annoyance can also be produced when an unprepared organism is forced to respond.

The third primary law, the *law of exercise*, was initially given importance equal to that of the law of effect. Use or exercise was said to strengthen connections, while disuse effectively weakened connections. Later experiments on the importance of exercise occurring in the absence of knowledge of consequences, however, convinced Thorndike otherwise. Exercise was important in strengthening connections only if each exercise (trial) was accompanied by an effective consequence. By itself exercise does not improve performance. The law of exercise was, therefore, subsequently regarded as a subsidiary law, dependent for its operation on the law of effect.

Additional subsidiary laws in Thorndike's system dealt with the factors responsible for responding in novel situations, with the determinants of the transfer of learning to similar situations, and with the phenomenon of associative shifting. *Associative shifting* is, according to Thorndike, a form of stimulus substitution in which, as in Pavlovian conditioning, a response gradually comes to be evoked by a new stimulus that has been added to the situation initially producing the response. Thorndike's classical example of associative shifting involved teaching a cat to stand up in response to a verbal command. Initially, a bit of fish is dangled before the cat, and the animal stands in response to the fish. Then, the verbal command "stand up" is added to the stimulus situation represented by the fish. Eventually, the fish stimulus can be removed, and the verbal command alone will evoke the response of standing. Though at first regarded as a subsidiary principle, associative shifting was later viewed as a distinct type of learning, which occurred independently of the law of effect.

Two new principles were added to Thorndike's connectionism in later years. Data obtained from human verbal learning experiments suggested that for a given consequence connections could be formed more easily in some situations than in others. If the response "belongs" to the situation, learning will occur more quickly; that is, the consequences will produce stronger connections in fewer trials. *Belongingness* is best illustrated by a situation described by Thorndike himself. Consider an experiment on language learning in which subjects are read sets of sentences each describing various individuals' occupations. "John is a butcher. Henry is a carpenter" (Hilgard, 1956, p. 28). Syntax ensures that "John" and "butcher" belong together, while "Henry" and "butcher" do not. In fact, though both the temporal contiguity and the consequences are the same for the two associations, the John–butcher connection is formed much more readily than the butcher–Henry connection. In a similar way, a particular response is much more easily connected to a given stimulus if the response initially belongs with the consequences that it produces. In a predatory cat, capture and feeding naturally follow a jump at the prey. In cats, therefore, the receipt of food might more readily alter jumping than some other consequence that does not belong with the jumping response. We will see this idea much more fully developed in more recent treatments of similar situations (see Chapter 10).

The *spread of effect* was a second phenomenon that assumed an important theoretical role in the later versions of connectionism. Consequences, either satisfying or annoying, apparently affect not only the connection that immediately precedes them, but also connections occurring either before or after the one that actually generated the rewarding (or punishing) outcome. It is as if the strengthening or weakening effect that a consequence has on the related S–R unit *spreads* to other nearby units as well. In a typical experiment on the spread of effect, subjects are presented lists of words. Each word is assigned a different number. Some portion of the word–number combinations are arbitrarily designated as right (and therefore rewarded), others as wrong (and therefore punished). Wrong (punished) pairs that are embedded within a series of correct (rewarded) pairs tend to occur with greater frequency, as if their connection has been strengthened. The same punished pairs embedded in a series of punished connections are weakened, presumably because of the absence of any offsetting spread of rewarding effect.

This gradually diminishing spread of effect, which decreases with increasing time or distance from the rewarded connection, suggests the modern notion of a *gradient of reward*. The phenomenon was important also because it constituted additional strong evidence of the importance of consequences. In doing so, it further verified the law of effect and re-emphasized Thorndike's position on the automatic and mechanical nature of learning.

Thorndike's views of animal and human learning set the theme for the experimental investigation of learning in America. We wil encounter many learning theorists who disagreed with Thorndike on various specifics; most of the questions addressed, however, were initially formulated by Thorndike. Though terminologies have become more and more varied, and empirical paradigms more and more specialized, research has focused on concepts of learning crystallized by E. L. Thorndike. Thorndike's priority was attested to by Pavlov himself:

> Some years after the beginning of the work with our new method I learned that somewhat similar experiments had been performed in America, and indeed not by physiologists but by psychologists. . . . I must acknowledge that the honor of having made the first steps along this path belongs to E. L. Thorndike. . . . [H]is book must be considered a classic [Pavlov, 1928, p. 23].

Much later, E. C. Tolman comments on the significance of the foundation laid by Thorndike:

> The psychology of animal learning . . . has been and still is primarily a matter of agreeing or disagreeing with Thorndike, or trying in minor ways to improve upon him. . . . All of us here in America have taken Thorndike, overtly or covertly, as our starting point [Tolman, 1938, p. 11].

THE GREAT AGE OF LEARNING THEORIES

Thorndike had characterized learning as the *gradual* formation of connnections between *stimuli and responses* brought about by the *consequences* associated with responding. Contained in this general statement are a number of issues that commanded the attention of the major learning theorists who followed. Is learning in fact a gradual process, or is the association formed instantly and completely with the first common occurrence of the relevant elements? What are these relevant elements? That is, are the connections actually formed between stimuli and responses or between other combinations of elements in the learning situation—for example between stimuli and other stimuli? Finally, are the consequences of responding the critical determinants of learning, as Thorndike maintained? If so, what makes a consequence effective—how does the law of effect work? A related question, which focused the work of Thorndike's successors, concerned the relationship between *instrumental conditioning* (in which receipt of the consequence depends on the occurrence of the response) and the newly discovered *classical (Pavlovian) conditioning* (in which "consequences" occur independently of the animal's responding). Are they representative of two different forms of learning? If so, how do they differ?

As opinions on these various issues diverged, major competing theories were generated, each elaborating a somewhat unique position. In the following pages we will consider these theories as posited by their major proponents. Included are Edwin Guthrie's contiguous conditioning, Clark Hull's behavior theory, Edward C. Tolman's purposive behaviorism, and B. F. Skinner's operant conditioning. Beginning approximately in the 1940s these four positions dominated the experimental psychology of learning.

Each of these positions shares some characteristics with all the learning theories that emerged following the ascendance of behaviorism in experimental psychology. In 1912, John B. Watson (1878–1958) first formally stated the tenets of *behaviorism*, which advocated the observation of behavior, rather than mental states, as a means of rendering psychology an objective science. In keeping with Watson's statements, behavior was eagerly accepted as the subject matter of psychology. Mental mediation was considered irrelevant, and objectivism (inherent in Thorndike's position well before) ruled the day. Accompanying Watson's view of behaviorism was an increasingly extreme environmentalism that allowed for no innate constituents of behavior—human or nonhuman. Here, too, psychology the science followed closely in the footsteps of its philosophical forebears. Locke's philosophical psychology explicitly assigned the source of all knowledge to experience. To objectify psychological inquiry, the behavioral tradition replaced knowledge with behavior. But the source of the effect (a change in behavior for the behaviorists, or the acquisition of knowledge for the philosophers) remained where Locke had so firmly placed it: in the experience provided the individual by the environment. Though now regarded as something of an overstatement, Watson's environmentalism served at the time to make the phenomena of learning fundamental to all of psychology. If psychology is the science of behavior and if all behavior is learned, learning must therefore be considered the pivotal process in the explanation of all psychological phenomena. For this reason theories of learning were often regarded as equivalent to complete theories of behavior.

GUTHRIE'S CONTIGUOUS CONDITIONING

Perhaps the most complete departure from Thorndike's view is contained in the pure associationism of Edwin R. Guthrie (1886–1959). Though Guthrie maintained conceptual emphasis on the occurrence of connections between stimuli and responses, he rejected both the law of effect and the law of exercise. Even Pavlovian reinforcement—the contiguous occurrence of two stimuli—one effective in producing a response and other neutral—found no place in Guthrie's system.

The cornerstone of Guthrie's theory—and the basis of all learning, in his view—consists of a process reminiscent of Thorndike's associative shifting. At once both lauded and criticized for its simplicity, Guthrie's view of learning was based on the single principle of *association by contiguity*. "A combination of stimuli which has accompanied a movement will on its recurrence tend to be followed by that movement" (Guthrie, 1935, p. 26). The single contiguous occurrence of a stimulus (or set of stimuli) with a response (movement) defines the necessary *and* sufficient condition for the formation of a learned connection. Guthrie, therefore, assumed that (1) no special consequences of responding are required; (2) new associations need *not* be predicated on the occurrence of *a priori* built-in connections (as in Pavlovian conditioning); and, perhaps most surprising, (3) repetition is irrelevant. The association is completely formed at full strength with a single pairing of stimulus and response. Additional trials have no bearing on associative strength. Learning is not a gradual process; nor is it dependent for its occurrence on what by that time was familiarly referred to as reinforcement.

Figure 2.2
Edwin R. Guthrie (1886–1959).
[The Imogen Cunningham Trust, San Francisco.]

Guthrie's theory commands an elegant simplicity, making it initially appealing to those who hold with Ockham's razor: "It is vain to do with more what can be done with fewer" (William of Ockham, c. 1430). Guthrie had no need for concepts such as drive, aversion, pain, reward, goal, and inhibition. Such simplicity becomes still more attractive when compared with the mounting and at times overburdening complexity that surrounded the Hullian system. Simplicity by itself, however, offers no advantage. The theory must also effectively account for the resultant complexity of the phenomena to be explained. This was Guthrie's task: to explain all of the observed phenomena of learning on the basis of a single principle—contiguity.

The most highly formalized statement of Guthrie's theory comes, surprisingly, from a student of Clark Hull. Virginia Voeks acquired her techniques of theory construction from Hull, psychology's acknowledged master; but she applied those techniques to the theoretical content outlined by Guthrie. Voeks (1950) formalized the four basic postulates of Guthrie's system. We are already familiar with *postulate 1, the principle of association*. The *single contiguous occurrence* of a stimulus pattern with a response defines the necessary and sufficient condition for the formation of an association. Without contiguity, learning cannot occur; moreover, no additional circumstances, whether drive states, reinforcement, or others, are required. Following the initial association, each future presentation of the stimulus pattern will elicit the response at full strength. Learning is said to be complete in *one trial*. *Postulate 2* states the *principle of postremity*. "A stimulus which has accompanied . . . two or more incompatible responses is a conditioned stimulus for only the last response made while that stimulus was present" (Voeks, 1950, p. 344). *Only* the response that was most recently associated with a given stimulus will occur with future presentations of that stimulus. As we shall see, using the principle of postremity in conjunction with the occurrence of incompatible responses to the same stimulus, Guthrie is able to account for the phenomenon of experimental extinction.

In postulate 3, the *principle of response probability*, Voeks emphasizes that the likelihood of any given response occurring increases as a function of the number of relevant stimuli present. Relevant cues are, of course, those that have been associated with the response in the past. The importance and necessity of postulate 3 can most easily be appreciated in conjunction with a knowledge of postulate 4. Postulate 4 states the *principle of dynamic situations*. With this statement we gain some feeling for Guthrie's concept of the stimulus. The effective stimulus (that which produces the response) for any response is not a single isolated event. Rather, it consists of a complex stimulus pattern composed of many identifiable elements. Any response occurs in the context of a complete stimulus configuration. This *stimulus complex* is, moreover, continuously changing. No two situations are ever exactly the same. The occurrence of the response itself may bring about a change in the stimulus complex. Fatigue, for example, may be added to the stimulus complex as a result of the prior occurrence of the response. The effective stimulus is, therefore, a dynamic, constantly changing flux of elements; hence the principle of dynamic situations. Given this dynamic flux of stimulus elements, what actually ensures the occurrence of the associated response? To answer this Voeks refers to postulate 3. The probability of occurrence of any given response increases as the proportion of stimuli present approximates the original stimulus complex. The addition of novel stimuli or the deletion of elements in the original stimulus set may decrease the likelihood of the response occurring.

These four postulates provide the conceptual basis of Guthrie's system. At times they seem to contradict much of what is superficially evident in the empirical data. Behavior change, for example, *does* appear to occur gradually. Similarly, the consequences that follow a response *are* highly correlated with an increase in the frequency of future occurrences of that response. Guthrie does not argue with these observed results. He merely proposes to account for them completely on the basis of his four postulates buttressed by empirical data that contradict the more familiar results.

Why does behavior change appear to occur gradually? If the association is complete in a single trial, why does the response follow each presentation of the stimulus pattern with increasing frequency as training proceeds? According to Guthrie, with each additional occurrence of the response more and more stimuli become part of the stimulus pattern. The larger the absolute size of the stimulus pattern, the less important become minor trial-to-trial fluctuations in stimulus elements. With progressively fewer fluctuations and larger stimulus patterns, the response becomes more likely (given postulate 3) on each successive trial. In Guthrie's words, "with successive practice periods more and more conditioners are enlisted, so that after twenty pairings there is a higher probability that the cue will have enough support from the presence of these additional newly conditioned stimuli to be effective" (Guthrie, 1935, p. 100). Voeks (1955) similarly points out that the artifactual appearance of incremental learning may result when data are grouped across a number of individuals. Some subjects may initially exhibit the required response on later trials than others. This yields a group incremental-like effect that is unrepresentative of the learning process in any one individual.

In a classic set of experiments, Voeks (1950) conditioned the human eyeblink response (originally stimulated by a puff of air) to occur following presentation of a buzz. Five groups of subjects underwent training, each under increasingly stable stimulus configurations. With the relevant stimuli (air puff and buzz) held constant for all groups, increasing stability in the remainder of the stimulus complex was positively correlated with rapid stability in response probability. The more stable the stimulus complex, the more sudden and permanent was the change in response probability. Under the most stable circumstances, subjects were required to breathe rhythmically prior to inhaling deeply while depressing a telegraph key with each hand. When both keys were depressed the buzz (CS) was automatically presented. These procedures were designed to minimize fluctuations in the stimulus compound generated by the behaving organism. Additional procedures stabilized a number of other aspects of the situation, including the individual's cognitive state. Results indicated that under such highly stable conditions 50 percent of the subjects exhibited no alternations in responding following their first correct response. That is, for these individuals learning was complete in a single trial. Moreover, the number of response alternations occurring increased as stability controls were progressively relaxed across groups.

Guthrie explains extinction on the basis of the conditioning of *incompatible responses* to the same stimulus complex. Unlearning, like learning, is not subject to strengthening or weakening; it, too, occurs in an all-or-nothing, one-trial fashion. *Unlearning, in fact, always involves learning something else.* Given that the sole condition required for the formation of an association is the contiguous occurrence of stimulus and response (postulate 1), why should the response ever fail to occur when the stimulus is presented? That is, why would extinction ever occur? If the initial response is either fatigued or otherwise prevented from occurring, and if an incompatible response occurs instead in the presence of the stimulus, then, according to postulate 2, only the second (last) response made in the situation can be associated with that situation. As Voeks (1950) explains it, "if the same stimulus pattern happens to be present while two incompatible responses are made, it will be cued to the postreme response only" (p. 348). The initially occurring response will now have automatically undergone extinction. In keeping with Guthrie's system, this is the only way to bring about the dissociation of two previously associated elements.

To account for the apparent strengthening effect of consequences without invoking the process of reinforcement or the law of effect as primary principles of learning, Guthrie focuses on the *mechanical arrangement* of the situation that prevails when reward is presented. Rewards always occur at the end of a series of responses. During the receipt of reinforcement, either the animal is exposed to a new set of stimuli introduced into the existing situation, or the animal is removed from the situation altogether. In either case, the transition to a new stimulus complex guarantees that the last response in the series is the response associated with the cues immediately preceding the receipt of reward. Exposure to a new stimulus pattern effectively removes the animal from the relevant cues for that response, thereby protecting the integrity of the association. "Instead of behavior being strengthened by reward, reward preserves it from disintegration" (Hilgard, 1956, p. 58). If no interference has occurred—that is, if no incompatible responses are evoked in the presence of those stimuli—when the subject is replaced into the situation the last response occurring in that situation tends to be repeated.

Supporters of Guthrie's pure association conducted a number of experiments to demonstrate that learning could occur in the *absence of reinforcement*. Parenthetically, it should be noted that Guthrie would have no objection to a purely empirical account of reinforcement that simply acknowledged the effect of consequences on the frequency of responding. As indicated earlier, Guthrie could not argue with the empirical results. The specific notion of reinforcement being challenged, however, was that of Clark Hull: reinforcement as the reduction of a physiological drive state (see the following discussion of Hull's theory). Presentation of non-nutritive saccharin, for example, following the occurrence of a response, acts as an effective consequence in spite of its inability to reduce the hunger drive. While it may be quite ineffective in reducing drive, it does provide the mechanical arrangement of conditions that will prevent an incompatible response from occurring in the presence of the relevant stimuli. Any outcome that removes the animal from the situation preserves the S–R association intact.

HULL'S BEHAVIOR THEORY

Science progresses through the experimental testing of theorems, which, in the ideal, are mathematically deduced from systems of formal postulates representing the theorist's basic premises. If the test of the derived theorem indicates agreement between prediction and empirical observation, the theorem has been demonstrated to be valid. This agreement in turn reflects upon the validity of the postulates from which the theorem was derived. If, on the other hand, prediction and results do not agree, the theorem is assumed to be a product of a faulty postulate. The postulate must then be either revised or extended in accord with the observed result. The process represents a self-correcting system in which the empirical test defines the standard of validity.

This process describes the conceptual methodology that guided the work of Clark Hull (1884–1952). Generally regarded as psychology's theoretician par excellence, Hull set about the task of formalizing, in accordance with the example set by Newton himself, a complete, objective theory of behavior. As such, Hull formalized the use of the *hypothetico-deductive method* in psychology, and he is therefore generally regarded as psychology's most rigorous formal theoretician. As Hull's student, Voeks took Hull's method and applied it to Guthrie's assumptions. Both theories therefore illustrate the use of the Hullian hypothetico-deductive method. The central concept in the Hullian system of behavior is that of *habit*. Habits are formed by the association of stimulus and response, and

Figure 2.3
Clark L. Hull (1884–1952). [From H. S. Langfeld, E. G. Boring, H. Werner, and R. M. Yerkes (Eds.), *A history of psychology in autobiography*, IV. Worcester, MA: Clark University Press, 1952. Reproduced by permission.]

the specific direction of behavior is therefore determined by the organism's experience. Though, as we shall see, numerous circumstances are required to predict the occurrence of a given behavior, in the final analysis the occurrence of behavior is based on the individual's experience.

Hull's theory is a complex system composed of seventeen basic *postulates* and seventeen derived *corollaries*. The former represent empirical or logical assumptions that are regarded initially as given; the latter constitute the theorems logically derived from these postulates and eventually subjected to empirical test. We will review only those elements of the theory essential to a general understanding of Hull's position. For a more complete account the reader is referred to what is regarded as the clearest full treatment of Hull's behavior theory, his book *Principles of Behavior*, published in 1943.

The conceptual basis of much that is contained in the Hullian system may seem quite familiar. For in it we see a highly detailed, greatly extended elaboration of Thorndike. With Thorndike, Hull emphasized the necessity and importance of the *law of effect*, the *gradual nature* of the learning process, and the importance of biological variables in the explanation of why consequences alter behavior. Much has been added that goes beyond Thorndike, but very little can be found that contradicts him. Recognizing the validity of data indicating that consequences were important in determining behavior, "Hull set himself the task of explaining ostensibly purposive behavior in terms of nonpurposeful, 'automatic,' or 'mechanical' principles" (Lowry, 1971, p. 184). For a deterministic science, behavior cannot actually be purposive—but it did *appear* to fulfill purpose. In seeking a physicalistic model with which to account for apparent purpose,

Hull turned to Darwin. Darwin, too, had faced the problem of finding a physical explanation for an apparently purposeful phenomenon. Organic change across generations appeared to serve an adaptive purpose. Darwin had successfully devised a physical account of the adaptations produced in organic evolution, and his account focused on the mechanism of natural selection. Determined to do the same for ontogenetic changes in behavior, Hull borrowed Darwin's model. Perhaps phylogenetic change could provide a useful analogue for the explanation of ontogenetic change. Note that Hull was *not* using evolutionary principles to explain behavioral change. He was instead extending the evolutionary *model* of change, that is, the logic of evolutionary change, into a different realm— the realm of behavioral ontogeny. Accordingly, Hull was to devise a mechanism by which certain responses were selected out of an existing pool of behavior (as genetic characters that facilitate reproductive success are selected from a much larger gene pool). The selected elements were then maintained to the relative exclusion of others. Darwin's mechanism of selection was reproductive success. Hull chose as his selecting mechanism *response-contingent reinforcement*—that is, stimulus consequences dependent for their occurrence upon the emission of a particular response.

To begin, Hull, like Darwin, needed *variability*. Any process of selection is predicated upon an existing range of elements from which to select. Moreover, the flexibility possible in the selection process depends on the amount of variability among elements. Since behavior appeared to be extremely flexible, Hull assumed extreme variability. This assumption was contained in his notion of the *behavioral tendency*. A given stimulus does not simply evoke a single specific response. Rather, the stimulus sets up a behavioral tendency consistent with the occurrence of a whole range of individual responses. Any one of these responses might be produced at a given time by the stimulus in question. Each individual response in the set has, moreover, a particular probability of occurrence. This probability represents that element's initial *reaction potential*. That response which is most adaptive will be selected out (by reinforcement) and will, therefore, have the greatest reaction potential. Of all the responses possible, given a particular behavioral tendency, the one with the greatest reaction potential will be the one that actually occurs. Each response has a measurable reaction potential, and by determining the factors that contribute to reaction potential it is possible to assign a probability value to the occurrence of any response in any situation—in effect, to predict behavior. This was Hull's task, and his theory essentially addressed interactions among factors contributing to reaction potential.

The most familiar formal statement of the theory makes use of seventeen postulates and seventeen corollaries. The first two of the postulates deal with the organism's innate response tendencies and with the internal contiguity of stimulus and response. Like Guthrie, Hull required contiguity; for Hull, however, much more was required in addition. Postulates 3 and 4 provide the cornerstones of the theory. Postulate 3 states the *principle of primary reinforcement*. With this statement Hull explains why Thorndike's law of effect works. Stimulus–response connections are strengthened when they occur in association with the *reduction* of a *physiological drive state*. For a hungry animal, eating alleviates a biological need, thereby removing the internal tension-producing stimuli generated by that need. Such reductions in drive stimuli are responsible for the ability of certain consequences to strengthen the connections that precede them. Primary reinforcement is therefore equivalent to drive reduction. Moreover, a neutral stimulus associated with a rapid reduction in drive will itself acquire reinforcing properties and is therefore the basis of *secondary reinforcement*.

For Hull, unlike Guthrie, learning was a gradual process. Postulate 4 describes the *law of habit formation*. *Habit* is defined as "a functional connection between *s* [stimulus] and *r* [response]" (Hull, 1943, p. 387). The strength of a habit increases as a function of *increasing numbers of reinforced trials*. Nothing else affects *habit strength* directly. Only reinforcement (drive reduction) produces an immediate and direct effect on the strength of a connection. As we shall see, however, habit strength is only one of the many factors that determine the reaction potential of a given response.

The next three postulates in Hull's system describe three additional factors contributing to reaction potential. Postulate 5 deals with *drive*. Drive actuates (energizes) behavior *and* produces increments in habit strength via drive reduction. Increases in habit strength in turn yield greater reaction potential. With no drive, there will be no energy for behavior. Moreover, with no drive, no learning can occur because no drive reduction (the sole determinant of habit strength) is possible. Another factor contributing to reaction potential is the *intensity* of the relevant stimulus. In postulate 6 Hull describes this effect as *stimulus intensity dynamism*. For any given level of habit strength, as the intensity of the stimulus increases, reaction potential increases. With learning (habit strength) held constant, therefore, an intense stimulus will render a response relatively more likely to occur than will a weaker stimulus. For Hull, *incentive*, described in postulate 7, was defined by the magnitude of the reinforcing stimulus. Larger amounts of food reinforcement, for example, constitute greater incentive. The greater the incentive motivation, the greater the reaction potential of a given response.

Postulate 8 summarizes all those factors which contribute to *increased reaction potential*. Formally, it reads:

$$_sE_R = D \cdot K \cdot V \cdot {_sH_R}$$

where reaction potential ($_sE_R$) is determined by drive (D), incentive (K), stimulus intensity dynamism (V), and, of course, habit strength ($_sH_R$). These factors characterize the essentials of the stimulus situation within which any response must occur.

The picture is, however, still more complicated. Many of the remaining postulates, for example, describe factors that *decrease reaction potential*. Inhibitory factors, which Hull termed *reactive inhibition* and *conditioned inhibition*, generate negative reaction potential. These detract from the overall excitatory effect of the factors (postulate 8) that serve to increase reaction potential. If the combined excitatory effects are exceeded by the combined inhibitory effects, the response will not occur, and *extinction* is said to result. To review how inhibitory factors detract from reaction potential let us consider *reactive inhibition* in more detail. Any time a response occurs, fatigue, pain or some expenditure of energy must also occur. Because any one of these may result, the act of engaging in the response itself slightly decreases the future likelihood of that response occurring. Reactive inhibition also subtracts from reaction potential in that it actually generates a need for inactivity. The "action" that reduces inhibition is *rest*; the natural means for reducing the *inhibitory drive*, therefore, makes all behavior (except rest) less likely to occur. In Hull's view, the reduction in response probability produced by nonreinforcement (extinction) occurs *not* because nonreinforcement directly weakens the strength of a connection but because it fails to increment habit strength. This in turn allows inhibitory factors to exert a relatively greater effect. The result, of course, is an overall decrease in reaction potential.

Hull's system is both more complete and far more quantitative than can be expressed in this short review. His goal was the complete explanation and prediction of behavior in precise quantitative terms. The system constitutes a complete nonteleological account of the adaptive character of behavioral change. Learning remains the central element. John Watson's radical behaviorism denied the subjective aspects of behavior; as a consequence, Watson was forced to reject Thorndike's law of effect, with its implicit notions of reward and purpose. The law of effect, unacceptable in Watson's behaviorism, became the very basis of Hull's system. Hull recognized the apparent purposefulness that characterized goal-directed behavior, and in fact adopted the law of effect as the basis of a selection process that provided a mechanistic account of purpose.

TOLMAN'S PURPOSIVE BEHAVIORISM

Edward C. Tolman (1886–1959) also sought to account for purpose in behavior within the framework of the learning process. In doing so, however, Tolman diverged greatly from both Thorndike and Hull, though along a path very different from the one taken by Guthrie. Tolman's theory of learning is a *cognitive approach* based on the establishment of

Figure 2.4
Edward Chace Tolman (1886–1959). [From H. S.
Langfeld, E. G. Boring, H. Werner, and R. M.
Yerkes (Eds.), *A history of psychology in
autobiography*, IV. Worcester, MA: Clark University
Press, 1952. Reproduced by permission.]

expectancies between particular cues (signs) and particular outcomes. The
organism learns that when it encounters a stimulus it can expect a particular event to follow shortly. Learning involves the establishment of *relationships* between cues in the environment and the animal's expectations. As
such, the relevant connection is *not* between stimulus and response (as
for Thorndike, Guthrie, and Hull) but between *stimuli* and other *stimuli*.
The set of expectations generated by a situation, and the relationship between that situation and its associated outcome produce in the organism a
cognitive map whereby the animal comes to know its environment. Learning is the acquisition of *meaning*.

The actual occurrence of the molar response is not required for the
establishment of the expectancy. Moreover, biological notions of reinforcement based, for example, on the existence of physiological needs
have no place in Tolman's system. Hull's principle of primary reinforcement by drive reduction and Thorndike's law of effect are both rejected
and replaced by far more cognitive notions. According to Tolman, biological drives play no part in learning; they act merely to energize, or activate,
behavior and have no effect on the strengthening or weakening of connections.

Moreover, for Tolman behavior was not "apparently" purposive; it was
in fact purposive. Molar behavior is goal-directed. That is, it is "regulated
in accordance with objectively determinable ends" (Hilgard, 1956, p. 186).
What is important in a behavioral event is not that it involves a particular
musculature but that it leads to a particular goal. In Tolman's words:

> For us, behavior has emergent patterns and meanings which are other than
> the patterns and meanings of the gland secretions and muscle contractions

which underlie it, though no doubt they are completely dependent on the latter [Tolman, 1967, p. 417].

[Behavior], no doubt, is strictly dependent upon an underlying manifold of physics and chemistry, but initially and as a matter of first identification, behavior as behavior reeks of purpose and of cognition [p. 12].

Hence Tolman's view is considered a *purposive behaviorism*. Though this may seem at first to inject subjective elements into behaviorism, Tolman's purposive behaviorism was no less objective for its assumptions of true purpose. Notwithstanding his use of a cognitive and teleological language, Tolman relied exclusively on the data of behavior. Any inferences drawn to cognition or purpose originate directly in observations of behavior change.

In rejecting Hull's principle of primary reinforcement, Tolman was obliged to provide an alternative account of the effects of consequences on behavior. This he did with his *principle of confirmation*. This principle maintains that when receipt of a goal object substantiates the organism's expectations, those expectations and the behaviors they guide will occur with greater frequency in the future. Confirmation strengthens expectancies and disconfirmation weakens them. Accordingly, though reinforcement (drive reduction) is superfluous to learning, the repeated "confirming" of expectancies about what leads to what defines the essential basis of learning.

Tolman's distinctive approach focused the theorists' attentions on a number of questions that represented central issues in the psychology of learning. Among these was the question "What is learned?" The debates on this issue were nowhere more evident than in the confrontations between the Hullian school and the Tolmanian school on the problem of *place versus response learning*. Do connections occur between stimulus and response, or do they occur between stimulus and stimulus? That is, does the organism learn a particular response in a given situation, or does the organism learn a cognitive route to the place where confirmation is evident? The latter view assumes that no one fixed muscular sequence results; rather, organisms engage in whatever response will get them to the place where they expect to find the goal object. One type of experiment designed to settle this issue compared "response learners" with "place learners." Deprived rats were situated in an elevated cross maze and required to find food in the maze. For one group (the response learners) food was always located to the animal's right. A right-turn response, therefore, was always required, though the actual location of the food in the maze might change. Figure 2.5 indicates that the response learners starting at S_2 (with the food at F_2) must make the same response as those starting at S_1 (with the food at F_1), though the food is actually located in a different place. This manipulation, therefore, requires subjects to learn a new place even though engaging in the same response. For the place learners, on the other hand, the food was always *located* at F_1. Starting at

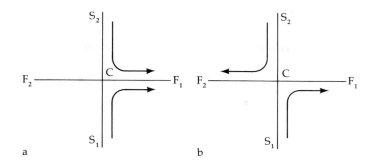

a   b

Figure 2.5
Place versus response learning. (a) Place learners theoretically learn
relationships between stimuli and therefore always run to the same
place (F_1). (b) Response learners, on the other hand, are assumed to
associate the stimulus with a particular response and therefore
should always engage in the same response (a right turn). [After J.
D. Chaplin and T. S. Krawiec, *Systems and theories of psychology,* 3rd
ed. Copyright © 1968, 1974 by Holt, Rinehart and Winston, Inc.;
copyright © 1960 by J. D. Chaplin and T. S. Krawiec. Redrawn by
permission of Holt, Rinehart and Winston, Inc.]

S_1, however, required a right-turn response, while starting at S_2 required
a left-turn response. For the place learners, therefore, place was held constant while the actual response changed. Which animals learned more
efficiently?—those that could reliably depend on the response (always
turn right) or those that could reliably depend on the place (always go
there)? Tolman's data indicated that the place learners were much more
successful than the response learners. Learning for all subjects in the
place group occurred within 8 trials, while in the response group the
criterion of 10 successive trials without error required as many as 72 trials.

A second major focus was the issue of *latent learning.* Latent learning is
covert learning, which can proceed without either an observed change in
behavior (unnecessary because of the S–S nature of the connection) or
any necessary reduction in a physiological drive state (which Hull would
have required). Hundreds of latent learning experiments were performed
to resolve this issue. Though no one experiment can be taken as representative, the description that follows captures the flavor of the problem.

Three groups of rats were tested in a modified T-maze. A *conventionally
rewarded group* received food with each successful completion of the maze.
A second, *no-reward group* was allowed to wander the maze *at random* but
never found food in the goal box. A third group, the *delayed-reward group,*
received no food reward for the first ten days of maze experience. These
subjects simply wandered the maze as did subjects in the no-reward
group. On the eleventh day, however, reward was introduced into the
goal box and presented contingent upon the successful completion of the
maze on each day thereafter. Figure 2.6 illustrates the results of the exper-

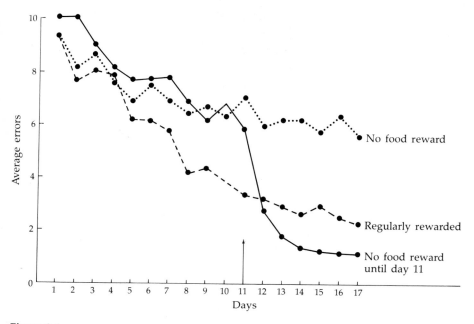

Figure 2.6
Evidence for latent learning. The delayed-reward group learned very quickly after
reward was introduced, suggesting that the unrewarded experience in the same maze
had produced some covert learning. [After E. C. Tolman and C. H. Honzik, Introduction
and removal of reward, and maze performance in rats, *University of California Publications
in Psychology, 4,* 257–275.]

iment. Note that little learning was observed (errors remained high) in the
no-reward group, while the standard gradual learning curve was evidenced in the behavior of the conventionally rewarded group. Of particular interest is the behavior of the delayed-reward group. On the early
(no-reward) trials, performance did *not* appear to improve substantially
with experience, as was expected. As soon as reward was introduced into
the situation, however, the animals' behavior changed dramatically—
much more quickly than would have been expected if the animals had
actually only begun to learn at that point. Hull, in fact, would have predicted that the performance of the delayed-reward group would parallel
that of the conventionally rewarded group except that in the former, improvement with experience should also be delayed until drive reduction
could begin to take effect (day 11). At that time, learning would begin and
would follow the same gradual progression already evident in the behavior of the conventionally rewarded group. This was not the case. The
dramatic abrupt change in the behavior of the delayed-reward group
suggested to Tolman that "latent learning" had taken place throughout.
While wandering the maze in the early days, the animals had begun to
acquire S–S connections, cognitive maps of the environment. Perform-

ance changed abruptly only because the animals had been learning all along. The presence of reward simply served to translate the learning into performance. Tolman concluded that even in the absence of both the systematic performance of the correct response and the occurrence of reinforcement via drive reduction, learning had taken place.

SKINNER'S OPERANT CONDITIONING

The work of B. F. Skinner (b. 1904) represents both the greatest divergence from the tradition of learning in American psychology (exemplified by the theorists discussed above) and the most significant force in altering that tradition from within the field. Though Skinner clearly shares in the heritage of Thorndike, his approach to the explanation of behavior change is unique. Rather than formulating a specific theoretical position, he is often regarded as an avowed *anti*theorist. Skinner prefers not to speak of learning at all, but refers instead simply to changes in behavior. It is characteristic of the early Skinnerian approach to scrupulously avoid the kinds of speculation couched in unobservables that are so often associated with theory construction. As a consequence, Skinner's system has developed to a large degree independently of the focal issues addressed by the theorists above. For example, because Skinner did not speak of unobservables such as "connections," the question of what the relevant connections are between is not treated in his system.

Skinner's approach is best characterized, not by his position on these traditional questions, but by two *methodological directives* that nullify many

Figure 2.7
Burrhus F. Skinner (b. 1904).
[The Bettmann Archive, Inc.]

of the questions. The first of these is Skinner's insistence on relying exclusively on phenomena that are *directly observable*. While Hull and Tolman, for example, speculated about why consequences strengthen responding, Skinner's stance does not go beyond (1) the empirical statement that consequences *do* strengthen behavior and (2) an account of the conditions under which this strengthening effect occurs. Skinner is consistent both in denying Hull his physiological unobservables and denying Tolman his cognitive unobservables. This brings us to Skinner's second methodological directive. Psychology must be regarded as an *independent science of behavior*, requiring neither the subjective mental constructs that characterized the prebehavioral science of consciousness nor the speculative physiological constructs that so captured the imaginations of Hull and others. Psychology need account for behavior only in terms of behavior.

Central to Skinner's system, and drawn more clearly here than in any of the other positions described, is the distinction between *operants* and *respondents*. *Respondents* are instances of behavior reminiscent of classical reflexes. A respondent is a response innately connected to a clearly specifiable stimulus. The stimulus is said by Skinner to *elicit* the response. That is, the correlation between presentation of the stimulus and the occurrence of the response is extremely high. As such, the frequency with which the response occurs is primarily a function of stimulus frequency. Moreover, respondents occur independently of their consequences. Irrespective of what outcome follows responding, if the stimulus is present the response is very likely to occur. *Operants* differ from respondents on all of the dimensions described above. Operant behavior is not reliably correlated with the occurrence of any single stimulus. Operant behavior "cannot be shown to be under the control of eliciting stimuli . . . no stimulus can be found that will elicit it" (Skinner, 1938, p. 20–21). Rather than being elicited, therefore, the operant response is, in Skinner's terminology, *emitted* by the organism. The environmental stimulus may eventually "set the occasion upon which a response will occur . . . but it does not elicit the response" (Skinner, 1938, p. 22).

> The kind of behavior that is correlated with specific eliciting stimuli may be called *respondent* behavior and a given correlation *a respondent*. The term is intended to carry the sense of a relation to a prior event. Such behavior as is not under this kind of control I shall call *operant*. . . . An operant is an identifiable part of behavior of which it may be said . . . that no correlated stimulus can be detected upon occasions when it is observed to occur. It is studied as an event appearing spontaneously with a given frequency [Skinner, 1938, pp. 20–21].

Though, as we shall see, the distinction between operants and respondents has become less and less clear, the notions of a variable response class and control by consequent events remain among the basic assumptions of the Skinnerian system.

A second central feature of Skinner's approach consists in the distinction between *two types of conditioning*. These describe the different procedures required to bring about the modification of operants versus respondents. Respondents become conditioned reflexes according to a procedure that Skinner called *Type S conditioning*. The essential feature of this procedure is the correlation of one stimulus with another stimulus, irrespective of the animal's responding. In Type S conditioning *(respondent conditioning)*, $stimulus_1$ bears a response-independent relation to $stimulus_2$, and the stimuli are presented whether or not a particular response occurs. Operants, on the other hand, become conditioned reflexes according to a procedure that Skinner called *Type R conditioning*. In Type R conditioning *(operant conditioning)*, behavior changes when the occurrence of a *response* is correlated with the subsequent occurrence of a particular stimulus. Occurrence of the stimulus in Type R conditioning is therefore *response-dependent* in that presentation of the stimulus depends on the animal's first engaging in the appropriate response. The response-dependent stimulus, termed the *reinforcer*, is presented only if the response occurs; presentation of the stimulus is said to be *contingent* upon the organism's producing the response. Because it takes place independently of responding and is instead defined by relations among stimuli, respondent conditioning is essentially equivalent to Pavlovian conditioning. Operant conditioning, by contrast, may be described as similar to Thorndikian conditioning in that, for both, the consequences of responding (presentation of the stimulus) modify the likelihood of the response's subsequent occurrence.

Similarly consistent with Thorndike's emphasis on consequences, operant conditioning has focused on the *law of effect*. Though the specific content of the law has evolved very differently in Skinner's system (see chapter 4), Thorndike's emphasis on the outcome of responding has been retained. Future occurrences of a response are determined by the consequences that have followed similar responses in the past. The *operant class* is defined as that group of responses which, by virtue of their similarity, are similarly affected by the consequences associated with any one member of the class. In effect, the operant must always be viewed as a group of responses rather than as an isolated behavioral event. While Skinner has clearly distinguished between two categories of behavior change—operant and respondent conditioning—the Skinnerian approach has assumed that for complex organisms operant conditioning is by far the more important of the two. The experimental analysis of the maintenance of operant behavior has, therefore, received the greatest empirical attention. The law of effect and its attendant notion of reinforcement have become the backbone of the Skinnerian system.

While the other psychologists treated thus far in the chapter borrowed heavily from Thorndike's methodology as well as from the substance of his work, Skinner did not. In fact, Skinner introduced a number of methodological advances that have subsequently revolutionized the psychology of learning. Among these are the in-depth analysis of the behavior of an *individual subject* observed under a number of different conditions; an emphasis on the extreme control of the animal's environment, and a reluctance to make reference to any unobservable factors in the explanation of behavior; a focus on the factors that maintain stability in behavior as opposed to those that induce changes in behavior; and, perhaps most important, the assessment of behavior as a *continuous process* rather than as an isolated event.

This final point requires some elaboration. Though Thorndike, Hull, Guthrie, and Tolman also generally assumed that behavior was a continuous process, they continued to study it in situations that effectively did isolate it as a discrete event. In the maze situation, for example, each running of the maze is regarded as the behavioral episode of interest. At the end of each trial, when the animal is taken out of the maze, the continuity of behavior is interrupted. Any major sequential properties of behavior, therefore, are left unobserved. Skinner, on the other hand, placed animals in a controlled environment (the Skinner box) in which the continuous occurrence of the response could be determined, not by the experimenter taking the animal in and out of the experimental situation, but by the prolonged and continuous effects of circumstances that prevail in the situation. Since the response could potentially occur at any time (not just when the experimenter allowed it to), Skinner was able to focus on the *rate*—number of responses per unit time—with which the response did occur. Thus in operant conditioning *response rate* became the relevant measure of interest. Viewing behavior explicitly as a continuous process and assessing that process in terms of the rate at which the response occurs (given free opportunity) opened the field to a whole new experimental domain—the domain of time itself.

It is to the notion of *time* that we must turn to realize Skinner's unique substantive contribution to the investigation of behavior change. The emphasis on contiguity has been important all along, but operant conditioning's analysis of temporal sequencing in behavior has gone beyond the notion of simple contiguity. Skinner drew psychology's attention to the idea that the sequencing of environmental events has critical effects on behavior apart from the absolute quality of those events or of their isolated association with behavior. That is, the *temporal sequencing of stimuli* is equally as important as the nature of the stimulus itself. The importance of patterning, or of the temporal order characterizing the presentation of stimuli, is embodied in Skinner's emphasis on *schedules of reinforcement.* Note first that reinforcement is a very different thing for Skinner than for Hull or Thorndike. Rather than inferring a specific physiological process (satisfaction or drive reduction), Skinner defined reinforcement empirically. By *reinforcement,* he meant nothing more than the observation that under certain conditions when a response is followed by a particular event, the effect of that event is to increase the future rate of occurrence of the response. This empirical result is reinforcement. Nothing more need be inferred. As such, reinforcement refers "both to a procedure and to an effect of the procedure. The procedure requires a particular form of an animal's behavior to be succeeded by a particular environmental event. The effect of the procedure is an increase in the rate of the particular form of behavior. The events are called reinforcers, and the forms of behavior are called responses" (Herrnstein, 1966, p. 33). Reinforcement is merely the presentation of an event that subsequently increases response rate.

Now, back to time. *Schedules of reinforcement* refer to periodic, patterned sequences of reinforcing stimuli. The schedule describes how the relevant (reinforcing) events are distributed over time, and what their relationship is to behavior. As we shall see in subsequent chapters, the data of operant conditioning have repeatedly indicated that the precise sequential nature of periodically occurring reinforcers can be an important determinant of the continuity characteristic of behavior in a given situation.

We have seen learning pass from the hands of the philosophers into those of the experimental psychologists, for a time to become the central concept in the explanation of behavior. In the 1940s and 1950s efforts to solve the puzzles of learning dominated experimental psychology. We have summarized some of the major theoretical attempts to solve these puzzles in essentially their ideal forms. In fact, when put to the empirical test in decades of research, all of these theories were found to be fraught with problems. The major theories and positions became one another's adversaries, with each theoretical camp attacking the weaknesses of the others. Conflicting results, inconclusive sets of "crucial experiments," and overburdening theoretical complexity resulted.[1] Many of the questions were left unanswered. Hull, Guthrie, and Tolman died, but the puzzles remained. Having almost exhausted the other views, experimental psychology turned to the more purely empirical approach of Skinner, and operant conditioning (also termed the experimental analysis of behavior) became the predominant approach to the study of behavior change.

RETROSPECTIVE: THE PROBLEM OF PURPOSE

The work of theorists discussed in this chapter has provided much of the direction of modern experimental psychology. Their common interests therefore represent a major domain of the new science. From its inception, objective psychology faced the problem (stated explicitly by Hull) of accounting for the widespread occurrence of apparently purposive, goal-directed behavior within the framework of a deterministic science. Much behavior appears to serve certain well-defined ends. The pigeon's key-peck functions to provide food. Human verbal behavior effectively

---

[1] Further analysis of these problems is beyond the scope of this chapter. For a more complete account of the issues debated by these workers, the reader is referred to the major text of the era, E. Hilgard's *Theories of Learning* (1956).

serves to attract the attention of others or to make the speaker's needs known. The consequences of an action (the end obtained) cannot, however, serve as the determinant of *that specific action*. If so, it would appear that the effect might precede the cause, and our assumption of causal determinism makes this impossible. To avoid this problem of "final causes" some mechanism must be found whereby the consequences of one action become the *antecedents* of future, similar actions. The efforts of the psychologists described in this chapter, therefore, converged on the quest for a mechanism of purposive behavior.

Earlier accounts of apparent purpose in the behavior of extremely primitive organisms had made use of response-independent mechanisms (Jennings, 1906; Löeb, 1918). Rather than focusing on the effects of consequences on future actions, these analyses focused on very simple response mechanisms such as tropisms and conditional reflexes. Jacques Löeb, for example, explained the apparently purposive locomotor behavior of various invertebrates on the basis of the *tropistic* or *forced movement theory* of orientation. A tropism is a "specific orienting response to a localized stimulus" (Maier and Schneirla, 1935), which orients the organism toward or away from a stimulus. Löeb maintained that behavior directed toward a stimulus ("goal-directed" behavior) was in fact forced by the effects of stimuli differentially impinging on bilaterally symmetrical sensory receptors. When stimuli impinge equally on all receptors (as from a light shining directly behind the organism), movement will continue in its existing direction. If, however, receptors on either side are unequally stimulated, the muscles of one side of the animal will respond more vigorously, and the organism will be forced to move toward or away from the source of stimulation. The animal will continue reorienting in this manner until the stimulus once again impinges equally on all receptors.

The mechanistic appeal of this approach, coupled with its success in explaining orientation in primitive organisms, promoted efforts to account for all goal-directed behavior (including the "higher mental processes" of humans) on the basis of automatic, tropistic responses. Similar efforts were directed at explaining the construction of goal-directed behavior out of flexible reflex chains. By and large, however, these efforts failed. The successful explanation of complex goal-directed behavior required something new, and the analysis of changes in behavior following response-dependent consequences provided the novel element.

The major theorists of the Great Age of Learning Theories represent the continuation of these efforts to account for purpose. At the hands of these individuals, however, the focus shifted away from tropisms and reflexes to control by consequences. For Skinner, Tolman, and Hull, purposive behavior was equivalent to behavior that could be modified by its immediate consequences. Principles of operant and instrumental conditioning were developed to provide the mechanism by which purposive behavior could be explained within the rubric of a deterministic science. Skinner (1953) writes:

Statements which use such words as "incentive" or "purpose" are usually reducible to statements about operant conditioning, and only a slight change is required to bring them within the framework of natural science. Instead of saying that a man behaves because of the consequences which are to follow his behavior, we simply say that he behaves because of the consequences which have followed similar behavior in the past [Skinner, 1953, p. 87].

In this way consequences become antecedents, and purpose becomes amenable to scientific analysis.

The questions asked by these workers are questions of behavioral ontogeny. As such, they focus on the factors that motivate and sustain changes in the behavior of an individual across a relatively short span of time, outlining the major parameters of purposive behavior. What, for example, is the effect of the patterning of consequences on future responding? When an organism is faced with alternative consequences, under what conditions will the selection of one alternative prevail to the exclusion of the other, and how are the effects of this selection manifest in future responding?

Numerous questions have, however, been left unanswered by this approach. Many of these, in fact, more appropriately represent questions of behavioral phylogeny. What, for example, are the attributes that define an effective consequence? Why do certain consequences more readily alter certain responses? Which responses (or which organisms) are amenable to change and which are not? In the chapters to follow we will review contemporary approaches to the analysis of purposive behavior, focusing on recent extensions of operant conditioning. Turning then to behavioral biology, we will address those aspects of behavioral phylogeny that complement our understanding of ontogenetic behavior change.

3 Habituation, Sensitization, Classical Conditioning

Though the preceding chapter emphasized American psychology's historical focus on associative learning processes, our systematic treatment of learning will begin with the phenomena of nonassociative learning. *Nonassociative learning* is said to occur when relatively permanent modifications in behavior take place with repetitive exposure to a single stimulus. Such changes in behavior presumably occur independently of associations between two or more distinct stimuli. Nonassociative learning phenomena had been described long before the major era of learning theory (Jennings, 1906; Sherrington, 1906), but for many years psychologists regarded them with little, if any interest. Learning theorists neglected to attempt to explain the relevant effects; many, in fact, disregarded the nonassociative processes as forms of learning. Instead, interest focused on classical and instrumental conditioning, while habituation and sensitization were often treated as confounding variables.

This situation has changed drastically within the last twenty years. Definitions of learning have broadened to include nonassociative as well as associative forms of behavior modification, and research on nonassociative learning processes has accelerated. This trend has been especially evident in the literature on habituation. Why? How could phenomena once regarded as of little importance—not really learning at all—become, not just bona fide forms of learning, but, in the eyes of some investigators, basic to all other learning processes? Frequently, scientists' interest in and enthusiasm for one class of events can obscure and detract from other, perhaps equally important events going on at the same time. Nonassociative learning, like conditioning, represents a relatively permanent modification in behavior as a result of experience. As we shall see, information appears to be stored, and behavior occurs differently in the future as a function of the effects of experience. By these criteria, nonassociative processes, too, qualify as learning.

Because the most vigorous experimental and theoretical efforts have been directed at the study of habituation, and because interaction between habituation and sensitization constitute a major theoretical focus, the chapter's treatment of nonassociative learning will be confined to habituation and sensitization. We will then turn to an account of what is traditionally regarded as the most basic form of associative learning: classical conditioning.

HABITUATION

Habituation has been broadly defined as "learning what not to do" (Razran, 1971, p. 29). Within this framework, discussion has initially centered on the adaptive value of habituation as a form of learning. In their natural environments organisms are continually bombarded with many different stimuli. A response to any one of these stimuli may be critically important. Sudden noises, for example, may signal the approach of a hungry predator. Yet both time and energy restrictions demand that the animal respond to some of these stimuli while ignoring others. How, then, does the individual select from among the many stimuli sensed at a given time the one most deserving of response? This may not always be a problem. Frequently, innate response hierarchies determine that if a particular stimulus is present, responding to that stimulus will prevail, even in the presence of equally prominent stimuli that might otherwise elicit a response. When faced with a stimulus signaling danger, for example, a hungry animal engaged in eating will stop and, depending on the nature of the signal, may either adopt a defensive threatening posture or attempt to flee. In some situations, however, the signaling value of the stimulus may be *ambiguous*. Rustling leaves may represent either an approaching predator or an alteration in wind conditions—two stimuli whose associated responses probably occupy very different positions in the organism's response hierarchy. To be on the safe side—in case it is the predator—the animal must initially respond. But the organism that continues to respond to an innocuous stimulus is wasting valuable time and energy engaging in uneconomical behavior. Klopfer (1973), for example, cites results indicating that some insectivorous birds must spend 90 percent of each winter day eating insects (one catch every 2.5 seconds) in order to maintain themselves. For such individuals, too much time spent responding to unimportant stimuli may mean starvation.

In fact, organisms do *not* continue to respond to potentially important, but situationally irrelevant stimuli. As repeated experience indicates that no predator is in the offing—this time it really is the leaves—escape or defensive responses will cease to occur. Time and energy can then safely be invested in responding to the next most important stimulus present (presumably insects, in the case of the insectivorous birds). The organism has, for that moment, effectively learned what not to do and may therefore turn to something else. This waning of responding under conditions of repeated stimulation is *habituation*. When a specific stimulus is presented over and over, the response initially produced by that stimulus will gradually *decrease* and may cease to occur altogether. In many such cases, habituation is said to have occurred, usually to the distinct advantage of the behaving organism.

Designating a particular decline in responding as a case of habituation learning, however, requires more than simply observing a response decrement. Not all observed decrements can be considered habituation; animals often cease to respond under other conditions as well. An animal repeatedly presented with food, which it then eats, will gradually engage in less and less eating behavior. The decrement in eating, however, is most likely due to the physiologically *satiating* effects of ingestion and is therefore not considered a learning phenomenon. Similarly, a failure to respond due either to *muscular fatigue* or to *sensory adaptation* is assumed to be a result of processes distinct from decremental learning. In neither case does the animal learn what not to do; rather it ceases to respond for reasons usually described as "peripheral"—involving neural receptor or effector processes rather than "central" learning processes, which are assumed to require higher-level neural integration. Experiments examining habituation must be careful to demonstrate that the observed failure to respond represents decremental learning and not some other, nonlearning, decremental process. A closer analysis of the nature and characteristics of habituation should indicate how such distinctions can be made.

Stimulus-Specificity of Habituation

The primary characteristic of habituation learning is that it is *stimulus-specific*. That is, a decrement in responding occurs only with the presentation of either the training stimulus itself (termed the *habituating stimulus*) or stimuli very similar to the habituating stimulus (see the discussion of generalization later in this section). Consider how the situation differs with either fatigue or satiation. In the case of fatigue, the presentation of any stimulus whose associated response involves use of the fatigued muscles should produce decremental responding. This would be expected irrespective of the nature of that stimulus. With complete satiation, too, the animal is physiologically unresponsive to food *in general*. Any foodstuff, regardless of the stimulus properties of the substance, should

be ineffective in eliciting eating.[1] Both fatigue and satiation might therefore be considered *response-specific* decremental processes, whereas
habituation, which occurs only with presentation of a specific stimulus or
class of stimuli, is *stimulus-specific*.

The stimulus-specificity of habituation is demonstrated clearly in Peeke
and Veno's (1973) studies of decrements in the aggressive behaviors directed toward adjacently territorial rivals in the three-spined stickleback.
The authors first comment on the adaptive value of such specificity. The
fish established in a neighboring, adjacent territory does initially constitute a stimulus to aggress. But continued aggressive display toward this
individual, who represents a neighbor not an intruder, constitutes a
maladaptive waste of energy and time. Habituation here is clearly adaptive, and the fish are known to respond accordingly. In time the neighbor
fails to elicit aggression. If, however, decrements in aggressive defense
are not specific to the neighbor but extend to all other conspecifics (members of the same species), the resident fish's territory will quickly be lost
to a highly aggressive intruding non-neighbor. Aggressive behavior in
general should not wane; rather, decrements should be seen only in aggressive behaviors elicited specifically by continued exposure to the
neighbor. To test the validity of their account, Peeke and Veno (1973)
placed "intruding" fish housed in glass tubes in specific locations of the
resident's tank. After 30 minutes of continuous exposure followed by a
15-minute rest period, subjects were re-exposed to one of the following
stimuli: (1) the same fish placed in the same location, (2) the same fish
placed in a different location, (3) a different fish placed in the same location, or (4) a different fish placed in a different location. Results, illustrated in Figure 3.1, indicate that minimal aggression was elicited by the
same fish in either the same or a different location (though more aggression was evident in the latter). By contrast, a different fish placed in either
the same or a different location evoked much more aggression. The
greatest reinstatement of responding occurred when both the individual
and the location were novel. Though the effects of generalization may be
confounded here with the effects of dishabituation (discussed later in this
chapter), in either case the data clearly indicate the stimulus-specific
character of habituation.

Rate of Habituation

In general, the rate at which a response habituates is assumed to be determined by the *intensity* of the habituating stimulus and by the *frequency*
with which that stimulus is presented. If a very intense stimulus is presented infrequently (with a long *interstimulus interval*), the response will

---

[1]Partial satiation with one food may be reversed if a novel preferred food is presented.
Complete satiation, however, should render the subject uninterested in all food.

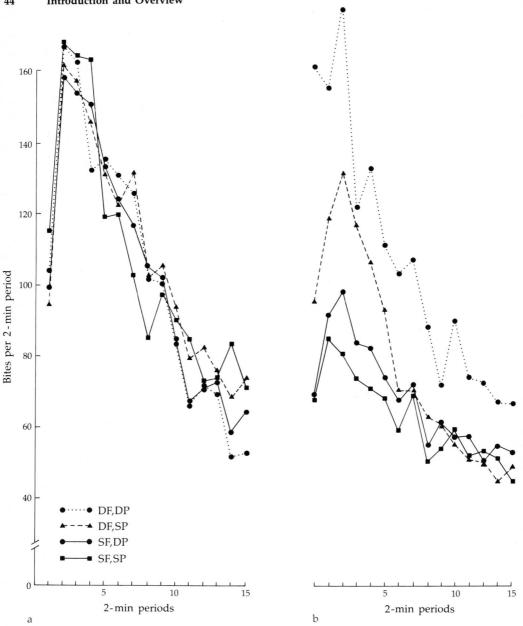

Figure 3.1
Stimulus-specificity in the habituation of the biting response of the three-spined stickleback. (a) Session 1. Responding during the initial training session habituated in all fish tested. (b) Session 2. The amount of responding seen in the same animal during the second session depended on the familiarity of the stimulus presented—whether the same fish in the same or a different place (SF, SP or SF, DP) or a different fish in the same or a different place (DF, SP or DF, DP). A different stimulus fish presented in a different place (DF, DP) elicited the most responding. [After Peeke and Veno, 1973.]

habituate slowly, if at all. Russell (1967), for example, repeatedly presented a shadow stimulus to guppies at intervals of either 15 seconds, 2 minutes, or 4 minutes. The defensive jerk response was found to habituate more rapidly and more completely with a 15-second interstimulus interval. Similarly, earthworms presented a weak electrical stimulus (150 mV) ceased responding roughly four times as quickly as those trained with a much stronger (300 mV) stimulus.

While these generalities have traditionally been taken as characteristic of the habituation process, more recent work has suggested that such general parametric relationships may not be as broadly representative of the habituation process as was originally assumed (see discussions in Hinde, 1970a; Peeke and Peeke, 1973). In many instances the effects of interstimulus interval and stimulus intensity may in fact be quite specific to the particular stimulus-response relationship under investigation. Peeke and Peeke (1970), for example, have investigated the habituation of aggressive responding to live rival males in the Siamese fighting fish, *Betta splendens*. Subjects receiving distributed experience (15 minutes of continuous exposure per day for a period of 20 days) habituated more rapidly than those receiving massed experience (1 hour of continuous exposure per day for 5 days). Here, therefore, increased frequency (massed presentation), resulted in slower habituation. A comparable procedure employing a different species of aggressive fish (convict cichlids) in a similar situation, however, yielded the opposite effect (Peeke, Herz, and Gallagher, 1971). Massed training produced more rapid habituation of both biting and aggressive display than did distributed training. Following Hinde (1970b), Peeke and Peeke (1973) have proposed that factors such as the naturalness of the stimulus-response relationship under study may alter the parametric effects of frequency and intensity.

The Interstimulus Interval

Methodological considerations also emphasize the difficulties of assessing the effects of parametric variations in interstimulus interval (ISI). Davis (1970) has pointed out that in most situations testing ISI effects, each stimulus is at once a training stimulus and a testing stimulus. That is, with each stimulus presentation an habituation effect is being measured (testing), *and* each subsequent stimulus presumably also enhances the process of habituation itself (training). Frequency differences in training are therefore completely confounded with frequency differences in testing; and subjects presented a shorter ISI during training also receive a shorter ISI during testing. Are the effects of manipulations in interstimulus interval specifically altering the habituation process that takes place during training, or are they artifacts of the ISI differences that continue to distinguish the groups during testing?

Davis set out to re-examine the effects on habituation of changes in the length of the interstimulus interval, using a procedure that separates ISI changes taking place during training from those occurring during testing. Training and testing were distinguished such that organisms trained with different interstimulus intervals were tested in identical situations. Habituation of the rat startle response, initially elicited by a 120-db tone, 50 msec in duration, was assessed using the following procedure:

1. During *prehabituation*, subjects received 75 exposures to the 50-msec tone at each of four ISI values. Tones separated by the four intervals (2, 4, 8, and 16 seconds) were presented in irregular order such that various intervals were interposed with one another throughout the prehabituation session.

2. On the following day, during the *habituation training session*, animals were divided into two groups. One group received 1000 tone presentations separated from one another by a constant 2-second ISI, while the second group received 1000 tones of the same pitch and intensity but separated by intervals of 16 seconds. Timing of the sessions was arranged so that habituation training ended at the same time for each group.

3. During the *posthabituation test session*, all subjects were again presented with 75 tones at each of the four initial ISI values. As in the first test session, the intervals occurred in irregular order.

During prehabituation, the traditional ISI result was obtained. More responding (increased startle frequency) occurred with the longer (16-second) interstimulus intervals. The greater the length of time since the previous stimulus, therefore, the more likely the response, and, correspondingly, the less the habituation. Performance exhibited by the two groups presented the 2-second versus the 16-second ISI during testing also conformed to traditional findings. Though little or no difference between the groups was apparent in responses to the first tone, substantial differences appeared as early as the second trial. Again, as expected, the shorter ISI group (2-second) engaged in far less responding. As Davis points out, these results suggest that the training effect is a sudden one, which need not build up gradually with repetitive experience.

Comparison of the data from the pre- and posthabituation test sessions clearly indicates that habituation did occur. For both the 2- and 16-second training groups, responding was significantly decreased in tests following repetitive stimulation. The most striking result was, however, the finding that responding during posthabituation tests was less in animals that had been trained with the *longer* (16-second) interstimulus interval. This suggests that in this situation greater habituation occurs with more *infrequent* stimulation. As shown in Figure 3.2, when procedures are used that separate training effects from testing effects in habituation of rat startle responding, unexpectedly, habituation is greater following training with *longer* interstimulus intervals. Effects of variations in ISI may therefore differ depending on the training regime employed.

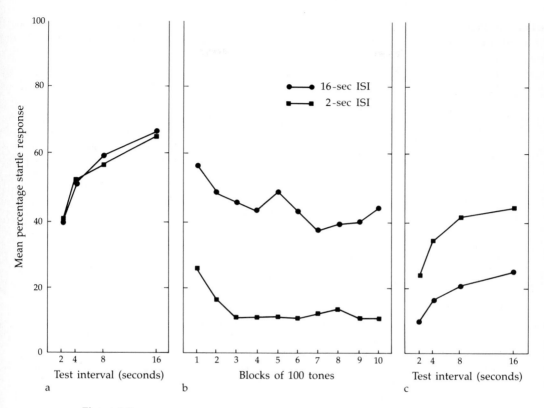

Figure 3.2
Separation of the effects of interstimulus interval during testing and training in habituation.
Results indicate that animals trained with the longer (16-sec) interstimulus interval
responded less during testing than animals trained with the shorter (2-sec) interstimulus
interval. (a) Prehabituation. (b) Habituation training. (c) 1-min posthabituation. [After M.
Davis, Effects of interstimulus interval length and variability on startle response habituation
in the rat. *Journal of Comparative and Physiological Psychology, 72*, 177–192. Copyright © 1970
by the American Psychological Association. Redrawn by permission.]

Generalization

As with the more traditionally recognized forms of learning, nonassociative learning owes much of its value to the fact that changes in responding are not confined to the conditions under which they were originally
produced. That is, behavioral changes initially occurring in the presence
of, or with exposure to, one stimulus *generalize* to other, similar stimulus
situations. Because individuals are rarely re-exposed to identical circumstances, generalization is an extremely adaptive feature of learning. It
essentially renders the acquired information useful for the future; without
generalization, learning would be to no avail. The effects of habituation to
a specific stimulus do generalize to similar stimuli. Balderrama and Maldonado (1971), for example, report generalization of habituation in the

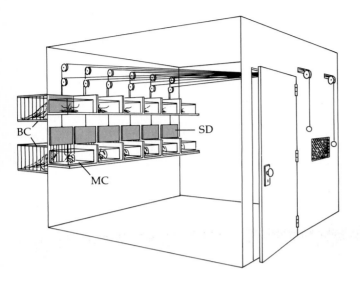

Figure 3.3
The apparatus used to measure habituation of the fright reaction of mantids presented with repeated exposure to predatory birds (BC, bird compartment; MC, mantid compartment; SD, slide screen). [After N. Balderrama and H. Maldonado, Habituation of the deimatic response in the mantid *(Stagmatoptera biocellata). Journal of Comparative and Physiological Psychology, 75,* 98–106. Copyright © 1971 by the American Psychological Association. Redrawn by permission.]

fright reaction of the praying mantis elicited by different species of birds. The apparatus used is pictured in Figure 3.3. Following habituation to a moderately frightening species (one resembling the insects' natural predator) presentations of a similar though highly frightening stimulus (the natural predator itself) resulted in more rapid habituation than that seen in naive insects receiving their first experience with the more frightening stimulus. As expected, more generalization was obtained with greater similarity between stimuli.

Recovery and Dishabituation

Some recovery from habituation is clearly as beneficial as the initial learning itself. The animal must be set to respond again later either to potentially harmful or to potentially beneficial stimuli. An organism that remains unresponsive for long may be at an extreme disadvantage. Though the degree of recovery evident following habituation varies dramatically both with training conditions and with the nature of the response in question, habituation, like many other forms of learning, is reversible.

Spontaneous recovery refers to the resumption of responding that occurs with re-presentation of the habituating stimulus following rest. If, after a response decrement has occurred, stimulation is withheld for a time, subsequent presentation of the stimulus will once again evoke a response. Very rapid recovery has been reported in many situations. Predatory responding in mantids, for example, is substantially recovered within five minutes following training; complete recovery is evident in as little as thirty minutes. In other situations spontaneous recovery takes considerably longer. Recovery measured at several intervals following habituation of the courtship response in the insect *Mormoniella vitripennis* is pictured in Figure 3.4. As indicated, more complete recovery typically occurs following longer intervals. Complete recovery may not occur for some responses. Over a period of six days, for example, teleost fish receiving continuous daily exposure to live brine shrimp enclosed in plastic tubes gradually cease to engage in predatory bites. Only partial recovery of predatory responding is observed after as much as ten days of rest (Peeke and Peeke, 1972). Chaffinches continuously exposed to a stuffed owl will

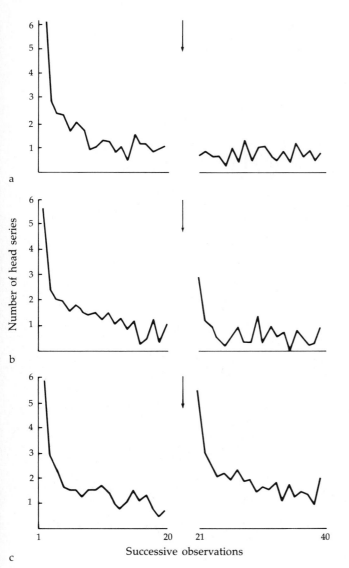

Figure 3.4
Degree of spontaneous recovery evident at various intervals following habituation of the courtship response in a hymenopteron insect. (a) 30-sec interval. (b) 60-min interval. (c) 24-hr interval. [After Barrass, 1961.]

initially emit "chink" calls while mobbing this replica of their natural predator. Following only thirty-minute period of exposure, the birds cease to call altogether. After a subsequent thirty-minute period of no stimulation, recovery occurs to levels of approximately 60 percent of the initial response index. Prolonged observation over a period of several days, however, indicates no evidence of any further recovery of responding (Hinde, 1960).

As indicated in Figure 3.5, the rate of recovery may vary with the intensity of the stimulus used during training. Recovery rates of the twitching response of earthworms, measured at various intervals following habituation, differ depending on the intensity of shock (the habituating stimulus) employed in training. Even after a period of 24 hours the recovery of responses habituated using a 150-mV shock is roughly 20 percent greater than the recovery of responses habituated with a 250-mV shock (Kuenzer, 1958).

Findings regarding variations in spontaneous recovery have led to speculation on the dimensions that might characterize the *retention* of habituation learning. If the response recovers very slowly, the organism has, for that period, retained the information gained during the training experience. Because no prolonged retention is presumed to characterize the peripheral processes of sensory adaptation and fatigue, retention and recovery are important definitive aspects of habituation. Interestingly, spontaneous recovery itself seems to be influenced by experience. Animals presented with repeated sessions of habituation followed by rest exhibit successively less responding, and, therefore, progressively more habituation with each session. Thompson and Spencer (1966) have re-

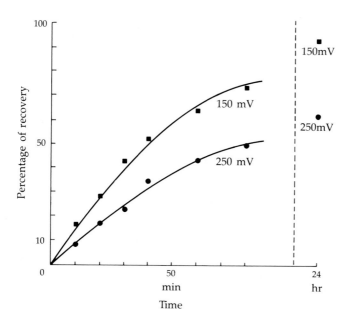

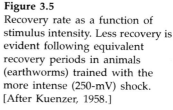

Figure 3.5
Recovery rate as a function of
stimulus intensity. Less recovery is
evident following equivalent
recovery periods in animals
(earthworms) trained with the
more intense (250-mV) shock.
[After Kuenzer, 1958.]

ferred to this as the *potentiation of habituation*. This phenomenon seems to suggest that the retained effects of experience accumulate with additional, prolonged exposure. Situations in which recovery occurs only very gradually and in which retention effects appear to accumulate emphasize the adaptive nature of the change taking place.

Discrepancies in the data on recovery times and on the characteristics of the initial response decrement have led to suggestions that the observed behavioral habituation curve may actually represent a number of distinct underlying decremental processes (see the discussion in Hinde, 1970b). Recent pharmacological data lend support to such notions. Pretraining injections of the anticholinergic drug scopolamine hydrobromide—a substance known to have disinhibitory effects on rat exploratory behavior—retard habituation of this response but have no effect on habituation of the rat startle response (Williams, Hamilton, and Carlton, 1974). Injected animals persist in prolonged exploratory responding, whereas under similar training conditions the startle response quickly habituates. Here it appears that distinct decremental processes may be differentially affected by the same substance. Similarly, Williams, Hamilton, and Carlton (1975) report differential habituation of exploratory behavior in rats as a function of age. Two groups of subjects were tested for habituation of startle and exploratory responses at 15–16 and 36–39 days of age. While the startle response habituated in both groups, only the older group exhibited habituation of exploratory behavior. It should be noted, however, that in both cases the older group engaged in far more initial responding than did the younger. Nonetheless, on the basis of both pharmacological and developmental distinctions between decremental processes, these authors have concluded that "to consider all instances of habituation in terms of a single physiological process is clearly an unwarranted oversimplification" (Williams, Hamilton, and Carlton, 1974, pp. 730–731).

We have seen that through rest and recovery the effects of habituation training can be reversed; the animal gradually comes to respond again to the habituating stimulus. In addition, a different and more immediate reversal of habituation can be brought about by the single presentation of a novel stimulus. If following the initial response decrement the subject is immediately exposed to the *single presentation* of a solitary novel stimulus, subsequent responding to the *habituating stimulus* will be quickly reinstated. That is, interpolated novel stimulation immediately restores the ability of the habituating stimulus to evoke the once prominent response. The subject once again responds to the habituating stimulus, whereas as recently as a few seconds earlier no response occurred. This immediate reversal of habituation produced by novel stimulation is termed *dishabituation*. The critical feature of the interpolated stimulus appears to be its novelty. When the habituating and novel stimuli represent the same stimulus modality, greater dishabituation is typically produced

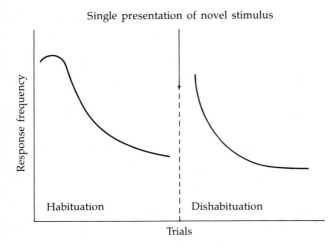

Single presentation of novel stimulus

Response frequency

Habituation

Dishabituation

Trials

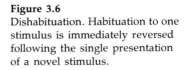

Figure 3.6
Dishabituation. Habituation to one stimulus is immediately reversed following the single presentation of a novel stimulus.

by a more intense stimulus. Data indicate that a stimulus of decreased intensity (less than that of the habituating stimulus) will also result in dishabituation. Moreover, the modality of the dishabituating (novel) stimulus need not be the same as that of the habituating stimulus. Habituation to a tactile stimulus can, for example, be immediately reversed by presentation of an electric shock or a loud noise. Figure 3.6 presents a diagram of dishabituation. Surprisingly, the amount of responding to the habituating stimulus produced by dishabituation can exceed the control levels that characterized responding *prior to* any habituation. After dishabituation the animal may actually respond more than it did before receiving any habituation training. As we shall see, this fact has suggested that dishabituation represents more than just a passive reversal of habituation. It instead apparently constitutes an independent incremental process that does not alter the habituation process but introduces superimposed response facilitation. Several authors have postulated that dishabituation represents a special instance of the more general incremental nonassociative process of sensitization. It is to this process that we now turn.

SENSITIZATION

Many accounts of habituation report that the early stages of repetitive stimulation are typically accompanied by rapid *increments* in responding, which then quickly decay or are concealed by habituation. Such response increments constitute sensitization learning. *Sensitization*, like habituation, represents a process of nonassociative behavior modification that occurs with repeated stimulation. However, sensitization effects are *incremental*, rather than decremental as in habituation. That is, successive stimulus presentations gradually result in a relatively permanent increase in responding. Razran (1971) has suggested that this induced increase may exist in either of two "modes": one in which the frequency or magnitude of the initial response increases with training (the more traditionally recognized mode, typically called sensitization) and a second in which new responses not in evidence prior to training occur with greater frequency following training. Razran (1971) applies the term *pseudoconditioning* to this second incremental mode.

Like habituation, sensitization can occur on a long-term as well as a short-term basis. Sensitization effects, moreover, apparently need not be confined to early, rapidly induced response increments. Gradual incremental effects not obviously accompanied by habituation have also been described. Prolonged sensitization of the frog wiping reflex, for example, has been demonstrated to occur over a twelve-day sequence of daily sessions of repeated tactile stimulation. Response frequencies obtained on the twelfth day were as much as seven times greater than those measured during the first training session (Franzisket, 1963). Interestingly, as indicated in Figure 3.7, when repeated tactile stimulation is administered each time to the exact same spot on the tactile receptive field of the frog, a response decrement (habituation) is obtained. If, however, the point of impact within the receptive field varies on each trial, increments (sensitization) in the frequency of wiping occur (Kimble and Ray, 1965).

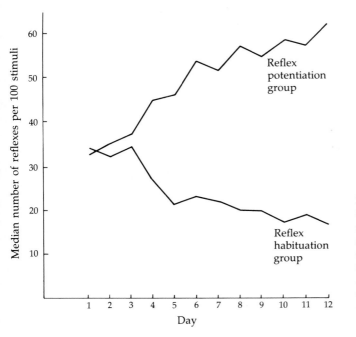

Figure 3.7
Sensitization of the frog wiping reflex. Repeated tactile stimulation administered to a different spot on each trial produces an increment in responding, while stimulation administered to the same spot on each trial produces a response decrement. [After Kimble and Ray, 1965.]

These data raise intriguing questions about the conditions under which sensitization rather than habituation might be expected. Both constitute nonassociative modifications in behavior produced by repetitive stimulation. Why in some situations does responding decrease, while in others responding increases? Clearly, both processes perform adaptive functions for the organism. Just as the animal is at times better off not responding to redundant and unimportant stimuli, so the tendency to respond vigorously and quickly in other situations may mean the difference between life and death. Consider, for example, a foraging bird that is alerted by sounds signaling the approach of a predator. The initial signal persists and becomes more intense as the predator nears. What was initially merely an orienting reflex on the part of the bird may recur with greater and greater strength, eventually resulting in an overt escape response. On future encounters with the same stimulus (the predator), escape responding may occur immediately as a result of the sensitizing effect of prior experience with the stimulus. The adaptive value of sensitized escape responding clearly maximizes the animal's chances of survival.

Experiments on pseudoconditioning as defined by Razran are, unfortunately, quite rare. This is in part owing to the fact that in most analyses of the effects of repetitive stimulation only a single response is monitored. Investigations of pseudoconditioning require, however, assessment of effects other than those evident in the response initially elicited. The importance of multiple response assessment for our understanding of interactions among various nonassociative learning processes is nicely illustrated by Szlep's (1964) work on habituation of prey-catching behavior in orb-weaving spiders (those that spin webs). In response to web vibrations, the spider, normally resting at the center of the web, distributes its legs at equal distances on the radii of the web, turns toward the vibratory focus in the periphery of the web, runs quickly in that direction, and, if prey is found there, engages in predatory attack. With repeated vibratory stimulation, these responses decrease in a sequential, orderly fashion. More important for our discussion here, however, is the finding that a number of novel response elements gradually emerge with more and more stimulation, and as the initial components of the prey-catching response wane. The plucking of the web by the spider, for example, was observed to occur with greater and greater frequency as the more familiar response components ceased to occur. It appears that nonassociative training in one stimulus–response system can facilitate the occurrence of novel responses to the original stimulus.

Dual-Process Theory

Major theoretical treatments of behavioral habituation have centered on interactions occurring between habituation and sensitization. It is here that we see the most sophisticated analyses of conditions that predict the occurrence of habituation or sensitization, or both. Groves and

Thompson (1970; see also Thompson, Groves, Teyler, and Roemer, 1973) have postulated the *dual-process theory*, which attempts to explain the effects of repetitive stimulation on the basis of two interacting, yet independent neural processes: habituation and sensitization. Dual-process theory assumes that each stimulus received by an organism has two distinct neurophysiological effects. It heightens the "general level of excitation" of the response system—that is, the "state" of the system—and it elicits a response in a specific stimulus–response pathway. Repetition of the stimulus alters these distinct neural systems in opposite ways. Stimulus repetition produces a decremental change in the responsivity of the stimulus–response pathway. This decremental change is termed habituation. In contrast, repetition has a generally incremental effect on the "state" of the system, indicative of the second neural process, termed by these authors sensitization. The effects of both processes are evident in the nonassociative alterations produced in overt behavior. Groves and Thompson emphasize that presentation of any stimulus of sufficient strength initiates both processes simultaneously. They further assume that the observed behavioral outcome of repetitive stimulation represents the additive interaction of these two independent processes. The presumed nature of this theoretical interaction is diagramed in Figure 3.8.

Both behavioral and neurophysiological data have further clarified the distinct characters of the two processes. As indicated in Figure 3.8, sensitization is typically regarded as an early-onset, transient or "phasic" process immediately initiating a short-lived increment in responding. The

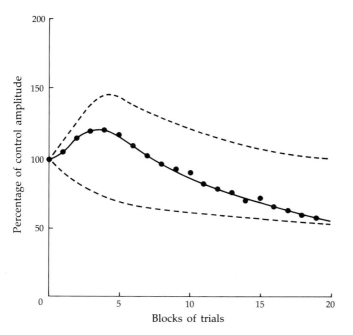

Figure 3.8
The interaction between habituation (lower dashed line) and sensitization (upper dashed line) proposed by dual-process theory. The middle line indicates the predicted behavioral outcome of the interaction. [After Thompson, Groves, Teyler, and Roemer, 1973.]

increment begins to decay during repetitive stimulation. Both the amount and duration of sensitization, however, are in part determined by stimulus intensity and interstimulus interval. Typically, more sensitization is observed to occur the greater the intensity and frequency of stimulation. The incremental effects of dishabituation (described earlier) are assumed by these authors to represent a special case of sensitization. The habituation process, by contrast, is characterized as a more long-term, "tonic" effect, which undergoes spontaneous decay only after stimulation has ceased. Though there is some disagreement on these points, Thompson et al. (1973) describe the extent of neural habituation as "directly related to stimulus frequency and inversely related to stimulus intensity" (p. 240). Increased frequency, therefore, has a similar effect on the two processes, while increased intensity affects the processes in opposite ways. While by far the bulk of the data has been collected on the habituation process, more recent attempts to support dual-process theory have focused both on the independent sensitization process and on the interaction of the two.

Interactions Between Habituation and Sensitization

Analyses of the conditions under which response strength will be determined by sensitization or, alternatively, by habituation have involved the assessment of differences in the decay rates presumed characteristic of the two processes. As already indicated, dual-process theory describes sensitization as a transient, rapidly decaying phenomenon—brief by comparison with the more permanent habituation process. As such, the effects of habituation should be retained for a longer period than the effects of sensitization. Davis (1972) has reasoned that response strength at the end of a training session theoretically reflects *both* retained sensitization and retained habituation. After a designated retention interval long enough to permit decay of the transient sensitization process, but short enough to allow for continued retention of habituation, response strength should be indicative of habituation alone. Davis predicts that under certain conditions habituation effects will actually become augmented, even in the absence of additional training, simply because all sensitization has decayed. Facilitation (by sensitization) will in time equal zero. Similarly, if asymptotically low levels of habituation are obtained, stimulation in subsequent sessions may reveal changes due to sensitization alone. In effect, a change in the behavioral manifestation of one process is expected, not because that process has itself changed, but because the behavioral index has been altered by changes in a second process. Results of this nature would, therefore, underline the independence of habituation and sensitization. To test his predictions Davis measured both incremental and decremental modifications in the rat startle response over prolonged training and retention periods. Animals received two training sessions a week for a period of four weeks. Each session consisted of a series of 50 120-db tones presented at 30-second intervals, and the two weekly sessions were separated by an interval of 24 hours. This procedure was repeated each week for four weeks, so that all animals were trained for a total of eight sessions, with intersession intervals alternately equal to 24 hours or six days.

As expected, the amplitude of the startle response decreased substantially during the first session, indicating that habituation was occurring (see Figure 3.9). Within each of the seven remaining sessions, however, responding *increased* across the 50 training trials. During the first 50-trial training sequence, therefore, responding decreased, while with each 50-trial sequence thereafter, responding increased. Increments were not cumulative across sessions; response amplitudes at the beginning of each session were comparably low. This suggests that while no prolonged retention of sensitization was occurring, stable retention of habituation was in evidence, and within-session increments occurred in the absence of further habituation. The independence of habituation and sensitization is suggested in the finding that the amplitude of the first response in each of sessions 2 through 8 was much *less* than that of the last response of the corresponding preceding session. The effects of habituation were, there-

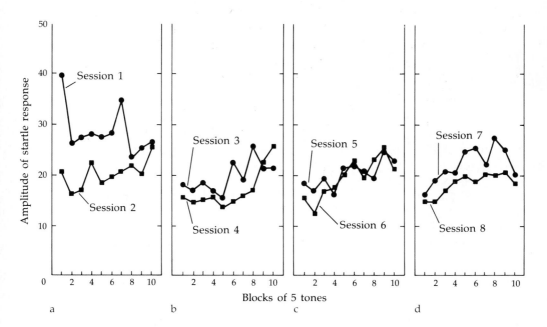

Figure 3.9
Within-session increments (sensitization) superimposed upon the retention of habituation in the rat startle response. (a) First week. (b) Second week. (c) Third week. (d) Fourth week. [After M. Davis, Differential retention of sensitization and habituation of the startle response in the rat. *Journal of Comparative and Physiological Psychology, 78,* 260–267. Copyright © 1972 by the American Psychological Association. Redrawn by permission.]

fore, more pronounced at the *beginning* of each succeeding session than they were at the *end* of the training session itself. This result held for both the 24-hour and 6-day intersession intervals. Even when the stimulus was re-presented with no further training and after six days of rest, responding was less than that evoked by the final stimulus of the previous session. Here, sensitization effects have decayed, permitting the full manifestation of the unconfounded process of habituation. Davis concludes that his results are largely consistent with dual-process theory. Clearly, two distinct processes are exerting independent, though interacting effects on the behavior of interest. One of these (sensitization) is incremental, develops rapidly, and decays quickly; the other (habituation) is decremental, stable, and quite prolonged.

More recently, again employing the rat startle paradigm, Davis (1974a, 1974b) has reported that the amount of background noise against which the auditory signal is presented (therefore the value of the signal-to-noise ratio) is an important determinant of the amount of habituation produced. Moreover, under certain conditions, increasing the noise while holding the signal constant can actually produce overall behavioral sensitization, eliminating any response decrement. Alterations in the startle response occurring during 100 presentations of a 100-db tone were observed in two groups of rats. For one group, the background noise level was set at 60 db, while for the other, noise levels equaled 80 db. The results, summarized in Figure 3.10, indicate that a change from 50 db to 30 db in the value of the signal-to-noise ratio produces a dramatic change in the effect of repetitive exposure to the signal. Under conditions of increased background noise (S/N = 30 db), response amplitudes evoked by the signal exhibited a marked increment across successive presentations. This is in contrast to the decremental effect obtained with decreased levels of background noise (S/N = 50 db). When training sessions with increased noise levels were repeated daily over a period of six days, incremental effects were observed within each session, but no apparent cumulative increment occurred. Davis (1974b) points out that the sensitization effects produced by increased noise are somewhat atypical of the process as described by dual-process theory. "When response increments occur they have mainly been confined to the first several stimulus exposures, after which response decrements typically set in. Under the present conditions a progressive increase in reflex strength occurred over a relatively long time period" (p. 573). Further research has demonstrated that the observed sensitization is noise-induced rather than tone-induced, and prolonged continuous exposure to 80-db noise alone produces a progressively accumulating increment in startle amplitude. Asymptotic increases in response amplitude were observed after approximately 30 minutes of continuous exposure. Moreover, the effects of 25 minutes of continuous 80-db noise were evident as long as 15 minutes following noise offset. Though Davis does note that habituation is in evidence following asymp-

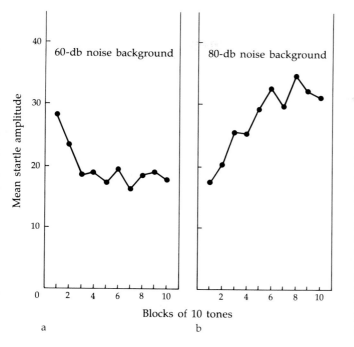

Figure 3.10
Response increments (sensitization) produced following an increase in background noise during presentation of a tone eliciting the startle response in the rat. (a) Habituation. (b) Sensitization. [After M. Davis, Sensitization of the rat startle response by noise. *Journal of Comparative and Physiological Psychology, 87,* 571–581. Copyright © 1974 by the American Psychological Association. Redrawn by permission.]

totic sensitization (again, therefore, confirming the assumption of two interacting processes), nonetheless, the time course of sensitization is much more protracted than expected by the descriptions provided by dual-process theory. Davis' data further indicate that decay need not proceed quickly after the initial stimulus exposures but may, in fact, follow a longer term that begins only after stimulation has ceased.

Similar accounts of sensitization at variance with those contained in dual-process theory have been observed in a number of neurophysiological preparations,[2] as well as in the overt behavior of the marine slug *Aplysia californica* (Pinsker, Hening, Carew, and Kandel, 1973). In *Aplysia* the effects of sensitization training were assessed against baseline habituation of the siphon withdrawal reflex (see Chapter 12) produced by ten successive tactile stimuli. Sensitization training, which followed the recovery of responsiveness, consisted of the presentation of four brief electric shocks per day for a period of four days. The retained effects of sensitization were assessed at one day, one week, and three weeks following training. As expected, responding was substantially facilitated as a consequence of sensitization training. More importantly, however, the effects of shock were retained up to three weeks following training. Tests at one day and

---

[2]Most neurophysiological preparations involve the direct electrical recording of neural activity from within the nervous system.

one week indicated significantly greater response strength than that observed for controls, while at three weeks responding persisted well above pretraining response levels evident in the experimental animals. The prolonged within-session increments in response strength and the extremely long-term retention of sensitization are both difficult to reconcile with dual-process theory descriptions of the nature of sensitization. Organismic differences may definitely come into play here (invertebrates are known for the occurrence of persistent central excitatory states [Dethier, 1969]), and the fact that such differences exist is an important consideration both for describing the nature of the sensitization process and for discussing its significance as a precursor of more complex forms of incremental associative learning.

CLASSICAL CONDITIONING

[U]nder natural circumstances the normal animal must respond not only to stimuli which themselves bring immediate benefit or harm, but also to other physical or chemical agencies . . . which in themselves only signal the approach of these stimuli. . . . The essential feature of the highest activity of the central nervous system . . . consists, not in the fact that innumerable signaling stimuli do initiate reflex reactions in the animal, but in the fact that under different conditions these same stimuli may initiate quite different reflex actions; and, conversely, the same reactions may be initiated by different stimuli [Pavlov, 1927, p. 15].

The great Russian physiologist Ivan Pavlov (1849–1936) refers here to two critical aspects of his revolutionary discovery of the mutability of the reflex—that is, classical conditioning. First, he points out that the ability to respond to signaling stimuli is adaptive for the organism because it allows the individual to *anticipate* significant changes in the environment. The individual essentially gains a head start on environmental change, made possible when a signal is correlated with events that are to come. It is as if one event, which itself might not have produced a response, becomes a signal for a stimulus of greater biological significance—one that ultimately demands a response. Pavlov (1927) cites the comparison between an animal whose defensive response anticipates the approach of the predator and one that responds defensively only after the predator has attacked. The former is far more likely to survive than the latter. Secondly, Pavlov emphasizes the flexibility that characterizes this reliance on signals. Behavioral anticipation can be effective only if the organism is able to take advantage of whatever stimuli happen to be predictive of the relevant event. The same signal can be used flexibly as an indicator of many different events. Similarly, as the environment changes such that one signaling stimulus no longer occurs reliably, novel stimuli may acquire new signaling value and therefore take on the essential predictive function.

Such flexibility is so familiar to the modern reader that it may be difficult to comprehend just how revolutionary were the observations made in Pavlov's laboratory at the turn of the century. At that time the study of skeletal and visceral reflexes was being pursued actively, preeminently in the works of Pavlov and C. S. Sherrington. And, though they viewed the reflex as a very complex event, in general it remained for them a rigidly mechanical relationship between a specific stimulus and a response whose occurrence depended on the presence of that stimulus and no other. Before Pavlov's discovery, therefore, the reflex was an inflexible event. For some time the reflex had been a tempting candidate for an objective and clearly measurable unit of behavior. Complex overt behavior, however, was extremely flexible. How could such a rigid, inflexible unit possibly help account for the undeniable changeability of overt behavior? What was the relationship between the apparent flexibility of behavior and this rigid mechanical reflex? Nowhere is the problematical rigidity of the reflex phrased more eloquently than in the words of William James:

> The dilemma in regard to the nervous system seems, in short, to be of the following kind. We may construct one which will react infallibly and certainly (based on rigid reflex action), but it will be capable of reacting to very few changes in the environment—it will fail to be adapted to all the rest. We may, on the other hand, construct a nervous system potentially adapted to respond to an infinite variety of minute features in the situation; but its fallibility will then be as great as its elaboration . . . [and] its hair-trigger organization makes of it a happy-go-lucky, hit-or-miss affair [James, 1890, p. 140].

Pavlov's discovery[3] added adaptive, yet controlled flexibility to the reflex relationship, and, in doing so, provided the basis for an objective account of the variability to which James refers. The astounding fact was that the rigid reflex was *not* so rigid after all. And no one made greater use of this fact than psychologists of the half-century that was to follow.

Pavlov assumed that the contiguity of stimulus with stimulus made this flexibility possible. Similar notions of association and contiguity had been a part of philosophical psychology for centuries. As Terrace (1973) points out, Pavlov effectively combined the traditional associationistic view of learning with the physiologically based notion of the reflex. The union of the two spawned the conditioned reflex. Paradoxically, the very rigidity

---

[3] An experimental instance of classical conditioning was reported in the United States at about the same time Pavlov's work was in progress and well before Pavlov's reports reached America. A graduate student at the University of Pennsylvania, E. B. Twitmyer, had discovered the conditionability of the patellar or knee-jerk reflex using the exact same experimental paradigm that Pavlov was later to make famous. In 1904, when Twitmyer presented his discovery at the meeting of the American Psychological Association, during a session chaired by the great American psychologist William James, its potentially revolutionary importance went completely unrecognized. Twitmyer subsequently abandoned his career in psychology. Ironically, that was the same year (1904) that Pavlov was to receive the Nobel Prize for his work in digestive physiology.

that had once been a problem, here provided the foundation for the union. One of the necessary prerequisites for the occurrence of classical conditioning is the association of two (or more) stimuli. The second, however, is a special, necessarily rigid relationship between stimulus and response—the traditional reflex. Pavlov in essence built his flexible reflexes out of inflexible ones. A rigid S–R connection provided the basis for the modification of stimulus function. Moreover, this was possible only through association. To see how, let us first examine the original classical conditioning paradigm exhaustively detailed by Ivan Pavlov.

Basic Principles

During the latter part of the nineteenth century, Pavlov had concentrated his scientific efforts on an understanding of the physiology of digestion. Food placed in the mouth of an unanesthetized, yet restrained dog initiated the secretion of various gastric juices. Pavlov noticed, however, that on occasion irregular secretion occurred *prior to* the presentation of food. Because the secretions were viewed as digestive reflexes, the occurrence of the reflex *before* the presentation of the stimulus constituted an extraordinary observation. Pavlov further noted that the secretion (saliva in this case) was often initiated by something as seemingly arbitrary as the sight of food or the sound of footsteps as the experimenter approached to present the food. Interest in these events so captured Pavlov's imagination that the focus of his career shifted from the explanation of digestive physiology to an attempt to understand what he came to call "psychic secretions." His efforts in this direction were amazingly thorough, and in time Pavlov's systemization of these observations became the standard classical conditioning paradigm. Much of the terminology of conditioning research today was developed by Pavlov.

Classical conditioning is regarded as the simplest form of associative learning.[4] A stimulus initially ineffective in producing a particular reaction acquires the ability to do so by being paired with an inherently effective stimulus—one that invariably elicits the response. This transfer of ability is *conditional upon* association with a rigidly established, built-in connection between stimulus and response. Elicitation of the response by the effective stimulus requires no special conditions. Simply present the stimulus and the response will occur. The reflex relationship is an unconditional one, and Pavlov therefore designated the effective stimulus the *unconditional stimulus* (UCS). The response reflexively produced by presentation of the UCS he termed the *unconditional response* (UCR). Conditional upon association with this built-in UCS–UCR compound, an otherwise insufficient stimulus, the *conditional stimulus* (CS), comes to

---

[4] Because of the extensive literature on classical conditioning, the following account is necessarily selective. For a more detailed analysis of many relevant issues, the reader is referred to Black and Prokasy (1972) and to Mackintosh (1974).

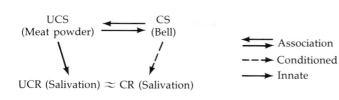

Figure 3.11
Pavlov's classical conditioning paradigm. Association of CS (bell) with UCS (meat powder) eventually enables the CS alone to evoke a response initially produced only by the UCS. This response then becomes the CR (salivation).

elicit a response functionally equivalent to, though measurably distinct from, the UCR, the *conditional response* (CR).[5] The CR may, for example, have a characteristically shorter latency or decreased amplitude when compared with the UCR; though again, the two responses can be said to perform the same function. It should be noted that the CS does initially produce some response in the organism. Depending on the nature of the stimulus, this response may be nothing more than an orienting reflex, occurring when the individual is innately alerted to subtle changes taking place in the environment. It is, however, critical that the CS be neutral with respect to the response to be conditioned. In Pavlov's original experiments, diagramed schematically in Figure 3.11, the digestive reflex of salivation provided the basis for conditioning. Placement of meat powder (the UCS) in a dog's mouth invariably elicited salivation (the UCR). Following a number of paired presentations of the meat powder with a stimulus initially ineffective in evoking salivation (the CS)—a bell or the ticking of a metronome—the CS acquired the ability to produce *by itself* a functional equivalent of the UCR, salivation (the CR). Following conditioning, therefore, the bell (or tick) can evoke salivation. Before, it could not. Note that though both the CR and the UCR are salivation, the two responses differ from one another in both quantity and quality of saliva produced. Note also the flexible and anticipatory character of conditioning. The CS now serves as a signal that meat powder will follow shortly. The animal has learned to anticipate—to respond sooner and to respond under different conditions, those signaled by the presence of the CS.[6]

Reinforcement in the classical conditioning paradigm refers simply to the temporal or spatial pairing of the two stimuli—CS and UCS. The relevant association in classical conditioning is therefore a stimulus–stimulus rela-

---

[5] The terms "conditional" and "unconditional" are now regarded as a more accurate translation of Pavlov's original usage. The Pavlovian procedure in effect describes the conditions under which the reflex can be altered. Modification is therefore conditional upon these sets of circumstances. Contemporary usage reserves these terms to refer specifically to Pavlov's work or to the Pavlovian paradigm; the derived terms "conditioned" and "unconditioned," however, are still appropriately used to refer to elements of the operant or instrumental conditioning paradigms.

[6] When we say the animal "anticipates," we mean, strictly speaking, only that it responds to the CS in a manner equivalent to its response to the UCS. The CS is correlated with the UCS, and the animal's responding is sensitive to this correlation. Whether or not the animal "mentally anticipates" the UCS is unknown.

tionship, and any time the two stimuli occur together, reinforcement is said to take place. Note that in classical conditioning, reinforcement occurs *independently of responding;* whether or not the animal responds to the CS, the UCS will follow. Virtually always in the early training trials, presentation of the CS is ineffective in producing the response of interest. Nonetheless, reinforcement occurs; the UCS follows quickly and independently of response parameters. As we shall see, this contrasts sharply with the response-dependent situation prevailing during operant conditioning. Here presentation of the reinforcing stimulus occurs only if the animal engages in a response.

The changes in behavior produced by classical conditioning are, of course, reversible. Repeated dissociation weakens the effectiveness of the conditional stimulus. In the process of *experimental extinction* the CS is repeatedly presented alone, resulting in a gradual decrease in the response-eliciting properties of the stimulus. The observed decrease need not, however, be complete. Moreover, numerous studies have indicated that even after the response-eliciting properties have returned to low pre-training baseline levels, future conditioning with that stimulus occurs more easily in the original subjects than in subjects that have never received training. As is the case with other forms of conditioning, the nature of the training procedure partly determines how long the animal will respond during extinction.

Temporal Relations Between Stimuli

Focus on the signaling function of the CS implies that the CS must in some manner *precede* the UCS if effective conditioning is to take place. In fact, a number of different temporal relationships may characterize stimulus pairing, and, interestingly, these seem to differ in their ability to sustain conditioning. The diagram presented in Figure 3.12 describes several distinct temporal relationships between CS and UCS possible in the conditioning paradigm. In each, the interval between stimuli, the duration of each event, and the interval between successive presentations of one stimulus (the intertrial interval) may differ. Here we are concerned

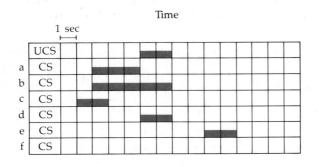

Figure 3.12
Temporal relations between CS and UCS in classical conditioning. (a and b) Delayed conditioning. (c) Trace conditioning. (d) Simultaneous conditioning. (e) Backward conditioning. (f) Temporal conditioning.

with the CS–UCS interval. All the situations described up to this point constitute *delayed conditioning* (a and b in the figure). In delayed conditioning, onset of the CS *always precedes* onset of the UCS, and the two stimuli are to some degree physically contiguous with one another. UCS either overlaps completely with CS (b), or UCS occurs simultaneously with CS offset (a). Delayed conditioning typically occurs quite easily, supporting the validity of the signaling interpretation suggested by Pavlov.

The efficiency of the delayed conditioning procedure is most evident when it is compared with the effects sustained by other temporal relationships that might exist between UCS and CS. In *trace conditioning* (c), CS precedes UCS, but here a measurable period of time must elapse between the two events. UCS onset occurs well after CS offset; there is no true contiguity between stimuli. It is therefore assumed that conditioning is based on some hypothetical stimulus "trace" that persists following CS offset. *Simultaneous conditioning* (d) refers to a situation in which CS and UCS are exactly concurrent with one another. UCS and CS duration, onset, and offset are equal. Interestingly, this situation of exact association, which may intuitively seem quite effective, generates little if any conditioning. Less surprising (especially from the signaling view) is the relative ineffectiveness of *backward conditioning* (e). In backward conditioning, UCS actually precedes CS, frequently with contiguity between UCS offset and CS onset. That sequencing is critical even when contiguity obtains again suggests the importance of the signaling function of the CS. This function is perhaps of no value if the event to be signaled has already occurred.

While delayed conditioning has traditionally been regarded as the most effective procedure, trace conditioning is also quite efficient, and any differences between the two appear to depend on the nature of the specific situation in question. In trace conditioning and delayed conditioning with equal CS–UCS intervals, the CS is equally correlated with UCS onset; only in delayed conditioning are the CS and UCS contiguous. As discussed later in this chapter, the effectiveness of both delay and trace procedures suggests the importance of correlation rather than contiguity in conditioning. Data indicate, however, that both are superior to either simultaneous or backward conditioning. The final segment of Figure 3.12 describes the *temporal conditioning* procedure (f). Here, no distinctly defined CS is present at all, but the UCS occurs repeatedly following a regular and predictable interval of time. It is assumed that the anticipatory cue for responding in temporal conditioning is the passage of time itself. The termination of the designated interval, presumably being monitored by the animal's internal timing sense, effectively comes to predict the next programmed occurrence of the UCS. In temporal conditioning, therefore, the major distinction between the UCR and the CR is one of response latency. Essentially the same response occurs, but it occurs at a different time. Prior to the conditioning, response latencies measured from an arbitrarily designated point (such as the middle of the interstimulus interval) are much longer than those observed after a number of training trials. Increased recognition of the importance of timing in behavior may render temporal conditioning and similar phenomena, such as entrainment,[7] of greater interest in the future.

Innumerable investigations of these temporal relationships as well as of parametric variations along dimensions such as stimulus duration, intensities of both the CS and the UCS, and the interval between CS onset and UCS onset, have attempted to outline the *general conditions* under which classical conditioning is optimized. The desire has been to identify those values that will sustain the most rapid, most vigorous, and most permanent modifications in behavior. Recent recognition of the importance of biological factors in conditioning has suggested, however, that a meaningful analysis of the conditions that optimize learning requires consideration of the relevant biological circumstances under which learning might be adaptive. Such circumstances are, by definition, very specific to the particular situation under consideration. General statements perhaps applicable in one context, therefore, cannot be assumed to extend unchanged to vastly different contexts. This view will be treated in more detail in Chapter 10; however, because of their relevance for many of the issues central to our understanding of classical conditioning, a preview of the focal arguments will be presented here. The issue at hand is the feasibility of backward conditioning.

As mentioned earlier, it is generally assumed that backward conditioning is at best a highly unreliable phenomenon, which perhaps does not exist at all. Keith-Lucas and Guttman (1975) have, however, recently reported an unusual instance of successful backward conditioning in the rat. This attempt differs in several respects from more conventional efforts to demonstrate backward conditioning. The most notable differences concern the nature of the conditional stimulus. Conditional stimuli typically used in backward conditioning studies are chosen arbitrarily and presented only for a very brief period of time. Keith-Lucas and Guttman instead employed a stimulus of more sustained duration and one chosen to simulate stimulus conditions in which backward conditioning might be adaptive in the animal's natural environment. Naive rats were presented with an "animal-like" CS (a toy hedgehog) that presumably approximated a potential predator. Conditioning was accomplished on a single trial during which electric shock was presented for 0.75 seconds while the animal, attracted to a particular part of the experimental chamber, was engaged in eating a sucrose pellet. The occurrence of shock initiated a backout period lasting until CS presentation. Subjects then received 1-minute exposure to the hedgehog at intervals of either 1, 5, 10, or 40 seconds following

---

[7]Entrainment refers to a situation in which the period of a biological rhythm such as a daily activity cycle is altered by the presentation of an external stimulus at regular intervals. The period of the biorhythm is modified to approximate that indicated by the occurrence of the external stimulus.

shock onset. In addition to these four experimental groups, two control groups were "trained" under identical conditions with the exception that one received no shock (CS alone) and the other received no hedgehog (UCS alone). Following the single training trial all animals were tested on the next day during a 10-minute period in which the toy hedgehog was placed in the experimental chamber with food nearby. A number of different responses, including taking the available food, were monitored photographically. Among these were approach responses, withdrawal responses, the amount of time spent in the presence of the CS, and, of course, whether or not the food was taken. Food-taking, approach, and time spent with the CS were regarded as reciprocal indices of avoidance. During the 10-minute testing period the hedgehog CS was presented first at one end (for 5 minutes) and then at the other end (again for 5 minutes) of the apparatus. Time spent in that half of the apparatus containing the CS was treated as a major measure of avoidance. Greater time spent in the presence of the hedgehog, for example, was indicative of less avoidance behavior.

Results of the tests indicated that a single hedgehog CS presented at either 1, 5, or 10 seconds following presentation of shock (the UCS) effectively modified the rats' behavior. Single-trial delayed backward conditioning was, therefore, in evidence. Experimental subjects (with the exception of those in the 40-second delay group) spent significantly less time than controls in the presence of the hedgehog. It should be noted that no differences existed among the various groups prior to conditioning. Other indices of avoidance also reflected the effectiveness of the hedgehog CS as an aversive stimulus: Greater retraction, less food taken, and reduced approach characterized all but the 40-second delay backward conditioning situations.

The authors interpret their success in obtaining backward conditioning on the basis of selection of CS parameters. In the natural environment, an abortive attack by a predator would likely be followed by cues (sight, smell, and others) associated with pain and escape. After such an experience, the cues would become signals for future attacks, therefore sustaining successful avoidance and allowing the animal to anticipate, behaviorally, the ensuing attack. Keith-Lucas and Guttman conclude that the nature of the signaling stimulus may in some situations be a more crucial determinant of association than the sequencing of stimuli.

> Underlying the concept of classical conditioning is the broader concept of signaling, usually understood as a functionally neutral stimulus (CS) preceding and predicting the occurrence of a biologically more important stimulus (US), in which the association is formed as the result of exposure to *this sequence* [italics ours]. However, it is quite evident that neither the present results nor those of any backward conditioning procedure can be explained on the basis of signaling so understood. Therefore, we must look elsewhere for an adequate explanatory context in which to place the present finding [Keith-Lucas and Guttman, 1975, pp. 474–475].

These authors look to "the adaptive specializations of learning" evident in the nature of the conditional stimulus. Note, however, that they have not advocated abandoning the notion of signaling altogether. On future trials the CS does serve as a signal to respond differently. Focus on the signaling function should not, however, obscure suggestions that the adaptive specializations characteristic of conditioning in this situation may render acquisition of the signaling function effective when stimulus sequencing is backward.

While these conclusions remain persuasive, they must be tempered by the results of subsequent work emphasizing the importance of experimental parameters in the success of backward conditioning. Mahoney and Ayers (1976) presented combinations of 0.4 seconds of electric shock (UCS) and 0.4 seconds of an auditory stimulus (CS) either simultaneously or in a forward or backward temporal order to albino rats. Again, only a single conditioning trial was presented, and controls received either the single UCS without a CS or one "trial" with the CS and UCS greatly separated in time. The effects of the single training trial were assessed in tests measuring the amount of licking from a drinking tube suppressed by presentation of the now aversive CS. As indexed by the amount of time required to complete 10 licks in the presence of the CS, significantly greater suppression was seen in backward conditioning, as compared with control groups. Much greater suppression was, however, evident in the forward and simultaneous conditioning groups. The authors conclude that success in obtaining backward (and simultaneous) conditioning may depend on the use of a single trial procedure. This again, however, need not invalidate the importance of a biologically relevant CS. Further work in the newly revived literature on backward conditioning should clarify this issue.

RESPONSE PARAMETERS IN CONDITIONING

Viewing classical conditioning as a mechanism whereby the organism comes to anticipate relevant environmental events might suggest that only certain responses can be modified in this manner. Under conditions that require a relatively discrete reaction, such as escape from a predator, the development of a reliable anticipatory response would seem ideal. If, however, the environmental change requires a continuous and prolonged interaction between the organism and its environment, such as when an animal engages in a prolonged search for food, simple anticipation may not suffice. Such considerations suggest that classical conditioning procedures may only be effective in modifying certain classes of responses. What is the nature of a response that can be altered by classical conditioning? How generally applicable are the procedures of classical conditioning for different response systems?

Traditional accounts of the generality of classical conditioning have assumed that the modification of autonomic responses occurs exclusively by means of classical conditioning. The modification of skeletal responses, on the other hand, is assumed to be produced only by response-contingent procedures, such as instrumental or operant conditioning, in which a change in behavior is required to produce a change in stimulation. *Autonomic* responses are responses that involve the contraction of smooth muscles operating under the control of the autonomic nervous system. The responses of glands (the salivary secretions of Pavlov's dogs), organs of the ingestive system, and the heart constitute autonomic responses. *Skeletal* responses, on the other hand, represent contractions of the skeletal muscles coordinated by the action of the skeletal nervous system. Limb movements and postural reflexes represent skeletal responses.

Historically, many theorists have maintained that classical and instrumental conditioning procedures represent fundamentally distinct learning processes. This position is in part based on the assumption that the hypothesized processes affect distinct response systems—the autonomic and the skeletal. Almost from its inception, however, the study of classical conditioning has challenged this assumption. The challenge emanates largely from two major classes of data: one demonstrating the modifiability of skeletal responses by means of classical procedures, and a second suggesting that autonomic responses can be altered instrumentally. As we shall see, however, both types of demonstration are open to alternative interpretations, and the issue remains an open one.

Early reports of the apparent effectiveness of classical procedures in altering skeletal responses quickly focused the issue. Pavlov himself reported the conditioning of leg flexion (a skeletal response) in dogs following repeated pairings of shock (the UCS) with a neutral stimulus. Similarly suggestive were successful modifications of the patellar (knee-jerk) reflex and the human eyeblink. Most examples of the classical conditioning of skeletal responses, however, have involved the use of *aversive stimulation*. This has raised the possibility that the occurrence of a conditional response actually serves to minimize the aversive effects of the UCS. Leg flexion following onset of a CS, for example, may serve to weaken the impact of the shock that is to follow. Under such circumstances, minimizing shock requires the occurrence of the response, and the response may therefore be strengthened instrumentally as a function of the consequences that follow. Interestingly, however, skeletal responses explicitly altered by instrumental procedures can be distinguished from those modified by classical procedures. Instrumentally conditioned eyeblinks, for example, differ in form from classically conditioned eyeblinks (King and Landis, 1943). The former are brisk and complete, while the latter are less pronounced and slower to develop. Therefore, while classical procedures may effectively alter skeletal responses, procedurally distinct differences in the modified result continue to suggest differences in some aspects of the modifying process. (See the discussion of similar findings in the "autoshaping" of the pigeon's key-peck in Chapter 4.)

Pavlov's position on the instrumental conditionability of glandular (and other autonomic) responses was clear from the outset. It could not be done. This conclusion was initially supported by several failures to demonstrate the feasibility of the instrumental modification of responses such as vasoconstriction and the Galvanic skin response (GSR). More recent data suggesting that autonomic responses may in fact be altered using instrumental procedures, however, render this side of the issue even more difficult to interpret. Beginning in the 1960s, studies appeared reporting the successful instrumental conditioning of autonomic responses including heart rate and GSR (Kimmel, 1967; Kimmel and Baxter, 1964; Kimmel and Kimmel, 1963). In each case the change in responding was brought about by the response-dependent presentation of a reinforcing stimulus. Critics, however, suggested that these attempts had actually modified concurrently occurring skeletal responses, and the autonomic changes represented secondary by-products of the modified occurrence of the skeletal response. Criticisms of this type would be difficult to answer in that many forms of stimulation do have complex effects involving several discrete responses. The most effective way to separate the concurrent actions of the two classes of responses entails the use of pharmacological agents such as curare to paralyze the skeletal musculature. Under these conditions only autonomic responses can occur, and mediation by overt skeletal responses is therefore impossible. Recent attempts to demonstrate the instrumental conditioning of autonomic responses in curarized animals have yielded extremely positive results. Heart rate, blood pressure, vasoconstriction, and intestinal responses (all autonomic) have all been modified by the presentation of response-contingent reinforcement in the apparent absence of mediation by the skeletal muscles. Unfortunately, several attempts to replicate these findings have failed. Similarly, because the possibility of central mediation[8] remains, no conclusive statement can be made about the instrumental flexibility of autonomic responses. It appears quite possible, however, that autonomic responses do not lie within the exclusive domain of classical conditioning. Similarly, skeletal responses appear subject to modification by classical conditioning. While differences may still exist between two distinct types of behavioral change, it is unlikely that the autonomic–skeletal distinction will constitute the basis for separation.

The Conditional Response

Given that a response can be classically conditioned, what is the nature of the conditional response, and how does it interact with other related re-

---

[8]Central mediation refers to the possibility that an autonomic state might be induced cognitively—for example, by thinking of a frightening situation.

sponses? Pavlov's early accounts of conditioning viewed the conditional response as literally the equivalent of the unconditional response. One major function of classical conditioning was to allow a response to occur under new conditions—in response to a previously ineffective stimulus. As such, classical conditioning was assumed to represent a process of *stimulus substitution,* not involving any modification in the form of the response itself. Instead, the change represented a change in the conditions that might produce the response. The dog that once had salivated only to food now (following conditioning) should salivate in exactly the same way, but in response to the CS. The same response was to occur under a different set of conditions. Hence the CS substitutes for the UCS with no change in the form of the response. More recent analyses have, however, indicated that this view is incorrect. Precise measurements have indicated that while similar, the CR does differ measurably from the UCR. Moreover, numerous elements of a response complex may be changed during conditioning. Which is to be regarded as the CR, and how might relationships among elements change as a function of conditioning?

While differences between conditional and unconditional responses have been documented in many conditioning situations (in Pavlov's original paradigm, for example, both amount and rate of salivation as well as the chemical composition of the saliva differentiated the CR from the UCR), the most extensive analyses have been performed on conditional versus unconditional eyeblink responses. In eyelid conditioning, the subject is presented a CS, usually a flash of light, followed by a puff of air to one eye. Measurements of the unmodified response (elicited by UCS alone) indicate that the UCR is an eyeblink that occurs with a latency of about 50 milliseconds following presentation of the stimulus. After conditioning, however, as indicated in Figure 3.13, eyeblinks evoked by the CS occur anywhere from 50 to 500 msec following CS onset. Clear latency differences can therefore distinguish the occurrence of the CR from the occurrence of the UCR. However, not all eyeblinks that follow the CS can be regarded as CR's. The CS, for example, can be shown to elicit an unconditional response prior to any pairing with the UCS. This initial response to the CS is called the *alpha response.* In eyeblink conditioning, the alpha response represents the eye's unconditional reaction to the CS of light. Grant and Norris (1947) report that alpha eyeblinks occur with a latency range of 50–120 msec (see Figure 3.13). Because alpha responses occur in the absence of conditioning, the same range of responses observed following conditioning can not be regarded as representative of CR's. Frequently the eyeblink response is photographed in a darkened room in which the experiment is conducted. Under these conditions the subject's eyes become dark-adapted during the experiment. The *beta response* (see Figure 3.13) represents another category of eyeblink that occurs when the eye is sensitized to light in the process of dark adaptation. Note how many more beta responses are indicated to occur under conditions of dark adaptation. Beta responses also must not be confused with

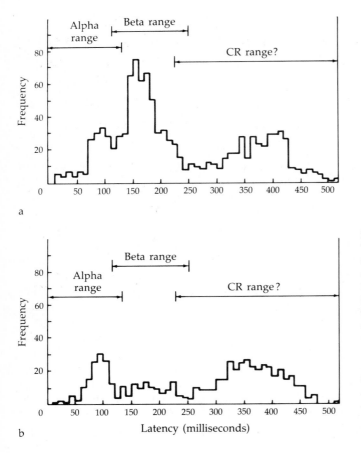

a

b

Latency (milliseconds)

Figure 3.13
The range of reactions evoked by the CS (light) during classical eyelid conditioning under both (a) dark-adapted and (b) nonadapted conditions. Only that range from 210 to 500 msec can be regarded as representing the conditional response. [Data from Grant and Norris, 1947. After G. A. Kimble, *Hilgard and Marquis' conditioning and Learning*, 2nd ed. New York: Appleton-Century-Crofts, 1961. Redrawn by permission of Prentice-Hall, Inc.]

CR's. Only eyeblinks that fall within the range of approximately 250–400 msec (and cannot be accounted for on any other basis), therefore, are assumed to constitute the conditional response. They are produced exclusively by the association between stimuli. Note, however, that the latency range of CR's can now be seen to be completely separate from that of UCR's, indicating clear differences in the nature of the response elicited by the CS versus the UCS. In effect, the CR is very likely not a simple equivalent of the UCR (see, however, the discussion in Mackintosh, 1974).

Numerous response elements that might be said to form a response complex can occur following presentation of any given stimulus. Food placed in a dog's mouth, for example, can produce far more than just salivation; responses such as chewing, stomach contractions, sniffing, and others may also occur. Hence a variety of CR's can be measured in any situation. Moreover, the distribution and timing of elements that occur following presentation of the CS (the CR), may be quite different from those that characterize the occurrence of the UCR. Newton and Gantt (1966), for example, report the acquisition of both leg flexion and heart rate CR's to a CS following pairing with shock. The changes in heart rate, however, occurred much more rapidly (in fewer trials) than the changes in leg flexion, suggesting clear differences between the UCR and CR complexes. Similarly, studies of heart rate conditioning indicate that while the UCR to shock is invariably an increase in heart rate, in response to presentation of the CS heart rate sometimes increases and sometimes decreases. Moreover, several other responses accompanying the change in heart rate—for example, increases in general activity and changes in respiration, may differentially affect the nature of the CR. Accelerations in heart rate CR's are seen to occur if presentation of the CS also produces running and jumping (de Toledo and Black, 1966). However, heart rate CR's may decelerate either when the CS is presented to unrestrained animals or when CS effects are measured in terms of the suppression of ongoing lever-pressing (Black and de Toledo, 1972). In both cases activity levels would be relatively low, and heart rate CR's decelerate.

Konorski (1967) has suggested that a distinction be drawn between two major classes of conditional responses. Diffuse "preparatory" CR's represent the subject's general motivational state, which has been conditioned to occur to CS following pairings of CS and UCS. Changes in heart rate and general activity constitute *preparatory* CR's. Precise *consummatory* CR's, on the other hand, are manifested by a specific reaction such as leg flexion, licking, or an eyeblink. Consummatory reactions are adaptive in highly specific ways—for example, in the acquisition of food or escape from danger. Such responses are, however, assumed to occur only within the context of a particular motivational state (the preparatory CR) also established by the CS. Both classes of conditioning occur in any classical conditioning situation, and all conditioning paradigms, therefore, involve at least two distinct classes of CR. Indeed, it has been observed that responses falling into the two classes begin to emerge at different times during training. Preparatory CR's occur following many fewer CS–UCS trials than do consummatory CR's. As previously indicated, for example, changes in heart rate are manifested in conditioning to a UCS of shock much sooner than changes in the occurrence of leg flexion. Clear distinction between the occurrence of predatory versus consummatory responses as CR's and their occurrence as UCR's has, however, not yet been achieved. Nonetheless, the distinction remains a plausible one, which may require both quantitative and functional separation between CR and UCR.

STIMULUS PARAMETERS IN CONDITIONING

We have introduced classical conditioning as the basic form of associative learning. Without the association between two stimuli, no change is expected to occur in the subject's behavior. Accordingly, experiments demonstrating true conditioning must ensure that these effects are specific to the associative relationship and do not occur as a function of other, nonassociative, aspects of the situation. Sensitization, for example, can also increase the likelihood of a response occurring. The effects of repeated presentation of a UCS alone, while not themselves based on an associative process, might easily be mistaken for associative conditioning.

Contingency Versus Contiguity

To clearly demonstrate true associative learning the experimenter must employ a number of appropriate control procedures designed to rule out behavior alterations resulting from something other than stimulus association. Rescorla (1967) has suggested that most of the traditionally used control procedures, such as presentation of the CS alone, are in fact inadequate for this purpose. Clearly, any single-stimulus control procedure is inadequate since it fails to account for the absolute amount of stimulation received by the animal (subjects in the experimental group receive both CS and UCS on each trial). More importantly, Rescorla has pointed out that the superficially definitive double-stimulus controls often used are also inadequate. In the *explicitly unpaired* control, for example, presentations of CS and UCS never occur concurrently; stimuli are typically presented with a minimum lapsed time always separating the occurrences of the two elements. Though the stimuli in this situation are in fact not positively associated with one another, Rescorla argues that a new systematic contingency does exist between the stimuli. Implicit in this argument is the distinction between *contiguity* (simple temporal pairing) and a true *contingency*. Any time the CS systematically provides any information about the occurrence of the UCS, a contingency is said to be operating, and an association can be formed. This includes conditions under which the CS is reliably correlated with the nonoccurrence of the UCS. That is, the CS predicts the *nonoccurrence* of the UCS. Such a *negative contingency*, potentially quite useful to the organism, constitutes an inhibitory conditioning procedure. The CS in this case signals that no UCS is coming; no anticipatory response occurs. This situation in fact prevails in the explicitly unpaired control. Because a relatively long minimal interval always separates presentation of the two stimuli, occurrence of the CS is reliably correlated with the nonoccurrence of the UCS for some time. Consistent information about some aspect of the UCS is contained in the occurrence of the CS, and behavior should change accordingly. Rescorla has termed this approach the *contingency view of conditioning*. It has the added advantage of placing equal emphasis on excitatory and inhibitory conditioning.

As Rescorla has suggested, the explicitly unpaired control does not control for the effects of contingency. It merely replaces one contingency with another. Similar objections are raised against the use of the *discriminative conditioning* control procedure. Here, one conditional stimulus (the CS+) is always paired with the UCS, while another (the CS−) is never so treated.

Substantial post-training differences between response-eliciting properties of the two "conditional" stimuli have traditionally been taken as evidence of the conditioning of the CS$^+$. The animal has successfully formed
a discrimination between the two stimuli. As in the case of the explicitly
unpaired procedure, however, here a contingency exists with respect to
both stimuli. The CS$^+$ reliably predicts occurrence of the UCS (a positive
contingency), while the systematically unpaired CS$^-$ predicts the repeated absence of the UCS (a negative contingency). Neither of the two
procedures described, therefore, allows the investigator to assess the effects of stimulation in the absence of any contingency at all.

Rescorla has proposed an alternative control procedure that avoids such
problems and can therefore be used as a neutral baseline against which
conditioning effects can be effectively evaluated. This is the *truly random
control*. The procedure consists of completely random and independent
presentation of the two stimulus elements. It differs from the explicitly
unpaired procedure in that with the truly random control occasional associations (pairings) between stimuli can be expected to occur by chance.
The CS, however, is not systematically correlated with the presence *or*
absence of the UCS. It is important to note that some behavioral change
may be in evidence with the use of the truly random control procedure.
Either sensitization or habituation, for example, may take place. The critical comparison is one that reveals differences in behavior produced by the
noncontingent (truly random) procedure versus those produced by the
contingent (conditioning) procedure. These are the differences indicative
of the occurrence of true associative learning.

The Correlational View

Up to this point we have not distinguished one reinforcing circumstance
from another. This is in keeping with traditional accounts of classical conditioning, which have for the most part assumed that simple contiguity is
the basic feature of the reinforcement process. Beyond the temporal dimensions already discussed, differences among distinct parameters of
reinforcement have been of little consequence. Numerous recent theoretical accounts of classical conditioning have, however, placed renewed emphasis on the signaling or *informational value* of the conditional stimulus.
As a result, unique findings have emerged clarifying the distinct conditions under which reinforcement will be differentially effective in sustaining learning. Mere contiguity is not enough; some instances of contiguity
work better than others. It now appears that contiguity is effective for
conditioning only if a *correlation* exists between the CS and UCS. A correlation exists if the CS reliably predicts occurrence of the UCS—if occurrence of UCS is conditional upon the presence of the CS. Rescorla (1968,
1972), for example, has shown that when the probability of the UCS in
the presence of a CS is held constant, the degree of conditioning may be

dramatically affected by manipulating the probability of the UCS *in the absence of the CS*. Rescorla found no conditioning when the probability of the UCS was equal in both the presence and absence of the CS—that is, when the UCS is equally likely to occur with or without the CS. Under such conditions the CS and UCS are paired but uncorrelated.

The distinction between contingency and contiguity discussed above suggests that contiguity *per se* may not be critical in determining the success of the conditioning process. Similar distinctions have been incorporated into many recent theoretical formulations. It seems reasonable to assume, for example, that if the signal provided by the CS (and therefore its predictive value with respect to the UCS) is either redundant or otherwise superfluous, contiguity of CS and UCS will be irrelevant. In such situations conditioning should *not* be expected to occur. It is perhaps because of just such cases that the theories devised to account for differences in the effectiveness of different reinforcing circumstances have centered on the signaling or informational explanation of classical conditioning.

Much of the literature supporting informational (signaling) accounts of classical conditioning describes situations involving *compound stimulation*. These are cases in which two (or more) conditional stimuli are presented together, and together acquire the ability to evoke a single conditional response. A moment's reflection should reveal that compound stimulation provides a realistic analogue of the conditions under which learning usually occurs. Rarely are organisms responding to a single stimulus. In fact, accurate evaluation of the single-CS conditioning procedure suggests that here, too, background stimulation is always present, potentially acting as a compound (Rescorla and Wagner, 1972). It has been within the context of such interactions among compound stimulus elements that the importance of informational signals has been rediscovered.

Wagner (1969) reports the results of an experiment in which three groups of rabbits received different degrees of conditioning of an eyeblink response initially elicited by electric shock. All animals received 200 trials on which the stimulus compound of light plus tone was followed by shock. One group was presented with an additional 200 trials on which light by itself was reinforced by shock, while in a second group 200 additional presentations of the uncompounded light went unreinforced. The first group, therefore, received only the reinforced stimulus compound (200 trials); the second received that plus 200 reinforced trials of light alone; and the third received the 200 reinforced trials with the stimulus compound plus 200 *unreinforced* trials of light alone. In both cases the 200 extra trials were interspersed among presentations of the 200 compound trials. All subjects subsequently underwent a series of 16 *reinforced test trials* in which the tone (the other element in the original stimulus compound) was for the first time presented alone. Wagner reasoned that although the tone had been followed by reinforcement the same number of times for all subjects, because the second element in the compound (the light) had undergone different degrees of conditioning, the groups should differ in the amount of conditioning sustained by the tone alone. That is, something more than simple contiguity was expected to determine the effectiveness of the tone. Specifically, for the group that received only the reinforced stimulus compound, both the light and tone were reliable cor-related with shock. Both light and tone might be moderately effective elicitors of the eyeblink response. For the group that received an addi-tional 200 reinforced trials with light alone, however, the shock was un-iquely correlated with the light (since the shock was preceded on all trials by the light but on only 200 trials by the tone). According to a correla-tional view, in this group the tone should be a weaker elicitor of the eye-blink response than in the first group. A simple contiguity view, however, would predict the tone to be equally effective for both. Finally, for the group that received an additional 200 unreinforced trials with light alone, the shock was uniquely correlated with the tone (since the tone was al-ways followed by shock, but the light was followed by shock on only half of the trials). The correlational view would predict that in this group the tone should serve as a more potent elicitor than in either of the other two groups.

Results, summarized in Figure 3.14, are consistent with these predic-tions. In the group that had received 200 additional light trials (I), and for which light was thus assumed to have high associative strength, very few CR's were elicited by the tone alone. By contrast, in the group in which the associative strength of the light had been weakened by 200 unrein-forced light-alone trials (III), far more conditioning was sustained by the tone alone. Recall that all animals received the same number of rein-

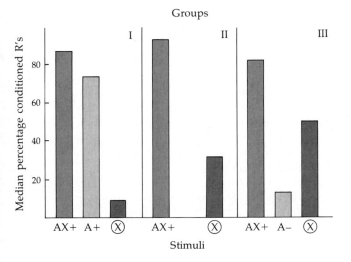

Figure 3.14
Effects of training with a compound conditioning stimulus (AX) on responding elicited by one element of the compound (X) as a function of training with the second element of the compound (A). [After R. A. Rescorla and A. R. Wagner, A theory of Pavlovian conditioning: Variations in the effectiveness of reinforcement and nonreinforcement. In A. H. Black and W. F. Prokasy (Eds.), *Classical conditioning II: Current research and theory.* New York: Appleton-Century Crofts, 1972. Redrawn by permission of Prentice-Hall, Inc.]

forced presentations of the light–tone compound. The effects of this experience apparently depended on the degree of correlation between the second element in the compound (the light) and reinforcement. When that correlation was high, the tone provided little additional input—the relevant event had already been signaled. When, however, the light–reinforcement correlation was low, and the tone was uniquely correlated with reinforcement, considerable conditioning occurred to the tone. Much of the literature on compound conditioning reveals that altering the correlation between one cue and reinforcement may determine the effectiveness of a second cue even though no differences exist in the amount of contiguity between the second cue and reinforcement (for example, see Egger and Miller, 1962).

The Rescorla–Wagner Model

Rescorla and Wagner (1972) have developed a model of classical conditioning that is perhaps the most clearly presented and widely cited of the recent accounts of conditions responsible for the differential effectiveness of reinforcement. The theory attempts to clarify specific conditions under which *associative strength* accrues to a stimulus when CS–UCS pairing has occurred. Under what conditions does contiguity result in the formation of an association? The model is based on the intuition that "the effect of a reinforcement . . . depends not upon that reinforcement itself but upon the relationship between that reinforcement and the reinforcement that the organism anticipated" (Rescorla, 1972, p. 11). The notion of anticipation implies that the organism may already have some information about (a basis on which to anticipate) the occurrence of the UCS. The effect of further reinforcement will depend in part on the existence of readily available information.

> Changes in associative strength of a stimulus as a result of a trial can be well predicted from the composite strength resulting from all stimuli present on that trial. If this composite strength is low, the ability of a reinforcement to produce increments in the strength of component stimuli will be high; if the composite strength is high, reinforcement will be relatively less effective. Similar generalizations appear to govern the effectiveness of a nonreinforced stimulus presentation. If the composite associative strength of a stimulus compound is high, then the degree to which a nonreinforced presentation will produce decrements in the associative strength of the components will be large; if the composite strength is low, the effect of a nonreinforcement will be reduced [Rescorla and Wagner, 1972, p. 73].

Also incorporated into the model, however, are dimensions emphasizing factors other than the informational value of the conditional stimulus—factors that may be of comparable importance in the development of a conditional response. It should be noted that the authors of the theory are attempting to explain not just the final level of performance that results from conditioning, but changes taking place *during* the process of conditioning itself. In addition to predicting post-training changes in performance, therefore, the theory also focuses on changes in the *associative strength* of a signal as learning proceeds.

At the outset, Rescorla and Wagner made several assumptions that outline the nature of the relevant parameters determining classical conditioning. The following are among the substantive assumptions of the theory:

1. Any given unconditional stimulus can support only a certain amount of conditioning. Beyond this point further instances of reinforcement will yield no further behavior change. This parameter, the *asymptote of learning*, will differ for each distinct UCS. It effectively places a ceiling on the magnitude of changes in associative strength.

2. The rate of learning supported by different UCS's—that is, how rapidly changes may develop—also differs with qualitative changes in the unconditional stimulus. Alterations of the type discussed in Chapter 10, involving qualitative differences in specific situations, can be incorporated into the model along these two dimensions.

3. When conditional stimuli occur in compound, the total associative strength of the compound is equal to the sum of the associative strengths of each element in the compound. Moreover, all conditional stimuli present at the time of reinforcement become, by definition, part of the total stimulus compound.

4. Changes in associative strength occurring with additional experience are determined by the *difference* between the prevailing strength of the compound at a given point in time and the asymptote of learning (maximal change possible) defined by a particular unconditional stimulus. Only a certain amount of change can occur, and increments in associative strength with each successive trial will, therefore, become progressively smaller because each additional change insures that less change is potentially possible. It is this final statement that most succinctly describes how the associative strength of a stimulus will be altered during the course of classical conditioning.[9]

Return for a moment to the more intuitive language of anticipation. If the organism's level of anticipation is already high (the difference between the asymptote of learning and associative strength is small), additional reinforcements will have little, if any, effect. If, on the other hand, little positive conditioning has already occurred, no signaling function is

---

[9]See Rescorla (1972) for a discussion of the necessary caution required in extending the informational language to the analysis of classical conditioning.

being served, and therefore anticipation is low, subsequent reinforcement (contiguity) should be quite effective in increasing associative strength.

In the experiments described earlier (Wagner, 1969), altering the associative strength of the compound by the addition of 200 trials, reinforced for one group (I) and unreinforced for another (III), drove the cumulative strength of the compound in opposite directions with respect to the asymptote of learning. For group I, light provided a disproportionate amount of the total strength of the compound, and the tone, therefore, was relatively ineffective. Two hundred extra reinforced trials had contributed much more to the attainment of the learning asymptote. In group III, the extra unreinforced light trials subtracted from the light's effectiveness in the compound, and the tone's contribution was correspondingly greater. In either case, the difference between the associative strength of the entire compound and the asymptote of learning is the critical determinant of conditioning. The effectiveness of the reinforcements applied to each element in the compound are, therefore, themselves determined by the amount of associative strength already contributed by other elements of that compound.

It is noteworthy that though contemporary accounts of classical conditioning are in accord with Pavlov's assignment of a signaling, or informational, function to the conditional stimulus, thinking on the means by which that function develops has changed considerably. Contiguity of CS and UCS is no longer thought of in absolute terms. Instead, contiguity must be considered in a larger, correlational context: Only when a CS and UCS are positively correlated will the CS become conditioned.[10] Thus a CS in close temporal contiguity (say, X sec) with a UCS may not be conditioned if the UCS is as likely (or more likely) to follow the *absence* of the CS within an equivalent period (X sec). At the same time, a CS that is less contiguous to the UCS (say, 2X sec) may be effectively conditioned if its occurrence increases the likelihood that the UCS will follow. We shall see that the correlational view of classical conditioning, inspired by the work of Rescorla and Wagner, has a parallel development in operant conditioning, especially in the area of conditioned reinforcement (Chapter 6).

---

[10]Use of the term "correlation" rather than "information" avoids some unnecessary connotations of the latter term. In discussing conditioned reinforcement (Chapter 6), for example, we will encounter "information theories" of conditioned reinforcement whose specific predictions are generally inconsistent with the facts of conditioning. Our use of "correlation," however, is comparable to Rescorla's (1972) use of "information" as applied to classical conditioning.

4 Operant Conditioning

Pavlovian conditioning deals with reflexive behavior—that is, responding that invariably follows a specific stimulus, such as blinking when a blast of air hits one's eyes. Operant (or instrumental) conditioning, on the other hand, deals primarily with nonreflexive behavior. For example, it is almost impossible for someone not to blink his eyes when a sudden blast of air hits them (an "elicited" reflex action), but it is possible for him to wink or not wink at a person passing in the hall (an "emitted" act). Of course, the emission of operant responses is not independent of environmental stimuli. Thus, for a person given to winking, the appearance of a close friend may set the occasion for a wink. It should be clear, however, that the appearance of the friend does not invariably produce a wink; that is, the wink is not a reflexive response to the sight of the friend. Pavlovian conditioning, then, deals with elicited responding, while operant conditioning deals with emitted responding. We stress, however, that the distinction between elicited and emitted responses is blurred, and the distinction between Pavlovian and operant conditioning is sometimes difficult to maintain.

The terms Pavlovian and operant conditioning also refer to the experimental *procedures* used in studying learning. The procedural distinction is more straightforward. It differentiates the two kinds of conditioning by the ordering of events in the learning process. While in Pavlovian conditioning the CS and UCS occur in a regular sequence independent of the organism's responses, in operant conditioning reinforcement is dependent upon (contingent on) what the organism does. Thus the sequence of events in classical conditioning might be tuning-fork sound (CS), blast of air at eyes (US), blinking (CR and UR). The critical relationship is between CS and US. In operant conditioning, however, the sequence might be sight of friend (discriminative stimulus), wink (operant response), friend's smile (reinforcer). Here the crucial relationship is between the response and the reinforcing stimulus that follows it.

Discriminative stimuli (S^D's) are stimuli that precede and accompany operant responses. Such stimuli are called "discriminative" because they set the occasion on which operant responses are reinforced. In effect, they tell the organism when responses may be effective in producing positive reinforcement or in avoiding punishment. The relationship between the three events described—discriminative stimuli, operant response, and reinforcing stimulus—has been termed the *three-term contingency*. The critical portion of the contingency defining operant conditioning, however, is that between the last two terms—the *operant response* and the *reinforcing stimulus* (hence a response–stimulus, or R–S, contingency).

Most vertebrate behavior is operant—that is, behavior *emitted* by the organism and strengthened by reinforcement according to the principles of operant conditioning (see Chapter 2). Thus students of behavior tend to spend more time investigating behavior maintained by operant than by classical conditioning. Consequently, we devote the next five chapters to a contemporary review of research and theory on operant behavior. Whenever relevant, we discuss the application of operant conditioning principles to the modification of human behavior in clinical and other applied settings.

Before providing an overview of operant conditioning in this chapter, we should mention that our discussion of classical conditioning is by no means complete. In this chapter—and in Chapter 8—we note some important interactions between the two kinds of conditioning. Moreover, when we turn to the behavioral biology of learning in Chapters 9 through 12, we will have more to say about classical conditioning, particularly in the realm of invertebrate learning. Having said that, we turn to the basic principles of operant conditioning.

BASIC CONCEPTS

The focal concept of operant conditioning is *reinforcement*. Reinforcement refers to the occurrence of a "reinforcing stimulus" or "reinforcer" defined as any event that increases the probability that the behavior it follows will recur in the future. For example, if a hungry cat rubs its body against the leg of its owner and receives a piece of salmon, the probability that the cat will perform this action in the future when it is hungry is likely to increase. If so, the salmon has served as a reinforcer.

As shown in Figure 4.1, there are two kinds of reinforcers: positive and negative. Whereas positive reinforcers make the actions they follow more

	Strengthens responding	Weakens responding
Presentation	Positive reinforcer	Punisher
Omission	Negative reinforcer	Negative punisher

Figure 4.1
A 2 × 2 table defining two types of reinforcers and punishers. For example, a punisher is a stimulus the presentation of which weakens the responding that produced it.

probable by their occurrence, negative reinforcers make the actions they follow more probable by their termination or nonoccurence. Thus a dog readily learns to jump over a hurdle in order to escape electric shock delivered through the floor of its cage. The electric shock is a negative reinforcer in that shock presentation increases the frequency of the response that terminates it (jumping the hurdle). This type of negative reinforcement is called *escape*. In a second type of negative reinforcement, *avoidance*, the organism may prevent the negative reinforcer from occurring. For example, if given the opportunity a dog will come to jump the hurdle so quickly at the start of the trial that it may *avoid* the shock altogether. Escape and avoidance are discussed further in Chapter 8. For now, however, it should be clear that negative reinforcers *increase* the future occurrences of behaviors that terminate them (as in escape or avoidance) just as positive reinforcers *increase* future occurrences of behaviors that produce them (see Figure 4.1). In a sense, it is difficult to distinguish between positive and negative reinforcement, since any example of positive reinforcement (for example, eating for a hungry organism) can be rephrased in terms of negative reinforcement (escape from deprivation or hunger) and any example of negative reinforcement (the dog jumping to escape shock) may be rephrased in terms of positive reinforcement (jumping to safety). The important point is that whether we are considering positive or negative reinforcement we are discussing events that strengthen the behavior they follow.

Negative reinforcement, therefore, must not be confused with *punishment*. Punishment weakens the behavior it follows such that response frequencies are decreased following the presentation of a punishing stimulus. For example, electric shock may be a punisher if it decreases the frequency of the response that produces it (such as remaining in the apparatus until the floor of the cage is electrified, instead of jumping). Thus punishment appears in Figure 4.1 in the cell noting that the *presentation* of an aversive stimulus weakens or suppresses the behavior.

Behavior may also be weakened by the *omission* of a positive reinforcer, as shown in the lower right-hand cell of Figure 4.1. A familiar example of such an omission procedure, also called *negative punishment*, occurs in the training of puppies or other young animals: A dog may receive a biscuit if it *does not* jump up on the person holding the treat; if it does jump, it is punished by not getting the biscuit.

MEASURING OPERANT BEHAVIOR

There are several ways in which responding may be measured, depending upon the kind of information the experimenter is interested in. Four measures are commonly employed: two types of time measurement, rate of responding, and probability of responding. One time measure is the *latency* or speed of responding—that is, the length of time between the presentation of the discriminative stimulus and the subject's response. For example, in an experiment involving avoidance conditioning, how long does it take a rat to jump off the floor after a buzzer signals that a shock is imminent? The second type of time measure is the *duration* or amount of time the subject spends engaged in a given response. In many cases the duration of time spent in an activity, particularly when other activities are available, is related to the reinforcing strength of that activity. In experiments measuring time, whether latency or duration, the response or activity must be chosen and defined carefully so that there is no ambiguity about its onset or termination.

Probably the most common response measure employed in studying operant behavior is *rate of responding*—that is, the number of responses per unit of time. Rate is a useful measure when a response must be emitted several times before reinforcement occurs, as in intermittent schedules of reinforcement. For example, in a variable-interval one-minute schedule (VI 1-min) responses are reinforced on the average of once every minute, although the actual interreinforcement intervals vary over a wide range (for example, from a few seconds to a few minutes). With such a schedule, rate of responding provides a more meaningful and useful measure than latency. Finally, *probability of responding* is frequently used to measure the relative effectiveness of one or more reinforcers in experiments on choice and in discrimination problems in which both correct and incorrect responses are available. In the typical choice experiment, for example, a pigeon may be given the opportunity to respond on either of two keys, each of which is associated with a different type or amount of reinforcement. The response measure is the proportion of the total number of responses that occurs to each of the two choices. Discrimination learning tests may be viewed as a subset of choice procedures. Here, however, responding to the discriminative stimulus on one of the two keys never produces reinforcement. In this case, then, we can talk about the probability of a correct response (number of correct responses over the total number of correct and incorrect responses).

Apparatus

Many kinds of apparatus have been developed to study learning. Each of them arranges an environment in which behavior has particular consequences under certain circumstances. The types of apparatus differ in the nature of the behavior required, the kinds of circumstances and consequences, and the ease with which the behavior may be measured. The traditionally most important pieces of apparatus are shown in Figure 4.2. Some, like the Lashley jumping stand, the T-maze, and the Skinner box, are particularly well suited for discrimination tasks—that is, those in which a subject must choose between two or more stimuli in order to obtain either positive or negative reinforcement. Other apparatuses shown, such as runways, puzzle boxes, shock chambers, and shuttle boxes, are useful for nondiscrimination tasks. These and other apparatuses have been designed to evaluate some particular ability or to study a particular response for a particular organism. Thus the T-maze shown is well suited for studying choice behavior in a rat or other small organism, which must turn left or right if it is to obtain food in the appropriate goal box.

The Skinner box is ideally suited to measure rate of responding. Response probability can be studied in choice or discrimination learning procedures if the Skinner box is equipped with two or more stimuli and two or more response manipulanda. For example, a typical pigeon chamber might contain two response keys on which different-colored lights or forms could be illuminated. The Skinner box and its variants permit precise measurement of some aspect of the organism's behavior, typically the rate of responding or the latency of each key-pecking response. Moreover, the device clearly separates the three elements of the three-term contingency: the discriminative stimulus, the response, and the reinforcer. The experimenter achieves complete control over the three most important elements of an experiment on operant conditioning: (1) occurrences of the discriminative stimulus and of the reinforcers, (2) the definition and measurement of the response, and (3) the relationship between the discriminative stimulus, the response, and the reinforcer.

The Skinner box evolved from earlier pieces of apparatus for studying learning. Experimental mazes have ranged from the simple to the complex. One of the most complex was adapted by Willard S. Small from the Hampton Court garden maze (Figure 4.3), a diversion of the English aristocracy. Later mazes have been simplified to bring the relationship between the stimuli in the maze, the subject's discrimination, and the reinforcers under better control. For example, Small's maze had many choice points; as the rats learned the maze it appeared that they were discriminating correct from incorrect choices at each choice point. In such a complex maze, however, it would have been quite difficult to specify which stimuli controlled the rat's behavior at each point. With the T-maze, however, there is only a single choice point, which can be provided with different cues (for example, a red and a green card, or a white and a black

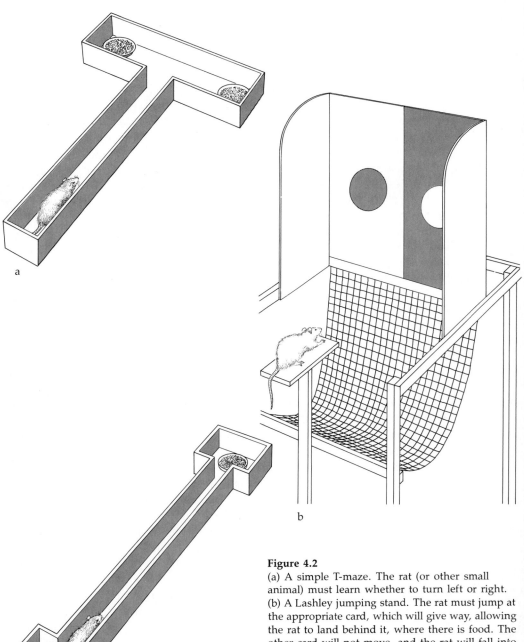

Figure 4.2
(a) A simple T-maze. The rat (or other small animal) must learn whether to turn left or right. (b) A Lashley jumping stand. The rat must jump at the appropriate card, which will give way, allowing the rat to land behind it, where there is food. The other card will not move, and the rat will fall into the net below. (c) A runway. Unlike the T-maze and the Lashley jumping stand, in which the subject must make the correct choice, the runway's dependent variable is the speed with which the subject reaches the goal box, which contains food.

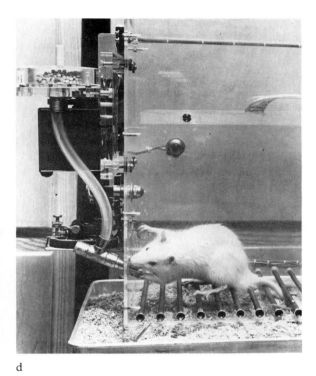

d

Figure 4.2 (cont.)
(d) A rat responding in a Skinner box. Choice can be studied in such an apparatus if two response levers have different consequences. The effect of these consequences on the subject's choice behavior—the number of presses on one lever relative to the number of presses on the other lever—is then assessed. [Courtesy of Pfizer, Inc.] (e) A puzzle box, used by Thorndike, Guthrie, and others to study instrumental behavior in the cat.

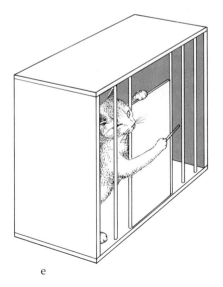

e

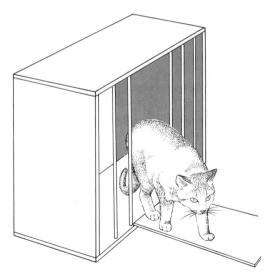

88

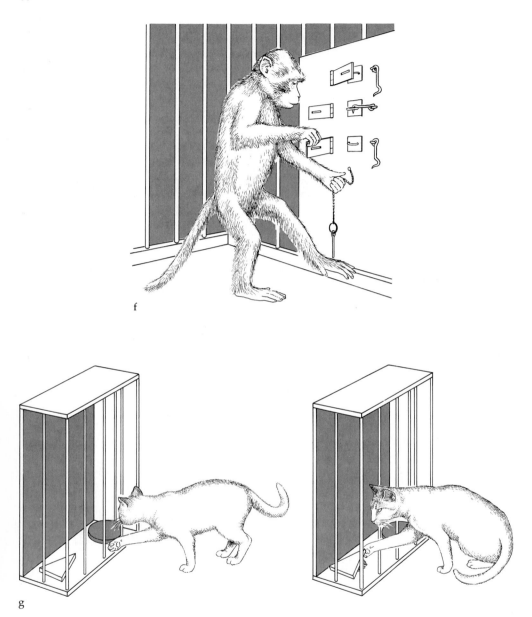

Figure 4.2 (cont.)
(f) A monkey at work on a mechanical puzzle. [After a photograph by Harry F. Harlow.]
(g) A cat responds to either of two distinctive stimuli. Food is found under only one of
the stimuli.

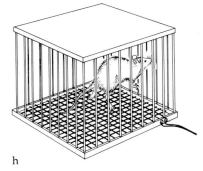

Figure 4.2 (cont.)
(h) In some experiments, animals must respond to avoid or escape an electric shock, delivered in this case through the grid floor of the chamber. (i) In a shuttle box the subject must run from the left compartment to the right compartment to avoid or escape a shock delivered through the grid floor of the left compartment. (j) Rats will press a bar when presses result in the delivery of an electric charge to certain portions of the brain. This intracranial self-stimulation (ICS) is delivered through an implanted electrode. [Courtesy of James Olds.] [Figures 4.2a, b, c, e, g, h, and i are redrawn after *Contemporary psychology* by E. Fantino and G. S. Reynolds. W. H. Freeman and Company. Copyright © 1975.]

h

i

j

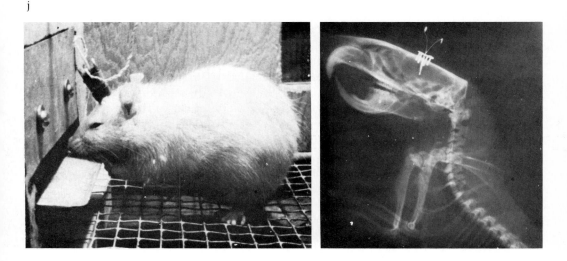

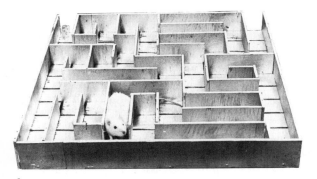

a

b

Figure 4.3
(a) A maze similar to that devised by Willard Stanton Small in 1901. The rat begins at the start and must learn to reach the goal to obtain food. (b) The Hampton Court Gardens maze in England from which Small patterned his maze. [British Crown Copyright: reproduced with permission of the Controller of Her Britannic Majesty's Stationery Office.]

floor) correlated with the reinforcement conditions in the goal box at the end of each arm. This not only facilitates the learning process but also permits the experimenters to study subtle discrimination (for example, between nearly equal colors or forms). An important disadvantage of every maze is that it necessitates a delay of reinforcement. Specifically, after the rat makes its choice it takes it a certain amount of time to run down the arm of the maze and reach reinforcement in the goal box. In most mazes the experimenter must manually return the rat to the start of the maze after each trial. Thus handling the rat may influence the results. Finally, the experimenter must remain near the maze during the experiment. Skinner reasoned that actual running by the rat is unnecessary, so he eliminated the alley leaving only a goal box. In the goal box, he replaced running with lever-pressing and arranged the presses to produce delivery of the reinforcer. Thus reinforcement may be delivered immediately after a response, and the animal need not be handled during the experiment. This automation had the important side benefit of permitting the experimenter to be studying the results (or be otherwise engaged) while the subject is working, rather than having to interrupt the experiment to carry the rat back to the starting point after each trial.

Subjects

Organisms from a wide variety of species have served as subjects in the operant conditioning laboratory, including some baboons, bats, bees, cats, chickens, crows, dolphins, ducklings, chimpanzees, dogs, fish, gerbils, humans, mice, monkeys, octopus, pigeons, porpoises, quail, rabbits, rats, sea lions, sheep, turtles, and vultures. The most popular in the past two decades of operant research has been the pigeon. The two most important reasons for the pigeon's popularity as a subject are the following: It has excellent color vision, permitting a wide array of visual cues to be utilized as discriminative stimuli, and it is capable of maintaining high rates of responding over sustained periods of time. Together, these facts mean that the experimenter can communicate with the pigeon readily, in the sense of providing distinctive S^D's for different reinforcement conditions, and measuring the pigeon's reaction in terms of differential rates of responding. Other advantages of pigeons include relatively cheap maintenance costs and the fact that they are readily handled and reasonably hearty organisms. Given that many investigators have acquired operant conditioning equipment specifically designed for use with pigeons, the pigeon's place in the future of operant conditioning remains secure. Extensive work with humans, monkeys, and rats, however, plus the diversity of organisms less frequently studied, does ensure that the principles generated from research with pigeons are tested with other species as well.

BASIC PHENOMENA

In this section we discuss the basic phenomena of operant conditioning, including acquisition and shaping, schedules of reinforcement, and extinction. Four additional topics, each of which represents an active area of research in contemporary operant conditioning, will be the subjects of the succeeding chapters on stimulus control, conditioned reinforcement, choice, and aversive control (Chapters 5–8).

Acquisition and Shaping

The reinforcement or punishment of previously acquired responses increases or decreases, respectively, their future rate of emission. But how does an organism acquire a novel response? For example, how may a dog be trained to fetch slippers or a chicken to play "Starry Night" on a toy piano? New behaviors may be acquired through a process called *shaping*.

The experimenter begins with responses that are already common in the organism's behavior repertoire and uses differential reinforcement to alter these responses such that they represent closer and closer approximations to the desired terminal behavior. For example, the experimenter may first provide a pigeon with food only when it happens to approach the side of the experimental chamber containing the response key. This should increase the frequency of remaining near the key and moving toward it when away. Next, the experimenter reinforces only certain ways of moving toward the key, ways that bring the pigeon's beak closer and closer to the key. Normally, any beak movement toward the key is reinforced. Ultimately, only pecking the key is reinforced. At each stage in this process, the experimenter is assisted by the variability the behavior displays when it is no longer reinforced: A pigeon that has received food after moving its beak close to the key will perform a flurry of different behaviors when reinforcement no longer follows this movement. Such behavioral variability increases the likelihood that the pigeon will emit a keypeck, and thus be reinforced. Use of the principle of *successive approximations* has enabled experimenters to shape behaviors that do not resemble, even remotely, those that the organism normally emits. Such shaping is of course the basis for complex animal-training demonstrations, such as those featuring trained seals or pigeons playing ping pong.

In Chapter 6 we will illustrate and analyze an extremely complex behavior chain mastered by the rat Barnabus of Brown University. Although we have been talking about chains as resulting from the successful application of shaping as a tool, there are also instances in which chains themselves may be utilized as a tool for shaping new behaviors. As an illustration of one such case we turn to the area of behavior modification with severely retarded children.

Modeling, Imitation, and Behavior Chains

Modeling therapy and imitation have been shown to be powerful tools for shaping desired behavior (for example, Bandura, 1969). Modeling has been used to induce imitation in a variety of situations, including teaching speech to severely retarded children (see Lovaas, Berberich, Perloff, and Schaeffer, 1966). What happens when the subject does not imitate, however? Baer, Peterson, and Sherman (1967) worked with three severely retarded children at the Kansas Neurological Institute who had *never* been seen to imitate the behavior of others during several days of observation. Baer and his co-workers first shaped an imitative tendency using a fading technique (elaborated in Chapter 5) in the following manner: One therapist would make a motor movement, such as lifting his arm while saying "do this"; the second experimenter lifted the child's arm in response and, in addition, immediately reinforced the arm-raising with food. The manual assistance was gradually faded out until the child was imitating on his own. The child could now imitate a sequence of over one hundred motor responses such as: "Walk and tap head with left arm," "Burp doll," "Place box inside of ring of beads," and so on. Importantly, all three subjects began to imitate new responses reliably on their first presentation—that is, prior to reinforcement of that response—showing that the children had developed an imitative repertoire. In other words, the children were not simply learning specific responses. Instead, they were learning to "Do as the experimenter does." The experimenter's behavior acquired control as a discriminative stimulus for emitting imitative behavior. Once the imitative tendency had been developed, modeling was used to establish other useful behaviors.

The experimenters were particularly concerned with speech. Would the children now imitate the model's verbal utterances? This proved more difficult. However, some success was achieved by embedding the word or sound in a response sequence consisting of a motor response followed by a word. With one subject, for example, the seated experimenter would say "Do this," get up and walk to the center of the room, then turn toward the subject and say, "Ah." As Baer et al. (1967) noted: "To such a demonstration subject 1 responded by leaving her seat, walking toward the center of the room, turning toward the experimenter, and then beginning a series of facial and vocal responses out of which eventually emerged an 'Ah' sufficiently similar to the experimenter's to merit reinforcement. This coupling of motor and vocal performances was maintained for several more demonstrations, during which the motor performance was made successively shorter and more economical of motion; finally, the experimenter was able to remain seated, say 'Do this,' say 'Ah,' and immediately evoke an imitation from the subject. Proceeding in this manner, simple sounds were shaped and then combined into longer or more complex sounds and finally into usable words" (p. 410).

Autoshaping

Much shaping in the contemporary operant laboratory no longer requires an observing experimenter. Through the technique of *autoshaping*, responding may often be shaped with an automated procedure. Such autoshaping is more than a handy technique, however. In addition, the phenomenon of autoshaping, first reported by Brown and Jenkins (1968), provides a good example of behavior that appears to be determined by principles of both operant and classical conditioning. In a typical autoshaping demonstration, a hungry pigeon that has never before been an experimental subject is placed in a standard pigeon chamber. A key in the chamber is illuminated repeatedly once every minute for 6 seconds. When the light turns off, food is presented to the pigeon. The light remains off for 54 seconds and then turns on again. In this procedure, then, reinforcement is delivered independently of the pigeon's behavior toward the key; that is, food is presented even when the bird does not peck the key. Nonetheless, the pigeon soon begins to peck the key once it is illuminated. The procedure is called "autoshaping" since the organism's key-pecking response is acquired without the usual shaping by differential reinforcement and successive approximations described earlier. All that is necessary for autoshaping is that the lighting of the key be associated with food. The autoshaping procedure is diagramed in the top half of Figure 4.4.

The determinants of the initial autoshaped reponse are not known with certainty; however, it is likely that classical conditioning is involved. After repeated pairings of the key light with the onset of reinforcement, the key light might become a conditioned stimulus (CS) for the response to the food (a key-peck). Once the first autoshaped response occurs, it produces immediate reinforcement. It is likely, therefore, that once autoshaped responding occurs it is maintained as well by operant conditioning.

More intriguing than autoshaping is the phenomenon of negative automaintenance first reported by Williams and Williams (1969). Williams and Williams's general procedure is diagramed in the lower half of Figure 4.4. Here pecks at the lighted key actually *prevent* the next scheduled presentation of food. In other words, when the pigeon responds the reinforcement is "avoided"; only when the bird fails to peck the lighted key does reinforcement occur at the end of the 6-second stimulus light duration. Surprisingly, some birds acquire the pecking response to such a degree that they rarely obtain food in the negative automaintenance procedure.

Obviously, the negative automaintenance phenomenon is considerably more puzzling than autoshaping. For, as noted, pecks in the typical autoshaping procedure actually cause reinforcement to be more immediate, since pecks at the stimulus light produce food immediately, whereas fail-

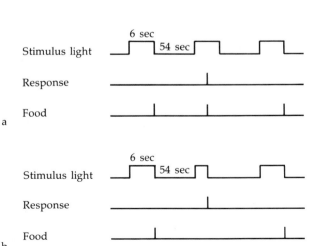

Figure 4.4
The temporal relations in the autoshaping and automaintenance procedures. (a) In autoshaping, a response in the presence of the light produces food immediately. In the absence of a response, food is presented automatically with the termination of the light. (b) Automaintenance is identical, with one crucial difference: a response during the light eliminates food presentation on that trial. Instead, the response turns off the light and begins a new trial. Pigeons acquire pecking even under these conditions. [After *Contemporary psychology* by E. Fantino and G. S. Reynolds, W. H. Freeman and Company. Copyright © 1975.]

ure to peck results in response-independent food only at the end of 6 seconds. In negative automaintenance, however, reinforcement occurs if and only if the organism fails to peck the stimulus light for its duration. What sustains responding in the negative automaintenance procedure? Again, there is no definitive answer at this time. Two likely sources of response strength have been identified, however. One is the same source that was identified for autoshaping, namely classical conditioning (again, resulting from the pairing of the stimulus light and food on those trials when the bird does not peck the light). The second source again appears to be operant conditioning. As in autoshaping, pecking the key does have one effect—turning off the key light—although food is not presented, as it is in autoshaping. On trials on which the subject does *not* peck the key for the duration of the stimulus light, the key light is turned off and food is simultaneously provided. Hence food is always preceded by the termination of the light. Stimulus events that are repeatedly paired with primary reinforcers, such as food, may themselves come to reinforce responding. Such stimuli are called *conditioned reinforcers.* It is possible, therefore, that the termination of the key light develops into a conditioned reinforcer by virtue of repeated pairing of light termination and food. This possibility was supported by Hursh, Navarick, and Fantino (1974), who showed that pigeons would cease to respond in a negative automaintenance procedure when a delay of several seconds was interposed between the peck and the termination of the key light. It appears that the prompt termination of the light indeed reinforced the key-pecking.[1] The role of stimulus change as a conditioned reinforcer—by virtue of its pairings with primary reinforcers—will be considered again later in this chapter when we discuss the intriguing phenomenon of responding for food in the presence of freely available food. For the time being, we note that it is likely that principles of both operant (response–reinforcer) and classical (stimulus–reinforcer) conditioning maintain behavior in autoshaping and negative automaintenance procedures.

Although we have been discussing autoshaping (also known as "sign tracking") and negative automaintenance studies carried out with pigeons, other organisms have been trained with these procedures as well. Peterson, Ackil, Frommer, and Hearst (1972), for example, demonstrated autoshaping in the rat, as did Wasserman, Hunter, Gutowski, and Bader (1975) with the chick. Negative automaintenance has also been found with rats (Stiers and Silberberg, 1974; Atnip, 1977; but see Locurto, Terrace and Gibbon, 1976, and Locurto, 1977, for some qualifications). We

---

[1]These results have been extended recently by Locurto (1977) with rats and a more complete experimental design. In the Hursh et al. study pecks not only delayed the end of the trial but also increased trial duration. Since autoshaped responding is weaker the longer the trial duration (Gibbon, Baldock, Locurto, Gold, and Terrace, 1977) their results might be explained in these terms. Locurto controlled for this possibility, however, and still obtained a decline in autoshaped responding when trial offset was delayed.

will have occasion to return to the important topic of autoshaping later in this chapter when discussing the nature of reinforcement. We have introduced it here as a method of shaping and also as an illustration of the fact that behavior may be multiply determined by classical and operant conditioning. Interactions of these two types of conditioning will be seen again when we examine aversive control in Chapter 8.

Schedules of Reinforcement

Although in some situations reinforcers occur each time an appropriate response occurs in the presence of the relevant discriminative stimulus (as when we insert a coin in a well-maintained jukebox), other reinforcers—both those we encounter in our everyday lives and those in laboratory experiments—do not occur on schedules of continuous reinforcement (CRF). Instead, they are obtained on intermittent schedules, in which only some responses are reinforced. For example, only some of our telephone calls are answered, and we may have to drive around the parking lot several times before we find a space. In the laboratory, which responses are reinforced is determined by the *schedule of reinforcement*. We shall begin by discussing the four most basic intermittent schedules of reinforcement: fixed interval (FI); fixed ratio (FR); variable interval (VI); and variable ratio (VR).

An FI schedule arranges reinforcement for the first response that occurs after a fixed interval of time has elapsed. Thus, in a fixed-interval 30-second schedule, only the first response that occurs after 30 seconds has elapsed is reinforced. The organism tends to make many nonreinforced responses during the fixed interval. Curve c in Figure 4.5 shows typical fixed-interval responding: Reinforcement is followed by a pause and then by a rapid acceleration of responding as the end of the interval approaches. This pattern of responding is known as an "FI scallop."

On an FR schedule, reinforcement occurs after the emission of a fixed number of responses. Curve b in Figure 4.5 shows typical performance on an FR schedule. Again, note the pause after reinforcement followed by a rapid "ratio run" until the next reinforcement occurs. The larger the FR requirement, the longer the pause tends to be. Indeed, with short ratios, little or no pausing occurs. Although the FI scallop and the FR ratio run are traditionally thought of as clearly distinct response patterns, in practice they often closely resemble one another (Schneider, 1969; Shull and Brownstein, 1970) as can be noted by comparing the form of curves b and d of Figure 4.5.

VI and VR schedules are analogous to FI and FR schedules, respectively, except that responses are reinforced after a variable rather than fixed amount of time has elapsed (VI) or a variable rather than a fixed number of responses has been emitted (VR). Thus a typical VI sequence might reinforce the first response after 50 seconds have elapsed since the

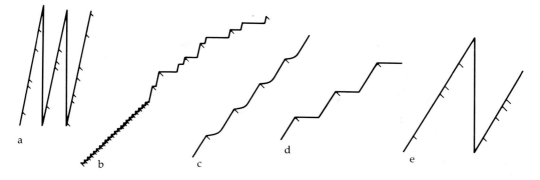

Figure 4.5

(a) A cumulative record of responding on a *variable-ratio schedule*, in which a certain number of responses is required for reinforcement. Unlike fixed-ratio schedules, the number of responses varies, and responding is maintained at a steady rate. (b) A cumulative record of responding on a *fixed-ratio schedule*, in which reinforcement is first delivered after every twenty-fifth response and later after every hundredth response. This record shows a break-and-run pattern. The break is known as an FR pause. Breaks sometimes occur during the performance, as when the ratio is abruptly increased from 25 to 100. (c and d) Typical cumulative records of responding on a *fixed-interval schedule*, in which the first response after the interval has elapsed is reinforced. One record (c) shows the gradual acceleration of responding within the fixed interval that is known as a fixed-interval "scallop." The other record (d) shows a break-and-run pattern more typical of behavior on well-practiced FI schedules. (e) A cumulative record of responding on a *variable-interval schedule*, in which the first response after each interval has elapsed is reinforced. Unlike fixed-interval schedules, however, the size of the interval varies, and responding is maintained at a steady rate. [After *Contemporary psychology* by E. Fantino and G. S. Reynolds. W. H. Freeman and Company. Copyright © 1975.]

last reinforcement, then after 70 seconds, then after 30 seconds, and so on, after 85, 80, 180, 5, 30, 20, and 50 seconds. The sequence would then be repeated again and again until the experiment was concluded. This particular VI schedule is a VI 60-second schedule because 60 seconds is the average of the ten different intervals comprising the VI sequence. Shown in curves e and a, respectively, of Figure 4.5, VI and VR schedules both maintain fairly constant rates of responding, since responses may be reinforced at almost any time. Thus the pauses characteristic of fixed schedules generally do not occur on variable schedules.

Rates of responding tend to be higher on VR schedules than on VI schedules since rapid responding is differentially reinforced on VR schedules but not on VI schedules. The faster the subject responds on a VR, the faster it collects reinforcement, since reinforcement is contingent upon the completion of a number of responses. On a VI, however, reinforcement is contingent upon the passage of time. Hence the subject does not appreciably affect its rate of reinforcement by responding at a higher rate. Consequently, VR schedules are very effective for generating high rates of uninterrupted responding. Not surprisingly, therefore, VR schedules are used in gambling houses and slot machines, such as the "one-arm bandit." The persistence of many gamblers in playing these machines is typical of behavior generated by VR schedules.

More complex reinforcement schedules may usually be reduced to variations or combinations of these four basic intermittent schedules. *Concurrent schedules*, as their name implies, are available simultaneously. For example, a VI one-min schedule might be arranged on the left key and a VI 3-min on the right key. In such a situation, the organism will tend to respond three times as often on the VI 1-min, a matching relation we will discuss in detail in Chapter 7. A *multiple schedule* also involves two or more schedules, but these are presented to the organism successively rather than simultaneously. Thus a multiple VI 1-min VI 3-min schedule would present the organism with the opportunity to respond on each of the two VI schedules, but in alternation, as determined by the experimenter. In multiple schedules each component schedule is associated with a distinct exteroceptive stimulus. If there were no discriminable difference between two components of a multiple schedule (except the schedule of reinforcement associated with each component), the schedule would not be called a multiple schedule but instead would be a *mixed schedule* of reinforcement. Thus, in a mixed VI 1-min VI 3-min schedule, for example, the VI 1-min and VI 3-min schedules alternate in the presence of the same discriminative stimulus.

Two schedules that have been used extensively in the study of conditioned reinforcement are *chain* and *tandem schedules*. Unlike multiple and mixed schedules, chain and tandem schedules provide reinforcement during only one component. Generally, reinforcement occurs only at the end of the last of two or more successive components. Thus, in a chain VI 1-min VI 3-min, the response that terminates the VI 1-min component advances the subject to the VI 3-min component. Only after the VI 3-min component is satisfied is primary reinforcement obtained. The chain schedule is similar to a multiple schedule in that a different exteroceptive stimulus is associated with each component or "link" of the chain. A tandem schedule, on the other hand, is similar to the mixed schedule in that the same exteroceptive stimulus is correlated with each component. The relations between multiple, mixed, chain, and tandem schedules are summarized in Figure 4.6.

Finally, we should also mention two useful schedules of reinforcement that differentially reinforce particular rates of responding. In the *differential reinforcement of low rate schedule (DRL)* organisms' responses are reinforced only when emitted at a sufficiently low rate. For example, on one type of DRL schedule only responses that follow one another by more than a specified number of seconds are eligible for reinforcement. Similarly, a DRH schedule *(differential reinforcement of high rates)* is one that

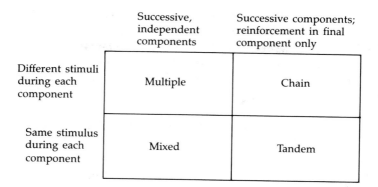

	Successive, independent components	Successive components; reinforcement in final component only
Different stimuli during each component	Multiple	Chain
Same stimulus during each component	Mixed	Tandem

Figure 4.6
A 2 × 2 table summarizing the relations between multiple, mixed, chain, and tandem schedules of reinforcement.

reinforces the emission of a given number of responses in a particular period of time. For example, the organism may be required to emit 25 responses within 15 seconds in order to obtain reinforcement. Finally, on a *differential reinforcement of other behavior schedule (DRO)*, failure to emit a particular response for a specified time is reinforced. Thus, on a DRO 30-sec, reinforcement occurs after 30 seconds have elapsed without a key-peck. The DRO differs from a comparable DRL 30-sec in that a key-peck is required after a 30-second pause in a DRL but not in the DRO. It should be stressed that, in all cases, reinforcement schedules have predictable, orderly—and profound—effects upon the organism's pattern and rate of responding.[2]

Extinction

Without reinforcement, responding decreases in frequency. The rate at which the phenomenon of extinction takes place depends in part on the reinforcement conditions in effect prior to extinction. Extinction after continuous reinforcement (when each response has been reinforced) is rapid because the organism has been shifted from a situation in which all of its responses are reinforced to a situation in which none of its responses is reinforced. The change in the situation is readily discriminable, and responding extinguishes rapidly. On the other hand, extinction following intermittent schedules is slower because there is less difference between the new and the old situations, especially in the case of extremely variable

---

[2]The classic book on schedules of reinforcement is that of Ferster and Skinner (1957). A recent treatment may be found in Zeiler (1977).

schedules. For example, a VR-500 schedule will contain some very long sequences of unreinforced responses—indeed, several thousand responses may occur between reinforcements. Thus it may take several hours of extinction before the new situation (no reinforcement) is discernably different from the old one. A broken slot machine may maintain thousands of unreinforced responses (coin insertions) by the gambler who has become accustomed to infrequent reinforcements. When a soda machine fails to operate, however, it is unlikely that one will insert more than two dimes, because a vending machine should operate on a continuous-reinforcement schedule.

The greater resistance to extinction of responding following intermittent (or "partial") reinforcement—known as the *partial-reinforcement effect*—has far-reaching practical implications for behavior. A mother who *occasionally* reinforces her child's undesirable temper tantrums by comforting the child is building stronger and more persistent tantrums than the mother who *always* comforts an unhappy child. The child with a history of intermittently reinforced tantrums will emit them seemingly endlessly in the future, even when the parent attempts to extinguish them by ignoring them. Common sense (and reinforcement principles) indicates that what the parents should be doing is reinforcing the child when he is quiet or otherwise behaving appropriately.

The partial-reinforcement effect is also known as "Humphreys' paradox" for reasons that shed light on Clark Hull's behavior theory, discussed in Chapter 2. For Hull, a key measure of response strength was resistance to extinction (a dependent variable), while a key factor in enhancing response strength was the number of reinforced trials (an independent variable). But Humphreys (1939) and Skinner (1938) each showed that resistance to extinction was increased, not decreased, when reinforcement was omitted on a number of trials. For Humphreys, this was a "paradox" since Hull's theory required the opposite. Hull revised his theory to account for the partial-reinforcement effect, but his resolution never proved fully satisfactory.

Even after extinction has been carried out to apparent completion, the tendency to emit a previously reinforced response readily surfaces under certain conditions. For example, if a day or so is allowed to elapse between the completion of extinction and the next opportunity to perform the response, we usually observe the phenomenon of *spontaneous recovery*— "spontaneous" because no further reinforcers have occurred. The response will once again be emitted at a rate reminiscent of that seen prior to extinction. Without further reinforcements, however, a spontaneously recovered response quickly extinguishes again. After additional experiences of this sort, spontaneous recovery gradually ceases to occur. Spontaneous recovery indicates that responding in the presence of a *new* opportunity for reinforcement has not yet been extinguished. For example, if you lose two quarters to a broken vending machine on a Monday, responding to the machine extinguishes. Yet you may hopefully insert another quarter into the machine on Tuesday.

Behavior therapists have long used extinction as a technique for modifying undesirable behavior. One of the early studies of extinction treatments was conducted by Ted Ayllon and Jack Michael in the psychiatric wards of a hospital in Saskatchewan, Canada (Ayllon and Michael, 1959). Like most of the early behavior modification studies, these conditioning techniques were utilized only because all other efforts had failed, and the patients' behaviors were considered fairly untreatable. The experimenters observed that the nurses were often responsible for their patients' abnormal behavior, inasmuch as they reinforced these behaviors with attention. The experimenters successfully demonstrated that by eliminating the reinforcing attention, a wide variety of bizarre behaviors could be eliminated.

For example, one group of subjects consisted of several men known as the "rubbish collectors" because they habitually hoarded newspapers and magazines by stuffing them into their clothing. The experimenters reasoned that the hoarding was being reinforced by the attention given the subjects when they were routinely "dejunked" by the nurses several times a day. This hypothesis was confirmed when the hoarding behavior disappeared after the nurses discontinued dejunking. The hoarding behavior underwent extinction because it was no longer reinforced by the nurses' attention. Had the nurses realized the effects of their previous behavior? No. In fact, they protested the efforts to disrupt the hoarding behavior. They felt that it was providing the hoarders with a needed "sense of security" and that to abolish it might cause more bizarre, less adaptive symptoms to emerge. What actually happened, however, was that once hoarding was no longer reinforced with attention, the rubbish collectors stopped hoarding newspapers and magazines and instead sat in the lounge and read them!

The important behavior therapy technique of *systematic desensitization* is believed to be largely effective because it involves extinction. Since this is one of the most important and highly regarded techniques of behavior modification, we will discuss it in some detail in the subsequent section.

APPLICATIONS IN BEHAVIOR THERAPY

The use of positive reinforcement in behavior therapy may be illustrated by the case of a 37-year-old woman who resisted eating to such an extent that her weight plummeted from 120 to 47 pounds in the course of a few years (Bachrach, Erwin, and Mohr, 1965). She was in danger of dying from malnutrition. Since there was no time for the kind of extended treatment that most forms of psychotherapy require, a new kind of therapy was tried in which the therapists concentrated on treating the symptom, refusing to eat, rather than trying to uncover and treat any underlying problem. Nor did they make any inferences or interpretations about the causes of her condition. They decided to apply the principles of positive reinforcement in an attempt to alter the woman's eating behavior before she went to her final reward.

The first step was to induce a response (eating) by selecting appropriate reinforcers. Among the pastimes the woman engaged in frequently were listening to music, reading, watching television, and conversation. Therefore the therapist made these reinforcers dependent upon eating behavior: when the patient did not eat, she was kept in a fairly barren room where none of these reinforcers were available. For example, nurses who had to come into the room to perform essential duties were instructed not to speak or otherwise pay attention to the patient. At meal times a therapist came in with a tray of food and sat silently with her, only talking with her if she touched her fork. Then the therapist reinforced responses that progressively approximated the desired behavior (eating). The behavioral requirement was successively raised from (1) touching her fork, to (2) lifting it, and finally, to (3) inserting food into her mouth. That is, the requirement for obtaining social reinforcement was gradually stiffened until eating was required for reinforcement. Eating was reinforced not only with companionship but also with wheeling in the television set and turning on the phonograph. Later, eating was reinforced with permission to go outside, and to receive special visitors. The patient was soon released in good health, weighing a reasonable 83 pounds. Follow-up studies indicated that she continued to maintain her weight gain. Her family was given some advice on operant-conditioning techniques so that mealtimes continued to be a rewarding occasion to the patient in her home environment.

Notice that the woman was cured without reference to her past history. In fact, the therapists avoided any talk about her background so that the effects of reinforcement would not be confounded with any potential effects of "working through" her problem. Later they did learn something of the history and causes of the woman's failure to eat. The patient had been extremely overweight as a child, and attempts to lose weight had been reinforced by her family and friends. As a result, she adjusted her eating habits so much that she became thin. In time, she married, but the marriage was an extremely unhappy one. She continued to curtail her eating until the doctor told her that she was much too thin and that if she lost any more weight he would recommend that she return to her parents. Her weight plummeted at once, and she went back home! Upon arriving home, her weight loss, which had previously been reinforced by social appreciation of her trim figure, was now reinforced by the concern manifested by family, friends, and doctors because of her refusal to eat. Thus, although events in the patient's history had truly been the source of her problem, the therapists' success in curing the disorder without delving into that history demonstrates that positive reinforcement may be effective even without "working through" the historical determinants of a behavioral problem.

Although most applications of operant conditioning to behavior therapy have involved positive reinforcement, it is sometimes more efficient, and even necessary, to utilize treatments based on punishment and negative reinforcement. Some techniques combine both positive reinforcement and punishment, as we shall see when discussing Lovaas' work later in this section. Techniques that use punishment predominantly are examples of *aversion therapy*. These therapies attempt to eliminate undesirable behavior by the use of aversive consequences such as electric shock or nausea (produced by an emetic). Our discussion of aversion therapy in dealing with temper tantrums, cigarette smoking, and other behavior problems, will be deferred until Chapter 8. At that time we will also see the use of a commonly employed negative punisher: the *time-out room*. Brief mention of time-out procedures is warranted here particularly since they also illustrate the use of negative reinforcement in attempting to modify behavior disorders. Placing a child in a time-out room when the child is emitting inappropriate behavior removes him from the opportunity to earn positive rewards, such as the social reinforcers available in play. In this sense, then, the time-out room serves as a negative punisher for inappropriate behavior. The effectiveness of time-out procedures may be maximized when release from the time-out room is made contingent upon appropriate behavior (such as being quiet). In this case, the opportunity to leave the time-out room is an example of negative reinforcement (at least insofar as being in the time-out room is aversive).

Dr. Ivar Lovaas of the University of California, Los Angeles, has had unprecedented success in treating self-destructive autistic children. Autistic children are marked by a profound lack of orientation to reality. They instead seem totally concerned with their own private world and with sources of self-stimulation (including self-destruction), to the exclusion of social interactions and stimulations from the external environment. Some children have been maintained in straight jackets in order to prevent them from harming or killing themselves, for example by repeatedly clawing at their eyes or smashing their heads against walls. Lovaas has shown that the treatment of an autistic child may resemble an attempt to build a person from scratch, combining the techniques of positive reinforcement, punishment, and other methods based on the principles of operant conditioning. Lovaas and his associates have succeeded in eliminating self-destructive behavior and replacing it with various social skills, including language.

In a pioneer study (Lovaas and Simmons, 1969), Lovaas theorized that the child's self-destructive behavior was being maintained by the attention given to it by concerned and loving parents and nurses. After all, it would appear a natural tendency to comfort the child engaged in self-destructive behavior. Under these conditions, self-destructive behavior may be reinforced and maintained by social attention. If so, it should be possible to extinguish the behavior by withholding attention—that is, by ignoring the self-destructive behavior. Lovaas and Simmons tested this hypothesis with two autistic boys. In each case, the self-destructive behavior extinguished as shown in Figure 4.7. The amount of time required for extinction was too great for it to be advisable as a normal treatment procedure, however. Obviously, in cases of severe self-destructive behavior, the child could seriously harm itself before self-destructive responding extinguished. Since extinction proved too slow to be a safe method for eliminating the self-destructive behavior, Lovaas initiated punishment in the form of painful electric shock. The punishment had an immediate suppressing effect on the frequency of self-destructive responses. It should be added, however, that when punishment was no longer made contingent upon the emission of self-destructive behavior, the behavior once again increased. If punishment is to be a really effective treatment for self-destructive behavior, therefore, its applicability must extend to other situations. Lovaas and his colleagues have shown that if the suppression of self-destructive behavior is to persist in new situations, at least two and preferably more experimenters must administer the shock, and they must do so in several different situations.

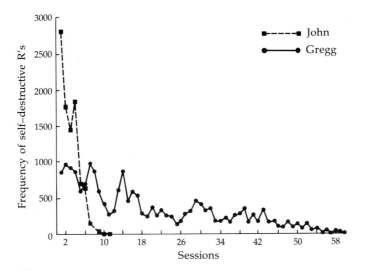

Figure 4.7
Extinction of the self-destructive behavior of two autistic boys.
[After O. I. Lovaas and J. Q. Simmons, Manipulation of
self-destruction in three retarded children. *Journal of Applied
Behavior Analysis, 2,* 143–157. Copyright © 1969 by the Society for
the Experimental Analysis of Behavior, Inc. Redrawn by permission.]

Lovaas and Simmons also showed that it was possible to intensify self-destructive behavior by communicating sympathy or understanding whenever the self-destructive responses were emitted. This finding supports the notion that by attempting to "understand" why the child is being self-destructive, parents, nurses, or therapists may be unwittingly providing attention and other social reinforcers that maintain self-destructive behavior. In other words, the traditional practice when dealing with autism, in which adults respond to self-destructive behavior with "warmth and understanding," appears actually to maintain rather than eliminate self-destructive behavior.

Once a child has stopped emitting self-destructive behavior, does his behavior change in other ways? Specifically, do undesirable side effects (or substitute symptoms) occur? Lovaas and his group have found just the opposite: desirable side effects, such as a decrease in the tendency to avoid others, occur instead. Equally important, now that the child has stopped his self-destructive behavior, the therapist is in a position to school the child in both social and intellectual skills. Thus Lovaas and his group have utilized positive reinforcement in order to instill important linguistic and social skills in children who have stopped emitting self-destructive behavior (see Lovaas et al., 1966; Lovaas, Koegel, Simmons, and Long, 1973).

Systematic Desensitization

One of the most widely used and thoroughly researched therapeutic techniques designed in accordance with laboratory research on behavioral change is *systematic desensitization*. Traditionally, systematic desensitization, used in the treatment of situational and pervasive anxiety, phobias, and other avoidance responses, has involved three treatment stages. First, the client is trained in progressive muscular relaxation skills. Theoretically, this newly acquired ability to achieve relaxation may *compete* with or *inhibit* the autonomic nervous system arousal (anxiety) associated with stimuli that elicit fear. This deep muscular relaxation is said to replace the tension present when the client is confronted with an anxiety-producing situation or thought (Wolpe, 1958).

The second stage involves the development of a stimulus hierarchy consisting of a series of discrete situational descriptions of anxiety-provoking stimuli presented in ascending order of arousal properties. All stimuli in the hierarchy are somewhat similar to the focal object of fear, and the steps of the hierarchy move the client progressively closer either to a real object or event (*in vivo* desensitization) or to an imagined fear-inducing object or event (*in vitro* desensitization).

The third stage involves the combination of the newly acquired relaxation response with the presentation of the fear-inducing items in the hierarchy. The client moves through the hierarchy while relaxed, and signals the therapist when any anxiety is experienced. The therapist then prompts the client to terminate the image and utilize his relaxation skills so as to associate relaxation instead of tension with the arousing stimulus item. For example, a person who is irrationally fearful while taking examinations may be taught relaxation procedures and then given a hierarchy in which an early item is, "Imagine yourself approaching the testing room one-half hour prior to the test." The terminal item might then be, "Imagine the test questions in front of you as you are asked to begin." The steps should not be too far apart so as to cause intense anxiety, which would prevent further progress through the hierarchy. The therapist must be careful to have the client terminate the scene or the actual approach if any anxiety arises from the presentation of a new item.

Until recently, the mechanism behind effective anxiety management with systematic desensitization was thought to be *reciprocal inhibition*. In other words, a competing behavior (relaxation) must occur in the presence of the fear-inducing stimulus such that it is eventually substituted for the maladaptive behavior (anxiety or avoidance). More recent research on the process of systematic desensitization, however, sheds doubt on the reciprocal inhibition hypothesis. Wolpin and Raines (1966), working with snake phobias, compared a group of subjects who received the ascending hierarchy of fear-inducing items *without* prior relaxation training, and another group who received the hierarchy while actually pairing muscle *tension* with the stimulus items. A third group began at the top of the hierarchy and was neither relaxed nor tensed. In other words, none of the subjects received typical systematic desensitization with relaxation training. Nonetheless, each of the three methods was effective. Other researchers (Schubot, 1966; Rachman, 1968; Nawas, Welsch, and Fishman, 1970; Miller and Nawas, 1970; Rimm and Medeiros, 1970; Sue, 1972; Silverstone and Salkind, 1973) have observed similar results. It appears, therefore, that while relaxation may help the process of desensitization, particularly with extremely phobic individuals, it is not an essential aspect of treatment.

Other findings also cast doubt on the reciprocal inhibition theory of systematic desensitization. Krapfl (1967) found that an ascending hierarchy is not necessary. Anxiety reduction occurs even when the client is presented the most anxiety-producing item first. Therefore the progressive matching of a competing response with more and more fearful items is not required. The effectiveness of another behavioral technique, *implosive therapy* (Stampfl and Levis, 1967), further detracts from the original hypothesis. In implosive therapy the client is asked to imagine a detailed confrontation with the anxiety-producing situation as vividly as possible. In this method no alternative responses are utilized, nor is the approach to the most fearful situation gradual. The successful results of this therapeutic approach, coupled with the data indicating that relaxation is not essential as an alternative response, detract from the traditional theory of systematic desensitization. The assumption that systematic desensitization depends upon the components of muscular relaxation, an ascending hierarchy, and reciprocal inhibition is cumbersome and generally not supported.

Several alternative hypotheses have been developed to explain the mechanism involved in systematic desensitization (for example, Goldfried, 1971; Valins and Ray, 1967; Nawas, Fishman, and Pucel, 1970; Ellis, 1962; London, 1964). It appears, however, that all of the findings reported in this discussion may be explained as examples of operant extinction (Gillan and Rachman, 1974). The client is asked to confront, either through imagery or in reality, the fear-producing stimulus. In effect, during treatment the client is placed in a nonthreatening situation very unlike those situations in which the fear-inducing stimulus has been encountered prior to therapy. Here the client experiences gradual approach to and contact with the stimulus repeatedly—*and in the absence of aversive consequences.* Without the anxiety response and the typical avoidance that results, the client confronts the problem situation in such a way that the lack of consequences alters behavior. This process is extinction. In addition, the client's rational behavior is reinforced by the therapist, friends, and family, thus increasing the probability that this new adaptive behavior will be maintained.

THE NATURE OF REINFORCEMENT

In Chapter 2 we discussed the "Great Age of Learning Theory," particularly the four positions—those of Guthrie, Tolman, Hull, and Skinner—that dominated the experimental psychology of learning in the 1940s and 1950s. As we indicated there, most of the central questions these theorists addressed were left unanswered. The central question concerning *why* consequences strengthen responding—really a question about the nature of reinforcement—remains unresolved, either in terms of an adequate theory of learning or in terms of the physiological basis of reinforcement. We have, however, advanced our knowledge of the conditions under which response strength is enhanced. This section examines the contemporary view of the optimal conditions for the occurrence of response strengthening by reinforcement.

Two important, related generalizations have grown out of recent work in operant conditioning. One states that events that bring the organism into the presence of higher rates of primary reinforcement, or at least closer in time to primary reinforcement, themselves serve as reinforcers. In order for response strengthening—the reinforcement effect—to occur reliably in the presence of a particular stimulus, for example, the occurrence of the stimulus should be associated with a higher rate of reinforcement than that occurring in its absence. In other words, a correlation between CS and UCS is necessary before conditioned responding occurs. We saw evidence for this in our discussion of classical conditioning in Chapter 3.

Much the same picture emerges in operant conditioning. As we shall see in our discussions of conditioned reinforcement and choice (Chapters 6 and 7), stimuli correlated with higher rates of reinforcement maintain higher rates of responding (Herrnstein, 1970), as do stimuli correlated with reductions in time to reinforcement (Fantino, 1977). It is important to note that, as in classical conditioning, it is not enough to consider only the *absolute* temporal relation between stimulus and reinforcer. Instead it is necessary to consider the relative relations and correlations as well. To review, we saw in Chapter 3 that contiguity of CS and UCS is no longer thought of in absolute terms. Contiguity is now considered in a larger, correlational context: Only when a UCS and CS are positively correlated will the CS become conditioned. We noted there that a CS in close temporal contiguity (say, X seconds) with a UCS may not be conditioned if the UCS is as likely (or more likely) to follow the *absence* of the CS within an equivalent period (X seconds). At the same time, a CS that is less contiguous to the UCS (say, 2X seconds) may be effectively conditioned if its occurrence increases the likelihood that the UCS will follow (as when the UCS is at least 4X seconds away in the absence of the CS). A similar story may be told for behavior maintained by operant conditioning. We shall see in Chapter 6, for example, that a stimulus serves as an effective conditioned reinforcer only to the extent that its occurrence is correlated with a reduction in time to primary reinforcement.

Autoshaping Studies

If a stimulus must be differentially correlated with positive reinforcement in order to itself be an effective reinforcer—whether a CS in classical conditioning or a conditioned reinforcer in operant conditioning—this correlation should also be necessary for autoshaping, since, as we suggested earlier, autoshaped responses are probably multiply determined by the two types of conditioning. Two types of evidence support this expectation. Gamzu and Schwartz (1973) studied autoshaped responding in several response-independent schedules of reinforcement. The basic schedules studied were variable-time 33-sec schedules (VT 33-sec). On such a schedule reinforcement occurs, independent of responding, on the average of every 33 seconds. A particular key color was associated with this schedule. When this schedule alternated with another equivalent VT 33-sec schedule associated with a different key color, little autoshaped responding occurred to either stimulus. In this case neither stimulus was differentially correlated with reinforcement, since the rate of reinforcement was equal in the presence of the two key colors. This result shows that key light–food pairings are insufficient to maintain auto-shaped responding. On the other hand, when the VT 33-sec schedule alternated with an extinction stimulus (one never correlated with food), a significant amount of autoshaped responding was sustained by the stimulus correlated with the VT 33-sec. Gamzu and Schwartz also found that the VT 33-sec schedule would sustain responding when it alternated with a VT 100-sec schedule. This latter finding indicates that autoshaped responding in the presence of the VT 33-sec schedule did not depend upon an alternating stimulus correlated with nonreinforcement. Instead these results suggest that any stimulus differentially correlated with rein-forcement will sustain responding, even when reinforcement is response-independent.

The second type of evidence comes from studies varying the duration of the intertrial interval in autoshaping procedures. A given stimulus maintains more autoshaped responding when it follows a longer intertrial interval (see Terrace, Gibbon, Farrell, and Baldock, 1975). This result is consistent with those we will encounter when discussing conditioned reinforcement (Chapter 6). Then we will see that conditioned reinforcers are those stimuli correlated with a reduction in time to reinforcement. Since a stimulus following a long intertrial interval is correlated with a greater reduction in time to reinforcement than the same stimulus follow-ing a short intertrial interval, it should be a more potent reinforcer. The autoshaping results suggest that such a stimulus also maintains a higher rate of responding in its presence. In general, a stimulus that precedes food sustains a higher rate of responding the closer in time it brings the organism to primary reinforcement.

The Premack Principle

We have just seen that the strength of a stimulus in maintaining behavior does not depend entirely on its absolute temporal relation to primary reinforcement. An even greater stride toward appreciating the relativistic nature of reinforcement was made by the theoretical and empirical work of David Premack. Two points should be made to set the stage for Pre-mack's findings. In the first place, we should make explicit that stimuli may have multiple functions. For example, a stimulus in a chain schedule serves both as an S^D for responding in its presence and as a conditioned reinforcer for responding in the prior component. Furthermore, some stimuli are primary reinforcers, such as food to a hungry organism or water to a thirsty one. This brings us to the second point: The traditional conception of reinforcement was that a limited number of reinforcing stimuli—such as those associated with hunger, thirst, sexual deprivation, and so on—existed for any organism and that other stimuli were not primary reinforcers. Premack's theory and research in the 1960s showed that this traditional conception was grossly oversimplified. In addition, the traditional conception was preventing us from realizing a more powerful and more generally valid conception of reinforcement.

Premack stressed that it was more useful to discuss reinforcers in terms of responses than in terms of stimuli. Thus, the reinforcer for operating vending machines may be thought of as eating (a response) rather than the sandwich itself (a stimulus), the reinforcer for the hungry rats' lever-pressing may be thought of as eating (a response) rather than the food itself (stimuli), and the reinforcer in sexual behavior may be thought of as sexual intercourse (a response) rather than the sexual partner or "object" (a stimulus). More importantly, Premack showed experimentally that the same event that serves as a reinforcer for some responses may be ineffective as a reinforcer for other responses. Reinforcers can often change places with the activities that produce them: A thirsty rat will run to get water, but a long-idle rat would actually drink in order to get a chance to run (Premack, 1962). In the first case, drinking reinforces running; in the second case, running reinforces drinking. In general, any behavior an organism performs can serve as a reinforcer for any other behavior that the organism performs less frequently. There is, therefore, a reinforcement hierarchy: Reinforcers at the top of the hierarchy are those behaviors that are performed with greatest likelihood, given the chance; those at the bottom of the hierarchy are those reinforcers that would be rarely engaged in even if the opportunity to do so were unlimited. In Premack's terms, for a given organism any response in the hierarchy may reinforce any response below it and may itself be reinforced by any response above it. Moreover, the position of a response in the hierarchy may be changed by depriving the organism of the opportunity to engage in that response. Thus, by depriving the organism of the chance to emit a naturally occurring response, the momentary value of that response in enhanced. As a consequence, that response will be a more general reinforcer in the sense that it will, temporarily at least, reinforce responses that are normally above it on the reinforcement hierarchy.

Evidence for the Premack principle has been developed in studies in both the animal and human laboratories. In a classic experiment (Premack, 1959), children were given the choice of eating candy or operating a pinball machine. It was found that children who preferred playing the pinball machine would increase their intake of candy if playing the pinball machine was contingent upon eating candy. If a child who preferred the pinball machine became sufficiently hungry, candy would come to reinforce pinball playing. Thus a shift in the relative probability of engaging in particular behaviors is accompanied by a shift in the reinforcing effects of these behaviors.

The Premack principle has long been applied by laymen. For example, when a parent requires a child to clean up his room before he can watch his favorite TV program, he is applying the Premack principle (or, more generally, the law of effect, described in Chapter 2). On the other hand, he is not doing so if he tells the child that he can watch the program provided he cleans his room afterward. The Premack principle has enjoyed successful application in the classroom as well as in the home. Pupils' writing abilities, for example, have been significantly increased by allowing the students the opportunity to play after successfully completing an assignment. In other settings the opportunity to engage in a highly preferred academic subject has been shown to improve performance in a less-preferred subject. Homme, deBaca, Devine, Steinhorst, and Rickert (1963) applied the Premack principle to the behavior of three-year-old nursery school children. They noted that the high-probability behaviors of their subjects included running around the room, screaming, working jigsaw puzzles, and pushing chairs. These activities were often continued even when the subjects were instructed to sit in their chairs. Homme et al. made these high-probability behaviors contingent on desired behaviors. For example, the behavior of sitting quietly in a chair looking at the blackboard was occasionally followed by the sounding of the bell and the instruction, "run and scream." The subjects would then jump up and run around the room screaming. Homme et al. utilized this procedure to achieve virtually perfect control after a few days.

Since the Premack principle stresses that any activity or set of stimuli may reinforce behavior, we are no longer tied to a conception of a fixed set of primary reinforcers. This liberation—and more recent elaborations by Timberlake and Allison (1974)—enables some complex phenomena to be better understood. We will look at one such phenomenon briefly.

Responding for Food with Food Already Present

Rats and pigeons with food continuously available to them will nonetheless acquire lever-pressing or key-pecking responses to obtain access to a second source of the same food. This phenomenon of responding for food in the presence of freely available food (Neuringer, 1969) appears surprising if one assumes that food is the only reinforcer in the situation. The results of an experiment by Wallace, Osborne, Norborg, and Fantino (1973) suggest that this phenomenon is due to the presence of conditioned reinforcers. The key-pecking response is reinforced not only by food (the unconditioned reinforcer) but also by the externally produced stimulus changes that accompany the presentation of food. When the pigeon pecks the key, the key light turns off, the food tray raises into position with an audible click, and then is illuminated. Since all these stimuli are closely associated with food, they tend to acquire the status of conditioned reinforcers. Figure 4.8 shows what happens when these stimulus changes are removed from the mechanical presentation of food and instead accompany pecks at the free food: the bird no longer pecks at the key (condition 2 in the figure). When the experimental conditions are

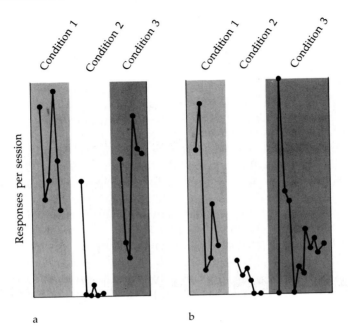

Figure 4.8
Extra responding by two pigeons (a and b) for stimulus change. In conditions 1 and 3, responses produced stimulus change in addition to food. In condition 2, responses produced food only, while pecks in the free-food cup produced stimulus change. The pattern of results shows that responding for food in the presence of freely available food depends upon the external stimulus changes that accompany such responding. [After R. F. Wallace, S. Osborne, J. Norborg, and E. Fantino, Stimulus change contemporaneous with food presentation maintains responding in the presence of free food. *Science, 12,* 1038–1039. Copyright © 1973 by the American Association for the Advancement of Science.]

again reversed, so that the stimulus changes once more accompany only the response-produced food (condition 3 in the figure), key-pecking is quickly resumed. It seems that the "extra" stimuli that accompany the food have become conditioned reinforcers of such strength that, in this situation, they influence the choice response.[3] In other words, the pigeon prefers food with external stimulus changes, rather than just food alone.

---

[3] We are assuming that the extra stimuli are conditioned reinforcers because they have been paired with food. It is also possible, however, that the stimulus change they provide is intrinsically reinforcing to some degree, a possibility not assessed by Wallace et al. (1973). In any case it is clear that the pigeon prefers the combination of food plus these stimulus changes to food alone, a conclusion also consistent with the results of Alferink, Crossman, and Cheney (1973), also with pigeons, and Osborne and Shelby (1975) with rats.

The phenomenon of responding for food in the presence of free food seems analogous to many human responses (for example, consider the premium put by many upon the "atmosphere" of a restaurant). This "contra-free-loading" phenomenon has been ably reviewed recently by Osborne (1977). More generally the research on contra-free-loading underscores the fact that behavior cannot be fully understood in terms of a fixed set of primary reinforcers.

Economical Distribution of Activities

With time and energy at a premium, activities should be distributed in as economical a way as possible. Indeed, for each organism in a given situation there should be an optimal "free-behavior point" (Staddon, In press; see also Rachlin and Burkhard, 1978) representing the distribution of activities under free conditions—that is, conditions without imposed contingencies. If a particular activity is restricted (for example, eating is restricted when food is scarce), more time should be spent on the activity when the opportunity arises, and that activity should be reinforcing. Traditional studies of deprivation and Premack's work indicate that this is in fact the case.

Recall that in Premack's terms, for a given organism, any response in the reinforcement hierarchy may reinforce any response below it and may itself be reinforced by any response above it (given the same schedule of reinforcement). Moreover, response deprivation leads to changes in the reinforcement hierarchy. Thus a thirsty rat will run to get water (drinking is higher than running in the hierarchy), but a long-idle rat will drink in order to gain access to a running wheel (running is now higher than drinking). In the first case, drinking reinforces running; in the second case, running reinforces drinking. Premack's theory need not be regarded as circular, since the reinforcement hierarchy may be determined independently of reinforcement contingencies. Thus, which activity should reinforce the other may first be determined in choice tests in which both activities are freely available. The behavior that is performed more frequently should serve as a reinforcer for the less frequent behavior but not *vice versa*. However, if the less frequent activity is restricted below its freely occurring rate, it should serve as a reinforcer. Assume, for example, that a particular student devotes two hours of his weekday evenings to studying and one hour to watching TV. Now a contingency is introduced such that three hours must be devoted to studying in order to watch TV for one hour. Watching TV should now reinforce studying, and the time spent studying should rise above two hours (the free-choice amount). Similarly, if a different contingency is introduced so that *less* studying is allowed than in free choice, say one hour of study for one hour of watching TV, studying should now reinforce TV watching and the amount of

TV watching should rise above one hour (the free-choice amount).[4] Timberlake and Allison (1974) proposed that responding in a given stiuation tends to reduce the conflict or "disequilibrium" between the optimal or free-behavior point, as measured in baseline sessions, and the terms of the contingency schedule.[5] They note:

> If it is assumed that conflict between the schedule-imposed behavior and the free-responding baseline determines instrumental preference, it is important to state precisely the circumstances necessary for this conflict. The concept of response deprivation provides such a statement. For a given instrumental schedule, the condition of response deprivation is defined to occur if the animal, by performing its baseline amount of the instrumental response, is unable to obtain access to its baseline amount of the contingent response [Timberlake and Allison, 1974, p. 152].

More formally, Timberlake and Allison stipulate that the condition of response deprivation is satisfied when

$$\frac{I}{C} > \frac{O_i}{O_c}$$

where I and C are the terms of the schedule and O_i and O_c are the baselines of the instrumental and contingent responses, respectively. The I term of the schedule is the instrumental requirement for access to the contingent activity, and C is the amount of access to the contingent activity (or the "payoff") earned by completing I. This response deprivation condition states that a given amount of access to the contingent activity (C) will reinforce the instrumental response whenever the ratio of I to C is greater than the baseline ratio (O_i/O_c). In the example just cited, the baseline rates of studying and TV watching were two hours and one hour, respectively. Thus TV watching should not reinforce studying as long as the ratio I/C is less than or equal to $O_i/O_c = 2/1 = 2.0$. When I/C is greater than 2.0, however, as when three hours of study are required for one hour of TV watching (I/C = 3.0), the response deprivation condition is satisfied and TV watching should reinforce studying.

------

[4]It should be emphasized that such reinforcement demonstrations are trivial unless the proper control group is employed. Specifically, if the student is prevented from studying and has no activities available other than watching TV, of course TV watching should be expected to increase. In our example we are assuming that the student has several other options available. Moreover, the effects of removing the opportunity to study on rate of TV watching could be assessed in a control group that had the study option removed altogether—in other words, without the imposition of a contingency. Only if TV watching rose more when a contingency was in effect would a true reinforcement effect be demonstrated. This issue is complex, however. For a discussion of appropriate control groups, see Timberlake (1977) or Bernstein (1973).

[5]See also Eisenberger, Karpman, and Trattner (1967).

Response deprivation theory implies that the organism should seek an equilibrium whereby response deprivation is reduced. When some responses are restricted by a contingency, then the organism should allocate its time among the available responses in an optimal way. In particular, it should achieve a distribution of times comparable to free-behavior (baseline) conditions but modified by the cost of making the requisite instrumental responses imposed by the contingencies. Formal models further quantifying and elaborating these relationships have been advanced recently by Rachlin and Burkhard (1978) and by Staddon (In press).

We have concluded our overview of the basic phenomena, theory, and applications of operant conditioning. In the four subsequent chapters we will discuss four active areas of research in contemporary operant conditioning.

II Research and Theory in Operant Behavior

5   Stimulus Control

If a response that has been conditioned in the presence of certain stimuli is emitted also when new stimuli are presented, we say that stimulus *generalization* has occurred (the response has generalized to the new stimuli). If the response is *not* emitted, *discrimination* has occurred (the new stimuli have been discriminated from the old ones). Generalization and discrimination reflect differing degrees of *stimulus control*, or covariation of stimuli and responses—generalization reflecting relatively imprecise stimulus control and discrimination reflecting relatively precise stimulus control. Thus a child who has been bitten by a brown Afghan hound is likely to be more frightened by an Irish setter than by a fox terrier and is less likely to fear a horse or a Siamese cat than either dog. Generalization and discrimination are matters of degree, which have been studied in the laboratory by measuring *generalization gradients*. Generalization gradients indicate the extent to which responses conditioned in the presence of one stimulus are emitted in the presence of (generalize to) other stimuli. Several important principles governing stimulus control have been found and clarified by these laboratory studies.

We should mention at the outset that virtually all of the research discussed in this chapter concerns stimulus control of behavior maintained by schedules of positive reinforcement. Little is known about the stimulus control of behavior maintained by schedules of negative reinforcement. We simply note here that what evidence there is suggests that the determinants of stimulus control of behavior maintained by positive and negative reinforcement are comparable (see Hearst, 1969a; Klein and Rilling, 1974; Rilling, 1977). This suggestion is consistent with our more general conclusion that behaviors maintained by positive and negative reinforcement follow the same general principles (see Chapter 8).

BASIC PRINCIPLES

Generalization Gradients

In a typical stimulus generalization experiment, the subject is trained on some intermittent schedule of reinforcement, and his responding is then extinguished in the presence of several stimuli, presented successively, including the one present during training. The subject's rate of responding is measured in the presence of each of these stimuli. Two procedural questions should be answered. In the first place, why is an intermittent schedule used? If continuous reinforcement were used, extinction would occur before there were many responses to measure. Only by pooling data from many subjects could a meaningful gradient be plotted. As Guttman and Kalish (1956) have shown, after responding is reinforced on an intermittent schedule, an individual organism will emit enough responses to generate meaningful, interpretable generalization gradients. Our second question is: Why switch to extinction to begin the generalization test? Why not measure generalization in the continued presence of the intermittent schedule of reinforcement? Since the generalization test assesses the effects of reinforced responding in the presence of the training stimulus on the tendency to respond to other (test) stimuli, it is important not to confound this response tendency with that generated directly by reinforced responding in the presence of the test stimuli. Such confounding of results is avoided by testing during extinction—a procedure known as the *extinction technique*. Of several alternative procedures, the most commonly used is the *maintained generalization procedure* (see D. Blough, 1967; P. Blough, 1972; Pierrel, 1958). In this procedure short test trials, during which responding is never reinforced, are interspersed with training trials, during which responding in the presence of the training stimulus is reinforced intermittently. Different test stimuli are presented on different test trials. Responding on these test trials provides the data for the generalization gradient.

Figure 5.1 shows typical generalization gradients obtained during extinction in the presence of different key lights (using the extinction technique), both before and after training in the presence of a particular discriminative stimulus (S^D)—here, a yellow key light. Rate of responding—the dependent variable—is measured as a function of the value of the stimulus along the particular stimulus dimension, here color. These rates are usually plotted in either of two ways. The most

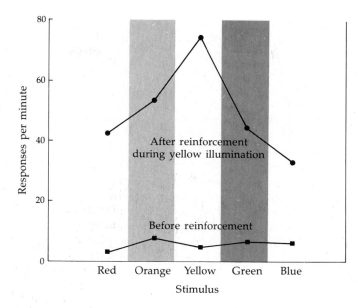

Figure 5.1
A typical generalization gradient. A pigeon whose key-pecks have
been reinforced when the key is yellow is presented with key lights
of several different colors in a generalization test conducted under
conditions of extinction. The generalization gradient has a peak at
yellow (the stimulus to which pecks have been reinforced
previously). The closer the color is to yellow, the more responding
occurs in its presence. [After G. S. Reynolds, *A primer of operant
conditioning.* 2nd ed. Copyright © 1968, 1975 by Scott Foresman
and Company. Redrawn by permission.]

straightforward plot is the *absolute generalization gradient*, which is based
on the total number of responses made to each test stimulus in extinction
(as in Figure 5.1). When it is desirable to make comparisons across conditions, or even across experiments, however, it is preferable to plot *relative
generalization gradients*, in which the number of responses to each test
stimulus is expressed as a proportion of the number of responses to the
S^D in extinction. The gradient in Figure 5.1 shows both generalization (to
a degree) and discrimination (to a degree): generalization, since the subject's tendency to respond to the S^D generalizes somewhat to the other
colors, and discrimination, since the subject responds at different rates to
different colors. The more physically similar the stimuli are to the S^D, the
greater the extent of the generalization. Although rate of responding has
been the most frequently used measure of generalization (at least in the
last decade), the degree of generalization may also be assessed by the
latency, probability, or *amplitude* of the generalized response.

Up to now we have been discussing stimulus control in procedures in which responses have been compared during extinction in the presence of a prior S^D (or S^+) alternating with novel stimuli; a higher rate of responding during the prior S^+ implies discrimination. Other important procedures for studying discrimination are those involving *differential reinforcement* in the presence of two or more stimuli. Typically, a stimulus in the presence of which reinforcement is unavailable (an S^-) is alternated with the S^+ in a discrimination task. When the S^+ and S^- are presented concurrently, the procedure is one of *simultaneous discrimination;* when they are presented successively, the procedure is one of *successive discrimination.* Examples of simultaneous discriminations include those involving subjects responding on concurrent schedules (Chapter 4) and human drivers turning at an intersection (where the correct and incorrect routes are stimultaneously available). Examples of successive discriminations include those involving subjects responding on multiple schedules (Chapter 4), and drivers selecting among turnpike exits. Discrimination is often superior when the stimuli are available simultaneously, probably because subjects have all the relevant cues present—a circumstance that tends to facilitate acquisition of difficult discriminations.

The study of generalization gradients produced by differential reinforcement often involves a successive discrimination procedure in which an S^+ and S^-, occupying different points on the same stimulus dimension, are presented to the subject in alternation. Following such training, a typical generalization gradient is measured based on responses to a variety of stimuli along the stimulus dimension of the S^+ and S^- (and generally including both of these stimuli).

Generalization gradients produced by differential reinforcement procedures typically differ in important ways from the gradient shown in Figure 5.1 (for generalization following nondifferential procedures). A typical *postdiscrimination gradient* is shown in Figure 5.2a. Three differences between this figure and Figure 5.1 are noteworthy: (1) The postdiscrimination gradient is "sharper"—that is, steeper or less flat; (2) the postdiscrimination gradient has a higher "peak," or maximum point—a phenomenon known as *behavioral contrast;* (3) the peak is shifted away from the S^+ in the direction opposite that of the S^-—a phenomenon known as *peak shift.* Each of these phenomena deserves further comment.

Postdiscrimination Gradients

An elegant study by Blough (1975), using a variant of the maintained generalization procedure, showed that the sharpness of the generalization gradient depends, in part, on how responding is sampled. Specifically, Blough studied responding on an FI 20-sec schedule and recorded responses in four 5-second periods: 0–5, 5–10, 10–15, and 15–20 seconds from the onset of the fixed interval. Unlike the typical fixed-interval

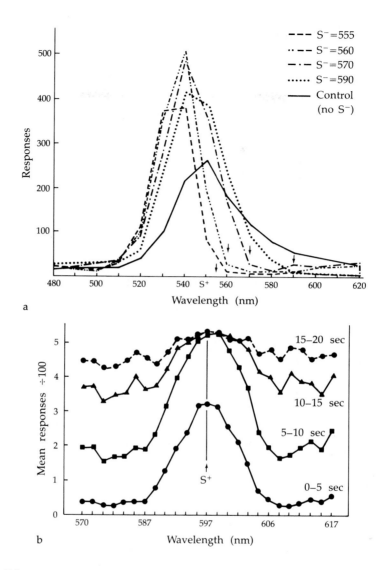

Figure 5.2
Postdiscrimination gradients showing behavioral contrast and peak shift. (a) Gradients represent responding after differential reinforcement for each of four groups, compared with that for a control group receiving nondifferential reinforcement. For all groups, including the control, responding had been reinforced in the presence of 550 nm (S$^+$). Pigeons in each of the four experimental groups had also received extinction in the presence of the S$^-$ shown on the graph. The generalization test was conducted in extinction. [After H. M. Hanson, Effects of discrimination training on stimulus generalization, *Journal of Experimental Psychology, 58,* 321–334. Copyright © 1958 by the American Psychological Association. Redrawn by permission.] (b) Responding by a single bird sampled over four 5-sec periods after onset of the fixed interval in an FI 20-sec schedule in which responding was reinforced at S$^+$ with 0.167 probability. Note that the generalization gradient is flatter toward the end of the interval. [After D. S. Blough, Steady state data and a quantitative model of operant generalization and discrimination. *Journal of Experimental Psychology, 104,* 3–21. Copyright © 1975 by the American Psychological Association. Redrawn by permission.]

schedule, however, responding was reinforced only 10 percent of the time that the interval was completed. This baseline schedule generated an above-zero rate of responding upon which the effects of additional positive (S^+) or negative (S^-) trials could be assessed. For example, Blough obtained a generalization gradient by increasing the percentage reinforcement in the presence of a particular wavelength (597 nm) to about 17 percent. Figure 5.2b shows the resultant gradients for each of the 5-second periods. Note that the gradients are peaked sharply in the period immediately following the onset of the fixed interval, with relatively little responding at wavelengths more than 10 nm from the S^+. In the final 10 seconds, however, a high rate of responding is maintained across all wavelengths, and, consequently, the gradient is relatively flat.

These results raise interesting methodological points: (1) The gradients obtained by averaging over the entire interval would reveal neither the sharp stimulus control present in the first half of the interval nor the relative absence of measurable stimulus control in the second half of the interval; (2) a schedule that generates a very high rate of responding, such as an FI 5-sec schedule, for example, might obscure stimulus control simply because of a "ceiling effect" of the type seen in the final five seconds of the FI 20-sec schedule in Figure 5.2b (15–20 sec. curve).[1]

We will be in a better position to discuss how stimulus control is sharpened by differential reinforcement when we have sketched the rich historical context in which it may be better understood. First, however, we turn to the other phenomena noted when comparing Figure 5.1 and 5.2: behavioral contrast and peak shift.

Behavioral Contrast

In the classical experiment on behavioral contrast (Reynolds, 1961a), pigeons were first studied on a multiple schedule in which two equal variable-interval three-minute (VI 3-min) schedules were alternated in the presence of different-colored (red and green) key lights. Following a number of such "baseline" sessions, one VI schedule was switched to extinction; hence the schedule was now *mult* VI 3-min EXT. Naturally, the rate of responding in the presence of the S^- (the key light now associated with extinction) declined rapidly. The interesting effect was a substantial *increase* in the rate of responding during the S^+ (the key light associated with the unchanged VI). This increase, an instance of *positive behavioral contrast*, is shown in Figure 5.3 (the curve labeled "VI-to-EXT"), which

---

[1]These results and others in Blough's paper support a quantitative model of (operant) stimulus control that is conceptually similar to the Rescorla–Wagner model of classical conditioning discussed in Chapter 3. Blough's model promises to be an influential one in shaping the future course of research and theory in stimulus control. The mathematically sophisticated reader with an interest in stimulus control is encouraged to read Blough (1975).

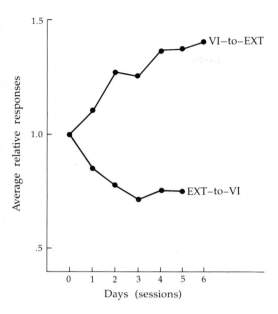

Figure 5.3
Positive behavioral contrast (upper curve) and negative behavioral contrast (lower curve). [After G. S. Reynolds, Behavioral contrast. *Journal of the Experimental Analysis of Behavior, 4,* 57–71. Copyright © 1961 by the Society for the Experimental Analysis of Behavior, Inc. Redrawn by permission.]

presents the rate of responding on the unchanged VI schedule on each session following the change in the other component. Rates are plotted relative to the baseline rate of responding on "day 0." Thus if the number of responses in the unchanged component was 1000 on day 0 and 1200 were emitted on day 1 (the first day in which the schedule in the *other* component was altered from VI to EXT), then 1200/1000 or 1.2 would be plotted on day 1 for the VI-to-EXT curve. Reynolds (1961a) labeled the increase occurring in the unchanged component "positive" since it was an increase, and "contrast" because it went in the direction opposite to the change in rate of responding during the other component. In other words, the lowered rate in the changed component does not generalize to the unchanged component; instead the response rate in the unchanged component is affected in the opposite direction. When reinforcement is increased in the changed component, *negative contrast* (a decrease in rate of responding during the unchanged component) is likely to occur, as shown by the bottom curve of Figure 5.3 (labeled "EXT-to-VI"), which represents responding after the EXT component was returned to VI 3-min.

In the past eighteen years literally hundreds of experiments have been conducted to clarify the determinants of behavioral contrast and to assess its permanence, its generality, and its molecular dynamics (for example, do the additional responses in positive contrast come at the beginning or end of each S+ presentation or both?). While the results of all these experiments, taken together, paint a complex picture, some important generalizations emerge from them that do provide an adequate summary of most, though not all, of the discrimination learning experiments on contrast.

Molecular Dynamics   A typical instance of behavioral contrast was shown in Figure 5.3. This figure tells us nothing, however, about the molecular dynamics of contrast. Do the additional responses that constitute positive contrast occur as soon as the transition from S^- to S^+ occurs, as one might expect if contrast reflected an excitatory process triggered by the removal of an aversive or inhibitory S^-? If so, the rate of responding *within* an S^+ component should appear as in Figure 5.4a. Alternatively, it is possible that the subject increases its rate of responding toward the *end* of the S^+ presentation, perhaps in anticipation of the imminent return to S^-. This "get it while you still can" pattern is illustrated in Figure 5.4b. Finally, the elevated responding might be distributed throughout the S^+ component, as shown in Figure 5.4c. In fact, all three patterns have been reported. While the pattern shown in panel (a) of the figure is perhaps most commonly observed (see Boneau and Axelrod, 1962; Malone and Staddon, 1973; Nevin and Shettleworth, 1966), those shown in panel (b) (see Buck, Rothstein, and Williams, 1975; Williams, 1976) and panel (c) (see Nevin and Shettleworth, 1966; Terrace, 1966a) have also been found. The kind of pattern shown in panel (a) is more apt to be a transient one, disappearing within 20 experimental sessions (though not in the Malone and Staddon study), while those shown in panels (b) and (c) are more apt

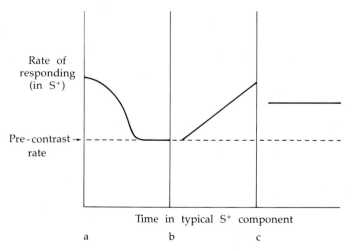

Figure 5.4
Three different patterns (a, b, c) of local response rate changes associated with positive behavioral contrast. Each has been found in different studies. In each case, responding is shown for the duration of the unchanged component.

to persist through an extended series of training sessions (Buck et al., 1975; Mackintosh, Little, and Lord, 1972; Nevin and Shettleworth, 1966; Terrace, 1966a). Presumably, these different patterns reflect different determinants, which may be unraveled in future research.

Factors Affecting Behavioral Contrast   There are at least five important factors that are significant determinants of behavioral contrast: (1) the difference in rate of reinforcement between S^+ and S^-; (2) the species studied; (3) the operant response selected for emission; (4) the degree of similarity between S^+ and S^-; and (5) the amount of temporal separation between S^+ and S^-.

Any stimulus correlated with a lower rate of reinforcement than the S^+ is likely to produce positive behavioral contrast when alternated with the S^+. Thus, changing a *mult* VI 1-min VI 1-min to a *mult* VI 1-min VI 3-min or to a *mult* VI 1-min EXT produces an increase in responding during the unchanged VI 1-min component. Indeed, the greater the increase in the proportion of the total number of reinforcements provided by the S^+, the greater the contrast effect (Reynolds, 1961c). Thus contrast tends to be greatest when one schedule is changed to extinction, in which case the proportion of reinforcement provided by the S^+ increases to 1.0.

Two marked changes occur when the schedule correlated with an S^+ is changed to extinction: The rate of reinforcement drops to zero at once, and the rate of responding drops to zero within a few sessions. How do we know whether the change in reinforcement rate or the change in response rate during the stimulus of the altered component (or S_C) is responsible for behavioral contrast? The two variables may be manipulated separately in a number of ways.

For example, reinforcements have been provided on schedules requiring little or no responding (a variable-time schedule in which reinforcements are given freely—that is, independently of responding—or a schedule that explicitly reinforces the absence of responding) and then discontinued. In this case, therefore, there is *no* simultaneous decline in the measured response rate in the altered component. Responding in the constant component nonetheless increases (behavioral contrast), suggesting that a change in reinforcement rate *per se* and not a change in response rate is crucial for producing contrast (see Reynolds, 1961a; Nevin and Shettleworth, 1966; Bloomfield, 1967).[2] While changes in response rate may occasionally result in contrast, even when reinforcement rate is unaffected (for example, Reynolds and Limpo, 1968; Wilkie, 1973), and while contrast may result from still other factors (as we shall see), an impressive body of evidence supports the following generalization:

---

[2] It is possible, of course, to argue that responses other than the measured one are declining and are in fact responsible for behavioral contrast. This position seems less straightforward and more difficult to assess than the one implicating rate of reinforcement.

Changes in rate of reinforcement during S_C result reliably in behavioral contrast.
Changes in rate of responding during S_C only sometimes result in behavioral contrast.

Most of the early work on behavioral contrast was done with the pigeon. According to laboratory lore, contrast was a more evanescent phenomenon when the rat was tested. Negative or variable findings (as when half of a group of six rats shows contrast, half does not) often went unpublished because of a lack of enthusiasm on the part of the investigators or the reviewers evaluating the paper. Finally, however, it became clear that whereas contrast appeared ubiquitous in the pigeon lab—and had been found with humans as well (see O'Brien, 1968; Waite and Osborne, 1972)—it was unreliable at best in the rat laboratory down the hall (see Mackintosh et al., 1972; Pear and Wilkie, 1971). More recent work in fact suggests that, given the right response, a pigeon may become rat-like in its tendency to demonstrate contrast (Hemmes, 1973; Westbrook, 1973). These studies did not find contrast when the operant was a lever-press instead of the usual key-peck. At the same time, recent work demonstrates reliable behavioral contrast (both positive and negative) in the rat (see Beninger and Kendall, 1975; Gutman, Sutterer, and Brush, 1975). Although much theorizing has been done about these interactions, no definitive conclusions may be drawn at this time.

One suggestion is worth noting, however. It may well be that species differences in contrast are at least in part due to different subjects' different predispositions to respond to different stimuli and emit different responses. Thus it is generally easier to demonstrate contrast with visual stimuli and key-pecking in pigeons than with auditory stimuli and lever-pressing. In general, when contrast is found with auditory stimuli signaling components, the extent of contrast is less than that found with visual stimuli (see de Villiers, 1977). When we discuss the theory of behavioral contrast, we will encounter the view that the extra responses generated when contrast occurs may be *elicited* (that is, Pavlovian conditioned) responses. If so, we would expect that species-specific factors would interact with the responses and stimuli used in the contrast experiment and affect the degree of contrast obtained. At this point, however, we can only note that contrast is influenced by the subject studied, the response it is required to emit, and the interaction of the two.

While the occurrence of contrast may depend upon the subjects and responses selected, it does not seem to depend upon the type of reinforcement schedules studied. For example, contrast has been obtained when any one of several reinforcement schedules is utilized in the changed component (for example, VI, VR, FR, DRO, DRL, and others). Although most studies have utilized VI schedules in the *unchanged* component, two early experiments showed that the use of VI's is not a necessary condition for contrast. Thus Reynolds (1961c) obtained positive contrast with FR 150 in the unchanged component, and Reynolds and Catania (1961) observed contrast when the constant component was either an FI 3-min or a DRL 21-sec schedule. Clearly, then, contrast is a robust phenomenon, the occurrence of which does not depend upon a narrow set of circumstances.

The degree of behavioral contrast found is a function of the extent of physical similarity between the S^+ and the S_C. In general, the more similar the two stimuli, the more contrast, up to a point. When the S_C and S^+ are identical, or nearly so, of course, the subject may not discriminate which component is in effect, and contrast will not occur. Excluding the limiting case of nearly identical S^+ and S_C, the degree of behavioral contrast appears to be an increasing function of similarity between S^+ and S_C (see Farthing, 1974; Hearst, 1969b; Kodera and Rilling, 1976). For example, Hearst (1969b) used a vertical line as S^+ and either no line, a horizontal line, a line displaced 60° from the vertical, or one displaced 30° from the vertical as an S^- (or S_C in contrast terminology). After training with the S^+ alone, Hearst divided his pigeons into four groups, each of which acquired a discrimination between S^+ and S^-. As shown in Figure 5.5, although all groups showed a strong contrast effect, the size of the effect increased with increasing similarity between S^+ and S^-. Other studies suggest that had Hearst included a discrimination group with an S^- displaced 15° or less from the vertical, the trend showed in Figure 5.5 would be reversed—that is, less contrast would be obtained (Mackintosh et al., 1972), consistent with our discussion earlier in this paragraph. No one study has explored contrast with an S^+ and a wide range of S^- from a single continuum, however.

Theory of Behavioral Contrast   Now that we have reviewed the factors determining behavioral contrast, it is time to summarize the theoretical status of contrast, a necessarily more speculative undertaking. Two

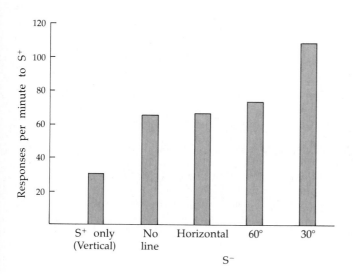

Figure 5.5
The effect of the similarity of S^+ and S^- on the magnitude of positive behavioral contrast. The terminal rate of responding to a vertical line is substantially greater when S^- is a line 30 degrees from vertical than when S^- is a horizontal line or a blank key. [Data from Hearst, 1969b. After N. J. Mackintosh, *The psychology of animal learning*. Copyright © 1974 by Academic Press, Inc. (London Ltd.). Redrawn by permission.]

generalizations have received considerable attention: One concerns the conditions required to generate the extra responses constituting (positive) contrast, and has a firm empirical base; the second addresses the nature of these extra responses.

As noted earlier, changes in rate of reinforcement during the changed component result in behavioral contrast. If reinforcement rate is increased, negative contrast occurs; if the rate is decreased, positive contrast results. But changes in reinforcement rate—while usually sufficient—are hardly *necessary* to produce contrast. For example, introducing punishment in one component of a *mult* VI X VI X generates positive contrast in the unchanged (that is, unpunished) component, a result first demonstrated by Brethower and Reynolds (1962) and illustrated in Figure 5.6 from a more recent experiment done at the University of California, San Diego. Similarly, response rates increase in the unchanged component when a *mult* VI VI is changed to *mult* VI DRH, so that a very high rate of responding is required for reinforcement in the changed component (see Hemmes and Eckerman, 1972). From data derived from choice experiments we know that interval schedules are preferred to DRH schedules providing the same mean rate of reinforcement (see Fantino, 1968; Moore and Fantino, 1975). Therefore interval schedules can be said to be of relatively greater value than DRH schedules. Thus data from

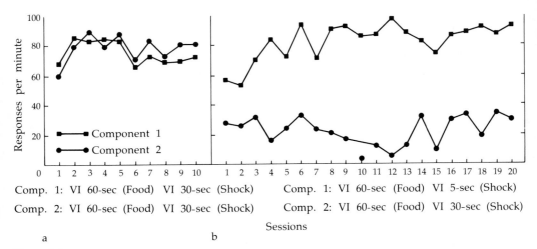

Comp. 1: VI 60-sec (Food) VI 30-sec (Shock)   Comp. 1: VI 60-sec (Food) VI 5-sec (Shock)
Comp. 2: VI 60-sec (Food) VI 30-sec (Shock)   Comp. 2: VI 60-sec (Food) VI 30-sec (Shock)

Sessions

a   b

Figure 5.6
Positive behavioral contrast induced by punishment. (a) In the baseline condition, two equal components alternate in a multiple schedule. In each, pecks are reinforced with food on a VI 60-sec schedule and are punished with shock on a VI 30-sec schedule. (b) In the positive contrast phase, the rate of punishment is increased in component 1 to VI 5-sec, but remains VI 30-sec in component 2 (the "unchanged component"). The rate of positive reinforcement is still maintained at VI 60-sec in each component. As expected, the rate of responding in component 1 decreases sharply when the rate of punishment is increased. The rate of responding in the unchanged component increases by 18 percent. [After J. Farley and E. Fantino, "Negative induction, behavioral contrast, and differential punishment," paper presented at 1976 meetings of the Psychonomic Society.]

studies finding contrast when punishment or high response rates are introduced are consistent with the data from studies of contrast manipulating rate of reinforcement, in the following sense: *Response rate in the unchanged VI component is enhanced whenever the schedule in the other component is decreased in value; response rate is depressed whenever the schedule in the other component is increased in value.* It is important to note that "value" need not be judged intuitively but may be measured independently in a choice procedure. This "value" hypothesis of behavioral contrast (Bloomfield, 1969; Premack, 1969), our first generalization regarding behavioral contrast theory, is consistent with almost all of the many studies of contrast.

The second generalization is considerably more speculative than the first but is sufficiently interesting—and has gained a sufficient number of adherents—to warrant brief mention. The extra pecks generated when positive behavioral contrast occurs may be pecks elicited by the higher-valued stimulus. In other words, the value hypothesis of behavioral contrast may itself be understood in terms of pecks elicited by the stimulus correlated with the higher-valued schedule. Recall that a stimulus differentially correlated with food will elicit key-pecking in the food-deprived pigeon ("autoshaping," described in Chapter 4). Moreover, Gamzu and Schwartz (1973) report that in a multiple schedule of noncontingent reinforcement (for example, *mult* VT X VT Y) substantial key-pecking was maintained in the component providing a higher rate of the response-independent reinforcers but not in the other component (for example, in the VT X component but not in the VT Y component if X < Y). When the rates of reinforcement were equal (X = Y), however, key-pecking was virtually eliminated. These results suggest that the extra key-pecks in the higher-valued schedule may be classically conditioned pecks directed at the response key when it is correlated with a relatively higher rate of reinforcement (a suggestion supported also by the results of Keller, 1974; Redford and Perkins, 1974, and Schwartz, Hamilton, and Silberberg, 1975; for a review of this "additivity theory" of contrast, see Schwartz and Gamzu, 1977). But how may the supposedly elicited pecks be distinguished from emitted responses in the typical response-dependent contrast procedure? Schwartz and Williams (1972) have shown that elicited pecks are typically of shorter duration than emitted pecks, making it possible to distinguish distributions of emitted and elicited pecks. If the extra ("added") pecks in positive behavioral contrast are elicited, then more short-duration pecks should occur when positive contrast occurs, and the peck-duration distributions should look like the hypothetical ones shown in Figure 5.7a.[3] The distributions on the left are from a VI X in a *mult* VI X

---

[3] Peck duration is defined in terms of how long the response key is depressed. When the response key is depressed sufficiently, an electric contact behind the key is opened. A computer records how long the contact remains open and stores this information in the appropriate 5-millisecond bin. The number of response durations at each 5-millisecond bin cumulated over a typical session defines the frequency distribution shown in Figure 5.7a.

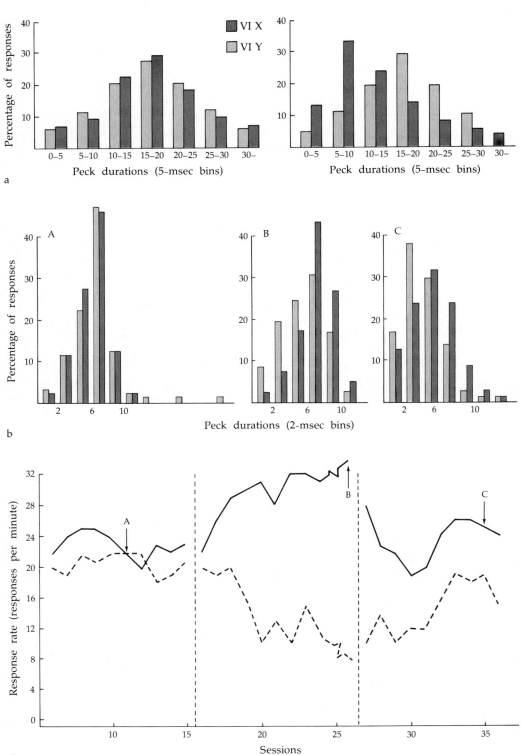

VI Y, while those on the right are from the same VI X after the schedule has been changed to *mult* VI X EXT.

The actual experiment, first done by Schwartz et al. (1975), will be considered in some detail. The experimenters used an elegant procedural feature employing two keys arranged to physically separate operant and elicited pecks. Pecks to the "operant key" were reinforced with food on a *mult* VI VI or *mult* VI EXT schedule. The operant key was illuminated by a white vertical line, regardless of the schedule in effect. Which schedule was in effect was signaled by the illumination of the second ("signal") key. Pecks at the signal key had no consequence but occurred with some regularity during the *mult* VI EXT condition when the signal indicated that the VI was in effect—that is, when the key light on the signal key was correlated with the presence of the food schedule on the operant key. Pecks to the signal key are autoshaped pecks and are presumably elicited, while pecks to the operant key are presumably emitted. According to additivity theory (Schwartz and Gamzu, 1977), when *mult* VI VI is changed to *mult* VI EXT, positive behavioral contrast should occur in the unchanged component owing to the occurrence of short-duration pecks elicited by the signal differentially correlated with reinforcement (Gamzu and Schwartz, 1973). Schwartz et al. (1975) *did* find an increase in short-duration pecks to the signal key when *mult* VI VI was changed to *mult* VI EXT but did *not* obtain contrast: The sum of pecks to the signal and operant keys during the unchanged component was not greater during *mult* VI EXT than during *mult* VI VI. Thus additivity theory may not offer a sufficient account of behavioral contrast, a possibility acknowledged by Schwartz et al. (1975).

Figure 5.7
(a) Hypothetical distributions of peck durations on a multiple VI X VI Y schedule. The duration of each key-peck is recorded and cumulated in 5-msec bins. The percentage of the total responses occurring at each bin duration, cumulated over a hypothetical session, is shown. In the left distribution, the VI schedules are equal (X = Y). In the right distribution, however, the VI Y schedule has been changed to extinction. According to additivity theory, the distribution of peck durations in the unchanged component (that is, during VI X) should shift so that a greater percentage of shorter pecks occurs, as shown in the right distribution. (b) Actual peck duration distributions for a typical pigeon. The shaded bars refer to the unchanged component, associated with VI 1-min; the clear bars refer to the changed component associated with VI 1-min in baseline panels (A and C) and with extinction during the contrast manipulation (B). Each pair of bars (one shaded, one clear) represents one 2-msec bin. The last bin is an overflow bin: all pecks too long to fit in any other bin are counted here. Data in each panel are cumulated over an entire session. (c) Response rates on the multiple schedule. The solid line refers to the unchanged component (always VI 1-min); the dashed line refers to the changed component (VI 1-min in the first and third panels, extinction in the middle panel). The increased response rate in the unchanged component (middle panel) represents behavioral contrast. Capital letters identify the sessions from which the frequency distributions of peck durations shown in (b) were obtained. [W. Whipple and E. Fantino, manuscript submitted for publication.]

Even if this experiment *had* found behavioral contrast, however, two potential problems would have remained unresolved and would have required an additional experiment. In the first place, Schwartz et al.'s (1975) pigeons spent most of their time responding to the operant key. Presumably, they were standing closer to it than to the signal key. Thus it is quite possible that the physical form of the pecks to the two keys may have differed because of the birds' relative position to the keys and that this difference in response topography—quite independent of any difference along the elicited versus emitted dimension—caused different peck durations. In the second place, whether or not contrast occurs with the two-key procedure employed by Schwartz et al. (1975) and whether or not the results support additivity theory in this setting, it does not follow that the results and interpretation necessarily apply to contrast in the standard one-key case. Both problems would, however, be eliminated if the same experiment were done with one key. Such an experiment has recently been completed by Whipple and Fantino. A robust behavioral contrast effect was obtained (Figure 5.7c), but there was no change in the frequency of short-duration pecks (Figure 5.7b). Thus the additivity theory of behavioral contrast, however appealing, remains unsupported, at least if short-duration pecks are taken as the defining property of elicited pecks. In addition to the empirical problems posed by the results shown in Figure 5.7b and c, the additivity hypothesis cannot readily explain why *negative* behavioral contrast occurs when, for example, *mult* VI 3-min VI 3-min is changed to *mult* VI 3-min VI 1-min (since no elicited pecks should be available, for later subtraction, in *mult* VI 3-min VI 3-min). Thus it appears unlikely that the value hypothesis of behavioral contrast, which appears consistent with almost all existent data, can itself be understood in terms of the generation of elicited short-duration pecks by higher-valued stimuli.

It should be added that while Schwartz and Gamzu's specific (and testable) version of additivity theory appears incorrect, more general versions of the theory still have adherents, at least for *positive* behavioral contrast. The popularity of additivity theory rests, in part, on its biological flavor. Stimuli having biological significance—such as those correlated with relatively high rates of reinforcement—are known to generate responding (Gamzu and Schwartz, 1973). It is plausible to assume that such responses may play an important role in behavioral contrast. Since biological interpretations of behavioral phenomena are becoming increasingly popular—and indeed the present book hopes to contribute to this trend—it is natural that the biological flavor of additivity theory would gain adherents (see Rachlin, 1973). Unfortunately, however, the evidence suggests that the theory is presently inadequate. Not only is the specific version in terms of peck duration insufficient (see also Ziriax and Silberberg, 1978) but other versions fail as well. For example, Rachlin's theory requires a pattern of responding in behavioral contrast such as that shown in Figure 5.4a, since he postulates a "biological" process that should generate responding ("excite pecks" in Rachlin's terminology) at the onset of the S^+. As we have seen, the response patterns shown in Figures 5.4b and 5.4c are also found with sufficient regularity (Buck et al., 1975, and others) to drastically limit the potential applicability of Rachlin's view.

Other types of findings have also limited the utility of additivity theory. For example, Hemmes (1973) changed a multiple VI 1-min VI 1-min schedule to a multiple VI 1-min EXT schedule when components were cued by different colored house lights. Since these stimuli were not localized on the key, autoshaped key-pecks could not add to operant key-pecks to produce contrast. Nonetheless, Hemmes obtained substantial positive contrast in the unchanged VI 1-min component when the other component was changed to extinction. More recently, Hamilton and Silberberg (1978) have also shown that contrast can occur independently of autoshaping in multiple schedules. Thus additivity theory does not presently appear to be a viable general theory of behavioral contrast.

The Peak Shift and Gradients of Not-Responding

Like behavioral contrast, the peak shift (Figure 5.2) occurs commonly in discrimination learning, as measured in subsequent generalization tests. Peak shifts have been reported for a variety of sensory continua and for a number of different species in many studies (Bloomfield, 1967; Ellis, 1970; Hanson, 1959; Pierrel and Sherman, 1960; for a review, see Purtle, 1973).

The peak shift may be understood readily if we accept the notion that gradients of *not-responding* occur about the S^- during discrimination learning. Just as the tendency to respond to S^+ generalizes symmetrically to points on either side of S^+ on a sensory continuum, so the tendency to *not-respond* to S^- may generalize symmetrically to points on either side of it. Thus if S^+ and S^- are on the same continuum, the tendency to respond to points on the continuum will be a joint function of the gradient of responding around S^+ and the gradient of not-responding around S^-. Since the difference between the tendencies to respond and not-respond will be greater for points on the side of the S^+ *away from* the S^-, more responses should occur to that side in generalization testing (see Figure 5.12). Moreover, depending on the shapes of the gradients around S^+ and S^-, the peak of the postdiscrimination gradient may be displaced away from the S^-, as in the peak shift.

Such gradients of not-responding around S^- have indeed been measured (see Jenkins and Harrison, 1962; Honig, Boneau, Burstein and Pennypacker, 1963). For example, Honig et al. (1963) measured stimulus control of not-responding to line orientation in pigeons after discrimination learning in which a blank key light was S^+ and a vertical line was S^-. Two such gradients, from two groups of pigeons, are shown in Figure 5.8 (cir-

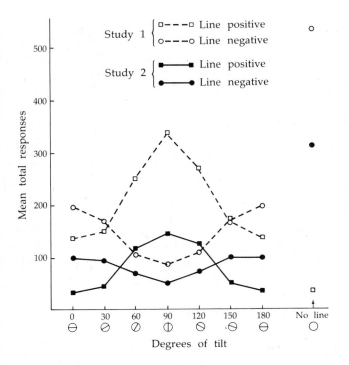

Figure 5.8

Gradients of not-responding around S⁻ following discrimination learning in which a blank key light was S⁺ and a vertical line was S⁻, for two groups of pigeons and in which the vertical line was S⁺ and the blank key S⁻ for two other groups. Mean total responses are plotted against line orientation. [After W. K. Honig, C. A. Boneau, K. R. Burstein, and H. S. Pennypacker. Positive and negative generalization gradients obtained after equivalent training conditions. *Journal of Comparative and Physiological Psychology*, 56, 111–116. Copyright © 1963 by the American Psychological Association. Redrawn by permission.]

cles), along with analogous data for training in which the vertical line was S⁺ and the blank key S (squares). Note that the gradients of not-responding are shallower (flatter) than the gradients of responding, a finding replicated by others. These gradients of not-responding are related not only to the peak shift but also to two more venerable discrimination phenomena, which we will discuss momentarily: *asymmetrical intensity gradients* and *transposition*.

Note that gradients of not-responding and peak shift, like behavioral contrast, may be demonstrated with stimuli other than those correlated with extinction. Thus Weisman (1969, 1970) found that pigeons generated gradients of not-responding around a stimulus correlated with either the longer of two VI schedules or schedules that require little or no responding (for example, DRL or DRO), and Desiderato (1969) obtained gradients of not-responding with shock. Similarly, peak shifts have been obtained away from the stimuli correlated with the longer of two VI schedules (Guttman, 1956), with DRL schedules (Terrace, 1968), and with aversive stimuli such as shock (see Grusec, 1968; Terrace, 1968).

Asymmetrical Intensity Gradients   Stimulus intensity dynamism, or "V" (Chapter 2), was the Hullian concept summarizing the relation between the intensity of a conditioned stimulus and the strength of conditioning:

the more intense the former, the stronger the latter. V was one of the factors that multiplied with habit strength to determine reaction potential. According to this concept, then, generalization gradients for intensity should be asymmetrical, with stimuli more intense than the S⁺ generating even more responding than the S⁺ itself—a result obtained in several investigations (see Heinemann and Chase, 1970; Razran, 1949) and illustrated in Figure 5.9. Heinemann and Chase suggested that monotonically increasing gradients (those showing consistent increases in responding with higher stimulus intensities) may characterize intensity generalization gradients, while the more conventionally observed peaked gradients are typical for other stimulus continua. But monotonic gradients are not a universal outcome in intensity generalization tests (see Ernst, Engberg, and Thomas, 1971), nor do they necessarily reflect the factor V. During discrimination training the subjects' responses are reinforced in the presence of S⁺ and not in the absence of S⁺—that is, not at (or near) the zero point on the intensity continuum. Thus a gradient of not-responding should develop with a peak around the zero point. The interaction of this gradient with the gradient of responding around S⁺ could produce asymmetrical postdiscrimination gradients for intensity such as that shown in Figure 5.9.

Such an analysis makes at least two testable predictions. In the first place, if a sufficiently wide range of test values were employed, responding should decline at points well above the S⁺ (since this analysis assumes that the gradient of responding around S⁺ is symmetrical). The findings of Ernst et al. (1971) confirm this prediction. These investigators found that with a narrow range of values (three) beyond the test stimulus, two of six pigeons showed monotonic gradients (for visual intensity), with maximal responding at the most intense value. With a wider range of test values, however (including six values above the S⁺), none of six subjects

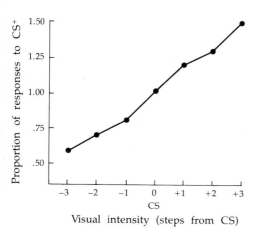

Figure 5.9
Proportion of responses to the CS⁺ as a function of intensity in a visual intensity generalization test. [Data from Razran, 1949. After N. J. Mackintosh, *The psychology of animal learning*. Copyright © 1974 by Academic Press, Inc. (London Ltd.). Redrawn by permission.]

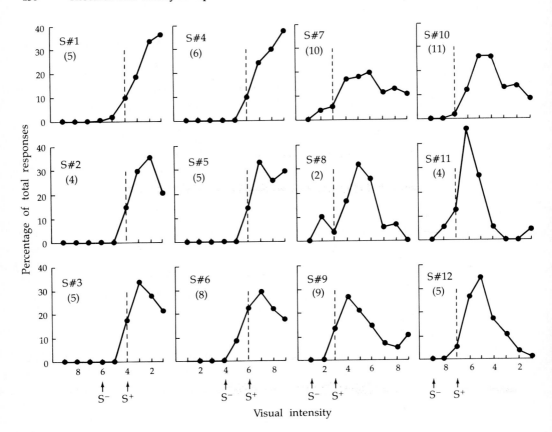

Figure 5.10
Relative generalization gradients of 12 pigeons plotted as percentage of total responses against intensity of visual stimuli. The vertical dashed line indicates the location of S⁺, and, to facilitate comparison, S⁻ is plotted to the left of S⁺ in all cases. The code numbers plotted on the abscissas correspond to the following intensity values (in mL): 1 = 70.00; 2 = 39.36; 3 = 22.14; 4 = 12.45; 5 = 7.00; 6 = 3.94; 7 = 2.21; 8 = 1.24; and 9 = 0.70 (1 mL = 3.18 cd/m²). The number in parentheses indicates sessions to criterion. [After A. J. Ernst, L. Engberg, and D. R. Thomas, On the form of stimulus generalization curves for visual intensity. *Journal of the Experimental Analysis of Behavior, 16,* 117–180. Copyright © 1971 by the Society for the Experimental Analysis of Behavior, Inc. Redrawn by permission.]

gave monotonic gradients. These results are shown in Figure 5.10. The second prediction is that it should be possible to generate asymmetrical intensity gradients with peaks *below* S⁺ following discrimination learning with an S⁻ *more intense* than the S⁺, a result also obtained in Thomas's laboratory at the University of Colorado (Thomas and Setzer, 1972) and shown in Figure 5.11.

Transposition   If an organism receives training with a white card as S⁺ and a gray card as S⁻ and is then required to choose between a gray card

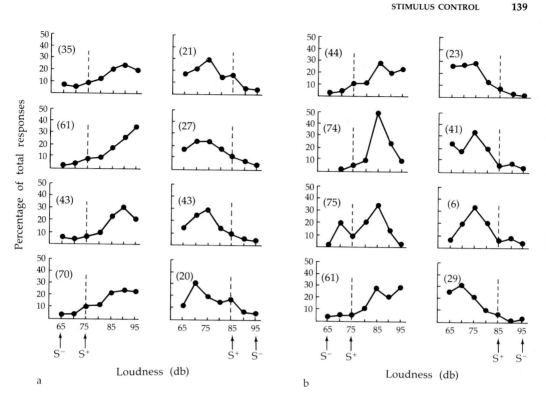

Figure 5.11
Relative generalization gradients. The number in parentheses indicates sessions to criterion. (a) In eight rats. (b) In eight guinea pigs. [After Thomas and Setzer, 1972.]

(the former S⁻) and a *black card*, which card will be chosen? In many experiments the lighter card (here the former S⁻) is chosen. This result is an example of *transposition*, so-called because the subject apparently "transposes" the relation learned in training to a new test situation characterized by the same relation. Thus, while the gray card in our example should control not-responding by virtue of being an S⁻, if the subject has learned more about the *relative* properties of the two stimuli that are correlated with reinforcement (in the example, the lighter stimulus) it will nonetheless choose the gray over the novel black card. The notion of interacting gradients of responding and not-responding can be applied to account nicely for transposition without *requiring* the assumption that relations are being learned.

The essence of Kenneth Spence's nonrelational theoretical treatment of transposition is shown in Figure 5.12. In the top portion, the brightness of the cards—in arbitrary units—is shown along the baseline, the gradient of responding (an "excitatory" gradient in Spence's terms) is curve A, the gradient of not-responding (an "inhibitory" gradient for Spence) is curve

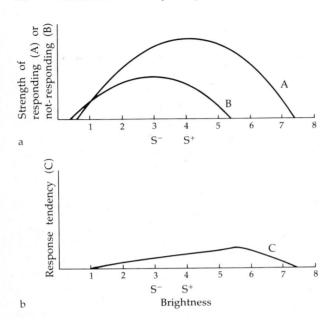

a

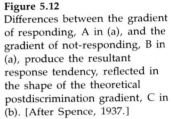

b

Brightness

Figure 5.12
Differences between the gradient of responding, A in (a), and the gradient of not-responding, B in (a), produce the resultant response tendency, reflected in the shape of the theoretical postdiscrimination gradient, C in (b). [After Spence, 1937.]

B. The difference in height between the curves corresponds to the resultant response tendency ("reaction tendency" in the Hull–Spence system). These differences are plotted against brightness to produce the theoretical postdiscrimination gradient at the bottom of the figure (C). Note that the tendency to respond is maximal above 5 and that the next greatest reaction occurs at 6; 5 and 6 are both lighter than the prior S^+ (4). Thus if given a choice between 4 and either 5 or 6, the subject should choose the lighter stimulus, not the S^+, thereby demonstrating transposition. Similarly, 3 (the previous S^-) should be chosen over any darker stimulus, again an instance of transposition. This theory also predicts when transposition should *not* occur ("transposition reversal"), as when 4 is compared with 7 or 8. In this sense Spence's theory provides a clear advantage over relational theories that do not specify when the subject should respond to absolute characteristics rather than to relative ones. With the possible exception of one study (Ehrenfreund, 1952; but see Riley's reappraisal, 1968), however, transposition reversal has not been found. Instead, as the former S^+ is compared with stimuli further and further out on the stimulus continuum (away from the S^-) the degree of transposition declines until chance responding is approached—that is, until the subject appears indifferent to the two stimuli in the transposition test (Riley, 1968). Such chance responding continues even when the stimuli are so far out on the continuum that Spence's theory requires reversal. The second shortcoming of Spence's theory of transposition comes from studies of transposition involving simultaneous discrimination learning. Here, there is less control of non-responding by S^-, as reflected by the lack of peak shift in the postdiscrimination generalization gradient (Rudolph, 1967; cited by Riley, 1968). If the postdiscrimination gradient peaks at the S^+, transposition should not occur, since the S^+ should be preferred to any other stimulus. In fact, however, transposition occurs (see Rudolph, 1967; Marsh, 1967).

Since Spence's theory, however ingenious, has proven inadequate, we may be left with accepting the fact of relational learning. The reader may question why Spence and others were reluctant to accept relational learning in the first place. Today most psychologists take for granted animals' ability to respond to relational, as well as to absolute, properties of stimuli. Indeed, where significant reinforcing stimuli confront the organism, we shall see (Chapter 7) that it is the relative rather than the absolute properties of reinforcement that affect behavior most directly. Moreover, evidence gathered since Spence formulated his theory points clearly to the occurrence of relational learning (see Lawrence and DeRivera, 1954; Riley, 1958). Finally, if the subject is responding to the relation between stimuli, we would expect transposition to be enhanced with the simultaneous (rather than successive) presentation of stimuli. This expectation has been confirmed in several studies (see Riley, Ring and Thomas, 1960).

In *successive* discrimination learning it may be that subjects must rely more on the absolute properties of the stimuli. Indeed, when transposition does occur after successive discrimination learning, its appearance is nicely correlated with the occurrence of peak shift. Honig (1962), for example, found that transposition occurred after successive discrimination learning (and subsequent generalization tests) only when the S^+ was compared with stimuli that had generated more responding in the generalization tests. Thus where successive discrimination learning is concerned, transposition appears to be a reflection of peak shift (as are the asymmetrical intensity gradients we discussed earlier).

Interactions of Stimulus Control Gradients

Studies by Terrace (1968) and Weisman (1969), among others, show that behavioral contrast, gradients of not-responding, and peak shift tend to occur (or not occur) under the same circumstances, suggesting that the same controlling variables may be operative in producing these phenomena. For example, in Weisman's study, only subjects that showed behavioral contrast (in the S^+) yielded gradients of not-responding (around the S^-), a correlation also found by Nevin (1968). Terrace (1968) found that subjects showing behavioral contrast also yielded peak shifts in subsequent generalization tests. Terrace's earlier work (1964, 1966a,b) also suggests that there is a strong correlation between the occurrence of behavioral contrast, peak shifts, and gradients of not-responding.

While behavioral contrast, peak shift, and gradients of not-responding seem to appear under similar conditions, it should not be inferred that they reflect the same underlying mechanism. In the first place, the occurrence of a gradient of not-responding need not lead to a peak shift (Hearst, 1969b). Second, some experimenters have found either behavioral contrast or peak shift without the other (see Dukhayyil and Lyons, 1973; Ellis, 1970; Rosen and Terrace, 1975). Finally, while the occurrence of peak shift is readily understood in terms of interacting gradients of responding and not-responding, behavioral contrast is *not*. For example, training with an S$^-$ should produce a gradient of not-responding, which should *subtract* from the gradient of responding, resulting in decreased responding to S$^+$—not the increase that actually occurs in positive behavioral contrast. Moreover, the more similar the S$^+$ and S$^-$, the fewer responses should occur to S$^+$. Instead, as we have seen, behavioral contrast actually increases the more similar the two stimuli.

To summarize, while contrast, peak shift, and gradients of not-responding often occur under the same conditions, they need not do so. Moreover, whereas stimulus control of not-responding appears to be a necessary, though not always sufficient, condition for the occurrence of peak shift, behavioral contrast occurs *in spite of* such control. When the schedule of reinforcement correlated with the stimulus is changed to extinction or otherwise devalued, a gradient of not-responding develops around the stimulus. This stimulus control of not-responding is reflected in a peak shift during generalization tests. The extent of the peak shift appears to depend on the similarity between the S$^+$ and S$^-$ (the greater the similarity, the greater the peak shift, up to a point). The peak shift is found reliably after successive, but not simultaneous, discrimination training.

The stimulus control of not-responding around the stimulus of the devalued schedule is usually insufficient to cause a decrease in rate of responding to the stimulus correlated with the unchanged schedule, although exceptions have been reported (see Reynolds, 1961b). The typical result is an increase in responding during the unchanged stimulus (behavioral contrast). The size of the contrast effect depends on the comparability of the alternating stimuli: the more contiguous temporally or the more similar physically, the greater the contrast effect. Note that while variation of physical similarity affects contrast and peak shift in the same way, variation of temporal contiguity does not: Unlike peak shift, which tends not to occur after simultaneous discriminations, contrast occurs readily with simultaneously available schedules (see Catania, 1963, 1966).

Thus behavioral contrast reflects a different effect of discrimination training than gradients of not-responding. In generalization tests both effects show up. As Figure 5.2 shows, the peak of the generalization gradient is shifted away from S⁻ (the peak shift, presumably reflecting stimulus control of not-responding around S⁻) and is also elevated relative to the control condition (presumably reflecting behavioral contrast).

THE SHARPENING OF STIMULUS CONTROL

Thus far we have discussed stimulus control after training with and without differential reinforcement and examined some of the properties and interactions of stimulus control gradients of both responding and not-responding. We have not addressed the important issue of the necessary and sufficient conditions for establishing stimulus control, nor how the postdiscrimination gradient may be sharpened so as to approach the maximum resolving power of the relevant sensory organs. Looking at the hypothetical generalization gradients in Figure 5.13, our first question is: What experience is necessary to change a flat generalization gradient (I) to the more typical one (III)? Our second and easier question is: How may the gradient be sharpened further until maximally precise stimulus control is exerted by S⁺ (II)? In discussing these questions, the interesting problem of *attention* will arise. After discussing the dynamics of attention, we will conclude the chapter by considering conceptual behavior. But perhaps the most complex and fundamentally important problem in stimulus control is not how stimulus control is elaborated and modulated in attention and in conceptual behavior but how it is established in the

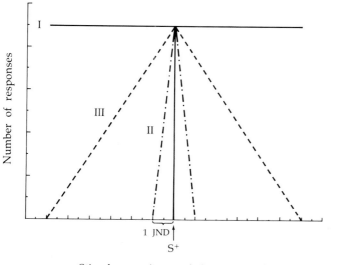

Stimulus continuum (arbitrary units)

Figure 5.13
Hypothetical generalization gradients. Gradient I represents no stimulus control. Gradient II represents the maximum possible stimulus control. Gradient III represents an intermediate amount of stimulus control. [After H. S. Terrace, Stimulus control. In W. K. Honig (Ed.), *Operant behavior: Areas of research and application*. New York: Appleton-Century-Crofts, 1966. Redrawn by permission of Prentice-Hall, Inc.]

first place. Two traditional conceptions of stimulus control—those of Lashley and of Hull and Spence—and some important experiments generated by the theories decades after they were formulated—have served to shape the contemporary view of the establishment of stimulus control.

The Hull–Spence and Lashley Theories

We have noted that for Clark Hull and Kenneth Spence the reinforcement of responses in the presence of a stimulus was the necessary and sufficient condition to establish response strength in the presence of that stimulus (S^+). Moreover, this response strength "spread" to other stimulus values in proportion to their proximity to the S^+. The result was the typical generalization gradient illustrated earlier in Figure 5.1 (Hull, 1943; Spence, 1937). Training with an S^-—as in differential reinforcement—also generated a gradient of not-responding,[4] which interacted with the gradient for responding to sharpen the postdiscrimination gradient (Spence, 1937). But such differential training was not *necessary* to produce a generalization gradient; reinforced responding in the presence of the S^+ was sufficient.

Lashley and Wade (1946) favored a very different interpretation. They claimed that in the absence of differential training the effects of reinforcing responses in the presence of an S^+ would generalize completely to other stimuli on the same continuum. For Lashley and Wade, generalization represented a "failure to discriminate" the distinguishing characteristics of the relevant stimuli. Successful discrimination was therefore likely to occur only after *differential reinforcement*—that is, reinforcement in the presence of one stimulus (the S^+) but not in the presence of another (the S^-). Simply reinforcing responses in the presence of a particular wavelength, for example, should be sufficient to establish only a flat gradient of responding on the wavelength dimension. Without differential reinforcement, no discrimination is learned. This prediction is strikingly different from that of Hull and Spence, who assumed that a generalization process occurred when responses were reinforced in the presence of a particular stimulus, resulting in a peaked generalization gradient around that stimulus. In order to choose between the two positions it therefore appears necessary to answer the following seemingly simple question: Does discrimination—as evidenced by a peaked generalization gradient—develop without differential reinforcement?

---

[4] In Hull–Spence terms—and in much of contemporary psychology—the terms "gradients of excitation" and "gradients of inhibition" are used instead of "gradients of responding" and "gradients of not-responding." We will avoid these terms, since the latter terms are more general. It should be clear, however, that the term "not-responding" is used to refer to the nonreinforced response only—that is, the response being measured and plotted in the gradient. The subject is indeed engaged in other measurable responses.

Experimental Evidence   Since we have seen clear evidence for a peaked generalization gradient in the absence of explicit differential training (for example, Figure 5.1) the argument would appear to be settled already in favor of Hull and Spence. The issue is, however, far more complex. Indeed, the ingenious arguments and experiments on this fundamental question give the flavor of psychological theory and experimental methodology at its best and have helped shape the contemporary view of stimulus control. We begin with the arguments that might have been offered by proponents of the Lashley–Wade theory to account for the apparently damaging finding of peaked generalization gradients for individual subjects in the absence of differential reinforcement (first reported by Guttman and Kalish, 1956). In the first place, Guttman and Kalish's pigeons had very likely received differential reinforcement with respect to wavelength prior to the start of the experiment. One of many potential sources of such differential reinforcement is the color of pigeon feed, which (a) is different from the color of cups in which it is placed, thus providing for differential reinforcement for pecks at grain in the cup,[5] and (b) consists of two or three kinds of grain, of different hue, one of which is usually preferred by an individual pigeon. In the second place, unintended differential training may have occurred once the experiment began. One source of such bootleg training depends upon the pigeon making occasional unreinforced pecks around the key, as it often does, especially during key-peck training. Since the background of the key is different from the key color (and typically is metallic gray), differential reinforcement of responding on the basis of color should occur.

Numerous experiments have evaluated each of these possibilities. In order to control for differential reinforcement prior to the experiment, subjects have been raised in monochromatic light (Peterson, 1962) or in darkness (Ganz and Riesen, 1962) and then tested for generalization. In Peterson's experiment ducklings were raised in sodium vapor light (589 nanometers) from the moment of hatching. They were trained to peck at the key (also lit with 589 nm) for water on a VI 3-min schedule. After 15 days of such training they were tested for generalization in an extinction test, during which they were both presented with the S⁺ and also received their first exposure to 8 additional wavelengths. Each of the four ducklings emitted flat generalization gradients, as shown in Figure 5.14, which also presents gradients for two subjects raised in normal (white) light. In a subsequent control experiment Peterson showed that the ducklings that had been reared in monochromatic light could be trained, with differential reinforcement, to show stimulus control by color, thereby ruling out the possibility of physiological deficit induced by the mono-

---

[5]Pecks at the grain (color A) are reinforced (by the grain), while pecks at the cup bottom (color B) miss the grain and are not reinforced.

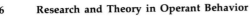

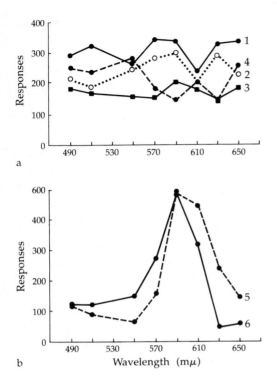

a

b

Wavelength (mμ)

Figure 5.14
Stimulus generalization gradients for individual ducklings. (a) Birds 1 to 4 were raised in a monochromatic environment. (b) Birds 5 and 6 were not. [After N. Peterson, Effect of monochromatic rearing on the control of responding by wavelength. *Science, 136,* 774–775. Copyright © 1962 by the American Association for the Advancement of Science. Redrawn by permission.]

chromatic rearing conditions (a possibility always present in such *isolation experiments;* see Chapter 9). Thus Peterson's experiment provides strong support for Lashley and the notion that differential reinforcement is a necessary condition for establishing stimulus control.

Ganz and Riesen's (1962) results are more equivocal, and have been interpreted both as favorable to Lashley (by Terrace, 1966) and as largely favorable to Hull–Spence (by Nevin, 1973). While their experiment was not conducted as a direct test of the Hull–Spence versus Lashley–Wade controversy, the results have been widely cited as relevant to it and should be considered here. After ten weeks of rearing in total darkness, infant monkeys received discrimination training in which key-presses in the presence of a monochromatic light (S+) were reinforced with sucrose on a continuous-reinforcement schedule and eventually on a VI 15-sec schedule, while presses in the dark (S−) were never reinforced. After an average of three months of such training, generalization testing was conducted for seven successive days, with interspersed reinforced responses during S+. As both Ganz and Riesen (1962) and Nevin (1973) point out, the Lashley–Wade hypothesis was weakened by the finding of steep gradients, averaged over seven days of testing, for the "hue-naive" monkeys. Indeed, their gradients were actually *steeper* than those of experienced controls (reared for their first ten weeks in normal illumination), which presumably had considerable opportunity for differential reinforcement of wavelengths. Yet, as Nevin has acknowledged, even this result does not conclusively refute Lashley's hypothesis, since the Ganz–Riesen procedure included differential training *during* generalization test sessions. Specifically, in a given test session, the monkey received trials in which responses to all seven stimuli (including the S$^+$) were nonreinforced *plus* trials in which responses to the S$^+$ were reinforced. Such differential training should be sufficient to establish a peaked generalization gradient in rather short order according to the Lashley theory. Moreover, the gradient was virtually flat—for the "hue-naive" subjects—on the first day of testing (a point emphasized by Terrace, 1966). By the second day a steep gradient had emerged, a result clearly compatible with the Lashley position. The fact that the gradients for the "hue-naive" subjects were ultimately steeper than those for the more experienced subjects is difficult to interpret in terms of either theory. It is possible, however, that sharper gradients of not-responding may have developed around the six S$^-$'s in the "hue-naive" group since they—unlike the control group—had never experienced reinforcement in the presence of these hues. Finally, it should be noted that the Lashley–Wade theory is often interpreted broadly to allow peaked gradients following differential reinforcement involving only one stimulus from the relevant sensory continuum—that is, interdimensional discrimination training.[6] Such differential reinforcement was provided for more than two months of daily sessions in the Ganz–Riesen (but not the Peterson) experiment. On balance, then, the Ganz–Riesen results are probably less compatible with the Hull–Spence theory than with Lashley's theory (and Peterson's results) but support neither view unequivocally.

More recent work with ducklings (Tracy, 1970) or quail and chickens (Rudolph, Honig and Gerry, 1969; Rudolph and Honig, 1972) reared in monochromatic light has tilted the weight of evidence towards the Hull–Spence point of view. This work has failed to find flat gradients, suggesting that, at least under some conditions, differential reinforcement is unnecessary for discrimination and the occurrence of peaked gradients. It is unclear why Peterson's results were so substantially different from those obtained by more recent investigators. Perhaps something about the experimental chambers used by Peterson made attending to stimulus dimensions other than color (for example, the shape or position of the key) more likely in his study than in the later ones. In any case, this work

---

[6]In this case the presence of a stimulus from a given sensory continuum is the S$^+$; its absence the S$^-$. More generally, *interdimensional discrimination training* involves S$^+$ and S$^-$ from two different stimulus dimensions. When both S$^+$ and S$^-$ are different values on the *same* stimulus dimension, the term *intradimensional discrimination training* has been used (see Honig, 1970).

underscores the importance of retesting important conclusions by repeating (replicating) important experiments.

Even when we can rule out pre-experimental differential reinforcement, however, we might expect peaked gradients after apparent nondifferential training due to unintended differential reinforcement during the experiment. Heinemann and Rudolph (1963) noted that with focused stimuli—such as the typical key light—a contrasting background provides a source of unintended differential reinforcement, a possibility already noted. They supported their argument by showing that generalization gradients became increasingly *flat* as the stimulus area used in training increased: When the key was surrounded by a similarly illuminated background, nonreinforced pecks around the key did not provide differential reinforcement with respect to the stimulus; hence the gradient was flatter or, with a sufficiently large background, flat. Heinemann and Rudolph's results lend plausibility to Lashley's position. Their experiment suggests that unintended differential reinforcement with respect to wavelength may occur routinely in studies using the standard apparatus containing a key light against a contrasting background. Thus studies showing discrimination in the apparent absence of differential reinforcement may actually have involved differential training. These results, however, do not *prove* that differential reinforcement is a *necessary* (as opposed to sufficient) condition for discrimination and for the occurrence of peaked generalization gradients.

Clearly, the question of whether sloped generalization gradients can occur in the absence of differential reinforcement is more complex than was first apparent. Moreover, whatever the answer to the question, the Hull–Spence and Lashley–Wade theories can both be made flexible enough to incorporate it, as we shall see. Indeed, the contemporary view of stimulus control includes aspects of each of these theories. Before summarizing the present status of these theories, however, we will discuss briefly a discrimination phenomenon that is important in its own right and that, together with phenomena already presented, clearly refutes an important portion of the Hull–Spence theory.

We saw earlier that the Hull–Spence theory cannot deal adequately with behavioral contrast, nor with some of the findings on transposition. In each case, these inadequacies resulted from predictions derived from gradients of not-responding. Another important phenomenon that creates a similar difficulty for the Hull–Spence theory is *errorless discrimination learning*. Terrace (1963a,b, 1966) trained difficult discriminations without error in pigeons with the following procedure. The S$^+$ and S$^-$ alternated. The S$^+$ assumed its final value in terms of intensity and duration (one or three minutes in different experiments) from the outset of training. The S$^-$, however, was faded in gradually. For example, the first time the S$^-$ was presented it was so low in intensity that the key was effectively dark. Since birds tend not to peck at dark keys, no pecks occurred during the 5 seconds of S$^-$ "exposure." On subsequent appearances, the duration of the S^- was progressively increased until it reached 30 seconds. Subsequently, the intensity of the S^- was gradually increased until it was a fully bright green light. The control pigeons were given the final discrimination abruptly. That is, they were exposed to the final intensity and duration of the S^- from the beginning of training. Those subjects which received the progressive (gradual) S^- training from the start made virtually no errors, that is, responses to the S^-, throughout training (in contrast to the thousands of errors typical of control subjects). Such errorless discrimination learning is incompatible with the Hull–Spence theory in the following way: Since there are no nonreinforced responses in the presence of the S^-, there should be no gradient of not-responding and, therefore, no sharp postdiscrimination gradient. Notwithstanding, sharp discriminations have been formed without error. The Lashley–Wade theory would be less troubled by errorless discrimination learning since this theory stresses the role of differential reinforcement in discrimination learning, and differential reinforcement occurs in the errorless learning procedure, at least in the sense that reinforcement occurs in the presence of the S^+ but not in the presence of the S^-. It should be noted, however, that the Hull–Spence theory may be salvaged with respect to errorless learning if we assume that responses other than key-pecks, such as approaches to the key, are extinguished in the presence of the S^-. If so, then a gradient of not-responding might indeed develop around the S^-, allowing a sharp postdiscrimination gradient. This counter argument is, however, somewhat speculative.

Resolution and Present Status   One reason the Hull–Spence theory has fared less well than Lashley's is that the former theory is far more specific. It makes a greater number of explicit predictions—a feature of a useful theory—and hence is demonstrably wrong more often. The Lashley–Wade theory, on the other hand, is often rather ambiguous in predicting what an organism will do in a particular situation. In fact, a number of other psychologists have interpreted Lashley and Wade in a variety of ways. Perhaps the soundest interpretation of the Lashley–Wade theory and the one consistent with most of the stimulus control literature is that discrimination will occur *even without differential reinforcement* providing the subject is sensitive to the correlation between reinforcement presentations and the aspect of the training situation that will happen to vary in generalization testing (Mackintosh, 1974). For example, the subject in a discrimination study may be presented with a round key lit with a yellow triangle. Pecks at the key produce reinforcement on a VI schedule. If the subject is tested for generalization of wavelength, will it produce a flat gradient or one peaking at yellow? It depends upon which aspect (or aspects) of the stimulus the subject was attending to. Only if the subject attended to the color of the triangle (as opposed to the roundness of the key or the shape of the triangle) should a peaked gradient be obtained, for only in this case has the subject associated color with reinforcement. This view can be circular unless we can specify what the pigeon attends to *prior* to the generalization test. When care is taken to avoid circularity, the view still appears consistent with most of the known facts about stimulus control and is supported by a comparison of stimulus control following different types of discrimination training (that is, following types of training that should promote or retard attention to a particular stimulus).

One way of making attention to relevant stimuli more likely is to provide intradimensional training, in which the S^+ and S^- are from the same stimulus dimension. If our interpretation of the Lashley–Wade theory is correct, sharper generalization gradients should be attained after intradimensional training than after interdimensional training, in which the S^+ and the S^- are from different stimulus dimensions or in which the S^- is the *absence* of a stimulus from the dimension containing the S^+. Indeed, intradimensional training does result in sharper generalization gradients than comparable interdimensional training (Jenkins and Harrison, 1960; 1962). Jenkins and Harrison's studies compared three types of procedures with pigeons. In nondifferential training, the S^+ was a 1000-Hz tone, and responding was reinforced on a VI 20-sec schedule in the presence of that tone. The tone and the VI reinforcement schedule were always available; hence the training was "nondifferential" with respect to the S^+. Here the subject might not be sensitive to the correlation between the tone and reinforcement. Indeed, Jenkins and Harrison found relatively flat generalization gradients in subsequent testing (Figure 5.15a). In an interdimensional training condition, the periods of tone and VI schedule alternated with periods in which both the tone and reinforcement availability were absent. In this condition, the pigeon is more likely to be sensitive to the correlation between the presence of the tone and the availability of reinforcement. As Figure 5.15b shows, a more clearly sloped generalization gradient was obtained in this condition. Finally, Jenkins and Harrison (1962) employed an intradimensional training condition in which the S^+ was still the 1000-Hz tone but the S^- was now a 950-Hz tone (instead of no tone). In this case much sharper generalization gradients were obtained than those shown in either portion of Figure 5.15.

The reader may have noted that the relatively flat gradients shown in Figure 5.15a, after nondifferential training, contrast sharply with the sloped wavelength gradients obtained by Guttman and Kalish with a similar nondifferential procedure, also with pigeons but with key lights. This difference may result from the fact that the tones are not located on the response key, so that the sort of bootleg discrimination training *during* the experiment, implicated by Heinemann and Rudolph's (1963) results with key lights, should not occur. It is also possible that lights are more salient than tones for pigeons, especially when the lights are focused spatially and most especially when they appear on the response key. It is also possible that the pigeon's pre-experimental history has provided less adventitious discrimination training with sound than with lights. Each of

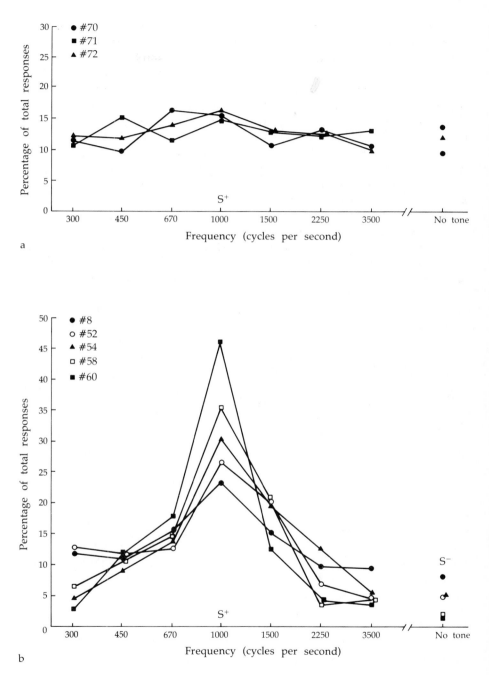

Figure 5.15
Relative generalization gradients of tonal frequency for each of eight pigeons following two training conditions. (a) S⁺ (1000 Hz) was present continuously. (b) S⁺ (1000 Hz) alternated with an S⁻ (no tone). [After Jenkins and Harrison, 1960.]

these possibilities could be assessed experimentally. Students are encouraged to ponder what experimental designs might be employed before reading on.

The pigeon's pre-experimental history with respect to tones could be manipulated explicitly, of course, perhaps by depriving the pigeon of water and giving it response-independent water in the presence of one tone—say, 3000 Hz—but not in the presence of another tone—say, 300 Hz—in a chamber different from the experimental one (with the S$^+$ and S$^-$ reversed for some subjects). Thus one tone would be differentially correlated with reward. If differing pre-experimental histories were a factor in producing different results in the Guttman and Kalish versus Jenkins and Harrison experiments, then a sloped gradient should be generated when the Jenkins and Harrison nondifferential procedure was replicated following this pretraining period.

It would be possible to localize the tones behind the response key in order to assess the possibility suggested by the Heinemann–Rudolph results (see Steinhauer, Davol, and Lee, 1977). A perhaps easier tactic would be to replicate the Guttman and Kalish experiment with diffuse light as the S$^+$ and no key light present. If flat wavelength gradients were obtained subsequently, the diffuseness of the tone in the Jenkins and Harrison experiment would be implicated as a factor producing their flat gradients. Use of a diffuse light would also constitute one condition in assessing the effects of the nature and location of stimuli upon generalization. Gradients from this group ("group I") could be compared with those from two other groups exposed to the following stimuli: group 2—a spatially focused light (for example, from a small bulb) not on the response key; group 3—a light on the response key. It is likely that the gradients for group 3 would be steep (replicating Guttman and Kalish), those from group 1 relatively flat, and those from group 2 intermediate.

Incidental stimuli—that is, cues incidental to those explicitly manipulated by the experimenter—can play an important role in the degree of stimulus control exerted by the intended effective stimulus. For Lashley–Wade adherents, incidental stimuli will weaken stimulus control to the extent that they mask the correlation between reinforcement presentations and the intended training stimulus. In the absence of discrimination training, several stimuli—possessing different attention-getting value for the subject—may be associated with reinforcement, and little or no control may be acquired by the stimulus that will later be varied in the generalization test. As noted earlier, intradimensional training should be more effective than interdimensional training in establishing stimulus control by the stimulus intended by the experimenter to be the relevant one.

For Hull and Spence, the complications posed by incidental stimuli enabled their theory to embrace some of the negative evidence that has been presented against it here. All the stimuli that are present when a response is reinforced should acquire some response strength. Without differential reinforcement, therefore, responding is likely to be controlled by stimuli from several dimensions. During the generalization tests several different values ("test stimuli") are presented along one of these dimensions (the "relevant" one, as defined by the experimenter). Stimulus control exerted by the incidental stimuli is likely to increase responding to all of the relevant test stimuli, thereby producing a relatively flat gradient. Thus, in the nondifferential training condition of the Jenkins and Harrison (1960) study, the lack of control by tone frequency may have resulted from more potent control by other stimuli in the experimental chamber (for example, visual stimuli such as the key light), which remain present during generalization testing on the tone-frequency dimension. During either type of discrimination training with differential reinforcement, control by the incidental stimuli is eliminated and control by tone frequency established.

Additional results are consistent with this analysis. For example, Van Houten and Rudolph (1972; see also Rudolph and Van Houten, unpublished data, in Mackintosh, 1977) repeated the nondifferential training condition of Jenkins and Harrison's (1960) study both with and without a lit key light. When the key light was present, as it had been in Jenkins and Harrison's research, the auditory generalization gradients were relatively flat, as in Figure 5.15a, replicating the earlier study. When training took place with an unlit key light, however, sloped generalization gradients were obtained, with a peak around the S^+ (a 1000-Hz tone). Thus these results suggest that stimulus control may be acquired by salient incidental cues, such as key lights, which prevent control by other incidental stimuli, such as tones. Which incidental stimuli acquire control probably depends on many factors, including the salience of the stimuli, the organism's prior experience, and the organism's phylogenetic response tendencies. With regard to the latter, for example, Hailman (1969) has shown that newly hatched laughing gull chicks show a strong tendency to peck at certain wavelengths of light, corresponding to important sign stimuli (see Chapter 9).

The role of prior experience can profoundly affect control by incidental stimuli. For example, Wagner, Logan, Haberlandt, and Price (1968) compared control of responding by a light stimulus in a light–tone compound for two groups of rats trained in a discrete-trial task in which lever-pressing was reinforced on 50 percent of the trials. The light was present on all trials for each group. For the *correlated* group, one tone was also present during trials with reinforcement available and a second tone during extinction trials. For the *uncorrelated* group, however, reinforcement was equally likely in the presence of either tone. Did the light—an incidental stimulus for both groups—acquire stimulus control of responding as measured during interspersed test trials with light but no tone? This result occurred only in the uncorrelated group. Thus incidental stimuli are likely to control responding only when no other stimulus is better correlated with reinforcement. As the reader will note, this view is similar to the version of the Lashley–Wade theory that we have adopted.

Assessment of Stimulus Control Theories

We can now answer the questions raised when looking at Figure 5.13. Differential reinforcement plays a critical role in sharpening stimulus control, with results ranging from complete lack of control by the stimulus dimension being tested, through moderately sloped postdiscrimination gradients, to gradients so sharp—after progressively finer discrimination training—they approach the maximal resolving power of the relevant sensory system. Discrimination may occur without nonreinforced responding in the presence of the S⁻, as the many reports of errorless discrimination learning have shown. The most important consequence of differential reinforcement (reinforcement in the presence of one stimulus but not in the presence of another) is a tendency not to respond to stimuli in the vicinity of the S⁻. A second effect of discrimination training is related to the first and involves changes in the height and shape of the generalization gradient. Not only is the postdiscrimination gradient sharper than the prediscrimination gradient, but it is higher (behavioral contrast) and shifted away from the S⁻ (peak shift). A third important effect of differential reinforcement involves elimination of a tendency to respond to incidental cues present in the experimental situation. In the absence of discrimination training, such cues may be correlated with reinforcement and may diminish or eliminate control by the intended S⁺. Of course, to the extent that "incidental" stimuli continue to be positively correlated with reinforcement, even during discrimination training, their effects on stimulus control will remain evident. As such, flat generalization gradients may be obtained even after discrimination training, a point illustrated in the next section on attention.

A strong version of the Lashley–Wade theory predicts that stimulus control will fail to occur without discrimination training. Since some evidence exists for steep gradients in the absence of explicit discrimination training, the theory must postulate unintended sources of differential reinforcement in these cases. In several instances these sources have been isolated experimentally, lending plausibility to the theory. In other instances the source of differential reinforcement is not apparent. A weaker but more tenable interpretation of the Lashley–Wade theory proposes that discrimination will occur whenever the subject is sensitive to a correlation between reinforcement and the S⁺. Without discrimination training this is less likely to occur, and the S⁺ may not exert stimulus control. Different types of discrimination training are more or less apt to emphasize this correlation and will result in more or less stimulus control by the S⁺. This version of the Lashley–Wade theory is no longer very different from the Hull–Spence view, particularly when the latter emphasizes the conditioning and extinction of incidental cues that may disrupt or enhance stimulus control, respectively.

The Hull–Spence theory is a victim of one of its greatest strengths: Unlike the Lashley–Wade theory and similar "relational" views of stimulus control, the Huil–Spence theory makes many straightforward and explicit—often quantitative—predictions. Some of the predictions derived from the theory are clearly incorrect. As we have seen, the theory's interacting gradients of excitation and inhibition err in implying the opposite of behavioral contrast, the absence of errorless discrimination learning, and the occurrence of transposition reversal. An additional basic problem, the occurrence, in some experiments, of flat gradients after nondifferential reinforcement training, may be accounted for in terms of control by incidental stimuli in the absence of discrimination training, a possibility that has been supported empirically. Thus, while flat gradients following nondifferential training are pro-Lashley and sloped gradients pro-Hull, each theory can account for negative findings, at least in an ad hoc fashion.

With appropriate selection of both the schedule of differential reinforcement and the psychophysical procedures used, the limits of stimulus control may be assessed reliably (see Blough, 1966; Blough and Blough, 1977; Stebbins, 1970). We should caution, however, against concluding prematurely that a subject cannot discriminate between two stimuli. Many organisms probably have discriminative abilities that are not developed fully until they experience differential consequences for differential responding in the presence of very similar stimuli. For many organisms there are a number of stimulus continua on which the organism may have the potential equivalent of the gourmet's cultured palate.

Given that several stimuli are present when a response is acquired, what factors, in addition to differential reinforcement, determine which will come to control responding? Or, in terms of incidental stimuli, which, if any, will acquire control over the reinforced response? To examine this question we turn to the problem of attention.

ATTENTION

Organisms attend more to stimuli differentially correlated with reinforcement. Thus hungry pigeons orient toward and peck a key light that precedes food (autoshaping), people attend to traffic lights, and people attend to people (for example, family members, professors, and police) who dispense reinforcement and punishment. There is more to the attention story, however. For any given organism and situation, different stimuli will be more readily attended to than others. Thus cats attend much more readily to movement than to color. And a motorist at a traffic light may be more likely to take his eyes off the light to gaze at a striking-looking woman walking along the sidewalk than to look at a lamp post or a dress shop.

How attention may be studied in the laboratory is an important question. One interesting answer is provided by Reynolds' study of attention in pigeons (1961d). In this study two compound stimuli were presented on a response key, each consisting of a form (circle or triangle) and background color (green or red). Pigeons' pecks were reinforced when the triangle was presented on the red background but not when the circle was presented on the green background. The two compound stimuli alternated on a multiple schedule. Pigeons quickly formed the discrimination, that is, they pecked at the triangle–red compound but not at the circle–green compound. What aspects of the S⁺ and S⁻ were Reynolds' two subjects attending to? Does each member of a compound have some control over responding (in the case of the S⁺) or over not-responding (in the case of the S⁻), or is attention directed only at one aspect of each? How may this be tested?

Reynolds next presented each of the four stimuli separately in an extinction procedure. Which positive component (S⁺) controlled responding, and which negative component (S⁻) controlled not-responding? The answer is given in Figure 5.16. For each subject, both aspects of the negative stimulus acquired control of not-responding. Interestingly, a different picture emerged for the positive stimulus: each pigeon was responding to just one component of the positive compound, and the component responded to differed for the two pigeons tested.

A related method for assessing attention following discrimination training with compound stimuli involves generalization testing. Assume, for example, that the positive compound stimulus in Reynolds' experiment had been a vertical line on a green background, while the negative stimulus consisted of stimuli from dimensions independent of angular orientation and hue (for example, a buzzer plus flickering of the chamber illumination). Stimulus control could be assessed by conducting independent generalization tests for both line orientation and wavelength. Sloped gradients imply stimulus control and therefore attention; flat gradients, lack of both. Or, in keeping with Reynolds' method, one could simply measure rate of responding to the vertical line presented without the green background and to the green background without the vertical line. Reynolds' method, while permitting a less complete analysis, is procedurally less complex.

General Principles and Phenomena

Reynolds' results should not be taken to mean that only one aspect of a stimulus compound is generally attended to. Other experiments have demonstrated that several aspects of a compound stimulus may exert stimulus control simultaneously (see Butter, 1963; Fink and Patton, 1953). Which stimulus of the compound commands more attention may usually be altered with appropriate training. Thus Johnson and Cumming (1968) trained pigeons with a vertical line on a green key as the S⁺ and a horizontal line on a red key as the S⁻. In testing, with the four stimuli

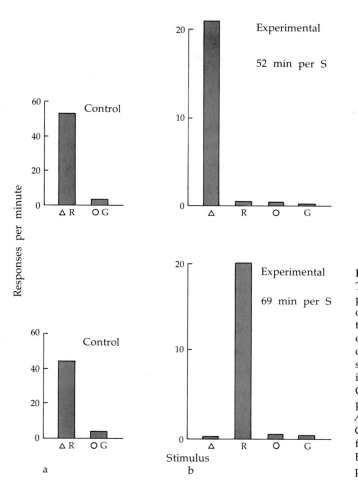

Figure 5.16
The rate of responding of two pigeons (a and b) in the presence of each of the key illuminations in the training phase of the experiment and in the test phase, during which each of the four stimuli was presented separately in an extinction procedure. [After G. S. Reynolds, Attention in the pigeon. *Journal of the Experimental Analysis of Behavior, 4,* 203–208. Copyright © 1961 by the Society for the Experimental Analysis of Behavior, Inc. Redrawn by permission.]

presented separately, each of the two pigeons showed control by color, not line (that is, each behaved like the pigeon in the bottom half of Figure 5.16 from Reynolds' experiment). In a subsequent portion of the study, pigeons were given several sessions of pretraining with simple line stimuli, again with the vertical as S⁺ and the horizontal as S⁻. When these birds were next exposed to compound stimulus training and testing, they responded predominantly to the vertical line and not the green key light. Thus the organism's experimental history (as well as its sensory capacities and genetic disposition) has clear effects upon attention.

Blocking and Overshadowing   The control of responding by a stimulus depends not only on its own salience and the history of reinforced responding in its presence but also upon the salience and reinforcement history of other stimuli present. This principle has been demonstrated already in the discussion of Johnson and Cumming's (1968) experiment on attention. We now discuss two related attentional phenomena of stimulus selection also involving compound stimuli. In *blocking*, the prior correlation of a stimulus with reinforcement prevents (hence "blocks") the development of effective control by a second stimulus when the two are presented together in compound. In a typical experiment, two groups of subjects might receive the following treatment:

	Pretraining	Training	Testing for stimulus control by
Experimental group	Light 1 (S⁺) *vs.* light 2 (S⁻)	Tone and light 1 (S⁺) *vs.* light 2 (S⁻)	Tone
Control group	None	Tone and light 1 (S⁺) *vs.* light 2 (S⁻)	Tone

If prior discrimination training between the two lights reduces stimulus control by the tone (relative to that shown by the control group), then "blocking" has been demonstrated. Miles (1970) found blocking in pigeons, using an experimental design similar to that just described, and several other investigators have demonstrated blocking with a variety of procedures, stimuli, and subjects (see Kamin, 1969; Williams, 1975).

In a test of *overshadowing*, stimulus control maintained by one member of a compound stimulus is compared with that exerted by the same member in isolation. For example:

	Training	Testing for stimulus control by
Experimental group	Light A and tone (S⁺) *vs.* light B (S⁻)	Light and tone (separately)
Control group	Light A (S⁺) *vs.* light B (S⁻)	Light

There are two bases for discrimination in the experimental group (presence of a tone and an intensity difference between lights) but only the light intensity difference for the control group. To the extent that the presence of the tone "overshadows" control by the light, the control group should show greater stimulus control by the light in testing. Overshadowing, like blocking, has been demonstrated with a number of subjects and stimuli in a variety of conditions in studies of both classical and instrumental conditioning (see D'Amato and Fazzaro, 1966; Miles and Jenkins, 1973; Pavlov, 1927). Our example was taken from a portion of a study by Miles and Jenkins. The researchers varied the intensity of light B over four values. As might be expected, the tone, but not the light, acquired significant stimulus control when the lights were only slightly different in intensity. Thus the tone overshadowed the light. When the lights were readily discriminable, however, the light overshadowed the tone.

Overshadowing is in part a function of stimulus salience. Thus Pavlov (1927) reported that a more intense CS will overshadow a less intense one. D'Amato and Fazzaro (1966) found that line orientation stimuli exerted little stimulus control over responding in their monkeys when a salient hue stimulus was also present. Thus overshadowing is an attentional phenomenon that can be understood in terms of stimulus properties. What makes a stimulus salient, of course, also depends upon the subject's prior experience with that and similar stimuli. The blocking phenomenon more obviously depends upon experience, for the simple reason that it explicitly manipulates the subject's experimental history in the pretraining phase. One context in which to understand how prior conditioning may affect stimulus control is offered by the Rescorla and Wagner (1972) theory discussed in Chapter 3. This theory posits that a given reinforcer can maintain only a certain degree of conditioning. Thus once reinforcement occurs in the presence of one stimulus, the stimulus will have acquired most or all of the associative strength that the reinforcer is capable of generating. This would leave little or no strength to accrue to a second stimulus that is later paired with the first in a compound.

The phenomena of overshadowing and blocking have helped shape the contemporary view of attention and stimulus control. Before summarizing this view, we shall discuss three other attentional phenomena: the feature-value effect, conditional stimulus control, and the transfer of stimulus control.

The Feature-Value Effect   So far our discussion of attention has produced few, if any, surprises. The *feature-value effect*, however, was greeted with puzzlement when reported by Jenkins and Sainsbury (1969, 1970). Their pigeons were given a response key illuminated alternately by a plain red light or by the same red light with small light spot (the "feature") located off-center on the key. For pigeons in one group ("feature-negative") the plain red stimulus was the S$^+$, while the spotted stimulus was the S$^-$. For the second group ("feature-positive") the spotted stimulus was the S$^+$ and the plain stimulus the S$^-$. Typical stimuli are sketched in Figure 5.17. Though these discriminations might appear to be equally simple, only pigeons in the feature-positive group formed a discrimination. Pigeons in the feature-negative group continued to respond equally often to the plain and spotted stimuli. In other words, the same feature that controlled behavior as the positive stimulus did not do so as the negative stimulus.

By examining where pecks occur on the key, we gain some insight into the feature-value effect. When the spotted stimulus is the S$^+$, pecks are

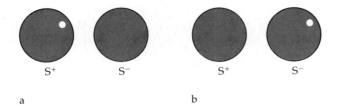

a   b

Figure 5.17
Typical stimuli used to demonstrate the feature-value effect. (a) In
the feature-positive case, the distinctive feature (the white spot) is
on the S$^+$ only. (b) In the feature-negative case, the distinctive
feature is on the S$^-$ only.

directed at the spot, not at the center of the key, since pecks at the spot
are uniquely correlated with reinforcement. When the plain stimulus is
the S$^+$, pecks are directed at the center of the key (which, of course, is
spotless). Since the center of both the S$^+$ and S$^-$ are spotless, however,
pecks occur to both centers and the discrimination is formed with difficulty at best. This analysis suggests that pigeons' attention is restricted to
what is in front of their beaks when pecking; that is, pigeons pecking at
the spotless centers do not attend to the presence or absence of a spot in
the periphery. If so, the feature-value effect should not occur when more
compact stimulus displays are employed, so that the negative feature
stimulates the pigeon no matter where it is pecking—a prediction confirmed by Sainsbury (1971).

A similar, but more general, explanation of the feature-value effect has
been proposed by Sainsbury (1973). He noted that in the feature-positive
case the probability of reinforcement for responding to the distinctive feature is one, whereas the probability of reinforcement for responding to
the common feature is less than one (one-half, assuming an equal number
of responses to S$^+$ and S$^-$). Since responding tends to maximize reinforcement, responses should be directed exclusively to the distinctive feature and the S$^+$–S$^-$ discrimination should be formed readily. In the
feature-negative case the probability of reinforcement for responding to
the distinctive feature is zero, whereas the probability of reinforcement
for responding to the common feature is greater than zero (again one-
half, assuming an equal number of responses to S$^+$ and S$^-$). In this case,
therefore, responses should be controlled by the common feature exclusively, thus hampering acquisition of the S$^+$–S$^-$ discrimination. Sainsbury
(1973) applied this analysis to the results of a feature-value experiment
with four- to five-year-old children. They showed the same effect as did
the pigeons in the earlier studies. Specifically, whereas all six children
reached a criterion of 90 percent-correct responses by the sixth session of
training in the feature-positive case, only one of six children did so in the

feature-negative case. When nine-year-old children were studied, how-ever, five of six reached criterion in the feature-negative case (again, all did so in the feature-positive condition). Subjects who do form the dis-crimination in the feature-negative case apparently look for the distinctive feature and then respond to the display lacking it, thus acquiring a two-link response chain.

Conditional Stimulus Control   Whether or not reinforcement can be ob-tained in the presence of a stimulus may depend on (be "conditional" on) the presence of a "higher-order" or a *supraordinate stimulus*. Such a stimulus cues which stimulus of a group, or which property of a stimulus compound, is correlated with reinforcement on that trial. For example, Reynolds and Limpo (1969) exposed pigeons sequentially to the following four compound stimuli: white triangle on red background; white triangle on green background; white circle on red background; white circle on green background. The supraordinate stimulus was the general illumina-tion provided by a lamp on the side of the chamber. When the lamp was blue, responding was reinforced if and only if the triangle was present; when the lamp was yellow, responding was reinforced only when the red background was present. Thus the lamp light cued whether reinforce-ment was correlated with responding to figure or ground, a cue the pi-geons quickly came to utilize appropriately.

Transferring Stimulus Control   In developing a discrimination between two stimuli, it is often convenient to utilize an existing discrimination and then transfer stimulus control from the old discrimination to the new one. Such transfer of control may be used to minimize errors (that is, re-sponses to the new S⁻). Assume a pigeon has formed a discrimination between a white horizontal (S⁺) and white vertical (S⁻) line, and you now want it to respond to a green (S⁺) but not a blue (S⁻) light. If the green illumination is gradually introduced onto the background of the white horizontal line, and the blue progressively illuminated behind the white vertical line, the pigeon will continue to respond at the same rate to the S⁺ and not respond to the S⁻. Then the white lines may be made progres-sively dimmer. At first, line orientation controls responding; but at some point, as the lines become dimmer, the colors come to control responding appropriately. Stimulus control transference of this sort was first reported by Terrace (1963b) in his study of errorless discrimination learning, dis-cussed earlier in this chapter. An interesting application of such *fading techniques* is in the treatment of homosexuals seeking therapy to transform their sexual interest from homosexual to heterosexual. Barlow and Agras (1973) observe that sexual deviation can be interpreted as an instance of abnormal stimulus control, since sexual arousal occurs to unusual stimulus objects. While many current treatments focus on the use of aver-sive control to suppress abnormal arousal, there is only mixed evidence that these treatments successfully eliminate deviant sexual behavior. Moreover, most of these techniques leave up to chance the development of normal heterosexual behavior, that is, they include no means of directly conditioning normal heterosexual responsiveness. Barlow and Agras attempted to alter directly the stimulus control of sexual arousal with a procedure based on Terrace's (with pigeons). In particular, they sought to alter the stimuli that control sexual arousal in homosexuals, who wished to be heterosexual, by fading in a more heterosexual stimulus as the arousal response (penile erection) was occuring. The therapists used two sets of colored slides, one that showed attractive nude males (to create sexual arousal) and one that showed attractive nude females (selected previously by the patient). The patient viewed the nude male slides until sexual arousal (penile erection) occurred. At this point, a slide of a nude female was faded in and the nude male was gradually faded out, as shown in Figure 5.18. The fading was done gradually so as not to disrupt sexual arousal. During this gradual stimulus change, the patient was instructed to see how long he could sustain his sexual arousal. After this process was repeated a number of times, the patient found the nude females by themselves to be sexually arousing. By the end of a few training sessions, the patient's responses to the nude females were those of a typical heterosexual male.

Did heterosexual responsiveness carry over to the nonlaboratory environment? Yes, for three of the four subjects treated. These three subjects replaced their homosexual tendencies and activities with heterosexual ones, even though two of them had *no* prior history of heterosexual intercourse. The remaining subject, who did not act upon his new heterosexual impulses, showed no permanent decline in homosexual arousal. As the authors note, this subject's failure to approach females suggests that he needs to learn the appropriate social behavior necessary to gratify his

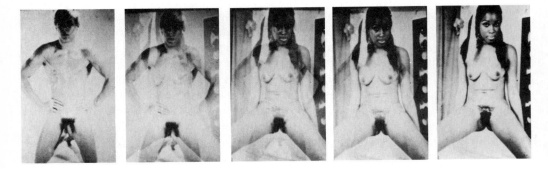

Figure 5.18
Five representative images from the series of sixteen images used during fading for one subject. These images were projected in color during the experiment. [Courtesy of Dr. David Barlow.]

heterosexual arousal and thus ensure positive environmental consequences—that is, reinforcement.

The Barlow and Agras technique and findings not only point to the
importance of stimulus control in abnormal behavior and the possibility of
using fading techniques to alter stimulus control but also stress the importance of having an alternative response available that is itself reinforcing
and that is incompatible with the undesired response. In the example just
cited, the reinforcement of heterosexual behavior was instrumental in
eliminating homosexual behavior.

An Overview of Attention

Organisms are often predisposed to attend to particular components of a
compound stimulus. Certain classes of stimuli may be more attention-
getting than others, either because of the organism's inherited sensory
capacities or its prior experience with members of these classes of stimuli.
The particular situation, or stimulus context, may also dictate which
stimuli are attended to. Thus a person who becomes nauseous after
snacking during a movie date is more likely to associate the illness with
the taste of the food than with the movie or his date. In the parlance of
stimulus control, the taste stimulus overshadows the other stimuli in the
situation. If the same person becomes sexually aroused, however, the
arousal will likely be associated with his date (or what's on the screen)
rather than with the snack. The importance of such stimulus–consequence interactions has been widely documented (for example, Revusky and Garcia, 1970) and will be discussed later, in Chapter 10. These
stimulus–consequence associations may be innately determined, or the
subject may have learned that certain stimuli and consequences tend to
occur together (and therefore *attribute* the consequence to the likely
stimulus). In either case, the previously formed associations may effectively block stimulus control by other stimuli in compounds paired with
the same consequences.

We also know that the more salient of two stimuli is more likely to
command attention. Estimating the salience of stimuli for a particular experimental subject *before* testing for attention is not always possible. As
suggested in a prior paragraph, a stimulus (for example, a particular
color) that is salient to one subject (a pigeon) may be less salient to
another (a cat) and may even be undetectable to still another (a rat).
Given that a stimulus is detectable, the more intense and centrally located
it is, the more likely it will be salient. In any case, salient stimuli may
prevent other stimuli in a compound from being attended to, as in overshadowing. Of course, the relation between stimulus salience and overshadowing is circular unless stimulus salience can be specified independent of the occurrence of overshadowing. Moreover, salience may itself
be a function of the organism's prior history. If reinforcement consistently

depends upon color discrimination, for example, color may become salient to an organism (such as a cat) for which it is normally not salient. This notion is similar to that of "acquired distinctiveness of cues" (Lawrence, 1949, 1950). Lawrence, a relational theorist (in the Lashley tradition) showed that differential reinforcement of responses in the presence of a class of cues facilitates use of these cues in solving subsequent problems. Stimuli that have become salient or distinctive owing to a history of differential reinforcement in their presence may overshadow stimuli that were previously more salient. In such cases, overshadowing is really an example of blocking, in which a stimulus commands attention as a result of differential reinforcement pretraining.

There are several more subtle attentional phenomena. One, the feature-value effect, was seen to depend upon several factors, including where the subject is looking while responding and the probability of reinforcement for responding to common versus distinctive features. Attention may be given conditionally when a supraordinate stimulus cues which property of a group of stimuli is correlated with reinforcement. Moreover, as we have seen, attention may be transferred from one stimulus to another without additional differential reinforcement if the original controlling stimuli are gradually faded out while the new controlling stimuli are being faded in progressively.

All the research on attention—more generally, on stimulus control—is consistent with the view that attention is directed at stimuli correlated with reinforcement and other biologically significant events. Thus the organism is predisposed to attend to stimuli that are important phylogenetically. These predispositions are modulated by the organism's history. Through differential reinforcement, organisms come to attend to previously neutral stimuli and to ignore most stimuli uncorrelated with reinforcement. Moreover, organisms tend to ignore stimuli that occur with others whose correlation with reinforcement has been established previously (blocking).

Finally, it is likely that, in most environments, attending to environmental stimuli is more highly correlated with reinforcement than not attending to them.[7] In that case, many organisms will tend to become more attentive with experience. Indeed, environments that maximize the correlation between attention and reinforcement may well produce more attentive organisms than those that do not. This distinction between environments with high versus low attention–reinforcer correlations may prove to be a critical one for distinguishing between behaviorally (or intellectually) stimulating and impoverished environments. A more modest implication of our proposition that general attentiveness may be enhanced by

---

[7]This, of course, is not true for stimuli that occur repetitively without consequence. As we know, habituation generally occurs to such stimuli (Chapter 3).

reinforcement is that training with differential reinforcement on one continuum should improve attention to stimuli on an independent continuum. Honig (1969) reported just that in an experiment with pigeons in which pigeons trained on a *color* discrimination showed steeper gradients of *line* orientation than control pigeons that had received nondifferential training with the same colors. Reinhold and Perkins (1955) found similar results with rats when the training and test stimuli were not even in the same sensory modality. Direct investigations of conditioned attentiveness may provide a useful perspective from which to view studies showing different degrees of stimulus control in the absence of training with differential reinforcement.

CONCEPTUAL BEHAVIOR

When a child correctly identifies novel members of a given class of stimuli, while discriminating nonmembers of the class, he is engaging in conceptual behavior. Conceptual behavior is usually a complex example of stimulus control in which the subject generalizes within a stimulus class but discriminates between classes. It is complex because the stimuli are usually multidimensional and because the subject may not be able to state the defining characteristics of class membership. Thus children may classify flowers, fruits, and vegetables with a high degree of accuracy even while they (and sometimes their adult mentors) are unable to state the defining characteristics of each. Indeed, Herrnstein and Loveland (1964) have shown that pigeons can be trained to emit adequate conceptual behavior even when the experimenters could not specify the defining characteristics of the stimulus class in physical terms.

In their study, pigeons' responses were reinforced on an intermittent schedule in the presence of color slides containing human beings but were never reinforced when the slides contained no humans. Pigeons eventually responded at high rates when novel slides including people (or parts of people) were presented, but at low rates when the novel slides did not include people. Over 1200 slides were used and contained people of different appearance and in different locations on the slides. The people sometimes appeared singly, sometimes in groups of different sizes. The people were of different colors and ages and adopted different postures; they were nude, semi-nude, or clothed. Often the people were partially obscured by intervening objects of all sorts, including trees and automobiles. Thus the experimenters were unable to specify in physical terms what defined the person in these pictures, although they, like the pigeons, could categorize the slides correctly. This work on pigeons' conceptual behavior has been extended recently by Herrnstein, Loveland, and Cable (1976), whose pigeons learned to discriminate pictures of bodies of water, trees, or a particular person in separate experiments.

Moreover, they discriminated pictures being seen for the first time almost as well as pictures seen in training.

Other studies have investigated acquisition of concepts such as sameness, difference, and oddity. Acquisition of such concepts depends on the subject responding to the relations between two or more objects, and not simply to the stimulus properties of single objects. Robinson (1955) trained chimps on a sameness–difference discrimination task in which two pairs of objects were presented on each trial. One pair consisted of two identical objects (for example, two triangles mounted side by side), while the other consisted of two different objects (for example, a circle and square mounted side by side). Only if the chimp picked up the pair with the physically identical forms did it obtain food. After the chimps mastered these sameness discriminations with various combinations of forms, they were tested with novel instances of the sameness problem (and with objects such as sink stoppers, scouring pads, and other household items that hardly resembled triangles and circles). Their accurate performance on these transfer tests showed that they had acquired the sameness–difference discrimination.

Pigeons also have been trained to make same–difference judgments (see Honig, 1965; Urcuioli and Nevin, 1975). These experiments involve stimuli presented concurrently on two keys. When the stimuli are the same, a "matching response" (for example, defined by a left key-peck) is reinforced; when the stimuli are different, an "oddity response" (defined by a right key-peck) is reinforced. In this procedure the solution requires that pigeons attend to both sameness (or matching) and difference (or oddity) on successive trials. Pigeons are not only able to do so but are also able to generalize the similarity–difference concept to novel stimuli and transfer tests.[8]

The importance of identifying controlling stimuli is nowhere more important than in treating abnormal behavior. Where irrational fears or "phobias" are concerned, for example, effective treatment requires adequate specification of the eliciting stimuli. The stimuli that set the occasion for deviant behavior are sometimes unexpected social stimuli. For example, the self-destructive behavior of psychotic children has been shown to be under stimulus control of such diverse stimuli as the presence of adults who reinforce the behavior by providing attention (Lovaas

---

[8] The area of conceptual behavior is one where it may be especially appropriate to note the importance of identifying the stimuli controlling responding. More generally, apparent instances of complex stimulus control may sometimes have simpler explanations. Perhaps the most famous such case involved the horse Clever Hans. Hans could count by tapping his hoof the appropriate number of times whenever his master called out a number. Psychologists investigated this legendary act and showed that Hans kept on tapping— beyond the appropriate count—if he could not see his audience. Apparently, viewers would unwittingly make anticipatory facial gestures when Hans reached the appropriate number, and it was these gestures that signaled the horse to stop. Hans was clever all right, but he had a head for faces, not figures.

and Simmons, 1969) and the presentation of demands, such as requests for simple gestures—for example, "point to the window." In the latter case the self-destructive behavior is negatively reinforced by escaping the demanding situation (see Carr, Newsom, and Binkoff, 1976). The possibility of multiple determination of self-destructive and other abnormal behaviors underscores the importance of assessing the controlling variables before deciding on a treatment.

Whether we are concerned with the behavior of pigeons or monkeys in the laboratory, or humans in applied settings, the adequate specification of stimuli controlling behavior is of fundamental importance for understanding and changing behavior. One major class of controlling stimuli consists of those which are consequences of behavior, or reinforcers. Whereas in this chapter we have been concerned with the first term in the three-term contingency (of stimulus, response, and reinforcers), in the next two chapters we will turn to a discussion of reinforcers, in the context first of conditioned reinforcement (Chapter 6) and then choice (Chapter 7).

6 Conditioned Reinforcement

As we noted in Chapter 4, stimuli that accompany reinforcers may themselves acquire conditioned reinforcing properties. In this chapter we will discuss the importance of conditioned reinforcement, the methods used to study it, and the conditions necessary and sufficient for establishing a stimulus as a conditioned reinforcer.

Conditioned reinforcement has held a prominent place in systematic theories of behavior (for example, Hull, 1943; Skinner, 1938, 1953) because it seemed clear that most behavior, especially among humans, was not maintained by unconditioned reinforcers. Since reinforcement was believed to maintain most behavior, actions that could not be attributed readily to unconditioned reinforcers were felt to depend on conditioned (or "secondary" or "derived") reinforcers, which came to be effective by being somehow associated with the unconditioned reinforcers. Early experiments with chimpanzees showed that conditioned reinforcers were especially useful in maintaining behavior that was separated in time from unconditioned reinforcers. As we shall see, the view that much behavior is critically dependent upon conditioned reinforcement is no longer viable. Nonetheless, the role of conditioned reinforcers in bridging delays between responses and unconditioned reinforcers remains an important one.

BEHAVIOR CHAINS

By properly scheduling conditioned reinforcers, elaborate chains of behavior, culminating in the presentation of only a single unconditioned reinforcer, may be shaped and maintained. For example, if chimpanzees are given poker chips that may be traded in for raisins (effective reinforcers for chimps), the poker chips become conditioned reinforcers; that is, they can then reinforce the chimps' responses (Cowles, 1937). Thus a chimp will pull a weighted handle in order to obtain a chip that may be exchanged later for a raisin. Note that the chip has two important functions: It is both a conditioned reinforcer (S^r) for the responding that obtains it (pulling the handle) and a discriminative stimulus (S^D) for responding reinforced by raisins (exchanging).

Wolfe (1936) introduced a delay between the acquisition of the chip and the opportunity to insert it into a slot machine (the "chimp-o-mat," pictured in Figure 6.1) for a grape. As long as the chimp could hold the chip, the delay had little decremental effect on responding. When a comparable delay occurred between the insertion of the chip into the chimp-o-mat and the delivery of the grape, however, the reinforcing value of the chip decreased markedly. Thus conditioned reinforcers help bridge the temporal gap between responding and primary reinforcement.

Far more complex behavior chains are commonplace, both in the laboratory and in animal training acts. At Brown University, for example, Bar-

Figure 6.1
The "chimp-o-mat." Chimps learn to earn tokens when the tokens can be exchanged for a primary reinforcer, such as grapes. Some chimps hoard the tokens, just as some humans hoard money. [Yerkes Regional Primate Research Center, Emory University, Henry Nisser.]

nabus the rat was trained to ascend a spiral staircase to a platform, in the presence of an appropriately illuminated light (the first of several S^D's), push down and cross a raised drawbridge to another platform, climb a ladder, pull a chain paw-over-paw to haul in an attached car, peddle the car over the bridge, ascend another staircase, run through a tube to an elevator door, enter the elevator, and raise a Brown University flag. When the banner was raised, the elevator descended to the ground floor. There, when a buzzer sounded, Barnabus ran to a lever, pressed it, and received a food pellet. (See the sketch of this apparatus in Figure 6.2.) Afterward, Barnabus waited for the light that signaled it was time to climb the spiral staircase again and reinitiate the chain.

Human behavior chains, still more complex than that mastered by Barnabus, are commonplace and seem to be acquired with such apparent ease that they often go unnoticed even as we engage in them. Consider

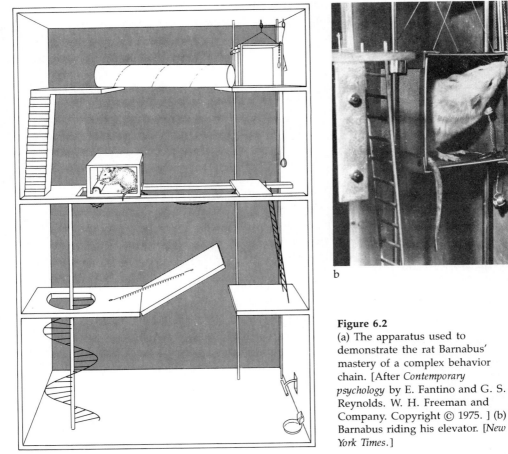

b

a

Figure 6.2
(a) The apparatus used to demonstrate the rat Barnabus' mastery of a complex behavior chain. [After *Contemporary psychology* by E. Fantino and G. S. Reynolds. W. H. Freeman and Company. Copyright © 1975.] (b) Barnabus riding his elevator. [*New York Times.*]

the straightforward activity of taking a friend to a new restaurant: phoning the friend, phoning the restaurant for reservations, obtaining directions, dressing, driving to the friend's house, driving to the restaurant, and so on. Each component in the chain—such as telephoning and driving—itself consists of a sequence of fairly complex activities. The behavior chain is reinforced by a good meal and conversation, each of which is more remote in time from the onset of the activity, and less certain in outcome, than the pellet that awaits the successful completion of Barnabus' rapid routine.

Yet we have chosen an example (going to a restaurant) that describes a payoff far more immediate than many human endeavors. Much of human behavior seems to comprise bits and pieces of complex response chains performed for reinforcers that are, apparently, far more remote: the premedical student, slavishly studying in the hope of gaining entrance into a medical school and, ultimately, a thriving and lucrative practice; Jimmy Carter, campaigning for the Democratic nomination, a very long shot more than a year before the national convention in 1976; the authors writing this book, knowing that one or two years would pass from the time these words were first written to the time they might be published and read. Performance on complex chains of behavior is dependent in part upon the reinforcer to which it ultimately leads. At the same time, this performance depends crucially on the events that occur as each component of the chain is completed. These two points are important, and their elaboration is essential for a proper grasp of both conditioned reinforcement and behavior chains.

If the ultimate reinforcer is indeed vital to adequate performance of behavior chains, it should be easy to show that the behavior would cease when the reinforcer is no longer available. Thus premed students might be expected to alter their course of study should the medical profession be abolished (in favor of faith-healing), most candidates stop campaigning once they have no chance to win the nomination, and authors generally refrain from writing texts unless they think a publisher might be found. In a complex chain (such as Barnabus') if the delivery of the food pellet were discontinued, the whole chain should be extinguished. The leverpress, the last response in the sequence, should be the last response to extinguish. Suppose we "break" Barnabus' chain in the middle, for example, by having running through the tube lead to a dead end, instead of to the elevator. In that event response components in the first part of the chain—such as lowering the drawbridge and peddling the car—would extinguish. But behaviors *following* the break would not be extinguished since they had not occurred. Thus, were Barnabus placed in front of the elevator—following complete extinction of the earlier response components—he would enter, raise the flag, ride down, and press the lever. If the food pellet no longer appeared, however, these later responses would also be extinguished.

The event that occurs as each component of the chain is completed sets the stage—serves as a discriminative stimulus (S^D)—for the behavior required in the next component. The *type* of event is important. In the first place, the more similar the event is to the reinforcer at the end of the chain the more potent it will be in maintaining behavior (see deLorge, 1971; Rose and Fantino, 1978); perhaps stimuli that are similar to the ultimate reinforcer make more salient the relation between responding early in the chain and the reinforcer ultimately produced. Successful completion of courses and chapters should be especially effective for the premed student and author, respectively, while delegate pledges and primary victories should serve a similar discriminative function for the candidate.

Secondly, the type of event occurring at the end of the component may be reinforcing in its own right, a point often overlooked in the analysis of complex behavioral sequences. Thus the student may find his course material interesting, independent of its relation to medical school; the candidate may enjoy a "political scrap"; some authors may be enamored of their own words; and the rat, caged most of the time, surely finds some activities reinforcing. In all of these cases, then, the stimuli (or events) associated with each response component of the chain are not only discriminative stimuli for responding in that component but are also reinforcers for responding in the prior component. If the response components making up the chain are sufficiently reinforcing, of course, the ultimate reinforcer will not be needed for performance of the chain. In the laboratory study of chains described in this chapter, responding throughout the components of the chain would clearly not occur without the final segment of the chain.

Thus behavior maintained on chained schedules is, in part, a function of how reinforcing each required component activity is. Of course, this factor also affects how quickly a behavior chain is acquired in the first place. An additional factor facilitating the acquisition of chains is how well learned the individual components are *before* the chain requirement is instituted. In the human behavior chains described earlier, the components—or building blocks of the chains—were already in the subject's behavior repertoire prior to the introduction to the chain: driving, using the telephone, asking directions, running for lower office (prior to the presidency), writing articles (prior to books), and so on. The behavior chains generated in animal training acts often involve novel activities for the organism in question (since laboratory animals tend to be exposed to less rich behavioral histories than humans); hence more elaborate training is generally required. Moreover, if the relation between the component activities and the ultimate reinforcer—say, food—is unclear, as it must be for lower organisms first acquiring an extended behavior chain (since language cannot be used to specify the task), it is essential to learn the components backward. Thus Barnabus first learned to press the lever when the buzzer sounded (and received food), he was then required to descend in the elevator (reinforced by reaching the box containing the lever and buzzer), and so on. In general, the responses at the end of the chain are most readily acquired and are most resistent to extinction.

Up to now we have discussed chains in a somewhat casual fashion. In particular, we have said little about the status of the component stimuli and activities comprising chains as conditioned reinforcers. Considerable light has been shed on this question in controlled laboratory studies. Before discussing this important work in some detail, we will review briefly other techniques for the study of conditioned reinforcement and describe the important variables affecting the strength of conditioned reinforcers.

EXPERIMENTAL TECHNIQUES

Conditioned reinforcement has been studied most frequently in one of three ways. In one technique (Bugelski, 1938; Skinner, 1938) responses during training produce primary reinforcement preceded by a neutral stimulus—that is, one with no obvious reinforcing or punishing properties. Tests to determine whether or not the neutral stimulus has become a conditioned reinforcer are carried out during extinction. The subject's rate of response (or the number of responses emitted before extinction is complete) when the neutral stimulus is produced by responding is compared with the rate observed when responding is totally ineffective (or the same comparisons are made across two groups of subjects, one receiving the neutral stimulus during extinction and one not). If, in extinction, the subject makes more responses or responds at a higher rate when its responses produce the neutral stimulus, the stimulus may be said to have acquired value as a conditioned reinforcer. One difficulty with this technique, however, is that stimulus generalization, and not conditioned reinforcement, may be responsible for the more persistent responding for the following important reason: The difference between training and extinction is less marked when the neutral stimulus continues to occur. If your car fails to start when you turn the ignition key, you are more likely to keep turning the key if some noise accompanies the turn than if your effort is greeted with silence. This does not mean that the noise is necessarily a conditioned reinforcer; rather, it makes the situation more comparable to those many occasions when your car has started.

Melching (1954) tested this criticism of the *extinction technique* in an experiment directly varying the similarity of acquisition and extinction. Rats in each of six groups were trained to press a lever for food on a continuous-reinforcement schedule. For rats in two groups, all responses produced a buzzer as well as food. For rats in a second pair of groups, the buzzer occurred on 50 percent of the trials. Finally, rats in the last two groups never heard the buzzer during acquisition. In extinction, the buzzer was presented after every response for one group in each pair but was

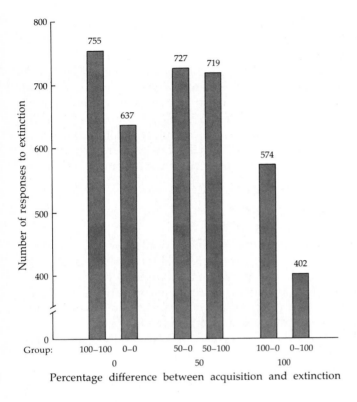

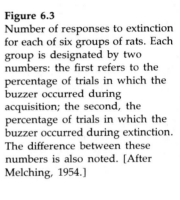

Figure 6.3
Number of responses to extinction for each of six groups of rats. Each group is designated by two numbers: the first refers to the percentage of trials in which the buzzer occurred during acquisition; the second, the percentage of trials in which the buzzer occurred during extinction. The difference between these numbers is also noted. [After Melching, 1954.]

never presented to rats in the other groups. The resulting numbers of responses made during extinction are shown in Figure 6.3. The data for groups 100–100 and 100–0 replicate the basic finding that we are trying to understand: buzzer presentations increase the number of responses in extinction (755 responses versus 574), But is this difference due to conditioned reinforcement or to generalization? Data from the other groups suggest that generalization is the process responsible. Groups 0–0 and 0–100, which did not receive the buzzer in acquisition, provide a comparison involving the same difference in generalization decrement between acquisition and extinction (as do groups 100–100 and 100–0) but without a difference in conditioned reinforcement (since the buzzer has never been paired with food). The difference between the number of responses made by rats in these groups (637 versus 402) is at least as great, suggesting that the differences for both pairs of groups reflect generalization. Finally, groups 50–0 and 50–100 provide a comparison involving a potential difference in conditioned reinforcement but with equal differences in generalization decrement. The similarity in the number of responses (727 versus 719) made by rats in these groups further supports the generalization interpretation. Thus these data provide no support for the notion that the buzzer was a conditioned reinforcer. More generally, the extinction technique is better suited for studying generalization than for studying conditioned reinforcement.

The *new-response technique* involves a similar acquisition procedure and also omits primary reinforcement in testing for conditioned reinforcement. During testing, the subject has the opportunity to emit a new response, the only consequence of which is presentation of the previously neutral stimulus. The extent to which the new response is acquired and maintained indicates the value of the conditioned reinforcer. One problem with this technique (which applies to the extinction technique as well) is that presentation of the neutral stimulus may activate behavior owing to the potentially frustrating effect of nonreinforcement in the presence of stimuli previously paired with reinforcement. Such frustration effects, well-known since the work of Amsel and Roussel (1952), may be controlled by using choice procedures in which one response leads to the stimulus being tested and the other does not. Any generalized activating effects of the stimulus might be apparent in the rate or vigor of subsequent responses but are much less likely to affect choice. For example, Saltzman (1949) fed rats in a distinctive goal box (at the end of a runway) and assessed whether access to the empty goal box would reinforce a particular turn at the choice point of a U-maze. Food was never presented during the 15 maze-learning trials. Saltzman did find a preference for the former goal box, demonstrating a conditioned reinforcement effect (although the problem of stimulus generalization could be raised again here). Within 10 trials, however, the rats were performing at chance level, suggesting that the conditioned reinforcement effect was transient indeed. This is not surprising: since food is never available in the U-maze, the rats may quickly learn that the maze is an S^- for running (just as the runway was an S^+). And this is the critical problem in new response techniques: The potency of the conditioned reinforcer wanes during extinction trials; it is therefore a poor reinforcer for the new response.

The third traditional technique for the study of conditioned reinforcement—*chain schedules*—avoids this difficulty by maintaining the effectiveness of the conditioned reinforcer with continuing presentation of primary reinforcement in its presence (see Ferster and Skinner, 1957; Gollub, 1977). A two-link chain, for example, involves two distinct schedules in each link. Responses in the first link produce a different stimulus in the presence of which responding on the second schedule results in primary reinforcement. This general procedure has at least one potential weakness: the effects of primary and conditioned reinforcement may be confounded. In other words, is responding in the initial link of the chain controlled by the stimulus change occurring at the end of the link or by the primary reinforcement obtained upon completion of the entire chain? We can answer this question by comparing performance on a chain FI FI schedule with performance on an equivalent tandem FI FI schedule. Re-

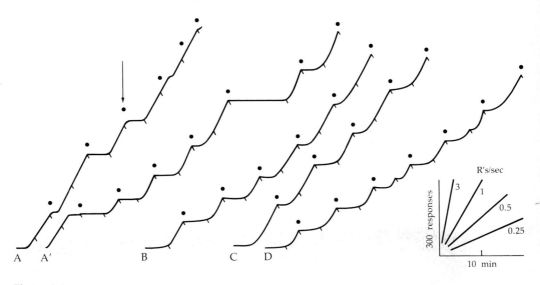

Figure 6.4
Performance on tandem and chain FI 3-min FI 2-min schedules. Record A is the transition from tandem to chained schedule (at the arrow). Record A' is the continuation of that session. Records B, C, and D show further development in the chained schedule: record B is from the second, C from the fourth, and D from the eighth session on the chained schedule. Pips indicate change from one schedule component to the next. Small dots above the record indicate food deliveries. [After R. T. Kelleher and L. R. Gollub, A review of positive conditioned reinforcement. *Journal of the Experimental Analysis of Behavior, 5,* 543– Copyright © 1962 by the Society for the Experimental Analysis of Behavior, Inc. Redrawn by permission.]

sponse requirements on the two schedules are identical, but the schedules differ in one critical respect: whereas different exteroceptive stimuli are correlated with each link of the chain, only a single exteroceptive stimulus is present throughout the tandem schedule.[1] Note that the first component on either schedule bears the same temporal relationship to reinforcement. Thus any difference in behavior in the first component of the two schedules must be due to the stimulus change occurring at the end of that component in the chain.

Typical behavior maintained by such tandem and chain schedules is sketched in Figure 6.4. Note that only one scallop, terminating with primary reinforcement, occurs on the tandem schedule. On the chain schedule, however, two scallops are produced: the organism's responding accelerates during the first FI until the stimulus associated with the second component is produced; then the organism pauses before again re-

---

[1]The relationship between tandem, chain, mixed, and multiple schedules was reviewed in Chapter 4 (see Figure 4.6).

sponding at an accelerated rate until food is obtained. Thus the *pattern* of responding in both links of the chain suggests that the stimulus change reinforces responding in the initial link. If responding in the initial link were controlled exclusively by the food, the pattern of responding should be equivalent to that found with the tandem schedule.

While chain schedules have been the most productive technique for studying conditioned reinforcement, interesting and important developments have been uncovered with the other techniques as well. In particular, the study of variables having major effects on the strength of conditioned reinforcement has profited by all three of the techniques we have outlined. It is to this study that we turn briefly.

STRENGTH OF CONDITIONED REINFORCERS

By "strength," "potency," or "value" of a reinforcing stimulus we mean how effective that stimulus is in maintaining behavior that produces it, how resistent to extinction that behavior is, and to what extent the stimulus will be chosen in a preference test including other reinforcing stimuli.

The same variables that determine how much of an effect a primary reinforcer has on behavior similarly affect the potency of conditioned reinforcers. Thus the number of pairings of a stimulus with primary reinforcers and the magnitude of those primary reinforcers will affect the strength of that stimulus as a conditioned reinforcer. The schedule of primary reinforcement in the presence of the conditioned reinforcer and the temporal interval between the onset of the conditioned and the primary reinforcers are also important.

Magnitude of Primary Reinforcement

The effects of the magnitude of primary reinforcement (that is, its amount or duration) on conditioned reinforcing strength have been studied in three ways. In the *between-subjects procedure*, different groups of subjects are exposed to treatments differing in the amount of reinforcement associated with the stimulus that is later assessed as a conditioned reinforcer. For example, Butter and Thomas (1958) gave rats 48 trials in which the click of a reinforcement mechanism was associated with either an 8 percent or 24 percent sucrose solution for each of two groups. In testing (with the new-response technique), a lever was introduced into the chamber that, when pressed, resulted in the presentation of click (but not sucrose). Rats in the 24 percent sucrose group emitted more presses than those in the 8 percent group.

D'Amato (1955) used a *within-subjects procedure* in which rats were first exposed to five food pellets in one distinctive goal box and only one pellet

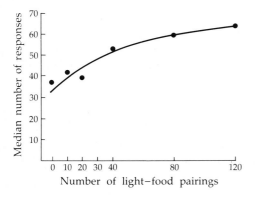

Figure 6.5
Median number of bar-presses in rats as a function of the number of light–food pairings during bar-press training. Data are from the testing phase in which no food was available, but bar-presses produced the light. [After P. J. Bersh, The influence of two variables upon the establishment of a secondary reinforcer for operant responses. *Journal of Experimental Psychology, 41*, 62–73. Copyright 1951 by the American Psychological Association. Redrawn by permission.]

in a different goal box. In testing—without primary reinforcement—the rats were given 15 trials with the five- and one-pellet boxes on either side of a T-maze. The rats chose the goal box that had been associated with five pellets, at a significantly higher rate than chance.

Neuringer (1967) used a within-subjects design and a *choice procedure*. Pigeons chose between two conditioned reinforcers, each of which was always associated with an FI 5-sec schedule of reinforcement. The two conditioned reinforcers differed in that one terminated in 2 sec of food reinforcement while the other ended in X sec of food. "X" was varied from 2 to 10 sec across conditions. Neuringer found that the pigeon's choice was very sensitive to the *relative magnitude* of *reinforcement*—that is, the value $X/(2 + X)$; the larger the X, the more often the pigeon chose the conditioned reinforcer terminating in X sec of reinforcement.[2]

Number of Pairings with Primary Reinforcement

Bersh (1951) studied the conditioned reinforcing strength of a stimulus as a function of the number of pairings of that stimulus with primary reinforcement. His results (measured as the median number of responses producing the stimulus) are shown in Figure 6.5. Note first that the function is an increasing one, as one might expect. That is, the greater the number of pairings, the more potent the conditioned reinforcer. Second, note that more than a tenfold increase in the number of conditioned–primary reinforcement pairings produces just a 50 percent increase in the number of responses. Bersh (1951) used a between-subjects design: such

---

[2]This procedure used by Neuringer is technically a concurrent-chains procedure since the schedule consists of concurrent initial links (choice phase) and either of two terminal links (the chosen conditioned reinforcer). We will describe this procedure more thoroughly when discussing choice in the next chapter.

designs are generally less sensitive to experimental manipulations than within-subjects designs. Larger effects of the number of primary reinforcements occurring in the presence of a conditioned reinforcer have been demonstrated in a within-subjects choice procedure (Fantino and Herrnstein, 1968).

Schedule of Primary Reinforcement

The strength of a conditioned reinforcer is affected profoundly by how primary reinforcement is scheduled in its presence. Two important generalizations can be made: (1) Intermittent presentations of primary reinforcement have a greater strengthening effect than continuous presentations, and (2) the more variable the intermittent presentations of primary reinforcement, the greater the strengthening effect upon the conditioned reinforcer.

The first generalization is supported by the results of Klein (1959), Armus and Garlich (1961), and Kendall (1974). Both Klein and Armus and Garlich used a between-subjects procedure in which the different groups received different percentages of primary reinforcement in the presence of the conditioned reinforcing stimulus. Thus in Klein's (1959) study each of six groups of rats received 120 trials in a runway, but with primary reinforcement percentages varying between 20 and 100 percent. Following these trials, the rats received an additional 20 trials without primary reinforcement in a T-maze in which one goal was neutral. The other was identical to the goal box used during training (that is, the box being tested for conditioned reinforcing strength). The percentage of choices of the conditioned reinforcer was greater the less frequently primary reinforcement had occurred in its presence. Similar results were found by Armus and Garlich (1961). These studies tested for conditioned reinforcing strength in extinction. Kendall's (1974) results—from a within-subjects design—suggest that, under certain circumstances, pigeons actually respond more to obtain a stimulus that is paired with food on 50 percent of the trials than one that is always paired with food, even when food is still being provided.

It should be acknowledged that some investigators, using a within-subjects design, have found greater conditioned reinforcing strength with continuous rather than intermittent schedules of primary reinforcement (see D'Amato, Lachman, and Kivy, 1958; Mason, 1957). If more test trials had been conducted in these studies, however, it is likely that the reverse result would have been obtained. In Mason's study, rats acquired two discriminations: in one, the positive stimulus was always associated with reinforcement; the second stimulus was associated with primary reinforcement on only 50 percent of the trials. In choice tests the two positive stimuli were paired in a new discrimination task for 10 (nonreinforced) trials. Seventeen of 20 subjects chose the stimulus that had been correlated with continuous reinforcement on more than half the trials. With additional trials, however, it is likely that subjects would have come to choose the stimulus that had been correlated with intermittent reinforcement, since its strength should be more resistant to extinction (an instance of generalization decrement being greater for the stimulus that had been correlated with continuous reinforcement).

Just as the intermittent presentation of primary reinforcement tends to strengthen the conditioned reinforcing potency of a stimulus correlated with these reinforcements, so does the variable presentation of these reinforcers (Davison, 1969, 1972; Fantino, 1965, 1967; Herrnstein, 1964b; Hursh and Fantino, 1973; Killeen, 1968). For example, Fantino (1967) showed that pigeons preferred a stimulus correlated with an FR 1 on 50 percent of the trials and an FR 99 on the other 50 percent, to one reliably paired with an FR 50. When primary reinforcement was withheld (Fantino, 1965), responding ceased in the presence of the conditioned reinforcers, but the choice responding that produced the conditioned reinforcers was maintained for some time afterward. Moreover, this responding continued to reflect preference for the variable conditioned reinforcer.

Why does the variable scheduling of primary reinforcement in the presence of a stimulus enhance the strength of that stimulus as a conditioned reinforcer? Apparently the short *interreinforcement interval* (IRI) between the onset of the conditioned reinforcer and the occurrence of the primary reinforcer is critical. Thus when the FR 1 and FR 99 are equally probable (technically, a *mixed* FR 1 FR 99 schedule), the subject receives both very long and very short IRI's. The stimulus correlated with the FR 50 is reliably associated with IRI's of intermediate length. The short IRI's of the mixed schedule exert sufficient strength to more than make up for any deleterious effects when the FR 99 occurs. Indeed, when the value of the constant FR is lowered from 50 to 25, the mixed FR 1 FR 99 is still preferred (though by a smaller margin). Only when the constant FR is lowered to 10 are the two schedules of comparable strength (Fantino, 1967).

These data make a more general point that will be evident throughout our discussion of both conditioned reinforcement and choice: Reinforcing events occurring relatively soon after a response, or relatively soon after the onset of a stimulus, have disproportionately greater effects on the strength of that response or stimulus than do events occurring later in time. There is additional, independent evidence that the length of the IRI is a critical determinant of conditioned reinforcing strength.

The Interreinforcement Interval

Jenkins (1950) and Bersh (1951) followed the onset of the neutral stimulus with primary reinforcement after intervals ranging from 0 to 80 seconds. Their experiments differed in that Jenkins used a trace procedure—the

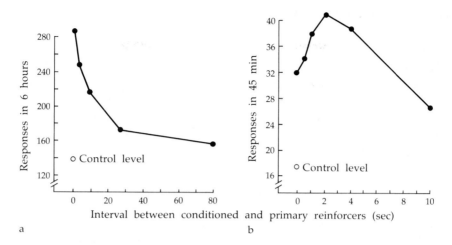

Figure 6.6
Number of responses as a function of the interval between the onset of a stimulus and the presentation of food in rats from each of two studies. (a) In Jenkins' study, the stimulus was a buzzer. [After W. O. Jenkins, A temporal gradient of derived reinforcement. *American Journal of Psychology, 63,* 237–243. Copyright 1950 by the University of Illinois Press. Redrawn by permission.] (b) In Bersh's study, the stimulus was a light. [After P. J. Bersh, The influence of two variables upon the establishment of a secondary reinforcer for operant responses. *Journal of Experimental Psychology, 41,* 62–73. Copyright 1951 by the American Psychological Association. Redrawn by permission.]

stimulus remained on for only 3 seconds—while Bersh used a delayed procedure—the stimulus remained on throughout the IRI and until after primary reinforcement occurred. The number of responses maintained in tests presenting the conditioned reinforcer alone is shown in Figure 6.6 as a function of the IRI. Note first that the strength of the conditioned reinforcer decreases as the IRI lengthens. Secondly, at very short IRI's, short intervals, such as 0.5 to 1.0 sec, appear superior to 0 sec. This intriguing finding may reflect either or both of the following: (1) optimal interstimulus intervals in classical conditioning typically exceed 0 sec, suggesting that conditioned reinforcing strength may be due to the association between stimuli formed by classical conditioning; (2) if the neutral stimulus and food are presented simultaneously, the subject may not attend to the neutral stimulus. Finally, note that the decline in conditioned reinforcing strength is sharpest for small IRI's and levels off somewhat after 10 or 20 sec. This finding is consistent with the results from the prior section (preference for variable over fixed schedules), suggesting that a given absolute difference in IRI will have a greater effect the sooner in the IRI the difference occurs.

CHAINED SCHEDULES

Up to now we have stressed the importance of conditioned reinforcement in helping to bridge delays between a response and the unconditioned reinforcement produced by that response. But we have not addressed a fundamental question: Do conditioned reinforcers maintain behavior when primary reinforcement is unavailable? Stated another way, does pairing a neutral stimulus with reinforcement impart reinforcing strength to that stimulus so that it will maintain behavior even when it does not signal that the original reinforcer is forthcoming? Does a conditioned reinforcer develop independent status as a reinforcer?

Work with the new-response and extinction techniques, reviewed earlier, suggests that the answer to this question is not "yes" or "no" but "not much." Conditioned reinforcement effects, when obtained with these procedures, appear to be quite transitory. However, two phenomena observed with chained schedules have been cited as evidence for the reinforcing potency of stimuli paired with primary reinforcers.

Chain Versus Tandem Schedules

The phenomenon of *response rate enhancement* was reported by Gollub (1958) when he compared responding in two-link tandem and chain fixed-interval schedules of reinforcement. When he changed the discriminative stimulus in the initial link of the tandem FI FI, thereby transforming the schedule into a chain, response rates eventually increased in the initial links. The increase in initial-link response rates may be attributed to conditioned reinforcement: the discriminative stimulus for responding in the tandem schedule had been paired with food at the end of each tandem schedule; through this pairing, the stimulus became a conditioned reinforcer, which enhanced responding in the initial link of the chain. This finding has been widely cited as evidence for what has been called the *pairing hypothesis* of conditioned reinforcement (see Fantino, 1977; Kelleher and Gollub, 1962). More recently, Wallace (1973) replicated Gollub's experiment but failed to obtain an increase in response rates in chain schedules above those seen in the tandem control. His data argue that the stimulus correlated with the terminal link of a chain schedule is not an effective conditioned reinforcer, at least for the schedules and procedures he employed. Taken together, the results from studies by Gollub (1958) and Wallace (1973) suggest that a terminal link of a chain schedule may serve as a conditioned reinforcer only under some conditions. (For example, Gollub's two subjects were exposed to the tandem schedule for nine months before being switched to the chains; in the Wallace study, twelve subjects were switched after 20 sessions.)

While the reinforcing potency of the stimuli in a chain schedule may be minimal, such stimuli do have discriminative functions: hence the stimuli comprising a chain control patterns of responding appropriate to the schedules correlated with their presence. Gollub (1958) showed that the discriminative function of the stimuli comprising chain schedules as well as their lack of reinforcing potency are clearly evident when he compared extended chain and tandem schedules. For example, consider the three following schedules: (1) a simple FI 5-min (with a blue key light throughout); (2) a chain FI 1 FI 1 FI 1 FI 1 FI 1 (with different key lights associated with each of the five links—say green, red, yellow, white, and blue); (3) a tandem FI 1 FI 1 FI 1 FI 1 FI 1 consisting of the same response requirements as the chain but with the same stimulus as the simple FI 5-min (a blue key light throughout). How do pigeons respond on the extended tandem and chain schedules?

The five-link tandem schedule generates behavior similar to that on a simple FI schedule; that is, the behavior is well maintained and manifests itself as a single scallop between primary reinforcements. Behavior is dramatically different on the five-link chain. Indeed, responding is so poorly maintained that pigeons tend to obtain on the order of one reinforcer per hour (instead of every 5 minutes) and usually stop responding altogether after extended training. Similar results have been obtained by Fantino (1969b) with rats. It appears as if the organism comes under stimulus control and stops responding because the stimuli presented during the early links of extended chains are correlated with (are cues for) nonreinforcement. In other words, the early stimuli in the chain tell the organism that it is *far* from reinforcement. Interestingly, responding on extended chains of this type decreases with more practice. The organism responding on a tandem schedule will initially continue to respond at a high rate when switched to a comparable chain; after a time, however, as stimulus control develops, responding gradually becomes strained in the early links. In extended chains, therefore, not only are the stimuli *not* conditioned reinforcers, but they actually serve as cues for nonreinforcement, and hence for nonresponding.

The reader may rightly be wondering how to reconcile the poorly maintained behavior on extended chain schedules with the facile performance on extended chains displayed by Barnabus and others, discussed at the outset of this chapter. In the first place, as we noted, each of the component activities performed by Barnabus was probably somewhat reinforcing in and of itself. More importantly, each response in Barnabus' chain was performed only once (per reinforcement), not repetitively as in the FI 1-min schedule. A corollary of this fact is that Barnabus moved immediately across components of the chain; he did not have to spend a minute or more in each component. Indeed, Gollub (1958) showed that the shorter each component of a chain, the more extended a chain could be constructed. In other words, there is a trade-off between component length and the number of components.

Paired Brief Stimuli

Gollub developed a schedule (a chain FI 1 FI 1 FI 1 FI 1 FI 1) that did not maintain behavior even though, by responding, the organism could obtain a reinforcer every 5 minutes. In contrast, Kelleher (1966) studied a schedule that provided a maximum of one reinforcer per hour but maintained behavior well. Pigeons had to satisfy fifteen consecutive FI 4-min schedules in order to obtain food. (Instead of writing FI 4 fifteen times, we will use the notation of such "second-order" schedules: FR 15 (FI 4). In words, the FI 4 must be satisfied fifteen successive times before food is obtained.) In one condition, the completion of each FI 4 produced a white light for 0.7 sec. Since this light was paired with food, it is called a *paired brief stimulus.* In a second condition, no stimulus occurred after the completion of each FI 4. In a third condition, a 0.7 sec stimulus change occurred following completion of each of the first fourteen FI 4 components, but did *not* also occur prior to food (that is, with the completion of the final FI 4 component). Hence these would be *unpaired brief stimuli.* Response rates were highest throughout the schedule in the paired brief stimulus conditions, suggesting that the paired brief stimulus was an effective conditioned reinforcer. Behavior in two of these conditions is shown in Figure 6.7.

The picture became complicated but intriguing when Stubbs (1971) published an extensive investigation of the effects of paired and unpaired brief stimuli on responding in second-order schedules. He found that the two types of brief stimuli produced comparable response rates for a wide range of stimuli and schedules. In addition, within components both types of stimuli maintained a pattern of responding similar to that maintained by primary reinforcement. Since the unpaired brief stimuli are presumably not conditioned reinforcers, their effectiveness in enhancing response rates calls into question the notion that the paired brief stimuli are effective conditioned reinforcers.

An alternative possibility was raised by Squires, Norborg, and Fantino (1975): Perhaps the enhanced response rates in second-order schedules result from the subjects' difficulty in discriminating between the components of the second-order schedule. Specifically, the salient brief stimuli in the early components resemble those prior to the final components. Perhaps the organism fails to distinguish between them and thus responds in the early components at a rate more appropriate to the later components. To test this possibility, Squires et al. (1975) used a procedure with two response keys. The pigeon advanced through the second-order schedule by responding on one key (the "main key") while brief stimuli occurred on a second ("brief-stimulus") key. A response to the final paired brief stimulus—the one occurring at the end of the final component—was required to obtain food. Responses to earlier brief stimuli—the ones occurring at the end of the earlier components—were unnecessary, or in one experiment were punished. If subjects can dis-

FR 15 (FI 4:W)

FR 15 (FI 4)

500 responses

FR 15 (FI 4:W)

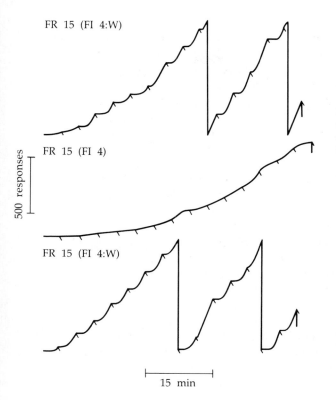

|— 15 min —|

Figure 6.7
Effects of omitting presentations of the paired brief stimulus (white light) at the end of each component of a chained schedule. Each cumulative response record shows a sequence of 15 consecutive FI 4 components; each sequence terminated with food reinforcement. Short diagonal strokes on the records designated FR 15 (FI 4:W) indicate 0.7-sec presentations of white light. Under the FR 15 (FI 4) schedule, there were no exteroceptive stimulus changes during the sequence; short diagonal strokes indicate the end of each FI 4 component. Note the lower rate of responding in the middle panel, in the condition without light presentations. [After R. T. Kelleher, Conditioned reinforcement in second-order schedules. *Journal of the Experimental Analysis of Behavior, 9,* 475–486. Copyright © 1966 by the Society for the Experimental Analysis of Behavior, Inc. Redrawn by permission.]

criminate between components of second-order schedules, they should not make premature brief-stimulus responses, especially when they are punished. Instead, the birds consistently responded to all brief stimuli.[3] Squires et al. (1975) suggested that when rate enhancements are observed in second-order schedules they may be due to the poor discrimination between the component immediately preceding food and the prior components of the schedule. This poor discrimination between components in turn results in response rates during the early components that are more appropriate to rates during the final component and are independent of any conditioned reinforcement effect. Where high response rates are also found with unpaired brief stimuli, a similar explanation makes

---

[3] One possibility is that these premature brief-stimulus responses are similar to the autoshaped pecks that occur, even when they prevent reinforcement, in negative automaintenance procedures (see Chapter 4). Subsequent work with auditory brief stimuli, selected so as not to elicit autoshaped pecks, has produced results similar to those of Squires et al: pigeons responded consistently to all brief stimuli. Thus the results of Squires et al. do not apparently reflect an autoshaping effect. Whether or not autoshaping is involved, however, the conclusion that early brief stimuli are poorly discriminated from late ones is tenable.

sense. The final component (in which food is obtained) begins after the last unpaired brief stimulus (which marks the end of the prior component). When such stimuli also occur after the first components of the second-order schedule, they make all components, beginning with the second, more closely resemble the final component. Since the unpaired stimuli are not paired with food, however, they may command less of the organism's attention and disrupt temporal control less than do paired brief stimuli. In such cases paired brief stimuli will produce more rate enhancement than unpaired brief stimuli. Again, however, this would not demonstrate conditioned reinforcement.[4]

Thus the most impressive evidence for the view that an arbitrary stimulus may become a potent conditioned reinforcer after a history of pairing with a known reinforcer—that from second-order schedules of paired brief stimuli—looks less impressive after empirical scrutiny. Instead, some of the apparent reinforcing effectiveness of paired brief stimuli results from the fact that such stimuli make it difficult for the subject to discriminate early (nonreinforced) components from the final (reinforced) component. Their effects resemble "conditioned confusers" more than "conditioned reinforcers" (Fantino, 1977). Stimuli are potent conditioned reinforcers—in the sense of maintaining responding that produces them—only when they signal the availability of primary reinforcement. We will make this statement more precise (and quantitative) in our discussion of theory. First, however, we will discuss an important application of conditioned reinforcement in behavior modification.

BEHAVIOR MODIFICATION: THE TOKEN ECONOMY

Recall that early experiments with chimpanzees showed that chips or "tokens" can become effective conditioned reinforcers (Cowles, 1937; Wolfe, 1936). The analysis of token reinforcement has blossomed in the past two decades, beginning with the experimental analysis of token reinforcement schedules with chimps (see Kelleher, 1957, 1958) and expanding to include behavior modification of inappropriate behaviors in psychiatric hospitals (Ayllon and Azrin, 1965, 1968), classrooms (Bushell, Wrobel and Michaelis, 1968; O'Leary and Drabman, 1971), correctional institutions (Cohen and Filipczak, 1971; Milan and McKee, 1976), and other applied settings (see Kazdin and Bootzin, 1972, for a review).

---

[4]More recent research has shown that after the rate enhancement due to temporal confusion is parceled out, a real, though small, conditioned reinforcement effect remains (Rose and Fantino, 1978). This qualification does not alter the conclusions stated thus far nor subsequently. Moreover, other recent evidence suggests that stimuli paired with primary reinforcement have some conditioned reinforcing strength that cannot be reduced to the discriminative effects of the stimuli (see Nevin and Mandell, 1978).

Token reinforcement procedures resemble second-order schedules of paired brief stimuli in that there is a *unit schedule*, specifying token delivery, and a *schedule for exchange*, specifying when behavior under the unit schedule is reinforced with food. In Kelleher's work the tokens were poker chips that the chimps could later exchange for foodstuff (similar procedures have been studied with rats, for example, by Waddell, Leander, Webbe, and Malagodi, 1972). The tokens maintained consistent response patterns and sustained rates of responding, as do the brief stimuli on second-order schedules. Extended pauses do occur, however, when the number of tokens is low and is hence correlated with nonreinforcement. When Kelleher (1958) presented chimps with a large number of response-independent tokens early in the schedule, however, responding was vigorously maintained. The analogy to the work of Squires et al. (1975) with pigeons and second-order schedules is clear: With a large number of tokens the stimulus conditions resemble those during the final components of the schedule, just as brief-stimulus presentations make all following components resemble the final one.

One of the most important and widely used techniques of behavior modification is the *token economy*, which has been employed successfully with school children, mental patients, and inmates of correctional institutions. The economy is based on the awarding of tokens, which can then be turned in for a variety of different reinforcers of the subject's choosing. For example, school children's classroom performance may be reinforced with tokens that are traded in later (at the end of the hour or day) for any one of a number of "back-up reinforcers," such as candy or toys, displayed in a "store," play privileges, and so forth. The opportunity to engage in activities that are chosen with high probability when freely available is often a particularly effective back-up reinforcer. Similarly, tokens may be awarded to severely retarded hospital patients in order to institute and maintain behaviors related to social responsiveness, work activities, and self-care behaviors (such as grooming, making one's own bed, self-feeding, continence, and so forth). Token economies have one and usually both of two aims: to institute and maintain desired behaviors during treatment conditions, and to maintain these behaviors after treatment is discontinued. The hope is that the activities themselves will ultimately take on reinforcing value or lead naturally to reinforcing events such as social approval (and hence become conditioned reinforcers). If the tokens are effective in instituting normal, productive behavior, then these behaviors themselves will be reinforcing and tokens will be progressively less necessary to maintain the behavior.

Since tokens are paired not with one but several different reinforcers, they are potent *generalized reinforcers*. There are several advantages to using generalized reinforcers, as well as some particular advantages to using tokens as the generalized reinforcers. The advantages of using generalized conditioned reinforcers have been listed by Kazdin and Bootzin. They note that conditioned reinforcers:

(1) bridge the delay between the target response and back-up reinforcement; (2) permit the reinforcement of a response at any time; (3) may be used to maintain performance over extended periods of time when the back-up reinforcer cannot be parceled out; (4) allow sequences of responses to be reinforced without interruption; (5) maintain their reinforcing properties because of their relative independence of deprivation states; (6) are less subject to satiation effects; (7) provide the same reinforcement for individuals who have different preferences in back-up reinforcers; and (8) may take on greater incentive value than a single primary reinforcer since, according to Ferster and DeMyer (1962), the effects resulting from association with each primary reinforcer may summate [Kazdin and Bootzin, 1972, p. 343].

Moreover, tokens have the following additional advantages (first noted by Ayllon and Azrin, 1968): (1) they are portable; (2) there is no limit to the number a subject may earn or possess; (3) they can be used to operate machines automatically dispensing reinforcers (such as the "chimp-o-mat" or vending machine); (4) the number of tokens earned is directly related to the amount of reinforcement the tokens may be exchanged for; (5) tokens are durable and can be made almost indestructible; (6) as with money, tokens may be unique and effectively nonduplicable, assuring that they will not be generated in an unauthorized manner.

Psychiatric Patients

In their token economy program at Anna State Hospital, Illinois, Ayllon and Azrin (1968) were able to institute and increase the frequency of basic work activities and self-care behaviors in severely retarded chronic schizophrenics. The target behaviors selected were those that were useful or necessary for the patient to function in a hospital environment. Tokens could be exchanged for the opportunity to engage in behaviors that occurred with high frequency when freely allowed (an application of the Premack principle, see Chapter 4). In a series of experiments, Ayllon and Azrin showed that the token economy was effective in maintaining the reinforced behaviors. These desired adaptive behaviors declined sharply in frequency when the reinforcement procedure was discontinued by ending the dispensing of tokens and making the reinforcing activities freely available. When reinforcement was again made contingent upon performance, however, performance returned to its prior level. These results are shown in Figure 6.8.

Ayllon and Azrin (1965; 1968) obtained similar results with self-care activities such as grooming (hair combing, appropriate dress), bathing (weekly), tooth brushing (daily), exercises, and bed making. Each of these activities, when performed at the appropriate time, earned a token. While the maintenance of such behaviors may seem a modest achievement, these were psychotic patients (primarily schizophrenic) who had been hospitalized continuously for an average of sixteen years (the range was

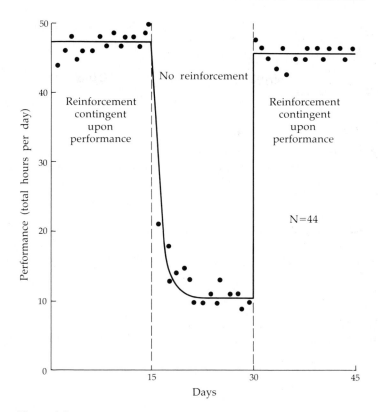

Figure 6.8
The total number of hours of on-ward performance by a group of 44
patients in a token-economy program. [After T. Ayllon and N. H.
Azrin, The measurement and reinforcement of behavior of psychotics.
Journal of the Experimental Analysis of Behavior, 8, 357–383. Copyright ©
1965 by the Society for the Experimental Analysis of Behavior, Inc.
Redrawn by permission.]

from one to thirty-seven years). Moreover, the lack of fundamental self-
care and work behavior can be a factor in prolonging hospitalization in
the chronic schizophrenic. Equally important, these are behaviors that
must be emitted with a degree of frequency and appropriateness if the
individual is discharged. Finally, when self-care behaviors are reinforced
in the token economy, other beneficial side effects may also occur. Atthowe and Krasner (1968), for example, found an increase in the social
interactions of their patients, although these interactions were not among
the target behaviors being reinforced.

The social interactions of chronic schizophrenics have also been directly
improved with token economies designed either to decrease the frequency of aggressive behaviors (see Steffy, Hart, Craw, Torney, and Mar-

lett, 1969) or to increase social interaction (Schaefer and Martin, 1966). In the latter study, not only were social interactions increased in frequency but apathy was reduced (apathy was defined operationally as engaging in a single behavior, for example, standing, without simultaneously engaging in any other behavior).

Classrooms

The application of token economies in the classroom has had two general aims: (1) to improve class management, by increasing attentiveness and decreasing misbehavior, and (2) to increase academic activities, such as study behavior. The classroom management problem is not a trivial one, as many a school teacher can testify. O'Leary and Becker (1967) showed that deviant behavior (that is, disruptive or inappropriate behavior) may constitute more than three-fourths of all behaviors for the average child in an elementary school adjustment class. When O'Leary and Becker introduced a token economy along with classroom rules, praise for appropriate behaviors, and ignoring of inappropriate behaviors, deviant behavior fell to 10 percent. Subsequent research showed that among the changes instituted by O'Leary and Becker, token reinforcement was the most effective in reducing the deviant behavior (O'Leary, Becker, Evans, and Saudargas, 1969).

Other researchers have increased academic activities, such as writing, reciting, and special projects, by reinforcing them with tokens that could be exchanged for special events, such as movies or field trips (Bushell, Wrobel, and Michaelis, 1968). Wolf, Giles, and Hall (1968) used token reinforcement to improve language, reading, and arithmetic skills. All of the eleven subjects in the study improved in the performance of their assignments. At the end of one year in the program, these students were earning significantly higher grades than controls and showed greater gains in an achievement test.

Correctional Institutions

One of the most successful applications of the token economy has been a juvenile-delinquent rehabilitation system developed by Harold Cohen (see Cohen and Filipczak, 1971). Cohen's CASE (Contingencies Applicable to Special Education) project successfully rehabilitated youthful inmates at one institution in Washington, D.C. Inmates acquired points, the equivalent of tokens, for engaging in specified educational behaviors. For example, points were awarded for correctly answering academic test questions. At any time the subject could turn in the points for such reinforcers as lounge privileges, soft drinks, or items from the outside world chosen from mail-order catalogs. Each point was worth a penny. The program was voluntary, and no inmate received points if he did not learn.

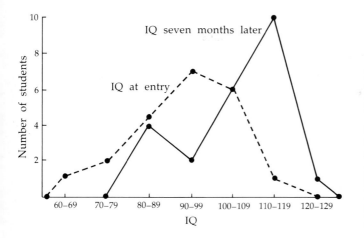

Figure 6.9
The distributions of IQ scores for 24 students in a Washington, D.C., reform school both before and after introduction of a remedial education program using monetary incentives to improve performance in academic subjects. [After H. L. Cohen and J. Filipczak, *A new learning environment.* San Francisco: Jossey-Bass, 1971.]

Not only was the program remarkably successful in demonstrably teaching the inmates verbal, arithmetic, and other skills, but it had unexpected side effects. Within six to eight months the average inmates' measured IQ increased by about 16 points (Figure 6.9). Furthermore, as learning progressed, it became its own reward: one of the most highly valued items came to be a private office where the inmate could better pursue his studies.

Problems

While the token economy has proven to be a remarkably effective application of reinforcement principles in a wide variety of studies—not limited to the three areas just discussed—there are difficulties associated with its use. One important class of problems involves the effective application of the token economy. The second involves the degree to which adaptive behaviors maintained effectively by a token economy will continue to occur when the token economy is no longer in effect.

Implementation   One serious problem in implementing the token economy concerns the behavior of the staff assigned to administer it. The staff may consist of several nurses and attendants in a hospital setting or a single teacher in a classroom. In either case, training is a vital and considerable task. In the first place, the staff must be trained to avoid the common habit of reinforcing inappropriate behavior with attention or other social reinforcers and instead ignore such behaviors while reinforcing appropriate ones. In the second place, once the desired adaptive behavior has been instituted and is well maintained, the staff must continue to reinforce it when appropriate; the tendency to ignore the nonproblem patient or student is strong, simply because staff (or teacher) time is so limited.

A second problem is presented by individuals who are apparently unresponsive to reinforcement procedures. Ayllon and Azrin (1965), for example, reported that almost one-fifth of the chronic schizophrenics in one of their experiments were largely unaffected by the reinforcement manipulation. Whether or not this reflects the failure to use sufficiently potent reinforcers (such as eating or sleeping), as Ayllon and Azrin suggest, or the intrinsic unresponsiveness of some psychotic individuals to environmental consequences is not known.

A third problem centers on some individuals' ability to obtain tokens or back-up reinforcers through unauthorized channels, such as stealing. Lieberman (1968) reports that one female schizophrenic obtained back-up reinforcers from patients in return for sexual favors, a phenomenon that has also been said to occur among chimps (Ruch and Zimbardo, 1971). While such behavior may circumvent the effective application of the token economy with respect to the person giving the sexual favors, it at least should not interfere with its effectiveness with respect to the person earning the reinforcers. As Kazdin and Bootzin (1972) note, contingencies may also be circumvented when either appropriate or inappropriate behaviors are emitted in the absence of staff members. To the extent that this is undesirable, target behaviors should be those that effect a change in the physical environment, which may be reinforced later. At the same time, intermittency of reinforcement may be desirable in many cases, as it should enhance the prospects for resistance to extinction and generalization when the token economy is no longer in effect. Indeed, the problem of generalization is perhaps the most significant one potentially limiting the utility of token economies.

Generalization   Will the effects generated by the token economy transfer to a new situation in which a token economy is not in effect? We stated earlier that the hope for the token economy is that the reinforced activities will themselves become reinforcing (for example, social interaction or reading) or lead naturally to other reinforcers (for example, grooming or work activities). If so, the activities should be maintained even when the token reinforcement is faded out or terminated. This is a critical consideration if the client is leaving an institution using a token economy and entering society at large. As Kazdin and Bootzin (1972) conclude in their evaluative review of token economies, the elimination of token reinforcement generally results in the return of the behavior to performance levels approaching pretreatment levels. They are quick to point out, however, that this conclusion is probably premature since:

> The relevant experiments have not been done. Most researchers have used the within-subject design with a reversal of effects to indicate that the reinforcement procedures were functionally related to the dependent variable. The goal of the research was not maintenance of desired behavior. In fact,

Bijou, Peterson, Harris, Allen, and Johnston (1969) cautioned researchers using an ABAB design not to wait too long before reversing, lest the behavior come under the control of new conditioned reinforcers and thus not reverse [Kazdin and Bootzin, 1972, p. 359].

If the goal is to maintain behavior change outside the institution rather than or in addition to evaluating the effectiveness of the token economy in a within-subjects experimental design, then generalization should be planned for. One effective way is to select behaviors that are likely to be maintained when there is no token economy. As Ayllon and Azrin (1968) have noted, the facts of extinction insure "that behavior cannot be expected to be maintained outside the training situation unless there is some reinforcement for it there. The law of extinction suggests, then, the following rule for selecting a response for training. *Relevance of Behavior Rule: 'Teach only those behaviors that will continue to be reinforced after training'* " (p. 49).

Certainly, behaviors typically reinforced in token economies are consistent with this rule (for example, self-care behaviors and social, work, and academic skills). If the relevance rule is adhered to and especially if token reinforcement is faded out gradually (as in Schaefer and Martin, 1969) behavior change is likely to be maintained.

THEORY OF CONDITIONED REINFORCEMENT

Thus far we have seen that conditioned reinforcement is an important process maintaining operant behavior only when the conditioned reinforcing stimulus is correlated with the availability of primary reinforcement. In addition, behavior will be reinforced by stimuli that the organism does not discriminate from those correlated with primary reinforcement (for example, the paired brief stimuli in the early components of a second-order schedule). For the sake of simplicity, we will not distinguish between these two cases henceforth. Instead, our present concern is to review briefly the primary theoretical conceptions of conditioned reinforcement. At the theoretical level our task is to better specify what we mean when we say that a stimulus is correlated with the availability of primary reinforcement. What operations produce effective conditioned reinforcers as measured by the responding of organisms? We will briefly describe three traditional hypotheses of conditioned reinforcement that have proved important, if ultimately inadequate, and then describe two more current alternatives.

Traditional Theories

Dinsmoor (1950) conducted an interesting experiment in which rats' barpresses in the presence of a light (the discriminative stimulus, or S^D) were reinforced with food. Following this training, extinction occurred. In one group, responding produced the S^D; for this group, then, the number of bar-presses emitted in extinction was a measure of the conditioned reinforcing strength of the former S^D. In the other group, the S^D was presented prior to responding, but responses in its presence were otherwise ineffective; for this group, the number of bar-presses emitted in extinction was a measure of the stimulus' discriminative strength. Dinsmoor found that the number of responses was comparable in the two groups, suggesting that the discriminative stimulus and conditioned reinforcing strength of a stimulus covary.

Schoenfeld, Antonitis, and Bersh (1950) have also sought to separate the discriminative and reinforcing functions of a stimulus by presenting a light *after* rats had obtained food. Though the light was contiguous with food, it should have no discriminative value. Would it nonetheless have value as a conditioned reinforcer? In an extinction test, Schoenfeld et al. found the light was not a conditioned reinforcer. As in Dinsmoor's study, therefore, the conditioned reinforcing and discriminative value of a stimulus were found to covary. These findings led Keller and Schoenfeld (1950) to formally state the *discriminative stimulus hypothesis* of conditioned reinforcement (first suggested by Skinner, 1938): "In order to act as a conditioned reinforcer for any response, a stimulus must have status as a discriminative stimulus for some response" (p. 236).

Although the discriminative stimulus hypothesis is generally correct— discriminative stimulus and conditioned reinforcer strengths do *tend* to covary—it has not proven to be a generally adequate theory of conditioned reinforcement. There are cases in which a stimulus will serve as an S^r even though it is no longer an S^D for responding in its presence (Duncan and Fantino, 1970; Fantino, 1965). For example, Fantino (1965) trained pigeons to respond on a chain VI FR schedule and then withheld primary reinforcement at the end of the chain. Responding in the initial link of the chain was maintained for some time after responding ceased in the presence of terminal-link FR schedule. In other words, the stimulus correlated with the terminal link was no longer an S^D for responding in its presence but continued to reinforce responding in the prior link of the chain (that is, was still a conditioned reinforcer). The results from the first four sessions of extinction are illustrated in Figure 6.10. Moreover, evidence *for* the discriminative stimulus hypothesis is ambiguous. For example, in the study by Schoenfeld et al. there is no evidence that the rats even noticed the stimulus, since they were presumably busy eating when it was presented. Thus the fact that it did not serve as an effective conditioned reinforcer is not surprising.

A hypothesis of conditioned reinforcement that also emphasizes the discriminative strength of a stimulus, but that avoids some of the problems of the discriminative stimulus hypothesis, is the *cue strength hypothesis* developed by Wyckoff (1959). He suggested that the strength of a conditioned reinforcer is a function of the probability of a response in its

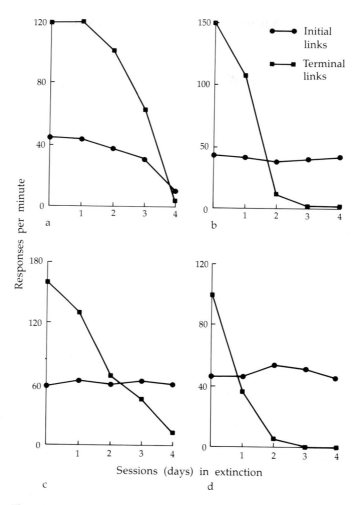

Figure 6.10
Rate of responding in both initial and terminal links for four pigeons
(a, b, c, and d) in each of four sessions of extinction. Session 0 was
the session prior to extinction. During extinction food was not
presented upon completion of the FR's. Yet responding was
maintained in the initial link by the stimulus correlated with the
terminal link. [After Fantino, 1965.]

presence. Moreover, the form of the general function relating conditioned
reinforcing value to cue strength should be a positively accelerated one
over some of its range—a restriction, required by the data of Prokasy
(1956) and others, that need not concern us here. As Nevin (1973) has
pointed out, an ideal preparation to evaluate Wyckoff's theory is a two-
component chain schedule in which the rate of responding in the initial

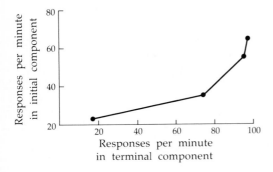

Figure 6.11
Rate of responding during the initial component of a two-component chain schedule, in relation to the rate of responding during the terminal component.The data were obtained at four different levels of deprivation. [Data from Fischer and Fantino, 1968. After J. A. Nevin, Conditioned reinforcement. In J. A. Nevin and G. S. Reynolds (Eds.), *The study of behavior.* Copyright © 1973 by Scott, Foresman and Company. Redrawn by permission.]

component is a measure of conditioned reinforcing value, while the rate of responding in the terminal component is a measure of cue strength. On the positive side are the data of Fischer and Fantino (1968), which, as Nevin shows, conform to Wyckoff's theory. These data are shown in Figure 6.11. Fischer and Fantino studied the responding of pigeons after extended training on chain VI 45-sec VI 45-sec schedules under four different levels of food deprivation. As deprivation increased, response rates increased in the terminal links. Crucial for Wyckoff's theory is the fact that the function relating response rates in the initial link to response rates in the terminal link was not only monotonically increasing but was positively accelerated.

Experiments that show an inverse relation between conditioned reinforcing value and cue strength are, of course, inconsistent with the cue strength hypothesis. Again, the best examples involve chain schedules. For example, pigeons will respond at moderate rates in the initial component to enter a terminal component in which responding may be emitted at a lower rate, as when reinforcement in the terminal component is response-independent (Ferster, 1953). Also, in a choice situation pigeons prefer to enter a terminal link in which reinforcement is available on an interval schedule (controlling moderate response rates) rather than to enter a terminal link in which high rates of responding are required (Fantino, 1968; Moore and Fantino, 1975). Moreover, Herrnstein (1964a) found no relation between the rates of responding in the initial and terminal links of chain schedules. Thus while conditioned reinforcing strength and cue strength covary in most cases, there are exceptions that render the cue strength hypothesis untenable as a general theory of conditioned reinforcement.[5]

The *pairing hypothesis* (after Hull, 1943) is probably the most viable of the traditional viewpoints of conditioned reinforcement. The hypothesis

---

[5] A more complete discussion of the cue strength hypothesis, arriving at a conclusion similar to ours, may be found in Nevin (1973).

is supported by the observation that a stimulus paired with primary rein-forcement acquires the properties of a reinforcer. But we now know that mere pairing, or contiguity, is not enough. For example, Rescorla (1968, 1972) has shown that Pavlovian fear conditioning will not occur if the probability of the unconditional stimulus (UCS) in the *absence* of the CS equals that in the presence of the CS. In other words, pairings of the CS and UCS are effective only so long as a correlation exists between them. The most striking evidence *for* the pairing hypothesis has come from second-order schedules. As noted earlier, however, the results of Squires et al. (1975) and Rose and Fantino (1978) show that pairing provides only a weak source of conditioned reinforcing strength.

Contemporary Theories

Having discussed the most influential of the older theories, we are now ready to discuss the current ones. At this point we will simply describe the two contemporary hypotheses. We will then evaluate them in the con-text of some interesting research on observing responses assessing the reinforcing potency of stimuli providing information about reinforcement.

The *information hypothesis of conditioned reinforcement* (Berlyne, 1960; Bloomfield, 1972; Rachlin, 1976) states that the conditioned reinforcing strength of a stimulus is a function of its informativeness about the availability of primary reinforcement. In other words, the more uncertainty about reinforcement the stimulus reduces, the more effective a con-ditioned reinforcer it will be. Hence this hypothesis has also been called the *uncertainty-reduction hypothesis.*

The *delay-reduction hypothesis* (Fantino, 1977) states that the conditioned reinforcing value of a stimulus takes into account how remote primary reinforcement has been prior to the onset of that stimulus: "the greater the percentage improvement, in terms of contiguity, to primary rein-forcement correlated with the onset of the stimulus, the greater its con-ditioned reinforcing strength. Thus a stimulus associated with an FI 30-sec schedule should be a stronger reinforcer if it is preceded by a 60-sec period of nonreinforcement than if it is preceded by a 10-sec period of nonreinforcement, since in the first case the onset of the 30-sec interval is correlated with a two-thirds reduction in time to primary reinforcement (of an original waiting time of 90 sec, only 30 sec—or one third—remains once the stimulus correlated with the interval schedule appears), but in the second case only with a one-fourth reduction in time to primary rein-forcement (of an original waiting time of 40 sec, 30 sec—or three-fourths—still remains once the stimulus correlated with the interval schedule appears)" (p. 314). These two hypotheses and the predictions they make may be best understood in the context of experiments on ob-serving, to which we now turn.

OBSERVING RESPONSES

In a typical observing response procedure, reinforcement is provided on either of two schedules of reinforcement but the same stimulus is associated with each. Thus the subject is faced with a *mixed* schedule. Observing responses may be made to convert the mixed schedule into a *multiple* schedule. In other words, when the subject makes a successful observing response, a stimulus, correlated with one of the two reinforcement schedules, is produced. Observing responses have no other consequence; that is, they are not required for primary reinforcement. Indeed, observing responses are usually made to a different key or lever than the responses on the reinforcement schedule; in some cases reinforcement is response-independent, and the observing response is the only one available. Under what conditions are observing responses emitted (or elicited, as the case may be), and what can the study of observing, intrinsically interesting in its own right, tell us about conditioned reinforcement? We will begin by making the observing paradigm more concrete, by discussing the results from a typical experiment. We will then be in a position to evaluate the information and delay-reduction hypotheses of conditioned reinforcement.

The observing-response procedure was developed by Wyckoff (1952, 1969), who alternated an FI 30-sec schedule with periods of extinction in the presence of a white key light. A pedal press—the observing response—turned the key red or green. The red or green light remained on until the subject got off the pedal. Thus the main dependent variable in this experiment was the proportion of time spent on the pedal. The procedure is diagramed in Figure 6.12. In one condition, red was associated with the FI 30-sec schedule and green with extinction; in a discrimination reversal condition, these schedule–key color correlations were reversed (red was associated with extinction, green with FI 30-sec); and, in an important control condition, there was no correlation between the schedules and the stimuli: the FI and extinction schedules were equiprobable (p = 0.5) in the presence of either red or green. Would pedal-pressing be maintained as well in this uncorrelated condition as in the correlated conditions? If so, pedal-pressing would appear to be maintained by stimulus change. However, if more pedal-presses occurred in the correlated conditions, then observing would appear to be maintained by the production of the discriminative stimuli correlated with the two schedules.

Wyckoff's central results are shown in Figure 6.13. Note that observing was poorly maintained in the uncorrelated condition, shown at the top of the figure (proportion of time spent observing less than 0.1). In this condition, of course, the subjects (pigeons) could not tell which schedule was in effect—hence their rate of key-pecking was equal in the FI and EXT components. The picture changes dramatically when we look at the bot-

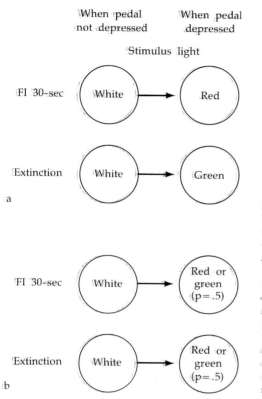

When pedal not depressed   When pedal depressed

Stimulus light

FI 30-sec — White → Red

Extinction — White → Green

a

FI 30-sec — White → Red or green (p = .5)

Extinction — White → Red or green (p = .5)

b

Figure 6.12
Typical observing-response procedure as developed by Wyckoff (1952, 1969). (a) In the correlated condition, the subject's observing response changes a mixed schedule into an analogous multiple schedule, as shown. The red and green stimulus lights are correlated with an FI 30-sec schedule and extinction, respectively. (b) In the uncorrelated condition, observing responses also produce a red or green light. In this case, however, the lights are uncorrelated with the schedules in effect. If a higher rate of observing occurs in the correlated condition, observing is said to be maintained by the production of the discriminative stimuli correlated with the two schedules and not by stimulus change.

tom half of the figure for behavior in the correlated condition. Here, observing is well maintained (proportion of time spent observing close to 0.5), and the subjects discriminate well between the two conditions (response rates in FI are fivefold those in EXT). Thus when the key lights were effective discriminative stimuli for the subjects, they also maintained observing. The results of Wyckoff's discrimination reversal condition, in which the key light correlated with the FI schedule was switched from red to green and that associated with extinction from green to red, also support the notion that effective discriminative stimuli maintain observing. These data (not shown in Figure 6.13) reveal a drop in observing (from 0.3 to less than 0.1) during the first reversal session, while the birds are still responding more to red (now EXT) than to green (now FI 30-sec). As the discrimination successfully reverses, however, so does rate of observing recover.

Wyckoff's results, and many subsequent ones (see Fantino, 1977, for a review), show that observing is not maintained primarily by stimulus change but by the production of stimuli correlated with the schedules of

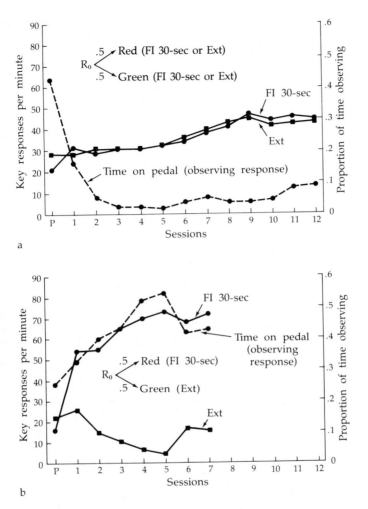

Figure 6.13
Results of Wycoff's observing-response experiment. (a) Data from uncorrelated condition. On any trial, an observing response was equally likely to produce a red or a green key, and each trial was equally likely to end with reinforcement. The first session (marked P) was a control session in which pedal responses had no consequences. (b) Data from correlated condition. Now on positive trials an observing response produced a red key, correlated with FI 30-sec; on negative trials an observing response produced a green key, correlated with extinction. [After Wyckoff, 1969.]

reinforcement in effect. But these results also raise several interesting questions:

1. Must the correlated stimuli be discriminative stimuli for a required response? Or will stimuli correlated with response-independent schedules of reinforcement maintain observing?

2. Do both of the correlated stimuli maintain observing, or does only the positive one? In Wyckoff's study, for example, was pedal-pressing maintained by the production of the stimulus correlated with extinction as well as that correlated with the FI schedule? This second question, we shall see, is crucial for evaluating both the information and delay-reduction hypotheses.

3. Will observing be maintained if *neither* stimulus is correlated with positive reinforcement? For example, if periods of response-independent shock are alternated with shock-free periods, will observing be maintained by the production of stimuli correlated with the shock-free and/or the shock periods? In other words, will information about aversive events maintain observing? According to the information hypothesis, it should.

The first question was answered by the results of several experiments showing that observing would be maintained even when the correlated stimuli were not discriminative stimuli for responding—that is, when all reinforcements were response-independent (see Jenkins and Boakes, 1973; Kendall, 1973a, 1973b). This result is not surprising: our review of the discriminative stimulus hypothesis of conditioned reinforcement already suggested that not all conditioned reinforcers were discriminative stimuli.

The second question has been the subject of much heated debate, many experiments, and a reasonably clear-cut resolution. As one proponent of the information hypothesis (Bloomfield, 1972) has put it, "the information hypothesis . . . requires that 'bad news' be just as much 'news' as 'good news' and so does not differentiate these two cases" (p. 194).

Several studies that have been cited widely as evidence for the proposition that "bad news" is reinforcing (see Lieberman, 1972; Schaub, 1969; Schaub and Honig, 1967) do not make a convincing case, since the procedures used make the results impossible to interpret with any certainty (for reviews, see Dinsmoor, Browne, and Lawrence, 1972, or Fantino, 1977). There *are* studies that employ straightforward procedures, however. One type of procedure, developed by Dinsmoor and his co-workers at Indiana University, separates the reinforcing effects of the positive and negative stimuli. In some sessions only the stimulus signifying "good news" may be observed; when the extinction schedule is in effect, observing is ineffective. During other sessions only the stimulus signifying "bad news" may be produced; when the reinforcement schedule is in effect, observing is ineffective. If the information hypothesis were correct, observing should be maintained as well when its only consequence is production of the stimulus correlated with extinction as when its consequence is production of the stimulus correlated with the schedule of positive reinforcement: the stimuli are equally informative. If the delay-reduction hypothesis were correct, however, observing should be maintained only if the positive stimulus were produced sometimes: only the

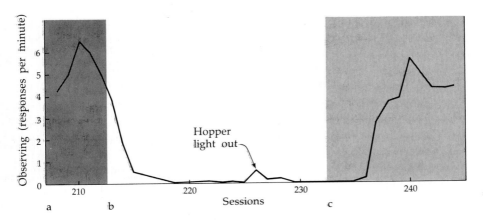

Figure 6.14
Rate of pecking the observing key on successive sessions by one pigeon when pecking
produced (a) S⁺ only, (b) S⁻ only, or (c) both stimuli. [After J. A. Dinsmoor, M. P. Browne,
and C. E. Lawrence, A test of the negative discriminative stimulus as a reinforcer of
observing. *Journal of the Experimental Analysis of Behavior, 18,* 75–85. Copyright © 1972 by the
Society for the Experimental Analysis of Behavior, Inc. Redrawn by permission.]

positive stimulus is correlated with the reduction in time to reinforcement. Dinsmoor et al. (1972) found that observing was eliminated when
the only consequence of pecking the observing key was the onset of the
stimulus correlated with extinction. When only the positive stimulus (correlated with a variable-interval schedule of reinforcement) could be observed, and when both positive and negative stimuli could be observed,
pecks at the observing key were well maintained. These results are
shown in Figure 6.14. Thus it appears that "bad news" is not reinforcing.

The conclusion that stimuli correlated with the absence of primary reinforcement will not reinforce observing is supported by many other recent
experiments, including those of Blanchard (1975), Mulvaney, Dinsmoor,
Jwaideh, and Hughes (1974), Jenkins and Boakes (1973), Kendall (1973a),
and Katz (1976). For example, Mulvaney et al. (1974) studied pigeons in
an observing procedure with three response keys. Periods during which
responding on the center key was reinforced with food on a VI schedule
alternated unpredictably with periods during which center-key responses
were not reinforced (extinction). Pecks at one side key intermittently produced either a positive stimulus on all three keys if the VI was in effect or
a negative stimulus on all three keys during extinction. Pecks on the other
side keys also produced intermittently the positive stimulus on all three
keys if the VI was in effect but had no consequence during extinction.[6]

---

[6]The consequences of observing are arranged on an intermittent schedule (usually a VI) so
that the absence of stimulus change after a few observing responses does not signal the
unavailable outcome.

Did more observing occur on the key from which both positive and negative information was available or on the key that did not convey the negative information? The subjects responded at a higher rate on the less informative side, suggesting that the negative stimulus was punishing, not reinforcing.

These findings have been extended by Auge (1973, 1974) and by Jwaideh and Mulvaney (1976), who have shown that an informative stimulus may not be reinforcing even when correlated with positive reinforcement. Specifically, if two schedules of positive reinforcement are alternated, only the stimulus correlated with the more positive schedule will maintain observing. For example, observing is maintained by the stimulus signaling the lesser of two delays to reinforcement but not by the stimulus signaling the greater delay (Auge, 1974). Such findings, of course, are incompatible with the information hypothesis. What does the delay-reduction hypothesis predict? When the subject does not observe, it remains in the presence of the mixed stimulus, correlated with both short and long delays to reinforcement and therefore with an intermediate average delay. The positive stimulus is correlated with the short delay and therefore a reduction in average time to reinforcement relative to the mixed stimulus. The negative stimulus is correlated with the longer delay and therefore an increase in average time to reinforcement relative to the mixed stimulus. Thus only the positive stimulus should maintain observing.

It should be clear that what defines positive and negative stimuli depends critically on the set of alternatives available. Given two different-valued alternatives, only stimuli correlated with the higher-valued alternative will reinforce observing. This result suggests an answer to our third question: Will observing be maintained if *neither* stimulus is correlated with positive reinforcement but one is more aversive than the other? Specifically, will information about aversive events maintain observing? Consider the following experiment: Periods during which response-independent shocks are delivered to an organism alternate with shock-free periods; no source of positive reinforcement is provided. Subjects may make observing responses in order to produce stimuli correlated with either the shock or the shock-free periods. Will the stimulus correlated with the shock-free periods maintain observing? If the effects on behavior of positive and aversive events are symmetrical, we would expect so. By the same token, the stimulus correlated with the shock periods should not maintain observing.

Although the experiment is yet to be done in the manner just outlined, an impressive series of experiments by Pietro Badia and his associates at Bowling Green University support these expectations. In several of Badia's experiments, rats were exposed to response-independent shocks occurring, say, on a VT 120-sec schedule (as in Harsh and Badia, 1975). If rats did not respond on a lever, shocks were not preceded by a signal. By lever-pressing, the rats converted the unsignaled condition to a signaled condition for one minute. During this one minute a light was on (the "correlated stimulus") and each shock was preceded by a 5-sec warning stimulus (a tone). At the end of the one minute the correlated stimulus terminated and future shocks were unsignaled. Subjects again had the option to reinstate the correlated condition by responding. Responding in no way affected the occurrence of shocks, only whether or not they were signaled. Note, too, the important point, to be developed later, that shocks never occur in the presence of the correlated stimulus when the tone is absent. Shocks occur only in the uncorrelated condition and in the presence of the correlated condition *plus* signal. Thus the correlated stimulus may actually serve as a "safety signal." One question this research addresses is whether or not such discriminable shock-free periods have reinforcing value.

The results from Badia's laboratory have shown unequivocally that rats have a strong preference for the condition in which shocks are signaled, often spending more than 90 percent of the time in the correlated condition. Indeed, even when the signaled shocks are four to nine times longer, or two to three times more intense, or two to eight times more frequent than the unsignaled shocks, rats prefer the correlated condition (Badia, Coker, and Harsh, 1973; Badia, Culbertson, and Harsh, 1973).[7]

Badia's group has considered three important views. The first is the information hypothesis, which proposes that information about shock onset should be inherently reinforcing (Bloomfield, 1972). As we have seen, the information hypothesis is disconfirmed in the case of behavior maintained by positive reinforcement. There, "bad news" is not reinforcing. The same conclusion is necessitated by work with aversive stimuli. Several studies have shown that stimuli correlated with shock-free periods will maintain observing but that stimuli correlated with shock periods will not (see DeFran, 1972; Dinsmoor, Flint, Smith, and Viemeister, 1969).[8] These results also argue against a second hypothesis, developed by Perkins (1955), which stresses that information about shock enables the organism to better prepare for it, thereby reducing the noxiousness of shock. Rachlin (1976), after reviewing studies of observing, has addressed this view:

> The findings demonstrate conclusively that animals prefer events such as food and shock to be signaled.

---

[7]Preference for signaled shocks has also been found with human subjects (Badia, Culbertson, and Harsh, 1974), although in this experiment shocks were either avoidable or escapable. Thus the signals helped subjects minimize their rates of shock and responding. Similar results occur in rats with both the avoidable (Badia, Culbertson, and Lewis, 1971) and escapable (Badia and Culbertson, 1972) shock procedures.

[8]These results might appear to contradict those from Badia's groups showing preference for signaled shock. As we shall see, it is not the signaled shocks *per se* but the discriminated shock-free periods in their absence ("signaled safety") that causes preference for the correlated condition.

Why are signaled events preferred to unsignaled events? In other words, why is information reinforcing? . . . One fairly obvious theory is that when an event is signaled it can be prepared for. That is, food may be more valuable if some salivation can take place before the food is ingested. Similarly, responses geared to withstanding shock, such as freezing or adjusting physiological processes, may make the shock less aversive [Rachlin, 1976, p. 248].

Preparatory-response theory is eminently reasonable, as Rachlin suggests. A problem with it, however, is its appeal to hypothetical unobservable states, which make the theory difficult to prove or disprove. More importantly, preparatory-response theory is not supported by the evidence. Indeed, the most damaging results for the theory are the same results, just cited, that argue against information theory: If stimuli correlated with shock periods, to which preparation may occur, do not maintain observing, while stimuli correlated with shock-free periods, which do not prepare the subject for shock, do maintain observing, then preparatory-response theory cannot be correct. There are additional empirical problems with preparatory-response theory, however, including the recent results of Badia, Harsh, Coker, and Abbott (1976). Before discussing their results, we should briefly outline the third important theory of preference for signaled shock conditions, namely, the safety analysis of Badia's group (see Badia and Culbertson, 1972; Badia, Harsh, and Coker, 1975).

The *safety analysis* stresses that a signaled shock condition is composed of aversive periods signaled by the 5-sec preshock periods (tones) and safety periods signaled by the presence of the correlated stimulus in the absence of the tone. The safety periods are considerably longer in duration than are the unsafe periods: the intershock interval is generally long relative to the signal duration; in the typical example we used from Harsh and Badia (1975), the average intershock interval was 120 sec and the signal duration was 5.5 sec. The safety periods also tend to occur much more immediately after the subject responds to enter the signaled shock condition. Thus the correlated stimulus may become reinforcing as a safety signal, a view consistent with the analysis of Seligman, Maier, and Solomon (1971). On the other hand, the unsignaled schedule is *always* unsafe since shocks may occur at any time throughout its duration. If so, when the subject responds to change the unsignaled condition to a signaled condition, it is leaving an unsafe period and entering one that is safe most of the time. According to this view, then, preference for the signaled condition is controlled not by the shock signals—nor information or preparation with regard to shock onset—but by the safety signal (that is, by the discriminated shock-free periods). This prediction, illustrated in Figure 6.15, is consistent with all of Badia's work, with the related studies of observing with positive reinforcement, and with research on Pavlovian fear conditioning (Rescorla, 1968; Weisman and Litner, 1971).

In order to test the safety analysis further, Badia et al. (1976) assessed whether preference for a signaled shock condition over an unsignaled one

	Stimulus state	Aversiveness	Duration
I	Uncorrelated condition	Moderately high	Always during uncorrelated condition
II	Shock signals (5-sec preshock tone plus 0.5-sec tone plus shock)	Maximal	5.5 sec in every 120 sec (on the average) during correlated condition
III	Correlated stimulus (in absence of shock signal)	Relatively neutral or "safe"	114.5 sec out of every 120 sec (on the average) during correlated condition

Figure 6.15
By switching from the uncorrelated condition (Stimulus state I) to the correlated condition, the subject is moving to a condition that is more aversive less than 5 percent of the time (Stimulus state II), but safe most of the time (Stimulus state III). Thus only when shocks in the signaled period are made much more frequent, intense, or long than in the unsignaled period do subjects choose to remain in the unsignaled condition. The values shown here are for a typical experiment from Badia's laboratory, in which shocks in both conditions are equivalent (same rate, duration, and intensity) and in which both the shock and safety signals are totally dependable.

is controlled by the signals predicting shock (the tones preceding shocks by 5 sec) or by the stimulus correlated with the absence of shock (the correlated stimulus, a light). If preparation for shock is responsible for the preference for signaled shock, then these signals should be critical, not the predictors of safety; if the preference is controlled by the production of stimuli correlated with discriminated shock-free periods, of course, the correlated stimulus should be critical.

In their first experiment, Badia et al. (1976) preceded all shocks in the signaled condition by the signals but varied the probability of a signal being followed by shock over a range of 0.02 to 1.0. Hence the signal was a necessary but not sufficient precursor of shock. The rats in the Badia et al. study chose the signaled condition when the signal was completely dependable (all signals followed by shock) and when the signal was extremely undependable (few signals followed by shock). Thus preference for the signaled condition occurred despite extreme variations in the dependability of a stimulus signaling shocks. This result suggests that preparation is not an important factor in choosing the signaled condition.

In their second experiment, Badia et al. (1976) followed all signals with shock. Now, however, some shocks occurred without a prior signal. These shocks occurred therefore in the presence of the correlated stimulus. Thus, in this experiment, the dependability of the correlated stimulus as a safety signal was varied. The results show that this variable is important: as dependability decreased, so did preference for the signaled condition. Taken together, these results show that the dependability of the safety signal is far more important than the dependability of the shock signal and together support the safety analysis. Finally, these results provide still more evidence against preparation and information theories.

Thus all of the work on observing points to the same conclusion: Only the more positively valued of two stimuli should maintain observing, since the less positive stimulus is correlated with an increase, not a reduction, in time to positive reinforcement (or a reduction, not an increase, in time to an aversive event). Less positive stimuli punish, rather than maintain, observing. More generally, such stimuli are not conditioned reinforcers. Conditioned reinforcers are those stimuli correlated with a reduction in time to reinforcement (or an increase in time to an aversive event). In other words, a stimulus correlated with a reduction in time to reinforcement (or with an increase in time to an aversive event) should maintain responding that produces it. Such a stimulus should also be chosen over one correlated with a smaller reduction in time to reinforcement in a preference test. Direct evidence for this latter prediction was not presented in this chapter. As we shall see, however, this prediction is supported by research on choice, which we encounter in the following chapter.

7   Choice Behavior

We are continually engaging in choice. The fact that you are reading these words results from a lifetime of choices made by you (and for you). At this moment you have dozens of response alternatives (some of which might become increasingly probable if this example were extended). Given the ubiquity and importance of choice, one might suppose that quite a bit is known about it. Indeed, not only has choice been widely studied but several rather powerful quantitative models have been developed to account for choice behavior in a variety of settings. One of these formulations, that of R. J. Herrnstein (1970, 1974), will be discussed in some detail later in the chapter. First we will review briefly some of the techniques for studying choice and discuss the use of choice procedures in measuring the behavioral effects of independent variables such as magnitude and delay of reward.

We should be clear at the outset that "choice" need not imply "free will" or "free choice." The term "choice" does acknowledge that there are many possible response alternatives at any given time. Which response actually occurs depends on the operation of important—and sometimes subtle—contextual factors, which are the subject of this chapter. All responses may be thought of as "choices" since there are always alternatives available. What distinguishes choice research from other research on animal behavior is that the experimenter makes two or more measurable alternatives explicitly available to the subject.

METHODS FOR STUDYING CHOICE

The subject in a choice experiment has two (or more) responses available simultaneously. These may be pressing one of two levers, buttons, pedals, or keys, entering one of two arms of a T-maze, or standing on one side or another of a chamber. Obviously, the number of potential responses is almost unlimited. For purposes of precise analysis, experimental paradigms are designed to limit the number of available response alternatives. The responses just listed have been used most frequently in recent studies of choice. The response selected by the experimenter varies with the organism being studied, the empirical question being investigated (and how it has been studied before), and the equipment available to the experimenter. Thus pigeons are seldom studied in mazes, but often peck concurrently available keys; rats are seldom required to press keys, but instead depress levers or run in T-mazes. (Some of the basic apparatus used in the study of learning and motivation were shown in Figure 4.2.) In most experiments the response alternatives have been comparable—for example, two levers or two keys—so that differences in the distribution of responses can be assumed to be due to factors other than characteristics of the two responses. Even with apparently identical responses, however, it is advisable to adjust the response devices so that they require the same minimum effort. As we have seen in our discussion of autoshaping (Chapter 4), the particular response selected may have a profound influence on the behavior being studied (a point that will be illustrated in the discussion of species-specific defense reactions in Chapter 9). Fortunately, in the study of choice with equivalent responses, the proportion of choices for one or two alternatives (as opposed to the absolute rate of responding), is unlikely to be seriously affected by the response selected.[1]

In some experiments choice is studied with a *discrete-trials procedure,* in which trials are separated (made discrete) by somehow eliminating the opportunity for the subject to respond between trials. In a T-maze, for example, the subject is removed from the goal box at the end of one trial and placed at the start of the T-maze when the next trial begins (an example of a T-maze experiment will be discussed shortly). In a Skinner box,

---

[1]The proportion of choices for one of two or more alternatives is the number of choices for that alternative divided by the total number of choices measured and is sometimes called the relative rate of responding. The absolute rate of responding, however, simply refers to the number of choices for one alternative divided by the total time available for responding. Thus if there are three response alternatives (A, B, and C) and the subject chooses A 30 times, B 15 times and C 5 times during a 10-minute session, its choice proportion (or relative rate of responding) for A is $30/(30 + 15 + 5) = 0.60$, while its absolute rate of responding for A is 30 responses/10 minutes = 3 responses/minute. Note that session time is not needed to calculate choice proportions, while choices of B and C are not needed to calculate the absolute rate of responding for A.

the lights may be dimmed and the response keys made ineffective. Some levers are retractable and can be withdrawn between trials. In *free-operant choice procedures* (also called "continuous choice procedures") the response alternatives are freely available continuously, and the subject may respond at its own rate. In these procedures, concurrent schedules of reinforcement are typically used, providing the subject with alternative regimes of reinforcement.

In addition to the number of responses made by the subject to each alternative, the amount of time spent responding on each alternative is often of interest, especially in free-operant choice experiments. Time spent in an activity is a bit more difficult to measure, however, than number of responses. One way is to have a cumulative timer operate from the time a response is made to one alternative until a response is made to the second alternative. A second timer cumulates time on the second alternative in the same fashion. Thus one of the two timers is always in operation (except during reinforcement), and the proportion of total session time (minus reinforcement time) spent on each alternative is readily obtained by dividing the time spent on one by the sum of the times spent on both. One problem with this technique is that any time the subject might spend wandering around the chamber will be counted as time spent on the alternative last responded to. An equally arbitrary but an intuitively more precise measure is that developed by Findley (1958). In a Findley concurrent schedule a distinctive stimulus is correlated with the availability of each component schedule, but both are arranged on the *same* response device. By responding on a *second* response device, the subject can change the schedule. Thus, in Findley's original study, the pigeons' pecks at one key (the *instrumental key*) produced food according to the schedule of reinforcement in effect on that key, while pecks on the other key (the *changeover key*) changed the schedule in effect on the instrumental key. For measuring the accumulating time spent on each, therefore, the Findley concurrent schedule has this advantage: the timers are precisely correlated with how much time is spent in the presence of each stimulus. If the subject now spends time wandering about the apparatus, it probably makes some sense to associate that time with the schedule in effect.

A more tangible advantage of the Findley procedure is that it separates the changeover and instrumental responses. In a standard (non-Findley) concurrent procedure, changeover and instrumental responses are made to the same keys. With the Findley procedure, however, changeover responses are physically separate. The Findley procedure's use may be illustrated by describing Brownstein and Pliskoff's (1968) elegant design in a study of choice involving *no* measured instrumental response. They studied pigeons' choice for schedules varying with respect to the rate of response-independent food deliveries occurring while each schedule was in effect. Only one response key was present. Responses on this key were not instrumental in obtaining food but simply changed the schedule in effect (the general illumination in the chamber was also changed, and a different color was correlated with each of the two schedules compared). Brownstein and Pliskoff found that pigeons emitted changeover responses such that the schedule associated with the higher rate of food delivery remained in effect most of the time. Indeed, they found that the proportion of time spent in the presence of a stimulus equaled the proportion of food delivered during that stimulus. Therefore if one schedule were a variable-time (VT) 15-sec and the other a VT 30-sec, the pigeons would tend to spend twice as much time in the presence of the stimulus correlated with the VT 15-sec. We will return to this important relation later.

Thus far we have discussed choice procedures with response alternatives leading to reinforcement. In such procedures the independent variable is generally some difference in either the scheduling of the reinforcers or the nature of the reinforcers themselves. An example of the former case would be the Brownstein and Pliskoff study of choice for different rates of response-independent reinforcement. An example of the latter would be a comparison of different reinforcers such as food and mirror-image stimulation in the Siamese fighting fish (see Chapter 9, Figure 9.8). It is possible, of course, to present two different reinforcers directly to the subject for choice. While this is an acceptable and convenient choice procedure, it may be fraught with problems when the consummatory responses differ, as in the Siamese fighting fish example. Does one measure the number of aggressive displays (to the mirror image) versus the number of brine shrimp consumed? The time spent displaying versus eating? Or what? Another problem is that different reinforcers may cause satiation at different rates. Sexual gratification, for example, may be a powerful reinforcer, but for many subjects once is enough, at least for a few minutes or hours; not so with eating peanuts. Also, different reinforcing activities may take different amounts of time. Thus a movie may last two hours, while a sliver of cheesecake may be wolfed right down. Which is more reinforcing? The problem has been discussed by Fantino and Navarick (1974):

> Assume we are interested in evaluating a person's preference for hot-fudge sundaes, peanuts, and hot onion soup. One obvious way to proceed would be to give the person experience with each of the three foods, deprive him for some time, and then present all three in a simple choice test. Leaving aside the problem that amount of deprivation is likely to interact with the food chosen, this simple choice procedure is fine for providing a crude measure of choice. For a more continuous, quantitative measure of choice, however, we need to know how much more reinforcing the chosen food is than the others. The answer we obtain will depend, of course, upon our method. An obvious measure, rate of eating, is fraught with problems. Hot onion soup, for example, may be the preferred food, but the person may eat it

more slowly than the others. Similarly, the amount of time spent engaged in eating the food may also be misleading: peanuts may be munched into the night, whereas the person is likely to satiate quickly on hot-fudge sundaes. One way around this problem is to study the rate of responding the person emits in order to obtain access to each of the three foods. This kind of simple concurrent schedule, in which relative response rates are used as a measure of choice, has become the standard operant choice procedure over the past fifteen years [Fantino and Navarick, 1974, p. 149].

In summary, it is often desirable to separate the choice response from the consummatory response. In this way the effects on our choice measure of differences in the nature of consummatory responses are minimized, and choice will more likely reflect the reinforcing potency of the consummatory responses.

CHOICE AS A TECHNIQUE

In addition to being intrinsically interesting, choice may serve as an effective, sensitive technique for studying the behavioral effects of numerous independent variables. Consider the effect of *amount of reinforcement* upon rate of responding. Assume we're trying to ascertain how much more a person will accomplish if paid $6 per hour rather than $3 per hour, or assess differing response rates in a pigeon whose pecks are reinforced by either 6 or 3 seconds of grain presentations every 2 minutes. Early studies looked at the effects of reinforcement amount (and reinforcement rate) on responding with nonchoice procedures in which rate of responding was determined first with one amount (or rate). Responding stabilized under these conditions, and then the effects of a different amount (or rate) were assessed. In most investigations, amount and rate of reinforcement were seen to exert only a small effect on rate of responding—that is, an effect that was statistically significant but behaviorally unimpressive.

Herrnstein (1961), studying rate of reinforcement, and Catania (1963a), studying amount, showed that much more pronounced effects of these variables could be demonstrated in a choice procedure. Each of their studies employed concurrent variable-interval (VI) schedules of reinforcement, and each VI schedule was associated with a different response key. In Herrnstein's study of reinforcement rate, the VI's on the two keys differed, while reinforcement duration was constant (each food presentation lasted 4 seconds). Reinforcement rate was therefore the variable of interest. In different conditions, different pairs of VI's were compared (for example, VI 1.8-min and VI 9-min; VI 4.5-min and VI 2.25-min) permitting Herrnstein to plot choice, the relative rate of responding on each key, against reinforcement rate for several different rates. In Catania's study of reinforcer duration, the VI's were identical (each was VI 2-min), but the reinforcer durations, and therefore the amount, produced by responding on the two VI's could differ (for example, 6 seconds versus 3 seconds).

In each study relative rates of responding on each key tended to match the relative rates (or durations) of reinforcement associated with that key. Catania's (1963a) results are shown in Figure 7.1, which plots rate of responding (in responses per minute) against duration of reinforcement (in seconds). The data from the choice procedure are shown with circles. Note that for all three pigeons the rates of responding in the choice procedure increase as food duration increases. For two of these pigeons (a and b) the circles fall along the diagonal describing a slope of 1.0. This means that increasing food duration by a certain amount increases responding by the same amount (at least over the range of durations studied). Thus as duration is doubled from 3 seconds to 6 seconds, response rates also double. The data are plotted in terms of absolute rates and durations so as to facilitate comparison with data from the nonchoice procedure. It is more conventional to plot choice data in terms of relative rates of responding (number of responses on one key divided by the sum of the rates of responding—called a "choice proportion") against relative duration of reinforcement (duration of reinforcement on one key divided by the sum of the durations of reinforcement). Had the data for Pigeons a and b been plotted in this way, they too would have fallen along the

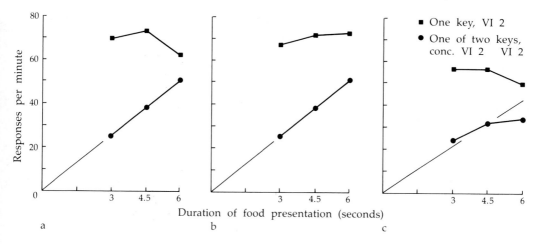

Figure 7.1
The rate of responding, for three pigeons (a, b, and c), maintained by three reinforcement durations. The squares show responding on a single key; the circles show responding on one of two keys. [After A. C. Catania, Concurrent performances: A baseline for the study of reinforcement magnitude. *Journal of the Experimental Analysis of Behavior, 6,* 299–300. Copyright © 1963 by the Society for the Experimental Analysis of Behavior, Inc. Redrawn by permission.]

diagonal, signifying that choice proportions tend to equal ("match") relative duration of reinforcement. We will see an example of matching (to relative rates of reinforcement) graphically in Figure 7.3. The squares in Figure 7.1 show Catania's results using a nonchoice procedure to study the relation between rate of responding (responses per minute) and reinforcer duration with the *same* pigeons as subjects. Results of the one-key procedure replicated those of prior studies: only a small effect of reinforcer duration on rate of responding emerged, far less pronounced than that seen with the two-key procedure. The important implication of this difference is that choice proportions are more sensitive to manipulations of the independent variable (in this case, reinforcer duration) than are response rates from nonchoice procedures.

In general, then, responding on concurrent schedules will be more affected by differences between the two schedules than responding on the same two schedules presented successively. Thus a subject confronted with a concurrent FR 10 FR 50 will respond exclusively to the stimulus correlated with the FR 10. When the same stimuli are arranged in a multiple FR 10 FR 50, however, responding will be maintained by both. Similarly, an avid sports fan may consistently choose to watch hockey rather than basketball when they are concurrently available on his TV set, but may watch basketball at almost the same high rate if it's the only sport available.

CHOICE AND REINFORCER MAGNITUDE

The results presented in Figure 7.1 show that choice proportions tend to match relative duration of reinforcement. While other studies using the same general procedure have shown that the data points tend to fall on a line whose slope is less than that of the diagonal (see Fantino, Squires, Delbrück, and Peterson, 1972; Schneider, 1973), as they do for one of the three pigeons described in Figure 7.1, this matching relation is a convenient approximation for our purposes. It should be stressed that matching of choice to relative reinforcer duration is dependent on the behavioral context in which choice takes place. Approximations to such matching can only be expected when choice is made on concurrent variable-interval schedules. If, instead, the two schedules leading to reinforcement were equal fixed-ratio or variable-ratio schedules, for example, matching to scheduled reinforcer duration clearly would not occur. Unlike interval schedules, in which schedule requirements may be satisfied by the passage of time, ratio schedules require cumulated responses. On ratio schedules, therefore, the subject would always respond on the schedule leading to the greater reinforcer duration. In that event "matching" to reinforcer duration would occur only in the sense that the subject would come to obtain all its reinforcement from the alternative with the greater duration (thus the choice proportion and the *obtained* relative reinforcer duration would both equal 1.0).

Although the actual experiment has not been done with ratio schedules, we can confidently predict exclusive choice for the greater reinforcer duration on the basis of (1) the exclusive responding for the shorter of two concurrent-ratio schedules, differing in terms of rate rather than duration of reinforcement, found by Herrnstein and Loveland (1975), (2) studies of reinforcer magnitude in the T-maze, and (3) the different characteristics of ratio and interval schedules. In the T-maze, for example, Logan (1965) and others have studied the effects of different reinforcer amounts in the two goal boxes of the maze. Logan studied hungry rats in a large number of conditions involving different delays and amounts of reinforcement. When the rat entered a goal box a timer began operating. If the timer was set at 5 seconds (5-second delay), at the end of 5 seconds a particular number of food pellets dropped into a food cup. For example, in one condition, rats obtained one pellet delayed one second in one goal box and three pellets delayed 5 seconds in the other goal box. Despite the greater delay, the rats came to choose the goal box providing three pellets on 100 percent of their choices. Only with sufficiently long delays (20 seconds or more) did rats come to choose reliably the goal box providing the single pellet. Logan's results show that both variables—delay and amount of reinforcement—have a profound effect on the rat's choice behavior in a T-maze. For our present purpose it is sufficient to note that rats will exclusively choose the larger reinforcer amount in a T-maze, given comparable delays of reinforcement.

The different characteristics of ratio and interval schedules are also important in explaining why we would expect exclusive responding for the shorter of two concurrent-ratio schedules but not for the shorter of two concurrent-interval schedules. Since it is important for the student to understand these two types of schedules, we will consider them here in some detail.

Concurrent-Interval and Concurrent-Ratio Schedules

With concurrent-interval schedules, the organism receives a higher rate of reinforcement for responding on both schedules. This is not so with concurrent-ratio schedules. On interval schedules, reinforcements become available with the passage of time. The equipment typically used to arrange, or "program," VI schedules is a VI timer, which consists of a tape with holes spaced irregularly on it. The tape is driven by a motor and moves at a constant speed until a hole is reached. At this point the motor is turned off and the tape stops moving. Reinforcement is now "available," and the next response on the key associated with this VI timer produces reinforcement. After reinforcement the motor is again activated and the tape moves again (until the next hole is reached). The spacing of the holes determines the intervals comprising the VI schedule (since the tape moves at a constant speed, a fixed distance on the tape corresponds to a fixed amount of time). If the holes are regularly spaced, the schedule is an FI (although FI's may also be programmed readily in other ways). Separate timers are typically associated with each of two or more concurrent-interval schedules. The tapes on these timers move with the passage of time. When reinforcement becomes available on one schedule (a hole in the appropriate tape is reached), the tape associated with that schedule stops moving but the other tape continues to move. Thus the subject responding on concurrent-interval schedules may make most of its responses on the schedule providing the higher rate of reinforcement but may receive additional reinforcements, which have become available with the passage of time, by occasionally responding on the schedule providing the lower rate of reinforcement.

With concurrent-ratio schedules, on the other hand, the two schedules do *not* advance simultaneously, since ratio requirements are met, not by the passage of time, but by the cumulative responses of the subject.[2] The equipment typically used to arrange VR schedules is a "VR programmer," which also contains a tape with irregularly spaced holes. Unlike the VI tape, however, the VR tape is driven by the subject's responses—each response advances the tape one unit. The spacing of the holes determines the ratios comprising the VR schedule (a fixed distance on the tape corresponds to a fixed number of responses). If the holes are regularly spaced, the schedule is an FR.

Consider a human subject responding on concurrent VI 1-min VI 1-min schedules with a $1 payoff on the left and a 25¢ payoff on the right. If the subject responds occasionally on both schedules, an average payoff of $1.25 per minute will be received. If the subject responded exclusively on the schedule providing dollar reinforcers, however, an average of only $1 per minute would be obtained. With concurrent VR 100 schedules, how- ever, the subject will receive $1 per 100 responses (on the average) by responding exclusively on the schedule providing dollars, but only $1.25 per 200 responses (or $0.625 per 100 responses) by responding on both.

Returning to the problem of choice and reinforcer magnitude, it is im- portant to stress that the question "How much more reinforcing is rein- forcer X (for example, 6 seconds food duration or $1) than reinforcer Y (for example, 1.5 seconds food duration or 25¢)?" has no simple invariant answer. Depending on how the question is approached experimentally, the answer may range anywhere from "not much," in the case of the one-schedule procedure, through "almost four times as much," in the concurrent VI case (approximating matching), to "indefinitely more," in the concurrent-ratio case (exclusive preference for the larger reinforcer).

---

[2]This assumes that both responses may not be effective on a strictly simultaneous basis (for example, by pressing one button with one finger and the second with another). This assumption is always met on conventional concurrent schedules.

CHOICE AND RATE OF REINFORCEMENT

We have already noted that relative response rates on concurrent variable-interval schedules tend to match relative rates of reinforcement. One of many findings supporting this generalization is shown in the graph in Figure 7.2, from Herrnstein's (1961) experiment. But how do response rates vary on each of the two VI schedules as the values of the VI's are changed? First, consider the following case: A concurrent VI 2-min VI 2-min (A) is changed to concurrent VI 2-min VI 3-min (B) and then to concurrent VI 2-min EXT (C). As we go from (A) to (C), rate of responding decreases on the second schedule. Obviously, the relative rate of responding on the first schedule (the VI 2-min) increases. Does the absolute rate of responding increase on this schedule as well? Yes. This increase is reminiscent of behavioral contrast in multiple schedules (Chapter 5).

Now we are prepared to entertain a more interesting question: Is the increase in responding on the unchanged VI 2-min schedule due primarily to the decrease in rate of *reinforcement* on the other key or to the attendant decrease in rate of *responding* on the other key (leaving the organism with more time to devote to the VI 2-min), or both? Catania (1963b) did an ingenious experiment to assess the separate contributions of each of these factors—that is, decreased responding and reinforcement—to the rate increase on the unchanged schedule. Catania devised a method for changing reinforcement rate and response rate independently. In this way, the extent to which changes in each of these rates affected rate of responding in the unchanged component could be assessed directly. This separation of effects was accomplished by signaling all reinforcements on one schedule as soon as the VI for that schedule arranged a reinforcement opportunity. Overall response rates on this "signaled VI schedule" were

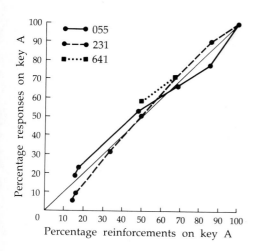

Figure 7.2
Relative frequency of responding to key A as a function of relative frequency of reinforcement on key A, for three pigeons. [After R. J. Herrnstein, Relative and absolute strength of response as a function of frequency of reinforcement. *Journal of the Experimental Analysis of Behavior, 4,* 267–272. Copyright © 1961 by the Society for the Experimental Analysis of Behavior, Inc. Redrawn by permission.]

close to zero or similar to those occurring during extinction. Yet the over-all rate of reinforcement for responding on this key was similar to that occurring on a normal (unsignaled) VI of the same value. If rate of re-sponding on the unchanged schedule were controlled, in part, by rate of reinforcement on the second (signaled) schedule, then response rate should increase when that second schedule was changed from either a normal or signaled VI to extinction but need not increase when the nor-mal VI was changed to a signaled VI. If rate of responding on the un-changed schedule were controlled, in part, by the time spent responding on the second schedule, however, then the rate on the unchanged schedule should increase when the normal VI was changed to either the signaled VI or extinction.

Catania found that rate of responding on one schedule was indepen-dent of rate of responding on the other VI schedule (within limits) but was very much dependent upon the rate of reinforcement on the other schedule. This led Catania to title his paper "Concurrent Performances: Reinforcement Interaction and Response Independence," a concise sum-mary of the results. *Reinforcement interaction* in concurrent schedules has subsequently been found by other investigators (see Guilkey, Shull, and Brownstein, 1975; Rachlin and Baum, 1972). *Response-independence*, how-ever, has proven to have less generality. For example, whereas Rachlin and Baum's results were consistent with Catania's, others suggest that response-independence occurs only under some conditions (see Catania, 1972; Guilkey et al., 1975; Pliskoff and Green, 1972). In other words, when rate of reinforcement is decreased on one of two concurrent schedules, rate of responding will reliably increase on the other schedule. While in some cases all of the increase may be attributed to reinforcement interaction, in others the increase depends as well on the greater amount of time allocated to the unchanged schedule. Indeed, Guilkey et al. (1975) raised an interesting possibility that may well account for response-independence when it does occur. In order to understand their account, however, we must first introduce a procedural feature that has been used in most of the experiments on concurrent schedules we have discussed thus far. Up to now, we have omitted it for the sake of clarity. This fea-ture, the *changeover delay* (COD), has interesting effects in its own right, both in reducing superstitious responding and in producing the matching function between rates of responding and reinforcement.

SUPERSTITION AND THE CHANGEOVER DELAY (COD)

Choices are often spatially separated (for instance, reading this book, going for a drive in the country, or even to the kitchen for a snack). Hence it normally takes some time to move from one alternative to another. In the operant chamber, however, spatial and temporal separations are typically minimal. The COD stipulates a minimal time interval between responding on one key and reinforcement on the other.[3] Without the COD, reinforcement may strengthen not only the response actually producing the reinforcer but also immediately preceding responses on the key associated with the other schedule as well as the act of "changing over" from responding on one schedule to the other. This may sound subtle, but it is intuitively plausible and empirically demonstrable. Let us examine the intuitive and empirical cases.

You may be aware there is something to the notion that watched pots seldom boil (at least, when they are supposed to). The reason the old saw seems true—at least among pot-watchers—is simple. Assume the liquid is going to take 2 minutes to boil, no matter how often it is watched (actually, if the watched pot is a covered one, it may take *longer* to boil the more doggedly the watcher uncovers it, but we will ignore this variable). Assume also that the pot-boiler is engaged in the concurrent activity of watching TV in the den next to the kitchen. The changeover response is walking from the den to the kitchen and vice versa. If on one occasion the person remains in the kitchen and peeks at the pot every 10 seconds or so, he will wind up having a dozen or so looks, only one of which is reinforced by boiling. If on another occasion the same individual spends the interval engrossed in an old Humphrey Bogart movie, he will find the liquid boiling on his first inspection. Although this instance of watching is reinforced, so is the prior nonwatching. Moreover, the longer the period of nonwatching, the higher the probability that looking will be reinforced. Each of these points has implications for responding on concurrent schedules that have been verified in a number of studies.

Catania and Cutts (1963) studied a concurrent VI 30-sec EXT schedule for one experimental session using Harvard college students as subjects. One button was correlated with extinction (the "extinction button"), the other with a VI 30-sec schedule of reinforcement (the "VI button"). Subjects were not told the schedule of reinforcement, but they were told to make one response each time a "pacing" light came on, which was 100 times per minute. For some subjects there was a 4.5-sec COD; for others there was no COD at first, but the COD was increased throughout the session from zero up to 15 seconds. Still other subjects never received a COD. Most of the subjects (there were 52 in all) responded on both buttons, at least at first. Only a few eventually stopped responding on the extinction button; most of these were subjects for whom the COD was increased throughout the session. No subject correctly verbalized the procedure in effect. Some, however, had elaborate hypotheses ("supersti-

---

[3] Actually, there are different ways of arranging changeover contingencies. For simplicity, we discuss only one.

tions") about the reinforcement schedule. One subject asked to be excused midway through the experiment because he had studied schedules of reinforcement in class and "knew" what the schedule was: "I press twice on the left button and once on the right." He was returned to the experiment.

One of the present authors (EF), then a beginning graduate student, had a more elaborate hypothesis. He "discovered" that 50 responses on one button (the extinction button, naturally) followed by 8 responses on the other produced reinforcement with a high probability. While this hypothesis was remarkably insensitive to the true role of the extinction button (that is, responses on the extinction button never produced reinforcement and sometimes delayed reinforcement for responding on the VI button), his behavior did show a curious, perhaps coincidental, sensitivity to the reinforcement contingency. It took 30 seconds to emit the 50 responses so that his length of stay on the extinction button equaled the mean of the VI schedule. The 8 responses on the VI button took 4.8 seconds or just the right number to satisfy the COD (and obtain reinforcement had it been arranged).

Catania and Cutts' results suggest that human subjects may require longer COD's than pigeons (which they also studied) to weaken control of changeover and prechangeover behavior by postchangeover reinforcement (for pigeons, a 1-sec COD may suffice). Others have suggested that rats may also require longer COD's than pigeons (see de Villiers, 1977). In any event, without a sufficiently long COD, reinforcement of one response will probably strengthen concurrent responses as well.

Given the role of the COD and the potentially confusing state of concurrent affairs in its absence, what role does it play in experiments relating relative rate of responding to relative rate (or amount) of reinforcement? If reinforcement strengthens concurrent responses when a COD is omitted, then responding on the schedule providing the lower rate of reinforcement may be unduly strengthened. In that event matching of responding to reinforcement might not be obtained; instead, subjects might be relatively more indifferent to the two schedules. Indeed, this is what occurs (Herrnstein, 1961).

When discussing pot-watching, we noted that the longer the duration of not watching, the higher the probability that a look at the pot would be reinforced. The same is true on concurrent VI schedules: the more time spent responding on VI A, the more probable reinforcement on VI B. Since COD's lower the rate of changeover, the probability of being reinforced after switching to a key is higher in concurrent VI's with COD's than without.Thus it may not be surprising that subjects respond at a particularly high rate (called a "COD burst") when changing over (Pliskoff, 1971; Silberberg and Fantino, 1970). The probability of reinforcement is highest immediately following completion of the short changeover period.

Now, if the COD is lengthened, so is the COD burst. Does matching (of response proportions to obtained reinforcement proportions) cease to occur when the COD is lengthened? If so, matching would be an uninteresting behavioral result, as it would occur only for a narrow range of COD values (since matching does not occur if the COD is absent or too short). Interestingly, matching obtains over a wide range of COD values (see Shull and Pliskoff, 1967, using rats; Silberberg and Fantino, 1970, with pigeons). In order to match with different COD lengths, the subject compensates for the longer COD burst on the nonpreferred key by changing over to it less often enough to preserve matching; that is, its overall rate of responding (or the overall time spent) on a schedule continues to match the relative rate of reinforcement on that schedule. The molecular dynamics whereby this is achieved are poorly understood. We can now return to Guilkey et al.'s (1975) account of why response-independence may occur on concurrent schedules. When the subject is responding on a concurrent VI VI (with a COD), it is emitting COD bursts that enhance overall response rates. When one schedule is changed to either a signaled VI or EXT, the subject allocates virtually all its time to the unchanged VI; overall response rates do not increase, however, since this responding does not include COD bursts. Guilkey et al. show that when manipulations that eliminate the COD burst in the concurrent VI VI case are used, response rates *do* increase on the unchanged VI when the other schedule is changed to a signaled VI.

Now that we have surveyed the basic principles of responding on concurrent schedules, we are ready to investigate an impressive but simple quantitative law that seeks to encompass these principles and account as well for *absolute* rates of responding on both single and concurrent schedules.

THE QUANTITATIVE LAW OF EFFECT

We have already seen that organisms tend to distribute their choice responses according to the relative rate at which these responses are reinforced (Herrnstein, 1961). In other words, the distribution of choices tends to match the distribution of reinforcements. In symbolic form:

$$\frac{R_1}{R_1 + R_2} = \frac{r_1}{r_1 + r_2} \tag{1}$$

where R denotes response rate, r denotes reinforcement rate, and the subscripts identify the two alternatives. A similar matching relation has been shown to hold for the amount of time a subject spends responding on one of two reinforced alternatives or engaged in one of two reinforced activities. The matching relation has provided an adequate approximation to choice in several different experiments with concurrent VI schedules: experiments with pigeons pecking keys (Catania, 1963b; Silberberg and Fantino, 1970), pressing treadles (McSweeney, 1975), or responding in a shuttle box choice procedure (Baum and Rachlin, 1969); with humans performing a vigilance task (Baum, 1975); with rats pressing levers (Graft, Lea, and Whitworth, 1977; Shull and Pliskoff, 1967); and several additional experiments.[4]

Equation (1), as written, is inapplicable to the absolute rate of responding for a single response. Obviously, a choice formulation that could also predict *absolute* response rate for each of two alternatives, and that could do so in the specific case of only one reinforced response (the typical single-response case) would be much more important than one restricted to the prediction of choice proportions (admittedly a substantial accomplishment in its own right). Equation (1) can be made applicable to absolute response rates. Let the constant k represent the maximum rate of responding characteristic of an individual subject in the given situation. The constant k is independent of the number of response alternatives available. Hence substituting in equation (1), $k = R_1 + R_2$ and

$$\frac{R_1}{k} = \frac{r_1}{r_1 + r_2}$$

Multiplying each side by k, we get:

$$R_1 = \frac{kr_1}{r_1 + r_2} \qquad (2a)$$

An analogous equation describes the rate of responding on the second of two alternatives:

$$R_2 = \frac{kr_2}{r_2 + r_1} \qquad (2b)$$

These equations have several interesting implications for behavior, some correct and others incorrect. In the first place, equation (2) implies that rate of responding should increase as the rate of reinforcement for that

---

[4] An excellent recent review is that of de Villiers (1977). It should be cautioned that, more often than not, equation (1) *overestimates* the actual choice proportions obtained. In other words, organisms tend to *undermatch* their choice proportions to the distribution of reinforcements. For a review and theoretical analysis see Myers and Myers (1977; also Myers, 1972). These systematic deviations from matching may be understood in the context of more general properties and do not necessarily impair the predictive utility of equation (1) (see Baum, 1974; de Villiers, 1977). For our purposes it is sufficient to assume that matching is a valid description of responding on concurrent variable-interval schedules. Henceforth, in this chapter, we do assume so.

response increases (R_1 increases as r_1 increases). Equation (2) also states that the absolute rate of responding decreases as reinforcement for an *alternative* response increases (R_1 decreases as r_2 increases). Each of these implications has been confirmed by the many studies we have reviewed earlier.

A third implication is empirically incorrect. When $r_2 = 0$, equation (2) requires that $R_1 = k$ (since $r_1/r_1 = 1$), regardless of the rate of reinforcement for R_1. Thus despite its ability to account for choice responding and despite its supportable implications about absolute response rates, equation (2) has limited generality; that is, it appears to hold only when both r_1 and r_2 are greater than zero. Can we do even better? Can equation (2) be modified so that it will continue to describe choice correctly and also account for behavior in the single-schedule case? Herrnstein (1970) came upon the solution while taking a break from work one day. He reasoned that there is, strictly speaking, no such thing as a single reinforcement schedule. Rather, there are almost inevitably other reinforced behaviors (as diverse as daydreaming, defecating, and other distractions) that may be emitted when the organism is responding on the only schedule provided by the experimenter. Other sources of reinforcement are likely to exist whether we are dealing with authors writing books, gourmets preparing food, chimps emitting language, or simply pigeons pecking keys. Thus even in the single-schedule case the organism has a choice between responding on that schedule or making an alternative response, unspecified by the experimenter. Responses on the specified schedule are reinforced on that schedule; the alternative responses are maintained by unspecified, and usually unmeasured, reinforcers. But if these "other" sources of reinforcement have the same effect on responding as do the explicitly programmed concurrent schedules, the former should also serve to lower response rates (recall that as r_2 increases, in equation (2a), R_1 decreases). What is missing from equation (2) is acknowledgement of these other sources of reinforcement. The term Herrnstein introduced for all sources of reinforcement other than those explicitly controlled by the experimenter was "r_0" (where "O" stands for "other"). Equation (2) now becomes:

$$R_1 = \frac{kr_1}{r_1 + r_2 + r_0} \tag{3}$$

where k now equals R_1 plus R_2 plus $\sum R_0$. Now, when $r_2 = 0$, $R_1 = kr_1/r_1 + r_0$, an increasing but negatively accelerated function that provides an admirable description of absolute response rate from a variety of single-schedule experimental procedures (see de Villiers, 1977; de Villiers and Herrnstein, 1976). Note that the closer r_0 is to zero, the more responding is controlled by r_1 and r_2: when r_0 equals zero, $R_1 + R_2$ sum to k, the maximum rate of responding for a given subject. The larger r_0 is, however, the less responding will be controlled by the explicit reinforcers, r_1 and r_2, and R_1 and R_2 will total less than k. In general, then, R_1 will be increased by increasing r_1 or by decreasing r_2 or r_0; R_1 is decreased by decreasing r_1 or by increasing r_2 or r_0.

Equation (3) also retains the positive qualities of equation (2); for example, it continues to require reinforcement interaction, and it continues to predict the matching relation for concurrent schedules (for if $R_1 = kr_1/r_1 + r_2 + r_0$ and $R_2 = kr_2/r_1 + r_2 + r_0$, then $R_1/R_1 + R_2 = r_1/r_1 + r_2$, since the denominators and k cancel out). Herrnstein (1970) has also applied a more general form of equation (3) to responding on multiple schedules. This extension requires the introduction of a final constant, m, which represents the degree of interaction between responding on one component and reinforcement in the other: when m = 1, interaction is maximal, as in a concurrent schedule; m = 0 denotes no interaction, as when there is great temporal separation between the two components. Herrnstein's equation becomes

$$R_1 = \frac{kr_1}{r_1 + mr_2 + r_0} \tag{4}$$

The equation accounts for contrast in multiple schedules: reductions in reinforcement frequency in the second component will result in a larger R_1 (providing m greater than zero). Note than in concurrent schedules, where m = 1, equation (4) reduces to equation (3).

Strengths and Limitations

We hope the reader is already impressed with the encouraging generality of equations (3) and (4). Their ability to make reasonably accurate quantitative predictions in a wide variety of experimental procedures makes the law of effect they express among the most significant developments in learning and motivation of the past two decades. Additional support for the law's generality will be provided briefly in this section. At the same time, some limitations of the law and some contradictory data will also be presented. One limitation we will note is the apparent inadequacy of equation (4) to describe data from multiple schedules. Hence, when not dealing with equation (4) directly, we shall restrict our attention to equation (3).

Although the law of effect, expressed by equation (3), is advantageously general, applying to both single and concurrent schedules and to both absolute and relative rates of responding, it achieves its generality at the expense of incorporating two parameters, k and r_0. The values of these parameters are not known prior to performing the experiment: they must be inferred from the data. In order for them to be convincing, therefore, it must be shown that they are intuitively plausible and, more importantly, that they behave in an orderly fashion. This means that k should be constant for an individual subject and response type across experiments; r_0 should vary as operations expected to vary it are performed. For example, deprivation should affect k and r_0 in different ways: k should remain constant (Herrnstein, 1974), while r_0 should decrease as deprivation (or drive) level is increased (Herrnstein, 1970). While many studies support the constancy of k, some do not (see McSweeney, 1975; also see de Villiers, 1977). Research on r_0 has yielded somewhat more clear-cut results.

The parameter r_0 may be varied, as suggested, by increasing deprivation for the explicit sources of reinforcement, say r_1 and r_2. In that event r_0 should decrease, since the relative value of r_1 and r_2 has increased (distractions should be minimized when deprivation is intense). This should be reflected in more responding ($R_1 + R_2$), and by a smaller value of r_0. Some support for this prediction with multiple schedules has been provided by Herrnstein and Loveland (1974). However, McSweeney (1975) failed to find an inverse relation between r_0 and deprivation in concurrent schedules. A more direct way to vary r_0 is to provide the organism with explicit free (noncontingent) reinforcers. Rachlin and Baum (1972) did so by giving pigeons, whose key-pecks were reinforced with food on a VI schedule, additional free food. As required by equation (3), the greater the rate of free food or the amount of free food per delivery, the more slowly the pigeons pecked.

It appears that r_0 is a crucial parameter for permitting the extension of Herrnstein's description of choice proportions (relative response rates) in concurrent schedules, represented by equation (1), to the more fundamental description of response strength represented by equation (3). The r_0 parameter also makes excellent intuitive sense. Most of the initial work suggests that r_0 behaves in an orderly and empirically predictable fashion when varied, but further study of this question is clearly needed.

The quantitative law of effect also has important limitations. Most of its empirical support has come from research on VI schedules, for which equations (1) to (4) were originally developed. It has had less success describing absolute response rates on FI schedules (see de Villiers, 1977) and relative response rates on most concurrent schedules *other* than concurrent VI VI (see Bacotti, 1977, for a review).[5] A second limitation involves the apparent inadequacy of equation (4), Herrnstein's extension to multi-

---

[5]On most concurrent schedules, other than VI VI, organisms respond much less often to the schedule providing the higher rate of reinforcement than required by equation (2). This undermatching tends to be more extreme than that found in concurrent VI VI schedules (see Footnote 4). As noted in the prior footnote, however, several instances of undermatching may be accommodated by Baum's (1974) generalization of the matching law. Moreover, if r_0 varies with different reinforcement schedules, other deviations from matching may also be understood (see de Villiers, 1977). At present, more research is needed to evaluate the possible relevance of equations (1) and (3) for concurrent schedules other than concurrent VI VI.

ple schedules. While this equation does an excellent job of describing the stable data from several experiments investigating behavioral contrast (see Lander and Irwin, 1968; Nevin, 1968; Reynolds, 1963), there are several demonstrations of behavioral contrast that equation (4) does not readily predict (see Premack, 1969; Terrace, 1972). More serious is the fact that some predictions derivable from equation (4) are not supported by the data. The conceptually simplest of these predictions is the implication that response rate on a multiple VI X VI X schedule will be less than that on a simple VI X. For if m > 0, reinforcements in one component should lower response rates in the other. The results of Spealman and Gollub (1974) are inconsistent with this implication: they found that pigeons did *not* respond at a higher rate when a VI 30-sec or VI 3-min schedule was presented in isolation than when it was part of a multiple schedule (multiple VI 30-sec VI 30-sec or multiple VI 3-min VI 3-min).

Alternative Formulations

Herrnstein's quantitative law of effect and more general versions of it (for example, Baum, 1974; Killeen, 1972; Staddon, 1972) are not the only formulations that can account for choice. We have emphasized Herrnstein's law here in part because we believe it is the most complete formulation, incorporating absolute rates of responding as well as relative rates, and because it has generated far and away the most research. Two other ambitious competing formulations are mentioned briefly (the interested reader should consult the references for details).

One is that of Shimp (1974), who agrees that organisms distribute their time on two or more alternatives according to their relative frequency of reinforcement. For Shimp, however, the basic unit is the length of the pause between responses, the *interresponse time* (IRT). Moreover, Shimp maintains that matching on concurrent schedules is a by-product of the organism's tendency to *maximize* reinforcement—that is, to select the alternative with the highest momentary probability of reinforcement at the time.[6] Thus, while, for Herrnstein, it suffices to say that organisms match relative response rates to relative reinforcement rates, for Shimp (1969,

---

[6]Consider a simplified example of what we mean by momentary reinforcement probabilities. If a subject is responding on a concurrent VR 50 FI 1-min schedule, the probability of reinforcement for a single response on the VR 50 remains fairly constant at one per 50 responses (or .02) throughout the session. The probability of a single response being reinforced on the FI 1-min, however, is zero for responses emitted within one minute following reinforcement on FI 1-min and abruptly rises to 1.0 at one minute. Thus, after reinforcement on the FI, subjects should respond exclusively on the VR schedule until something approaching one minute elapses, (just how long depends upon the subject's temporal discrimination), whereupon the probability of a reinforced response on the FI schedule exceeds that for responding on the VR (.02). At this point, the subject should change over to the FI. A similar, but more complex (mathematically), analysis applies to the more typically studied case of concurrent VI schedules.

1974) such matching is in turn a result of emitting IRT's that maximize momentary reinforcement probabilities. While it is not yet possible to settle this question definitively, the following conclusions appear warranted: (1) Organisms are indeed sensitive to momentary reinforcement probabilities (see Fantino and Duncan, 1972; Shimp, 1966; Williams, 1972); and (2) matching may nonetheless occur in the absence of measurable momentary maximizing (Herrnstein, reported in de Villiers, 1977; Heyman, 1979; Nevin, 1969).

A second alternative formulation, that of Catania (1973), makes empirical predictions so similar to those of equation (3) that it will be even more difficult to decide between them. We simply note that Catania avoids both the reliance on unspecified sources of reinforcement (r_0) and the assumption that there is a maximum rate of responding characteristic of a given subject for a given response form (k in equation 3). He achieves the same result by postulating *inhibitory* effects of reinforcers. Just as r_0 has intuitive appeal and empirical support, so does the notion that reinforcement has inhibitory as well as excitatory properties (see Catania, 1973; Williams, 1976). Williams, for example, has shown that the strengthening effect of a reinforcer is reduced when other reinforcers follow it closely in time.

CHOICE FOR SCHEDULES OF REINFORCEMENT

Up to now we have been discussing choice for concurrent schedules differing in rate or amount of reinforcement. While simple concurrent schedules appear to provide reasonable measures of choice for some pairs of schedules, the method is always flawed by a confounding feature. When two very discrepant schedules or two different reinforcers are utilized, *the measure of choice is confounded with the rate of responding produced by the schedules themselves.* Suppose we encounter a young man who goes hiking once every weekend and who also spends his lunch hour jogging as part of a weight-regulation program. We could not infer that he prefers jogging to hiking simply because the response is made more frequently (five times a week rather than one) and more vigorously. Rather, the demand characteristics and intrinsic nature of the activities require that jogging be more frequent and vigorous. Taking a different example, a young married couple will probably spend more time eating than making love (frequency of eating in meals per week greater than making love in intercourses per week) but may actually enjoy making love more (especially if the couple is inept in the kitchen).

In a similar way, schedules of reinforcement tend to control distinct rates and patterns of responding, as we saw in Chapter 4. Thus when FI and VR schedules are compared for choice in a simple concurrent design, it cannot be determined to what extent responding represents choice for one schedule over another and to what extent behavior is controlled by the nature of FI and VR schedules. For example, response rates on VR schedules tend to be much higher than those maintained by typical FI schedules. If we were to take the relative rates of responding on simple concurrent schedules as our measure of choice, we would be stacking the deck in favor of the VR schedule. Such a choice measure would be even more obviously inappropriate if we were comparing choice between a ratio schedule and a schedule that *required* low rates of responding (such as a DRL). Perhaps to avoid such confounding of choice with the response rates generated by the schedules being chosen, Autor (1960, 1969) developed the concurrent-chains procedure diagramed in Figure 7.3. Scores of studies have used the concurrent-chains procedure to assess choice in recent years (see Fantino, 1977, for a review). Our present concern is twofold. In the first place, does matching, which occurs in simple concurrent VI VI schedules, also occur in the concurrent-chains procedure? In addition to helping us further assess choice for concurrent VI VI schedules, research with concurrent chains can assess choice for a number of conditions that could not be studied meaningfully with simple concurrent schedules. We will deal with these two concerns in turn.

The concurrent-chains procedure measures choice by the rate of responding emitted during the choice phase, consisting of two equal, concurrently available, VI schedules, each leading to a different schedule outcome (the "outcome phase"). Since the concurrent VI schedules are

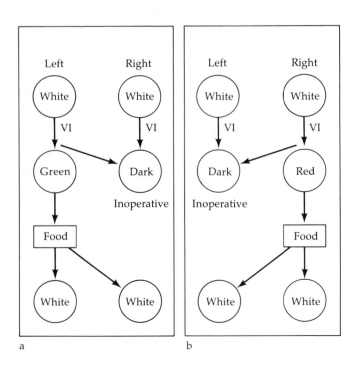

a   b

Figure 7.3
The concurrent-chains procedure. (a) The sequence of events when responses on the left key are reinforced. (b) The analogous sequence on the right key. Responses in the presence of the colored lights (the stimuli of the terminal links) are reinforced with food according to some schedule of reinforcement (generally, the independent variable). The measure of choice is the relative rate of responding in the presence of the concurrently available white lights. Typically, equal VI schedules arrange access to the terminal links. [After E. Fantino, Choice and rate of reinforcement. *Journal of the Experimental Analysis of Behavior, 12,* 723–730. Copyright © 1969 by the Society for the Experimental Analysis of Behavior, Inc. Redrawn by permission.]

equal, differences in response rates may reasonably be assumed to reflect differences in the reinforcing effectiveness of the outcomes being chosen—that is, the schedules of reinforcement associated with the terminal links of the chain (Figure 7.3). The independent variable is the difference between the schedules of reinforcement in the terminal links (that is, the difference in the two outcomes). The dependent variable is the measure of choice: the number of responses made on the VI leading to one outcome divided by the total number of responses made on both VI's. Since choice is arranged on concurrent VI schedules, entry into the two terminal links generally occurs at the same rate, even if one is clearly preferred. This ensures that the two outcomes will be encountered about equally often. Thus the effects of number of reinforcements are not confounded with those of the intended independent variable. As Figure 7.3 shows, once the subject enters the terminal link on one schedule, the other schedule becomes inoperative. Responses during the terminal links are reinforced with food according to the schedules of reinforcement in effect there. The choice stage is typically reinstated after the subject obtains a single reinforcement in the outcome phase.

Now that we have introduced the procedure, we are ready to assess whether matching obtains between the relative rates of responding in the choice phase and the relative rates of reinforcement in the outcome phase. Early work with the concurrent-chains procedure suggested that matching does occur, at least with VI and VR schedules in the terminal links. Specifically, both Autor (1960) and Herrnstein (1964a) found matching with pigeons pecking at keys. Herrnstein's results for each of four pigeons are shown in Figure 7.4.

If we let t_{2L} and t_{2R} represent the average durations of the left and right outcome phases, respectively (the "2" refers to the second or terminal link), the matching relation may be written:

$$\frac{R_L}{R_L + R_R} = \frac{1/t_{2L}}{1/t_{2L} + 1/t_{2R}} \tag{5}$$

This is analogous to equation (1) for matching with simple concurrent schedules.[7] R_L and R_R represent the number of responses during the choice phase on the left and right key, respectively.

If equation (5) were valid, at least for VI schedules in the terminal links, our story would be gratifyingly simple: the same matching relation would describe choice measured either in the presence of two different

---

[7]Whereas r_1 and r_2 represent rate of reinforcement in equation (1), their use in equation (5) would be ambiguous since they might refer to the rate of entering the terminal links, the rate of reinforcement during the outcome phase, or the rate of reinforcement during the entire chain. The reciprocals of t_{2L} and t_{2R} specify the rate of reinforcement during the outcome phase.

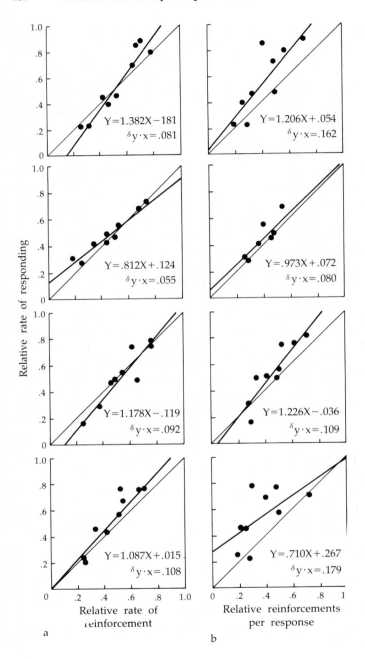

Figure 7.4
Relative rate of responding as a function of (a) relative rate of primary reinforcement and (b) relative probability of primary reinforcement. The diagonal line from the origin to (1.0, 1.0) represents the locus of perfect matching between relative response rates and relative reinforcements. The other line represents the linear regression line through the data points. Each graph shows the calculated linear equation and the standard deviation around the regression line. [After R. J. Herrnstein, Secondary reinforcement and rate of primary reinforcement. *Journal of the Experimental Analysis of Behavior, 7*, 27–36. Copyright © 1964 by the Society for the Experimental Analysis of Behavior, Inc. Redrawn by permission.]

schedules (concurrent choice), or in the presence of two equal schedules, each leading to one of two different alternatives (concurrent-chains choice). Upon reflection, however, we see that equation (5) cannot be generally valid, even when restricted to VI schedules. Consider a person choosing between two favorite reinforcers—for example, a plain yogurt or a honey yogurt (the reader may substitute his or her own imaginary reinforcers, providing they are both favorites but one is slightly preferred to the other. Indulge yourself; the imaginary reinforcers need not be foods, and the example is clearer the more reinforcing the alternatives). The two reinforcers are behind latched doors, each of which opens on VI schedules. The response is turning the doorknob. Suppose the equal VI schedules were short, say 10 seconds (on the average, after responding on one of these doorknobs for 10 seconds, the door unlatches). We maintain you will respond for 10 seconds exclusively on the knob leading to the preferred reinforcer (even though by responding on both you would open one door—you don't know which one—on the average after just 5 seconds); for you would probably be willing to spend a few extra seconds responding in order to ensure access to the preferred outcome. On the other hand, what if the equal VI schedules were VI 1-hour schedules? Wouldn't you be more likely to respond on both knobs now? Since one outcome is only slightly preferred, it would seem that the responding organism might change over from door to door, thus obtaining an outcome in 30 minutes, on the average (instead of 60 minutes, if responding exclusively for the preferred outcome). Preference now might be closer to 50:50. More responding might still occur for the preferred outcome, but the organism would be apt to change over occasionally and emit a COD burst on the other door. These intuitions are illustrated in Figure 7.5. What is their relevance for the validity of equation (5)? Simply, that choice should not be invariant when the length of the choice phase is varied. The shorter the choice phase, the greater the preference for the outcome providing the higher rate of reinforcement. Matching should be expected only for a particular value of choice phase durations. Since the length of the choice phase is not included in equation (5), this equation would thus be incomplete.

This argument has been tested with pigeons in several experiments (see Fantino, 1977, for a review). The results from all confirm our intuition that *the strength of preference is a function of the length of the choice phase*. The first study to manipulate the length of the choice phase did so with pigeons responding for terminal-link outcomes of VI 30-sec and VI 90-sec. The equal VI's scheduling entry into the terminal links were either VI 40-sec, VI 120-sec, or VI 600-sec. Choice for the VI 30-sec schedule was almost exclusive (average of 0.95) with the shortest choice phase, closer to matching (0.81) with the intermediate-duration choice phase, and closer to indifference (0.60) with the longest choice phase (Fantino, 1969a).

While we would have been grateful had matching provided an adequate description of choice for schedules of reinforcement, just as it does for simple concurrent VI's, the situation is by no means hopelessly complex. Indeed, the results with the concurrent-chains procedure are

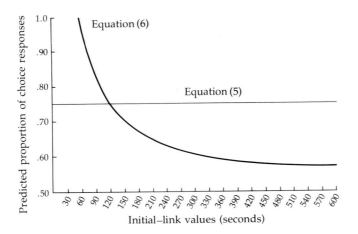

Figure 7.5
In a concurrent-chains procedure with equal initial-link values and
terminal values of VI 30-sec and VI 90-sec, the proportion of choice
responses for the VI 30-sec reinforcement schedule can be expected
to decrease with increasing initial-link values, as shown by the
equation (6) curve. The horizontal line shows that, according to
equation (5), choice is independent of initial-link size. [After E.
Fantino, Choice and rate of reinforcement. *Journal of the Experimental
Analysis of Behavior, 12*, 723–730. Copyright © 1969 by the Society for
the Experimental Analysis of Behavior, Inc. Redrawn by permission.]

consistent with those from the observing-response studies we reviewed
in the preceding chapter. Recall the conclusion from that chapter: A
stimulus is a conditioned reinforcer to the extent that its onset is correlated with a reduction in time to reinforcement. The same delay-reduction
hypothesis is consistent with choice in the concurrent-chains procedure.
To see this we need only calculate how far in time from primary reinforcement the organism is during the choice phase. For we already know
how far reinforcement is when the left and right terminal links are entered: the values of t_{2L} and t_{2R}, respectively. Let T stand for the average
overall time to primary reinforcement from the outset of the choice phase.
The delay reduction correlated with the onset of t_{2L} (entering the terminal
link on the left) then equals $(T - t_{2L})$; similarly, the delay reduction correlated with the onset of t_{2R} equals $(T - t_{2R})$. If the organism's choice responding matches the delay reductions correlated with each outcome,
then the following equation should describe choice:

$$\frac{R_L}{R_L + R_R} = \frac{T - t_{2L}}{(T - t_{2L}) + (T - t_{2R})} \quad \text{(when } t_{2L} < T, t_{2R} < T) \qquad (6)$$

$$= 1 \quad \text{(when } t_{2L} < T, t_{2R} > T)$$

$$= 0 \quad \text{(when } t_{2L} > T, t_{2R} < T)$$

Note that when either outcome represents an *increase* in average delay to reinforcement (either $t_{2L} > T$ or $t_{2R} > T$), equation (6) requires the subject to respond exclusively for the other outcome. In other words, equation (6) specifies when the organism should choose one outcome exclusively.[8]

Let us illustrate by returning to the case in which t_{2L} equals 30 sec and t_{2R} equals 90 sec. T equals the average time in the choice phase plus the average time in the outcome phase. When the equal VI's in the choice phase are VI 120-sec schedules, the average time in the choice phase equals 60 sec. The average time in the outcome phase also equals 60 sec. Thus T equals 120 sec and equation (6) requires a choice proportion of 0.75 [since $T - t_{2L} = 90$, $T - t_{2R} = 30$, and $90/(90 + 30) = 0.75$]. Note that this is the same choice proportion required by equation (5) for matching to relative rates of reinforcement. The picture changes with shorter or longer VI's in the choice phase, however. Thus when the equal VI's are 600 sec, T equals 300 plus 60, or 360; the choice proportion required by equation (6) is now equal to 0.55 [since $T - t_{2L} = 360 - 30$, $T - t_{2R} = 360 - 90$, and $330/(330 + 270) = 0.55$]; and when the equal VI's are 40 sec, T equals 20 plus 60, or 80, and the choice proportion required by equation (6) is 1.0 (since $t_{2R} > T$, the outcome on the right actually represents a delay *increase*; only t_{2L} represents a delay reduction and it should be chosen exclusively). Note that equation (5) continues to require a choice proportion of 0.75. As we saw earlier, the results are consistent with the delay reduction model (equation 6).[9]

Another implication of equation (6) relates to the duration of the outcome phase (t_{2L} and t_{2R}). For a given choice phase (say, concurrent VI 1-min initial links), how does choice vary as t_{2L} and t_{2R} are increased while maintaining a constant ratio to one another? Assume, for example, we study the following three pairs of outcome values: (1) $t_{2L} = 10$, $t_{2R} = 20$; (2) $t_{2L} = 20$, $t_{2R} = 40$; (3) $t_{2L} = 40$, $t_{2R} = 80$. It can readily be shown that equation (6) requires choice proportions of 0.58, 0.67, and 0.83 in 1, 2, and 3, respectively. Thus increasing the duration of the terminal links (while maintaining a constant ratio between them) relative to the choice phase has the same effect as decreasing choice phase duration relative to that of the terminal links: Preference for the favored alternative should increase. Equation (5), on the other hand, requires a constant choice proportion of 0.67. The results from several studies of choice for either VI or FI schedules show that preference indeed increases when the duration of

---

[8] Note that t_{2L} and t_{2R} cannot *both* be greater than T.

[9] Equation (6) has itself been modified by Squires and Fantino (1971) to account for choice when the initial links are *unequal* VI's. This extension is also valuable because the Squires–Fantino formula requires matching of choice to rate of reinforcement when there are no terminal links—that is, when $t_{2R} = t_{2L} = 0$. The Squires–Fantino formula, therefore, reduces to equation (1) in the case of simple concurrent choice. We will not discuss this formulation further here. For the sake of clarity, we discuss the simpler, unmodified version (equation 6) since both make similar quantitative predictions with equal initial links and most studies with concurrent-chains schedules have used equal initial links.

the terminal links is increased while a constant ratio is maintained between them (see MacEwen, 1972; Williams and Fantino, 1978).

In summary, choice for different VI schedules, as measured in the concurrent-chains procedure, is a function of the reduction in average delay to reinforcement correlated with one VI relative to the reduction in average delay correlated with the other. For a given pair of outcomes, the shorter the choice phase the larger the preference for the favored outcome. Similarly, for a given choice phase duration, the longer the outcome durations (providing a constant ratio is maintained between them) the larger the preference for the favored outcome. This delay-reduction formulation is also consistent with the literature on observing, reviewed in the previous chapter. Thus it appears encouragingly general. It does have its limitations, however: Precise quantitative predictions are made by equation (6) only when both outcomes are VI schedules. It is useful only in making ordinal predictions—that is, whether one outcome will be preferred to another when the outcome consists of schedules other than VI's. There are also some interesting limitations—which apply to equation (5) as well—that depend upon more molecular characteristics of choice, to which we now turn.

Molecular Characteristics of Choice

Up to now we have discussed VI schedules as if it is their mean value that is critical, rather than the distribution of intervals comprising the VI. When averaged, these of course equal the mean value. If such a molar assumption were correct, equation (6) should be able to deal with FI outcomes, or even with choice comparing FI and VI outcomes. However, we have already noted (Chapter 6) that immediate events have more impact than less immediate ones in altering the strength of the stimulus in effect. In terms of choice for reinforcement schedules, this means that short interreinforcement intervals (IRI's) should be weighted more heavily than longer ones, and the organism should prefer a VI X-sec schedule to a FI X-sec schedule. Suppose we compare a VI 15-sec and FI 15-sec schedule as outcomes of a concurrent-chains schedule. The VI 15-sec schedule consists of some IRI's that are considerably longer and shorter than 15 sec. If the occasional short IRI's contained in the VI 15-sec schedule have a disproportionate effect on choice, the organism should prefer the VI despite the fact that equation (6)—as well as equation (5)—requires indifference between them. Herrnstein (1964b) tested this notion, finding that the VI 15-sec was strongly preferred to the FI 15-sec schedule. Comparable results have been found by Bower, McLean, and Meacham (1966), Davison (1969, 1972), Killeen (1968), and several others. For example, as noted earlier, Fantino (1967) found strong preference for an outcome that was FR 1 on half the trials and FR 99 on the other half, to one that was always FR 50. Indeed, the constant FR had to be reduced to about FR 10 before pigeons were indifferent to it and the outcome that alternated randomly between FR 1 and FR 99. Clearly, then, it is inappropriate to assume that variable schedules are functionally equivalent to the mean of their component IRI's. Thus formulations such as equations (5) and (6), which have been developed to account for choice between VI schedules, should not be expected to apply to other schedules in any precise fashion.[10]

We have just seen that the distribution of IRI's comprising a schedule—not considered by molar views such as those represented in equations (5) and (6)—can have profound effects on choice. These equations also fail to consider the nature of events during a given IRI, some of which affect choice. For example, under certain conditions, requiring the organism to respond at a high rate in one terminal link (but not in the other) can weaken choice (see Moore and Fantino, 1975, for a review). In addition, under certain conditions, segmenting one of two outcomes into a chain schedule can have a profound weakening effect upon choice for that outcome. Duncan and Fantino (1972), for example, compared a simple FI 2X in one terminal link with a chain FI X FI X in the other and found a strong preference for the simple FI 2X. This preference increased as X increased, a result shown in Figure 7.6, which also illustrates the procedure. Apparently the subjective or "psychological" delay to primary reinforcement is greater in a chain schedule, a finding consistent with our survey of chain schedules in the previous chapter (see Gollub, 1958).

It should be noted that a problem exists in interpreting the degree of preference in Duncan and Fantino's (1972) study. As the open circles at the bottom of Figure 7.6 show, the pigeons obtained a slightly higher rate of reinforcement on the FI schedule as opposed to the chain schedule. This resulted from the fact that the pigeon did not always advance immediately from the first to the second link of the chain. Thus the length of the chain FI X FI X was slightly larger than the length of the simple FI 2X. Wallace (1973) avoided this problem by assessing choice between response-independent schedules: chain FT X FT X and a simple FT 2X. On such schedules no response was required to move from one link of the chain to the other nor to obtain food. Thus the two schedules were identical both in terms of response requirements (none) and in terms of the effective IRI. Wallace found a clear and consistent preference for the simple FT schedule, in keeping with Duncan and Fantino's (1972) results. Nonetheless, preferences were far smaller than in the earlier study. These results are shown in Figure 7.7.

---

[10]The issues here are thorny and involve questions such as the transitivity of choice. For example, if an organism chooses schedule A over schedule C with a choice proportion of 0.75 and schedule B over schedule C, also with a choice proportion of 0.75, will the organism be indifferent to schedules A and B (that is, choice proportions approximating 0.50)? Not always—if they are different types of schedules—a finding that spells trouble for general choice formulations (see Fantino and Navarick, 1974; Navarick and Fantino, 1974, 1975).

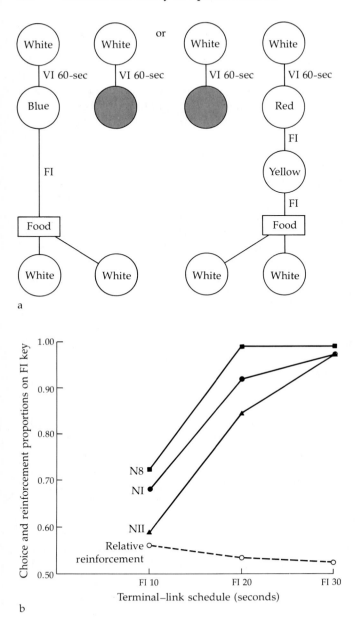

a

b

Figure 7.6
(a) The experimental procedure used by Duncan and Fantino. The left portion of the figure indicates the sequence of events when responses on the left key were reinforced; the right portion indicates the sequence of events when responses on the right key were reinforced. The terminal links consisted of a simple FI schedule on one of the keys and a chain FI FI schedule on the other key. (b) The mean choice proportions for each bird on the FI key are plotted as a function of the size of the intervals in the terminal links. The open circles indicate the relative rate of reinforcement on the FI key. [After B. Duncan and E. Fantino, The psychological distance to reward. *Journal of the Experimental Analysis of Behavior,* *18,* 23–24. Copyright © 1972 by the Society for the Experimental Analysis of Behavior, Inc. Redrawn by permission.]

The results considered in this section suggest that while the mean IRI is a crucial determinant of choice, the distribution of IRI's comprising a schedule and events *during* the IRI's must also be considered in any complete account of choice. Despite these limitations, the delay-reduction hypothesis set forth in equation (6) is consistent with most of the research

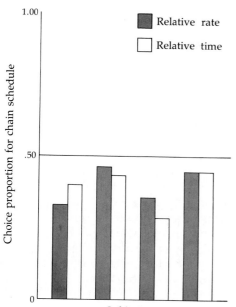

Figure 7.7
Choice proportion for a chain FT FT schedule
compared with a simple FT schedule having the same
total interreinforcement interval, plotted in terms of
both relative time and relative rate of responding in
the initial links (concurrent variable-interval
schedules). The simple FT schedule was preferred by
all four pigeons in the experiment. [After Wallace,
1973.]

in choice for reinforcement schedules from the concurrent-chains literature and on observing responses when only the mean size of the IRI is
manipulated. As such, it has promising generality. The finding that limits
it most seriously is itself fascinating: the disproportionate effects on choice
of reinforcers occurring soon after choice. Indeed, this is the crux of the
problem of self-control, a fitting topic to conclude any discussion of
choice.

SELF-CONTROL

Self-control generally reduces to a choice between an immediate small
reward (for example, a mint for a dieting model, a cigarette for a chain
smoker, or an extra hour of sleep for a lazy author) and a delayed large
reward (for example, a trim figure, better health, or a chapter of a manuscript completed). Selection of the immediate small reward is often considered "impulsive," while selection of the delayed larger reward is considered evidence for "self-control." While self-control was once thought
to be exclusively the province of humans and other higher primates, research in the last dozen years has shown that lower organisms may exhibit self-control as well. It is our thesis that self-control and impulsiveness
are governed by the same general laws that govern all choice behavior.
Specifically, self-control and impulsiveness are special cases of choice,

which, as we noted at the outset of this chapter, refers to the multiple response alternatives possible at a given time. Thus self-control and impulsiveness, like choice in general, do not imply "free will," and the factors that determine which response actually occurs are the same factors that determine choice behavior in the general case. When self-control is viewed in this way, it is perhaps not surprising that response alternatives may be arranged so that even organisms such as pigeons exhibit self-control.

The data in Figure 7.8 show the results of an early study of self-control in pigeons. Pigeons could obtain reinforcement either by pecking a key immediately after it was illuminated with a red light or by postponing their pecks until the light turned green. When the pigeon pecked at the red key, reinforcement was followed by a period of extinction; when the pigeon waited until the light turned green, reinforcement could be obtained without penalty. Although Figure 7.8 shows that the pigeons did not often exhibit self-control by delaying, their tendency to do so increased in proportion to the advantages of delaying. In other words, pigeons exhibited self-control more frequently when it was more advantageous to do so. Although these data (Fantino, 1966) do show that self-control may occur, the degree of self-control was limited, and even these results were obtained only after several months of training with the procedure. It is possible to demonstrate more robust self-control using a dif-

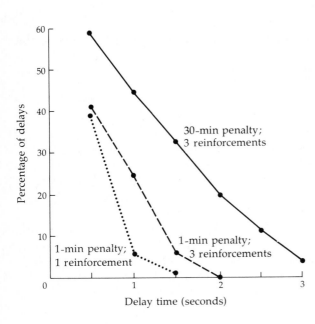

Figure 7.8
Data from an experiment in rudimentary self-control in the pigeon.
Food—followed by a penalty—could be obtained immediately by pecking a red key. If the pigeon waited until the key turned from red to green, a peck would produce food without a subsequent penalty. The advantage to delay was greatest when the penalty for not delaying was 30 min of darkness (during which there was no opportunity to earn food) and the pigeon could earn three reinforcements if it waited for the green key light. The advantage to delay was least when there was only a 1-min penalty and one reinforcement. The figure shows that the percentage of trials on which pigeons delayed in each condition is a function of the length of time (from 1/2 to 3 sec) they had to wait for the change from red to green. Comparison of the three curves shows that the pigeons delayed more, the greater the advantage to delay. [Data from Fantino, 1966.]

ferent procedure—one that mimics a time-honored and effective self-control technique employed by humans. Consider the classic example of Ulysses, who tied himself to the mast of a ship in order to avoid being tempted by the Sirens. He determined at a distance that the avoidance of crashing upon the rocks outweighed the pleasure of approaching the Sirens, and he realized that the closer he got to the Sirens the less likely he would be able to resist them. Thus he tied himself to the mast so that he would be committed to his original decision not to be tempted. Many of us follow the same logic when we put an alarm clock out of easy reach so that we will not be able to turn it off without rising from bed the following morning. This is done when the consequences of one behavior—getting to work on time—are valued more highly than the consequences of another—getting more sleep. In the morning this preference may be reversed; the out-of-reach alarm, however, forces us to get out of bed.

Ainslie (1974) gave pigeons the opportunity to commit themselves in advance to waiting for the larger delayed reinforcer. The basic sequence of key illumination was green to dark to red. The key remained red for 3 seconds if the bird did not peck, after which the bird obtained 4 seconds of food. Pecks at red, however, produced 2 seconds of food immediately. The procedure is shown in Figure 7.9. Once confronted with the red key light, birds tended to peck it on more than 95 percent of the trials, thereby producing the small immediate reinforcer. The novel twist was that pecks at green prevented red from occurring. Thus pecks at green *committed* the pigeon to the delayed larger reinforcer. Some of Ainslie's pigeons consistently pecked green in this condition, thereby demonstrating self-control. It should be added that Ainslie employed several control groups. In the most important one, pecks at the green light did not prevent onset of the red light; in this condition, responding to green declined, supporting the notion that pecks at green, in the experimental condition, were reinforced by avoidance of red and production of the larger reinforcer.

Ainslie's study shows that choice for a larger delayed reward over a smaller immediate reward is facilitated by allowing the subject to commit itself in advance to the larger reward. This advance commitment is necessary since the subject is much more likely to choose the smaller reward once it is immediately available. The advance commitment occurs because at the time the commitment is made the larger reward is preferred. As the rewards become temporally close, a reversal of preference occurs: Immediacy of reward becomes more important than magnitude. Fantino and Navarick (1974) have considered such preference reversals in human self-control:

> For example, consider a reluctant dieter faced with the choice of a delectable hot-fudge sundae, a scoop of orange sherbet, or no dessert at all. His choice is based on taste and caloric content. If he is asked to order his dessert 24 hours before the meal is to be served, he may well choose neither, since the caloric dimension may be more important to him at this time. As the meal

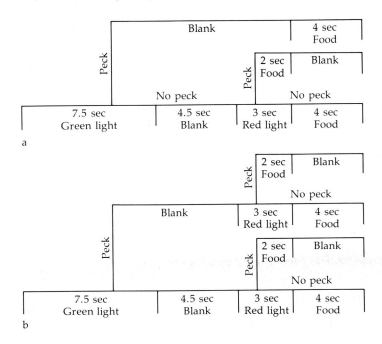

Figure 7.9
The conditions of Ainslie's self-control experiment. Events proceed in a
horizontal line. A response caused a vertical move to a different
horizontal line. (a) Experimental condition. (b) Control condition. [After
G. W. Ainslie, Impulse control in pigeons, *Journal of the Experimental
Analysis of Behavior, 21,* 485–489. Copyright © 1974 by the Society for the
Experimental Analysis of Behavior, Inc. Redrawn by permission.]

approaches, however, taste becomes more important and preference may
shift from omitting dessert to ordering sherbet. When the sundae and sherbet are physically presented for choice at the actual meal, however, selection
of the sundae becomes more likely, since the taste dimension should be
most important at this time [as long as the eater is still hungry] [Fantino and
Navarick, 1974, pp. 148–149].

If commitment occurs in Ainslie's procedure because preference
changes with time, then it should be possible to get similar preference
reversals by having the subject choose at different times—that is, at different temporal distance from reinforcement—between two rewards, as in
the weight reduction versus taste comparison. Indeed, Rachlin and Green
(1972) demonstrated such preference reversals. In their study, preference
for the small immediate reward over the large delayed reward was reversed by adding a constant amount of delay to both rewards: When the
added delays were both long, subjects chose the larger (more delayed)

reward; when the added delays were short, they chose the more immediate (smaller) reward. Rachlin and Green interpreted their results in
terms of a matching model proposed by Baum and Rachlin (1969) in
which

$$\frac{V_1}{V_2} = \frac{A_1}{A_2} = \frac{D_2}{D_1} = \frac{R_1}{R_2} \tag{7}$$

where V represents the value of an alternative, A the amount of reinforcement, D the delay of reinforcement, and R the number of choice
responses.

It should be evident that such a model is consistent with the preference
reversals found by Rachlin and Green (1972) and Ainslie's (1974) results
on commitment. For example, let $A_1 = 6$ sec of reinforcement, $A_2 = 3$ sec,
$D_1 = 10$ sec, and $D_2 = 0$ sec. In that event, $V_1/V_2 = 0$, and the subject
should behave impulsively (select A_2). In other words, all or most of the
organism's choice responses should be those producing the immediate
smaller reward ($R_2 > R_1$). Now add 20 sec to each delay so that $D_1 = 30$
sec, and $D_2 = 20$ sec (A_1 and A_2 remain 6 and 3 sec, respectively). Equation (7) now requires that the subject choose A_1 (display self-control)
since $V_1/V_2 = 2(2/3) = 1.33$, that is $R_1 > R_2$. As Rachlin and Green acknowledge, however, other choice models, including that represented by
equation (6), are also consistent with these results.[11]

Navarick and Fantino (1976) noted that a simple procedural variation
could differentiate between the adequacy of equations (6) and (7): Let the
delays of reinforcement (D_1 and D_2) associated with A_1 and A_2 (with $A_1 >$
A_2) be *equal*, and vary the size of these equal delays. Now equation (7)
requires a constant preference for the larger reward (since $D_1 = D_2$, R_1/R_2
simply $= A_1/A_2$), whereas equation (6) requires *increasing* preference for
the larger reward as the absolute size of the equal delays is increased.
Navarick and Fantino's results conclusively supported equation (6).

Thus the work on commitment and self-control points to two important, although tentative, conclusions: (1) As Rachlin and Green (1972)
maintain, self-control appears to be a special case of choice behavior, controlled by the same laws that govern choice, and (2) the same choice
model that successfully accounts for choice in concurrent-chains
schedules and observing responses—the delay-reduction hypothesis represented by equation (6)—appears to account for self-control as well. It
is likely that our knowledge of choice and of self-control will continue to
advance hand in hand.

---

[11] Actually, modification of equation (6) is necessary to apply it with differing reinforcer
magnitude. The details need not concern us here, however (see Navarick and Fantino,
1976).

8   Aversive Control

Up to this point we have studied how behavior is maintained by positive reinforcers. The study of aversive stimuli, or punishers—those stimuli which reduce the frequency of responses they follow—and negative reinforcers—those which make responding more probable by their offset or nonoccurrence—has been dealt with only sparingly, in Chapters 4 and 6. (See Figure 4.1 for a review of the relationship between positive reinforcement, negative reinforcement, and punishment.) In this chapter we will consider how well the principles that have evolved from the study of positive reinforcers apply to punishers and negative reinforcers.

The comparison of positive reinforcement, on the one hand, and punishment and negative reinforcement, on the other, is complicated by some procedural differences necessitated by the use of aversive stimuli. For example, the study of punishment requires that behavior be maintained in the first place, usually by positive reinforcement. Thus while the study of positive reinforcement typically does not involve a superimposed schedule of punishment, the study of punishment does typically involve a superimposed schedule of positive reinforcement. A second complication arises from an intrinsic difference between positive and negative reinforcement: Whereas in positive reinforcement the reinforcing simulus is generally not present while its effect is being measured (that is, the to-be-reinforced response occurs in the absence of the reinforcer), in negative reinforcement the to-be-reinforced response often occurs in the presence of the reinforcing stimulus. (Recall that it is the *termination* of a stimulus that constitutes negative reinforcement and the *presentation* of a stimulus that constitutes positive reinforcement.) The negatively reinforcing stimulus—for example, electric shock—may constrain the behavior available for selection and strengthening by reinforcement or may have other interfering effects.

When behavioral differences resulting from these procedural differences are taken into account, however, comparisons between behavior maintained by positive reinforcement and behavior maintained by negative reinforcement and punishment may be made. The principal generalization that will emerge from our review of aversive control is that a remarkable symmetry exists between the effects of behavior maintained by positive reinforcement and negative reinforcement. Moreover, the effects of both types of reinforcement are equivalent but opposite to those of punishment. Specifically, positive and negative reinforcement both make the responding they follow more probable, in the same way that punishment makes the responding it follows less probable.

PUNISHMENT: AN EMPIRICAL OVERVIEW

As we noted in Chapter 4, a punisher is a stimulus, the presentation of which weakens the responding that produced it. The definition of punishment as an event that decreases the probability of the preceding response is symmetrical with that of reinforcement, an event that increases the probability of the preceding response. These symmetrical definitions suggest that punishment and reinforcement are symmetrical processes. Evaluation of this symmetry is an important part of contemporary research and theory in punishment. Before considering this issue in detail, we briefly review the factors involved in the maintenance of punished behavior, the parameters of punishment, the effects of discontinuing punishment, the effects of punishment as a discriminative stimulus, and the effects of response-independent punishment in the conditioned suppression paradigm. Where appropriate we relate the empirical findings to the theoretical issue of the symmetry of reinforcement and punishment.

Maintenance of Punished Behavior

As already noted, the study of punishment is necessarily more complex than the study of reinforcement. This can be appreciated by considering the following question: Why should a subject continue to emit a punished response? Obviously, in order to study the effects of punishment on continuing behavior, one must first maintain behavior. The maintenance of behavior in the face of punishment is readily arranged by using a schedule of positive reinforcement. A schedule of punishment may then be superimposed upon the baseline schedule of positive reinforcement. In that case, however, we are assessing the effects of punishment on behavior maintained by a schedule of positive reinforcement. The situation becomes more complex, but this poses no major conceptual problem as long as we realize that the effects of reinforcement on behavior are typically studied without an additional explicit schedule. Thus when comparing the effects of punishment and reinforcement we should expect some differences that merely reflect this procedural asymmetry.

A large number of punishment studies maintaining behavior with different schedules of positive reinforcement have been conducted in the past twenty years, beginning with the classic study by Azrin (1959) with pigeons. Azrin punished every key-peck maintained on an FR 25 schedule of reinforcement with electric shock. The intensity of the electric shock was varied from 0 volts (the prepunishment level) to 120 volts. Cumulative records from typical sessions are shown in Figure 8.1. Note that punishment does not affect the ongoing rate of responding; that is, the rate of responding between the postreinforcement pause and the next reinforcement remains reasonably constant. Instead, punishment affects the *pause* following reinforcement: the pause increases with increasing punishment, much as the pause following reinforcement increases with

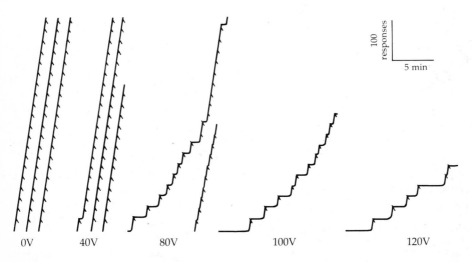

Figure 8.1
Cumulative response records indicating the effect of various punishment intensities (in volts) on performance maintained by an FR 25 schedule of food reinforcement (reinforcements are indicated by the oblique blips). The punishment was delivered immediately following every response. One complete daily session is shown for each of the values of punishment. [After N. H. Azrin, Punishment and recovery during fixed-time performance. *Journal of the Experimental Analysis of Behavior, 2,* 301–305. Copyright © 1959 by the Society for the Experimental Analysis of Behavior, Inc. Redrawn by permission.]

increments in FR size in the study of positive reinforcement (Chapter 4). In other words, the form of fixed-ratio responding is unaffected by punishment. Research on punished behavior maintained by fixed-ratio schedules of reinforcement, together with studies of punishment's effects on behavior maintained by FI schedules (for example, Weiner, 1962, with human subjects), suggests that punishment exerts its greatest effect on the period following reinforcement (that is, before the organism resumes responding).

On variable schedules, such as VI's, however, while the pattern of constant responding throughout the interreinforcement interval is unaffected, the overall rate of responding is reduced (see Azrin, 1960). In general, the effects of punishment are similar to those of satiation, which also increases pausing after reinforcement on fixed schedules and decreases rate of responding on variable schedules. If so, we should be able to reverse the effects of punishment by increasing deprivation. Indeed, Azrin, Holz, and Hake (1963) did just that in studying the effects of food deprivation on pigeons' key-pecking maintained by a VI 3-min schedule of positive reinforcement and punished by intense electric shock on an FR 100 schedule. The results, shown in Figure 8.2, demonstrate that with moderate deprivation (85 percent of free-feeding body weight) the suppressive effects of punishment are virtually complete, whereas with intense deprivation (60 percent of body weight) the effects of punishment are minimized. Again, the rate of responding throughout the interreinforcement interval remains constant for a given level of deprivation. The

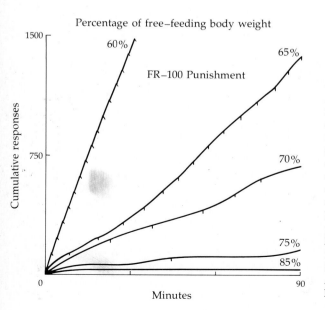

Figure 8.2
Effect of food deprivation during fixed-ratio punishment of responding maintained by a VI 3-min schedule of food reinforcement. Every hundredth response was punished by an intense shock (160 V) at the moment indicated by the short oblique lines on the response curves. [After N. H. Azrin, W. C. Holz, and D. F. Hake, Fixed-ratio punishment. *Journal of the Experimental Analysis of Behavior, 6,* 141–148. Copyright © 1963 by the Society for the Experimental Analysis of Behavior, Inc. Redrawn by permission.]

greater the deprivation, the less punishment affects the overall rate of responding.

Parameters of Punishment

We have seen that the effects of punishment on responding depend critically on the schedule of reinforcement and deprivation used to maintain responding. The effects of punishment also depend, of course, on aspects of the punisher itself—that is, on the parameters of punishment—as we saw in Figure 8.1. The effects of three critical parameters will be summarized here: (1) the intensity of punishment, (2) the schedule of punishment, and (3) the manner in which punishment is introduced. Numerous studies have shown a direct relationship between intensity of the punishing stimulus and the degree of response suppression produced by it (providing, of course, that other factors are held constant—for example, manner of introduction, schedules of punishment and food reinforcement, and degree of food deprivation). The effects of punishment range from small and transitory changes with mild punishers to complete and irreversible changes with very severe punishers (see Azrin, 1960; Appel and Peterson, 1965). With sufficiently intense punishment, punished responding is virtually eliminated and may never recover, even if punishment is discontinued (Appel, 1961; Storms, Boroczi, and Broen, 1962). Of course, as long as the subject emits no responses, its behavior cannot be influenced by the fact that punishment has been discontinued. With shock intensities less than those necessary for complete suppression, however, recovery is complete once punishment is discontinued. The parallel to positive reinforcement may be clear: When positive reinforcement is reinstated following prolonged extinction, complete recovery quickly occurs if the subject ever does emit the response required by the reinforcement schedule.

The suppressive effects of punishment are maximal when punishment is applied immediately following the response (Azrin, 1956; Cohen, 1968). Again the symmetry with positive reinforcement is clear: The effectiveness of reinforcement is progressively weakened as the delay between response and reinforcer is lengthened (Grice, 1948; Skinner, 1938). The symmetry argument also suggests that *continuous punishment* (FR 1) should suppress behavior more effectively than *intermittent punishment*. Indeed, Azrin, Holz, and Hake (1963) found this to be the case in a study that manipulated the value of a fixed-ratio schedule of punishment (electric shock presentations). Since the schedule maintaining pigeons' keypecking in this study was a VI schedule, the effects of punishment were expressed in terms of suppression of overall response rates. As the results shown in Figure 8.3 indicate, the degree of suppression produced by the schedule varied directly as a function of the ratio of punished to unpunished responses. Thus increasing the rate of punishment (by decreas-

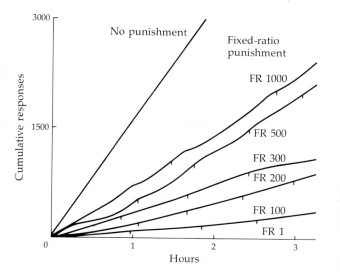

Cumulative responses

3000

1500

0

No punishment

Fixed-ratio
punishment

FR 1000

FR 500

FR 300

FR 200

FR 100

FR 1

1   2   3

Hours

Figure 8.3
Stable performance during
fixed-ratio punishment at several
fixed-ratio values from FR 1 to FR
1000. The oblique lines on the
response curve indicate the
delivery of electric shock (240 V).
Responding is maintained by food
reinforcements (not indicated on
the graph) delivered according to
a VI 3-min schedule. [After N. H.
Azrin, W. C. Holz, and D. F.
Hake, Fixed-ratio punishment.
*Journal of the Experimental Analysis
of Behavior, 6,* 141–148. Copyright
© 1963 by the Society for the
Experimental Analysis of
Behavior, Inc. Redrawn by
permission.]

ing the value of the FR schedule) has the same effect as increasing the
intensity of punishment: The more frequent or more intense the punishment, the greater the suppression of responding.

When punishment is arranged on a fixed-interval schedule, a negatively accelerated response curve is generated; that is, responding *decreases* as the moment for the scheduled punishment approaches (Azrin,
1956; an interesting exception to this generalization appears later in the
chapter, in the discussion of self-punitive behavior). This, of course, is
just the opposite of what occurs with FI schedules of reinforcement, and
it is just what would be expected if punishment and reinforcement have
symmetrical (though opposite) effects on behavior.

Finally, the manner in which punishment is introduced is a third important variable in determining the effectiveness of punishment. For example, Azrin et al. (1963) showed that a punishment of moderate intensity
which produced only partial and transient suppression when introduced
gradually (by beginning with low-intensity shock and progressively increasing the intensity over successive presentations), would completely
suppress responding when introduced suddenly. Similarly, the order of
presenting different shock intensities can influence the results of studies
intended to assess the effects of different shock intensities on responding.
To obtain replicable results it is best to increase the intensity gradually
and then decrease it, obtaining curves for the ascending and descending
orders. If, instead, shock intensities are selected at random, a moderate
shock value that represents a sudden increase in intensity may produce
more severe suppression than higher values of shock that happen to follow intense shock. These issues, as well as a more complete consideration
of punishment parameters, are discussed in Fantino (1973).

Punishment as a Discriminative Stimulus

If punishment tends to be associated with the availability of reinforcement—that is, if punishment is a discriminative stimulus (S^D) for reinforcement—then punishment may actually enhance responding rather than suppress it. Just such an enhancement effect has been demonstrated by several investigators, including Holz and Azrin (1961) with pigeons and Ayllon and Azrin (1968) with humans. Holz and Azrin first conducted two sessions, one in which both punishment and reinforcement were presented, and another in which neither punishment nor reinforcement occurred. Following these sessions an extinction session was conducted in which punishment (electric shock) followed every response. As the results in Figure 8.4 show, the reintroduction of punishment actually increased the rate of responding over that generated without punishment. The correlation of punishment and positive reinforcement in the earlier sessions (in which either both occurred or neither occurred) established punishment as an S^D for reinforcement. Thus the effects of a punishing stimulus are not invariant. In order to predict reliably what effect a stimulus will have one needs to know the experimental history of the organism with respect to that stimulus.

Note, too, that the effect is reversible: when punishment is again removed, as Figure 8.4 shows, response rates again decline. Thus the *removal* of punishment, though generally resulting in an increase in response rate, may have no effect (as noted earlier) if the subject does not respond (as after intense punishment). On the other hand, removal of punishment may actually reduce responding if the punishment functions

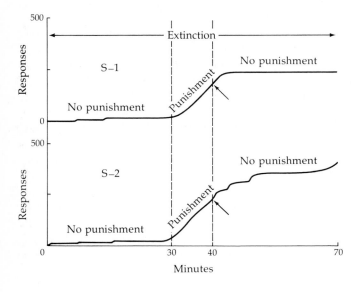

Figure 8.4
Cumulative-response records for two subjects showing an increase in responding following presentation of punishment. In both cases the sessions shown occurred in extinction, following maintenance on a VI schedule of food reinforcement with punishment. [After W. C. Holz and N. H. Azrin, Discriminative properties of punishment. *Journal of the Experimental Analysis of Behavior, 4*, 225–232. Copyright © 1961 by the Society for the Experimental Analysis of Behavior, Inc. Redrawn by permission.]

as an S^D for reinforcement. Of course, the more typical outcome is an increase in response rate with punishment removal. One can predict which will occur only with knowledge of the subject's experimental history and within the complete context of the experimental procedures being studied.

Conditioned Suppression

The pairing of conditioned with unconditioned stimuli in everyday life produces conditioned emotional reactions. One of the first explanations of the conditioning of emotional reactions was made by Watson and Rayner (1920). As a UCS they used a sudden loud noise, which elicits crying and trembling in young children. The CS was a white rat. Before conditioning, the experimenters demonstrated that the subject, a child named Albert, would try to play with the rat. This showed that the rat was not already an aversive stimulus. Next, they paired touching the rat and the sight of the rat with the loud noise. After several pairings, a clear emotional reaction developed: young Albert would whimper and recoil at the sight of the rat he had once trusted as a playmate.

Many experiments seeking to assess the conditioning of emotional responses have used a *conditioned suppression* paradigm. In this paradigm a stimulus that is typically neutral at the beginning of the experiment is intermittently presented to the subject. When this originally neutral stimulus is terminated, electric shock is delivered to the subject independently of its behavior. Responding is maintained by a schedule of positive reinforcement. After several pairings of the neutral stimulus and the electric shock, presentation of the stimulus comes to lower the rate of responding as measured by a *suppression ratio*, which divides rate of responding in the presence of the stimulus by the rate of responding in its absence. For example, if the stimulus is totally effective in suppressing behavior, the suppression ratio is zero; if the stimulus is an ineffective suppressor, however, the ratio is 1.0. Conditioned suppression has been found with several species of organisms, including humans, pigeons, rats, and monkeys. In the first study of conditioned suppression Estes and Skinner (1941) maintained rats' lever-pressing behavior on a FI 4-min schedule of food reinforcement on which they superimposed a 3-min conditioned stimulus terminating in shock. The Estes and Skinner study was titled, "Some quantitative properties of anxiety," for, until recently, it was thought that the aversive nature of the preshock stimulus was responsible for suppression. Specifically, after several pairings of the stimulus and shock, the stimulus was thought to evoke an emotional response, such as anxiety, or fear, which disrupted the behavior maintained by positive reinforcement.

The more recent experiments of Azrin and Hake (1969) and Meltzer and Brahlek (1970) call into question the interpretation of conditioned suppression in terms of anxiety or fear. For example, Azrin and Hake studied the effects of unconditioned stimuli such as water (to a thirsty organism), food (to a hungry organism), or intracranial stimulation (in the "reward" centers of the brain) on responding maintained by a different positive reinforcer. Surprisingly, they found that when any one of these three positive reinforcers was used as the unconditioned stimulus in the conditioned suppression paradigm, suppression indeed occurred in the presence of the conditioned stimulus. For example, when the conditioned suppression procedure was utilized with food instead of shock as the unconditioned stimulus, suppression (of responding for water or intracranial stimulation) occurred in the presence of the prefood stimulus. Azrin and Hake interpret their results—known as "positive" conditioned suppression, since the UCS is a positive reinforcer—as being due to the energizing effects of some type of emotional preparedness. It appears that any strong UCS may suppress a particular operant, perhaps by eliciting responses that compete with performance of the operant. Unfortunately, it is often difficult to specify the competing response. This will be made clear in our discussion of Kelly (1973), in this section, and later in the chapter when discussing the problem of evaluating competing-response theories.

It must be stressed, however, that competing responses have sometimes been implicated directly in positive conditioned suppression, as shown in an elegant series of studies by Vincent LoLordo and his students (see LoLordo, 1971; LoLordo, McMillan, and Riley, 1974). These studies also make the important point that suppression is not a *necessary* outcome when response-independent food is superimposed on a schedule of response-dependent reinforcement. For example, LoLordo (1971) maintained pigeons' key-pecking on a VI schedule; on this schedule he superimposed response-independent food, which was preceded by a 20-sec stimulus change (the prereward stimulus or the "CS") on the key. LoLordo obtained facilitation rather than suppression with this procedure. Similar facilitation was also found by Herrnstein and Morse (1957), whose result has sometimes been referred to as the "joy" or "conditioned elation" effect. LoLordo reasoned that autoshaped pecks were directed at the CS and that these autopecks added to the baseline pecks maintained by the response-dependent schedule to produce facilitation. If so, facilitation should not occur with an auditory CS unlikely to generate autopecks, an inference confirmed by LoLordo et al. (1974). More interestingly, suppression rather than facilitation should occur when the autoshaped response is different from the baseline response. Specifically, if the baseline response were treadle-pressing and the CS were a stimulus change on the key, autopecks should be directed at the key, perhaps resulting in a suppression of treadle-pressing during the CS. LoLordo et al. also confirmed this prediction. Whether suppression or facilitation occurs when response-independent food is superimposed on a schedule of response-dependent reinforcement turns out to depend on several factors, including the stimuli and responses selected. In the remainder of this section we return to a consideration of research demonstrating suppression.

Positive conditioned suppression is one of two major pieces of evidence suggesting that conditioned suppression is not necessarily the result of fear or anxiety, as was once thought. Positive conditioned suppression instead shows that suppression may occur to any salient prefood stimulus. The second type of evidence comes from extensive experimentation that has failed to implicate a unitary entity such as that suggested by the labels "fear" or "anxiety" in conditioned suppression. For example, Brady, Kelly, and Plumlee (1969) simultaneously recorded changes in blood pressure, heart rate, and lever-pressing rate in rhesus monkeys in a conditioned suppression procedure in which 3-min clicker presentations were followed by electric shock (responding was maintained by food on an intermittent schedule). Over the course of the first 5 to 10 clicker–shock pairings, subjects' blood pressure and heart rate tended to decrease during the clicker. On subsequent trials, however, large and systematic *increases* occurred for both cardiovascular responses, as shown for one subject in Figure 8.5. Note that the conditioned suppression, as measured by the rate of lever-pressing, was complete by the third trial, or well in advance of the large increase in the cardiovascular measures. Clearly it would be difficult to "explain" the suppression of lever-pressing in terms of the physiological events here measured. Similarly, deToledo and Black (1966) found that changes in rats' heart rates developed more slowly than suppression in a conditioned suppression paradigm and that the heart rate changes were more variable and of shorter duration than the suppression effect. Finally, Kelly (1973) studied positive conditioned suppression with monkeys and found long-term prereward suppression that was independent of cardiovascular activity. Kelly concluded that his results weakened the notion that positive conditioned suppression was caused by competing responses elicited by the prereward stimulus. These and other studies (see Blackman, 1977 for a review) support the conclusion that conditioned suppression—whether to preaversive or prereward stimuli—is relatively independent of the physiological measures recorded thus far. Since these are measures commonly used as indicators of fear or anxiety, it appears that these labels themselves have little relevance for conditioned suppression. Thus far, at any rate, these labels have had little utility in helping us to understand the variables controlling conditioned suppression.

CURRENT THEORIES OF PUNISHMENT

The symmetrical definitions of reinforcement (an event that increases the probability of the preceding response) and punishment (an event that decreases the probability of the preceding response) have suggested to vari-

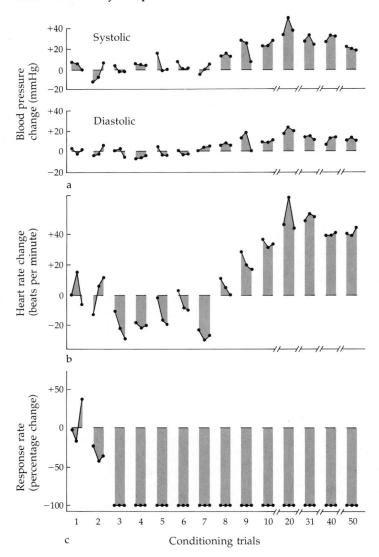

Figure 8.5
Minute-by-minute changes in (a) blood pressure, (b) heart rate, and
(c) lever-pressing response rate for a monkey on successive 3-min
clicker–shock trials during acquisition of the conditioned emotional
response. The zero points represent control values calculated from the
3-min interval immediately preceding the clicker. [After Brady, Kelly,
and Plumlee, 1969.]

ous researchers the possibility that punishment and reinforcement are
symmetrical processes. Proponents of such a *symmetrical law of effect* (for
example, Azrin and Holz, 1966; Church, 1969; Estes, 1969; Fantino, 1973;

Rachlin and Herrnstein, 1969; Smith, 1974), though differing on the nature of the reinforcement process, agree that whatever the process responsible for increased responding due to reinforcement, the same process, working in reverse, is responsible for decreased responding due to punishment. This has been called the *single-process theory of punishment* (see Navarick and Fantino, 1974).

Others have argued that punishment results from a combination of processes, not equivalent to those operating in reinforcement (for example, Bolles, 1967; Rescorla and Solomon, 1967; Skinner, 1938; Mowrer, 1947). A popular theory that argues that punishment and reinforcement are not symmetrical is the *competing-response theory of punishment* (also called the competing response-elicitation theory), according to which reduction in punished responding results from the strengthening of alternative responses (see Bolles, 1967). Indeed, Bolles has concluded that "punishment is not effective in altering behavior unless the reaction to punishment itself competes with the response we wish to punish" (p. 433). According to Bolles's argument, punishment does not directly weaken the behavior it follows (the way reinforcement strengthens the behavior *it* follows), but rather elicits responses, including fear, that generally interfere with the punished response. For example, the natural reaction to grasping a red-hot piece of charcoal is withdrawal. The heat will serve as an effective punisher for grasping hot charcoal because punishment elicits a response (dropping the coal) that is incompatible with the punished response (grasping the coal). Or the sight of hot coals may elicit fear, which will also interfere with grasping the coals. However, if the behavior elicited by punishment happens to be compatible with the punished response, punishment may actually *facilitate* that response. For example, slapping a crying baby may facilitate further crying rather than suppressing it.

An elegant study supporting competing-response theory was carried out with rats by Fowler and Miller (1963), who reinforced traversing a runway with food. In addition, rats were shocked in the goal box as soon as they obtained the food. Some received shock in the hind paws—said to elicit a forward lurch—and others in the fore paws—said to elicit a backward flinch. As training progressed, subjects shocked in the hind paws ran faster, while those shocked in the fore paws ran progressively slower than a control group receiving no shock. Thus the response elicited by the shock tended to influence the running response in a manner consistent with the competing-response theory. When shock elicits a response that competes with running, as does fore-paw shock, punishment suppresses running; when shock elicits a response that is compatible with running, as does hind-paw shock, punishment facilitates running.

Another important supporting argument for the competing-response view comes from the observation—most notably by Estes (1944)—that noncontingent aversive events (such as response-independent shocks) suppress behavior about as well as contingent ones (that is, supposed punishers). If this observation is generally correct, it could suggest that aversive events suppress behavior because they elicit competing responses. As Fantino (1973) has noted, Estes (1944) found that:

> The effect of electric shock was independent of whether it was received for bar-pressing or whether it was presented when the animal was not pressing the bar. He found the same degree of suppression and the same degree of recovery of the response whether or not the shock followed the response. This experiment was a major factor in generating the belief that the effects of punishment were nonspecific, that is, that punishment depresses responding in the situation in general without having a specific effect on the response that produced the punishment. If this were the case, of course, we would have a dramatically different situation than we have with positive reinforcement (e.g., Ferster and Skinner, 1957). This notion fits in very well with the hypothesis that all punishment does on those occasions when it appears to reduce the probability of a response is to generate behavior that is itself incompatible with the punished response. In this case, for example, the shocks, whether or not they follow the bar-press, are believed to create a general emotional state with concomitant emotional responses, such as freezing, that interfere with an integrated response such as a bar-press [Fantino, 1973, p. 259].

This observation does not have general validity, however. In Estes's pioneer study the onset of shocks coincided with the onset of extinction and was therefore perfectly correlated with the absence of reinforcement. We have already seen (Figure 8.4) that punishment can have important discriminative properties. In Estes's experiment the response-dependent and response-independent shocks should have been effective cues for nonreward and should have suppressed behavior for this reason alone. Viewed in this light, the fact that no additional suppressive effect of the response-dependent shocks was found is not conclusive. More importantly, shocks were applied for only 10 minutes, a period during which punishment is most likely to produce transient emotional states. Many more recent investigations have shown conclusively that with additional exposure the far greater suppressive effects of response-dependent, as opposed to response-independent, shocks become evident (for example, Azrin, 1956; Schuster and Rachlin, 1968; see Fantino, 1973, or Mackintosh, 1974, for a review).

The results from a study by Schuster and Rachlin of the effects of shock on pigeons' key-pecking are illustrated in Figure 8.6. The study employed a concurrent-chains procedure, described in Chapter 7, in which pecks at either key in the choice phase produced identical VI schedules with food reinforcement in the terminal links. In one terminal link response-contingent shocks were scheduled, while in the other terminal link shocks were response-independent. As shown in Figure 8.6, Schuster and

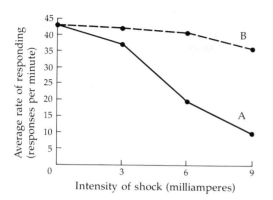

Figure 8.6
The effects of response-dependent shocks (curve A) and response-independent shocks (curve B) on pigeons' key-pecking. The rate of delivery of the independent shocks was 120 per minute. [Data from Schuster and Rachlin, 1968. Redrawn after *Behavior and learning* by H. Rachlin, W. H. Freeman and Company. Copyright © 1976.]

Rachlin found that response-contingent shocks produced much more response suppression. The pigeons' choice, however, was a function of the relative rate of shock associated with each terminal link. In other words, pigeons preferred the terminal-link schedule arranging the lowest rate of shock, whether shocks were response-dependent or response-independent. Each of these findings parallels the findings with positive reinforcement: pigeons' responding in the terminal link will be higher for response-dependent than for response-independent reinforcement; pigeons' choice behavior, however is a function of the relative rates of reinforcement obtained in the terminal link, irrespective of whether or not these reinforcements are dependent on responding (see Killeen, 1968b; Neuringer, 1969).

The finding that punishment (e.g., response-dependent shocks) appears to produce effects that are far more striking than the effects produced by comparable response-independent shocks weakens one of the two main cornerstones of the competing response-elicitation theory of punishment—that is, the notion that noncontingent aversive events suppress behavior about as well as punishers. We acknowledge, however, that competing responses may be elicited by aversive stimuli and contribute to response suppression. But the effects of such competing responses appear to be symmetrical to those that are elicited by positive stimuli. Thus the fact that competing responses may play a part in response suppression caused by punishment does not weaken the symmetry of reinforcement and punishment. As both Fantino (1973) and Mackintosh (1974) have argued, similar considerations apply to reinforcement. Indeed, as Mackintosh has noted:

> Presentation of an appetitive reinforcer contingent upon the occurrence of one response, or upon the omission of another, is not always sufficient to insure a reliable increase or decrease in probability of that response. . . .

The most reasonable account of many of these failures of the positive law of effect . . . point to the possibilities of Pavlovian processes of reinforcement overriding the instrumental contingency. If subjects are required to make a response to obtain a particular reinforcer that happens to be incompatible with the responses elicited by that reinforcer, or if they are required to suppress a response that is in fact elicited by the reinforcer, then Pavlovian conditioning will interfere with instrumental learning. It is reasonable to suppose that similar effects will occur with such an effective UCS as electric shock. Punishment, therefore, may be ineffective if the punished response is one elicited by the punishing stimulus, and avoidance learning may be ineffective if the required avoidance response is incompatible with the response elicited by shock [Mackintosh, 1974, p. 287].

The second cornerstone of competing response-elicitation theory of punishment is the assertion that punishment will be ineffective in suppressing behavior unless the reaction elicited by the punisher competes with the punished response. The large body of results showing greater suppression with response-dependent shock (as in Figure 8.6) argues against the necessity of this assumption. For it is not always clear why the reaction to punishment should be substantially different in the response-dependent and the response-independent cases. Why should competing responses occur in one case but not in the other? More importantly, how may the competing response be specified? Usually, competing responses are *not* observed. Instead, occurrence of a competing response is inferred from the absence of the punished response. Competing-response theories in effect state a relation between two dependent variables (the presumed competing response, elicited by the aversive stimulus, and the punished response) rather than directly between the independent variable (the aversive stimulus) and the dependent variable (the punished response). Thus such theories—along with other theories postulating mediating variables—tend to be less accountable to the data. Additional problems with the competing-response approach have been noted by Fantino (1973) and Mackintosh (1974). It appears that while competing-response theory may provide insight into isolated cases of response suppression, it has little utility as a general theory of punishment. Moreover, it does not provide a basis for rejecting the symmetry of reinforcement and punishment. As one of us has concluded elsewhere, "although punishment has not been studied as extensively as positive reinforcement, the evidence thus far obtained points to the likelihood that the principles that apply to positive reinforcement . . . apply to punishment as well. Indeed, the work summarized here points to a remarkable symmetry between the effects of reward and punishment" (Fantino, 1973, p. 261). Research in the subsequent five years has been consistent with this conclusion (see Farley and Fantino, 1978; Hutton and Lewis, in press).

AVERSION THERAPY

The use of punishment in therapy situations was avoided for years, largely because of the misconception that punishment did not have an enduring suppressive effect on behavior. This misconception followed the influential theorizing of Skinner (1953) and others, which was in turn based on some early empirical work (for example, Skinner, 1938; Estes, 1944). Indeed, the use of punishment in the control of behavior was thought to be ineffective, immoral, and unethical. The research summarized in this chapter, however, shows that punishment is as effective in suppressing behavior as reinforcement is in strengthening it. One of us has reviewed Skinner's position and the ethics of aversive control elsewhere (Fantino, 1973). Today the ethical use of punishment is accepted as an effective tool in voluntary therapy for behavior problems. Recall also that in Chapter 4 punishment was seen as an invaluable tool in the elimination of self-destructive behavior by autistic children. Here we will look briefly at the use of punishment in aversion therapy.

As its name implies, *aversion therapy* attempts to eliminate undesirable behavior by the use of aversive consequences such as electric shock, nausea (produced by an emetic), or time-out from positive reinforcement. As an example of the latter, *time-out rooms* were used by Wolf, Risley, and Mees (1964) to eliminate temper tantrums in an autistic child who had been emitting severe tantrums for several years. The situation was arranged so that whenever the child emitted a temper tantrum he was placed in a time-out room, where he had to remain until he was quiet for a period of time. At the outset this failed to reduce the frequency of tantrums, as the attendants offered elaborate, sympathetic explanations to the child when placing him in the room, thereby no doubt negating the effects of punishment. Indeed, when the attendants stopped offering explanations and simply placed the child in the time-out room during a tantrum, the frequency of tantrums showed a sharp decline. An important by-product of the elimination of tantrums was that other aberrant behavior could now be treated, and Wolf was able to institute a successful language program using principles of reinforcement and punishment.

In a pioneer study, Kushner (1965) treated a young man with a panty fetish (and attendant impotence) using aversion therapy. (A fetish is an habitual tendency to become sexually aroused by a certain type of inanimate object.) Kushner was aware that fetishes are rarely cured with traditional therapies. Indeed, Freud and other psychoanalytic therapists have cautioned that "cure" would result in the emergence of other, still more undesirable symptoms—such as impotence, sadism, or homosexuality. Nonetheless, Kushner decided to treat the fetish by utilizing electric shock, taking care not to allow the effects of shock to generalize to legitimate sex objects. A variety of stimuli related to panties (including thinking of panties) were paired with shock. Over the course of some 40 sessions (about three per week) the subject reported a complete cure. Indeed, by the second session there were changes in the patient's evaluation of the "attractiveness of panties." The patient remained cured over a two-year follow-up period. In addition, his impotence was cured by means of systematic desensitization (see Chapter 4). It should be added that the patient in this study sought treatment for his fetish and impotence. He was eager to be "cured." Aversion therapy is less likely to be effective with patients who are less committed to treatment, for the aversive aspects of the treatment sessions may cause the patient to avoid them.

Aversion therapy has proven to be effective in producing clear, permanent decrements in cigarette smoking, at least for many subjects (see Dericco, Brigham, and Garlington, 1977). In the study by Dericco et al. electric shocks were presented to subjects contingent upon their lighting a cigarette, holding a burning cigarette, and smoking it. Subjects whose smoking behavior was totally suppressed after this treatment were still nonsmokers at the six-month follow-up interval. Aversion therapy has been less successful in modifying the behavior of homosexuals and alcoholics.[1] A major part of the problem is that many homosexuals and alcoholics are treated in one environment but then return to the same environment in which they first acquired their habits (a problem that poses some difficulty for ex-smokers as well). Behavior modification, in general, and aversion therapy, in particular, will be effective only so long as the environment does not continue to provide reinforcement for the reacquisition and maintenance of the behavior that has been eliminated. Temper tantrums and fetishes, once eliminated, are less likely to be reinforced and reacquired. Alcohol consumption may have immediate reinforcing effects, however, which make its reacquisition more likely. With respect to homosexuality, as we noted earlier (Chapter 5), the existence of alternative (heterosexual) routes to sexual reinforcement is critical.

NEGATIVE REINFORCEMENT

Negative reinforcers are those which make responding more probable by their offset or nonoccurrence. Thus they differ from positive reinforcers in that responding is increased by their removal or prevention rather than by their presentation. While this distinction is often easy to maintain, there is actually only a fine line between positive and negative reinforcement. For example, is a swim on a blistering summer's day positively reinforcing because it is cooling (positive stimulation is added) or nega-

---

[1] For a review of the use of aversion therapy in the treatment of homosexuals, see Marks (1976). For its use in the treatment of alcoholism see Nathan (1976).

tively reinforcing because the bather feels "less hot" (negative stimulation is removed)? Is eating positively reinforcing because of the gustatory stimulation it provides or negatively reinforcing because the eater feels "less hungry"? In the laboratory studies we will be discussing, fortunately, we will be dealing with relatively straightforward cases of negative reinforcement.

When offset of an aversive stimulus is contingent upon responding, we designate the negative reinforcement operation *escape*. When nonoccurrence or postponement of an aversive stimulus is contingent upon responding, we designate the negative reinforcement operation *avoidance*. Since avoidance has probably given rise to more studies of aversive control, and certainly more theory and controversy, than punishment and escape combined, we will devote more attention to it than we did to punishment. Escape being a far simpler procedure yielding more straightforward effects, we will discuss it briefly first.

Although we will follow a long-standing tradition by treating escape and avoidance as separate problems, they can readily be viewed as points along a continuum of negative reinforcement procedures (Hineline, 1977). In escape, responding changes the situation from one containing the aversive stimulus to one without the aversive stimulus for some period of time. In avoidance, responding changes the situation from one associated with a certain rate of aversive stimulation to one with a lower rate. For both escape and avoidance procedures reduction in the rate of aversive stimulation appears to be the variable controlling responding. Escape is generally acquired more rapidly, since the change from the presence to the absence of the aversive stimulus is highly discriminable. As we shall see, avoidance procedures that enhance the discriminability of response-produced decreases in the rate of aversive stimulation are better maintained than those that do not.

ESCAPE

If a dog is placed in a cage with an electrified grid, it will readily come to jump over a hurdle or make other responses to escape the electric shock. In general, subjects learn to escape aversive stimulation about as readily as they learn to obtain positive stimulation. The ease with which the escape response is acquired depends upon the nature and intensity of aversive stimulation, the nature of the escape response, the schedule of escape responding, and the type of subject. Working in favor of rapid acquisition is the fact that aversive stimulation ordinarily generates activity (providing it is not so intense that it immobilizes the organism, in which case escape responding may not be acquired) and therefore increases the probability that the subject will happen to make the correct response. This is a particularly advantageous feature of escape learning, since it provides the experimenter with a wide array of behaviors from which to select in shaping successive approximations to the correct response. On the other hand, aversive stimuli such as shocks may elicit behaviors that are incompatible with the correct response. To the extent that the rat jumps or freezes in response to electric shock, for example, it will be unable to press a lever or turn a wheel. Thus the presence of aversive stimulation may either facilitate or retard acquisition of an escape response. Moreover, the presence of aversive stimulation makes the typical escape procedures different from typical procedures using positive reinforcement: In positive reinforcement the correct response is acquired in the absence of the reinforcer (it produces the reinforcer); in escape the correct response is acquired in the presence of the negative reinforcer (it terminates the reinforcer). Another fundamental difference between negative and positive reinforcement procedures concerns deprivation: In the typical appetitive reinforcement case, the subject is maintained at roughly the same level of deprivation throughout the testing sessions; in the typical escape and avoidance cases, when the subject makes the correct response it removes or prevents the source of motivation—that is, the aversive stimulus. These differences make it difficult to make direct comparisons between the ease of acquiring responses maintained by positive versus negative reinforcement. Despite this cautionary note, we will make a few comparisons between escape and positively reinforced behavior in presenting the basic generalizations about escape that have emerged from its study.

In large measure, and to the extent that comparison is valid, behavior maintained on an escape procedure is comparable to that maintained by positive reinforcement (see Fantino, 1973 for a review). For example, the pattern of escape responding maintained by basic schedules of negative reinforcement is similar to that maintained by basic schedules of positive reinforcement. Amount of reinforcement in escape may be thought of as degree of shock reduction (a function of shock intensity) or duration of the shock-free period. As with positive reinforcement, there appears to be a positive relation between rate or speed of escape responding and amount of (negative) reinforcement (see Fantino, 1973; de Villiers, 1977; Dinsmoor and Winograd, 1958; Winograd, 1965). However, behavior is less well maintained on intermittent schedules of escape from shock than on comparable intermittent schedules of food reinforcement, at least for rats and pigeons. An intermittent schedule of shock-escape is analogous to one of positive reinforcement except that the reinforcer is termination of shock. Thus in an FR 10 schedule of escape from electric shock, ten responses must be emitted before the shock is terminated. Hendry and Hendry (1963), with rats, and Hineline and Rachlin (1969), with pigeons, have shown that subjects would not complete FR schedules once the ratio requirement was raised to moderate levels (around FR 8 to FR 20) that readily maintain behavior with positive reinforcement. It is likely that in

Figure 8.7
"Breakfast in bed." A rat that has learned to avoid grid shock by lying on its back while pressing the response lever with its hind foot to produce food pellets. [Courtesy of Dr. Nathan Azrin.]

the intermittent escape procedures, unsuccessful escape responses are sometimes followed by shock. The more intermittent the schedule of escape, the more likely such apparent punishment is to occur and the more the escape response will be suppressed. In addition, as already mentioned, the shocks themselves may elicit responses incompatible with the sustained emission of an operant response on, say, a fixed-ratio schedule. Data (from the first author's lab) replicating Hendry and Hendry's general finding with intermittent fixed-ratio schedules of escape indicate that rats will acquire an escape response on an FR 4 but not on an FR 8. The animals acquired the habit of lying on their backs, a position that minimized the effectiveness of shock (because of the insulating properties of rat fur), rather than press the lever eight times to terminate the shock. Such lying down on the job has also been reported by Azrin and Holz and is shown in Figure 8.7.

In general, in rats and pigeons if responding must be maintained for several seconds before an escape requirement is satisfied, responding may become variable or cease altogether, probably owing to interference by competing responses elicited by the shock. Squirrel monkeys, however, are able to maintain adequate performance on FR schedules of escape (Azrin, Holz, Hake, and Ayllon, 1963). On the basis of what limited evidence is available, there is no reason to reject the null hypothesis that behavior maintained by negative reinforcement in escape procedures requires the same set of principles as behavior maintained by positive reinforcement. As we turn to avoidance procedures, however, we see that there is a diversity of opinion regarding the principles of negative reinforcement.

AVOIDANCE

There are a multitude of procedures that have been labeled avoidance procedures. The two main categories of procedures are those involving discrete trials with an exteroceptive CS signaling the opportunity to make an avoidance response (called "discrete-trial" or "discriminated avoidance"), and those without an explicit CS (called "free-operant avoidance" or "continuous avoidance" or "Sidman avoidance"). Although there are many variations of these basic procedures (a few of which we will have occasion to mention) it will suffice to understand these two clearly.

Discrete-Trial Avoidance

In discrete-trial avoidance the CS is often a light or tone (but may be any exteroceptive stimulus), the UCS is electric shock (but may be any aversive stimulus), and the response is typically a lever-press (but many responses, especially running, have been studied). Responses are only effective when a "trial" has begun—that is, after the onset of the CS. If the subject does not respond before the CS–UCS interval has elapsed, the UCS comes on. In the procedure diagramed in Figure 8.8, the CS and UCS remain on until the response is made (effectively an "escape" response), though in some experiments the UCS is short and terminates independently of responding (such a UCS is, in a sense, "inescapable"). If the subject responds before the CS–UCS interval elapses, the response both terminates the CS and prevents the onset of the UCS. In either case, CS termination constitutes the end of the trial and begins the intertrial interval (ITI). After the ITI elapses, the CS comes on again, marking the beginning of a new trial. In the diagram, three hypothetical trials are shown. An avoidance response is made only on the second trial (the fourth response shown). The second and fifth responses terminate the CS

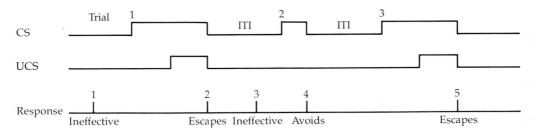

Figure 8.8
A discrete-trial avoidance procedure. Typically, the ITI (intertrial interval) is considerably longer than the CS–UCS interval. For example, the CS–UCS interval may be 5 sec and the ITI 60 sec. Owing to space considerations, a short ITI is pictured here.

and UCS on the first and third trials, respectively. The other responses are emitted during the ITI and are ineffective. While responses during the ITI are often numerous early in training, few responses are made during the ITI in later sessions (see Keehn, 1966).

In rats, avoidance learning is a surprisingly slow, tedious process, at least when the standard responses, such as lever-pressing, chain-pulling, and wheel-turning are used. Yet these same responses are readily acquired by rats with positive reinforcement or with escape. Pigeons are even more stubborn nonavoiders, especially when the avoidance response is a key-peck. The reader may suspect why rats and pigeons avoid so poorly in these situations. Before confirming this insight, however, let us see how the most common of subjects, the rat, behaves in an avoidance task in which the response to be acquired is that most common of responses (in the rat lab), the lever-press. What variables appear to determine the rat's slow rate of response acquisition in this task?

One proposal was that avoidance learning may depend on the nature of the *escape* response on trials in which shock is not avoided. Rats quickly learn to escape shock. Indeed, they may crouch over the lever through the ITI and especially through the CS–UCS interval and press the lever as soon as the shock is turned on. Reliable avoidance, however, may not occur for several hundred trials. One reason avoidance behavior may eventually emerge over the many trials is that the escape response may "move forward" in time until it occurs before the shock, and hence avoids the shock (Solomon and Brush, 1956). Two types of empirical observations reduce the plausibility of this interpretation. In one type of study the escape response is eliminated and shocks that the rat fails to avoid are brief and inescapable. If the rat typically learns the escape response, which then becomes the avoidance response, inescapable shock procedures should result in slower acquisition of avoidance than those using escapable shock. Instead, when shocks are inescapable, lever-press avoidance is acquired at a rate comparable to that seen when escape is possible (Hurwitz, 1964; D'Amato, Keller and DiCara, 1964). The second type of experiment has used different escape and avoidance responses (see Mowrer and Lamoreaux, 1946; Bolles, 1970). For example, if a rat is required to press a lever to avoid shock, its rate of avoidance will be about the same whether the escape response is also a lever-press or whether it is a different response, such as a chain-pull. Both types of experiments show that lever-press avoidance is not acquired because the escape response (nonexistent in the first set of studies and different in the second set) moves forward in time until it "emerges" as the avoidance response.

If the escape response is not critical, what is? Other likely candidates have been investigated in parametric studies and have been found wanting also. These include the durations of the CS–UCS interval and the ITI, and the intensity of the UCS. While decreasing the ITI (Pearl, 1963; Cole and Fantino, 1966) and *decreasing* shock intensity (D'Amato and Fazzaro,

1966; Bolles and Warren, 1965) both enhance the rate of avoidance conditioning with the lever-press, the effect is behaviorally unimpressive. Moreover, in other studies *increasing* shock intensity enhances lever-pressing (Riess, 1970), particularly the maintenance of an already acquired response (D'Amato, Fazzaro, and Etkin, 1967). More generally, the relation between avoidance conditioning and either ITI duration or UCS intensity may differ depending upon the response and type of organism used (see Fantino, 1973 for a review). Effects of the CS–UCS interval on avoidance are also variable and unimpressive. Moreover, the longer the CS–UCS interval, the more of an opportunity the subject has to avoid the UCS (Bitterman, 1965). This greater opportunity to respond rather than any differences in conditioning may explain the somewhat more rapid acquisition of lever-press avoidance with longer CS–UCS intervals found by Hoffman and Fleshler (1962) and Cole and Fantino (1966). In order to control for this possibility, it is therefore desirable to utilize different CS–UCS intervals in training but then to conduct tests with equal CS–UCS intervals. When this is done, no significant effects of training with longer CS–UCS intervals are evident in avoidance conditioning, with either lever-pressing (Cole and Fantino, 1966) or other responses, such as wheel-turning or running (Anderson, 1969).

In summary, by employing a large enough number of subjects it is possible to find effects of shock intensity, ITI duration, and even CS–UCS duration on rate of avoidance conditioning. The effects are small, however; even when optimal ITI and CS–UCS durations and UCS intensity values are used simultaneously, lever-press avoidance develops slowly.

The most potent variable affecting avoidance acquisition and maintenance is the *nature of the response*. Thus whereas lever-pressing, wheel-turning, and chain-pulling are acquired with difficulty, other responses are rapidly acquired. In a runway a rat is required to move from one end to the other while the CS is on in order to avoid shock. The rat typically requires only five to ten trials to learn the avoidance response in the runway. Pigeons acquire a runway response within 120 trials (Macphail, 1968), whereas they are notoriously poor at key-peck avoidance. Similarly, if a rat must jump onto a platform to avoid shock, it learns to do so within two or three trials (Baum, 1965, 1969). What do jumping and running have in common? Both involve gross bodily movements that bring the subject to a different location. Moreover, jumping and running are both frequently occurring responses to shock; lever-pressing is not.

The techniques for producing rapid avoidance learning utilize responses that have a high probability of occurring in the presence of the UCS. Not only is the lever-press unlikely to occur in response to shock, but it shares topographical features with crouching or freezing over the lever. Crouching and freezing are both high-probability responses to shock. Since the rat is in the vicinity of the lever at the end of a trial (having made a lever-press, which terminated the shock) it will probably remain there during the ITI. After several CS–UCS pairings the rat is likely to freeze when the CS starts a new trial. Freezing makes the lever-press improbable. The onset of the UCS disrupts freezing, however, allowing the UCS to be terminated swiftly. If this response *topography* analysis (developed originally by Meyer, Cho, and Wesemann, 1960) is correct, it follows that lever-press avoidance should be facilitated if freezing is somehow prevented. Two experiments support this view. In one, lever-press avoidance was enhanced when freezing was minimized by the administration of d-amphetamine (Krieckhaus, Miller, and Zimmerman, 1965). In the second, rats were required to run from one box to another before pressing the lever (Fantino, Sharp, and Cole, 1966). The results of this experiment are shown in Figure 8.9. The rats whose data are represented by curve A have only 5 seconds to run from one box to the other and press the lever after the onset of the CS (a door between the two boxes drops open). These rats acquire the lever-press rapidly, whereas control rats (whose data are represented by curve B), which begin the trial in the same box with the lever and also have 5 seconds to press it, do not. After 80 trials, the requirements for the two groups of rats were reversed. As one would expect from the results of the first part of the experiment, the rats that were now required to run acquired the lever-press rapidly. But the rats that had learned to run and press no longer pressed when only pressing was required. Rats in this condition showed no trace of their earlier learning, indicating that they had learned the specific run and lever-press sequence during the 80-trial training period.

The lever-press can apparently be facilitated by embedding the pressing requirement in a response sequence that makes freezing less likely.

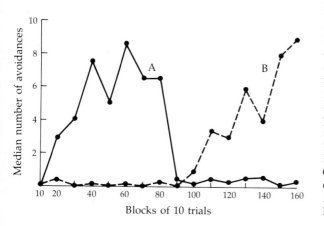

Median number of avoidances

Blocks of 10 trials

Figure 8.9
In the first 80 trials, rats in group A learn to run from one chamber to another and to press a bar, all within 5 sec, in order to avoid shock; whereas rats in group B fail to avoid shock even though they need only press the bar. When the conditions are reversed for the two groups, the results reverse also. Interestingly, rats in group A that have been successfully avoiding shock after running and pressing fail to avoid shock when they need merely press. [After E. Fantino, D. Sharp, and M. Cole, Factors facilitating lever-press avoidance. *Journal of Comparative and Physiological Psychology,* 62, 214–217. Copyright © 1966 by the American Psychological Association. Redrawn by permission.]

The fact that the attempt was successful underscores both the importance of paying attention to specific response factors and the possibility of facilitating "problem behaviors" by embedding them in a sequence of more simple, probable behaviors. Donald Baer and his associates at the University of Kansas adopted a similar strategy in getting severe retardates to emit vocal imitations, as we saw in Chapter 4.

In the typical lever-press avoidance experiment the lever must be released after a press before the next press can be effective. Thus if the subject remains crouched over the lever, in the depressed position, throughout the ITI and the subsequent CS–UCS interval, it will receive shock at the end of the CS–UCS interval. Early in training rats often display this topography, which suggests that simply holding the lever (as opposed to releasing it and pressing it) is compatible with simultaneously freezing. Supporting this suggestion are the results of J. D. Keehn and his collaborators (Keehn and Walsh 1970; Keehn, 1967), who showed that lever-holding is rapidly acquired as an avoidance response.

The importance of the response used in avoidance has also been emphasized by Robert Bolles of the University of Washington, who placed the importance of response topography within the context of evolution. Bolles (1970) advanced the premise that animals must enter their natural environments with defensive reactions already available in their behavior repertoires that are adequate for most potentially aversive or damaging situations. He predicted that avoidance responses would be rapidly acquired in the laboratory only if the required response is a part of the subject's species-specific defense reaction (SSDR). For the rat this repertoire includes fleeing, freezing, and hiding. Thus laboratory avoidance responses such as jumping out of a box or running in the shuttle box are rapidly acquired because they are part of the SSDR repertoire. On the other hand, responses such as wheel-turning, chain-pulling, and lever-pressing are not part of that repertoire and are therefore difficult to acquire.

We can accept the foregoing comments on the SSDR, of course, without concluding that all responses in the SSDR need be innate (see our discussion of the learning versus instinct issue in Chapter 9). Rather, the range of flexibility possible in avoidance is limited to a particular class of behaviors (the SSDR's). Within that class, however, flexibility exists. We maintain that those responses which are highly probable in the presence of a particular UCS (such as shock) will be more rapidly acquired than those which are less probable. Even this more conservative statement should, however, be applied with caution. It is all too easy, after the fact, to make intuitive guesses as to what is a "natural" or a "highly probable" response and what is not. What is needed is careful parametric work in which the probabilities of various responses to a given UCS are ascertained *prior* to studying the efficacy of these responses in avoidance. Although such work has not been undertaken systematically, it is likely that the more probable a response is to a noxious UCS (for a given subject) the more readily it will be acquired when its emission avoids the UCS.

If so, it would be of further interest to determine if the response hierarchy continued to predict ease of avoidance acquisition when the hierarchy was altered by experience interpolated between the initial determination of the hierarchy and avoidance training. For example, if a less probable response in the presence of the UCS were made more probable by having it produce positive reinforcement (but not affect the UCS), will this response subsequently be acquired more readily than some initially more probable ones in the avoidance test? Such evidence would underscore the role of experience in modulating the SSDR hierarchy. However, if the initially determined response hierarchy continued to be the best predictor of avoidance acquisition, the role of later experience would appear to be considerably less important. As we shall see, work in the areas of self-punitive behavior and "learned helplessness" have already implicated the central importance of experience in modulating responses to aversive stimulation.

The work on response–reinforcer interactions and avoidance learning stresses that the effectiveness of a given reinforcer (here, the avoidance of shock) is very much dependent on (hence "interacts" with) the nature of the response. This conclusion is similar to that suggested by the literature on taste aversion discussed in Chapter 10. There we will see that different (potential) punishers are differentially effective with different stimuli in suppressing eating and drinking. Whereas the taste-aversion work emphasizes stimulus–reinforcer—or stimulus–punisher—interactions, research on avoidance has emphasized response–reinforcer interactions.

Free-Operant Avoidance

The free-operant avoidance paradigm (see Figure 8.10) usually employs no exteroceptive CS. The oldest and most frequently used procedure in this paradigm was devised by Sidman (1953). In the absence of responding, brief, inescapable shocks occur periodically. The interval between shocks is known as the shock–shock ("S–S") interval. Any time a response occurs, it postpones the next shock for the duration of a second important interval: the response–shock ("R–S") interval. Assume first that the S–S and R–S intervals each equal 10 sec, as in Figure 8.10a. In the absence of responding, shocks occur every 10 sec (6 per min). Responding will tend to lower the rate of shocks received by postponing onset of the next S–S interval. How a given number of responses are distributed in time, therefore, may critically affect the degree of shock reduction. Assume first that the subject averages one response every 10 sec. If the responses are bunched together, as in Figure 8.10b, the shock rate will be near the 6 per min maximum. If the responses are spaced every 10 sec, however, as in Figure 8.10c, all shocks will be avoided. In practice, sub-

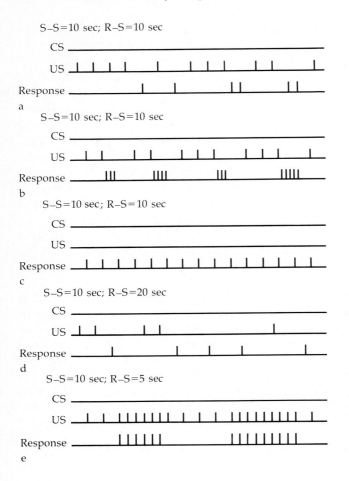

Figure 8.10
Five free-operant avoidance procedures. In (a), (b), and (c) the shock–shock (S–S) and response–shock (R–S) intervals each equal 10 sec, but the subject's hypothetical pattern of responding differs, resulting in different patterns of shock presentations. In (d) the R–S interval is increased to 20 sec, and in (e) it is reduced to 5 sec. Note that there is no CS in typical free-operant avoidance.

jects respond at a rate that results in intermediate shock rates (see Clark and Hull, 1966; Hineline, 1977). Of course, if subjects respond at a higher rate (for example, averaging one response every 1 or 2 sec) few shocks will be received even if most responses have little effect on postponing shock.

Now consider unequal R–S and S–S intervals. If we keep the S–S interval at 10 sec and increase the R–S interval to 20 sec (as in Figure 8.10d) fewer responses are needed to avoid shocks, since each response postpones the next shock by 20 sec, or twice the S–S interval. Both Sidman (1962) and Leaf (1965) have shown that acquisition of avoidance is enhanced when the R–S is greater than the S–S. Finally, the R–S interval may actually be smaller than the S–S interval, for example, S–S = 10 sec, R–S = 5 sec (as in Figure 8.10e). In this case, a response soon after a shock actually brings the next shock closer in time than if no response

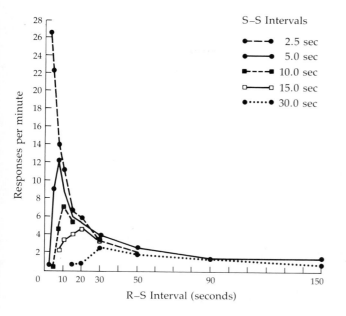

S–S Intervals

●– – –●   2.5 sec

●———●   5.0 sec

■– – –■   10.0 sec

□———□   15.0 sec

●·····●   30.0 sec

Responses per minute

R–S Interval (seconds)

Figure 8.11
Rate of avoidance responding by one rat plotted against the response–shock interval, for each of five different shock–shock intervals. [After M. Sidman, Two temporal parameters in the maintenance of avoidance behavior of the white rat. *Journal of Comparative and Physiological Psychology, 46,* 253–261. Copyright 1953 by the American Psychological Association. Redrawn by permission.]

occurred. Although subjects could, in theory, avoid all shocks by responding at least once every 5 sec, they rarely do so. Instead, as we shall see, responding is generally maintained poorly when the R–S interval is shorter than the S–S interval.[2]

Figure 8.11 shows the typical performance of a rat on a free-operant avoidance procedure with varying S–S and R–S intervals. Rate of responding (in responses per min) is plotted on the ordinate and length of the R–S interval on the abscissa. Each curve represents response rates with different S–S intervals. Note that rate of responding decreases with increasing R–S intervals as long as the R–S interval is longer than the S–S interval. When the R–S interval is significantly longer than the S–S interval, all shocks may be avoided even with low response rates. Why do response rates also decline with R–S intervals that are shorter than the S–S interval? Because responses bring impending shock potentially closer in time (as already noted, a response transfers scheduling of the next shock from the S–S interval to the R–S interval; thus a response soon after a shock actually reduces time to the next scheduled shock). Of course, all

---

[2]Some of the major variations of the free-operant avoidance procedure we have outlined here include cases in which exteroceptive stimuli are available and correlated with impending (but still avoidable) shocks and those in which the shocks occur irregularly with respect to time (variable rather than fixed S–S intervals). We will discuss important experiments employing each of these features when we consider the reinforcer in avoidance behavior (for example, Sidman, 1955; Herrnstein and Hineline, 1966).

shocks may be avoided if the subject always emits a response before the R–S interval time expires. With short R–S intervals, however, this is a stringent requirement; thus subjects' response rates go down and shocks are often arranged by the longer S–S interval. The decline of response rates when the R–S interval is shorter than the S–S interval may be better understood if we realize that such a procedure actually involves a type of delayed punishment. This follows from the fact that some responses actually make shocks occur more immediately than they would in the absence of responding. Consider the extreme case of an R–S interval equal to zero. This constitutes a normal punishment procedure: responses produce immediate shock. Obviously, in this case no responding should occur.

The decline in response rates for a given R–S interval when the S–S interval is increased is straightforward: The longer the S–S interval the lower the response rate necessary to reduce shock density. When the S–S interval is zero, shock is presented continuously in the absence of responding. By responding, the subject escapes the shock for the length of the R–S interval. Unlike typical escape procedures, however, this procedure permits the subject to avoid all shocks by always responding before the next R–S interval elapses.

Having discussed the basic factors governing avoidance responding in both discrete-trial and free-operant avoidance procedures, we turn next to the interesting question of what maintains responding in such procedures. What is the reinforcer in avoidance? This question is important not only because it is so fundamental to an appreciation of avoidance but also because it has provided an arena of controversy into which proponents of diverse theoretical views and traditions have eagerly entered. In attempting to answer this question, we will have occasion to discuss some of the more important research employing each of the main classes of avoidance procedures introduced in this section.

The Reinforcer in Avoidance

Given that organisms do learn avoidance, what is reinforcing their avoidance responding? We will consider three plausible—and *not* mutually exclusive—hypotheses around which avoidance theory has revolved. After having considered these hypotheses and the historically important research evaluating them we will be in a better position to frame an answer to the question of what reinforces avoidance. Two of the three hypotheses stipulate that a reduction in fear is critical.[3] One hypo-

---

[3]Such hypotheses are somewhat impractical since they rely on a mediating variable ("fear") and since fear is not a unitary entity (recall our discussion of conditioned suppression). Nonetheless, at least one of these hypotheses has been highly influential in generating research and theory in avoidance. Hence they deserve our attention here. Moreover, an impractical theory is not necessarily a wrong one!

thesis—which we will call the *apparatus-fear hypothesis*—attempts to explain why typical avoidance learning is so difficult under some conditions as well as why it finally does occur. According to the apparatus-fear hypothesis, the shock apparatus is highly aversive and fear-inducing. With some procedures, such as chain-pull or lever-press avoidance, even when the organism avoids shock it remains in the aversive chamber. Hence little decrement in fear results and the reinforcement is relatively small. In one-way shuttle box avoidance or in ledge-jump procedures, however, an avoidance response not only prevents the shock but also removes the organism from the area where shocks are administered. Hence there should be a large decrement in fear and a relatively large reinforcing effect.

A second hypothesis, also involving fear-reduction, is the *two-factor theory of avoidance* (see Mowrer, 1947; Dinsmoor, 1954). According to two-factor theory, the reinforcer for avoidance is the termination of the CS. The CS becomes aversive since it is paired with the UCS on trials when the organism fails to avoid the UCS. Thus in the typical case involving a light CS and a shock UCS, light–shock pairings (on nonavoidance trials) result in the conditioning of fear to the CS. This classical conditioning component constitutes one factor in avoidance. When the avoidance response is emitted, it is reinforced by the termination of the CS. This operant conditioning component constitutes the second factor in avoidance. According to two-factor theory, then, subjects are escaping the fear-inducing CS rather than avoiding the UCS.

A third hypothesis stipulates that the absence of the UCS (UCS avoidance) reinforces avoidance. A more general version of this hypothesis, termed *shock-frequency reduction theory* (since shock is the UCS typically used in avoidance research) states that reinforced responses are those which reduce the frequency of shock (see Sidman, 1962; Herrnstein and Hineline, 1966), particularly shocks scheduled to occur immediately.

The reader might consider which of the hypotheses is most promising and how each might be tested. If the apparatus-fear hypothesis were correct, we would expect that rats would have less trouble acquiring lever-press avoidance if subjects were permitted to leave the apparatus following an avoidance response. Wahlsten, Cole, Sharp, and Fantino (1968) tested this notion. Avoidance responses not only prevented shock but also opened a door allowing the rats to enter an adjacent "safe" chamber. At the end of the intertrial interval the rat was removed from the safe box and returned to the shock box for the next trial. Rats in this experimental group acquired the avoidance response much more rapidly than those from a control group, which could not escape the shock chamber. Thus far, the results look very good for the apparatus-fear hypothesis. The two groups differed, however, not only in terms of whether escape from apparatus cues was possible but also in terms of the amount of handling required to return them to the shock chamber. A second control group was also not allowed to escape from the shock chamber; these animals were, however, handled prior to the onset of a trial in the same way as rats in the experimental group (experimental subjects, of course, had to be handled in order to remove them from the safe box and return them to the shock box at the start of a trial). Subjects in the handled control group also displayed rapid avoidance, demonstrating that handling a subject immediately prior to the start of a trial greatly improves avoidance performance. This result is compatible with the SSDR and response topography notions, considered earlier, since handling is likely to disrupt freezing. Thus the study provided no positive evidence for the apparatus-fear hypothesis.

More recently, however, Baron, DeWaard, and Lipson (1977) have provided such evidence. They demonstrated that avoidance responding is enhanced when responding not only prevents shock but also allows rats access to a safe place (in this study, a shelf introduced into the apparatus during shock-free periods subsequent to an avoidance response). Baron et al. note that their results support a conditioned-reinforcement interpretation. In introducing their experiment the authors note, "if reductions in shock density are the sole basis for the reinforcement of avoidance behavior, there is little reason to expect different outcomes when shock-free periods are spent inside and outside the aversive environment. By comparison, if termination of stimuli correlated with shocks is reinforcing, then escape from the aversive environment should add to the reinforcing potential of shock-free periods" (p. 40). Baron et al.'s results support the notion that stimuli associated with a decrease in shock density acquire conditioned reinforcing properties. Thus the poor avoidance learning shown by rats in the typical lever-press situation may be attributed in large part to the aversiveness of the shock situation and to the similarity of conditions prevailing before and after successful avoidance responding. It should be cautioned, however, that this conclusion must be regarded as tentative since there are alternative interpretations of Baron et al.'s results. In the first place, the study did not control for the possible reinforcing potency of jumping on the ledge, independent of the avoidance contingency. Probably a more serious reservation hinges on analysis of the avoidance response in rats that did and those that did not have the shelf to jump to. The effective avoidance response when the shelf was available was the lever-press plus jumping, but only the lever-press when the shelf was unavailable. Since jumping is believed to be part of the rat's SSDR to shock, the opportunity to make this response may have facilitated lever-pressing. Recall that Fantino et al. (1966) found that running facilitated lever-press avoidance (Figure 8.9), although in that case running *preceded* lever-pressing.

In most experiments with lever-press avoidance, subjects are not permitted to escape from the shock apparatus when they successfully avoid shock. Hence most studies of the reinforcer in avoidance have assessed the role played by CS-termination (implicated by two-factor theory) and UCS-avoidance (implicated by shock-frequency reduction theory).[4] It is difficult to evaluate whether CS-termination or UCS-avoidance is more critical, since in the typical avoidance procedure responses both terminate the CS and enable the organism to avoid the UCS. The first experiments to pit these two variables against one another compared the performance of rats that could avoid the UCS but could not terminate the CS with the performance of rats that could terminate the CS but not avoid the UCS (Kamin, 1956, 1957). The results from each of these two groups were compared with those from a "normal" avoidance group (for which responses both terminated the CS *and* avoided the UCS) and from a classical conditioning group (in which responses were totally ineffective). The principal findings are shown in Figure 8.12. Simply terminating the CS was not an effective consequence for maintaining avoidance responding, a finding inconsistent with the predictions of two-factor theory. Avoiding the UCS, however, did maintain considerable avoidance responding, partially supporting the shock frequency-reduction theory. We say "partially" because the degree of avoidance maintained by rats in the "avoid UCS" group was far less than for rats in the "normal" group for which responses terminated the CS and avoided the UCS. We will return to this important point shortly. A similar experiment was reported a decade later by Bolles, Stokes, and Younger (1966). These researchers replicated Kamin's basic finding that UCS-avoidance was the critical factor maintaining avoidance responding and that CS-termination alone produced only a small (but statistically significant) effect.[5]

A final point about the data in Figure 8.12 should be noted. While early in training the termination of the CS appears to be more effective than the

---

[4]Two-factor theory has much in common with the apparatus-fear hypothesis, of course, since both stress postresponse stimulus changes and the importance of terminating aversive stimuli. Whereas the apparatus-fear hypothesis implicates general cues, however, two-factor theory isolates the role of the CS.

[5]Two-factor theory was, however, so strong in the 1950s that the results shown in Figure 8.12 were actually used to support the theory! Proponents of two-factor theory emphasized the early learning shown by the "terminate CS" group. Today we are most impressed with the small size of this effect and its transience. Note that within 70 trials performance of the "terminate CS" group has declined to the point where it approximates that for the classical conditioning control group, which neither escapes the CS nor avoids the UCS. It should be added, however, that the lack of avoidance in the "terminate CS" group does not by itself seriously weaken two-factor theory. On the contrary, on trials in which the subject responds, shock occurs in the absence of the CS, thereby disrupting the CS–UCS pairings (the correlation of CS *onset* and the subsequent occurrence of shock remains intact, however). Consequently, the continued presence of the CS may not be an aversive stimulus. This counterargument is weakend, however, by results discussed later in this section suggesting that the main function of the CS is that of a discriminative stimulus—for the avoidance response—rather than that of a negative reinforcer (whose termination would be reinforcing, as required by two-factor theory). In any case, the results in Figure 8.12 support shock-frequency reduction theory over two-factor theory because of the successful avoidance in the "avoid UCS" group.

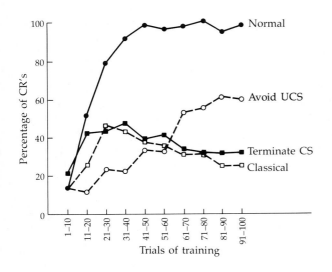

Figure 8.12
Percentage of conditioned responses (CR's) in an avoidance experiment as a function of training trials for four groups of rats distinguished by the effects of their CR's as follows: "avoid UCS" avoided shock (UCS), but did not terminate the CS; "terminate CS" did not avoid the UCS, but did terminate the CS; "classical" did neither, that is, responding was ineffective; "normal" avoided the UCS and terminated the CS. [After Kamin, 1957.]

avoidance of the UCS, the situation is progressively reversed. Thus these data describe a shift of controlling relationships as training progresses.

These experiments, as well as others, suggest that avoidance is maintained by UCS-avoidance, as shock-frequency reduction theory requires. One serious problem remains, however, before we can conclude with confidence that UCS-avoidance is an important variable having behaviorally impressive (as opposed to merely statistically significant) effects on avoidance learning: Organisms permitted to avoid the UCS but not terminate the CS are much poorer avoiders than organisms permitted to do both (as was clear from Figure 8.12). An ingenious study by D'Amato, Fazzaro, and Etkin (1968) solved this problem by demonstrating that CS-termination reinforces avoidance only to the extent that CS-termination functions as a cue for UCS-avoidance. D'Amato et al. arranged for a cue other than CS-termination to occur immediately after a successful avoidance response. For example, if the CS was a set of three small lights, the cue following a successful avoidance response was a burst of white noise; for other subjects, the CS was noise and the cue for successful avoidance was the set of lights. This cue was never paired with the UCS and therefore would not be a fear-eliciting stimulus. The CS was paired with the UCS on trials without a successful avoidance, but on those trials, of course, the cue for successful avoidance did not occur. At the same time, avoidance responses did not terminate the CS, which remained in effect for a time equal to the CS–UCS interval. D'Amato et al.'s rats readily acquired and maintained avoidance responding when it produced the cue, suggesting that the facilitation of avoidance by CS-termination results from its correlation with the avoidance of shock. Stated another way, the response-produced decrease in shock frequency is made more discriminable by CS-termination.

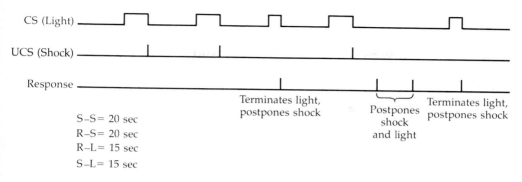

CS (Light)

UCS (Shock)

Response

Terminates light,
postpones shock

Postpones
shock
and light

Terminates light,
postpones shock

S–S = 20 sec
R–S = 20 sec
R–L = 15 sec
S–L = 15 sec

Figure 8.13
Free-operant avoidance with a warning light (CS).

Similar results have been reported by Bolles and Grossen (1969).[6] Taken together, these results allow us to dismiss the traditional version of two-factor avoidance theory. Prior work pointing to the reinforcing function of CS-termination reflected primarily the fact that CS-termination was an effective cue for the avoidance of shock. CS-termination may also be associated with fear-reduction, as traditional two-factor theory requires, but this possible role of CS-termination does not appear to be important for the acquisition or maintenance of avoidance responding.

A similar conclusion applies to studies of free-operant avoidance. For example, experiments by Sidman and his colleagues (see Sidman, 1955; Sidman, 1957; Sidman and Boren, 1957a, 1957b; Ulrich, Holz, and Azrin, 1964; Grabowski and Thompson, 1972) have investigated the aversiveness of preshock cues or "warning stimuli" preceding shocks in modified free-operant avoidance procedures. Recall that we introduced the standard free-operant avoidance procedure as one not involving any exteroceptive CS. See Figure 8.10. In Sidman (1955), the S–S and R–S intervals were each 20 sec, but a 5-sec warning light preceded each shock. This light could itself be postponed by a response for 15 sec. Thus the "response-light interval" (R–L) was 15 sec. In the absence of a response the light came on 15 sec following a shock; thus the "shock-light interval" (S–L) was also 15 sec. The procedure is diagrammed in Figure 8.13. Note

---

[6]Additional results suggest that stimuli correlated with the absence of shock—or "safety signals"—reinforce avoidance (see Denny and Weisman, 1964; Denny, 1971; Dinsmoor and Sears, 1973). Recent extensions of two-factor theory stress the role of these safety signals rather than CS-termination (Dinsmoor, 1977). For our purposes there is little to distinguish such two-factor theories from shock-frequency reduction theory in that one stresses the onset of a stimulus correlated with the absence of shock and the other the absence of shock itself. In practice the two views become virtually indistinguishable and we shall not attempt to distinguish them here. The important point is that the safety signal, like CS-termination, probably enhances avoidance acquisition by delineating the shock-free period, making it more discriminable.

that in the absence of responding, light onset occurs 15 sec after the prior shock; 5 sec later a brief shock is delivered, terminating the light and beginning the new S–L and S–S intervals. If responding occurs only after light onset, a response terminates the light, postpones the shock, and begins the new R–L and R–S intervals. But a response during the S–L and R–L interval could postpone the warning stimulus (and postpone the shock as well, of course). If the warning stimulus were sufficiently aversive, we would expect subjects to avoid it. The cats and rats in Sidman's study avoided it infrequently, however. Instead, the probability of a response in the 5 sec prior to a scheduled light onset was quite low relative to the probability of a response during the light.

Both Field and Boren (1963), studying rats, and Grabowski and Thompson (1972) studying monkeys, employed a different type of procedure, which sheds additional light on the role of the warning stimulus in free-operant avoidance. Their procedure involved a series of warning stimuli (in different conditions, either visual, auditory, or both) that were progressively correlated with shock delivery. For example, in one case eleven stimuli were differentially correlated in time and space with shock, as shown in Figure 8.14. When the pilot light most distant from the response lever was lit, shock was 100 sec away. As successive 10-sec segments transpired without a response, successive lights came on, each bearing a progressively closer temporal relationship to shock. The eleventh light—directly above the response lever—was lit during a 5-sec preshock interval. In the absence of responding, shocks occurred every 5 sec and the eleventh light remained on continuously. Each response cumulated 10 sec of shock-free time (up to 100 sec) and turned on the

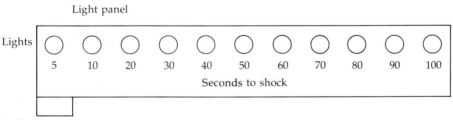

Figure 8.14
The procedure used by Field and Boren (1963) to illuminate the role played by the warning stimulus in free-operant avoidance. When the light most distant from the response lever was lit, shock was 100 sec away. As successive 10-sec segments transpired without a response, successive lights came on, each bearing a closer temporal relationship to shock. The eleventh light (directly above the response lever) was lit during a 5-sec preshock interval. Each response increased the temporal distance to shock by 10 sec and moved the light to one position further from the response lever. In the absence of responding (in the presence of the preshock light), shocks occurred every 5 sec.

light correlated with the temporal distance from shock actually in effect at that instant. Thus the subjects could effectively "adjust" their distance from shock. If the stimuli close to shock were aversive, subjects might be expected to respond so as to remain in the presence of stimuli relatively distant from shock—that is, the first few lights (those farthest from the response lever). If the lights merely served a discriminative function, setting the occasion for avoidance responses, however, the subjects might be expected to remain in the presence of stimuli relatively close to shock— that is, the last few lights. The results favored the latter alternative: subjects tended to remain 30 to 50 sec away from shock. In a control condition in which the schedule was identical but no warning stimuli were available, subjects typically kept shock 90 to 100 sec away. Thus it appears that the importance of warning stimuli in maintaining avoidance responding rests more with their discriminative function than with any aversive role they may also play.

If the role of the warning stimulus is indeed primarily a discriminative one, then the more salient or discriminable the warning stimulus the closer to shock subjects might permit themselves to remain. Just the opposite might be expected if the primary function of the warning stimulus is reinforcing avoidance, through acquired aversiveness. Field and Boren (1963) varied the discriminability of their stimuli and found that with more highly discriminable stimuli responding shifted so that the rats remained in the presence of stimuli more closely correlated with shock. This result supported the view that the primary function of the warning stimulus is a discriminative one rather than a reinforcing one.

What if responding to the preshock stimulus cannot postpone shock? If the primary role of warning stimuli is a discriminative one, responding in this case should extinguish and avoidance responding should occur prior to light onset. Sidman and Boren (1957a) did such an experiment and obtained the expected results: responding was maintained during the dark—a discriminative stimulus for shock postponement—but only at very low levels during the light—a warning stimulus for impending unavoidable shock. All of the results discussed, then, support the conclusion that warning stimuli serve primarily as discriminative stimuli for responding to avoid shock. Results from other experiments (for example, Sidman and Boren, 1957b) are also consistent with this conclusion (see Hineline, 1977, for an excellent review).

Shock-Frequency Reduction Theory

If shock-frequency reduction theory is correct, responding will be strengthened as long as it reduces the frequency of shocks received to a level below that received in the absence of responding. The avoidance procedures we have been dealing with thus far represent an end point on the frequency-reduction continuum: in the absence of an avoidance response, shock occurs with a probability equal to 1.0; an avoidance response reduces the probability of shock to zero. The probabilities of receiving shock following a response, or in the absence of a response, may assume any value between 0.0 and 1.0, however, as illustrated in the following table (see also Gibbon, Berryman, and Thompson, 1974).

	A	B	C
Probability of shock if response	0.0	1.0	X
Probability of shock if no response	1.0	0.0	Y

In the typical discrete-trial avoidance procedure (A), the probability of shock given a response during the CS—P[S|R]—is 0.0, while shock is certain if the response is not made, that is, the probability of shock in the absence of a response—P[S|$\overline{\text{R}}$]—is 1.0. Logically, these probabilities may be independently varied between 0.0 and 1.0. Another extreme point is that described in (B), where the probabilities are reversed: here a response *produces* the shock, which otherwise does not occur. This situation is an example of punishment: avoidance of shock depends on the absence of response. What if both P[S|R] and P[S|$\overline{\text{R}}$] equal 1.0? Then shock is certain regardless of what the subject does. When both P[S|R] and P[S|$\overline{\text{R}}$] are 0.0, shock never occurs. According to shock-frequency reduction theory, responding should be maintained as long as P[S|R] < P[S|$\overline{\text{R}}$], or whenever X < Y in (C) in the table. For only then does responding reduce shock frequency. This proposition has been supported empirically in several experiments beginning with the important study by Herrnstein and Hineline (1966).

Rats in Herrnstein and Hineline's study could respond to reduce shock frequency, the overall rate of shocks per time. In the absence of responding, shocks occurred at one rate (for example, 9 shocks per minute). A response switched the rat to a lower rate of shock (for example, 6 shocks per minute) for a period of time, after which the higher shock rate was reinstated.[7] The subjects maintained responding even when the shock schedules produced shock frequencies as close as 9 versus 6 shocks per minute. Importantly, response rates increased as the difference in shock frequencies increased; that is, the greater the shock-frequency reduction, the higher the rate of responding. When responding produced no reduction in shock frequency, it extinguished. In other words, responding was maintained only when it was correlated with a reduction in shock-frequency. These results parallel those in which responding is reinforced when it is correlated with positive reinforcement (Chapters 4 and 6) and comparable findings in the classical conditioning literature (Chapter 3).

---

[7] Actually, transfer to the higher shock rate occurred whenever a shock was received on the low-rate schedule.

Two interesting features of Herrnstein and Hineline's procedure should be pointed out: (1) no exteroceptive stimuli indicated which shock schedule was in effect, and (2) the shocks were delivered randomly in time. Thus it is unclear how two-factor theory could account for avoidance responding in Herrnstein and Hineline's experiment. Specifically, there is no CS whose termination could have reinforced avoidance. Even covert (internal) stimuli, related to the passage of time, cannot be readily invoked, since shocks occurred randomly in time (but see Dinsmoor, 1977, for a different point of view). Instead, Herrnstein and Hineline's results provide direct support for the view that shock-frequency reduction reinforces avoidance.

The shock-frequency reduction theory of avoidance behavior has been supported in several other studies (for example, deVilliers, 1972, 1974; Clark and Hull, 1966; see Hineline, 1977, as well). One appealing aspect of the theory is that it permits us to describe the relation between response frequency and reinforcement in the same way whether reinforcement is positive or negative. Just as rate of responding is a positive function of rate of positive reinforcement, so rate of avoidance responding is a positive function of rate of negative reinforcement.

This symmetry between the effects of positive and negative reinforcement is the second important symmetry we have encountered in this chapter. Recall that punishment and reinforcement have symmetrical effects on behavior, though opposite in sign. Taken together, these symmetries mean that the effect of either positive or negative reinforcement should be equivalent but opposite to that of punishment. That is, reinforcers, whether positive or negative, make behavior more probable; punishers make behavior less probable.

Recall that in discussing positive reinforcement in Chapters 6 and 7 we noted that events occurring soon after a response have disproportionately greater effects on responding than those occurring later. For example, in studies of choice between interval schedules, short interreinforcement times enhance preference above and beyond their contribution to rate of reinforcement. Thus a VI 15-sec schedule is strongly preferred to an FI 15-sec (Herrnstein, 1964b) and a mixed FR 1 FR 99 schedule (in which the FR 1 and FR 99 are equiprobable) is preferred to a simple FR 50, or even an FR 25 (Fantino, 1967). Indeed, in Fantino's study the fixed FR had to be lowered to FR 10 before pigeons reliably chose it over the mixed FR 1 FR 99. Equally striking are the results from studies of self-control: Immediate reward is generally preferred to delayed reward even if the overall rate of reinforcement is higher in the delayed case (see Chapter 7). If positive and negative reinforcement are symmetrical, immediate negative reinforcement should also have disproportionately greater effects on responding than delayed negative reinforcement. Here, too, by disproportionate effects we mean effects that are larger than expected simply on the basis of relative shock-frequency reduction. For example, suppose response A delays shock for 10 sec, following which five unavoidable shocks are presented (one every 2 sec), while response B is followed by an immediate shock but avoids the five subsequent shocks. If neither response is made, all six shocks occur. This example pits immediate negative reinforcement (available only by making response A) against shock-frequency reduction (five shocks in 20 sec avoided by response B but only one shock in 20 sec avoided by response A). While the precise experiment suggested by this example has not been done, several experiments by Philip Hineline and his colleagues at Temple University (see Hineline, 1977) suggest that response A will be maintained but *not* response B. Moreover, response B will not be maintained even if it is the only response available (Lambert, Bersh, Hineline, and Smith, 1973). In general, shock-delay is more potent than shock-frequency reduction in maintaining responding. Indeed, as our example and the results of Lambert et al. suggest, a response will not be effectively maintained by shock-frequency reduction if the same response also produces an immediate shock.[8] This situation is analogous to that with positive reinforcement: Immediate reinforcers (or, more generally, short response–reinforcer intervals) enhance responding above and beyond their contribution to rate of reinforcement.

The Role of Pavlovian Processes in Avoidance

As we have amply documented, traditional two-factor theory no longer provides an adequate description of the acquisition and maintenance of avoidance responding. The important role of the CS appears to be that of a discriminative stimulus rather than a negatively reinforcing stimulus. We have seen that avoidance responding will be acquired and maintained even in the absence of a CS and when shocks are presented randomly in time. Moreover, Taub and Berman (1963, 1968) have shown that monkeys will learn and maintain a lever-press response in a free-operant avoidance task even in the absence of proprioceptive and exteroceptive feedback, which presumably mediate fear and its reduction. These results are also difficult to reconcile with traditional two-factory theory. Finally, in reviewing the avoidance literature, Rescorla and Solomon (1967) acknowledge that the avoidance response can occur in the absence of measurable fear. In their important review, Rescorla and Solomon argued that while Pavlovian conditioning of internal events, such as fear, was not *necessary* for avoidance conditioning, fear and other internal events, such as hope and frustration, may nonetheless have potent effects on instrumental responding. This statement is one of a *weak two-factor theory*.

---

[8]Such a response is analogous to a self-control response in that the response produces an immediate cost but long-term benefits (see Chapter 7).

Without getting embroiled in the question of internal events as response mediators, we readily agree that Pavlovian processes have clear effects on instrumentally conditioned behavior, in general, and in avoidance responding, in particular. Thus while Pavlovian processes do not play the central role in avoidance required by two-factor theory, it is nonetheless possible to show that they may have an effect on avoidance responding. For example, both Rescorla (1966), studying dogs in the shuttle box, and Weisman and Litner (1969), studying rats in a wheel-turning task, assessed the effects of superimposing conditioned stimuli (CS's) bearing different relationships to shock on a baseline task involving unsignaled shock avoidance. In both studies a positive CS (positively correlated with the shock by prior CS–UCS pairings), a negative CS (negatively correlated with shock in that subjects were exposed to each but never together), and a neutral CS (the UCS was just as likely to occur during the CS as during its absence) were used. The results from both studies show that the positive CS sharply enhanced avoidance responding, the negative CS sharply suppressed avoidance responding, and the neutral CS had no effect. Moreover, although a negative CS *lowers* rate of avoidance responding, when presented noncontingently, Weisman and Litner went on to show that their negative CS (a 5-sec tone correlated with the omission of shock) would *reinforce* appropriate rates of responding when its presentation was made contingent on either high or low rates of responding (DRH and DRL schedules, respectively—see Chapter 4). These results are shown in Figure 8.15. Note that when a high response rate was required to produce the tone, response rates almost doubled; when a low response rate was required, however, response rates were halved. Thus the tone, a *conditioned inhibitor*, in Pavlovian terms, was an effective reinforcer.

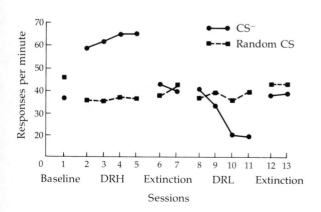

Figure 8.15
The effect of presenting a stimulus (CS⁻), previously established as a signal for the omission of shock, contingent upon different patterns of free-operant avoidance responding. On a DRH schedule the stimulus increased the rate of responding; on a DRL schedule it decreased the rate of responding. [After R. G. Weisman and J. S. Litner, The course of Pavlovian excitation and inhibition of fear in rats. *Journal of Comparative and Physiological Psychology,* 69, 667–672. Copyright © 1969 by the American Psychological Association. Redrawn by permission.]

The reader may appreciate the methodological elegance of Weisman and Litner's study. Had they tested for a reinforcement effect merely by employing a DRH schedule, critics could argue that any rate enhancement was due, not to the contingency between response rates and the CS, but to excitatory effects of the CS presentations. Similarly, had they used only a DRL schedule, any rate suppression could have been attributed to the CS presentations, which had been shown to lower response rates when presented noncontingently. Since both enhancement and suppression were demonstrated, however, depending on the direction of the contingency, the importance of the contingency was isolated. Thus we may conclude that a stimulus correlated with the omission of shock may reinforce responding when it is contingent upon responding and will depress responding when presented noncontingently. It should be cautioned, however, that the effects of cues superimposed on avoidance responding after Pavlovian conditioning may be transitory and inconsistent across studies. Pomerleau (1970), for example, showed that, depending on the duration of a cue paired with shock, either enhancement or suppression of ongoing responding may occur.

We have seen previously that shock-frequency reduction is the principal reinforcer of avoidance behavior and that the termination of the warning stimulus plays only an indirect role in maintaining avoidance. In both discrete trials and free-operant avoidance, the CS is an S^D for responding to avoid the UCS, while CS-termination is a cue that the UCS has indeed been avoided. The results reviewed in this section suggest further that given an ongoing rate of avoidance responding, a cue correlated with UCS omission may affect responding in a complex way. When the cue is presented noncontingently, responding will be depressed (presumably since avoidance responding is unnecessary—that is, not reinforced—during the CS^-); when presented contingently, however, the CS^- reinforces responding. Such results show that Pavlovian conditioning can affect avoidance responding. Its effects are not usually apparent in the typical avoidance experiment, presumably since responding is primarily under control of shock-frequency reduction. When shock-frequency reduction is being manipulated, its effects may mask any due to ongoing Pavlovian processes. Moreover, as we have indicated, the role of Pavlovian processes in avoidance may be quite complex.

In summary, shock-frequency reduction theory emerges as the best account of avoidance behavior among those considered. It does not tell the whole story, however, as the results of Baron et al. (1977) and others reviewed in the prior sections demonstrate. Specifically, it is necessary to consider response-produced stimulus changes as well as response-produced decrements in shock frequency (Hineline, 1977). The emphasis placed by the older avoidance theories on CS-termination and apparatus-fear reduction had an important grain of truth: *Stimulus changes correlated with situation transitions to lower densities of shock will also reinforce responding by enhancing the discriminability of response-produced decrements in shock frequency.*

Extinction of Avoidance and Self-Punitive Behavior

Under certain conditions avoidance behavior is extremely resistant to extinction (see Solomon, Kamin, and Wynne, 1953). Such resistance is at times so thorough that Solomon et al. (1953), studying dogs, postulated a type of "traumatic avoidance learning" in which changes in behavior are largely irreversible. Moreover, animals that have acquired an avoidance or escape response may continue to emit the response even when shocks are made response-dependent—when they occur if and only if the response is made. This effect has been called *self-punitive behavior* and the *vicious-circle effect*, for reasons we will discuss shortly. Such self-punitive behavior has been demonstrated after discrete-trial negative reinforcement procedures (see Brown, 1969) and after free-operant negative reinforcement procedures (see Byrd, 1969) in a large number of experiments with several different organisms (including cats, goldfish, rats, squirrel monkeys, and humans). This work underscores the central importance of previously acquired responses on subsequent behavior and may be relevant to self-punitive (masochistic) behavior in humans (Rose and Fantino, 1977). We begin our discussion of self-punitive behavior with two prototype studies, one using free-operant avoidance and the other discrete-trial escape.

Byrd (1969) studied two cats in a free-operant avoidance procedure in which the R–S interval was 60 sec and the S–S interval 5 sec. After the cats acquired a rate of avoidance responding sufficiently high so that they rarely received shocks, the experimenter *added* response-independent shocks every 15 min (irrespective of the cats' performance). Thus an FT 15-min schedule of shock presentations was now superimposed on the basic avoidance schedule.[9] The next step was removing the avoidance schedule, leaving only the FT 15-min shock presentations. Now, of course, the cats' responses were wholly ineffective. Nonetheless, response rates increased for each of the cats. Following 33 sessions of exposure to the FT 15-min schedule, the schedule was changed to FI 15-min. Now all shock presentations were response-dependent. The subject would not get shocked if it did not respond. Both cats maintained responding, however, producing close to the maximal rate of shocks possible. Similar results have been reported by Byrd (1972), McKearney (1968, 1970), Morse and Kelleher (1970), Stretch, Orloff, and Dalrymple (1968) and many others. While the necessary and sufficient conditions for producing behavior whose only consequence is painful electric shock remain

---

[9]Recall that FT stands for "fixed-time" and that an FT schedule is the same as an FI schedule except that it is a response-independent schedule of reinforcement.

uncertain, it is clear that the organism's experimental history is critical. Most studies have employed a history of avoidance responding, as in Byrd's study. In all cases, it appears that training procedures must either generate levels of responding high enough to compete with the suppressive effects of punishment (once response-contingent shocks are introduced) or they must generate patterned responding that obscures the correlation of periods of not-responding and subsequent periods of shock reduction (Hutchinson, 1977). Self-punitive behavior in the free-operant case may be better understood by analyzing the factors controlling self-punitive behavior in the simpler discrete-trials case.

Discrete-trial experiments on self-punitive behavior after negative reinforcement generally begin with placing the subject, usually a rat, in a start box above an electrified runway. In training, when the subject is dropped onto the runway, the grate is electrified and the rat must run the length of the runway to a "safe box" in order to escape shock. Following training, the rats are divided into two groups, each of which receives extinction trials. For subjects in one group (the "regular extinction" group) the runway is not electrified. For subjects in the other group (the "punished extinction" group), however, the midsection of the runway is electrified. If these subjects remain in the start box, they do not receive shock. If they traverse the runway, however, they do receive shock until they reach the safe box. Whereas subjects in the regular extinction group stop running after very few trials, those in the punished extinction group continue to run rapidly for many trials.

According to the *vicious-circle hypothesis*, such self-punitive behavior results from fear responses that are conditioned to the start box and runway cues (Mowrer, 1947). In the punished extinction condition the subjects become fearful when dropped into the start box, they run and quickly re-experience painful shock, and then escape to the safe box. The fear motivates the running, the running produces shock, and the shock strengthens the fear in a "vicious circle" (Brown, 1969). An alternative hypothesis has eschewed reliance on fear as an intervening variable in interpreting self-punitive behavior. The *discrimination hypothesis*, framed by Church (1963) and Tinsley and Renner (1975), among others, states that resistance to extinction will be enhanced the greater the similarity between conditions in pretraining (acquisition) and testing (extinction). This similarity may be manipulated in at least two general ways: by changing the degree of contingency between the response and its consequences (as in the change from avoidance to either punishment or response-independent shocks) and by changing the frequency or location of events (as by altering the rate of shock or by delivering shock in the goal box instead of the runway). For example, since the delivery of shock in the runway during extinction makes the situation similar to that in acquisition, behavior (here, running) acquired during acquisition is likely to recur. But once running occurs, it is reinforced by shock offset (upon goal-box entry). Two procedural features in concert with the similarity of events in acquisition and extinction conspire to enhance the likelihood that the running response will be maintained (Fowler, 1971; Mackintosh, 1974). In the first place, the response (running) that escapes the shock in extinction is identical to, or at least compatible with, the response that is punished (running). Thus the same response is both punished and reinforced on each trial—with reinforcement (escape) occurring last. More importantly, the studies that have reported the self-punitive effect have applied a shock of fixed duration to a section of the alley. Thus, given that the subject runs, the faster it runs the more rapidly it will traverse the offending section and escape from shock. Not only is running—the response required in acquisition—still reinforced, but the subject tends to receive greater punishment by slowing down. Indeed, studies that have employed fixed-duration shocks—in which the subject's behavior cannot affect the shock received once the shock has begun—have found that shocks suppress running (see Campbell, Smith, and Misanin, 1966).

Finally, other studies have manipulated variables that affect the similarity of acquisition and extinction. According to the discrimination hypothesis, of course, running should extinguish more rapidly the greater the differences between acquisition and extinction. The following observations support this view: (1) More responding occurs if shock in extinction is delivered in a section of the runway near the start box than if delivered in a section of the runway near the goal box (Campbell et al. 1966); (2) extinction is rapid if shock is delivered in the goal box (Kintz and Bruning, 1967); (3) humans will discontinue self-punitive behavior when they are instructed that a self-punitive contingency is in effect (Tinsley and Renner, 1975) or when conditions in extinction are otherwise altered sharply (see Rose and Fantino, 1977); (4) when response-independent shocks are presented in extinction, responding is strengthened (see Coulson, Coulson, and Gardner, 1970, with rats, and Wallace and Scobie, 1977, with goldfish). This last observation makes an important point: Since shock itself is part of the stimulus complex controlling responding in acquisition, its presentation in extinction should continue to exert control over the same response; hence the presence or absence of shock will be a major factor in the extinction of responding. Recall that in Byrd's (1969) study of self-punitive behavior in free-operant avoidance cats were exposed to a noncontingent schedule of shock presentations (FT 15-min) following avoidance training, but before the introduction of the contingent schedule of shock presentations (FI 15-min). By changing the procedure in this gradual way, Byrd minimized the discriminability of the changes in the contingency between response and shock. The vicious-circle hypothesis, with additional complicating assumptions, can probably account for most of the findings discussed in the last two paragraphs. Indeed, the two hypotheses make similar predictions in most cases (see Rands and Dean, 1977). There appears to be no need, however, to retain the former in favor of the more direct discrimination hypothesis.

The phenomenon of self-punitive behavior in both the free-operant and discrete-trials case is consistent with the discrimination hypothesis. Specifically, a response that was negatively reinforced in training by producing either escape or avoidance of shock will continue to be maintained when it no longer produces negative reinforcement, providing the discriminability of the change in the response–shock contingency is low. This will occur most readily when shocks are present in the extinction situation. Self-punitive behavior will be enhanced if the same response that produces "punishment" is also instrumental in escaping or minimizing the punishing stimulus; in that event the response provides negative reinforcement, as it did during acquisition. Once the variables controlling self-punitive behavior are understood, it becomes clear that self-punitive behavior is neither more nor less self-punitive than food-reinforced lever-pressing is self-reinforcing. In that sense the label "self-punitive" is misleading, if not a misnomer, in that it obscures the actual nature of the controlling relationships.

More generally, the resistance of an avoidance response to extinction will be a direct function of the similarity of conditions in acquisition and extinction. A striking example of resistance to extinction in a negative reinforcement procedure was provided by Herrnstein and Hineline's (1966) study discussed earlier. Recall that in their study avoidance responding was a direct function of shock-frequency reduction. They also found that responses that produced a large decrease in shock frequency extinguished rapidly once they were no longer effective in reducing shock frequency (extinction). On the other hand, when the response-contingent decrease in shock frequency was minimal, about 17,000 responses were made in extinction!

Herrnstein and Hineline's results, as well as those from a large number of additional studies, allow us to conclude that responses extinguish in much the same manner after either positive or negative reinforcement: Resistance to extinction is enhanced the more similar the conditions in acquisition and extinction. In the positive case, however, the typical extinction procedure tends to ensure that extinction conditions will be readily discriminated, resulting in fairly rapid extinction. Here, for example, food is typically withheld in extinction. In extinction after negative reinforcement, however, response-independent shocks are sometimes presented, making discrimination more difficult and retarding extinction. When the analogous operation is performed after positive reinforcement—providing response-independent food during extinction—resistance to extinction is also enhanced (Rescorla and Skucy, 1969). Moreover, after positive reinforcement, responding no longer produces food in extinction. But in the more typical extinction procedure after avoidance, responding is still followed by the absence of shock, making the situation comparable to that prevailing prior to extinction. When the previously successful avoidance response produces shock in extinction, however, turning the avoidance contingency into a punishment contingency, the response extinguishes rapidly.[10]

Learned Helplessness

We have seen that a response acquired in a negative reinforcement procedure may persist in extinction, if the discriminability of the change from acquisition to extinction is low. Just the reverse appears true in the phenomenon of *learned helplessness*. In this case, "acquisition" consists of training with extinction in which unavoidable and inescapable (hence noncontingent) shocks are presented. The subject eventually stops making would-be instrumental responses in the situation. Then, when an escape procedure is introduced, a straightforward escape response is not acquired. Thus in learned helplessness the typical order of acquisition and extinction is reversed. Learned helplessness has been found in a large number of experiments, originating from Richard Solomon's laboratory at the University of Pennsylvania and continuing at several other laboratories, most prominently Steven Maier's at the University of Colorado and Jay Weiss' at The Rockefeller University (see Maier, Seligman, and Solomon, 1969; Maier, 1970; Maier and Seligman, 1976; Maier, Albin, and Testa, 1973; Seligman and Maier, 1967; Glazer and Weiss, 1976a, 1976b; Baker, 1976; Overmier and Seligman, 1967). In a prototype experiment, Seligman and Maier (1967) presented dogs with a series of intense unsignaled noncontingent electric shocks—that is, shocks that were inescapable. Following this pretraining, the dogs were exposed to a discrete-trial avoidance procedure using a shuttle box. Once the CS came on, the dog had 10 seconds to jump over a barrier separating the two parts of the box in order to avoid shock. If the dog failed to emit the avoidance response, the CS remained on and shock was presented, both for an additional 50 seconds, unless the dog escaped by jumping to safety. The dogs generally failed to acquire the avoidance response and usually did not even escape the shock! Comparable findings have been demonstrated with other subjects, including rats and goldfish. Of course, subjects not pretrained with uncontrollable shocks learn rapidly to escape and then to avoid shocks in the shuttle box. Clearly the pretraining has had a profound effect on subsequent acquisition of escape and avoidance. What is responsible?

----

[10]This rapid extinction will take place as long as response-independent shocks are not also presented. As just discussed, such noncontingent shocks make discrimination of extinction conditions difficult and tend to enhance resistance to extinction (see Wallace and Scobie, 1977; Byrd, 1969).

One interpretation is that subjects in the learned helplessness procedure are apparently sensitive to the fact that there is no correlation between their responses and noxious stimulation. According to this interpretation, subjects have emitted their high-probability responses in the presence of the uncontrollable UCS's and these responses have been extinguished. When avoidance or escape training begins, the subjects still fail to respond and still receive the UCS. Nothing has changed! Subjects that have received escape training *prior* to training with uncontrollable shock *do* reacquire an escape response (see Seligman, Rosellini, and Kozak, 1975). These subjects have already learned that their responding sometimes affects noxious events.

The explanation of learned helplessness based on sensitivity to correlations between responding and subsequent events is not only plausible but dovetails nicely with the explanation of self-punitive behavior. Recent work suggests, however, that it is by no means a complete explanation of most demonstrations of learned helplessness. In particular, Jay Weiss and his associates have amassed persuasive data arguing for a reinterpretation of learned helplessness (especially Glazer and Weiss, 1976a, 1976b). They note that most demonstrations of learned helplessness do not appear to have the characteristics of learned behaviors. As they point out, a major requirement for showing that a response is learned is that it will persist over time. But the original demonstration of learned helplessness produced temporary deficits which were not shown by some subjects when tested after only 48 hours (see Overmier and Seligman, 1967). In addition, the size of any learned helplessness effect should be a function of the degree to which the test situation resembles that in which the uncontrollable shocks have been given. Surprisingly, the degree of resemblance does not have a clear effect on the size of the deficit or on the proportion of the subjects showing a deficit (Maier et al., 1969).

A recent experiment by Altenor, Kay, and Richter (1977) has shown that pretraining with one type of uncontrollable UCS produces just as great a deficit when testing is conducted with a *different* UCS as when it is conducted with the same UCS. Altenor et al. (1977) pretreated rats with either shock or underwater exposure. Half of the rats in each group were permitted to escape (the control group) and half were not (the experimental group). The duration of uncontrollable shocks for the rats in the experimental-shock group was matched to that received by the rats in the control-shock group, which in turn was a function of the control rats' latencies to depress a nose lever. Similarly, the duration of underwater exposure for rats in both the experimental-water and control-water groups was determined by the latency of rats in the control group to traverse an underwater maze. In *testing*, half of the rats from each of the four pretreatment groups received either 20 shock-escape trials in a two-way shuttle box or 20 water-escape trials in an underwater maze.

Altenor et al. found that subjects in both of the experimental groups were slower to escape, in testing, than the control subjects (which had been pretrained with escapable noxious stimuli). Moreover, the learned helplessness effect, while small for all subjects, appeared to be no smaller when the aversive stimulus was changed between pretraining and testing than when it was unchanged. These results suggest that whatever is learned in pretraining generalizes surprisingly well to novel noxious stimuli.

Glazer and Weiss interpret transient performance deficits in terms of a short-lived neurochemical change, presumably in central neurotransmitter activity, which results in a "motor activation deficit." They point out, however, that some demonstrations of learned helplessness have appeared to be relatively long-term, suggesting a different explanation (see Seligman et al., 1975; Maier et al., 1973; Weiss and Glazer, 1975). For example, Seligman et al. (1975), found that rats previously exposed to inescapable shocks of moderate intensity showed a deficit in acquiring a response to avoid or escape shock as long as one week later. All of the demonstrations of a *long-term deficit* involve lower levels of longer-duration (at least 5 sec) shock than those showing a transitory deficit. Glazer and Weiss suggest that what is acquired is not "learned" helplessness nor sensitivity to the lack of correlation between responding and subsequent events but rather some activity that later interferes with the response required (for negative reinforcement) in testing. Specifically, Glazer and Weiss (1976b) postulate that the competing behavior learned is *inactivity* (or some behavior, such as gripping the grid floor, that makes the subject appear inactive). They suggested that the same inescapable shock treatment that produces a performance deficit with one type of response may actually facilitate the acquisition of responses compatible with those acquired in response to inescapable shock. In support of their hypothesis Glazer and Weiss showed that rats given long-duration, moderate-intensity shocks will indeed show a long-term performance deficit when tested for avoidance and escape acquisition with lever-press, running, or jumping responses. When a response more compatible with relative inactivity was studied, however (a nose-push by a rat restrained inside a tube), rats actually acquired the avoidance–escape response in fewer trials than rats without pretraining.

Some of Glazer and Weiss's data are shown in Figure 8.16. The top half of the figure shows results exemplifying the learned helplessness phenomenon (or the "long-term interference effect" in Glazer and Weiss's terms). In this study triplets of rats, one from each of three groups, were studied simultaneously. In pretraining, the rat from the escape group turned a wheel to escape shock. The rat from the yoked group received shock whenever the rat from the escape group did; these shocks were thus inescapable for the yoked rat. The rat from the control group re-

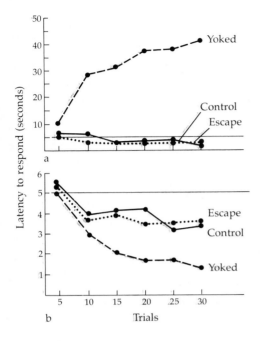

a

b   Trials

Figure 8.16
Mean latency to perform the correct avoidance or escape response after onset of the warning signal in two different tasks for rats given different pretraining. (Latency is plotted in blocks of 5 trials, with the last trial in each block indicated on the abscissa.) The escape animals were allowed to escape from shock during a shock session 72 hours before the test. The yoked animals were matched to escape subjects, so that they received the same shocks as escape subjects, but were unable to escape from them; that is, they received inescapable shock 72 hours before the test. The control animals received no shock before the test. Part (a) shows results in an FR 3 lever-press task, as used by Seligman and Beagley (1975), and part (b) shows results in a nosing task. [After H. I. Glazer and J. M. Weiss, Long-term interference effect: An alternative to "learned helplessness." *Journal of Experimental Psychology: Animal Behavior Processes, 2,* 202–213. Copyright © 1976 by the American Psychological Association. Redrawn by permission.]

ceived no shock. Seven triplets of rats were then tested in a lever-press task requiring three lever-presses (FR 3) to avoid or terminate shock, a procedure previously used by Seligman and Beagley (1975). The other seven triplets were tested with the nosing response. Latencies shorter than 5 sec represent avoidance, longer ones, escape. Note that the yoked rats in the top half of the figure became progressively slower in escaping shock as testing continued. A dramatically different set of results was obtained with the nose-pressing response. Here the yoked rats' latencies were shorter than those of rats in the escape and control groups.

A strong point of the Glazer and Weiss study just described is the fact that the experimenters obtained the learned helplessness phenomenon under the same conditions that earlier studies had (for example, Seligman and Beagley, 1975), thus supporting the notion that they were dealing with the same phenomenon. With the identical procedure but with a different response—selected on the basis of their interference theory—they were able to obtain the opposite pattern of results. It is too soon to tell if the Glazer–Weiss explanation of a transitory interference effect produced by motor activation deficits (mediated by central neurotransmitter disturbances, produced by high-intensity electric shocks) and a long-term interference effect involving learned inactivity will prove adequate for a relatively complete understanding of the learned helplessness phenomenon. While it appears that "learned helplessness" is indeed a misnomer—at least in most situations studied to date—the Glazer–Weiss explanation must be regarded as tentative at this time.[11]

Our tour of aversive control is now complete. Although the nature of punishment and negative reinforcement dictate procedural complexities that make comparisons with positive reinforcement difficult, it seems fair to conclude by simply restating a generalization that has held up remarkably well throughout this chapter: (1) The same principles that permit us to describe behavior maintained by positive reinforcement appear to apply with little or no modification to negative reinforcement as well; (2) the effects of either positive or negative reinforcement are equivalent but opposite to that of punishment. That is, reinforcers (both positive and negative) make behavior more probable in the same way that punishers make behavior less probable.

---

[11]There is disagreement, for example, as to whether motor activation deficits should last even 24 hours. Altenor et al. (1977), for example, do not accept this possibility as an explanation of their learned helplessness demonstration. Moreover, the uncontrollable shocks used during pretraining in their study were of the correct intensity and duration to produce transitory, rather than long-term, effects according to Glazer and Weiss's specifications. Moreover, Maier and Seligman (1976) have raised a number of objections to earlier explanations of the learned helplessness phenomenon in terms of motor activation deficits. Finally, Jackson, Maier, and Rapaport (1978) found that while exposure to inescapable shock produces activity deficits, in accordance with Glazer and Weiss's explanation, they also found additional performance deficits which are not readily explained in terms of activity deficits.

III The Biological Perspective

9 Species-Specific Behavior Patterns

Under appropriately warm and humid conditions in the late spring, the common garden snail *(Helix pomatia)* initiates one of spring's most romantic courtship sequences. Each member of the mating pair engages in an identical protracted behavior series, made all the more dramatic by the fact that the snails are *simultaneous hermaphrodites*. Each member of the pair possesses a complete set of both male and female reproductive organs, and during copulation each simultaneously deposits sperm into the vagina of the other. The sequence begins when the normally horizontally oriented snails meet and adopt an *upright vertical posture* facing each other, with lips and tentacles in contact, and with the soles of the molluscan feet pressed tightly together. This position is pictured in Figure 9.1. Each animal then curves its forward head region downward and injects a tiny sharp needle of calcium into its partner's sole. The needle is appropriately termed a "love dart." It apparently serves no direct reproductive function; however, it is only after dart-shooting has taken place that copulation can occur. Following the exchange of love darts, the snails reassume the upright vertical posture, expose genital openings to one another, and simultaneously insert the penis into the vagina. Interestingly, copulation must occur simultaneously; if one individual attempts to insert the penis before the other, successful copulation will not occur. Following copulation, the snails will remain immobile in the upright posture with soles in contact. While each component of the sequence may persist literally for hours, the final stage of immobility typically lasts longest. During this stage the

Figure 9.1
The upright vertical posture in the courtship sequence of the land snail *Helix pomatia*.
[Courtesy of Hans Pfletschinger—Peter Arnold, Inc.]

sperm, enclosed in a sperm pocket, or spermatophore, are transported to a storage cell to be used later to fertilize the eggs. Four to six weeks after copulation as many as seventy fertilized eggs are deposited into warm, moist underground nests, there to develop into young snails.

The land snail's mating behavior represents a highly stereotyped species-specific sequence of responses. The precise ordering of components within the sequence is critical for successful reproduction. Copulation cannot occur unless the shooting of the love darts has taken place; similarly, if dart-shooting occurs but copulation is prevented, an immediate decline in mating behavior results. In either case the sequence has been interrupted. What is the function of the reproductively inert love dart? What role does it play in the coordination of the sequence? How important is the completion of each component of the sequence in initiating subsequent behaviors? Recent data have suggested that the dart may serve a regulatory or coordinating function and that control of the orderly sequence results from the action of a neural program guaranteeing precise behavioral ordering independent of further environmental input. Its species-typical stereotypy, its obvious adaptive value, and its independence of environmental feedback suggest that the snail's mating behavior represents a fixed action pattern (discussed later in the chapter), perhaps initiated in two animals simultaneously by the abrupt insertion of a small love dart.

Throughout much of the book we have focused on the development of behavior occurring within the lifetime of an individual organism. We have seen, for example, that certain behaviors are reinforced and made more probable, while others are punished and made less probable. Much can be learned, however, about all behavior by appreciating the principles of *phylogeny*. As indicated in Chapter 1, these principles describe the evolutionary development across generations of behaviors characteristic of a given species. Phylogenetic analysis is most easily accomplished and has traditionally been most successful when applied to behaviors that, like the snail's courtship, have the following characteristics: (1) they are adaptive, (2) they are displayed uniformly by all members of a given species, and (3) they remain largely unmodified by changes in environmental input. Behaviors (or sequences of behavior) to which these characteristics apply have been termed *species-specific behaviors*, and they are frequently referred to as innate. For the psychologist the study of species-specific behaviors is central to an understanding of both the ontogenetic and phylogenetic development of behavior. Our treatment of the analysis of species-specific behavior patterns will begin with a historical survey of the investigations that have addressed the question of phylogeny in behavior, and conclude with a review of data bearing on the current understanding of species-specific behaviors.

THE CONCEPT OF INSTINCT

An historical survey of the study of species-specific behaviors essentially represents the history of the concept of *instinct*. Historically, instinctive behaviors have been thought of as relatively complex sequences of responses that have evolved within the species over many generations. While there are many definitions of instinct, one, which guided investigations of instinct early in this century and which can be dated to the time of the Stoics in 300 B.C., defines instinctive behavior as behavior that is unlearned, adaptive, and uniform within a species. Instinctive behavior is therefore species-specific. Modern interest in instinctive behavior was stimulated in the late nineteenth and early twentieth centuries by the widespread acceptance of Charles Darwin's theory of evolution by natural selection. Evolutionary theory initially focused on an explanation of the diversity of morphological characteristics that distinguish animal species.

The study of morphological evolution stressed the importance of the adaptive function of any developing characteristic. This emphasis on adaptation in turn quickly suggested that behavior, too, would logically fall within the domain of evolutionary theory. Just as evolutionary principles could explain the structures characteristic of a given species, so those same principles might account for the behavior characteristic of a given species. Some, in fact, date the modern effort to account for behavior within the theory of evolution from Darwin's own publication in 1872 of *The Expression of Emotions in Man and Animals.* Those behaviors which were "evolutionary in origin" came to be called instincts.

Under the influence of Darwin, two distinct groups drew heavily on the concept of instinct: the early American psychologists and the European ethologists. However, at the hands of both, and at a time when little was known about the evolutionary determinants of animal behavior, the term "instinct" came to be wrongly used as an explanation of behavior rather than merely a category of behavior satisfying a particular definition and obeying certain principles. In psychology, instincts were invented in great numbers, and the coining of a term was often mistaken for an explanation of the behavior designated by that term. The great American social psychologist William McDougall was, for example, extreme in his abuse of the concept of instinct. He claimed that all behavior—including human—had instinctive origins. Because science was ignorant of the basis of instinctive control, however, (evolutionary theory itself was in its infancy) all McDougall could effectively do was to list instincts. Accordingly, one was pugnacious, or parental, or gregarious because one had a fighting instinct, a parental instinct, or an instinct to congregate. Such labeling, of course, tells us nothing about what factors actually control the behavior in question. The lists of instincts grew, and different theorists' lists differed extensively, often being contradictory. Indeed, when the different lists were compiled, the total number of instincts came to several thousand. "Instinct" was being used merely as a label to handle misunderstood complexity. To merely label behaviors such as "suspicion" and "sociability" as "instinctive impulses" is hardly useful in understanding the behaviors to which the terms were applied. At the time, however, the possibility for postulating instincts seemed to be limited only by the imagination and thoroughness of the theorist. Though the usages of the concept of instinct by ethologists and psychologists differed greatly, when the reliance on the concept was challenged by the early behaviorists in the 1920s, the challenge extended to both groups.

The Anti-Instinct Revolt

The rise of American behaviorism brought an emphasis on experience and the environment as the principle determinants of behavior. The disparity between this view and that of the instinct theorists led to an "anti-instinct" revolt among the behaviorists. An important body of experiments, critical of the early instinct view and representative of the behaviorists' emphasis on experience, was performed in the 1930s by Zing Yang Kuo. Kuo's interest in aggression led him to ask if cats have an instinctive tendency to kill rats. To answer this question he raised some kittens alone, away from other kittens, but each in the presence of one rat pup; others he raised in isolation, exposed neither to other rats nor to cats; a third group of kittens was raised with cats and rats in a normal rat-killing environment. In such a "normal" environment, the kitten was brought up by its mother cat and was exposed to the sight of its mother and other cats killing rats. Kuo reasoned that if rat-killing were an instinct, all of the cats should kill rats irrespective of differences in their environmental rearing conditions. Indeed, when given the opportunity to do so, most of the kittens raised in the normal rat-killing environment killed rats by the age of four months. When given the same opportunity, however, less than half of the kittens raised in isolation killed rats. Most of the nonkillers eventually learned to kill after being allowed to watch other cats kill. Finally, kittens that were raised with a single rat pup did not kill rats when given the opportunity. Only one of eighteen cats raised with rats was finally trained to kill, although three others learned to kill rats of an unfamiliar strain. Kuo concluded that these animals were not rat-killers by instinct, nor was it easy to instruct them in the art of rat-killing. Similar results have been obtained with cats stalking birds, with dogs attacking rabbits, and with rats killing mice. Moreover, cats raised with a single rat (and most dogs raised with a single rabbit) displayed behavioral signs of affection for their cage mate. If the rabbit or rat were taken away from the dog or cat, the dog or cat would make a whining sound as if it "missed" the other animal. This observation led Kuo to ask sarcastically whether or not the results showed that cats have a rat-*loving* instinct.

In a subsequent study, Kuo raised groups of kittens and rat pups together. Under these conditions behavioral signs of either aggression or affection between the kittens and rats were largely absent. From all appearances, it seemed that the animals displayed a mutual indifference to one another. Once the rats had offspring of their own, however, the situation changed. Twelve of seventeen cats were seen eating the young rat pups when the mother rat (with whom they had been raised) was absent. What was the difference between the new rat pups and the older rats? Why did the cats attack the offspring but not the adult rat? The same cats that ate rat pups would also eat shaved adult rats. Kuo separated the cats and rats and found that, even after four months, the cats would not kill the normal adult rats. The cats were then given imitation training (observing other cats killing and eating rats), but to largely no avail. Of the sixteen cats tested, six tried to kill rats and only three of these succeeded even after imitation training. Yet these same cats routinely killed and ate shaved adult rats. Thus the cats' behavior was clearly under *stimulus con-*

trol, with the relevant stimulus being the rat's fur. These experiments clearly demonstrated the conditions under which rat-killing behavior reliably occurred, in addition to those under which it reliably failed to occur. The studies also demonstrate the profound influence of early experience upon the development of later behavior. The fact that the cats kill and devour only shaved rats, suggests that the eating of shaved rats is a continuation of their earlier behavior of eating naturally hairless newborn rats. Kuo concluded:

> In reviewing the results of this study, one is impressed with the fact that the behavior of the cat toward the rat is much more complex and much more variable than most psychologists would have thought. . . . We have presented the actual behavior picture of the cat towards the rat in terms of stimulus and response together with the life history of the cat. Do we need to add that such responses are instinctive, such and such are learned by trial and error, and such and such are due to insight or ideation? Do we need to add that in our findings the cat shows instincts of rat-killing and rat-eating as well as the instinct to love the rat? Do we need to resort to such concepts as modification of instinct, periodicity of instinct, waning of instinct, and the like in order to explain the results of our study? [Kuo, 1931, p. 32]

Kuo's answer was clearly no.

An important consequence of the anti-instinct revolt was the realization that the notion of instinct should not be used as an explanatory principle in the absence of any deeper understanding of the factors actually giving rise to the behavior labeled as instinctive. To merely name something is not to explain it. To respond, for example, to the question, "Why do cats kill rats?" with answer, "Due to an instinct for aggression," is often nothing more than an admission of ignorance.

While the anti-instinct revolt made several important points, it also has had some unfortunate consequences. Most significantly, hereditary factors were wrongly deemphasized to the point that many investigators assumed that the environment could explain all differences in behavior in all organisms. The importance of the organism's natural environment and the relevance of evolution in behavior were ignored, and often psychologists completely discounted the potential importance of organismic variables. This unfortunate backlash took many years to correct.

Interaction of Heredity and Environment

In the 1950s, comparative and physiological psychologists decried the contrived dichotomy between "heredity" and "environment" or between "learned" and "unlearned" behaviors as generally useless for an understanding of behavior. Instead they argued, as did Kuo before them, that one should study the interaction of environmental and organismic factors in the stimulation of behavior. Behavior patterns *develop* as a result of the constant interplay between an organism, in part representing a genetic endowment, and an environment, which in a molecular sense partially controls the nature of that genetic endowment. More recently, Whalen (1971) has argued persuasively that:

> Behavior thus emerges from genes *acting in environments*. Primary gene actions in enzyme and metabolic activity are themselves not independent of the environment. In fact, genes without environments would not yield organisms, much less behaving organisms [Whalen, 1971, p. 57, italics in original].
>
>   . . . *all* behaviors are under joint genetic and environmental control. "Learned" behaviors are not considered to be different in kind from the instincts. In this way, the similarities of all behaviors are emphasized [p. 60, italics in original].

Renewed interest in and emphasis on a more scientifically workable concept of instinct has accompanied modern advances in evolutionary biology. Perhaps because of an historical aversion to the term "instinct," however, the terms "innate" and "species-specific" enjoy more current usage. Differences in the species-specific behaviors that characterize distinct animal groups are said to be *innate*. Notwithstanding the change in terminology, the flavor of the newer approach is captured in Whalen's statement. The genes are viewed as the regulators of a programmed developmental sequence. The realization of the program, however, must occur in an environmental context; inputs from the environment can to a greater or lesser extent modify the expression of the developmental sequence prescribed by the genes. Some developmental programs are more open to variations in environmental input than others. Species-specific responses remain one category of behavior characterized by a developmental program that is relatively less open to modification by the variety of contextual factors typically encountered by individuals of a given species. It is important to note that labeling a particular behavior as innate or species-specific provides no complete explanation. Ideally, we shall eventually understand how in each case a genetically based program of development finds expression in interaction with a particular range of environments. Because such understanding lies in the future, however, the concept of innateness remains controversial. Some modern investigators prefer that no such term remain in use (see the discussion in Lorenz, 1965). However, no consensus has been reached, and in the following section we shall describe one sense of the term "innate" regarded by many as acceptable current usage.

As indicated above (and discussed further in Chapter 13), all behavior exhibited by an individual must develop as a result of a complex integration of genetic and environmental information—a developmental interaction that begins with conception and may continue until death. What, then, is the meaning of the term "innate"? It is actually inappropriate to state that a particular behavior is genetically determined, since in development all behavior is both genetically and environmentally determined. (For the same reasons, of course, it is inappropriate to maintain that a given behavior is learned.) The term "innate" can, however, be appropriately applied to behavior through an analysis of the *differences* in behavior that characterize distinct populations of individuals. If the behavioral differences among populations (or individuals) can be reliably attributed to genetic differences known to differentiate the populations, then behavior can be said to be innate. Here the term simply indicates that behaviors develop differently as a function of genetic differences among groups. In such cases, therefore, differences in the genotype must be employed to explain the behavioral differences in question. This is true of morphological characteristics as well as of behavior. Eye color, for example, cannot be said to be genetically determined. Rather, differences in eye color among different populations are the result of the genetic diversity that distinguishes those populations. If differences in behavior among populations can be attributed to genetic rather than environmental differences among them, the term "innate" is appropriate.

The *calling song* of the male cricket, for example, serves to attract sexually receptive females to the male's nest. In many of the over 3,000 species of cricket, song consists of a series of sounds (each of which is termed a chirp) produced when a hardened scraper on one wing is passed across a toothed ridge, or file, on the other wing (see Figure 9.2). Each distinct species, however, produces a unique temporal patterning of chirps uniformly displayed by all the males in that species. Moreover, the females of each species are attracted only by the songs of the males of their own species. Several species-specific chirp patterns are diagramed in Figure 9.3. The uniformity with which the songs are produced within a species, the consistent differences between species, and the clear adaptive value of the successful song suggest that cricket song may be regarded as an innate response. The accurate application of the concept of innateness in the context described here, would, however, require experimental demonstration that the differences in the songs of various species are the result of genetic differences among those species.

The work of Bentley and Hoy (1972, 1974) and their colleagues analyzing the genetics, neurophysiology, and ontogeny of cricket song provides such a demonstration. Neurophysiological analysis indicates, for example, that networks of nerve cells in the cricket's brain can be stimulated to produce the entire calling pattern characteristic of a given species. This neural pattern is, moreover, produced even after the responding neurons have been completely isolated from any further environmental input. These results suggest that differences among species cannot be due to differences in the type of environmental feedback (either proprioceptive or acoustical) received during singing. In such an isolated system, no feedback is possible. Developmental studies also point to the irrelevance

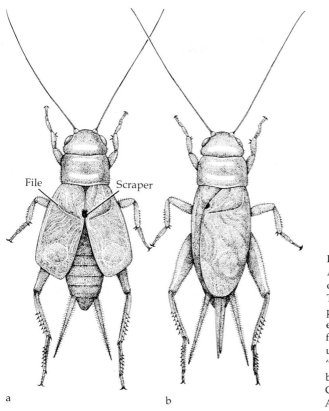

File   Scraper

a   b

Figure 9.2
A singing cricket in the (a) wings-
open and (b) wings-closed position.
The elements of song (chirps) are
produced when the scraper on the
edge of one wing passes across the
file (a series of ridges) on the
underside of the other wing. [After
"The Neurobiology of Cricket Song"
by David Bentley and Ronald R. Hoy.
Copyright © 1974 by Scientific
American, Inc. All rights reserved.]

of environmental differences in producing song differences between
species. Immature crickets develop through a series of ten stages, separated from one another by the molting of the insect's exoskeleton. With
each stage, the immature cricket becomes progressively more adult-like in
form. Immature crickets, however, are never observed to sing; only after
the insect reaches full maturity does singing occur. Nonetheless, stimulation of the immature cricket's brain does result in the neural pattern associated with song. The young crickets are therefore capable of singing well
before any songs are produced. This again suggests that acoustical feedback during development (absent because developing crickets do not
sing) is unnecessary for the development of the organized song pattern.

In other studies (Bentley and Hoy, 1970) crickets of the same species
were raised under a variety of different environmental conditions. These
included variations in temperature, diet, population density, and acoustical experience. In the latter condition, some groups heard no songs, some
heard the songs of their own species, and others were exposed to the
songs of other species. In all cases, when the insects were tested at matur-

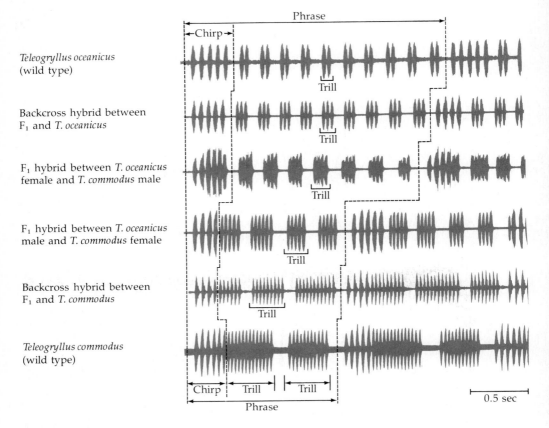

Figure 9.3
Song patterns of several hybrid cricket species illustrate the species-specific organization
of cricket song. Dotted lines indicate the form of the repeating phrase of the particular
species shown. [Courtesy of David Bentley.]

ity all produced identical species-specific songs. Environmental variation,
therefore, was ineffective in producing differences in song among members of the same species. These data strongly suggest that differences in
song patterns between species are due, not to environmental changes,
but to the genetic differences that distinguish those species.

Manipulation of genes would therefore be predicted to alter the patterning of cricket song. Genetic manipulations can be produced when individuals of one species of cricket (which sings a particular song) are
mated with individuals of a different species (which sings a different
song). The hybrid offspring resulting from such a mating represent a mixture of the genotypes of the two parent species. If differences in song are
the result of genetic differences among species, hybridization should produce distinctive changes in the calling song. Hybridization studies

(Bentley and Hoy, 1972) in fact have indicated that each unique genetic mixture produces a group of individuals that sing a unique calling song. Moreover, all the individuals of each distinct genotype sing the same song. The genetic changes produced, therefore, have uniform effects within the group. The patterns of song pictured in Figure 9.3 represent the differences in song that characterize the offspring of various hybrid pairs. Factors responsible for the development of distinct songs in different cricket species appear, therefore, to be encoded in the genes. Interestingly, the female's response to the male's calling song is also altered by genetic manipulation. Most females will respond only to the songs of the males of their own species. When presented with the songs of various species of males in the apparatus diagramed in Figure 9.4, the females of a particular hybrid cross repeatedly preferred the songs of the males of the same hybrid cross (their brothers) over the songs produced by the males of either of the two parent species. Species-specific differences in both the production of song by the males and the recognition of song by the females, therefore, result from genetic differences among species (Hoy, Hahn, and Paul, 1977). While the development of song in any individual requires a sequence of subtle interactions between hereditary and environmental factors, pronounced species-specific *differences* in song are produced by differences in genetic rather than environmental inputs. In this sense, cricket song can be accurately referred to as innate.

Behaviors that are innate or species-specific are so because the organisms that exhibit those behaviors share a common genetic heritage.

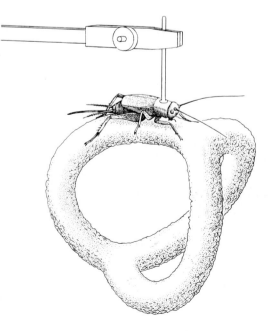

Figure 9.4
The Y-maze used to test the preference of the female cricket presented with the songs of various species of males. The female makes a choice as she encounters a fork in the Y, which she holds as she walks along. [After "The Neurobiology of Cricket Song" by David Bentley and Ronald R. Hoy. Copyright © 1974 by Scientific American, Inc. All rights reserved.]

Moreover, variations in the environment in which the individuals normally develop are uncorrelated with differences in the behaviors that develop. The basis for both the stereotypy and the range of specificity is presumably the same as that underlying any morphological character common to a group of genetically isolated individuals: phylogenetic evolution. Like morphological characters, species-specific behaviors have been molded across generations by the evolutionary mechanism of natural selection. Hence knowledge of the *theory of evolution by natural selection* is essential to our understanding of the origin and occurrence of species-specific behavior patterns. Before examining innate behavior in greater detail, therefore, we shall briefly review the basic principles of evolutionary theory. For a more complete treatment of the principles of evolution the reader is referred to Mayr (1970); Emlen (1973); Savage (1977); and Dobzhansky, Ayala, Stebbins, and Valentine (1977).

EVOLUTION

The basic tenet of evolutionary theory is *genetic change*. Living organisms exist as they do today as the result of gradual sequential changes that have taken place in their ancestral lineages. Therefore an understanding of both the behavioral and morphological characteristics that typify living groups rests in the nature of the ancestral changes that have given rise to those groups.

Modern understanding of the nature of evolutionary change was initiated in 1859 with the publication of Charles Darwin's *The Origin of Species by Natural Selection*. In this classic work Darwin did not introduce the idea of evolution; rather, he postulated a theoretical process by which evolutionary change is guided and maintained. What mechanism determines the kinds of changes that will take place and persist? Darwin maintained that the primary mechanism directing evolutionary change is *natural selection*. Natural selection has been defined as the differential reproductive success of individuals within a population, which results from genetic differences among those individuals. In effect, some members of a population leave more offspring that live to reproduce than others.

The natural environment contains only limited amounts of the resources, such as food, shelter, and mates, necessary for life. It is the task of each organism to extract these resources from the environment as efficiently as possible. Because the supply is limited and the number of consuming individuals is so large, there is usually not enough to go around. In the natural state resources are quite scarce. That set of vital resources available in a stable environment defines its carrying capacity: the number of individuals whose existence can be sustained by the environment without detriment to the quality of life. The number of individuals produced usually far exceeds the carrying capacity of the environment, and therefore many organisms will die before reproducing. Those individuals that fail to reproduce have been selected out by natural forces governing access to resources. Individuals better able to extract these vital resources from the environment are more likely to survive and therefore more likely to reproduce and perpetuate their kind. Moreover, perpetuation of the characteristics of the successful individual takes place through the re-productive transmission of genetic information.

The key to successful perpetuation is not simply survival but *differential reproductive success*. Organisms that live a full life but fail to successfully reproduce, fail to make a contribution to the gene pool. Hence their characteristics are not transmitted to future generations. Those charac-teristics are therefore gradually removed from the population, and genet-ically based characteristics that remain dominate evolutionary trends. Re-productive success is actually a very general concept. It refers to far more than simply being able to mate successfully. For example, only those ani-mals that successfully evade their hungry predators will live to find a mate and reproduce. Similarly, the mother bird that abandons her helpless offspring is negating her existing contribution to the evolutionary process. True, she has reproduced and the offspring have hatched. But they re-present her contribution to the gene pool, and it is not until that contribu-tion itself is perpetuated—until the offspring themselves live to repro-duce—that her evolutionary "responsibility" is fulfilled. The demands of reproductive success can therefore persist after the young arrive. To be successful in evolutionary terms the individual must feed, protect, and nurture those offspring as long as they are dependent. In fact, the final criterion for success in reproduction lies in ensuring that one's offspring's genes, and therefore one's own, enter the gene pool.

Any process of selection implies the existence of a pool of items from which to select. Natural selection is no exception. It does not produce or initiate change; rather, it perpetuates changes that already exist. As such, natural selection maintains what is already there. The process of natural selection is therefore predicated upon the prior existence of *variability*. *Dif-ferential* reproductive success implies inequality, and variability guarantees this inequality. As such, variability, too, is essential to evolution. If all organisms were exactly alike, selection would produce no change. One "choice" would have no different implications from any other. In evolu-tion, variability is introduced by *mutation* and augmented by the process of *sexual reproduction*. The tremendous reproductive potentials of most or-ganisms and the genetic recombination assured by sexual reproduction generate the raw material of morphological and behavior diversity on which selection operates.

The attainment of reproductive success defines *adaptation*. Adaptation is, in effect, the function of evolution. This function is, however, an ex-tremely relative one. What is required to extract those vital resources from the environment is dictated by the environment itself, and adaptation can only be viewed within the context of what would be most efficient in *that* environment. Water, for example, will be most efficiently obtained in very different ways in a desert than in a tropical rain forest. Similarly, the efficient acquisition of a mate might occur in very different ways in a highly social versus a solitary cannibalistic species. What constitutes the "best" will differ from situation to situation. In the next chapter we will see how the specific demands of the natural environment govern the nature of the learning processes exhibited by organisms in that environment. For the moment, however, let us return to an examination of instinct to see how stereotyped and species-specific behavior patterns can greatly aid in the realization of reproductive success. When this occurs, the behaviors themselves are maintained and perpetuated in the process of organic evolution.

THE GENETICS OF BEHAVIOR

Modern evolutionary biology has made increasingly clear the relationship between genetics and evolution. The integration of population genetics, molecular biology, ecology, and Darwinian evolutionary theory in fact provides the dominant framework for modern research in evolution. Any evolutionary change has its basis in fluctuations in the population gene pool. If behavior has an evolutionary basis, therefore, it must in theory be possible to engage in a genetic analysis of the evolution of behavior. The recently maturing field of *behavioral genetics* has devoted itself to just such analyses. The promise of this area has been to account for how evolution produces phylogenetic change in behavior through modifications in the population gene pool. Population differences in the behavioral phenotype[1] then serve as indirect evidence of differences in population gene pools that might underlie behavioral diversity. Walter Rothenbuhler's (1967) analysis of the *hygienic behavior* of different strains of honeybees provides an excellent example of the genetic analysis of a complex behavior pattern.

Some laboratory-bred strains of honeybees are unusually susceptible to a particular bacterial infection. When once contracted by a colony, the disease spreads quickly through a population, killing the larval forms encapsulated in the cells of the hive. Other very closely related strains of the same species are apparently resistant to the disease. Rothenbuhler has demonstrated that the basis of this increased resistance is a behavioral

---

[1]The genotype refers to the actual genetic information contained in coded form in the sequence of nucleotide bases on the DNA molecule. Chromosomes are composed of DNA, and the structure of each organism's DNA defines the coded genetic program of development for that individual. The phenotype, on the other hand, refers simply to any observable characteristic of the organism—for example, eye color, courtship behavior, height, or learning ability. Rarely are genotypes directly measurable, and the phenotype must often be taken as a partial indirect index of the genotype.

one. Resistant bees prevent the spread of the infection by quickly removing dead and diseased larvae from the cells, thereby checking bacterial spread at an early stage. Mendelian analysis of hygienic (nest-cleaning) behavior suggests that behavioral differences in the susceptibility of the two strains are produced by differences in only a very few genes.

To assess the source of the strain differences, Rothenbuhler crossed a genetically pure resistant strain of bees (nest-cleaners) with a pure susceptible strain. The product of this cross, the first filial (F_1) generation of progeny, consisted entirely of bees heterozygous[2] for this trait. When tested, these bees proved to be quite susceptible to the infection. As the product of the union of two genetically pure strains, individuals in the F_1 generation each had one gene form producing resistance and one gene form producing susceptibility. Since the progeny were in fact susceptible, the gene form for susceptibility must have been a dominant one. Nest-cleaning (removal of the diseased larvae) therefore must be a recessive behavioral character whose expression is masked by a dominant form inhibiting nest-cleaning. To determine exactly how many genes are involved in producing the behavioral differences between strains, Rothenbuhler then took males (drone bees) of the F_1 generation and bred them back to the pure recessive queen bee. If only one gene were involved in producing the strain differences in hygienic behavior, one-half of the progeny resulting from this backcross should be hygienic (and therefore pure recessive); the remaining one-half should be heterozygous with, of course, susceptibility emerging as the dominant trait. The results of this backcross unexpectedly produced six colonies of bees that were hygienic; they effectively removed diseased larvae. Nine colonies, however, uncapped the sealed cells but failed to remove the infected larvae. The fourteen remaining bee colonies were completely susceptible; that is, they neither uncapped cells nor removed infected larvae. These proportions suggested that differences in the complete response sequence might result from the combined action of two genes: one regulating the behavior of uncapping the cells and the other regulating the removal of the diseased larvae. If this were the case, the fourteen susceptible phenotypes should in fact represent distinct genotypes. Rothenbuhler reasoned that bees incapable of uncapping the cells might actually be able to remove larvae, but fail to do so because the cells remain sealed. Of the fourteen susceptible groups,

---

[2]Most organisms have two copies of each gene. These two copies may occur in any one of a number of different forms called *alleles*. Alternatively, for a given gene the two copies may occur in identical form; the individual is then said to be *homozygous* for this character. If the two copies of a given gene are composed of different alleles, the individual is said to be *heterozygous* for the character represented. Different alleles for the character blood type are, for example, responsible for the numerous different blood types seen in human beings. One allele may represent a dominant form and mask the expression of other alleles with which it is paired. In such a case a heterozygous individual with one dominant allele will be phenotypically indistinguishable from a genetically homozygous individual with two identical dominant alleles.

therefore, 50 percent would hygienically remove larvae if the cells were uncapped; the remaining 50 percent would do neither. To test this possibility, Rothenbuhler himself uncapped cells for the bees to see how the fourteen susceptible groups would respond if half the job were done for them. As predicted, approximately one-half of these groups proceeded to remove larvae; the other half failed to remove infected larvae even from the unsealed cells. The former were presumably heterozygous dominant for inhibiting uncapping (and therefore left the cells sealed), while at the same time homozygous recessive for removal (and therefore did remove larvae from the uncapped cells). The latter, the completely susceptible groups, were very likely heterozygous for both uncapping and removal, and therefore dominant gene forms inhibiting those behaviors masked the expression of the recessive gene forms regulating the occurrence of the behaviors, and neither response occurred. Through an elegant case of behavioral genetic analysis, Rothenbuhler has demonstrated that the differences in the complex hygienic behavior of different strains of honeybees are in fact attributable to differential behavioral regulation by as few as two genes.

THE ETHOLOGICAL APPROACH

The modern analysis of species-specific behavior is based on the science of ethology. *Ethology* is the study of behavior from a biological perspective, encompassing physiological and ecological as well as evolutionary analysis. A conceptually based biology of behavior emerged early in the twentieth Century with the work of Oskar Heinroth, Konrad Lorenz, Wallace Craig, Niko Tinbergen, and others. Motivated by the persuasive Darwinian framework, these men sought a theoretically based biology of behavior. While many of the early concepts have been either modified or discarded in accord with modern developments in the related fields of neurophysiology, ecology, and genetics, the framework developed by the early ethologists has remained a central part of the study of species-specific behavior.

Virtually all of the early concepts were derived from observations of the behavior of animals in their natural environments. Moreover, ethologists extended their interests to the behavior of all organisms, including insects, fish, and birds, as well as mammals. Consequently, the striking diversity of behavior across the animal kingdom itself became a question of interest. The ethologists' naturalistic observations, the diversity they addressed, and their attempts at explanation crystallized the major issues of concern to ethology; these issues remain central to the explanation of species-specific behavior.

Their extensive naturalistic observations quickly drew the ethologists' attention to the importance of *function* in behavior. A series of vital tasks faces the organism in the wild. Among these, for example, are the location of mates and food, escape from predators, and protection and nurturance of offspring. Each of these tasks may be critical to the reproductive success of the organism, and each is ultimately solved behaviorally. If behavior serves critical functions in the organism's adaptation to the demands of the environment, behavior can therefore be assessed in terms of selective advantage. The functions of various ritualized behavior patterns, such as the elaborate courtship displays of birds, became a focal concern for the ethologists.

Detailed descriptions of naturally occurring behavior in many types of organisms suggested that comparisons of the behaviors of various species might reveal the phylogeny of behavior. How might behavior have evolved among closely related species that share a common ancestry? Differences in the courtship behaviors of various species of gulls, for example, might be representative of evolutionary changes in the courtship behaviors of ancestral species. Using comparisons among existing species, therefore, the ethologists speculated on how behavior might have evolved in the extinct ancestors of these species. Both the interest in function and the striking differences among various species led to much ethological theory on the nature of the physiological mechanisms that underlie species-specific behavior. Before reviewing the theoretical models devised by early ethologists, however, we will turn to a summary of the methods used to address these issues.

Techniques

Ethologists have used three main experimental tools, each reflecting some aspect of the general ethological orientation. First among these is the *ethogram*. An ethogram is a catalog or complete detailed description of an organism's behavior in the natural state. A precise descriptive analysis is an essential element in understanding the problems posed by ethology. Without the equivalent of a modest ethogram, it would be difficult for either the ethologist or the psychologist to perform any experiment efficiently and effectively. Assume, for example, that you have encountered a new organism that exhibits an unusual pattern of bowing when it meets a conspecific. With the opportunity to observe the individual unobtrusively in its natural setting, you may obtain a wealth of information that can be very useful in analyzing both the phylogeny and the ontogeny of the behavior. Detailed observation of this behavior in the field may reveal many related responses in the animal's repertoire. More importantly, observation may indicate the specific natural conditions under which the behavior occurs, revealing the range and types of stimuli to which the animal is responsive. Does bowing occur in the presence of all conspecifics, only males, only females, or only juveniles? Do contextual factors such as the presence of food in the immediate situation, seasonal change, or the presence of other individuals alter the effectiveness of a given stimulus? Answers to these questions may provide the basis for plausible hypotheses regarding the function served by the behavior. Moreover, the detailed description of the form of the response can reveal subtle differences in bowing exhibited by closely related species. Comparison among these species may then be used to infer the phylogeny of the response.

In the last several years psychologists have realized that ethograms may be invaluable in laboratory work too. An animal's ability to perform in a learning situation depends upon the particular stimuli, responses, and reinforcers selected by the experimenter. It is inaccurate to assume, for example, that all reinforcers are equally effective in strengthening a given response, or that all responses are equally strengthened by a given reinforcer. Instead, the interactions between stimuli, responses, and reinforcers, though subtle, are often critical. Invariably, they depend upon natural tendencies to respond revealed by observation or experimentation. Knowledge of the animal's behavior in the field, therefore, can be equally useful in the analysis of that behavior in the laboratory. The testing of hypotheses generated by field observation requires that the organism be brought into the laboratory and observed under rigorously controlled experimental conditions. Only in this way can the animal's responses to a particular stimulus situation be precisely measured, while the effects of extraneous variables are minimized. The ethological approach therefore also helps ensure that findings obtained in the laboratory are not idiosyncratic and unrepresentative of the animal's behavior in its natural setting.

A second technique used by ethologists is the *isolation study* (also called the deprivation experiment). Kuo's experiments on cats raised in isolation and the analysis of the effects of variations in acoustical experience on the development of cricket song (both described earlier) represent isolation studies. The isolation technique represents an attempt to raise an organism in the absence of variations in environmental experience, thereby evaluating the importance of a particular type of experience in the development of behavior. If the behavior develops normally, that experience is then judged nonessential for the development of the behavior. Abnormalities or differences in behavior following isolation, however, suggest that variations in experience may alter the behavioral outcome. Kuo, for example, questioned whether or not the experience of seeing cats kill rats was essential for the development of rat-killing in the isolated cat. Once such a question is answered in the affirmative, further work can pinpoint which aspects of the experience are critical.

The isolation technique has at least two problems. First, isolation may produce its effect by damaging the organism. Early experiments, for example, used the isolation technique to determine the effects of visual deprivation in infancy upon the monkey's subsequent perception. While deprivation was found to have dramtically debilitating effects on visual perception, this result occurred for the relatively trivial reason that the monkeys' visual systems had deteriorated in the absence of exposure to light. Thus early visual experience was necessary for the normal development of pattern perception, not because the absence of such experience restricted visual learning, but because the absence of exposure to light permanently impaired the functioning of the visual system. In later experiments monkeys were raised in diffuse, nonpatterned light. Under these conditions deprivation had no obvious effects on the visual system but did produce certain perceptual deficits. The second potential pitfall of the isolation technique is the frequently held assumption that learning cannot occur in an isolated organism. Any emerging behavior must therefore be unlearned or innate. The problem here is that the organism can learn a wealth of behavior from stimuli provided by the organism itself; that is, the animal may receive proprioceptive feedback from its own movements. Thus the fact that there has been no other organism present cannot be taken to mean that any resultant behavior is unaffected by environmental variation. In general, then, one should be cautious in designing or interpreting studies using the isolation technique.

A third ethological technique involves the use of *models*. A model is an artificial replica of the critical stimulating features correlated with the occurrence of the behavior in question. Models can be altered to resemble the essential stimulus features to varying degrees. Tinbergen, for example, observing that during mating season the male stickleback will attack any other male stickleback intruding on its territory, has asked, "What feature of an intruding male is responsible for the attack?" Utilizing a series of models, such as those in Figure 9.5, Tinbergen ascertained that

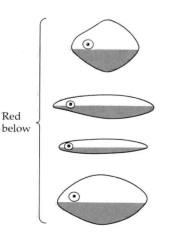

Red below

Figure 9.5
The series of models employed by Tinbergen to release attack in the male stickleback. Accurate renditions of the fish lacking a red underside were ineffective, whereas very crude imitations with red below successfully released attack. [After Tinbergen, 1951.]

the critical stimulating feature was the red patch on the male's underside. Tinbergen constructed a series of models of different colorations and shapes and presented them to his male sticklebacks. He found that the stickleback would attack a wooden square with a big red spot on it, but did not attack a model that looked like a male stickleback in every detail except that its red patch was missing. Thus Tinbergen was able to demonstrate that the red patch was the controlling stimulus for the attack, illustrating the use of models in the analysis of species-specific behavior.

ETHOLOGICAL THEORY

The focus of ethological theory has been to identify those natural conditions under which the occurrence of a particular behavior will augment reproductive success. What features of the environment ensure the occurrence of the response at the appropriate time, and, given these circumstances, how is the response brought about? Further, why do functionally similar behaviors, such as various forms of courtship, differ so dramatically from species to species? Though the specific principles brought to bear on these questions have developed dramatically over the years, early ethological theory was devised to address just such issues.

Sign Stimuli

Detailed description of the behavior of many organisms observed in their natural settings has revealed that particular sequences of behavior virtually always occur in the presence of specific stimuli. Moreover, such sequences are seen to undergo very little change from instance to instance. The search for biological mechanisms by which these "automatic" sequences might be explained became the ethologists' major task. Efforts began with the identification of those biologically relevant features of the natural environment in whose presence the response was virtually assured. In many situations, relatively simple configural stimuli were observed to "release" the behaviors in question, and the uniquely effective stimulus was therefore termed a *releaser* or *sign stimulus*. The red patch on the male stickleback's underside constitutes a sign stimulus for attack. Similarly, the orange breast of the European robin releases territorial aggression in another robin. As we have already noted, not all features of the naturally occurring configurations are essential in initiating the sequence. A fish shape is ineffective in stimulating attack in the stickleback, while a red patch by itself quickly provokes attack.

Sign stimuli, however, do not exert their effects independently of *context*. A male stickleback will attack another male that enters its territory. If, however, the stickleback encounters another male in the latter's territory, the intruding fish will flee. The red spot, therefore, not only signals territorial attack by a defending male but also flight from another male's territory. Thus the context in which the sign stimulus is presented is crucial in determining which of a number of possible responses will occur; the stickleback's behavior is subtly controlled by an interaction between the sign stimulus and its location in the environment.

Sign stimuli play important roles in interspecies communication as well. Their adaptive nature can be seen rather dramatically in the case of certain species of moth and butterfly (see Figure 9.6) that have evolved large owl-like eyes on their wings. Because owls and hawks are their natural predators, insectivorous birds fly away from rapidly moving stimuli resembling the eyes of owls and hawks. Appropriate displays have evolved, therefore, among certain insect species that would otherwise constitute food for these insectivorous birds. In the moth *Automeris coresus*, for example, a sudden spreading of the wings exposes owl-like eyespots on the hind wing. Because they provide great selective advantage to the moth, the owl-like patterns have been perpetuated (Manning, 1971). It is apparent that these species of moth and butterfly have evolved in such a way as to guarantee their protection from major predators—that is, the insectivorous birds. But why isn't this interaction maladaptive from the point of view of the bird? Certain releasing functions such as fleeing from predator-like stimuli are so important to the organism that it is to the individual's advantage to respond to these stimuli in a nondiscriminating fashion. The birds do not discriminate between actual owl eyes and those on insects' wings, and instead flee from both. The responses to these releasers represent a type of "false alarm." However, while the bird may occasionally pass up eating a delectable and harmless butterfly, in the long run this loss is far less important than the danger of flying into the clutches of a hungry owl.

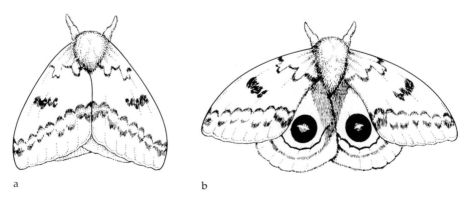

a   b

Figure 9.6
The moth *Automeris coresus* (a) at rest and (b) exposing its eyespots in response to tactile stimulation. [After Blest, 1957.]

As suggested by the stickleback's behavior, sign stimuli are often critical in intraspecific communication as well. The courtship patterns of many species provide excellent examples. Male sexual displays that attract a female's attention very likely will develop a selective advantage. Similarly, females that are more responsive to these behaviors are more likely to reproduce. Courtship patterns like that of the female finch shown in Figure 9.7 are highly responsive to evolutionary pressures and are known to differentiate even very closely related species. They effectively allow an organism to identify correctly the most biologically compatible mate: Offspring of interspecies matings (hybrids) are far less likely to reproduce successfully than are those of intraspecies matings. Thus distinguishing structural or behavioral features can serve as sign stimuli that assist in reproductive isolation. These are likely to be favored by natural selection.

Lorenz and Tinbergen (see Tinbergen, 1951) have coined the term *social*

Figure 9.7
Courtship postures used by the female chaffinch in soliciting for copulation. [After Hinde, 1970.]

releaser to describe that class of releasers which communicate information to other organisms, including fellow members of one's own species. One example of the effects of a social releaser is provided by the aggressive behavior of the male Siamese fighting fish *(Betta splendens)*. When confronted by either another male Betta, its own mirror image, or an appropriate model, the fighting fish engages in a highly stereotyped pattern of aggressive behavior consisting of a deepening of body and fin color, gill membrane extension, and frontal approach toward the other *Betta*, accompanied by undulating movements. Under appropriate conditions two confined male *Bettas* may combat until exhaustion or death. Moreover, the Siamese fighting fish will learn a response in order to obtain this social releaser for aggressive display. Fantino, Weigele, and Lancy (1972) deprived fish of both food and the opportunity to display and found that at moderate levels of deprivation (48 to 120 hours) for both rewards the fish chose the response that produced its mirror image more frequently than the response that produced food. With sufficiently high levels of deprivation (for example, 240 hours) food was preferred. These results, shown in Figure 9.8, suggest that the effectiveness of social releasers can depend critically upon the state of the organism's internal environment. In fact, there is rarely a perfect one-to-one relation between sign stimuli and the behaviors they release. Despite these qualifications, however, a remarkable specificity exists between sign stimuli and behavior.

In the presence of certain sign stimuli the appropriate behavior may be released even when other aspects of the situation are unusual. The study

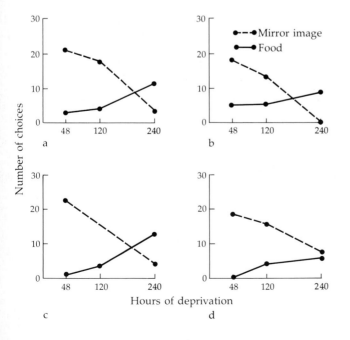

Figure 9.8
The effect of levels of food deprivation on the choice of food versus aggressive display (to a mirror image) in four Siamese fighting fish (a, b, c, d). [After Fantino, Weigele, and Lancy, 1972.]

of models has shown that once the appropriate sign stimulus has been isolated, the rest of the stimulus configuration is largely irrelevant; as long as the sign stimulus is present, the behavior will be released. What if the sign stimulus itself is manipulated? For example, what if the organism is presented with a stimulus that resembles the sign stimulus but is actually more salient than the normally occurring sign stimulus? Utilizing models, ethologists have found that stimuli stronger (along the relevant dimension) than the naturally appearing sign stimulus may be more effective in releasing behavior. For example, oyster catchers and other birds prefer to sit on a huge *supernormal* egg rather than on a normal-sized egg (as shown in Figure 9.9). In the case of the stickleback models (shown in Figure 9.5) the larger the red spot on the males' belly, the stronger the releaser, and the more vigorous the response. A final example, reported by Tinbergen, is provided by the case of the herring gull chick, which obtains food by pecking a red spot on the parent's bill. When the chick pecks at the red spot, the parent regurgitates food to the chick. When presented with models of bills like those shown in Figure 9.10, the chick does *not* give the strongest pecking response to the most realistic-looking bill. Instead, models that are longer and contain more red than normal will be more effective releasing stimuli. On the other hand, something that looks very beak-like (at least to humans) but is short and lacks redness will release very little responding on the part of the chick.

This aspect of sign stimuli—the greater effectiveness of supernormal releasing stimuli—poses an intriguing problem. Since natural selection is presumably responsible for shaping instinctive behavior, how could a situation arise in which stimuli that do not occur in nature are more effective than those that do? While there is no definitive answer to this question, it is clear that natural selection would have virtually no opportunity to select against the tendency to respond to supernormal stimuli. Since sign stimuli are generally associated with functions that are vital to survival, in many instances the selection process may have resulted in the tendency to respond more vigorously the stronger the relevant stimulus.

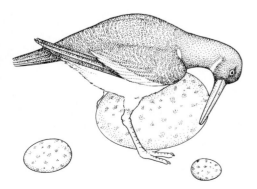

Figure 9.9
An oyster catcher attempting to incubate a supernormal egg in preference either to its own normal egg (at right) or to a herring gull's egg (at left). [After Tinbergen, 1951.]

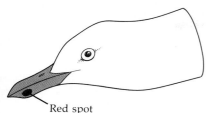

Red spot

a

b

Figure 9.10
(a) The realistic model of a herring gull's head does not release as strong a pecking response in the chick as (b) the thinner, supernormal model, which is completely colored red with three white bars. [After Tinbergen and Perdeck, 1950.]

Again, "false alarms" generally do not have serious consequences for the species.

Up to now we have concentrated exclusively on visual sign stimuli. There are, however, many examples of sign stimuli occurring in other sensory modalities. For example, Schleidt (1961), studying the involvement of audition in the development of parental behavior in turkey hens, has shown that the "cheeping" call of the young is a sign stimulus for normal parental behavior. Schleidt found that deaf turkey hens that cannot hear the cheeping call (though they can see the chicks perfectly well) will generally kill their offspring.

Fixed Action Patterns

The effectiveness of a sign stimulus depends on its ability to produce an extremely stereotyped behavior pattern. Ethologists termed such stereotyped sequences *fixed action patterns.* Fixed action patterns are species-specific; that is, they are displayed uniformly by all members of the species (though occasionally a given response may be seen either only in males or only in females). In addition, the motor patterns occur in identical fashion each time they are displayed by a particular individual. The form of the response sequence is therefore quite constant. "When the inner readiness to act [a motivational state] coincides with the appropriate releasing stimulus situation, then a particular fixed action pattern will run its course almost automatically" (Eibl-Eibesfeldt, 1974, p. 17). For the ethologists, therefore, the fixed action pattern became the unit of species-specific behavior. Eibl-Eibesfeldt describes the following example of a fixed action pattern in the spider:

> While constructing a cocoon, the spider *Cupiennius salei* first produces a base plate, then a raised rim that provides the opening into which the eggs are

deposited. Having laid the eggs, the female closes this opening. If she is interrupted while spinning her cocoon, after the base plate has been completed, she will not produce a new base plate half an hour later when she builds a new cocoon, but instead spins only a few threads and then continues with construction of the rim, so that the bottom of the cocoon remains open. If one adds the number of spinning movements she performed for the previous base plate and for the new substitute cocoon, the number roughly equals the number normally used to build a complete cocoon. She has available, so to speak, a limited number of spinning movements— approximately 6400 dabbing movements. This number of movements is performed, even if, under abnormal circumstances, she is no longer able to secrete any threads. This has happened when the glands dry up as a result of hot lights used during filming. In such instances the spider still produces her behavior program. After the appropriate number of ineffectual dabbing movements she will lay her eggs, which will then drop to the ground. Then she continues as if she were closing the rudimentary cocoon. . . .

The spider is therefore not affected by the success of her efforts. This can also be seen when the same spider is placed upon a half-completed structure. The existing structure is not taken into account. Instead, she continues as if she were sitting on her own cocoon [Eibl-Eibesfeldt, 1974, p. 18].

The ethologists further recognized that fixed action patterns (FAP's) are often made more adaptable by virtue of orienting movements, or *taxes,* superimposed upon the stereotyped sequence. Taxes allow for the immediate orientation of the movements comprising the fixed action pattern and therefore serve to coordinate the occurrence of the FAP as the pattern proceeds. Together, the occurrence of orienting movements superimposed upon the FAP represents instinctive activity. Perhaps the classic example of the unity of the two elements into an instinctive pattern is the egg-rolling behavior of the graylag goose pictured in Figure 9.11.

If a graylag goose is presented with an egg outside its nest it will reach out with its bill over and beyond the egg and pull it in with the underside of the bill, balancing it carefully back into the nest. This behavior may be broken down into two components. If one removes the egg after the rolling movement has been started, then the movement continues in vacuo. The bird behaves as if the egg were still there. However, the lateral balancing movements cease and the neck is pulled back in a straight line to the nest. This movement, which once released will continue in the absence of additional external stimuli, is the fixed action pattern. The lateral balancing movements are the orienting movements or taxis components, which are also inborn but are discontinued in the absence of the releasing stimuli [Eibl-Eibesfeldt, 1974, p. 19].

As the description indicates, the distinctive feature of the FAP component (pulling the neck straight back with the head bowed) is that once stimulated it will continue in the absence of any further environmental input.

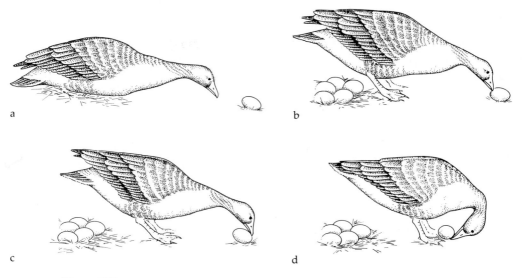

a

b

c

d

Figure 9.11
The egg-rolling behavior of the graylag goose illustrates the unity of fixed action patterns and orienting taxes in the instinctive behavior described by ethologists. [After Lorenz and Tinbergen, 1938.]

The Hydraulic Model

The ethologists assumed that the specificity with which a particular stimulus feature (the sign stimulus) produced a species-specific behavior sequence (the fixed action pattern) was assured by the organization of the animal's nervous system. The adaptive value of the occurrence of the fixed action pattern under biologically relevant conditions increased the reproductive success of the individual that behaved in this way. As a result, in phylogeny neural structures came to be organized such that under a particular set of circumstances this and only this sequence would occur. Among the major theoretical efforts of the ethologists were accounts of how nervous systems might be structured to assure such complex stimulus–response specificity. Investigators' attentions centered on two key questions: (1) How does the specificity between sign stimulus and fixed action pattern result from the organization of neural structure representing a particular response system? and (2) Given the diversity of stimulation present at any one time in the natural environment, why is one response system activated while others remain quiet?

In the 1930s specific knowledge of the neurophysiological organization of behavior was lacking. Ethologists therefore relied on the construction of theoretical models to represent the logical schema by which neural systems might be structured. Among the most prominent of these attempts was Konrad Lorenz' *hydraulic model* (also called the energy model). Lorenz' model is schematized in Figure 9.12. In general, the model states that *action-specific energy*—instinctual energy reserved for the performance of a particular behavior—builds up in specific centers, or reservoirs (R), in the central nervous system. The energy accumulation sets up a corresponding drive state within the organism. When the organism encounters a sign stimulus, or releaser (Sp), the stimulus activates an *innate releasing mechanism* (components V and S in the figure), thereby dissipating the action-specific energy that led to the instinctive behavior sequence. The innate releasing mechanism (IRM) is assumed to be a neurosensory mechanism that allows the accumulating action-specific energy to be discharged specifically to the effectors required in the performance of the sequence (Tr). The IRM is thus seen to "recognize" and respond exclusively to the sign stimulus; the model stresses specificity between the releaser and the FAP, a specificity assured by the organization of the IRM. According to one metaphor, the IRM acts as if it were a lock on the instinctual energy; the releasing stimulus fits the lock, opens it, and allows the energy to be dissipated in the performance of the species-specific behavior. Specificity is therefore provided by the structure of the IRM. In the absence of the appropriate stimulus, the IRM performs an inhibitory function, blocking the discharge of energy until the biologically appropri-

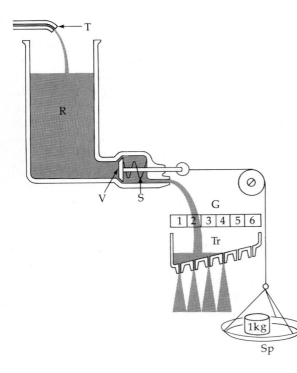

Figure 9.12
Lorenz' hydraulic model. With the accumulation of action-specific energy, presentation of a sign stimulus triggers the IRM leading to the performance of an instinctive behavior sequence. [After Lorenz, 1950.]

ate moment. Only at this time would the occurrence of the fixed action pattern result in increased reproductive success. The nervous system has therefore evolved equipped with mechanisms that prevent the response from occurring at any other time.

Ethologists proposed the concept of a response-specific pool of energy to explain the phenomenom of *vacuum activity*. Vacuum activity is species-specific behavior that occurs in the apparent absence of stimulation (hence in a psychological vacuum). Tinbergen cites the example of the stickleback performing a zigzag dance in an empty tank after sufficient sexual deprivation. Similarly, Hinde (1958) has noted that canaries deprived of nest-building material may eventually perform nest-weaving movements in the nonexistent nest. Finally, Lorenz (1970) reports that the starling, deprived of food, may perform an entire sequence of fly-catching behavior, including searching for, catching, and killing a nonexistent fly. The energy model stipulates that as the action-specific energy builds up, the IRM will be unlocked "spontaneously"—that is, in the absence of a releaser, presumably by the overwhelming build-up and eventual overflow of energy specific to that particular response.

In situations as complex as those which face organisms in their natural environments, the individual is not likely to encounter one sign stimulus at a time. Rather, several may be presented simultaneously, or contextual factors may render the sign ambiguous. Under such circumstances sign stimuli may trigger incompatible or "conflicting" response tendencies. What will the organism do in such situations? How are these "neural conflicts" to be settled, and can the observed outcomes be explained by the ethologists' hydraulic model?

If competing, conflicting releasers are present, organisms have been observed to engage in behavior that is apparently irrelevant to either stimulus. Such responses have been termed *displacement activities*. Responses produced in this way are thought to be incomplete innate patterns of behavior, more appropriate to releasers not present in the situation. When, for example, two male sticklebacks meet at the border of their respective territories, both fish will engage in "displacement digging." Each appears to displace its tendency either to attack or to flee with the seemingly irrelevant behavior of digging. Displacement digging can also be produced by punishing the stickleback for attacking an appropriate model in its own territory. When the model is presented to the stickleback and actually used to hit him, the stickleback first fights, then stops fighting and begins to dig. After a time, however, the fish will fight again. This suggests that digging occurs when the tendency to flee (caused by the punishment) is equal to the tendency to fight (released by the presence of an appropriate sign stimulus in the stickleback's territory).

Displacement activities—of which displacement digging is only one example—are fairly common. Ethologists have also reported instances of "displacement fanning" occurring during the stickleback's courtship sequence. In courtship the male stickleback performs a zigzag dance designed to lure the female stickleback into the nest, where she lays her eggs (ejaculation for the male requires the presence of the female's eggs as well as of the female herself). If the female does not respond to the zigzag dance, the male makes nest-ventilating movements called "fanning." The amount of "displacement fanning" has been used as a reliable index of the male stickleback's sexual motivation. Other instances of displacement activity include courtship preening and courtship feeding, both prevalent in many birds. These are preening or feeding activities that seem to be displaced from more direct sexual activities. Efforts to explain displacement activities within the framework of the hydraulic model described the action-specific energy as "sparking over" from the mutually inhibited drives into another channel appropriate to the displacement activity. In this way the activity is released in the absence of its innately associated sign stimulus. In the case of displacement digging in the stickleback, when the tendencies to fight and flee are equivalent the mutually exclusive behaviors cancel each other. Energy from those tendencies then sparks over into channels associated with digging, and digging occurs.

Alternatives to the Hydraulic Model

There are a number of explanations of displacement and vacuum activities more parsimonious than those proposed by the energy model. Richard Andrew (1956) has pointed out that displacement activities in fact do occur in the presence of the stimuli that normally releases them. For example, the phenomenon of displacement drinking in conflict situations may be explained by the fact that conflict produces dryness of the throat, which in turn leads to drinking. The activity is not capricious. Nor does it require explanation in terms of energy "sparking over" from the prepotent conflicting response centers. Andrew has also shown that birds in conflict situations adopt postures similar to those adopted by birds trying to cool themselves off after being in heated environments. Presumably the "displacement postures" are a response to the increase in body temperature generated by the conflict.

Several other examples could be cited to support the contention that displacement activities are influenced by the prevailing stimuli. In these cases displacement activity is a normal behavioral reaction to peripheral stimulation, such as dryness of the throat. In other cases in which displacement activity occurs instead of either of two mutually exclusive prepotent responses, the emitted response may simply be the next most probable response. For example, digging behavior in the stickleback is a likely response for the organism any time it is at the edge of its territory. Normally, however, in the presence of the red patch either attacking or fleeing another male stickleback is more probable than digging. At the boundary of two territories the prepotent but mutually exclusive responses of attacking and fleeing become much less likely because they effectively cancel one another. In fact, neither occurs, and the next most probable response in the situation—in this case digging—results instead.

One critical question facing the energy model is whether displacement activity is truly independent of external stimulus events or whether it is instead actually modulated by such stimuli. The "sparking over" hypothesis suggests that displacement behavior should be independent of prevailing external stimulus conditions. However, the results of Rowell's (1961) studies of displacement preening in chaffinches placed in conflict situations cast doubt on this hypothesis. On some occasions Rowell put water on the birds' plumage, while on other occasions he placed a sticky substance on the birds' beaks. If displacement preening were independent of prevailing external stimulus conditions, the type of preening exhibited should depend only upon the conflict situation and not upon the nature or location of the applied substance. Instead, Rowell found that preening was a function of the kinds and intensities of stimuli normally producing characteristic forms of grooming. Although preening did increase during conflict, the type of preening that occurred depended upon the nature of the applied substance: when water was put on the plumage the bird preened; when a sticky substance was placed on the beak the bird engaged in a bill-wiping response. These results, along with others suggesting that displacement behavior occurs in response to prevailing stimulus conditions, argue against the sufficiency of the "sparking over" hypothesis.

The picture is much the same when the discussion turns to vacuum activities. Here, too, as several ethologists have themselves suggested (see Thorpe, 1948; Hinde, 1970), the external stimulus conditions may be more important than earlier interpretations had implied. Under strong sexual deprivation, for example, organisms may mount an inappropriate sexual object. If mounting is viewed as normally occurring in response to a large configuration of stimuli, including internal hormonal changes, its occurrence in the absence of one particular source of stimulation (the "normal" or "appropriate" sex object) appears less anomalous. Moreover, the classification of behavior as vacuum activity has the added disadvantage of discouraging further investigation of stimulus conditions possibly responsible for the behavior.

While the energy model itself has been largely discounted, several of its component concepts have proven to be quite useful outside the framework of the complete model. Among those which stand as workable constructs are the notions of the innate releasing mechanism and the fixed action pattern. All remain very much a part of modern theories of species-specific behavior.

As we have seen, most modern treatments view species-specific behavior as consisting of complex sequences of responding whose final outcome is adaptive to the organism. That is, species-specific behavior provides for the more efficient completion of some function that facilitates reproductive success. The sequential patterning characteristic of such behavior is assumed to be genetically based, and a given sequence occurs by virtue of the genetic programming of behaviors in time. Recall that the definitive feature of a fixed action pattern is that at some point following the initiation of the response sequence, further orderly patterning proceeds independently of environmental input. Presumably, at this point, contextual variations are irrelevant, and the genetic program itself guides the final sequencing of behavior.

Recent investigations of the physiological control of orderly sequencing in behavior have given the ethologists' characterizations of innate releasing mechanisms and fixed action patterns renewed validity. Consider the former as neural aggregates selectively programmed to activate an organized motor sequence. The fixed action pattern therefore becomes the resulting molar behavior sequence. Willows and Hoyle's (1969; Willows, 1971) analysis of the stereotyped escape response in the marine mollusk *Tritonia diomedia* is representative of this growing trend in behavioral research. The escape sequence, which on description nicely fits the classical ethological definition of a fixed action pattern, is pictured in Figure 9.13.

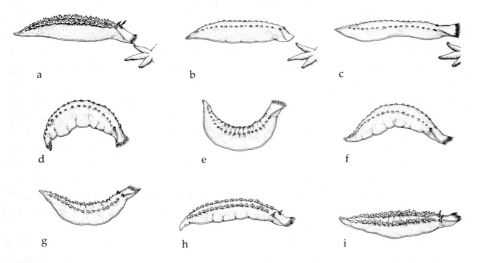

Figure 9.13
Stereotyped escape response of *Tritonia diomedia*. When one of the animals, (a) cruising normally, comes in contact with a starfish, (b) it first pulls in extended parts of its body. (c) Next there is an elongation and enlargement of head and tail regions into paddle-like structures. The animal then begins a series of (d) ventral and (e) dorsal flexions resulting in a vigorous swimming movement. (f–i) The response ends with a series of gradually weakening upward bends, with short intervals of relaxation between them. [After "Giant Brain Cells in Mollusks" by A. O. D. Willows. Copyright © 1971 by Scientific American, Inc. All rights reserved.]

Following initial chemotactic stimulation by some species of starfish, *Tritonia* (a giant sea slug) contracts its gill tufts and elongates both ends of its already flat body. Then follows an alternating series of dorsal and ventral flexions of the muscles on the body walls of the animal's back and underside. This response sequence, which lasts for approximately 30 seconds, effectively propels the organism away from the dangerous predatory starfish. The chemotactic stimulus is a releaser that activates an orderly sequence of responding. If the neural sequence involved in regulating the response is an IRM, we can assume that following the initiating action of the releaser a genetically programmed closed system of neural output proceeds unmodulated by further environmental input.

Tritonia's nervous system is composed of a relatively small number of very large neurons. The size of the neuron cell bodies may range up to as much as a millimeter in diameter. The shapes and positions of these cells within the nervous system are, moreover, quite consistent across animals. These features make the neurophysiological analysis of complex response sequences much more feasible than would be the case in most organisms. Willows has in fact identified groups of neurons whose firing patterns are well correlated with specific elements of the response sequence. By manipulating various aspects of the relationships among nerve cells, he can determine both the contribution of each individual cell and the importance of interactions among cell groups in organizing the complete behavior sequence. Recordings collected with the animal mobile and able to respond while the brain has been immobilized on a raised platform, as pictured in Figure 9.14, indicate that an initial burst of cellular activity correlated with elongation of the body stimulates further firing in three distinct cell groups. One group, the *dorsal flexion neurons* (DFN), fire continuously for a short time, during which the animal engages in a dorsal flexion. Cessation of activity in the DFN cells is followed by the initiation of firing in a second group of cells, the *ventral flexion neurons* (VFN). Here, sustained activity is accompanied by contraction of the muscles on the ventral body surface. The active phases of these two cell groups alternate repeatedly over an extended period, during which the animal responds with alternate dorsal and ventral flexions. A third group of cells, the *general excitor neurons* (GEN), fire continuously throughout the entire sequence that follows the initial releasing burst. Taken together, these cell groups and their interactions constitute a central innate releasing mechanism regulating the occurrence of the escape sequence.

Reciprocal communication among cell groups apparently serves to organize the sequential patterning of the responding independently of input from the periphery. The initial burst need not persist throughout the sequence; it rather provides the initial impetus. In analyzing the relationships among cell groups, Willows (1971) has focused on the following questions: What initiates firing in the DFN and VFN groups; given that each fires for only a short period, what turns each group off; what is the role of the general excitor neurons; and finally, in Willow's own words,

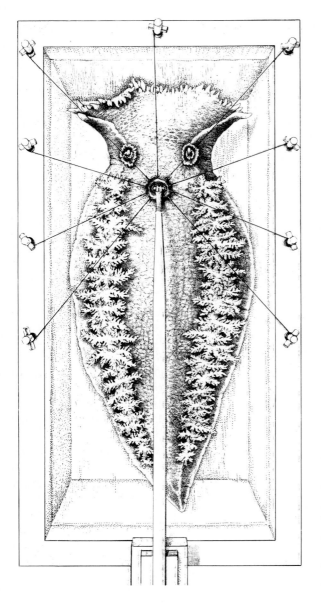

Figure 9.14
Records of the neural activity associated with *Tritonia's* escape response are obtained by suspending the animal in shallow water and immobilizing its brain on a small platform immediately above. [After "Giant Brain Cells in Mollusks" by A. O. D. Willows. Copyright © 1971 by Scientific American, Inc. All rights reserved.]

"does the brain drive the entire sequence of movements in accordance with a built-in general plan *or does the behavior simply consist in a chain of reflexes, each one successively giving rise to the next?"* (p. 74). If the former were the case, the escape response would constitute a true fixed action pattern sustained by the combined actions of the cell groups constituting the innate releasing mechanism. Willows has postulated that sustained action in the GEN group reinitiates output in the other two groups. These two groups periodically start and stop, but a pattern of ongoing stimulation is maintained by the GEN cells. Willows has performed additional experiments that completely isolate these segments of the still viable nervous system, thereby negating any possibility of guided sequencing by environmental or proprioceptive feedback. The cell groups composing the IRM are neurally isolated, and no environmental input is possible. Even under these conditions an initial externally produced burst of activity in turn stimulates patterned firing of the three cell groups described. None is receiving any input from the environment, and the initial external input need not persist, but only briefly initiates action. Yet the pattern ensues as if the organizational framework for behavior were contained within the programmed output of the cell groups themselves. While active, the DFN group may inhibit activity in the VFN cell group. Activity in the VFN cells has the opposite effect, thus ensuring that the animal will not attempt to engage in incompatible muscular contractions at the same time. More importantly, an analogue of the entire behavior sequence plays itself out in the neurons in the absence of input from the environment. This, then, constitutes the definitive feature of a fixed action pattern. Neural analysis of *Tritonia*'s sequential escape pattern appears to indicate that the response sequencing (the FAP) results from the interconnected action of groups of neurons (an IRM) whose coordinated firing imparts patterned organization onto the actions of connected muscles.

THE DEVELOPMENT OF SPECIES-SPECIFIC BEHAVIOR

Species-specific behavior, like all behavior, develops under the regulation of a genetic program that expresses itself in a particular environment. The genes themselves are nothing more than DNA; in the pathway from a DNA molecule to a complex behaving organism lies an amazingly complex developmental interaction.

Earlier we made the statement that some developmental programs are more open to variations in environmental input than others. The process controlling gene–environment interaction can be viewed as a continuum in which the timing and the degree of specificity required of environmental inputs range from extremely precise to quite flexible. What constitutes a functionally acceptable input can be (at one extreme) either a very clearly specified event or (at the other) any one from among a very general class of events. Species-specific behaviors must be placed on the high-specific end of the continuum. As we shall see in Chapter 10, many types of learning processes fall more appropriately at intermediate points, while still other types demonstrate extremes of flexibility. The nature of the evolutionary forces that mold behavior will determine where on the continuum a particular behavior sequence falls. Species-specific behaviors that can employ only highly specific environmental inputs are also those which must be perfectly executed on first exposure. This, of course, would be the case with predatory escape sequences such as that described for the sea slug. Similarly, alarm calls and the escape responses they elicit occur normally even in birds raised in total auditory isolation. However, in the same organism prolonged experience may be required for the development of territorial songs and other less immediately essential vocalizations. Experience may also modify the conditions that give rise to even such relatively simple behaviors as alarm calls, as we next see.

The first time a bird hears an alarm call, it flees. A question that immediately arises is how the bird giving the alarm call is able to recognize a potential predator. Alarm calls have been studied extensively with geese and other game birds in experiments using the ambiguous goose–hawk figure shown in Figure 9.15. Note that when the figure is seen as moving to the left it resembles the shadow of a goose; when moving to the right it resembles the shadow of a hawk overhead. It has been known for some time that the hawk-like figure constitutes a sign stimulus for the release of an alarm call in geese and other fowl. A model of the same figure facing the opposite direction (the goose-like direction) is, however, not a stimulus for an alarm call. The relationship between a hawk-like stimulus flying overhead and the resultant alarm call is, however, not nearly so specific as was originally thought. Rather, learning appears to be involved. Studies in which models are presented to geese raised in isolation show that the goose emits an alarm call to almost any form moving overhead at an appropriate speed. This nondiscriminating response is adaptive in that it is essential to flee successfully from a predator even at the cost of occasionally fleeing nonpredators. Obviously, however, it is more adaptive to learn to flee only in response to predators. In time, the goose apparently develops indifference to familiar forms flying overhead and

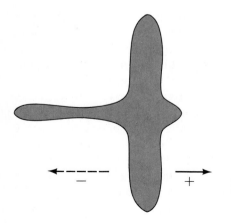

Figure 9.15
The goose/hawk model used to investigate alarm calls elicited by a predator. [After Tinbergen, 1948.]

stops emitting alarm calls to them. The goose has essentially learned to withhold the alarm call when it encounters stimuli that have in the past flown overhead without adverse consequence. Thus the initial tendency to sound an alarm call in response to any object flying overhead at the appropriate speed is modified through experience so that alarm calls eventually occur only when danger is imminent.

Studies have shown that newly hatched chicks and turkeys will rapidly adapt to the sight of *either* goose or hawk models flying overhead. The geese used in the earlier work were experienced and apparently had already habituated to the goose-like forms. In the natural environment, geese often fly overhead without consequence and the alarm call habituates. Hawks are a scarcer commodity, however, and habituation has less of an opportunity to occur. Thus the experienced geese in the earlier studies emitted alarm calls to the hawk model but not to the goose model.

Once again we see how behavior develops through a complex interaction between organism and environment. The organism's genetic endowment predisposes it to respond to particular stimuli. This response may then be modified or elaborated by the organism's further interactions with its environment. Perhaps the most elegant example of the complex interplay can be found in Daniel Lehrman's comprehensive study of parental behavior in the ring dove.

The Lehrman Experiments

The ring dove's reproductive cycle consists of several successive components (courtship, nest-building, egg-laying, incubation of the eggs, and feeding of the young), which are executed with precision and stereotypy. Lehrman's work (see Lehrman, 1964) has demonstrated that each stage in the cycle of reproductive behavior is determined by the interaction of stimuli in both the internal and external environments. When two experienced breeders who have never mated with one another are paired, *courtship* behavior occurs on the first day and is characterized by the "bowing coo" of the male, depicted in Figure 9.16. The doves then participate in *nest-building* for the next week or so, during which time they also copulate. As the week of nest-building progresses, the female dove becomes increasingly attached to the nest. If a human hand examines the nest, for example, the female will doggedly remain on the nest, perhaps slapping the human with her wing. Once this occurs, *egg-laying* is imminent. Somewhere between the seventh and eleventh day, the female produces her first egg, usually between four and five o'clock in the afternoon. Forty hours later, she lays her second egg. *Incubation* of the egg is accomplished during the next 2 weeks with both parents participating in alternation: the female always sits for 18 hours, while the male sits for the remaining 6 hours of the day. The female simply gets up from the nest after 18 hours have elapsed; regardless of what the male is doing at the time, he im-

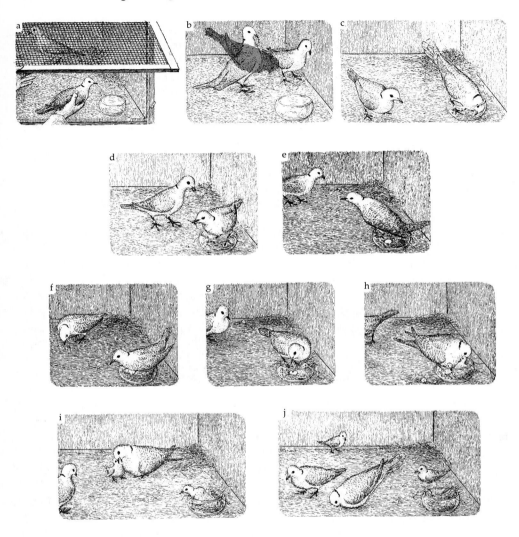

Figure 9.16
(a) The cycle of reproductive behavior in the ring dove begins soon after the male and female are introduced into a cage containing nesting material and an empty glass bowl. (b) Courtship activity, on the first day, is characterized by the "bowing coo" of thé male. (c) The male and then the female utter a distinctive "nest call" to indicate their selection of a nesting site. (d) There follows a week or more of cooperation in nest-building, (e) culminating in the laying of two eggs at precise times of day. (f) The cycle continues as the adult birds take turns incubating the eggs, (g) which hatch after about 14 days. (h) The newly hatched squabs are fed "crop-milk," a liquid secreted in the gullets of the adults. (i) The parents continue to feed them, though reluctantly, as the young birds learn to peck grain for themselves. (j) When the squabs are between two and three weeks old, the adults ignore them and start to court once again, and a new cycle begins. [After "The Reproductive Behavior of Ring Doves" by Daniel S. Lehrman. Copyright © 1964 by Scientific American, Inc. All rights reserved.]

mediately darts over and sits on the eggs for the ensuing 6-hour period. Once the eggs hatch, the young birds must be fed. The final 2-to-3 weeks of the 6-to-7 week reproductive cycle are therefore spent in the *feeding* of the young. During incubation of the eggs, the walls of the parents' crops become thick and the inside layers begin to sluff off, falling into and eventually filling the crop. In feeding, the parent regurgitates the crop milk, which the young then ingest. As the 2-week period comes to an end, however, the parents become increasingly unconcerned with the feeding requests of the young. During the same period the young doves develop the ability to peck for grain on the cage floor. Within a week or two the adult male once again begins to strut about, his bowing and cooing signaling renewed courtship and the advent of a new reproductive cycle.

Lehrman investigated the determinants—both internal and external—of each behavior in the reproductive cycle. He found, for example, that the entire process of nest-building and egg-laying must be completed before incubation of the eggs can occur. A pair of doves presented with a nest they had not built and eggs they had not laid would only incubate the eggs if they had been together for a period of at least 7 days, and during that time had constructed a nest. A single dove given a nest and eggs will never incubate. Therefore it appears that the doves must be together and have access to one another for several days before incubation can occur. Moreover, two doves that have been together for a time but have not received nest-building material will, when subsequently given a ready-made nest and eggs, tear the nest apart and rebuild it. Following this, incubation begins, suggesting that the initiation of incubation is critically dependent upon the prior experiencing of both courtship and nest-building.

Lehrman has further demonstrated the critical part played by hormonal stimuli in sustaining the behavioral succession of the reproductive cycle. The secretion of hormones induced by environmental events (including behavior) must precede certain stages of the cycle. In the male, *progesterone*, necessary for the incubation of the eggs, is stimulated by the prior nest-building behavior. Similarly, nest-building in the female is dependent upon secretion of the hormone *estrogen*, which is itself stimulated by the courtship ritual. The effects of hormonal secretion induced by preceding environmental events may be mimicked by the direct injection of hormones. Thus doves that have not experienced courtship and nest-building will nonetheless incubate eggs if first injected with *progesterone*.

In summary, Lehrman has shown that each of the successive components of the cycle of reproductive behavior is determined by a different set of interacting stimulus conditions and hormonal states. Behavior occurring at each point in the cycle is influenced both by external stimuli and by hormonal regulation. At the same time, the hormones that modulate behavior are themselves influenced by events in the external environment, including behavioral ones. The interactions that control the cycle of reproductive behavior in the ring dove are schematized in Figure 9.17 (from Lehrman, 1964).

Specific Hungers

According to Lorenz (1966), hunger, flight, sex, and aggression are the "master instincts" in the "great parliament of instincts." Much ingestive behavior, for example, is adaptive, unlearned, and uniform within the species, and therefore can be described as species-specific. In many organisms, however, the functions served even by Lorenz' master instincts develop differently as a function of different environmental inputs.

The phenomenon of *specific hungers* for years served as a classic example of innate food preferences. An organism deprived of a particular nutrient in an otherwise adequate diet appeared to seek out the appropriate food necessary to relieve the deficiency. Modern analyses of specific hungers, however, illustrate that in some organisms selection of appropriate nutrients requires a complex interplay of genetic and environmental factors. Human infants given the opportunity to self-select their own diets in "cafeteria-style" experiments do remarkably well at choosing a nutritionally sound, well-balanced diet. Davis (1928), for example, offered newly weaned human infants their choice of a wide variety of foodstuffs for a period of several months. While the infants might choose a disproportionate amount of some foods on some days, over the course of the experiment the infants selected an adequate balanced diet and experienced normal growth and health. Davis did not offer the infants harmful or inadequate foods, however, so that the selection was biased in a healthy direction. Other studies have shown, however, that organisms in cafeteria-style experiments will avoid harmful foods (though there are exceptions). Similar results have in fact been obtained with swine, rats, deer and other organisms. The cafeteria-style experiments also showed that organisms exhibit specific hungers for foods containing nutrients in which the organism is deficient. Depriving the organism of several of the B vit-

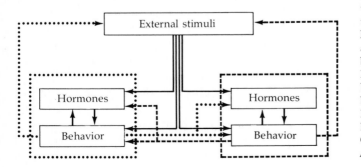

Figure 9.17
Interactions that appear to govern the reproductive behavior cycle of the ring dove are suggested here. Hormones regulate behavior and are themselves affected by behavioral and other stimuli. Moreover, the behavior of each bird affects the hormones and behavior of its mate. [After "The Reproductive Behavior of Ring Doves" by Daniel S. Lehrman. Copyright © 1964 by Scientific American, Inc. All rights reserved.]

amins, protein, carbohydrates, fats, and other substances, leads to a compensatory increase in the intake of food substances that will eliminate the deficiency.

There are, however, limitations on how optimal the self-selection of diets can be. In the first place, in many organisms the inexperienced are vulnerable. Newly weaned rats do not self-select well, nor do female deer pregnant for the first time. A second limitation to efficient self-selection involves cases in which experience actually *interferes* with development of specific hungers. Young and Chaplin (1945) performed an experiment in which rats learned to select a preferred sugar-flavored foodstuff over a protein (casein) -enriched food by choosing one arm of a maze. Once the rats had learned to choose the sugar side of the T-maze, they continued to do so whenever tested in the T-maze, even after they had been deprived of protein. Interestingly, the same animals switched to a protein preference when tested in a new apparatus. When moved back to the original maze, however, the sugar preference again interfered with protein selection. In rats, therefore, the experience of having tasted the protein-enriched food and having learned to choose it in the new apparatus did not transfer to the old apparatus. There, the old habit of choosing the sugar continued to mask the specific hunger. A third limitation to efficient self-selection is revealed by the finding that some substances have no apparent specific hungers associated with their deficiency. For example, whereas deficiencies in several of the B vitamins give rise to specific hungers, deficiencies in vitamins A and D do not. A vitamin A-deprived organism presented with a choice between a vitamin A-enriched food and one lacking vitamin A is usually indifferent.

Despite these limitations, self-selection generally works, and nutritional deficiencies frequently give rise to adaptive specific hungers. What, then is the mechanism for specific hungers? For some time it was assumed that the bodily deficiency created by the missing nutrient set up a corresponding motivational state or drive, which directed behavior toward relieving the deficiency. It was thought that the organism learned to prefer the taste associated with recovery from the deficiency. One problem with this interpretation is that the deficiency is often not immediately remedied in ingestion of the appropriate food. How the system was equipped to associate recovery from the deficiency with the ingestion of the responsible food therefore remained unclear.

One early hypothesis concerning the mechanism underlying specific hungers proposed that peripheral nerves were more sensitive to the needed item. It was therefore suggested that a change in receptor sensitivity for the deficient substance occurred. This theory was, however, put to rest with Pfaffman and Bare's (1950) demonstration that the neural threshold was unchanged by salt deprivation or by adrenalectomy (removal of the adrenal gland resulting in salt imbalance). These authors showed that an adrenalectomized rat detects salt at the same levels of concentration as does a normal rat. Thus the mechanism underlying specific hungers requires more complexity than the peripheral explanation in terms of changes in receptor thresholds can provide.

Others explained specific hungers as the representation of an innate ingestive response to the deficiency. It was thought that organisms came into the world equipped with a tendency to seek out foods relieving vital deficiencies. Experiments using pure nutrients quickly shed light on this hypothesis. Any inborn taste preferences should be expressed only for naturally occurring substances. The effects of evolution can only be manifest on substances encountered in the natural environment. Any inborn taste preferences should therefore be directed toward natural foods, not toward pure nutrients. Addressing this point, Richter provided adult rats with an assortment of minerals, vitamins, carbohydrates, and proteins in forms that do not occur as natural foods. Not only did the animals select a well-balanced diet from these pure nutrients but they also actually selected a better diet than animals offered lab-chow chosen by a dietician (Richter, Holt, and Barelare, 1938). Richter's experiment suggests that the rats' performance is not due to inborn preferences because his animals were self-selecting on the basis of completely novel tastes.

Though most experiments had been performend on omnivorous organisms that naturally ingest a wide variety of substances, here it appeared that specific hungers were dependent upon experience. Most investigators believed that somehow the organism learned to associate the taste of a food containing the deficient nutrient with the partial recovery from the deficiency. Consequently, the organism would eat more of that food until the deficiency was eliminated. When faced with a similar deficiency in the future, the organism would immediately choose the food previously associated with recovery. One problem with this view was that the deficiency was often not remedied for some time after appropriate selection. It was not clear, therefore, how the system was equipped to associate recovery from the deficiency with the earlier ingestion of the responsible food. Moreover, many other behaviors, including ingestion of other substances, might have occurred in the interim. How would the organism correctly single out the one food responsible for recovery? Finally, the explanation in terms of recovery faced an additional problem, referred to as "preference after recovery." If a deficiency is rectified either by injection or by allowing the organism to ingest the appropriate nutrient, and the same organism is *later* given a choice between the old deficient food and a new food, it will choose the new food. But this new food cannot be chosen for its prior association with recovery, since recovery had occurred before its ingestion.

The Rozin Experiments

A series of experiments by Paul Rozin and his associates (Rozin, 1976) have made considerable progress in the direction of solving the riddle of specific hungers in many organisms. Rozin subjected rats to thiamin-deficient diets for twenty-one days. As expected, they became weak and anorexic. The rats were then given a choice between the deficient diet and a thiamin-supplemented diet. As expected on the basis of the older work, the deficient rats chose the thiamin-supplemented diet. In a second experiment, Rozin placed thiamin in the old deficient food and presented the thiamin-deprived rat with a choice of the familiar food now enriched with thiamin and some new food lacking thiamin. If the organism were seeking out thiamin—if it had a "thiamin sensor" of some kind—it obviously should choose the familiar, now thiamin-enriched food. Instead, the rats immediately chose the new food whether or not it contained thiamin.

One possible explanation of this finding is that the organism has developed an *aversion* to the deficient food ("hates old"). Alternatively, it may be that the organism will choose any new food encountered—that the organism with a nutritional deficiency becomes *neophilic* ("loves new"). The neophilia hypothesis is consistent with the interpretation that the organism tries out a variety of new foods and learns to choose the one that helps rectify the deficiency. Rozin tested the two hypotheses in an experiment in which thiamin-deficient rats were given a choice of three foods. Two of the choices were the standard pair: a new food and the familiar thiamin-deficient food. According to either hypothesis ("loves new" or "hates old") the organism should choose the new food. In addition, however, Rozin presented his subjects with a third alternative consisting of an old familiar food that had never been associated with deficiency (that is, a food that the organism had ingested prior to the thiamin-deficient regimen). Consider the possible outcomes of these three choices. If the thiamin-deficient animal has developed neophilia, it should still choose a new food as it does in the two-choice situation, while displaying indifference between the two familiar foods. On the other hand, if the organism has developed an aversion to the deficient familiar food, it should spurn that food and restrict its ingestion exclusively to the new food and the safe familiar food. Rozin's results are in fact more consistent with the latter (learned aversion) hypothesis. The findings indicate that rats prefer the familiar safe food and avoid the familiar deficient food, apparently having developed an aversion to the deficient food. Rozin also found that the familiar safe food was preferred over the new food, indicating that the rats were somehow *neophobic*, not neophilic. Given the two foods that were nonaversive, the rats tended to prefer the familiar one.

Rozin's experiments show that at least some specific hungers result from the development of an aversion to deficient foods. In a sense, then, for rats the phrase "specific hunger" is a misnomer; a more appropriate phrase would be "specific aversion." These results also explain the phenomenon of "preference after recovery" referred to earlier. "Preference after recovery" was enigmatic because the organism was thought to be seeking a food to correct an already remedied deficiency. Now we can see that the organism is merely continuing to shun a diet for which it has developed an aversion.

Rozin's results do not, however, by themselves solve all of the riddles associated with specific hungers. For example, recall that baby rats do not self-select well. How, then, do rat pups tend to eat only safe foods? It appears that they do so in part because of their sensitivity to relevant social, gustatory, and olfactory cues. Rat pups tend to stay near their parents. The parents have learned which foods to eat, and since the rat pups happen to be in the same area they are likely to eat the same foods. By the time they are on their own, therefore, they have already learned to eat many "safe familiar foods." They will then choose these familiar foods over novel ones. These social factors were implicated in an elegant series of experiments by Bennett Galef and his associates (Galef and Clark, 1971a, 1971b; Galef, 1976, 1977). In one type of experiment adult rats were offered a highly palatable but poisoned food and a relatively unpalatable safe food. The rats quickly learned to feed on the relatively unpalatable safe food. Interestingly, when a litter of pups born subsequently was old enough to eat solid food, these pups also chose the relatively unpalatable food. Subsequent work has shown that the social cues discussed so far constitute a sufficient but *unnecessary* mechanism for generating the rat pups' taste preferences. A second mechanism involves gustatory cues transmitted in the lactating mother's milk. The fact that the milk is flavored by the mother's safe diet is apparently sufficient to produce preference for solid foods with similar gustatory cues (Galef and Clark, 1972; Galef and Sherry, 1973). More recently, the role of olfactory cues, including those contained in the mother's anal excretions, have been implicated in feeder site selection (see Leon and Moltz, 1972; Galef and Heiber, 1976). Thus there are several mechanisms enabling the vulnerable rat pup to develop safe eating habits despite its inability to self-select well in the absence of the kinds of cues identified by Galef and others.

A more difficult question remains. Why should the organism develop an aversion for food at all? As Rozin and Kalat (1971) have pointed out, many events may have intervened between ingestion of a deficient or poisoned food and the resultant sickness. We will obtain a partial answer to this question in the next chapter when we discuss a series of ingenious experiments conducted by John Garcia, having implications not only for the study of specific hungers but for reinforcement theory in general.

Research on specific hungers points once again to the interplay between structural and environmental factors in the development of behavior. In retrospect, it should have been clear all along that a "generalist" or omnivore such as the rat should be flexible in its eating habits—that is, rely on learning. Taste preferences are more likely to be under relatively inflexible genetic control among "specialists" who eat only particular foods (Rozin, 1976). More will be said about generalists and specialists in the next chapter.

Throughout this chapter we have seen that behavior develops through a complex interaction between organism and environment. The organism's evolutionary history predisposes it to respond to particular types of stimuli. Under certain conditions such as those represented by fixed action patterns, differences in ontogenetic experiences have little effect on altering behavior and behavior remains stereotyped and inflexible. In the next chapter we will review behavior sequences characterized by much more flexibility. Here the interaction between ontogeny and phylogeny is even clearer. Moreover, here it becomes more obvious that neither the ontogeny nor the phylogeny of behavior can be fully explained without a knowledge of both.

10 The Natural History of Learning

The coping behavior of an organism in the artificial (laboratory) niche can only be understood in terms of its behavior in its natural (evolutionary) niche [Garcia, Clarke, and Hankins, 1973, p. 1].

Statements such as this have begun to appear with increasing regularity in the psychological literature. Collectively, they represent a growing awareness on the part of behavioral psychologists that complete understanding of an animal's behavior in any situation is predicated upon a knowledge of that animal's behavior in the natural environment. This view constitutes a significant departure from the more traditional approach of experimental animal psychology, which has relied almost exclusively on data collected within the "artificial" (laboratory) setting. Some comment on the rationale for the newer view is therefore in order.

In the previous chapter we observed that in some cases behavior occurs in a highly stereotyped, species-specific fashion suggestive of strong evolutionary and hence genetic input. In such cases behavior has developed phylogenetically as a result of the adaptive advantage that it extends to individual members of the species in question. That is, the behavior serves some biologically relevant function, which ultimately contributes to the reproductive success of the individual and therefore ensures its own perpetuation. The logical extension of this view conceptualizes *all behavior,* "learned" as well as "innate," as the product of an evolutionary process guided by the mechanism of reproductive success. The various propensities to learn exhibited by an organism have themselves evolved. Each has, moreover, evolved to accord with specific natural situations that face specific individuals at specific times. As such, "when individual reproductive success depends heavily on learned ability, selection will strongly favor those individuals that possess mechanisms that help this learning happen easily, quickly, accurately, and reliably" (Alcock, 1975, p. 234). Species differ in what they are able to learn; moreover, these differences represent distinct learning processes suited to accommodate specific environmental demands. Learning may therefore occur only in those situations in which it promotes adaptive fitness. The natural environment that defines the context for survival for a group of individuals will determine when, where, how, and if learning will occur. In this, learning processes are like all other evolved biological processes. The character of the process is molded by forces of selection produced by a very specific set of environmental constraints.

THE NATURAL ENVIRONMENT

To understand fully the logic and implications of the naturalistic approach to learning it is necessary to form an accurate conceptualization of the construct "the natural environment." Roughly equivalent to the more technical term "ecological niche," the natural environment refers to the complex *set* of *selection pressures*, unique for each individual, imposed by the environment. In order to exist and to perpetuate itself each organism must have access to vital resources such as food, water, living space, light, mates, prey, and so on. Access to these resources is structured by the natural environment. The resources are often limited and obtainable, with much effort, only in very specific ways. The well-adapted species consists of individuals characterized by efficient means of extracting these vital resources. These individuals stand the best chance of successfully reproducing. Efficient exploitation of natural resources, and hence survival, is therefore contingent upon meeting the demands of the environment that provides those resources.

Note, however, that the natural environment is *not* a unitary concept. That is, it does not refer to a single entity. On the contrary, basic to the notion of the natural environment is the concept of diversity. Approximately 1,400,000 unique species of living organism are known to exist. Each is composed of numerous unique individuals. Such great diversity persists just because the globe comprises an undetermined number of distinct microenvironments, each defining a singular set of selection pressures, which in their singularity demand and perpetuate diversity. In fact, no two natural environments are exactly alike.

The naturalistic approach summarized here contains several implications of importance for the study of learning. First, similarities and differences in learning abilities among species do not necessarily depend on differences in behavioral or sensory-motor complexity or differences in relative phylogenetic position. While such factors may covary with the nature of the various learning processes, many are dictated by differences in the specific environmental demands placed on distinct groups— demands that reflect each species' unique ecological niche. Second, even within a species we may at times expect to see individual learning abilities vary drastically *from situation to situation*. A given species' membership cannot be characterized across the board as composed of generally "good learners" or generally "bad learners." Ontogenetic behavioral flexibility may, for example, be quite useful for a particular group in the selection of nutritive foodstuffs, while at the same time and for the same individuals flexibility in the selection of a mate may be damagingly maladaptive. Such individuals might therefore be expected to learn well in a foraging (food-searching) situation but show a complete lack of behavioral flexibility in their selection of a potential mate. In neither case can the particular situation be assumed to be representative of the group's general learning ability. Third, in certain situations or at certain times learning may simply *fail to occur*. The situations will, of course, be those in which behavioral flexibility either is of no benefit or is actually maladaptive in the natural context. Similarly, learning may fail to occur in completely artificial situations—that is, those that have no analogue in the natural history of the species. While many arbitrary behaviors are acquired in the artificial setting of the laboratory, as we have noted elsewhere (Chapter 8), some responses may be relatively unaffected by particular reinforcers. This may be expected in situations in which the required response is an unnatural one or one set in an unnatural context. The species has never confronted such situations in the wild, and learning abilities could therefore never have evolved to accommodate them. Brower (1971) recounts an amusing case of a toad completely unable to learn not to eat buckshot:

> In a moment of relaxation during a critical series of feeding experiments one summer evening in southern Florida, I had reason to become extremely annoyed with my student research assistant. Perhaps our field work earlier that hot day could be blamed, but in retrospect it seems more likely that the liberal arts tradition had prompted my student to do a little side experimenting on his own. Buckshot in a bowl in one corner of the laboratory proved just too great a temptation; soon they were rolling in front of one of our particularly cooperative experimental subjects, a southern toad, *Bufo terrestris*. This animal proceeded to eat one buckshot after another until weighing so much that it could hardly jump. Since we had planned to use this toad in an experiment the next night, my ire continued to rise. But then I suddenly realized the importance of the contradiction between this toad's apparent inability to stop eating the useless food and the rapidity with which our other experimental toads had learned to reject bumblebees on sight. Why did our toad just keep on eating the buckshot? [Brower, 1971, p. 66].

. . . From what we have learned, we can conclude that the toad was unable to habituate to the stimuli presented by the rolling buckshot. Given the rather limited mental endowment of toads, and viewed in the correct ecological perspective, this is not unreasonable. Natural selection operating upon toads has undoubtedly favored strong orientation and attacking behavior toward any moving object within a general size range. The result is that these animals spend most of their time catching living insects. In their natural environment buckshot does not occur and nonliving objects generally do not move. All the toad really requires under these circumstances is an ability to become conditioned to avoid insects which are noxious, and this it clearly can do.

Thus the apparent inability of the toad to habituate to buckshot is not really surprising. Indeed, . . . the toad's repertoire of feeding behavior seems ideally suited to its existence [pp. 75–76].

Natural selection literally means selection by the forces of nature. The view of behavior as a biological process, coupled with a recognition of the critical role played by natural selection in molding all biological processes, requires focusing on the distinctive natural history of each organism. This is the appropriate context within which to couch the explanation of behavior. If learned behavior occurs as it does in specific situations because it allows the organism to meet the demands of that situation more efficiently, and if the environment is in fact the final selector of all behavioral characters that persist, then a complete analysis of learned behavior must be based on an understanding of the natural context within which that behavior occurs.

GUSTATORY LEARNING, FORAGING, AND PREDATION

Much of the recent emphasis in American psychology on the importance of natural behavioral tendencies in learning can be traced to John Garcia's initially anomalous findings on taste aversion learning in rats. These findings came to the attention of psychologists in the late 1960s, and since that time they have challenged several basic assumptions that have for decades provided the foundation of American learning theory. The nature of these anomalies is, moreover, consistent with various reconceptualizations of learning initially generated at about the same time by behavioral biologists (for example, Lorenz, 1965). The parallels between the two movements and the growing recognition of the validity and widespread applicability of Garcia's work have raised serious questions regarding psychology's traditional views of learning. In this section we will review Garcia's early findings, thereby illustrating the nature of the challenge. We will then review the empirical and conceptual extensions of these and similar findings, focusing on the role of learning in foraging strategies and in the interactions between predators and their naturally occurring prey. Feeding behavior constitutes one behavioral category that has evolved to meet a very specific set of demands on which survival depends. Under what kinds of circumstances and in what ways might learning processes aid in satisfying these demands?

Taste Aversion Learning

Garcia's early work (for example, Garcia and Koelling, 1966; Garcia and Ervin, 1968) concerned itself with an analysis of the conditions under which rats will learn to avoid various ingestibles. The behavioral phenomena have more recently been collectively labeled *taste aversion learning*. Garcia and Koelling (1966) attempted to suppress drinking by presenting aversive consequences contingent upon the occurrence of drinking. Animals initially underwent acquisition training in which drinking was reinforced in the presence of both tasty (saccharin-flavored) water and a display of visual and auditory stimuli consisting of gurgling noises and flashing lights. This procedure ensured equivalent training with both sets of cues. Animals then underwent suppression training in which one-half of the initial population of rats received only tasty water, while the other half drank unflavored water accompanied only by the audiovisual cues. For one-half of the rats in each of these groups licking was followed by an immediate electric shock. The consequence of ingestion for the remaining half was the sensation of nausea (toxicosis produced either chemically or by X-ray irradiation). Thus there were four main groups of rats, each receiving one of the following four treatments: bright-noisy water paired with electric shock; bright-noisy water paired with nausea; flavored water paired with shock; or flavored water paired with nausea. Following a number of trials under these conditions, water intake was measured for all groups. The main results are shown in Figure 10.1. It is evident that punishment was indeed effective both for rats made nauseous after drinking the flavored water and for rats shocked while drinking the bright-noisy water. The important finding, however, is that these same "punishers" (toxicosis and electric shock) were ineffective in suppressing drinking in either of the other two groups. Shock was ineffective in the presence of the gustatory cue, while nausea did not suppress drinking in the presence of the audiovisual cue. In each case rats ingested close to their normal fluid intake. The design and results of these experiments are summarized in Figure 10.2. As indicated, the effectiveness of conditioning clearly depended on which stimuli were paired with which consequence.

It has been suggested that this anomalous finding is due in large measure to the fact that the nausea resulting from poisoning follows a very different time course than the pain caused by shock. In addition to lasting longer, nausea may have a very gradual onset, increase slowly, and last for several hours before eventually declining. It may be that shock would

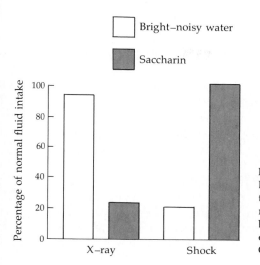

Figure 10.1
Differential suppression of drinking as a function of the type of cue and consequence used. X-ray induced nausea paired with saccharin and shock paired with bright-noisy water were the only combinations that effectively suppressed drinking. [After Revusky and Garcia, 1970.]

be equally effective in suppressing the drinking of saccharin-flavored water it if too were given in a massive amount with a gradual onset, a duration of several hours, and a gradual offset. In order to test this interpretation, Green, Bouzas, and Rachlin (1972) performed an experiment with just such a shock procedure. They found that the shock con-

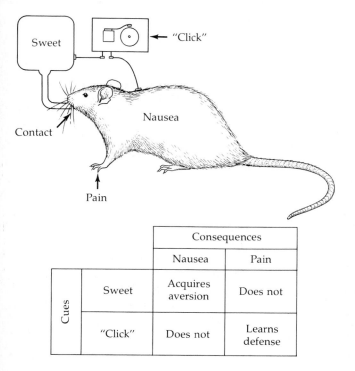

		Consequences	
		Nausea	Pain
Cues	Sweet	Acquires aversion	Does not
	"Click"	Does not	Learns defense

Figure 10.2
The double dissociation design in which two cues are pitted against two reinforcers. Conditioning is not obtained readily in all four cells, indicating the biased association mechanism of the rat. [After Garcia, Clarke, and Hankins, 1973.]

tinued to be ineffective in significantly reducing the intake of the flavored water, and in this situation was clearly inferior to toxicosis as a punisher.

Experiments on taste aversion learning in the bobwhite quail illustrate the species-specific character of such interactions. Garcia's results indicate that rats require *gustatory* cues to learn to avoid toxic substances in food. Wilcoxon, Dragoin, and Kral (1971) have indicated, however, that quail, a diurnal and highly visually oriented species, make excellent use of *visual* cues in the development of food aversions. Three groups of quail were offered water that was either colored dark blue, made sour by the addition of small amounts of hydrochloric acid, or both. One-half hour following ingestion the animals received a single injection of a nausea-inducing drug. The results of subsequent tests with treated water indicated that successful aversive conditioning occurred in all three groups of quail. Quail, therefore, unlike rats, can benefit from the experience of a visual cue paired with a gastrointestinal consequence. Interestingly, when the double cue was split for testing—that is, when quail trained with sour blue water were tested with the two cues presented separately—removal of the visual cue virtually eliminated the effects of conditioning. Visual cues for the quail therefore appear to be actually far more salient than gustatory cues (an example of "overshadowing"—see Chapter 5).

These studies and others stimulated by them have provided the initial impetus behind the growing objection in learning theory to the *principle of equipotentiality* (Seligman and Hager, 1972), which has heretofore formed the basis of many psychologists' view of learning. The principle embodies the notion that learning represents a general process (see further discussion in Chapter 13) in which the elements of the learning situation—that is, stimulus, response, and reinforcer—can be arbitrarily chosen. As long as the general relationship among elements obtains, the specific quality of those elements is irrelevant. "In effect, in any operant situation, the stimulus, the response, and the reinforcer are completely arbitrary and interchangeable. No one of them bears any biologically built-in fixed connection to the others" (Teitelbaum, 1966, p. 567).

The Garcia-type result is clearly at variance with the assumption of equipotentiality. It definitely does matter what the quality of those elements is. Moreover, it matters in ways determined by the function that behavior has evolved to perform under specific natural circumstances. Subsequent work in food aversion learning and analyses of behavioral change in other functional categories of behavior have accentuated the validity of the naturalistic approach. This approach, of course, begins with the now familiar assumptions described earlier. Behavior represents a biological process shaped by natural selection, and evolved, therefore, to perform an adaptive function. This function is itself defined by the unique set of selection pressures that constitute each individual's natural environment. As such, "behavior comes in biologically meaningful 'chunks' (p. 6) . . . shaped to some consummatory survival purpose by natural selection in the species' history. Within these biological constraints behavior has some plasticity" (Garcia, et al., 1973, p. 21). The nature and degree of plasticity are determined by that biologically meaningful function, itself defined by the organism's unique adaptive circumstance—its ecological niche. Of his own sick rats Garcia concludes: "The sick rat acts as if 'it must have been something I ate,' because he has been wired to learn which flavor led to the illness. In his natural niche, *plasticity within constraint* [Garcia's italics] is more efficient than a random net capable of associating any combination of stimuli on the basis of intensity, recency, frequency, and effect" (Garcia, et al., 1973, p. 35).

Much of the work on food aversion learning can be conceptualized as representing a laboratory-based case of a more general natural phenomenon: The environment is replete with numerous inedible and toxic substances. The organism (usually hungry) must somehow select for ingestion only those substances that are edible, nontoxic, and nutritive. Many potential ingestibles are in fact best avoided. Garcia's work strongly suggests that in some situations learning may provide the basis for this selection, and that the evolutionary process predisposes the individual to readily learn to avoid those stimulus compounds that naturally occur in conjunction with toxic or otherwise aversive consequences. Recent work generated by the more traditional view, however, suggests that rats, at least, are more capable of associating exteroceptive stimulus compounds with sickness than Garcia's results indicate. Rudy, Iwens, and Best (1977) and Rudy, Rosenberg, and Sandell (1977) have shown that rats are quite capable of associating *novel* exteroceptive stimuli with sickness. Thus it may not be necessary to interpret Garcia's findings in terms of natural predispositions to associate certain stimuli and sickness. However, consider again from the ecological point of view the extremely adaptive character of a very flexible response to novelty.

Taste Aversion Learning in the Wild

Numerous descriptions of the foraging and hunting behavior of animals in the wild support the conclusions of laboratory investigations on the importance of learning in the avoidance of nonpalatable or toxic ingestibles. Some of the most interesting involve the phenomenon of *Müllerian mimicry*. Müllerian mimicry, diagramed in Figure 10.3, refers to the common or similar *warning coloration* that occurs among unrelated species all of which are poisonous or highly unpalatable to potential predators. Many poisonous groups, from snakes to butterflies, are, for example, brightly colored in some combination or simple arrangement of black, white, red, orange, and yellow. These combined cues mean "I am toxic." The use of common signals by many unrelated species is presumably adaptive because it permits more efficient generalization of avoidance reactions on the part of predators. Predators learn that certain color com-

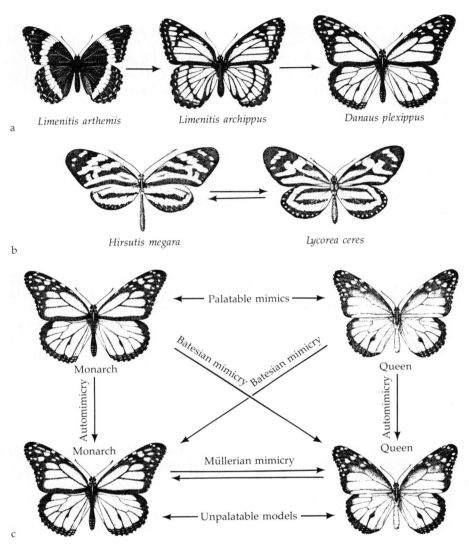

a   *Limenitis arthemis*   *Limenitis archippus*   *Danaus plexippus*

b   *Hirsutis megara*   *Lycorea ceres*

Palatable mimics

Monarch   Queen

Batesian mimicry   Batesian mimicry

Automimicry   Automimicry

Monarch   Queen

Müllerian mimicry

Unpalatable models

c

Figure 10.3
(a) Batesian mimicry. A palatable butterfly evolves to appear like an unpalatable one.
(b) Müllerian mimicry. Two species of unpalatable butterfly appear very similar, thereby
advertising a common warning coloration. (c) A combination of three types of mimicry.
[From "Ecological Chemistry" by Lincoln Brower. Copyright © 1969 by Scientific American,
Inc. All rights reserved.]

binations constitute a cue for unpalatability, and they respond by avoiding
these combinations no matter where they occur. A fascinating example of
Müllerian mimicry is provided by two species of South American butterfly that, in the areas where they coinhabit the continent, are actually

more similar to one another than they are to members of their own species inhabiting adjacent areas. While both species are unpalatable, one is much more so than the other. In any area in which the two occur together they are virtually indistinguishable, even to the trained eye. "Over most of tropical America they are found together, changing now to this pattern, now to that, but always in strict parallel with each other. When two *Heliconius* species look alike, the cost of advertisement—the number of butterflies that would have to be tasted and maimed or killed in every generation to educate and re-educate their predators—is distributed between the two species and both benefit" (Turner, 1975, p. 31). By virtue of the learning that it supports in the predator, therefore, Müllerian mimicry is beneficial both to prey species, and, of course, to the predator as well. The predator need not undergo unpleasant food aversion learning anew with each new potentially unpalatable species encountered. The common warning coloration becomes a discriminative stimulus for avoiding the aversive consequences of ingesting a toxic substance.

Two other forms of mimicry (see Figure 10.3), Batesian mimicry and automimicry, also illustrate natural conditions under which learning can be involved in the development of taste aversion reactions. In *Batesian mimicry,* a species that is not at all dangerous or unpalatable mimics or evolves similarly to one that is. In *automimicry,* palatable and therefore perfectly edible members of one species benefit from their genetically based similarity to conspecifics (members of the *same* species). Both types of mimicry are excellently illustrated by observations of the monarch butterfly's antipredator adaptations to insectivorous birds such as blue jays.

Monarch butterflies have long been regarded as an unpalatable species. Lincoln Brower and his colleagues have, however, demonstrated that the monarch's distastefulness is in fact dependent on what the animal has eaten while in the larval stage of metamorphosis. Those individuals that, as caterpillars, ingested certain species of poisonous milkweed plant actually become poisonous following ingestion. The insects themselves are unaffected by the poison. However, blue jays fed monarchs reared on poisonous milkweed respond, as pictured in Figure 10.4, by quickly vomiting. Monarchs raised on cabbage or some other nontoxic plant are quite palatable to the birds. The nonpoisonous monarchs become, therefore, *automimics* of their poisonous conspecifics. In fact, most populations of monarchs are mixed, containing both palatable and unpalatable individuals. This is clearly to the advantage of the palatable individuals. Blue jays that have once consumed a toxic monarch associate its coloration with the nauseating consequences of ingestion and thereafter generalize the learned avoidance response to all individuals exhibiting similar coloration. This of course, would include the toxic monarch's palatable conspecifics.

Laboratory investigations indicate that most wild-caught blue jays reject proffered monarchs on sight. If, however, the birds are made hungry

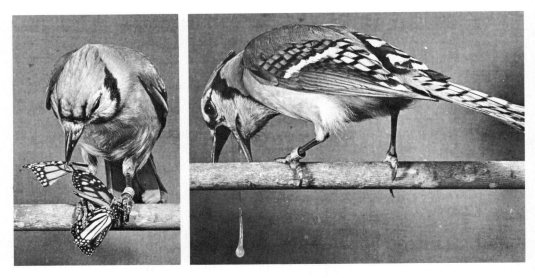

a   b

Figure 10.4
A blue jay (a) ingesting an unpalatable monarch butterfly and (b) quickly vomiting in
response. Birds that have had such experience will subsequently reject this and all similar
butterflies on sight. [Courtesy of Lincoln Brower.]

enough, they will eventually again taste a monarch. When the insect
presented is nontoxic—has never ingested poisonous plants—the once rejecting birds "will eat up to six in a row without hesitation, and will continue to eat them day after day" (Brower, 1971, p. 70). If the same birds
are later offered toxic monarchs, the resultant acceptance induces intense
retching and vomiting. The birds thereafter reject all monarchs. "After
one emetic experience, the blue jays reject monarchs on sight for several
days. Moreover, the conditioning to the monarch's visual stimuli is so
strong that some birds actually retched at the sight of another monarch
offered 24 hours later" (Brower, 1971, p. 70).

The adaptive advantage conferred on palatable monarchs by the automimicry of unpalatable conspecifics is shared by any species of palatable butterfly sufficiently similar to the monarchs. This, of course, would
constitute *Batesian mimicry,* and the monarchs are in fact known to have
several Batesian mimics. The close phylogenetic relatives of the viceroy
butterfly are colored in black or brown with clear white band-like mark-
ings. The viceroy itself, however, is a perfect Batesian mimic of the
monarch. As such, its coloration is characterized by far less black and the
noticeable addition of bright orange plus white speckles. Here again the
viceroy's coloration has diverged from that of its close relatives in response to the adaptive advantage conferred by the evolution of a color

scheme that will exploit the predator's capacity to generalize. Blue jays experienced with unpalatable monarchs are known to reject viceroys, as well, on sight. Studies that have constructed generalization gradients using butterflies varying in similarity to an unpalatable model suggest that the learning taking place in these situations in fact represents naturally occurring stimulus generalization. As you would expect, the more dissimilar the stimulus, the more likely the insect is to be eaten, and hence the less the generalization. When, however, extremely unpalatable training insects are used, the birds will reject *all* proffered insects regardless of their visual similarity to the model. Perhaps here less subtle cues, such as shape or the presence of wings, are sufficient to support generalization, given the extremely aversive consequences.

Consider once again the comparison between rats and bobwhite quail described earlier. Like the rats, blue jays require initial taste cues for the establishment of a food aversion reaction. Only secondarily through association with taste do the color cues become signals to avoid. Quail, however, appear capable of forming a direct association between visual cue and consequence. What kinds of specific environmental factors might be responsible for the differently evolved abilities of the rats and jays versus the quail? Garcia, McGowan, and Green (1972) have provided a plausible ecological rationale for the differences described.

> The blue jay, like the rat, is an opportunistic predator, scavenger, and forager of animal and plant sources. Adaptation to similar niches may lead to the similar associative mechanisms in both species. On the other hand, the bobwhite is able to associate visual cues (CS) directly (as well as flavors) to visceral illness (US) in a one-step process. This bird is much more dependent upon seeds and grains where the actual food and flavor are packaged in a rough and relatively tasteless seed coat. These speculations can only be tested by comparing these species in situations where the relevant ecological variables are experimentally manipulated [Garcia, McGowen, and Green, 1972, p. 20].

Learning to Locate Food

Given the prevalence of antipredator adaptations such as mimicry and the use of poisons, learning what not to eat can be extremely adaptive. Numerous other antipredator adaptations—for example, the cryptic (camouflaging) coloration of the edible moths pictured in Figure 10.5— render the opposite problem equally challenging: How does a predator locate and recognize an appropriate prey object? Several authors (Tinbergen, 1960; Krebs, 1973) have suggested that here, too, learning may play an important role.

Suppose the density of an animal's accustomed prey changes drastically. If the prey has become much less readily available and (perhaps because of its crypticity) suddenly very difficult to locate, the predator

Figure 10.5
The cryptic coloration of the salt and pepper moths renders predatory birds unable to detect the presence of the moth on the tree. (a) On the dark bark of an oak tree near Liverpool, the black form is better camouflaged than the typical light form. (b) On the light-colored, lichened bark of an oak tree in rural Wales, the typical light-peppered moth is almost invisible. [Courtesy of J. A. Bishop and Laurence M. Cook.]

that persists in pursuing such inaccessible individuals is wasting valuable time and energy. For a predator whose prey population is likely to fluctuate, and for one capable of eating many different types of prey objects, therefore, behavioral flexibility in foraging and hunting behavior would be very adaptive. That is, when prey densities do change, the predator can learn to distribute its hunting energies more efficiently in searching instead for a more available morsel.

Before turning to a more detailed analysis of modifications in predatory behavior, we shall consider the possible kinds of feeding strategies of the animals under consideration. In hunting and foraging, as in other behavioral categories, flexibility may not always be adaptive. The question again becomes: What kinds of feeding strategies might be most efficiently realized through the operation of a learning mechanism? Perhaps the most important dimension to consider here is that of the *generalist–specialist continuum*. Let us begin with the *specialist*. A specialist feeder restricts itself to one or a very few kinds of food. Typically, this individual is exceptionally well adapted for recognizing and taking that particular food object. With no other nutritive resources available, the animal has no other alternative. The koala bear, whose complete nutritive intake is provided by the leaves of a single species of eucalyptus tree, is an extreme specialist. Specialists are not likely to learn their choice of food. Because their food is so restricted (and presumably, therefore, relatively abundant and evenly distributed) they can simply be genetically programmed to take that single food which is both most readily available and best suited to meeting their metabolic needs. "The problem of food choice rarely arises, since the world is pretty well categorized as food and not food; natural selection rather than the individual organism makes the significant food choices" (Rozin, 1976, p. 24).

Learning is much more likely to come into play in the foraging behavior of a *generalist*. A generalist feeder eats many different kinds of food, any one of which is likely to be less constantly available and less homogeneously distributed than the food supply of a specialist. Many generalists, such as the rat, the blue jay, the cockroach, and the human, will in effect eat anything with nutritional value. The rat's tendency to sample such a broad range of possible food items is perhaps responsible for its well developed capacity for food aversion learning. Though generalists obviously require a certain vital set of nutrients, the form in which these nutrients are obtained can be extremely variable. It is therefore to the generalists' advantage that the behaviors involved in recognizing and selecting these foods be just as variable.

Let us return now to a consideration of changes in the density of one among the many prey objects available to a *generalist predator*. If predatory behavior were simply a function of fluctuations in prey density—that is, if predators simply took a particular food type according to how much was available at any given time—then, as the density of the prey species either increased or decreased, you would expect to see a linearly related increase or decrease in the frequency with which the predator captures the prey. In many predators, however, this is not the case. Krebs (1973) notes that, instead, in the early stages of a change in prey density the predator's behavior lags behind changes in prey density (too few prey are taken relative to that expected purely on the basis of prey density). In the latter stages, however, the predator's behavior is accelerated with respect to prey density (that is, a greater proportion of prey are taken than would be predicted on the basis of the density change alone). This discrepancy between changes in prey density and changes in the frequency with which the predator takes the prey is diagramed schematically in Figure 10.6. The sudden acceleration in the curve that describes the predator's nonlinear response is assumed to be the result of learning.

> [The] extent to which the predator learns about a particular prey is a result of the interaction between learning and forgetting, and only when the prey density is high enough will the predator learn more rapidly than it forgets. At this point the attack rate will suddenly increase [Krebs, 1973, p. 78].

It is as if more frequent encounters with one type of prey augment the ease and rate of learning to capture that prey.

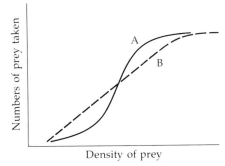

Figure 10.6
The difference between near linear increases in prey density (B) and the frequency with which a particular prey type is taken from the population (A). [After Krebs, 1973.]

Several hypotheses have been advanced to explain how learning might contribute to more efficient predation. Perhaps the most thoroughly examined of these is the hypothesis of *search image formation*, initially suggested by L. Tinbergen. Focusing on the observation that many prey species have evolved antipredator adaptations (such as crypticity) that make them very difficult for a predator to detect, Tinbergen reasoned that learning might facilitate predation through experience that instructs the predator in what to look for. Vaguely defined, search image formation involves "learning to see" particular characteristics of prey objects that have been encountered frequently in the past. In describing Tinbergen's early experiments on birds' facility in detecting cryptic insects, Krebs (1973) writes: "As the prey density increased with time . . . the birds came across the prey by chance more and more often. As a result of these chance encounters, the bird learned to recognize the prey against a background and the rate of predation suddenly increased" (p. 28). Hence search image formation has been characterized as a form of *perceptual learning* in which the animal learns to attend specifically to stimulus attributes that, by virtue of frequent chance encounters, have in the past been associated with feeding. Croze (1970) has analyzed search image formation using field observations of the crow's response to variously colored mussel shells. Both hand-reared and wild crows were exposed to shells covering pieces of meat. The shells were cryptically colored in shades of muted reds, blacks, and yellows, resembling the pebbles normally found on the beach. After two or three experiences in which the birds were directed to shells of one color, crows thereafter selectively chose only shells of that color. Experience had presumably rendered those shells less cryptic than the remaining shell colors, which the birds still failed to discriminate from the pebbles.

Dawkins (1971) tested search image formation in domestic chicks using colored grains of rice presented on either matching or contrasting backgrounds. Test stimuli are pictured in Figure 10.7. Some test stimuli were highly cryptic (for example, green on green), and responses to those were compared with responses elicited by conspicuous stimuli (those in which the rice color did not match the color of the background, for example, green on orange). While the chicks typically took cryptic grain at a much slower rate at the beginning of a test, after several minutes eating rates for cryptic grains increased quite rapidly, and in time approximated or exceeded eating rates observed for the conspicuously colored grain. Dawkins concludes that the chicks quickly learned to recognize and detect cryptically colored grain.

The same author also reports that when chicks are given sequential tests with both conspicuous and cryptic grain, "the chick's ability to see cryptic grains can be altered in opposite directions by feeding them on either cryptic or conspicuous grains immediately beforehand" (Dawkins, 1971, p. 571). Chicks were fed in two five-minute sequences per day over a period of eight days. Those animals that had received conspicuous training first found a sample of cryptic grain *much less quickly* that did chicks that had had their initial experience with cryptic grain. These results are interpreted as supporting the view that the predator or forager has learned to perceive the prey or food object more clearly as a result of prior experience. Krebs (1973) has suggested that the process underlying the

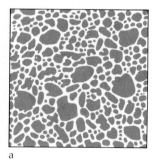

a

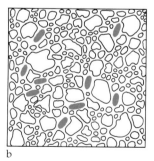

b

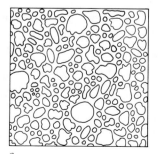

c

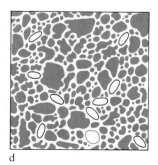

d

Figure 10.7
Food stimuli used by Dawkins to measure the formation of a search image. (a and b) Cryptic and conspicuous green rice. (c and d) Cryptic and conspicuous orange rice. [After Dawkins, 1971.]

formation of search images might be quite similar to that responsible for the acquisition of selective attention (see Chapter 5).

While search image formation remains a plausible account of learned predation, other accounts suggest that in some situations predators learn to *concentrate their hunting in the most profitable areas*—presumably those in which prey density is highest or where larger or more nutritive prey are most abundant. This approach assumes no change in the organism's perception of the prey. Rather, when one area differs from another as to prey density, prey size, ease of capture, or some other significant variable, the predator learns to spend the majority of its hunting time in the most profitable region. The animal presumably samples numerous areas and, as a result of this experience, learns to hunt in the area that yields the greatest gain. The experimental analyses of both time and response matching described in Chapter 7 can essentially be viewed as providing a laboratory analogue to hunting the most profitable area. Recall that in matching experiments the animal (usually a pigeon) distributes either its responding or its time so as to match the relative rate of reinforcement available on a particular manipulandum. Again, the animal appears sensitive to how much benefit results from responding in a particular place and distributes its time so as to net the greatest profit.

Several authors have pointed out that it may not be necessary to choose between the hypotheses of search image formation and hunting the most profitable area. Again, depending on the ecological circumstances, the individual may employ either one or both types of learning to the extent that either or both contribute to the animal's overall reproductive success. Some situations will dictate the use of search image formation; some may dictate the use of hunting the most profitable area. In other situations the greatest adaptive benefit may accrue from the use of both learning strategies.

HOMING AND MIGRATION

The means by which many organisms navigate over considerable distance to return to a familiar point, such as a home ground or winter area, has remained a topic of perpetual interest in the field of animal behavior. Prolonged time courses and extended distances characterize the migratory activities of many birds, fish, and insects. Moreover, as we shall see, the navigational systems of some organisms employ information unavailable to the human senses. These intriguing features have stimulated numerous efforts to explain homing and migration.

Homing is defined in terms of long-distance orientation to breeding or nesting areas. Such orientation may occur from any of a number of unfixed locations but is always directed toward a fixed end point. Examples of homing at distances of up to as much as three to four hundred miles have been cited, but it is usually the case that the greater the distance from the roost, the smaller the percentage of animals that successfully complete the flight. *Migration*, on the other hand, refers to the long-distance, bidirectional navigation characteristic of a species at a particular time of year, or at a particular point in the individual's development. Unlike homing, migration usually implies long-distance orientation to and from fixed reference points. That is, the animals always travel from one fixed location to another, invariably returning to their original point of departure. One American migratory bird, the blackpoll warbler, for example, after breeding in the forests of Alaska, migrates all the way to South America on a journey that includes a nonstop flight over water of more than 2400 miles. The extreme effort that animals expend in migration attests to the strength of the migratory tendency. The two-year-old salmon, for example, migrates to the sea from the stream or river where it was spawned. This journey may often involve a distance of over a thousand miles. After another two-year period, the salmon manages to return again to the very same stream or river of its origin. Some migrations, such as that of the sea cod, are even more striking: Although the fertilized cod eggs drift many miles before hatching, the fully developed adult still reaches the specific spawning area some four years later! The precise stimuli controlling these migrations have yet to be identified. In salmon migration, however, as in homing, we do know that cues associated with the position of the sun are important. The nature of water currents, surprisingly enough, does not appear to be critical. Yet even when the sky is overcast the salmon can orient to a certain extent—a fact suggesting the operation of additional cues.

The Ontogeny of Pigeon Homing

Among the most thoroughly studied examples of navigation is the amazing homing ability of the pigeon. An elegant combination of field and laboratory techniques has recently revealed the involvement of previously unknown sensory dimensions, as well as the importance of learning and early experience, in the development of homing in pigeons (Keeton, 1974a). Pigeon homing is thought to be an example of true navigation. In true navigation an animal located at point A attempting to relocate at point B is hypothesized to require two pieces of information: (1) the relationship between where it is (point A) and where it is to go (point B, home) and (2) a directional reference point that enables it to distinguish one direction from another. If the information described in (1) indicates that home is, for example, northeast of its present location, the information provided by its directional referent, (2), allows it to distinguish one direction from another and therefore to select the appropriate direction of travel—that is, that which will enable relocation at point B. Based on the relationship between points A and B, the animal will alter its angle of flight with respect to its directional referent. According to this scheme the animal must essentially do what a human would do using a map and a compass. The map provides the relationship between points A and B, and the compass provides a directional referent. This hypothesis has therefore been termed the *map and compass hypothesis.*

Pigeons are known to be able to relocate over distances of several hundreds of miles in the absence of landmark cues. Birds fitted with contact lenses that eliminate vision beyond 100 yards orient homeward normally. Similarly, birds carried to a release site (the point from which the animal is released) under anesthesia also subsequently home normally. The animal does not therefore learn its way home by piloting according to the cues provided by familiar visible landmarks. As we shall see, however, the pigeon's ability to navigate is critically dependent on experiential factors.

Research indicates that homing pigeons frequently use the sun as a directional referent (Keeton, 1974b). They do not, however, fly directly toward the sun, but appear to select another direction based on the position of the sun, flying at a given angle with reference to the sun. Because of its continual apparent motion the sun cannot reliably be used to indicate absolute direction (by itself even a stationary cue for absolute direction would be of value if the organism were always required to go in only one direction). The sun is not, for example, always in the East; it is in the East only at a certain time of day. To use the directional information contained in the sun's position, therefore, the birds must have some type of internal timing mechanism that allows them to time the continual movement of the sun and compensate for changes in the sun's position (and therefore the direction it indicates) with changes in time.

Clock shifting experiments have shown both that the birds do use the sun as a directional referent and that they are able to time changes in the sun's position. In clock shifting experiments birds are placed in an artificially lighted room in which the lights are turned on and off out of phase with the rising and setting of the sun. If, for example, the lights go on when it is actually noon, real time (6 hours after sunrise), the birds' sunrise occurs approximately 6 hours later than the actual sunrise. The birds' sun is therefore 6 hours out of phase with the real sun, and their internal 24-hour clock is off by one quarter (6 hours). When birds that have been clock-shifted in this manner for some period of time are released to home under normal daylight conditions, they make a one-quarter circle (90 degree) error in their selection of direction. William Keeton (1974b) describes the following situation: "[P]retend that before we release each pigeon we whisper in its ear 'Home is due north.' Now the bird must use its sun compass to locate north. Its internal clock says it is 6:00 A.M., when the sun should be in the east; hence north should be approximately 90 degrees counterclockwise from the sun. Remember, however, that the bird's clock is six hours slow; it is actually noon, when the sun is in the south.

Hence the bird's choice of a bearing 90 degrees counterclockwise from the sun sends it east, not north" (p. 102).

Keeton and his colleagues at Cornell University have recently re-evaluated the question of how essential the sun is to the birds' homing abilities (Keeton, 1969). How is it, for example, that many birds home at night or under extremely overcast weather conditions when in each case the sun is invisible? Keeton has hypothesized that the birds may also obtain directional information from the earth's *magnetic field*. A bar magnet placed on the pigeon's back will distort the magnetic field surrounding the animal's head. Data presented in Figure 10.8 indicate that when birds are required to home with bar magnets in place on overcast days, they orient randomly. They are unable to navigate home. Interestingly, however, the magnets have no effect on sunny days. Similarly, when devices such as those pictured in Figure 10.9 (which reverse the direction of the magnetic field passing through the bird's head) are placed on the pigeon's head, the animal reverses its homing direction accordingly as if its directional referent had been altered (Walcott and Green, 1974). Again, however, this reversal only occurs when the sun is hidden from view. The birds apparently use the information contained in the earth's magnetic field as a back-up system for directional reference when the sun is hidden from view. If the sun is visible, the birds gain directional information using the sun compass. If the sun is invisible, however, the birds fly in a

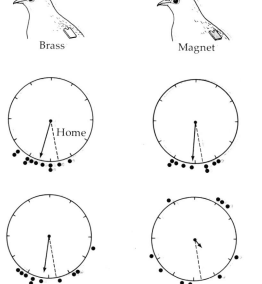

Figure 10.8
Pigeons with bar magnets attached to their backs are disoriented when released from an unfamiliar site under overcast conditions. If the sun is visible, however, the same birds fly normally even with magnets attached. Control pigeons with brass bars attached to their backs orient normally under conditions of bright sun as well as conditions of total overcast. The dots indicate the direction in which the bird was last seen flying, while the broken lines indicate the true home bearing. The mean directional tendency of all birds in a group is indicated by the arrow. [From "The Mystery of Pigeon Homing" by William Keeton. Copyright © 1974 by Scientific American, Inc. All rights reserved.]

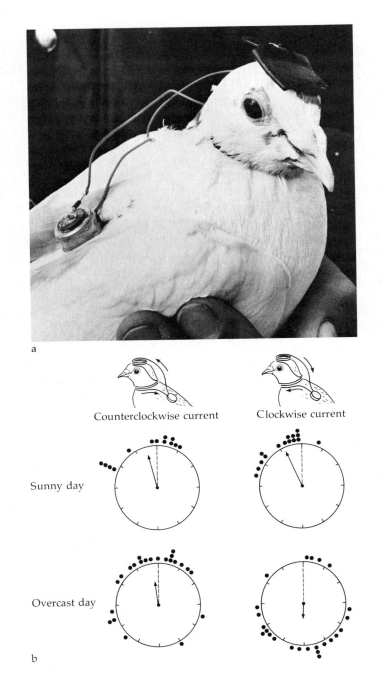

a

Counterclockwise current   Clockwise current

Sunny day

Overcast day

b

Figure 10.9
(a) Helmholtz coils fitted on the pigeon's head and neck can be used to reverse the direction of the magnetic field passing through the bird's head. [Courtesy of Ralph Morse.]
(b) Pigeons with Helmholtz coils in which the current flows counterclockwise fly almost directly homeward on both sunny and overcast days. When the current in the coils is made to flow clockwise, the birds still fly normally homeward on sunny days, but on overcast days they fly almost 180 degrees off course. [From "The Mystery of Pigeon Homing" by William Keeton. Copyright © 1974 by Scientific American, Inc. All rights reserved.]

particular direction with reference to magnetic north, effectively using a magnetic compass. Because the position of magnetic north does not change with time, no time compensation is required when the magnetic compass is in use, and at such times clock shifting will have no effect.

More recent experiments have further indicated that the use of the sun compass is not under rigid genetic control. Rather, it appears that an effective relationship between the sun's position, the bird's internal clock, and geographic direction is formed on the basis of a learning process. Birds homing in the southern hemisphere, for example, learn a different relationship and appear to compensate for changes in the sun's position with time by correcting in a counterclockwise rather than a clockwise direction. Wiltschko, Wiltschko, and Keeton (1976) have demonstrated the importance of ontogenetic experience in the formation of this relationship. These authors reared pigeons from the age of 24 days under permanently clock-shifted conditions. Young birds that had never seen the sun were placed in light-tight rooms in which the lights came on 6 hours after sunrise and went off 6 hours after sunset. As in the clock shifting experiments described earlier, therefore, the birds' internal clocks were 6 hours out of phase with real sun time. Unlike the birds described earlier, however, these birds were raised under clock-shifted conditions and had never known anything else. It is important to note, however, that these birds did have visual experience with the sun. During the period of overlap between the birds' time and real sun time—that is, part of the day after the birds' artificial sunrise but before true sunset—the pigeons were placed in an outdoor arena with full exposure to the sun. Surprisingly, comparisons of the flight directions of these birds with those of control birds that had never been clock-shifted revealed no differences. The permanently clock-shifted birds did not alter their direction of flight in response to a mis-set clock. They flew as if their clocks were indistinguishable from those of control birds. Comparison of the flights of permanently clock-shifted birds with those clock-shifted for only 5 days (the more usual procedure) indicated that while permanently clock-shifted birds again flew normally, as expected from the results of previous studies, the short-term clock-shifted pigeons departed in a direction approximately 90 degrees in error.

These experiments then attempted to accommodate the permanently clock-shifted birds to the natural day, that is to "normalize" their clocks, by confining them for five days in a room where the lighting cycle was identical to that of the natural day. When these now "normal" birds were first released to home, they behaved as if they had been temporarily clock-shifted, flying 90 degrees in error. After a number of flights under normal sun, however, the birds gradually began to fly normally again. Moreover, following a year's normalization under real sun time, temporary 6-hour clock shifting had comparable effects on both the formerly permanently clock-shifted birds and normal birds. The authors interpret their results as indicating that the pigeons synchronize their clocks on the basis of their early experience with relevant environmental cues. Experience, in a sense, teaches them how to use the sun compass by allowing for an accurate coupling of the internal clock with the position of the sun. By virtue of the permanent clock shift, "they had learned to read a southerly sun as an early morning sun, a westerly sun as a midday sun, etc. Thus pigeons apparently have no inherent ability to interpret the sun's azimuth at a given time as indicating a given direction; instead the sun compass must be established by experience" (Wiltschko, Wiltschko, and Keeton, 1976, p. 241).

Though much less is known about the processes by which the pigeons structure a map, current hypotheses suggest that learning may be an important factor here, too. Pigeons may have learned their location relative to home on the basis of a hypothetical sensitivity to local geographic factors and/or to site-distinguishing odors. The phenomenon of *release-site bias* suggests the importance of physical factors specific to a particular terrain in the choice of a directional bearing. Release-site bias refers to the fact that birds released to fly home from a site as much as 200 miles away will initially depart in an inappropriate direction. After flying as much as 10 miles away from the release site, the flight direction is oriented more directly homeward, and the birds eventually home correctly. This initial "error" is, however, seen in all birds departing from that site, and the degree of initial deviation is characteristic of the particular location. The bias remains whether birds are relying on the sun or the magnetic compass, and comparable biases are seen in all birds independently of whether or not they have flown from that site before. Keeton (1973) has hypothesized that release site biases represent "distortions" of the pigeon's map resulting from peculiarities in the geophysical characteristics of particular areas. Understanding how such irregularities alter homing may provide cues about how the birds normally use geophysical cues to form a map.

In order for such a hypothesis to be valid, the pigeon must initially have sensory receptors that render it sensitive to such subtle cues. In fact, experiments using techniques devised in the psychological learning lab have revealed heretofore unknown sensory dimensions to which the birds are sensitive. Birds have been placed in a classical conditioning situation in which the receipt of electrical shock is preceded by a previously neutral stimulus. Changes in the bird's heart rate normally follow shock. If the bird is sensitive to the neutral stimulus, after a number of pairings of shock and the stimulus in question, heart rate changes should occur following presentation of the neutral stimulus and prior to the presentation of shock. Through such procedures it has been demonstrated that birds are sensitive to cues quite unfamiliar to us. Among these are the plane of polarized light, infrasound (atmospheric changes in pressure of less than one cycle per second), and changes in barometric pressure. In addition, the birds have been found to have unusually sensitive olfactory abilities. In fact, birds that are released from a completely unfamiliar site are very deficient in homing if they have been deprived of olfactory cues. Odor landscapes may, therefore, be very important in determining the characteristics of the map (Hartwick, Foa, and Papi, 1977; Benvenuti, Fiaschi, Fiore, and Papi, 1973).

Interestingly, however, such procedures have revealed no apparent ability in the birds to detect magnetic fields. The birds clearly use magnetic information, but the means by which they extract this information from the environment is unknown. Experiments are now in progress using an operant conditioning paradigm to assess the pigeons magnetic sensitivity in the lab. Pigeons are placed in a long rectangular box that can be tilted horizontally up and down. The birds are required to peck a key for food under circumstances in which the gravitational field produced by different tilts constitutes a discriminative stimulus for food. Attempts are then made to distort the gravitational field using magnetic currents. The extent to which this distortion produces changes in pecking behavior may reveal the impact of magnetically induced distortions of gravitational cues. Laboratory analyses of the birds' sensory abilities coupled with experiments on the nature of homing in the wild represent a balanced combination of approaches. Together such efforts may ultimately reveal how pigeons acquire information relevant to the use of both the map and the compass in the highly adaptive process of homing.

IMPRINTING

The phenomenon that has perhaps been most responsible for the recent broadening of both the psychologists' and the biologists' views on learning is *imprinting*. Imprinting has initiated a heuristic restructuring of many conceptualizations of learning by requiring early on that they take as their starting point the organism's natural environment. Writing of his early rediscovery of imprinting, Konrad Lorenz states: "At that period, like most of my contemporaries and indeed like most present-day behaviorists, I more or less equated learning with the process of classical conditioning by reinforcement. From that point of view imprinting does indeed seem very different from learning" (quoted in Hess, 1973, p. ix). The clear distinctions between imprinting and the more traditionally recognized forms of learning, however, did not simply brand imprinting as different. Rather, they gradually drew attention to important dimensions of learning not evident in other, more familiar, learning processes. These dimensions, which we shall review shortly, have become central to our basic understanding of a variety of learning situations.

For a time psychologists mounted concentrated efforts to bring imprinting into the fold—to make it consistent with the standard, laboratory-based examples of learning. This, of course, involved bringing imprinting itself into the laboratory. After largely initiating the laboratory trend, Eck-hard Hess has more recently advocated a recentering of attention on those factors which initially made imprinting appear so different—factors whose influence is most evident in the natural setting.

> I then began looking at real imprinting events occurring out in nature be-tween newly hatched ducklings and their own parent. As a result of doing this I found that in nature there are a whole host of innate factors which work together to guarantee the formation of an optimal parent-young bond. I found that the situation was extremely different from that which is usually found in experimental laboratory studies of imprinting. . . . In these labora-tory situations the introduction of abnormal variables into the life of hatch-ling ducklings and chicks had led to widely differing results and theoretical formulations upon the nature of imprinting.
>
> So, after 25 years of doing research on imprinting, I have become con-vinced that much of the imprinting process, particularly in the natural situa-tion, has a complex innate substrate [Hess, 1973, p. xii].

Hess now maintains that to study imprinting in ignorance of its occur-rence in the natural setting is, in fact, not to study imprinting at all. Only by using imprinting as it occurs in nature as your "reference point"—in effect, as your baseline—can you then proceed to a more controlled labo-ratory analysis of the phenomenon. "The control is always the actual natural parent–offspring relation in a feral setting" (Hess, 1973, p. 427). This view is, of course, quite consistent with the natural history approach described earlier. Because imprinting has been subjected to both labora-tory and field analyses, it provides, as Hess suggests, an especially in-structive example of how the two approaches, *when used independently*, can result in two very different accounts of the same events. In keeping with the emphasis of this chapter, we shall focus on those characteristics which have emerged largely from work done in the field.

Imprinting has been defined as a learning process "in which innate so-cial responses that can be elicited by and directed to a wide variety of objects come to be elicited by and directed to only the classes of objects experienced in a limited neonatal period" (Salzen, 1970, p. 150). The most familiar example of imprinting is *filial imprinting*: the *following response* of young precocial birds.[1] The birds essentially follow and form filial attach-ment to the first object they encounter during a certain period following hatching. The geese in Figure 10.10 have imprinted on the Austrian ethologist Konrad Lorenz. The following response represents the forma-tion of a strong social attachment to the maternal figure (the object fol-lowed). In general, however, imprinting includes any instance in which

---

[1]*Precocial* animals are those that are relatively mature at or shortly after the time of birth or hatching. They require far less parental care than *altricial* animals, which are extremely help-less and more dependent on parental care to survive after birth or hatching.

Figure 10.10
The Nobel Prize-winning ethologist
Konrad Lorenz is pictured here being
followed by a gaggle of young geese
that have imprinted on him. [Courtesy
of T. McAvoy, *Life Magazine*, © 1955
Time Inc.]

an object acquires significance as a result of some kind of early social
exposure. Imprinting can be regarded as another example of *perceptual* or
exposure learning. That is, rather than acquiring new responses, the organism learns perceptual relationships; it "learns the details of its environment" (Salzen, 1970, p. 161). As with the previously described case of
perceptual learning—search image formation—here, too, stimuli gain distinctive significance through exposure. Thereafter, responses that previously might have occurred to any one of a number of stimuli now occur in
very greatly restricted, discriminated contexts. The animal has learned the
appropriate stimuli.

Sexual Imprinting

Several unique features of imprinting clearly distinguish it from the more
traditionally recognized laboratory examples of learning. First, imprinting

may have extremely *long-lasting effects,* evident only much later in the animal's life, and involving behaviors that are not themselves present at the time of the initial imprinting experience. The most thoroughly investigated case of the effects of early imprinting experience on later adult behavior is that of *sexual imprinting.* Recall that filial imprinting (the following response) is defined as the social attachment formed between newly hatched birds[2] and their maternal object. This attachment is manifest shortly after post-hatching exposure to the maternal figure; the birds immediately follow the object on which they were imprinted. Sexual imprinting, on the other hand, refers to the establishment of sexual preferences later in life, when the birds are sexually mature and engaged in the task of choosing a mate. These preferences are in fact formed during the period of filial imprinting. They constitute the long-lasting consequences that emerge only much later on. It appears as if long-lasting social bonds, ultimately determining mate preferences, are formed as a result of early experience that has taught the organism the attributes of an appropriate stimulus.

Experiments on *cross-fostering,* in which young birds are raised by (and presumably imprinted on) foster parents of another species, reveal how strong these learned preferences can be. Schutz (1971) raised mallard ducklings with foster parents of another species. When the birds were older, they were released on a lake containing as many as thirty species of geese and ducks. Most of the male mallards, when sexually mature, attempted to mate with members of the species with which they had been raised, and not with available members of their own species. Interestingly, the results were much less clear-cut with female mallards. In females, the consequences of early imprinting experience had a much less pronounced effect on recognition and selection of mates. Females tended to select members of their own species regardless of rearing conditions. This may reflect the fact that in many of the species tested the males and females have a *very different physical appearance.*[3] In mallards, the male, unlike the female, is very brightly colored. The males of different species differ more than the females of different species. The female, therefore, may not need to learn the male's appearance; she may need only be able to innately distinguish the gross features of the male's distinctive coloration. The male, on the other hand, must discriminate the drably colored female from other, similarly drab females of other species. Predictably, learning appears to provide the basis for the male's much more subtle discrimination. The validity of this interpretation is supported by data on imprinting in doves. Male and female doves look very much alike.

---

[2]Our continual reference to birds reflects merely where the bulk of the research has been done. In fact, as we shall see, mammals, fish, and numerous other organisms are now known to exhibit imprinting-like phenomena.

[3]A condition referred to as sexual dimorphism.

Both are drably colored, like many other species of bird with which they may come into contact. Cross-fostering experiments on doves indicate that sexual preferences in *both males and females* are acquired during the early imprinting experience. In species like doves, where the female cannot rely on the distinctiveness of the male, she, too, must learn her mate preference. She apparently does so on the basis of the early filial imprinting experience.

The role of the imprinting experience in establishing nonfilial social bonds reveals a second characteristic of imprinting that distinguishes it from other more traditional forms of learning. This is its *irreversibility*. In many situations, once sexual preferences are determined by the early filial imprinting experience, those preferences are fixed for life. Even after as much as seven years of "counter experience" in which male birds imprinted on a different species were forced to pair repeatedly with members of their own species, sexual preferences established by imprinting persisted. In spite of so much intervening experience, as soon as the males were once again given a choice between a conspecific (same-species) female and a female of the foster parent species, they chose the latter. These experiments also indicate that the conventionally recognized reinforcement for sexual behavior (copulation) is insufficient to alter the established preference. Apparently, the early filial imprinting experience determines what stimuli will reinforce sexual behavior. Even extended copulation with the less preferred, conspecific female was insufficient in reversing the preference for females of the foster parent species. The preference for the foster species persisted despite the occurrence of conventional sexual reward associated with the conspecific.

Several treatments of imprinting have suggested that the consequences of early perceptual learning are to impart special significance to certain features of the environment. The reports of sexual imprinting attest to this, as do numerous experiments demonstrating that the successfully imprinted stimulus will later serve as a reinforcer in other contexts (see Hoffman and Ratner, 1973). Imprinting effectively narrows "the range of stimuli with reinforcing properties" (Hinde, 1970, p. 519). Momentary visual presentation of the imprinting stimulus, for example, is sufficient to maintain a pecking response in imprinted ducklings. Correct responding in a T-maze has been similarly shown to persist when made contingent upon presentation of an imprinted stimulus. The function of perceptual learning may therefore be to specify the behaviorally significant properties of a general class of stimuli. Specific members of that class thereby differentially acquire the ability to reinforce.

The Sensitive Period

Perhaps the most intriguing of the distinguishing characteristics of the imprinting process, and that which most clearly differentiates it from other forms of learning, is the occurrence of the sensitive period. The literature on imprinting has indicated that the same experience can have very different effects on an organism depending on the time at which the experience occurs. That period during which the individual is exceptionally susceptible or sensitive to the effects of a particular experience is termed the *sensitive period*. Early experiments by Hess on the filial imprinting of ducks indicate that exposure from 13 to 16 hours following hatching results in the strongest imprinting (see Figure 10.11). The animal's imprintability is greatly reduced following the offset of the sensitive period: If exposure occurs too late, the animal's behavior (in, for example, choice of mate later on) may be permanently impaired.

Though the factors responsible for the onset and offset of the sensitive period in ducks have been the object of much controversy (see review by Bateson, 1966), most researchers now agree that there is an optimal period of susceptibility during which the organism is uniquely able to incorporate certain kinds of experience. It is, moreover, widely assumed that such time-dependent susceptibilities are *biologically based* developmental phenomena. Differential sensitivities arise because of developmental differences in the biological functioning of behavioral systems. At some developmental stage the physiological structure and functioning of the organism is radically different from that which might characterize later stages. Though recent physiological data (for example, Salinger, Schwartz, and Wilkerson, 1977a, 1977b) have challenged this view, it is widely held that such developmental sensitivities occur only in young organisms. The effects of early experience, therefore, must coincide with

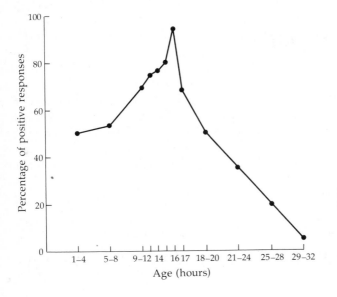

Figure 10.11
Hypothesized duration of the critical period for imprinting in mallard ducks. [From "Imprinting in Animals" by Eckhard H. Hess. Copyright © 1958 by Scientific American, Inc. All rights reserved.]

a particular period of time, the sensitive period. If the organism does not undergo the relevant experience at this time, normal development may be permanently impaired; the organism will be unable to incorporate the effects of similar experiences that might come later on.

Hess has pointed out that the characteristics of sensitive periods may differ in different situations. Sensitive periods may vary both in duration and in the degree to which stimulation is absolutely essential at the indicated time. These differences are not rigidly defined but, as Hess suggests, perhaps represent points on a continuum that in reality comprises many gradations of the more general phenomenon of the sensitive period. During the *critical period*, for example, susceptibility is rigidly restricted to a very brief period of time, and the consequences of experience occurring at this time are permanent. Similarly, a lack of relevant experience during a critical period produces permanent abnormality. The filial and sexual imprinting processes occurring in some birds are assumed to represent the operation of true critical periods. As such, the processes that govern the acquisition of early experience are qualitatively different from those that characterize the more traditionally recognized processes of associative learning. The latter apparently do not involve the operation of a critical period.

An *optimal period*, by contrast, is characterized by much less rigidity than a true critical period. Sensitivity to certain kinds of experience is heightened at this time, but the nature of the relevant experience may be much more general, and the effects of either exposure or deprivation are much less permanent. The experience can, in fact, be incorporated at other times, but with much greater effort and perhaps far less completely. It is as if the optimal period defines a time of *maximal sensitivity*, though some lessened sensitivity occurs at other times as well. Hess' classification of types of developmental susceptibilities reflects an important general point. That so many different manifestations of the phenomenon exist indicates the extremely widespread occurrence of sensitive periods. What was once a peculiarity of imprinting is now recognized to be an integral part of many learning phenomena, and perhaps of any developmental sequence in which future functioning is affected by the progressive incorporation of early experience.

The Function of Imprinting

Up to this point we have emphasized the view that learning processes develop in a manner that serves some function critical for the life history of the species. Imprinting is no exception. It is clearly a learning phenomenon—but one that is rigidly controlled by innate factors. Both the flexibility and the rigidity evident in the imprinting situation assure the realization of some evolutionarily vital function. What is the function of imprinting, and how does the unique interplay of *learned and innate components* work to serve this function? The answer to the first question has become rather straightforward; the answer to the second remains one of the most difficult tasks faced in the study of animal behavior.

Imprinting functions in the development of *species recognition*. In both filial and sexual imprinting, the organism has learned what object to direct certain critical responses to. In either situation the correct choice is a member of the same species, and in both cases exposure during the critical period "teaches" the individual what stimuli to use in identifying another organism as a conspecific. The consequences of making an error are grave. If the young bird habitually directs food-getting (begging) responses to a different-species "parent," the request is likely to go unheeded, and the animal may starve to death. Similarly, if a male duck directs courtship to the female of another species and if his attentions are returned at all, the product of the mating will likely be a nonviable hybrid, incapable for one reason or another of furthering either of the parent species.

Here one may ask, if species recognition is so critical, why should the opportunity for error through experience be introduced at all? Why are there not simply built-in inflexible species recognition mechanisms (FAP's) that genetically ensure a correct response, leaving no room for error? If species recognition were of sole importance, this might be quite sufficient. Suppose, however, that the precise recognition of individuals is also important, and considerable variability exists in the species-specific characteristic. Frequently, the individual must be able to recognize one particular member of its species (its own parent, in the case of filial imprinting), distinguishing among various members of its species on the basis of subtle characteristics. Such demands would require that the individual be capable of forming rapid discriminations among the extremely subtle and diverse signals that indicate individual distinctiveness. An increased reliance on learning would allow for the formation of rapid, precise, and very adaptive discriminations, produced much more rapidly than phylogenetic change would permit.

Because the function of species recognition is so important, natural selection has placed certain restrictions on the flexibility of the imprinting process. The critical period is obviously one of these. Learning takes place at a time when the individual most likely to be encountered is a member of one's own species. This guarantees that the learner will incorporate the "correct" set of species characteristics. Restrictions are also placed on the nature of what constitutes an incorporable stimulus. Some imprinting models simply either do not alter behavior at all, or the change produced may be a very transient one. This feature is especially evident in the case of sexual imprinting. Mallards can only be successfully cross-fostered with certain other species. They will sexually imprint on *geese*, for example, but very little sexual imprinting results if the foster parent model is either a coot or a domestic chicken. Learning apparently cannot occur in response to some kinds of stimulation. It moreover appears that the ease with which imprinting occurs is determined by similarity to one's own species. Little imprinting occurs in response to stimuli whose characteristics are vastly different from those of a conspecific. When, for example, birds are raised by mixed-species foster parents (one conspecific and one heterospecific) and then later tested for mate preference, they typically prefer the conspecific *independently of sex* (Immelman, 1972). We will see other examples of this type of rigidity when we examine the development of birdsong—a phenomenon that in many species closely resembles an imprinting process.

Nonvisual Imprinting

Our discussion of imprinting thus far has focused on situations in which exposure has been largely visual in nature. As will be evident in the next section, however, imprinting-like phenomena can also be based on nonvisual exposure—that is, on information received via some other sensory modality. Both *auditory* and *olfactory imprinting,* for example, are now known to occur. Goats and European shrews form a filial attachment to the maternal object on the basis of olfactory signals to which they are exposed during a critical period. Note that both of these organisms are mammals; as mentioned earlier, imprinting is not a learning phenomenon restricted to birds. In the shrew (a rat-like animal in appearance) the mother initiates the formation of a caravan in which the closest offspring (there may be as many as five or six) grasps her fur. Each of the others grasps the fur of the sibling in front of it, and in this way the young are prevented from straying from the protective presence of their parent. Research indicates that the young identify the object to be grasped as a result of a process of olfactory imprinting. The young shrews become imprinted on the odor of the animal that nurses them during the period of from 8 to 14 days following birth. Olfactory exposure prior to this time has no effect. If the young are exposed to olfactory stimulation during the critical period, therefore, only objects with this odor can stimulate the formation of caravans. A cloth imbued with the imprinted odor can itself become the object of caravan formation. Moreover, when returned to their biological parents, cross-fostered shrews imprinted on the odor of a foster parent will *not* grasp the alien-scented fur of their own biological parent.

Recent research on the following response in ducklings has indicated that *prehatching auditory imprinting* may enhance the effectiveness and ease of later visual imprinting. Imprinting in the wild, therefore, may be a multi-modal sensory experience. Work by both Hess and Gilbert Gottlieb (performed using techniques such as those illustrated in Figure 10.12) has suggested that the prehatching vocal (and therefore auditory) interactions between the mother duck and the unhatched duckling can substantially

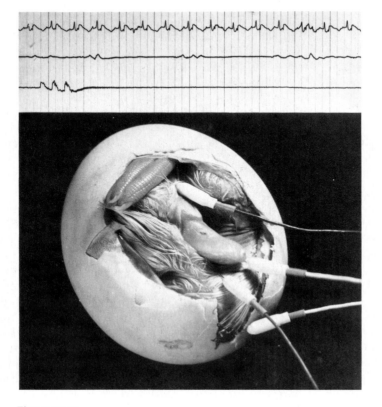

Figure 10.12
Peking duck embryo with recording electrodes in place on the day
before hatching. Heart beat is shown on the top line, oral activity
(bill-clapping) on the middle line, and vocalizations on the bottom line.
Note that bill-clapping and vocalization are independent measures,
since the embryo can vocalize without making overt bill movements.
[From Gottlieb, 1968.]

alter the character of the posthatching filial imprinting experience. In effect, the imprinting process has already begun in another modality,
perhaps with an independent set of critical periods, and in response to
exposure to an independent set of stimuli.

Ducklings respond preferentially to the calls of conspecifics, both parents and siblings (Gottlieb, 1971). Moreover, if ducklings are exposed to
the calls of a conspecific prior to the elicitation of the following response,
subsequent presentation of a vocal model (one providing both visual *and*
auditory stimulation) enhances the occurrence of imprinting. The magnitude of this effect, however, depends on the nature of the prior auditory
exposure. Imprinting in birds that had previously heard conspecific calls
was enhanced when the vocal model emitted those same conspecific calls.
By contrast, birds exposed to the calls of a different species underwent

less enhancement when later exposed to imprinting models emitting the same heterospecific (different-species) calls. Interestingly, however, whether mere exposure or actually actively following the sound is important during this period of prior exposure depends on the ecological context of the species in question. *Surface nesting species,* such as mallards, will actively *follow* a sound *before* the onset of the critical period for visual stimulation. Following seems to be necessary to produce the later facilitating effects of vocalizations on the visual phase of the process. In *hole-nesting species,* such as wood ducks, however, whose nests are maintained in darkness, auditory exposure with *no* active following is sufficient to produce the subsequent preference for *following* a vocalizing visual stimulus. This comparison again points to the importance of a consideration of differing ecological contexts (in this case surface-nesting versus hole-nesting) in determining the basic character of specific learning processes.

Naturalistic Studies of Imprinting

In keeping with his recent suggestion that the examination of imprinting in the wild is essential for an understanding of the nature of the learning process, Hess (1973) has enumerated a number of striking differences between laboratory imprinting and naturally occurring imprinting. He mentions, for example, that while laboratory imprinting has repeatedly been observed to be readily reversible, naturally occurring imprinting evidences "zero reversibility." Similarly, in the laboratory both duration of incubation and hatching time of eggs are quite variable, and therefore do not occur in synchronous fashion within a given clutch of eggs. By contrast, in the wild both incubation and hatching are much more constant and synchronous (within a few hours of one another), even though the female actually lays the eggs over a period of several days. These differences suggest that the quality of the experience presented to developing ducklings is very different in the laboratory and in the field. Such differences, moreover, apparently have profound effects on the nature of the posthatching imprinting experience itself. Hess has demonstrated that seasonally changing environmental factors, such as temperature and humidity, and *prehatching parent–offspring vocal interactions,* now known to be important in the occurrence of later visual imprinting, are critical in producing the adaptive synchronous hatching evident in the wild. Synchronous hatching is, of course, beneficial because it ensures that the several chicks hatched from a given clutch of eggs will all reach comparable stages of locomotor maturation, as well as the critical period for imprinting, at the same time. This makes the mother's tasks of keeping the family together, feeding, and protecting her offspring much easier.

The term "vocal interactions" implies that not only is the mother duck vocalizing to her chicks, but also that they are responding in turn, vocalizing to her. Both occur before hatching has taken place. Hess has devised an elegant combination of laboratory and field techniques to observe the character of the naturally occurring vocal exchanges, and then to analyze the impact of these vocalizations on both the synchrony of hatching and on the subsequent occurrence of filial imprinting. Figure 10.13 depicts the procedures employed. Nest boxes are constructed in the wild for the

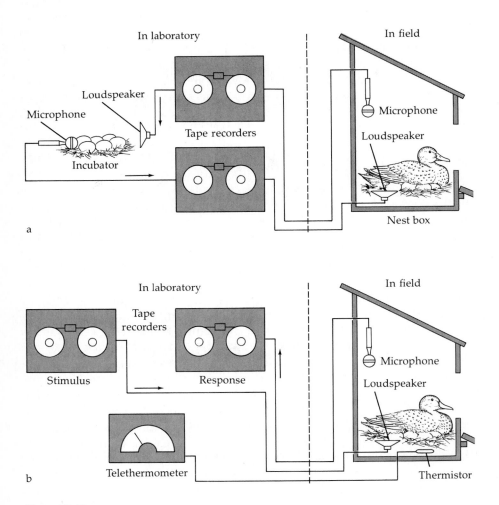

Figure 10.13
Conditions devised to measure vocal interactions between a female duck sitting in the field and unhatched ducklings incubating in the lab. (a) Speakers and microphones transmit sounds from the ducklings in the lab to the incubating female in the wild. Microphones positioned near the female permit the ducklings to hear her vocalizations as well. (b) The various recorded duckling sounds are presented to the incubating female in the field to assess her response to systematic changes in the sounds produced by the unhatched ducklings. [From "Imprinting in the Laboratory" by Eckhard H. Hess. Copyright © 1972 by Scientific American, Inc. All rights reserved.]

incubating female duck. These are equipped with tape recorders, microphones, and speakers to both receive and transmit vocalizations. Following unobtrusive field observations of the naturally occurring vocal interactions, further analyses have involved the reciprocal connection of eggs incubating under controlled conditions in the lab with the vocalizing female sitting in the field. In this procedure eggs undergoing controlled observation in the lab will receive exactly the vocal stimulation that would normally be occurring in the wild. Such observations indicate that the female mallard duck begins to engage in "cluck-like sounds" a few days before hatching is scheduled to take place. This vocal output in fact increases substantially as the time of hatching approaches. In the appropriate stage of her reproductive cycle, the female appears to vocalize in response to the emergence of incipient vocalizations produced by the developing embryos. The ducklings, in turn, begin to respond reciprocally to the occurrence of maternal vocalizations. The frequency of the duckling's response during the period of maternal vocalizations also increases considerably as the time of hatching approaches. Maternal vocalizations peak at two times during the cycle. Maximal frequencies occur first at the time of hatching itself, and then again at the time of the exodus from the nest—"when the female leads the hatchlings off the nest" (Hess, 1973, p. 443). This suggests that female mallards are vocalizing vigorously at the time of filial imprinting. The fact that the two events (the occurrence of filial imprinting and maximal vocalizations) are coextensive, plus the fact that each female appears to emit "her own typical vocalization pattern," further suggests that vocal interactions predispose the young to the formation of an immediate and irreversible parent–offspring social attachment during the critical period. The uniqueness of the maternal vocal pattern yields a stimulus that can be used by the ducklings to discriminate their own mother from all the other maternal figures potentially available. Other nearby mothers of the same species may look very much alike, but they apparently sound different. "The pre-hatching communication may possibly set the stage for a very strong imprinting to the female mallard, in spite of the fact that the young duckling in the egg certainly cannot follow the parent object" (Hess, 1973, p. 448).

Typically, none of this potentially vital communication is provided in the more traditional laboratory imprinting setting. Does its presence in the wild actually alter the imprinting process? Hess has presented evidence that requires an answer in the affirmative. Ducklings that had developed under natural conditions and that were hatched by a female mallard (rather than in a laboratory incubator) were removed from their mothers well before the occurrence of the nest exodus. "None of these ducklings responded to any sort of laboratory imprinting procedure, despite the fact that they had had no previous opportunity to follow the female. . . . However, we have found subsequently that in some cases it is possible to have such young follow in an apparatus. In these cases, the ducklings were ones that were removed from the nest box in the middle of the night

... and they followed a decoy *if it emitted the call of a female mallard"* (Hess, 1973, pp. 448–449, italics ours).

Hess's work has clearly demonstrated the value of the laboratory analysis of a complex process such as imprinting conducted against a backdrop of well-controlled, detailed observations of the behavior as it occurs in the natural setting. This includes, of course, the species-specific ecological context that defines this setting. As we shall see in the next section, the study of the development of singing in various species of birds has begun to provide another persuasive example of the essential validity of this approach.

SONG LEARNING IN BIRDS

Learning processes reminiscent of imprinting phenomena are evident in the development of singing in many species of passerine birds.[4] The development of birdsong has for a number of reasons become a major focus of research in recent years. Like imprinting, song learning may involve novel aspects, such as the operation of critical periods, that require a re-evaluation of our assumptions about the nature of various learning processes. Birdsong development can, moreover, be readily analyzed within the context of the natural circumstances that prevail for the species under investigation. Song learning in fact occurs under so many different sets of circumstances that ecological comparisons among different species of songbird are both feasible and quite informative. These comparisons may reveal why different learning strategies characterized by different degrees of flexibility have evolved in response to different ecological demands. The development of birdsong has provided perhaps the most systematically studied instance of how natural influences exert ultimately genetic control over the nature of the learning process. Within this context, a number of parallels can be drawn between the development of singing in passerine birds and the development of language in humans (Marler, 1970b, 1975).

It is important to emphasize at this point that song development does not necessarily represent the manifestation of a single learning process. Rather, singing defines a class of behaviors serving a territorial or reproductive function whereby one individual communicates to another. Learning may or may not be involved in the efficient realization of this function. Its involvement will, of course, be determined by the nature of the situation within which the function must be performed. As we shall see, varying degrees of learning are evident in comparisons of even closely related species whose natural environments differ in important ways. When they do occur, therefore, the learning processes that take part in

---

[4]Passerine birds are altricial perching songbirds such as finches, sparrows, mockingbirds, and cardinals.

song development may be quite distinct from one situation to the next. These differences reflect the different ecological demands defined by different environments. Thus the role that learning plays and the nature of the learning process can both be expected to vary with ecological circumstances. This by now should be a familiar theme. As already noted, one of the major advantages of studying the development of birdsong is the unusually large number of comparisons possible across species and circumstances. This divergence in strategies of development permits conclusions regarding how learning must of necessity occur differently (or not at all) in response to distinct environmental demands. In a recent review of the literature on the development of birdsong, Jerram Brown writes: "The interaction between genetic factors and experience in the learning process is probably nowhere more conspicuous and so easily studied" (Brown, 1975, p. 658).

Developmental Stages in Singing

Most passerine birds are classified as altricial species. They undergo a relatively prolonged period of extreme dependence on parental nurturance. They remain in their nests for weeks after hatching, and during this time the young birds are largely incapable either of feeding themselves or of performing efficient locomotor activities. Singing, too, is underdeveloped and often absent in young passerine birds, though they may engage in numerous simple calls. True song is usually defined by "loud, sustained, complex vocalizations" (Nottebohm, 1972, p. 117). Such true singing typically occurs later, with the onset of sexual maturity, and within the contexts of courtship, mating, and territorial defense. The normal fully developed song, termed the *primary* or *full song*, is, therefore, only exhibited by adult birds as much as eight months to a year after hatching. However, the primary song often does not emerge abruptly. Rather, its occurrence may be preceded by a number of developmental stages during which various approximations to the adult song appear and gradually become progressively more like the final adult song. In some species of finch and sparrow, for example, early, premature singing begins with *subsong* (as early as two months post-hatch). While sharing some characteristics of the primary song, subsong lacks both complexity and qualitative specificity. These features gradually emerge during a transitional *rehearsed* or *plastic song* stage, which finally culminates in the production, at the time of sexual maturity, of the adult primary song. Frequently, this is the song that is sung for the remainder of the bird's life. In many species, especially those characterized by gradual transitions from one phase to the next, the nature of the experience that occurs during these early months provides the critical basis for the emergence of the normal adult song. It is in these instances that factors associated with learning are most pronounced.

Figure 10.14
The white-crowned sparrow.

Among the most thoroughly studied instances of song development is that of the white-crowned sparrow *(Zonotrichia leucophrys)*, pictured in Figure 10.14. Song development in this species, in which only the males sing, follows the developmental program outlined above. The resulting primary song, pictured in Figure 10.15a, consists of a repeated phrase composed of two major components. The first, a sustained *whistle,* while somewhat individualized, is generally quite characteristic of the genus and occurs as part of virtually all white-crowned sparrow songs. It can be used to identify the bird as a sparrow. The second component, the *trill,* is acoustically far more complex and is characterized by much greater variability than the whistle. Geographically distinct populations of white-crowned sparrows are known to produce distinctly different song patterns. Such regional variations in song pattern are termed *dialects;* a given dialect distinguishes the members of a particular population, whose song pattern clearly differs from the dialects characterizing same-species members of a different regional population. All songs retain certain species-specific, white-crowned sparrow, attributes. However, the occurrence of dialectic differences among distinct populations, coupled with similarities among the members of one regional group, strongly suggests that learning and the social transmission of dialects play critical roles in the song development of the white-crowned sparrow.

The work of Peter Marler and his colleagues at the Rockefeller University has in fact indicated that both *experience* and *practice* are essential for the progressive emergence of the primary song in this species. Birds removed from nests in the wild at 2 or 3 days of age can be maintained in soundproof chambers for various periods during development. Singing

Figure 10.15
Song development in the white-crowned sparrow. (a) Normal development through subsong and full-song stages follows exposure to the appropriate model during the critical period. (b) Acoustical isolation (the absence of appropriate model) impairs development of the dialect characteristics in full song. Song still, however, exhibits species-specific characteristics. (c) Deafening prior to the onset of subsong results in extremely abnormal song, exhibiting neither species-specific nor dialect characteristics. [From Alcock, 1975.]

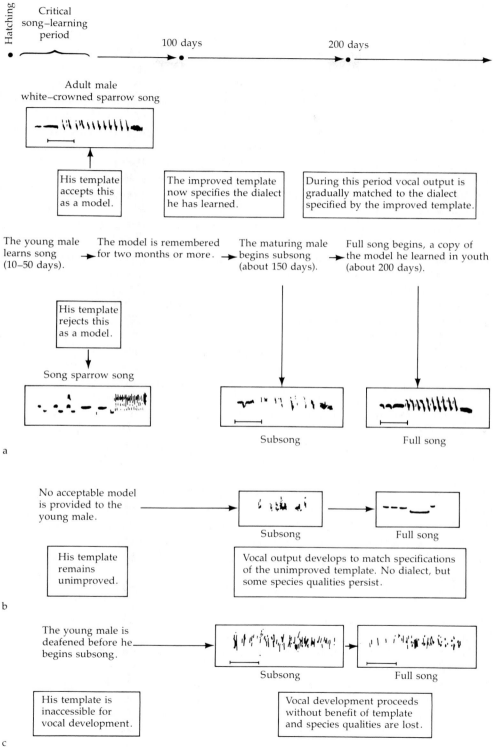

Hatching

Critical
song–learning
period

100 days

200 days

Adult male
white–crowned sparrow song

His template
accepts this
as a model.

The improved template
now specifies the dialect
he has learned.

During this period vocal output is
gradually matched to the dialect
specified by the improved template.

The young male
learns song
(10–50 days).

The model is remembered
for two months or more.

The maturing male
begins subsong
(about 150 days).

Full song begins, a copy of
the model he learned in youth
(about 200 days).

His template
rejects this
as a model.

Song sparrow song

Subsong

Full song

a

No acceptable model
is provided to the
young male.

Subsong

Full song

His template
remains
unimproved.

Vocal output develops to match specifications
of the unimproved template. No dialect, but
some species qualities persist.

b

The young male is
deafened before he
begins subsong.

Subsong

Full song

His template is
inaccessible for
vocal development.

Vocal development proceeds
without benefit of template
and species qualities are lost.

c

behavior is then assessed months later (at approximately 10 months of age), when the primary song would normally be expected to emerge. Males captured from the wild and isolated at about 100 days of age exhibited no disruption of song development when tested at maturity. The normal primary song emerged on time and was characterized by dialect patterns corresponding to those exhibited by the population from which the birds were taken. As indicated in Figure 10.15b, however, birds isolated completely from post-hatch day 5 later produced highly abnormal songs. Adult singing stabilized much later than normal, and virtually all of the fine detail characteristic of the home dialect was lacking. "In one bird a syllable trill was completely lacking and the song consisted only of broken whistles" (Marler, 1970a, p. 6).

Experiments coupling isolation with systematic exposure to recordings of adult male white-crowned sparrow models have revealed that a *critical period* for song learning occurs in the white-crowned sparrow. If the young bird is exposed to the recorded model during the period of time from 10 to 50 days after hatching, the normal primary song emerges at approximately 8 months of age when the bird has reached sexual maturity. Isolation either before or after this period has *no effect* on the later emergence of the primary song. If no relevant exposure occurs during the critical period, however, the song is permanently impaired (see Figure 10.15b). No amount of subsequent exposure can reverse the resulting deficit. When, however, the birds are exposed to the song of a white-crowned sparrow model during the critical period, the dialectic characteristics of the emerging primary song are identical to those of the model, even if the model's dialect differed from that of the population from which the developing birds were taken. Under a set of rather constrained circumstances, white-crowned sparrows appear to learn their dialects.

Marler's results further indicate that exposure is a necessary but, interestingly, *not* a sufficient condition for the learning of the normal song in this species. Sparrows that are *deafened following* normal exposure during the critical period still fail to sing normally. Figure 10.16 compares sound spectrograms of white-crowned sparrows maintained under various conditions of exposure and deafening. Deafening appears to impede learning even when it occurs in conjunction with exposure during the critical period. Moreover, the song of a deafened bird is more abnormal than that which develops following acoustical isolation but in the absence of deafening. That this result is not merely an artifact of the deafening procedure is shown by the behavior of birds deafened *after* they have already produced the normal adult song. These animals continue to sing normally despite their deafness. Thus, once the primary song is learned, it is produced normally even by a deaf sparrow. Hearing is, however, required for the development of the song in the uninitiated bird. It is as if the bird must practice and benefit from hearing its own product. That product presumably constitutes the feedback that provides the basis for further modifications in the song.

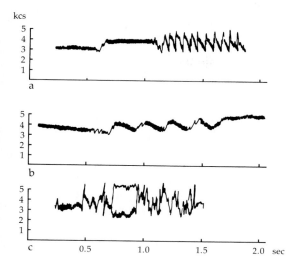

Figure 10.16
Comparison of the songs produced by white-crowned sparrows (a) reared normally (wild bird), (b) reared in isolation (hand-reared bird), and (c) deafened prior to the occurrence of subsong (deaf bird). [Courtesy of M. Konishi.]

Biological Constraints on Song Development

We mentioned earlier that the birds learn only under rather restricted circumstances. These biological constraints, together with several unique features of white-crowned sparrow song learning, exemplify the nature of genetic control exerted over the learning process. Marler's results indicate that both experience during the critical period and feedback are essential for normal song development. Further experiments in which young white-crowned sparrows were exposed to different kinds of experience, however, reveal that the *nature of the experience* is equally as important as the timing. Birds taken from their nests prior to the onset of the critical period were isolated and then exposed to the normal song of the song sparrow (*Melospiza melodia*). Exposure occurred during two daily sessions from day 7 to day 28—therefore within the critical period. This procedure was virtually identical to that employed when the subjects were provided conspecific models, and the pattern of song development was again observed as the birds reached maturity. In birds exposed to the song sparrow model, development occurred slowly and *none* of the features of the song sparrow's song were incorporated as a result of the exposure. Moreover, the songs that did emerge were very abnormal. They approximated the degree of disruption evidenced by birds raised in complete isolation. White-crowned sparrows appear, therefore, to be restricted in the nature of the experience that they are able to benefit from. Several different species have been used as models, and in each case the normal development of song is impaired. The birds must be exposed to the song of a white-crowned sparrow (not necessarily of the same dialect) in order to benefit from the effects of experience. Within these constraints, however, song is flexible.

In many areas populations of white-crowned sparrows and populations of song sparrows are *sympatric* with one another. That is, the ecological niches of the two species overlap to some extent, and individuals of each group are likely to encounter one another. Consider in this context how maladaptive it would be if the white-crowned sparrow were capable of learning the song sparrow's song. Exposure is a likely event because the species are sympatric, and if the white-crowned sparrow could "benefit" from this exposure, the song learned would probably not perform the essential functions of adult singing. Song would not be used as a signal for territorial defense because intruding white-crowned sparrows would not respond to the unfamiliar song. Similarly, seasonally receptive female birds would not react to the song as a courtship signal. If receptive female song sparrows responded to the song sparrow-like communications generated by the male white-crowned sparrow, any ensuing mating would likely result in the production of a poorly adapted hybrid. In this context, it is to the white-crowned sparrow's advantage to be unable to incorporate certain kinds of information.

Similar biological constraints seem to operate on the *continued flexibility* (beyond the time of sexual maturity) of the white-crowned sparrow's singing behavior. Once the final adult song becomes *crystallized* at about 8 to 10 months of age, no further learning can take place. The bird's song pattern is set for the rest of its life. Attempts to further modify song patterns following adult crystallization have been quite unsuccessful. The period during which learning can play a significant role in the development of song seems itself to be genetically fixed. Once the period of flexibility has passed, no further learning can take place; that is, no additional acoustical information can be incorporated into the song.

It should be emphasized that the development of song in the white-crowned sparrow is *not* necessarily representative of birdsong learning in general. Crystallization following sexual maturity and full song development is, for example, not generally typical. Marler and Waser (1977) report that while temporary deafening has profound initial effects on song development in canaries throughout their first singing season, a substantial increase in repertoire size is evident during the second season. The rigid crystallization evident in the white-crowned sparrow does not occur here. Strategies range all the way from no involvement by learning to situations (as with the mockingbird) in which the types of constraints evident in white-crowned sparrow song learning do not appear to operate.

Learning is, moreover, not necessarily associated with song complexity. Many songbirds exhibiting songs more acoustically complex than that of the white-crowned sparrow sing the adult song at the appropriate time, regardless of the bird's previous experience. Of far greater significance than complexity in explaining the role of learning are the ecological demands that the species must meet. The emergence of song in brood parasites, for example, typically involves no learning. *Brood parasites* are birds, like the cuckoo, that lay their eggs in the nests of birds of another species. The *host species* therefore essentially becomes the unknowing foster parent of the parasitic bird, feeding and nurturing it as if it were its own off-spring. If the offspring of the brood parasite learned its song through exposure to models provided by the first song it heard during some criti-cal period, it would very likely develop the wrong song—that of the host species. Because, by disrupting courtship signaling, this might severely impair adult reproductive behavior, learning in this situation would be quite maladaptive. Experiments in fact indicate that the reproductive ef-fects of song in most brood parasites emerge normally even when the birds are raised in complete isolation from adults. To this species' benefit, learning is not involved.

Cowbirds are known to parasitize the broods of as many as 200 distinct species of host. Recent reports (King and West, 1977) indicate that female cowbirds reared in auditory as well as visual isolation respond with ap-propriate copulatory postures when presented (at 8 months of age) with the courtship song of the male of the species. No response is evoked by the songs of either the red-winged blackbird or the Baltimore oriole. In-terestingly, however, females will respond even more vigorously than normal to the abnormally developed song of male cowbirds reared in acoustical isolation. The authors suggest that the abnormal male song re-presents a *supernormal stimulus* (see Chapter 9) for innate mate recognition in this species. The normal male song contains information relevant to contexts (territoriality and aggression) other than mate identification. When these (for the purposes of the female cowbird) extraneous features are absent due to abnormal rearing conditions, the receptive female may respond to unambiguous signals clearly defining species-specific mate recognition in the cowbird.

Immelman (1969) has demonstrated that the emergence of song in sev-eral species of finch represents a much greater degree of flexibility than that described for the white-crowned sparrow. Zebra finches can incorpo-rate information provided by exposure to a different species model. When raised by parents of another species, these finches learned and, as adults, sang the song of their foster parents. Here, too, however, some degree of specificity is indicated. Birds raised by nonsinging females within earshot of the songs of both conspecific males and males of another species of finch developed songs containing elements of only the conspecific "mod-els." Given a choice, therefore, finches, too, appear predisposed to model their own species. Even more flexible and amenable to experiential input are the songs of birds that in the wild mimic the songs of other species. Mockingbirds are notable in this group, which also includes some species of starlings and bower birds. Here, the songs may actually be composed of chains of near-perfect imitations of the phrases typical of a number of other species of bird. Many aspects of the song, however, are species-specific and can be used to indicate that the bird in question is definitely a mockingbird and not a member of the mimicked species. Temporal characteristics of the song are important in this regard. Mockingbirds repeat each different species' pattern (there may be several) from four to six times before switching to another pattern. While much less systematic investigation has been made of the ontogeny of song development in species that imitate in this fashion, it is quite plausible that learning plays a very large and much less constrained role in such situations.

A final intriguing example of song development occurs in situations in which the relevant exposure is provided, not by an adult male of the same species, nor by the members of a different species, but by the bird's own mate. In *duetting birds* (Thorpe, 1972) the male and female sing together (either simultaneously or in alternation). Duetting is believed to function in maintaining the courtship bond between the birds (many duetting birds pair for life), and in providing the basis for joint aggressive vocal displays in which the two birds sing together to ward off potential intruders and defend their mutual territory. Even within species, individuals vary considerably in the characteristics of their duets, suggesting that learning may take place in the co-development of duetting. Within a pair, each bird usually sings its own distinct part, with minimal exchange of parts taking place. If, however, one member of the pair dies or is removed, the remaining member will sing both parts. Especially in cases where the members of the pair sing alternating parts, the tonal and temporal parameters of the duet are quite intricate. They are, moreover, assumed to develop in conjunction with "a long period of complex and accurate learning" (Hooker and Hooker, 1969, p. 203).

Theories of Song Learning

A number of theories of song learning have been suggested to account for the amazing diversity characteristic of song development. Marler has suggested that, in the white-crowned sparrow, during the practice period of rehearsed song the bird is in effect matching the product of its own efforts with the characteristics of a *neural template*. The template is itself of variable flexibility and actually serves as an *internal referent* to a greater or lesser degree provided by the bird's experience. The referent tells the bird what the final song should sound like. When the match is near perfect, song learning crystallizes and no further modification is required. The origin and nature of this hypothesized template (to date no direct evidence supports its existence) vary from species to species. Experience presumably plays an important role in molding the template in the white-crowned sparrow. In species like the song sparrow, however, which require no model, the template is fixed (see, however, Kroodsma, 1977). The model is genetically given, and only practice is required to improve the match (while song sparrows require no model, deafening does disrupt the emergence of their song). The white-crowned sparrow's template is somewhat fixed in that the bird requires a conspecific model. Beyond this, however, experience refines the template to conform to the characteristics of the regional population dialect. A still more flexible template theoretically characterizes those species (for example, mockingbirds) that can accept any model as a basis for template formation. Here, too, however, practice—and therefore the chance to match via auditory feedback—may be essential.

Nottebohm (1972) has proposed an alternative theory of song development based, not on trial and error template matching, but on the feedback-based coordination of an ordered developmental program. He suggests that subsong does not perform a communicative function, but provides the raw material from which a number of more complex song components develop. At each stage of development the vocalizations available (initially, perhaps, simple calls) provide the basis for the shaping of more complex vocalizations. Feedback plays a coordinating role, integrating the various elements into a progressively more complex product—ultimately, the primary song. Song learning, by this analysis, constitutes a "highly programmed sequence" in which "each step in the development both circumscribes and potentiates the next step" (Nottebohm, 1972, p. 48). No template is required, and, rather than performing a matching function, subsong practice allows for a progressive accumulation of elements out of which coordinated song is formed. Note how such a process would permit the development of species-specific songs that nonetheless retain the mark of the individual. The simplest and earliest elements of subsong (which may be highly invariant within the species) provide common units for all individuals. This species-specific base should result in the development of complex song that retains many of the species' typical qualities. The unique developmental sequence that characterizes each animal, on the other hand, provides an individual distinctiveness superimposed on the species-specific base. Nottebohm's theory suggests that in those cases (unlike that of the white-crowned sparrow) in which relevant exposure to a model occurs *during* the subsong and plastic song periods, the species-typical song base may provide a guide for the young bird's selection of an appropriate model. In the wild, a young bird is very likely to be exposed to the songs of numerous other species. The successful development of song, however, usually requires some sort of selective attention to conspecific models. By building on a species-typical base, young birds may recognize appropriate models on the basis of their similarity to the developing song that they themselves have produced. The model then serves to facilitate the production of finer detail and more precision in an already developing process.

THE NATURAL HISTORY APPROACH

Though much remains to be explained, the amazing diversity of learning strategies exemplified in the development of song in passerine birds has provided further elaboration of three important concepts. These three, also evident in the literature on food acquisition and food aversion learning and in the literature on imprinting, have greatly broadened our notions of learning: (1) Intricate interactions occur between ontogenetic and phylogenetic factors in learning. The nature of these interactions is determined by the ecological demands placed on the species in question. (2) Learning processes occur with tremendous diversity, which is governed by the nature of the situation that renders learning of adaptive benefit. (3) Only by understanding how learning functions to maximize reproductive success in the organism's natural environment can we arrive at complete explanations of the nature of behavior change. For it is here that the demands for survival are defined.

As indicated earlier, many of the findings of the natural history approach contrast sharply with those of the approaches presented in previous chapters. The latter take little note of species differences and frequently examine behavior change in situations often described as arbitrary. That is, they are not intended to model the environment in which the organism has evolved. Efforts are, moreover, focused on the generality rather than the diversity of learning. What are the implications of the approach presented in this chapter for the more traditional psychological analysis of behavior change? While these issues are treated in more detail in Chapter 13, we must at this point indicate that ontogenetic generalities such as those formulated by the experimental analysis of behavior must surely be possible. They represent a distinct realm of inquiry. Their utility, however, depends on the extent to which they are compatible with and complement phylogenetic principles, which also govern behavior change. To the extent that principles of behavioral analysis represent common features of the ontogeny of behavior change, generalities are possible. We must ask what common environmental features prevalent in many animal groups have been tapped by traditional experimental analysis. This, however, presupposes some existing knowledge of the prevailing natural situation. Experimental analysis must therefore proceed against the backdrop of a naturalistic data base. Given the appropriate grounding, however, principles of ontogenetic behavior change will emerge as an essential element in our understanding of learning.

11 Invertebrate Learning I: Protozoa, Coelenterates, Platyhelminthes

Species-specific behavior patterns and behavioral plasticity—both discussed in the preceding chapters—have often been regarded as mutually exclusive behavioral categories. A given instance of behavior is traditionally classed as *either* learned *or* innate. The behavior is said to be learned if it occurs as a function of environmental changes encountered during the individual's lifetime; it is said to be innate if it appears to result from variations in the evolutionary history of the species to which the individual belongs. More recently, however, as we have seen in Chapter 10, psychologists as well as biologists have stressed that no behavior sequence can be fully understood without considering the *interaction* of ontogenetic and phylogenetic factors. Both play necessary roles in the completion of an integrated sequence of behavior.

Like species-specific behaviors, learning abilities, too, have evolved to serve different functions in differing species. The remaining chapters deal with the *phylogeny of learning:* how learning occurs at different times and in different ways as a function of the evolutionary history of the species in question. In this and the next chapter we will review the evidence on the learning abilities of various groups of widely divergent organisms, considering, where possible, the kinds of interactions that may be expected to occur between phylogenetic and ontogenetic factors in the modification of behavior.

The animals with which we will be dealing in this and the next chapter have been called the "forgotten majority" (Corning and Lahue, 1972) in the literature of animal learning—the *invertebrates*.[1] Though invertebrates constitute well over 90 percent of the species in the animal kingdom, the representation of invertebrates in the animal learning literature falls far short of that figure. (Only 5 percent of all papers published in the *Journal of Comparative and Physiological Psychology* from 1950 to 1970 dealt with invertebrates.) This is the case despite both the initial impetus provided by early work on invertebrate learning and the numerous advantages associated with the study of invertebrates.

Investigations of learning in invertebrates date from the very inception of the scientific study of learning in America. Even before Pavlov's work on classical conditioning had reached the English-speaking world, much effort had already been directed toward the analysis of behavior change in "lower" organisms (see Jennings, 1906). This fascinating pursuit was all but forgotten, however, in the flurry of behavior studies monopolized, until recently, by the rat. Much of the rat research was guided by the implicit assumption that behavioral laws discovered by studying one organism are applicable to most other organisms as well; animal subjects were therefore selected largely for convenience. The rat's particular sensory and motor capacities and the parameters of deprivation and reinforcement used ensured performance in a variety of laboratory apparatuses. These paradigms provided an impressive empirical basis on which to build. Moreover, once a large body of data had been collected describing the behavior of the rat, it become an even more convenient subject. When the pigeon was discovered to have important methodological advantages over the rat, it, too, was studied extensively. The notion that the ecology and phylogeny of the organism under investigation must provide the basis for an accurate interpretation of behavior change went largely unnoticed. The rat and pigeon dominated research on learning to the exclusion of most other nonhuman vertebrates and of virtually all invertebrates.

In fact, the comparative study of different types of organisms may contribute significantly to our understanding of the nature of behavioral flexibility. More recently, the advantages and importance of understanding behavior change in invertebrates have resurfaced, and work has resumed. Invertebrates occur with tremendous diversity, and a great deal of morphological data tracing their evolutionary origins is already available. Use of the comparative method to describe the phylogeny of behavioral plasticity requires the analysis of learning abilities across a wide array of closely related species. Because of their diversity and because of the

---

[1]The group to which all vertebrates belong—the subphylum Vertebrata—is generally divided into five major classes of animals. These are the fish (there are actually three classes of fish), the amphibians, the reptiles, the birds, and the mammals. Virtually all other living organisms are invertebrates.

wealth of data already available on lines of evolutionary descent within groups, invertebrates may yield important information on the evolution of learning. In addition, the nervous systems of invertebrates have undergone clear structural changes during evolution. By assessing the types of plasticity possible in the various systems represented, we may discover how various kinds of learning are related to changes in neural development. This task is often made easier in the study of invertebrates because certain invertebrates confer special advantages on the experimental paradigm itself. Much of our knowledge of neural transmission, for example, came more quickly because squids have giant axons, which made the task of investigation easier. We will see in Chapter 12 that a similar structural advantage in the marine mollusc *Aplysia* may facilitate an analysis of the cellular changes that occur during learning.

As we have already noted, many of the principles devised by psychologists to account for behavioral flexibility derive from investigations of the behaviors of rats and pigeons in a few restricted situations. In large part these situations comprise variations on the operant (or instrumental) and classical conditioning paradigms described earlier in the book. To what extent are these principles specific either to the organisms studied or to the situation in which these organisms were placed? By extending these principles to the world of the invertebrates we may examine their generality across the animal kingdom. Moreover, new principles may emerge, which, while basic to both vertebrate and invertebrate learning, might have remained unnoticed in the complexity of vertebrate behavior. Rightly or wrongly, researchers tend to be far more careful in recognizing and evaluating the assumptions they make regarding the behavior of less familiar organisms. Once made explicit at the more primitive level, however, our general assumptions regarding behavior change may then be evaluated critically at the more familiar level. The results of extending our basic conceptualizations of learning to invertebrate organisms may ultimately require serious reconsideration of our notions of behavior change in all organisms.

Finally, the human species' ever-growing awareness of its own ecological relatedness to other species has made behavioral investigations of invertebrates of practical importance. Invertebrates comprise the majority of our neighbors. What they do affects us, and what they do may at times depend on what they are capable of learning. Recent data, for example, suggest that certain groups of insects *learn* to avoid the pesticides that have been developed to aid in their control. The fact is that most organisms *are* invertebrates. Our understanding of the behavior of organisms and the kinds of changes it may undergo should not be generated by or restricted to two or three specialized (and perhaps unrepresentative) biological lines. General principles, if they are to be truly general, must be applicable to all organisms.

PHYLOGENETIC DIVERSITY IN LEARNING

Recent attempts to extend evolutionary and ecological analyses to the study of behavior have emphasized that, like the evolution of morphological characteristics, the evolution of behavior does *not* occur according to an orderly progression of development across widely diverse organisms. Rather, the nature of the change evident in evolution is determined by the particular adaptive demands exerted by the organism's environment (see Chapter 10). These are unique for all organisms, and they constitute the source of the behavioral uniqueness that evolution confers on organisms. The evolution of learning is no exception (Hodos and Campbell, 1969). Learning abilities are not necessarily greater as we proceed from "simple" organisms to more "complex" organisms. There is no linear evolutionary progression of intelligence culminating in the tremendous intellectual abilities of *Homo sapiens*. While humans undoubtedly are the most flexible, and therefore the most intelligent, animals on earth, this does not mean that any organism more closely related to humans is necessarily more intelligent than any of their more distant phylogenetic kin. A dog may fail to learn a task that is relatively easy for an octopus. It certainly is the case that some organisms appear to exhibit more behavioral flexibility than others, and phylogenetic history may provide the basic prerequisites for the evolution of flexibility in a given species. But learning differences are not due solely to phylogenetic position. The demands exerted by the particular environment in which a species has evolved define if and when learning will be useful. In an evolutionary sense, all organisms are faced with the same task—that of adaptation. If adaptation requires behavioral plasticity, the successful organism will be capable of changing its behavior.

The following review of the learning abilities of invertebrates will in general be ordered according to the organizational scheme defined by the phylogenetic scale. This is employed only as a convenience and is not intended to convey the course of the evolution of learning abilities. We in fact know very little about the paths by which learning mechanisms have evolved. We do know, however, that such abilities will have developed to the extent that they confer an adaptive advantage on an organism required to meet the demands of a particular environment. As we review the animal phyla represented, refer back to the quotation at the beginning of Chapter 10 and speculate on the kinds of environmental demands placed on a given population that might make the appearance of one form of learning more adaptive than another.

The data presented in the remainder of this chapter will be organized according to traditionally recognized categories of learning. Keep in mind, however, that these may not be the only kinds of learning of which the organisms in question are capable. Moreover, demonstration that an animal is capable of behavior change within the context of a laboratory paradigm need not necessarily suggest that the animal's natural environment requires the use of such a capacity. The order of our presentation more accurately reflects the predominant experimental paradigms within which learning has been approached in these organisms. These, in turn, have been handed down from work on vertebrates, and for this reason may occasionally be difficult to apply to invertebrates. In addition, as we have seen in Chapter 10, many instances of behavior modification occurring under more natural circumstances in vertebrates are difficult to place in any one of the standard categories of learning. In invertebrates, too, we can expect that the abilities of the organism may at times exceed the boundaries of the situations designed to reveal those abilities.

PROTOZOA

Protozoa are single-celled organisms of tremendously diverse form, which exist, quite literally, everywhere some kind of moisture exists. Figure 11.1 suggests the extent of this diversity. Once characterized as unicellular, protozoans are now more properly referred to as *acellular* organisms: Rather than consisting of only one cell, they differ from metazoan (multicellular) organisms in that they are not divided into cells at all. The difference between "unicellular" and "acellular" becomes clear when a protozoan is compared with a single cell taken from a metazoan organism. The metazoan cell is highly specialized to perform one isolated function that serves the larger organ or tissue system of which the cell is a part. It in fact does, and is equipped to do, little else. It is clearly a unitary element, part of a much larger system. By contrast, the protozoan is far more complex both anatomically and behaviorally. It performs numerous physiological and behavioral functions independently of other units. In fact, rather than being a unitary element in a larger system, it is a complete behaving organism interacting with a relatively complex environment.

The nature of these interactions is of some import in addressing the issue of whether acellular organisms learn. If, for example, the protozoan's commerce with its environment is very simple—that is, if the environment remains relatively constant and places few unusual demands on the individual—why should it ever need to learn? In such a homogeneous environment the capacity for behavior modification might be of minimal adaptive value. The following passage from H. S. Jennings' *Behavior of the Lower Organisms* illustrates that simplicity is not the rule in the protozoan's interaction with its environment. (Jennings' account refers to the diagram in Figure 11.2.)

> I had attempted to cut an Amoeba in two with the tip of a fine glass rod. The posterior third of the animal, in the form of a wrinkled ball, remained attached to the rest of the body by only a slender cord—the remains of the ectosarc. The Amoeba began to creep away, dragging with it this ball. This

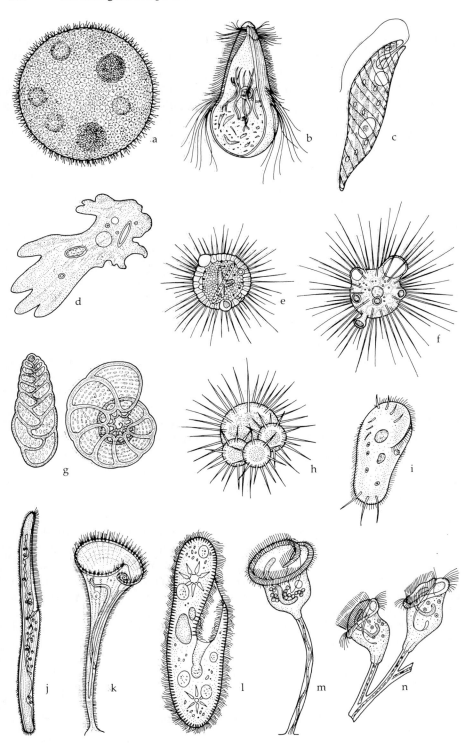

Figure 11.1
Examples of members of the phylum Protozoa. These acellular organisms exhibit tremendous diversity in form as well as behavior. (a) Flagellata, *Volvox globator.* (b) Flagellata, *Trichonympha collaris.* (c) Flagellata, *Euglena spirogyra.* (d) Sarcodina, *Amoeba proteus.* (e) Sarcodina, *Actinosphaerium eichornii.* (f) Sarcodina, *Actinophrys sol.* (g) Foraminiferan shells. (h) Sarcodina, *Globigerina.* (i) Ciliata, *Stylonychia mytilus.* (j) Ciliata, *Spirostomum ambiguum.* (k) Ciliata, *Stentor coeruleus.* (l) Ciliata, *Paramecium aurelia.* (m) Ciliata, *Vorticella.* (n) Ciliata, *Carchesium polypinium.* [After Corning and Von Burg, 1973.]

Amoeba may be called *a*, while the ball will be designated *b* [see Figure 11.2]. A larger Amoeba (*c*) approached, moving at right angles to the path of the first specimen. Its path accidentally brought it in contact with the ball *b*, which was dragging past its front. Amoeba *c* thereupon turned, followed Amoeba *a*, and began to engulf the ball *b*. A cavity was formed in the anterior part of Amoeba *c*, reaching back nearly or quite to its middle, and much more than sufficient to contain the ball *b*. Amoeba *a* now turned into a new path; Amoeba *c* followed [Figure 11.2, at 4]. After the pursuit had lasted for some time the ball *b* had become completely enveloped by Amoeba *c*. The cord connecting the ball with Ameoba *a* broke, and the latter went on its way, disappearing from our account. Now the anterior opening of the cavity in Amoeba *c* became partly closed, leaving only a slender canal

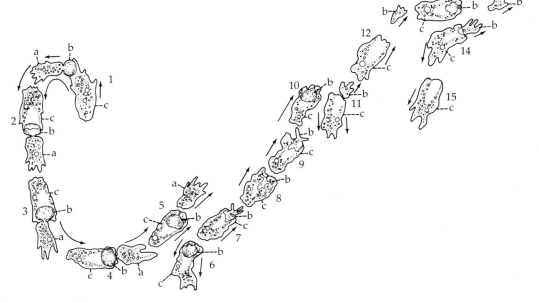

Figure 11.2
Jennings' depiction of the predatory pursuit of one amoeba by another. [After Jennings, 1906.]

(5). The ball *b* was thus completely enclosed, together with a quantity of water. There was no adhesion between the protoplasm of *b* and *c*; on the contrary, as the sequel will show clearly, both remained independent, *c* merely enclosing *b*.

Now the large Amoeba *c* stopped, then began to move in another direction [Figure 11.2, at 5–6], carrying with it its meal. But the meal—the ball *b*—now began to show signs of life, sent out pseudopodia, and became very active; we shall therefore speak of it henceforth as Amoeba *b*. It began to creep out through the still open canal, sending forth its pseudopodia to the outside (7). Thereupon Amoeba *c* sent forth its pseudopodia in the same direction, and after creeping in that direction several times its own length, again enclosed *b* (7, 8). The latter again partly escaped (9), and was again engulfed completely (10). Amoeba *c* now started again in the opposite direction (11), whereupon Amoeba *b*, by a few rapid movements, escaped from the posterior end of Amoeba *c*, and was free—being completely separated from *c* (11, 12). Thereupon *c* reversed its course (12), overtook *b*, engulfed it completely again (13), and started away. Amoeba *b* now contracted into a ball and remained quiet for a time. Apparently the drama was over. Amoeba *c* went on its way for about five minutes without any sign of life in *b*. In the movements of *c* the ball became gradually transferred to its posterior end, until there was only a thin layer of protoplasm between *b* and the outer water. Now *b* began to move again, sent pseudopodia through the thin wall to the outside, and then passed bodily out into the water (14). This time Amoeba *c* did not return and recapture *b*. The two Amoebae moved in opposite directions and became completely separated. The whole performance occupied about fifteen minutes [Jennings, 1906, p. 17].

Such behavior is evidently quite complex.

Associative Conditioning

The current resurgence of interest in the subject of protozoan learning was heralded by the work of Beatrice Gelber and the ensuing Gelber–Jensen exchange (see Corning and Von Burg, 1973). The debate centered on the question of whether or not associative learning had in fact been clearly demonstrated in the experiments reported by Gelber. In her initial study, Gelber (1952) exposed cultures of the advanced protozoan *Paramecium* (see Figure 11.1e) to a series of training sessions in which on every third trial a wire coated with bacteria (food for a paramecium) was dipped into the medium containing the organisms. On the other two trials of each three-trial sequence, *no additional bacteria* coated the wire, and the number of paramecia entering a 3-mm area surrounding the length of the wire was measured. One control group received an equal number of "training" trials with no food placed on the wire. An additional control group received no exposure to the wire at all. Comparison of the experimental (reinforced with food) and the control (never receiving food) groups (see Figure 11.3) indicated that progressively more of the

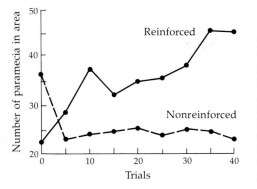

Figure 11.3
The number of paramecia entering the area in which food reinforcement is presented increases with training. No comparable increase is observed in animals that have never received reinforcement. [After B. Gelber, Investigations of the behavior of *Paramecium aurelia*: I. Modification of behavior after training with reinforcement. *Journal of Comparative and Physiological Psychology, 45,* 58–65. Copyright 1952 by the American Psychological Association. Redrawn by permission.]

experimental animals were counted in the 3-mm area surrounding the length of the wire.

Jensen (1957, 1965) has objected to a learning interpretation of these results and instead maintains that the observed behavior change can be more simply accounted for on the basis of the creation of bacteria-rich zones, which remain in the medium even after the coated wire is removed. Bacterial concentrations would naturally be higher in the areas in which the wire was repeatedly inserted. Large numbers of paramecia would therefore be attracted to those areas, creating the illusion of a conditioned response to the wire in the absence of the reinforcing stimulus (food). Jensen supports these objections with observations indicating that, in situations similar to those used by Gelber, higher concentrations of bacteria *are* found in the central regions of the medium into which the wire is dipped. Moreover, when given the alternative, paramecia do aggregate in pools containing a bacteria-rich medium and not in those without bacteria. Jensen's argument is given further support by an experiment (Katz and Deterline, 1958) in which vigorous stirring of the medium in an effort to equalize food concentrations across the total area all but eliminated the "approach" response in the reinforced group.

This evidence would seem to have put the issue to rest. However, subsequent experiments by Gelber (1957), which included gentle stirring of the culture, again supported the conditioning interpretation. In tests in which the wire coated with food was inserted in the periphery of the dish, while during testing the bare wire was inserted in the center, the protozoa aggregated at the centrally located bare wire on unreinforced trials. When the food was inserted in one area but the bare wire was inserted in another, following training the experimental animals continued to aggregate near the wire rather than in the area that might contain higher food concentrations. In addition, McConnell and Jacobsen (1970) point out that experiments using vigorous stirring to eliminate both food gradients and acquisition effects should not be taken as definitive. Because of the tremendously disruptive effect such stirring might have, all behavioral effects exhibited by the animals might be obscured. "The vigorous stirring that these authors employed to dissipate any concentration of bacteria surely would have either seriously injured many of the animals or disoriented them considerably. If one 'vigorously stirred' a rat in a maze immediately after it had learned the maze, then *at once* put the rat back at the starting point, might one not readily demonstrate that rats are incapable of learning?" (McConnell and Jacobsen, 1970, p. 436) To date, the Gelber–Jensen debate remains unresolved.

Investigations of associative avoidance conditioning in protozoa have yielded similarly equivocal conclusions. Following early experiments indicating that various protozoa learn to avoid aversive stimuli by selectively collecting in signaled safe areas, numerous failures to obtain similar results were reported. Bergström's (1968, 1969) attempts are both the most recent and the most convincing. In experiments using the ciliate *Tetrahymena*, a close relative of Paramecium, four groups of animals were exposed to light and/or shock. The experimental group received 15 trials on which the onset of light preceded shock by 0.5 sec. Three control groups consisted of one with shock only, one with light only, and a third that received neither light nor shock. All subjects were subsequently tested on light-only avoidance trials, and results, pictured in Figure 11.4, indicate that a smaller proportion of the subjects that had received light–shock pairing were found located in the lighted compartments. Bergström also reports the surprising finding that retention of the avoidance reaction persisted throughout several cycles of cell division.

Notice that one critical control group is missing in the Bergström design. Only the experimental animals received repeated presentations of *both* stimuli. If the effect is to be regarded as a case of associative learning, it must be shown to be the relationship between the two stimuli, and not the total amount of stimulation, that is critical. A fourth group presented with both light and shock, but independently and in random order, should exhibit no conditioning (see the discussion of appropriate control procedures in Chapter 3). Attempts to repeat this experiment, incorporating the appropriate control group, indicate that neither experimental nor control animals exhibit any differential responding to light. For a more complete account of attempts to demonstrate associative learning in protozoa, see Corning and Von Burg (1973).

Habituation

Recently obtained data on habituation represent a far more conclusive demonstration of the protozoan learning capacity. That something like what we now call habituation appears to exist in protozoa is suggested by Jennings' (1906) early work on the "adaptability" of ciliates to repeated tactile strokes, which initially elicit a strong contraction response. Jen-

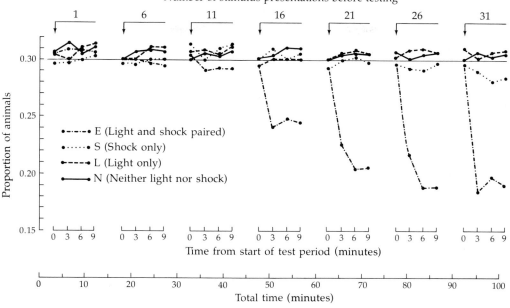

Figure 11.4
Conditioned aversion in a ciliated protozoan. With increased training, a progressively smaller proportion of individuals in the experimental (light–shock paired) group were found in the lighted part of the test chamber. [After Bergström, 1968.]

nings found that with repeated stimulation the number of strokes required to produce contraction increased. At first, only one was required, but after many trials the animals became much less responsive and as many as 20 or 30 strokes might be required. The modern rekindling of interest in the habituation phenomenon has been accompanied by a parallel rekindling of research efforts directed at demonstrating habituation in the protozoan. Much of this work is predicated on the persuasiveness of Jennings' early reports.

Harden (reviewed by Corning and Von Burg, 1973) used a loudspeaker attached to dishes containing about 100 *Stentor coeruleus* (see Figure 11.1k) to administer repeated mechanical stimulation. Each group received 30 such stimuli separated from one another by an interval of 1 minute. During the intertrial interval a continuous photographic record was kept, indicating the number of animals contracting immediately following each stimulus. Control subjects were photographed at 1-minute intervals in the absence of any mechanical stimulation. Approximately 50 percent of the animals in experimental groups contracted on initial stimulation. After 30 presentations, however, this number decreased to as little as 10 to 15 percent of the population. Roughly 40 percent of these subjects contracted in response to light stimulation administered immediately following completion of the 30-trial sequence of mechanical stimuli, indicating that simple fatigue was not responsible for the decrease in responding. Retention of habituation was tested under a number of conditions and, while no retention was observed in subjects retested at 24-hour intervals, subjects retested at 1-hour intervals exhibited less initial responding on retesting. Moreover, responding in these animals returned to baseline more rapidly than that of animals undergoing habituation for the first time. Additional water-change control groups were tested to assess the effects of possible alterations in the chemical medium to which the animals might be responding directly. No evidence for chemical mediation was obtained.

Independent accounts of response decrements in *Stentor* as a function of repeated mechanical stimulation have been reported by Wood (1970a, 1970b). Stimulation once per minute over a period of one hour resulted in a roughly 60 percent drop in response probability (see Figure 11.5). Spontaneous recovery was observed, and some retention was evident up to six hours following initial testing. Moreover, administration of a more intense mechanical stimulus was effective in eliciting contraction.

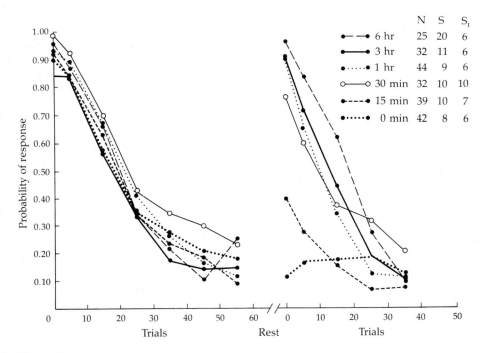

Figure 11.5
Response decrements obtained in the protozoan *Stentor coeruleus* with repeated mechanical stimulation. Both recovery and retention are evident at various intervals following training. [After Wood, 1970a.]

   More recently, Wood (1973) has demonstrated that prior habituation to mechanical stimulation does not alter *Stentor's* subsequent sensitivity to photic stimulation (see Figure 11.6). With repeated photic stimulation, however, response decrements can be produced in this modality as well. Furthermore, habituation to the light stimulus has no effect on subsequent sensitivity to mechanical stimulation. In each case, habituation seems to occur independently in one modality or the other, indicating that the resulting decrements are stimulus–specific—that is, they occur *only* in conjunction with the training stimulus. Such discriminative properties would be expected if learning is in fact taking place.

   Intracellular electrophysiological recordings taken throughout the course of behavioral habituation sessions yielded extremely interesting results (Wood, 1970c). Contractions occurring in response to both mechanical and photic stimulation were correlated with the occurrence of identical all-or-nothing electrical potentials (spikes), which *remained unaltered* as the response decrement proceeded. Despite drastically reduced responding, the frequency of spike potentials was unchanged. Both types of stimulation also produced a much smaller prepotential (a decremental electrical potential, which is not all-or-nothing), which in both cases preceded the occurrence of the spike. Unlike the spike potentials, the prepotentials associated with the two modalities were clearly different from one another and, according to Wood (1973), represent different processes. Moreover, when repeated mechanical stimulation occurs, the associated prepotential is characterized by a gradual decrease in amplitude and an increase in latency, both correlated with the decrement in contraction responding. Given the stimulus-specificity of behavioral habituation, Wood has concluded that the electrophysiological data suggest that habituation

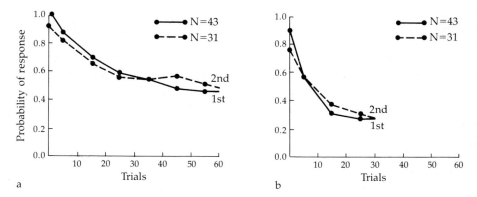

Figure 11.6
(a) Comparison of responding to mechanical stimuli produced either just prior to (1st) or just after (2nd) repeated presentation of a light. (b) Comparison of responding to light produced either just prior to (1st) or just after (2nd) repeated mechanical stimulation. [After Wood, 1973.]

in *Stentor* is produced by a stimulus-specific alteration in receptor function that occurs with repeated stimulation. While these observations cannot, by themselves, be used to conclude anything about the physiological basis of habituation in multicellular organisms, they provide convincing evidence of the existence of behavioral plasticity in the protozoan.

Traditionally, if an instance of behavior change is to be regarded as evidence of learning, the change must be retained for some period of time following training. That is, the organism must leave the situation with new information of benefit at some later time when faced with a similar situation. Habituation is no exception (see Chapter 3). If the protozoan is actually learning in the habituation paradigm, therefore, it should be possible to demonstrate that the information learned is retained over some period of time. Just how long this period of time must be is open to some question. On the basis of the length of its lifespan alone, for example, it would be unreasonable to expect the protozoan to retain information over periods comparable to those normally used to demonstrate mammalian or avian retention. Some interval more in accord with characteristics of the organisms' life cycle and metabolic rate is presumably more appropriate. Habituation data obtained from the ciliate *Spirostomum* (see Figure 11.1j) indicate response decrements similar to those described for *Stentor* (see Applewhite and Morowitz, 1967). Moreover, the *Spirostomum* studies show that significant retention can be obtained at intervals of from 1 to 2 minutes following initial training (Applewhite, 1968). Other investigators report retention at intervals as great as 10 minutes, but none at intervals of 30 minutes or greater. Wood, however, has reported unusually long-term retention occurring up to 6 hours following training in *Stentor*. Applewhite (1968) has demonstrated that retention at 15-second intervals is nonlocal in character. That is, when trained individual *Spirostomum* were transected, both halves of the organism exhibited equal retention of habituation. For a complete account of the theoretical mechanisms proposed by Applewhite and his co-workers to account for cellular habituation in *Spirostomum* see Applewhite and Gardner (1971).

By far the most controversial question in protozoan habituation learning concerns the presence or absence of *dishabituation*. Recall (see Chapter 3) that dishabituation is assumed to be a special case of an independent excitatory process normally superimposed upon the habituation process. The status of dishabituation, therefore, need not reflect on the validity of the habituation process being described in protozoa. Nonetheless, reports by several investigators (Eisenstein and Peretz, 1973; Wood, 1970a) describe fruitless efforts to obtain dishabituation. Following habituation in *Stentor* resulting from repeated strong mechanical stimulation, Wood (1970a), for example, was unable to produce dishabituation using a weaker mechanical stimulus. Additional trials with the stronger (habituating) stimulus, subsequent to the presentation of the weaker (novel) stimulus, yielded no evidence of an increment in responding produced as a function of the interpolated novel stimulation. Eisenstein and Peretz (1973) suggest that dishabituation may be impossible in the acellular system. They propose that neural synapses may be required to support the kind of plasticity represented by dishabituation.

Data collected more recently on *Spirostomum*, however, suggest otherwise (Beck, 1976). Animals initially received weak repetitive vibratory stimulation, which resulted in a decrement in contraction responding. Subjects were then administered a more intense vibratory stimulus (the dishabituating stimulus) on every fourth trial. Response probabilities measured on the three trials following the first dishabituation trial were substantially greater than those recorded during the final three trials of habituation. Moreover, the change in responding produced by the dishabituating stimulus itself became progressively less pronounced with continued dishabituation. Such *habituation of dishabituation* is characteristic of dishabituation in more advanced organisms (Thompson and Spencer, 1966). Note the procedural difference between this study and that reported by Wood (1970a). Wood used a weaker dishabituating stimulus, while Beck used a stronger dishabituating stimulus. Theoretically, either manipulation should be effective in producing dishabituation, though with a stronger stimulus increased responding could simply result from the increase in the intensity of stimulation (and not novelty per se). Definitive evidence for dishabituation in the protozoa must therefore await a demonstration that dishabituation in *Spirostomum* occurs as a function of weaker as well as stronger novel stimulation.

Many of the studies mentioned up to this point have focused on behavior change occurring in a group of protozoa. Though group studies are typically required by the small size of the organisms, this strategy eliminates the possibility of systematic analysis of behavior change occurring progressively within a single individual. Instead, dependent measures are often equivalent to the proportion of animals responding in a group that may contain from one hundred to several thousand members. The work of Hamilton, Thompson, and Eisenstein (1974) is therefore somewhat unique in its emphasis on the detailed description of individual protozoan behavior as habituation proceeds. These data reflect both the tremendous behavioral diversity possible in the protozoa and the complexity of even the most simple form of learning.

Individual *Spirostomum ambiguum*, selected for study on the basis of their size (they may reach as much as 3 mm in length) were placed on specially adapted microscope slides and presented with 10 minutes of intermittent vibratory stimulation. Following this habituation sequence, animals received a number of additional stimuli at 2-, 5-, and 10-minute intervals to assess the retention of habituation training. Vibratory stimulation may evoke one of two responses in *Spirostomum*: Either the animal might contract, thereby decreasing its overall length by as much as one-half, or the animal might engage in an avoidance reaction characterized by the reversal of the motion of the hairlike cilia, resulting in movement in the opposite (posterior) direction. Hamilton et al. (1974) measured both responses to vibratory stimulation, along with a number of other behavioral characteristics. Among these were the animals' vertical versus horizontal posture, body shape (bent or straight), duration and direction of swimming behavior, and the occurrence of "probing"—an exploratory response in which the animal, while stationary, rotates its anterior and posterior ends before proceeding on. Presentation of the first few stimuli in the habituation sequence indicated that individual *Spirostomum* differ in their initial contractile responsiveness to vibratory stimulation. High, low, and medium responders were identified and, more importantly, these differences in contractile responsiveness were correlated with systematic differences in the effects of repetitive stimulation (see Figure 11.7). High responders habituated to repeated stimuli, as expected; medium responders habituated slightly, though much less than the former group; and low responders exhibited an *increase* in the probability of contraction responding as a consequence of repeated stimulation. The habituation procedure actually resulted in a facilitation of responding, reminiscent of sensitization, in organisms initially relatively unresponsive to vibratory stimulation. The separation between groups was evident in retention as well. Interestingly, these differences in amount of habituation were not reflected in the likelihood of avoidance responding. Any one group engaged in as much avoidance responding as the others, and the frequency of avoidance did not change with continued stimulation. When avoidance responding did occur, however, the *magnitude* (distance traveled or response duration) of that responding showed a significant decrease with

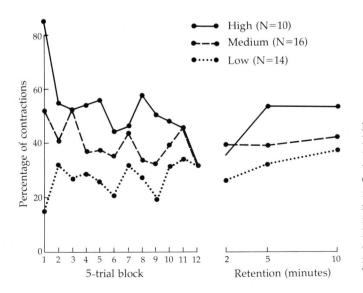

Figure 11.7
Individual protozoa may differ in their initial responsiveness to vibratory stimulation. Comparisons of the effects of repeated stimulation on high, medium, and low responders indicate that the nature of habituation in these organisms depends in part upon initial response levels. [After Hamilton, Thompson, and Eisenstein, 1974.]

repeated stimulation in all categories of responders. The other behavioral characters monitored did not prove to be good predictors of habituation versus facilitation; but in all groups a number of interactions between behaviors occurred, altering the probability of contraction. Vertically oriented animals, for example, were more likely to contract on stimulation than horizontally oriented animals. On the other hand, vertical orientation decreased the likelihood of eliciting an avoidance reaction. Similarly, a bent posture was correlated with an increase in contraction probability but a decrease in the frequency of avoidance responding. If the animal was probing as the stimulus was presented, contraction was far more likely than if the animal was swimming (in either direction) as the stimulus occurred.

The authors conclude that habituation as well as facilitation processes occur in all *Spirostomum*. However, one or the other process will dominate depending upon individual responsiveness to the stimulus in question. Such a conclusion is quite consistent with the dual process theory of habituation based on data collected from vertebrates (see Chapter 3). More importantly, the findings of Hamilton et al. (1974) underline the complexity of behavioral plasticity in the protozoan. Even in a "simple" organism, a traditionally "simple" form of learning is in fact quite complex.

COELENTERATES

The phylum Coelenterata consists of a group of extremely primitive aquatic intertebrates, which provide an especially intriguing source of information on the phylogenetic development of learning. These animals exist in two states: the sessile (stationary) forms—corals, hydra, and sea anemones; and the free-swimming forms—jellyfish. Figure 11.8 presents a diagram of a sea anemone. Coelenterates are unique in that they contain the most primitive functionally organized nervous system in the animal kingdom. They are the first animals to possess a true nervous system. In addition, coelenterates represent a significant developmental stage in the evolution of neural organization because their nervous systems are characterized by *none* of the centralization that typifies the nervous systems of virtually all more advanced organisms. That is, coelenterates have no *central* nervous system. In most coelenterates there is no evidence of either the aggregation of neuron cell bodies into ganglia or of the occurrence of well-defined tracts of fibers connecting one section of the animal to another. Instead, the coelenterate system consists of one or more *nerve nets,* each a morphologically diffuse system of interconnected neurons—with synapses—evenly distributed in selected areas of the animal. Though organized very differently, the individual coelenterate neurons seem to function in a manner analogous to the more highly organized

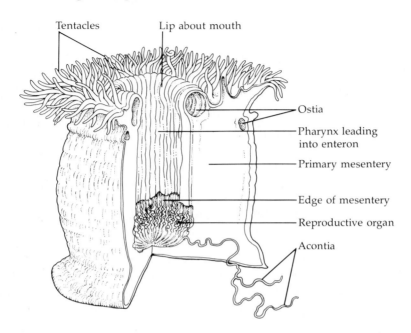

Figure 11.8
The sea anemone *Metridium marginatum*. [Redrawn with permission of Macmillan Publishing
Co., Inc., from *Invertebrate zoology,* 2nd ed., by R. W. Hegner and J. G. Engemann. Copyright
© 1968 by Macmillan Publishing Co., Inc.]

elements of advanced nervous systems. Both decremental and all-or-
nothing (spike) neural activity have been reported in coelenterates, and
the possibility of chemical synaptic transmission is good (for a more complete account of the anatomy and physiology of the coelenterate nervous
system, see Bullock and Horridge, 1965; Rushforth, 1973).

Perhaps because of the coelenterate's unusual nervous system, experimental analyses of the feasibility of learning in these organisms began
early, before the turn of the century. Efforts were initially concentrated on
the more sessile forms, especially hydra and sea anemones. It is difficult
to assess the extent to which these early studies demonstrate learning in
coelenterates. This is partly because the reports are not couched in the
language of modern learning theory (many came well before Pavlov's
terminology had reached the English-speaking world) and partly because
the investigators often did not employ what are today regarded as necessary control procedures to eliminate alternative explanations of behavior
change. The early work is nonetheless quite valuable in accurately depict-
ing surprisingly complex behavior sequences in these organisms. More
comprehensive reviews of the earlier work on coelenterates can be found in
Jennings (1906) and, more recently, in Ross (1965) and Rushforth (1973).

Gee's (1913) work on modifiable behavior patterns in *Anthopleura zantho-grammica* (a California shore anemone) will serve as a representative case.

Gee repeatedly presented a piece of filter paper soaked in meat juice to the anemones alternately with pieces of meat alone. "After a few times, the filter paper was refused, though the meat continued to be accepted" (Gee, 1913, p. 312). Eventually the meat alone was refused as well. Subsequent presentation of the meat juice and filter paper to the tentacles on the *opposite side* of the animal's mouth was, however, immediately accepted. This was taken by some investigators as evidence of what today might be called habituation of the response to filter paper alone, distinct (because of the opposite tentacle response) from satiation or generalized fatigue. Gee, however, went on to investigate the role of the copious amounts of mucous secreted by the animal during the process of ingestion. Following repeated presentations of food and subsequent refusal by one group of tentacles, Gee presented food to the tentacles of the other side not just once but several times. Initially the food was accepted by the tentacles of the opposite side, but the food was rejected much more quickly than it had been on the original side of stimulation. Gee attributed this accelerated refusal to the mucous secretion stimulated by ingestion. The original series of trials produced mucous, which diffused in the water to the tentacles of the opposite side. Then, when the opposite tentacles were themselves directly stimulated, the food was refused more quickly owing to the effects of the diffused mucous plus that stimulated by the direct food presentations to the opposite side. Though repeatedly stimulated tentacles remain unresponsive even after removal of the secreted mucous (a finding suggestive of true habituation) Gee appears to favor the conclusion that the refusals on the originally stimulated side were the result of a decline in the reactivity of the tentacles produced by the gradual accumulation of mucous secreted during ingestion (and therefore not true habituation). At this early juncture the ability of coelenterates to engage in simple learning was left in considerable doubt.

Associative Conditioning

Sea anemones and hydra are typically characterized as sessile (stationary) coelenterates. That is, they are very inactive organisms with extremely limited behavioral repertoires. The paucity and simplicity of their behavior is traditionally assumed to mirror the relative simplicity and diffuseness of their nervous systems. Again, we must ask the ecological question: Why should they be able to learn? in the face of such behavioral simplicity, what adaptive advantage would be gained by behavioral plasticity? Recent reports suggest that the behavior of some species of sea anemones certainly warrants further investigation of learning. The complex swimming response of the Puget Sound anemone *Stomphia coccinea*, described in Figure 11.9, constitutes a striking example. Chemical stimula-

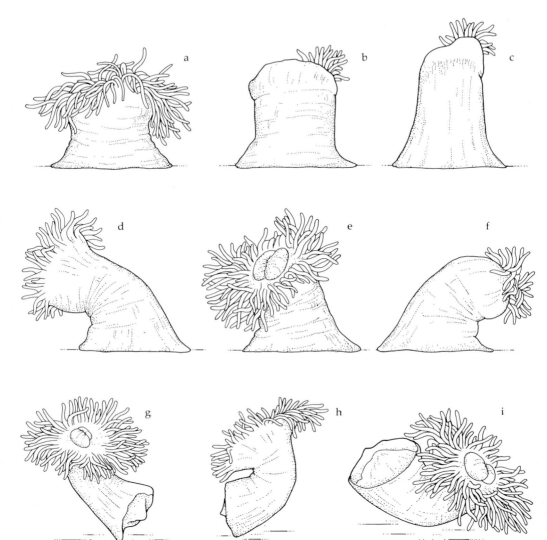

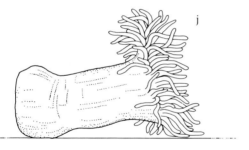

Figure 11.9
The swimming response of the anemone
Stomphia coccinea. (a) Normal position.
(b and c) Contraction following contact with starfish.
(d–f) Lateral bending prior to detachment.
(g–i) Lateral bending during swimming.
(j) Inactivity after swimming. [After Sund, 1958.]

tion from certain species of starfish or mollusc initiates the following sequence: the anemone first contracts, elongates while contracted, reopens, detaches the pedal disk (foot) from its substrate, and begins a series of longitudinal contractions occurring at a frequency of about one per second. These propel the animal quickly for some distance, after which the anemone remains inactive for a short period before reattaching at a new location. The swimming response is complete within a few minutes. It is likely that the response constitutes a defensive escape from potential predators.

Ross (1965) has pointed out that a demonstration of the capacity for associative learning in sea anemones might best be approached using such complex response sequences, and he has therefore attempted to classically condition the swimming response of *Stomphia*. Using the swimming response as the unconditional response, Ross paired a number of different conditional stimuli with the starfish UCS in a delayed conditioning paradigm. Among the conditional stimuli tested were a pipe cleaner dipped in extract of clam and gentle pressure applied to the base of the animal. Subjects received about twelve trials per day, on an average of one per hour. Probe trials on which the subjects received the conditional stimulus alone failed to show any evidence of conditioning. No animal swam in response to the CS alone. The pressure stimulus did seem, however, to have some suppressive effect on the ability of the starfish chemical to elicit swimming. This suggested that inhibitory conditioning might be a more appropriate paradigm, and in a second experiment Ross attempted to inhibit occurrence of the swimming response by the presentation of strong mechanical stimulation to the animal's base. The starfish extract became the conditional stimulus, followed in two seconds by a UCS of mechanical stimulation. The latency to swim is typically much longer than the latency of the UCR (immediate contraction) to mechanical stimulation. The 2-second interstimulus interval therefore ensured that the contraction response would effectively prevent occurrence of the swimming response elicited by the starfish chemical. After five days of trials on which the contraction response blocked swimming, subjects received tests in which the starfish CS was presented alone. On the first test trial all eight experimental subjects responded with contraction as if they had received mechanical stimulation (the UCS). Thus with repeated pairings of chemical and mechanical stimulation the long latency response normally produced by the starfish chemical was prevented. When the chemical was presented alone, the contraction response, normally only elicited by pressure, occurred instead. Moreover, with repeated presentation of the CS alone, the swimming response was gradually restored. In addition, subjects that had received relatively fewer inhibitory conditioning trials during training were the first to resume swimming during extinction; similarly, the subject receiving the greatest number of conditioning trials never swam during extinction. Both CS-alone and UCS-alone control subjects were tested, and in neither case did animals contract during mock extinction when the starfish stimulus was presented alone.

Though these studies are highly suggestive of associative conditioning in the coelenterate, they cannot be taken as conclusive. The Ross experiment, for example, employed no dual-stimulus control procedure (see Chapter 3) and, perhaps more important, Ross himself has been unable to replicate the results just described. Decisive demonstration of associative conditioning in the sea anemone is yet to come. What are the chances of arriving at such a demonstration? There is no consensus among investigators. Just how important is the central nervous system in associating two stimuli such that the response initially evoked only by one can now be produced by the other as well? Ross has reasoned largely on the basis of the group's evolutionary success. "It seems almost axiomatic that individuals belonging to any successful animal stocks must have some capacity for modifying their behavior adaptively to reinforced experiences if the stock is to survive. We are dealing here with a stock that has survived and that is very successful by any standards" (Ross, 1965, p. 101).

Habituation

More conclusive results on learning in the sessile coelenterates have been obtained using the habituation paradigm. From the perspective of adaptation, habituation would be an extremely useful form of behavior modification for an inactive organism. Sudden, potentially significant changes in stimulation require responding. Alterations in water turbulence, for example, might be produced by an approaching predator. Evolution does not tolerate mistakes. The animal must initially respond "to be on the (evolutionary) safe side." As repeated experience reveals that the stimulus was an innocuous one (not a predator, just another wave), responding not only becomes unnecessary but may even be maladaptive in that it prevents the organism from engaging in some other adaptive behavior such as seeking food (see Chapter 3). Most animals would at this point have at least two options: (1) move away from the repeatedly occurring but nonsignificant stimulus, or (2) learn that it clearly is nonsignificant and therefore requires no response—that is, habituate. For a sessile organism unable (or unlikely) to do the former, the ability to opt for the latter would be very useful indeed. Recent literature on coelenterate habituation supports this analysis.

Rushforth, Burnett, and Maynard (1963) have reported the habituation of the contraction response elicited by mechanical agitation in the sessile coelenterate *Hydra pirardi*. With 2-second periods of agitation occurring every 16 seconds, the proportion of individuals contracting during the 2 seconds immediately subsequent to each trial decreased to an asymptotic value of 0.2 after about 5 or 6 hours of exposure (see Figure 11.10). Values

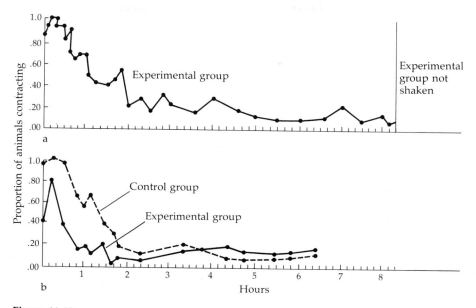

Figure 11.10
(a) Habituation to repeated mechanical stimulation in the coelenterate *Hydra pirardi*.
(b) One hour following initial training, experimental animals ceased responding sooner
than controls, which had received no prior training. [After Rushforth, 1965.]

of 0.3 were measured within 2 hours. Moreover, the presentation of intense light immediately following asymptotic habituation to agitation
produced close to 100 percent contraction on each of 20 exposures. This
suggests that the decrements obtained following repeated agitation were
not due to muscular fatigue. Rushforth (1973) instead infers a true process
of habituation.

The effects of prior habituation training in hydra seem also to be retained over short periods of time. Animals that had undergone one series
of habituation trials were allowed to rest for one hour and were then
rehabituated (Rushforth, 1965, 1971). When compared with controls exposed to only a single habituation session, experimental animals ceased
responding much more quickly during the second (rehabituation) series
of trials. Rushforth then used the restoration of responding as a function
of time as an additional index of the retention of habituation. Subjects
were tested for initial sensitivity to agitation, habituated for a period of six
hours, and then retested at various intervals following the end of habituation. Figure 11.11 summarizes these results. The lowest levels of sensitivity, and therefore the greatest retention of habituation, were observed
immediately following the end of the habituation session. After as much
as three hours of recovery time, however, sensitivity to mechanical agita-

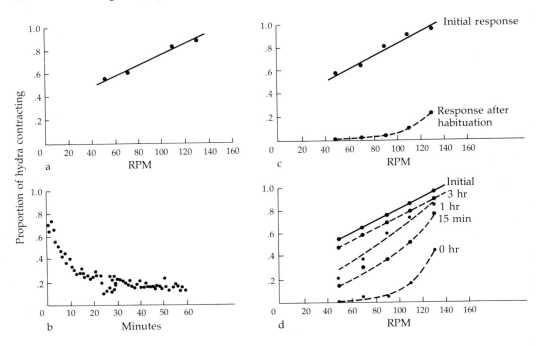

Figure 11.11
Retention of habituation in *Hydra*. (a) Initial sensitivity to mechanical stimulation.
(b) Habituation to repeated stimulation. (c) The effect of habituation on sensitivity to
mechanical stimulation. (d) Recovery of pretraining levels of sensitivity at various intervals
following habituation training. [After Corning and Ratner, 1967.]

tion was still below initial response levels. Four hours following habituation, responding was indistinguishable from that observed prior to the six-hour habituation session. After a period of four hours, therefore, recovery was complete. These data do, however, represent the retention of habituation at intervals of up to four hours in *Hydra*.

The process of habituation within the individual coelenterate has been described in the Pacific shore anemone *Anthopleura elegantissima* (Logan, 1975). Repeated presentations of the moderate-intensity stream of fresh water produced decrements in the frequency and magnitude of the contraction response in as few as 20–30 trials. Similar results were obtained repeatedly with a number of individuals, and the occurrence of habituation was generally unaffected by whether or not the animals were given time on each trial to recover from the effects of the previous stimulus. The author also reports that less habituation was observed with water streams of longer duration, and that the retention of habituation was apparent during subsequent rehabituation tests. Figure 11.12 illustrates a case of initial habituation followed after an interval of one hour by rehabituation. That prior learning has been retained is suggested by the more rapid re-

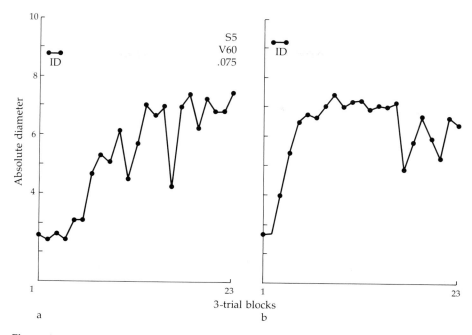

Figure 11.12
(a) Habituation and (b) rehabituation to repeated water-stream stimulation in the sea anemone *Anthopleura elegantissima*. The decrement occurs more quickly one hour after initial training (ID, initial diameter).

sponse decrement occurring in rehabituation following the spontaneous recovery of responding. More recent results of similar tests indicate that the retention of habituation in *Anthopleura* may persist up to four days following initial habituation (Logan and Beck, 1978). It would appear that capacity of the coelenterate nerve net to retain a behavior change may be comparable to that of the central nervous system of more complex organisms.

Further results of these experiments indicate that direct tactile stimulation with a glass rod immediately following habituation to the water stream invariably elicits contraction. Motor fatigue, therefore, apparently is not responsible for the obtained response decrements. The dishabituating effects of novel stimulation were measured on an additional five trials, and in over half of the tests responding to the water stream was reinstated by the novel stimulation.

The data on retention suggest that the observed effects are not being produced by a process of sensory adaptation. Even more convincing evidence of habituation, however, is provided by numerous changes in the topography of contraction responding that occurred during testing. Recall that alterations in response topography (see Chapter 3) accompany habituation in many organisms (invertebrates as well as vertebrates) and are assumed to reflect the discriminative nature of the habituation process. The occurrence of such changes in the anemones, as well, supports the notion that the process described in these animals is similar to the kind of habituation familiar in animals with central nervous systems. They, moreover, attest to the behavioral ingenuity of these primitive coelenterates. Subjects were, for example, frequently observed to reorient the expanded horizontal surface (the circular area containing the tentacles, in Figure 11.8) in a vertical direction, as if turning away from the water stream. Others might open their mouths "widely" in a posture typically seen during the reception of food; a few actually overtly moved out from under the impact of the water stream. Not only, then is the coelenterate system capable of habituation, but as one response is modified a number of others may change as well.

PLATYHELMINTHES

Planaria are representative of the class of organisms (phylum Platyhelminthes) exhibiting the most primitive bilateral symmetry in the animal kingdom. A representative individual is pictured in Figure 11.13. These unsegmented flatworms are also the first organisms to possess an enlarged anterior collection of neurons, which might be thought of as a primitive brain. Additional neural advances, such as a predominance, for the first time, of polarized neurons (those that transmit information in only one direction), and the occurrence of the first specialized sensory receptors among metazoans (multicellular organisms) indicate that this group represents the beginnings of developmental trends more fully realized in almost all advanced organisms. Advanced neural organization

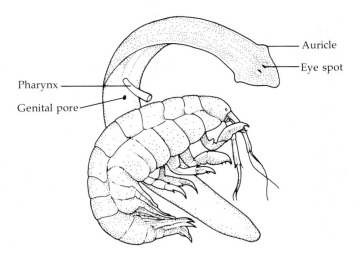

Pharynx
Genital pore
Auricle
Eye spot

Figure 11.13
A planarian feeding on a small shrimp-like animal. [Redrawn with permission of Macmillan Publishing Co., Inc., from *Invertebrate zoology,* 2nd ed., by R. W. Hegner and J. G. Engemann. Copyright © 1968 by Macmillan Publishing Co., Inc.]

coupled with refined sensory capacities would presumably allow for the more efficient integration of information in planaria. Partly for these reasons a great deal of research has been directed toward the study of learning in the planarian.

The animals typically studied are cannibalistic flatworms whose behavior is closely regulated by circadian (daily) and possibly semilunar cycles of activity (Best, 1965). Most respond negatively to light, increase activity levels in the presence of high temperatures, exhibit spontaneous alternation in turning responses, and, as they move, secrete mucous trails to which other closely related, cannibalistic species are attracted. Both their cannibalism and their ability to regenerate transected pieces have provided methodological rationale for their widespread use in studies of the biological correlates of behavior modification. In regeneration, for example, both the structure and function of transected sections are restored after removal. Experiments can then be performed that demonstrate that animals trained prior to transection regenerate into "offspring" that behave differently as a function of training. Similarly, memory can apparently be transferred through cannibalism (McConnell, 1962). The extensive literature resulting from attempts to demonstrate learning in planaria and the controversies aroused by it have been comprehensively reviewed by Corning and Ratner (1967), Corning and Riccio (1970), and Corning and Kelly (1973).

Classical Conditioning

Associative learning has not been clearly demonstrated in coelenterates. The planaria represent the beginnings of neural centralization. Is this structural modification in the nervous system accompanied by the development of more complex, associative learning abilities?

The prototypic experimental paradigm in studies of planarian conditioning employs either light or shock as the conditional or unconditional stimulus. Using light as the CS and shock as the UCS, Vattano and Hullett (1964), for example, described the performance of planaria trained under either delayed, backward, or simultaneous conditioning procedures. Controls received unpaired presentations of light and shock. Two distinct behaviors, cephalic (head) turns and contractions (both evoked by shock) were monitored. Results on the number of cephalic turns exhibited in extinction following the various training sessions are somewhat equivocal. The only significant differences occurred between some of the delayed conditioning groups and the simultaneous conditioning group. On the basis of classical conditioning results obtained with vertebrates, one would, of course, expect similar differences between delayed conditioning groups and both unpaired and backward conditioning controls. Clearer results were obtained with the contraction response. The number of contractions occurring in extinction was significantly greater for all delayed conditioning groups than for any of the groups subjected to other conditioning procedures or for the unpaired controls.

Many such studies have been published, some asserting and some denying the potential for learning in the planarian. Subtle procedural differences across studies coupled with equivocal results and numerous failures to replicate earlier results have left the topic of learning in the planarian in something of a state of controversy (Corning and Riccio, 1970). The controversy focuses primarily on the question of associative learning.

Jacobson, Horowitz, and Fried (1967) have combined several previously used procedures in an attempt to overcome procedural discrepancies and distinguish behavior changes representing "true conditioning" in planaria from those reflecting either pseudoconditioning or sensitization. These authors define pseudoconditioning as an "enhanced responsiveness to the CS which is *not* dependent upon pairing of CS and US in a forward temporal order" (p. 73); sensitization is defined as "enhanced responsiveness to the CS which *does* depend on pairing of CS and US in a forward temporal order but which represents an augmentation of UR's rather than of CR's to the CS" (p. 73). Results describing both contraction and turning responses indicate that delayed conditioning groups exhibited significantly more contractions to light (the CS) in extinction following training with a UCS of shock than either backward or simultaneous conditioning groups or groups receiving the CS alone. No significant differences were obtained among these four groups when compared on the turning measure.

Data were also collected on subjects trained under a differential conditioning procedure in which light served as the CS^+ and vibration the CS^- for one-half of the subjects, with the conditions reversed for the remaining half. Results indicated differential responding to the two stimuli. With 15 light presentations intermingled with 15 vibratory presentations in a constant irregular sequence, contractions occurred singificantly more often in response to the CS that had been paired with shock (CS^+). The stimulus that never occurred with shock failed to elicit contractions reliably. As indicated in Figure 11.14, when the CS^+–CS^- relations were reversed for each subject, the direction of differential responding reversed accordingly. Differential responding was also observed in exinction with the CS^+ and CS^-, both presented in the absence of shock. The validity of these data is augmented by the use of blind testing procedures and reliability checks of observational judgments. Similarly, positive results have been obtained, using a mass training classical conditioning procedure, by Corning and Freed (1968). They report "clear differences" between light–shock delayed conditioning groups and either random light–shock or light-only controls. Jacobson and his co-workers have concluded that, though some pseudoconditioning was seen, these effects were sufficiently distinct from those produced by delayed conditioning to warrant the label of "true conditioning" applied to the latter. Support for this conclusion is provided by studies that report the observation of traditional classical

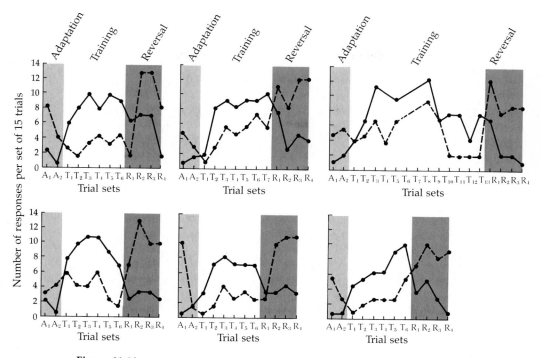

Figure 11.14
Conditioned responses to light (solid line) and vibration (dashed line) during differential conditioning with shock in six planaria. [After A. Jacobson, S. Horowitz, and C. Fried, Classical conditioning, pseudo-conditioning, or sensitization in the planarian. *Journal of Comparative and Physiological Psychology*, 64, 73–79. Copyright © 1967 by the American Psychological Association. Redrawn by permission.]

conditioning phenomena such as the partial reinforcement effect and spontaneous recovery in the behavior of planaria.

Even within the classical conditioning literature, however, anomalous findings restrict the unequivocal acceptance of Jacobson's conclusions. Crawford (1967), for example, again using combinations of light and shock, has compared the performance of pseudoconditioning, backward, and delayed conditioning groups in both acquisition and extinction. The delayed conditioning group performed significantly better than either of the other two groups during acquisition. However, during extinction, performance of the backward conditioning group was greatly elevated over that seen during the final acquisition trials and did not differ from extinction responding exhibited by the delayed conditioning groups. Crawford maintains that these results are interpretable either as true conditioning or as sensitization. A number of other investigators report failures to see "training" effects evident in standard extinction measures (for example, James and Halas, 1964).

Brown (1967) has reported a series of experiments that cast similar doubts on a classical conditioning interpretation of the planarian literature. In these studies planaria were presented two consecutive sequences of 15 trials each; the sequences were separated by an interval of 20 to 25 minutes. On each trial the worms received three seconds of light, the last one-third of which was accompanied by an electric shock. Baseline responding to light alone provided a standard against which the effects of light–shock pairing were to be compared. Light–shock pairings did produce increased responding during the first 2 seconds of light presentation. However, because both light and shock reflexively elicit a reaction from the planarian, Brown reasoned that any obtained increments in responding must be evident in retention measures if we are to conclude that conditioning has occurred. The animal must show that it will respond differently in the future on the basis of its past experience. Brown accordingly noted how long it took for light-only responding (extinction) to return to baseline following light–shock pairings and whether any savings were evident in the *second* 15-trial sequence. That is, did the animal learn more quickly in the second session on the basis of information acquired and retained from the initial training experience? Results indicate no retention evident with either of the measures employed. The author's conclusions are generally negative on the conditionability of planaria.

Several specific factors have been suggested to account for some of the anomalous findings discussed here. The presence of slime (mucous trails secreted by the worms), for example, appears to be critical. Preferences have been noted for slimed versus nonslimed portions of an apparatus (McConnell, 1967), and Riccio and Corning (1969) found that slime can alter the worms' reactivity to light. The animals apparently became more reactive when slime is present. Other factors of potential importance are the subjects' housing medium, the presence of other animals, the species of the individuals being tested, diurnal cycles, and subtle changes in physiological responsivity to repeated stimulus presentations (Corning and Riccio, 1970). The efforts of Jacobson et al. to control many of these factors suggest that the positive results obtained by these investigators represent a valid assessment of classical conditioning in the planarian.

Instrumental Conditioning

Results obtained from response-dependent paradigms are also somewhat inconsistent. Working on planaria within an instrumental conditioning framework, Crawford (1967) reports the results of several studies in which worms were required to traverse an alley to obtain food. Many of these efforts indicated significantly faster alley-running times in control worms trained *without* benefit of food reinforcement. In one experiment systematically assessing the confounding effects of both handling and satiation in the absence of training, *faster* running times were evident in all groups, and again subjects that had received food reinforcement in the alley performed significantly more poorly (running times were substantially greater) than controls. In spite of several conditioning failures, this investigator has concluded that "under proper conditions runway acquisition in the planarian can be demonstrated" (Crawford, 1967, p. 237).

More conclusive results have been obtained using submersion as a reinforcer. Best (1965) devised a maze consisting of three wells connected by waterproof tunnels. The entire maze was first drained of water, the worms' choice of the lighted over the dark well was then reinforced by refilling the maze with water. The proportion of correct responses (selecting the lighted well) increased steadily during the early trials. As training proceeded, however, more incorrect choices occurred, and the animals eventually refused to traverse the maze at all (they apparently learned to avoid a generally aversive situation). Greater stability in the initial learning was evident when animals were retested in a less confining maze. Corning (1964) has suggested that in many instrumental situations like this one, repeated testing across trials may have negative effects that gradually cancel the behavior change initially produced by reinforcement.

Learning demonstrations in the free-operant paradigm appear to be more successful. Crawford and Skeen (1967), for example, have replicated and extended earlier positive findings indicating operant conditioning in the planarian (Lee, 1963). Animals were placed individually in small cylindrical containers and trained to interrupt a photobeam that turned off an intense overhead light for a period of 60 seconds. Subjects were tested in matched pairs, with one member of each pair designated as the yoked control. Both animals, therefore, received the same amount of reinforcement (light offset), but only for the experimental ("light escape") worms was light offset contingent upon responding. By the end of a four-hour session, the response-contingent group was engaging in significantly more cumulated responses than the yoked controls.

The most convincing demonstrations of complex learning in planaria have employed an early, though recently restored, technique developed by P. Van Oye (1920). Use of the *Van Oye Maze*, as it has come to be called (Wells, 1967), avoids many of the potential sources of error, such as handling, stimulus traces left by previous subjects, and the use of unnatural modes of stimulation prevalent in many planaria conditioning studies. The Van Oye Maze is a water-filled container which provides continuous housing for the worms, and into which various types of stimuli can be introduced. A typical training sequence using the Van Oye technique is pictured in Figure 11.15. A stimulus object, usually food, is suspended from a glass rod, which can be lowered into the water at various depths (a). The organisms are required to reach the surface of the water, move across the surface until they reach the rod, and then descend the rod to obtain food (b). Results such as those presented in Figure 11.16 indicate that, even with controls that eliminate the possibility of chemical gra-

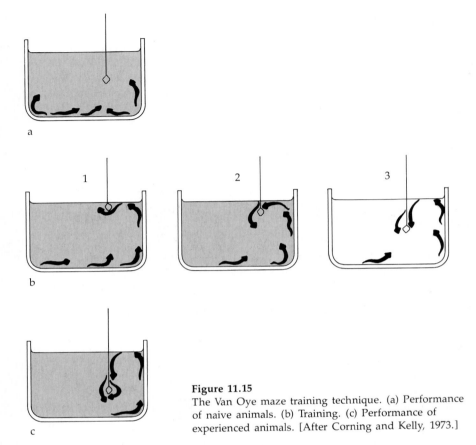

Figure 11.15
The Van Oye maze training technique. (a) Performance
of naive animals. (b) Training. (c) Performance of
experienced animals. [After Corning and Kelly, 1973.]

dients radiating from the food, when tested in the maze following removal of the food, significantly more experimental than control animals
reached the unbaited goal (Wells, Jennings, and Davis, 1966). Wells (1967)
also reports having used the Van Oye Maze in "stimulus pairing" tests in
which planaria were exposed to continuous darkness except during a
daily one-hour training period, throughout which a light was on and food
was available. After 25 such trials, significantly more experimental than
control worms responded to light alone by moving down to the unbaited
end of the glass rod. These results are frequently cited (Corning and Riccio, 1970) as the most conclusive demonstration that planaria can in fact
engage in instrumental associative learning.

Reactive Inhibition

The greatest accord on the issue of associative learning in planaria surrounds the phenomenon of reactive inhibition. Though it is rather uncon-
ventional to do so, McConnell (1966) includes Hullian reactive inhibition
in his list of behavioral events representing learning. McConnell justifies

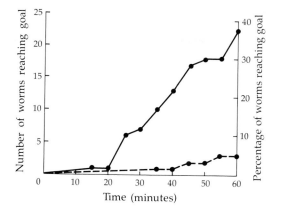

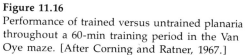

Figure 11.16
Performance of trained versus untrained planaria throughout a 60-min training period in the Van Oye maze. [After Corning and Ratner, 1967.]

his position on the grounds that "some form of memory" is involved in the phenomenon. Any time a response occurs, the accompanying muscular strain, pain, fatigue, or injury generates reactive inhibition. Any response will produce reactive inhibition, which then acts as a "barrier" to future responding. The inhibitory effect is assumed to dissipate spontaneously with time, and if enough time passes between responses the occurrence of one response will have no detrimental effect on subsequent responses.

The reactive inhibition construct has been enlisted as an explanation of the occurrence of spontaneous alternation following forced turns in planaria. Aderman and Dawson (1970) compared the behavior of goldfish and planaria across several situations in a forced-choice alternation paradigm. Members of each species were tested in proportionally sized maze patterns in which choice at a T-shaped test point was preceded by five forced turns. All subjects received four unreinforced trials of forced turns either to the left or to the right. Distances between turns were progressively increased prior to the choice point for some subjects and progressively decreased prior to the choice point for others. Results have indicated that alternation beyond chance levels does not occur with progressively increasing distances between turns. However, with progressively decreasing distances between turns, presumably each of insufficient length to allow time for the dissipation of reactive inhibition, the animal's choice behavior at the test point was predictable well beyond chance levels. Subjects (both fish and worms) reliably turned in the direction opposite to that dictated by the forced-choice trials.

Habituation

Perhaps because attention has been focused on the associative learning abilities of planaria, there has been a surprising lack of interest in the planaria's capacity for nonassociative learning. Changes in responding as a function of repeated stimulation have frequently been observed during the course of conditioning experiments; however, because the intent of these studies has been to focus on a different phenomenon, they rarely constitute well-controlled demonstrations of habituation or sensitization.

Westerman (1963), in an effort to specifically assess the habituation of the contraction response in planaria, repeatedly presented animals with 3-second periods of illumination. Subjects received 25 trials per day over a period of as many as 20 days. During this time the percentage of animals contracting in response to light dropped to as little as 5 percent. Moreover, regenerated portions of animals that had been trained to a habituation criterion of 50 trials without a response "rehabituated" more quickly than cut sections of naive animals. Learning not only survived regeneration but in addition the information apparently was retained over the period required for regeneration. Westerman in fact reports the retention of habituation at intervals of up to 7 weeks following training.

Using a different species of planarian, Applewhite (1971) has demonstrated habituation of responding to tactile stimulation presented with a 100 micron wire. Again, response decrements were obtained, and, more importantly, savings were observed in the individuals regenerated from parts of the originally trained subjects. That is, the regenerated animals actually habituated more quickly than the initial ("parent") subjects. When habituated for the first time, however, regenerated parts of untrained "parents" failed to show any savings. The effect is therefore specific to the occurrence of an initial training session in the "parent" worm. Applewhite also reports generalization of habituation in these flatworms. Animals that had habituated to tactile stimulation on the anterior end also failed to respond to tactile stimulation presented to the posterior end. In addition to demonstrating generalization, these results eliminate sensory adaptation as an explanation of the obtained response decrement.

The planarian controversy seems recently to have abated somewhat. Corning and Kelly (1973) reflect the views of the proponents of planarian learning in maintaining that most of the inconsistencies have been "attributed to procedural deviations and to an inadequate knowledge of factors that influence planarian behavior." They assert that "much of the debate stemmed for *a priori* notions about what level of animal can learn" (p. 217). Consideration of the differing ecologies represented by the various species investigated suggests an additional source of inconsistency. It has become increasingly clear that situationally specific factors restrict learning at times. Ecological demands dictate such restrictions on learning (see Chapter 10), and it is possible that the range of restrictions is greater for some species than for others. The literature on learning in the platyhelminthes covers a wide range of species. Discrepant results may involve comparisons between species of differing ecologies, such that what constitutes a viable learning context for one does not for another. It may be that some flatworms are unable to learn in some situations. Inspection of Table 11.1 (compiled by Corning and Kelly, 1973), which summarizes the frequency of positive and negative results obtained from various learning paradigms, suggests, however, that negative findings cannot be regarded as generally representative. The conclusion that associative learning has been clearly demonstrated in species representing the simplest degree of neural centralization seems far more appropriate.

Table 11.1
Positive and Negative Results of Learning Studies in Planarians [From Corning and Kelly, 1973.]

Positive	Negative
A. Habituation	
Applewhite and Morowitz (1967)	Bennett and Calvin (1964)
Applewhite (1971)	Brown (1964)
Dilk (1937)	
Freed (1966)	
Togrol et al. (1966a, b)	
Walter (1908)	
Westerman (1963)	
B. Classical conditioning: acquisition measures	
Applewhite and Morowitz (1967)	Bennett and Calvin (1964)[a]
Barnes and Katzung (1963)	Brown (1964)
Baxter and Kimmel (1963)	Brown (1967a)
Bennett and Calvin (1964)[a]	Brown et al. (1966a)
Brown and Parke (1967)	Brown et al. (1966b)
Chapouthier (1967)	Cummings and Moreland (1959)
Cherkashin and Sheiman (1967)	Halas et al. (1962b)
Cherkashin et al. (1967)	
Corning and John (1961)	
Cornwell (1961)	
Cornwell et al. (1961)	
Crawford (1967)	
Crawford and King (1966)	
Crawford et al. (1965)	
Crawford et al. (1966)	
Fantl and Nevin (1965)	
Freed (1966)	
Griffard (1963)[a]	
Guilliams and Harris (1971)	
Halas et al. (1962)[a]	
Hartrey et al. (1964)	
Hyden et al. (1969)	
Jacobson (1967)	
Jacobson et al. (1966)	
Jacobson et al. (1967)	
John (1964)	
Kimmel and Yaremko (1966)	
King et al. (1965)	
McConnell (1967a)	
McConnell and Mpitsos (1965)	
McConnell et al. (1959)	

(continued)

Table 11.1 (*continued*)

Positive	Negative
McConnell et al. (1960)	
Thompson and McConnell (1955)	
Walker (1966)	
Walker and Milton (1966)	
Yaremko and Kimmel (1969)	

C. Classical conditioning: extinction measures

Positive	Negative
Corning and John (1961)	Baxter and Kimmel (1963)
Crawford (1967)	Brown (1964)
Crawford and King (1966)	Brown (1967a)
Crawford et al. (1965)	Brown and Beck (1964)
Crawford et al. (1966)	Cornwell (1960)
Hullett and Homzie (1966)[a]	Crawford (1967)
Jacobson (1967)	Halas et al. (1961)
Jacobson et al. (1967)	James and Halas (1964)
Kimmel and Yaremko (1966)	
Vattano and Hullett (1964)	
Yaremko and Kimmel (1969)	

D. Differential conditioning

Positive	Negative
Block and McConnell (1967)	Kimmel and Harrell (1964)[a]
Fantl and Nevin (1965)	Kimmel and Harrell (1966)[a]
Griffard and Peirce (1964)	
Jacobson (1967)	
Jacobson et al. (1967)	
Kimmel and Harrell (1964)[a]	
Kimmel and Harrell (1964)[a]	

E. Instrumental paradigms

1. Instrumental avoidance

Positive	Negative
Dilk (1937)	
Hovey (1929)	
Lacey (1971)	
Ragland and Ragland (1965)	
Soest (1937)	
Tushmalova (1967)	

2. Mazes

Positive	Negative
Best (1963)	Bennett and Calvin (1964)
Best (1965)	
Best and Rubinstein (1962)	
Chapouthier (1968)	
Corning (1964)	
Corning (1966)	
Ernhart and Sherrick (1959)	
Haynes et al. (1965)	
Humpheries and McConnell (1964)	
Jacobson and Jacobson (1963)	
McConnell (1966b)	
Pickett et al. (1964)	
Roe (1963)	
Van Oye (1920)	
Wells (1967)	
Wells et al. (1966)	

[a] Equivocal findings or interpretations.

12 Invertebrate Learning II:
Annelids, Molluscs, Arthropods

Our discussion of invertebrate learning will continue in this chapter with a consideration of three additional major groups of invertebrates: annelids, molluscs, and arthropods.[1] Most distinctions drawn between the groups treated in Chapter 11 and the groups treated here are based largely on taxonomic convenience. In fact, our knowledge of invertebrate learning is far too incomplete to construct any major lines of evolutionary divergence based on learning abilities. However, few investigators would challenge the conclusion that associative learning is clearly possible in many representatives of the phyla discussed in this chapter. The questions asked about these groups therefore become more precise. Rather than asking if learning is possible in a particular species, investigations focus on questions such as how the nature of learning mechanisms might be revealed in the neurophysiology of the organism, what the parametric characteristics of behavior change might be (are they different from those typical of vertebrates?), and, given a recognized potential to learn, under what circumstances might learning actually play a role in the organism's natural history.

Such questions are more meaningfully addressed to the groups reviewed in this chapter largely because far more consensus surrounds the

---

[1] The six groups reviewed in Chapters 11 and 12 by no means exhaust the literature on invertebrate learning. For a more widespread treatment of these and other groups see *Invertebrate Learning*, Volumes I, II, and III (1973, 1973, 1975), edited by Corning, Dyal, and Willows.

answer to the initially more important question, "Can they learn at all?" In addition, far more is known about the behavioral characteristics of these organisms under natural circumstances. If we deviate, therefore, from the format that characterized the previous chapter, it is because the available literature demands such deviation. As we shall see, for example, especially with the arthropods, we can adhere much less closely to the traditional psychological learning paradigms discussed to this point. Most organisms on earth are members of this group, and they can be found in virtually any habitat on earth. Consequently, they offer exceptional promise for appreciating the relationship between plasticity in behavior and specific ecological circumstances. The cephalopod molluscs are perhaps the most intelligent of the invertebrates, while their cousins, the gastropods (including snails and slugs), have permitted the demonstration of unparalleled correlations between behavior change and observed neural change. We will discuss the molluscs and arthropods extensively after first turning briefly to yet another group of worms: the annelids.

ANNELIDS

Annelids are segmented worms exhibiting far more structural complexity than the planaria discussed earlier. The segmentation of the annelids (termed *metamerism*) is such that the worms are essentially a series of very similar repeating sections, terminating at the anterior end in a distinct head. Each section contains a separate neural ganglion, apparently coordinating the local activity of that segment. At the anterior end, in the head, rests a primitive brain, the *supraesophageal ganglion*. This large anterior ganglion joins the interconnected segmental ganglia (the ventral nerve cord) in a manner very suggestive of the central nervous systems of vertebrates.

Behavioral analyses of learning phenomena have been conducted to varying degrees in each of the three major classes of annelid worms pictured in Figure 12.1. These are the *polychaetes* (nereid marine worms), the *oligochaetes* (earthworms), and the *hirudinea* (leeches). By far the most work has been done in polychaetes and oligochaetes, and, once again, the most conclusive results come from the simplest of learning paradigms.

Habituation

Habituation of the withdrawal reflex has been clearly demonstrated in the polychaetes (Clark, 1965; Evans, 1965), though the characteristics of the process vary considerably among several species. For example, the intertidal species, regularly exposed to natural changes in lighting conditions, which accompany the ebb and flow of the tides, are very reactive to such changes and habituate to light quite slowly. By contrast, subtidal species (those living in deeper waters, and therefore not regularly exposed to a

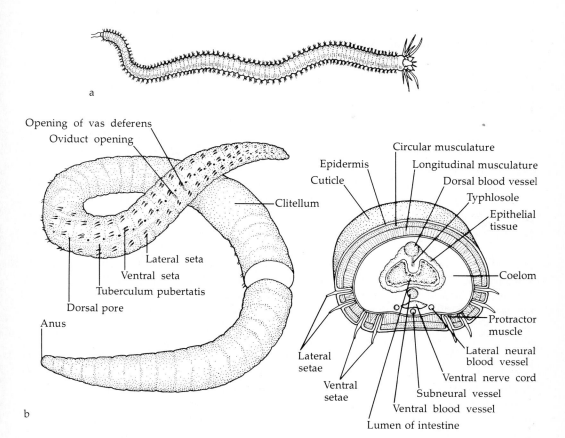

a

Opening of vas deferens
Oviduct opening

Circular musculature
Epidermis
Cuticle
Longitudinal musculature
Dorsal blood vessel
Typhlosole
Epithelial tissue

Clitellum

Lateral seta
Ventral seta
Tuberculum pubertatis

Dorsal pore

Anus

Coelom

Protractor muscle

Lateral setae

Ventral setae

Lateral neural blood vessel
Ventral nerve cord
Subneural vessel
Ventral blood vessel

Lumen of intestine

b

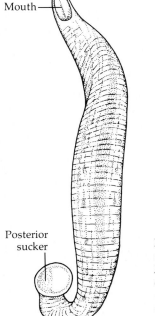

Mouth

Posterior sucker

c

Figure 12.1
(a) The nereid marine worm. [After N. R. F. Maier and T. C. Schneirla, *Principles of animal psychology*, New York: Dover Publications, Inc., 1964.]
(b) The anatomy of the earthworm. [From *Biology Today*, CRM, 1972.]
(c) The medicinal leech. [Redrawn by permission of Macmillan Publishing Co., Inc., from *Invertebrate zoology*, 2nd ed., by R. W. Hegner and J. G. Engemann. Copyright © 1968 by Macmillan Publishing Co., Inc.]

fluctuating light environment) exhibit greatly reduced responsivity to changes in natural lighting conditions and habituate rapidly to light (Clark, 1965). Similarly, the presentation of a tactile stimulus to either end of a worm, which easily produces habituation in most species, results in no habituation at all in the carnivorous polychaete *Nereis pelagica*. This finding is in keeping with current theoretical views of habituation that emphasize the differential habituation of orienting versus consummatory responses (Ratner, 1967). Consummatory responses are said to habituate much less rapidly, if at all. In addition, even within species different responses to the same stimulus habituate at different rates, and habituation can be shown to occur to a variety of classes of stimuli.

In most species of polychaetes, removal of the supraesophageal ganglion (the primitive "brain") has little if any effect on the habituation process. Clark (1965) maintains that these findings suggest that habituation is "mediated at the level of the segmental ganglia and . . . [should be] rightly regarded as the simplest learning process manifested by the animals" (p. 135). The same author also suggests that the *a priori* assignment of the seat of coordinated behavior, associative plasticity, and memory to the supraesophageal ganglion may be premature. He calls attention to the possibility that in annelids the ganglion functions as a predominantly endocrine organ, regulating behavior largely through hormones and pheromones.[2] The supraesophageal ganglion, therefore, would participate in learning to a degree only equivalent to that of any of the ventral chain ganglia.

Habituation has also been recently demonstrated in the second major class of annelids, represented here by the leech. Ratner (1972) reports data on the habituation of movement in response to repeated changes in illumination in *Macrobdella decora*. With light onset beginning every 20 seconds and lasting for two seconds, subjects reached the habituation criterion of 8 trials without a response in as few as 30 trials. Retention tests conducted both 24 and 48 hours following original training indicated fewer responses made in each successive habituation session when compared with either the original session or the immediately preceding session. Habituation of the leeches' response to a change in water current was also observed, and in both cases topographic changes in responding were noted analogous to those reported in earthworms (see the following discussion). Moreover, as is usually the case with habituation, the longer the intertrial interval, the greater the number of trials required to reach the habituation criterion.

In oligochaetes, notably *Lumbricus terrestris*, the common earthworm, habituation has also been repeatedly demonstrated (Gardner, 1968; Ratner and Stein, 1965). Gardner's work provides a thorough documentation of

---

[2] Pheromones are externally secreted hormones (chemical signals) that serve important communicative functions in many **invertebrates**. Recent investigations have extended their importance to vertebrates as well (Thiessen and Rice, 1976).

habituation, while also describing several associated phenomena helpful in identifying the observed response decrement as the familiar habituation seen in vertebrates. Two easily distinguishable components of the earthworm's response to vibratory stimulation are the initial *withdrawal response* and the subsequent *hooking response*. The latter consists of a "rapid contraction of the posterior of the animal with simultaneous ventral hooking of approximately the last 15 segments of the worm" (p. 315). Gardner found that these two response components habituate at different rates, with significantly more rapid habituation occurring for the withdrawal component. These results are pictured in Figure 12.2. Unlike the case with vertebrates (Thompson and Spencer, 1966), *overhabituation*, the presentation of additional training trials after the complete cessation of responding, has no effect on the recovery rates of either response component in the earthworm. Finally, a savings retention score computed following rehabituation at varying intervals revealed no differential recovery rates for the two components. For both, retention was greatest after 12 hours; however, a significant savings over baseline levels of responding was indicated as much as four days after the original habituation. Interestingly, no comparable long-term retention effects have been observed in either of the other major groups of annelids. Such discrepancies among closely related groups may suggest the evolutionary divergence of major aspects of the habituation process.

Ratner (1967, 1970) has suggested that the type of change in *response topography* described by Gardner (the differential habituation of the two-component earthworm withdrawal response) should be considered a general characteristic of the habituation process for all phyla. Successive stimulus presentations presumably affect not only the strength of re-

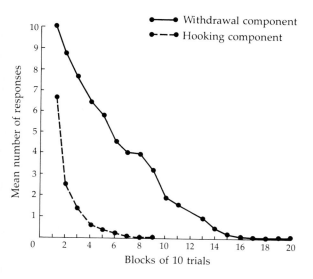

Figure 12.2
Habituation in two distinct components of the defensive response of the earthworm. [After L. E. Gardner, Retention and overhabituation of a dual-component response in *Lumbricus terrestris sp. Journal of Comparative and Physiological Psychology, 66*, 315–318. Copyright © 1968 by the American Psychological Association. Redrawn by permission.]

sponding but also the form of the organism's response. New responses may actually emerge, and the character of the habituating response is altered. Ratner mentions latency and duration of responding as among those aspects of response topography possibly undergoing progressive change during habituation. Finer-grained analyses of behavior habituation may require attention to multi-component changes in the topography of responding.

Classical Conditioning

Though all three classes of annelids have been studied in classical conditioning paradigms, the bulk of the evidence has been collected on earthworms. Commonly employed UCS–UCR relationships are withdrawal to increases in illumination, withdrawal to tactile stimulation or to electric shock, and approach responses to nutritive substances. In the situation employing the *Ratner–Miller conditioning ring* (Ratner and Miller, 1959), shown in Figure 12.3, the worm is placed in a moistened closed plastic circular tube, which has been vented with holes. The tube rests on a wooden base located beneath a light source, which provides the increase in illumination used as the UCS. Mild vibration of the wooden base serves as the CS, and a withdrawal response, originally elicited by the UCS, serves as the CR. Results indicate that experimental (forward conditioning) groups achieve asymptotic 80 percent CR responding in 58 to 80 trials. The percentage of CR's exhibited by pseudo conditioning and sensitization controls at no point exceeds the base rate occurrence of the response in question. Extinction occurs rapidly; however, (as is the case with many vertebrates) partial reinforcement during training does result in greater

Light source
at 18''

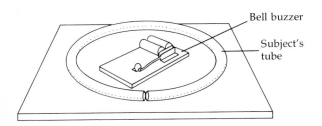

Bell buzzer

Subject's
tube

Figure 12.3
The conditioning ring used to assess classical conditioning in the earthworm. [After S. C. Ratner and K. R. Miller, Classical conditioning in earthworms, *Lumbricus terrestris. Journal of Comparative and Physiological Psychology, 52,* 102–105. Copyright © 1959 by the American Psychological Association. Redrawn by permission.]

resistance to extinction (Wyers, Peeke, and Herz, 1964). The manipulation of temporal variables such as the interstimulus and intertrial intervals generates results in accord with the findings of many other conditioning experiments. As observed with many other organisms (but see Chapter 3), the "optimal" CS–UCS interval for earthworms in this situation is 0.5 seconds, and several studies (Ratner, 1962; Ratner and Miller, 1959; Ratner and Stein, 1965) indicate that shorter intertrial intervals result in weaker conditioning. This may be due to increased habituation of the unconditioned response, possibly resulting from the more frequently occurring trials that characterize the use of short intertrial intervals.

A final variable of major interest in earthworm classical conditioning studies is the effect of decerebration (removal of the brain). As with habituation, learning can proceed following removal of the supraesophageal ganglion (Ratner and Stein, 1965). However, the conditioning of decerebrate worms requires much shorter intertrial intervals than those found to be effective in the intact worm.

It seems that, though extraneous environmental variables such as temperature change (Herz, Peeke, and Wyers, 1964; Reynierse, 1968) may have contributed to discrepant results in some cases, reliable and valid classical conditioning has been demonstrated in the earthworm.

The same cannot be said, however, of the polychaetes (marine worms). The few studies that have been done on polychaetes describe only equivocal cases of classical conditioning. Moreover, even these are open to alternative interpretation. Evans' (1966a, 1966b) work on nonassociative behavior modification in polychaetes attests to the questionable nature of the associative "learning" exhibited by these animals. Four groups of *Nereis diversicolor* were placed in tubes containing 70 percent seawater in an attempt to classically condition a "food seeking response." The conditional stimulus was an increase in illumination, normally ineffective in eliciting the UCR. The animals, deprived of food for 2 weeks prior to the beginning of the experiment, each received 6 trials per day for 8 successive days. Daily CS presentations were separated by intervals of at least one-half hour. Subjects underwent one of the following manipulations: a forward conditioning procedure in which food was paired with the CS except on every sixth trial; a trace conditioning procedure in which food was presented about 5 minutes after termination of the CS; or one of two CS-only procedures whose differences need not concern us. Evans had assumed that no true conditioning could occur over a trace interval of 5 minutes. Results indicated, however, that the percentage of subjects responding and the mean reaction times were significantly above baseline for both the forward and trace conditioning groups. Moreover, the performance of the trace conditioning subjects was indistinguishable from that of the forward conditioning subjects. Because it was assumed that true association could not occur with trace intervals of 5 minutes, these findings were interpreted largely in terms of the sensitizing effect of food.

Comparable results were obtained using sudden decreases in illumination as the CS during the conditioning of a withdrawal reflex elicited by a UCS of shock. Reactivity of both forward and backward conditioning groups increased over trials, while the reactivity of the CS-only group declined (habituation). Any behavior modification seen in the conditioning groups was again attributed to sensitization. Evans (1966b) concludes that "there is no evidence that N. diversicolor can learn to associate a sudden decrease in illumination with the presentation of food" (p. 117) and that the increased reactivity produced by the sensitizing effects of food can serve to explain the result of these and earlier attempts to classically condition polychaetes.

Although a few attempts have been made to demonstrate simple learning in leeches (Gee, 1912), the most advanced of the annelids, only one recent study has met with any success using a classical conditioning paradigm. Henderson and Strong (1972) examined the conditionability of an anterior-posterior contraction response in Macrobdella ditetra to a CS of light. The animals were tested in an ellipsoidal tube immersed in water and fitted with stainless steel electrodes for shock (UCS) presentation. Both experimental and explicitly unpaired control groups received 250 "acquisition" trials in sessions of 25 each for 10 successive days. The unpaired controls received either CS or UCS on a random schedule with the second stimulus occurring 15 seconds subsequent to the initial random presentation. The intertrial interval also equaled 15 seconds, and these animals therefore received twice as many discrete nonoverlapping stimulus presentations as did the experimental animals, whose minimal intertrial interval was 30 seconds. Significant differences were obtained in acquisition scores, with the experimental (forward conditioning) groups exhibiting a higher percentage of CR's than the unpaired controls. In addition, for the experimental animals, the higher the UCS intensity the greater the percentage of CR's elicited.

Extinction was rapid for all experimental animals, occurring usually within 10 trials, and spontaneous recovery was observed (again, as in vertebrates) at the beginning of a second extinction session. The authors maintain that they have demonstrated "clear classical conditioning in the leech." They also report, however, communications wtih Thompson discussing failures to condition leeches in a number of different procedural contexts.

Instrumental Conditioning

The bulk of the literature on annelid learning deals with attempts to train the worms in more complex alley and maze learning situations. The large number of studies perhaps reflects the greater degree of inconclusiveness existing at this level. The most frequently employed procedure, very similar to that originally used by Yerkes (1912), makes use of a T- or Y-maze such as that shown in Figure 12.4. Here, an approach response is preceded by a "defensive response" made to prodding, shock, or some other aversive stimulus. The worm is essentially goaded down the alley to the choice point and adjacent goal boxes, one of which contains the reward. The reward usually consists of return to the damp, dark home box. An increase in the number of correct responses (choosing the rewarded goal box) is taken as evidence of learning. Ratner (1967), however, has convincingly criticized this procedure as more indicative of the experimenter's increased facilitation in guiding the animals than of the worm's acquired ability to traverse the maze. He discounts the findings of any study in which prodding confounds the training procedure. In support of this position, Kirk and Thompson (1967) found no evidence of approach learning in a straight alley paradigm in which the only prodding was electric shock delivered through a grid at the beginning of the alley.

Investigations of approach learning using procedures not involving prodding (Ratner, 1964; Reynierse and Ratner, 1964) and passive avoidance studies employing shock to inhibit forward-going alley responses (Evans, 1963, 1966b) are also open to alternative interpretation. Regarding the latter, both experimental subjects and control subjects receiving no shock inhibit any forward-going (approach) response that places the organism in an open area (Ratner, 1964). Rather than learning, therefore, all subjects appear to avoid open areas innately. In approach learning decreased running times were recorded when subjects were run to a goal area containing moist sphagnum moss, whereas increased running times were observed in response to either a black or a white empty goal box. If moist sphagnum moss is viewed as a reinforcer, these data imply instrumental conditioning. Reynierse, Halliday, and Nelson (1968), however, maintain that any such result can be accounted for on the basis of nonassociative stimulus change occurring independently of reinforcement. These authors tested earthworms in straight alleys terminating in either a flat plastic surface or a plastic box filled with moist sphagnum moss (iden-

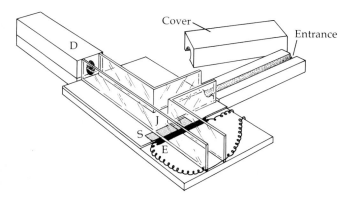

Figure 12.4
The T-maze employed in Yerkes' classic studies investigating instrumental learning in earthworms (D, dark chamber; E, electrodes; J, junction of alleys; S, sandpaper). [After Yerkes, 1912.]

tical to the subject's home container). Results indicated a significant interaction between the goal condition and the type of confinement subjects
had received 30 minutes prior to the acquisition trials. Faster running
times "occurred when confinement and goal conditions were the same"
(p. 161), that is, either both were plastic surfaces or both were moss-filled
boxes. In a second experiment, the distance at which the goal box was
placed below the alley was found to affect running times significantly,
regardless of the goal condition. For both types of goal, running times
were faster with the goal 1 inch as opposed to 4 inches below the alley.
The systematically varied factor of assumed goal box reinforcement was
uncorrelated with increasing responding. The authors conclude that
though the effects of the nonassociative factors involved in stimulus
change are themselves poorly understood, more experimental attention
should be directed toward them before interpretations in terms of associative learning can be invoked.

A final factor affecting tests of associative learning in annelids has recently received much deserved attention. This is the effect of *stimulus
traces* left in the apparatus by the secretion of *pheromones* by the previous
subject. Aversive stimulation elicits the secretion of an alarm pheromone
by *Lumbricus terrestris* (Rosenkoetter and Boice, 1975). This substance is a
highly specific, externally secreted chemical signal that communicates
alarm to other members of the same species. Ressler, Cialdini, Ghoca,
and Kleist (1968) report that the earthworm's mucous-like alarm pheromone is "highly aversive to other members of the same species" (p.
597). Out of 24 test subjects, none were observed to cross a plexiglass
plate on which another worm had previously been shocked. Eight out of
12 subjects crossed control plates containing no pheromone. The negative
effects of the pheromone appeared to be extremely persistent. An undis-
turbed deposit was reported to be "as potent three months after secretion
as it was a few hours after secretion and even more potent than when still
wet immediately after it had been secreted" (p. 599). In addition, the
pheromone did not appear soluble in cold water. The authors express
doubts that, even when they are used in instrumental conditioning
studies, most typically employed cleaning procedures would be successful in eliminating the alarm pheromone.

Some demonstrations of instrumental learning in annelids cannot,
however, be discounted by the confounding effects of pheromones. Ray
(1968) signaled the onset of bright light (an aversive UCS) with presentation of a weak vibratory stimulus (CS). During the interval between CS
onset and UCS onset, subjects (earthworms) could avoid receiving the
aversive light by entering a moist dark area. Latencies to respond to the CS
decreased rapidly with training, while the percentage of successful avoidance responses increased to 70–75 percent by the eighth daily trial. Here
alarm pheromones secreted in response to the aversive light should become less of a factor as training proceeds. With more successful avoidance

the occurrence of the aversive stimulus decreases substantially and little if any pheromone should be released. The possibility does remain, however, that to the extent that the CS itself becomes aversive, pheromones might be secreted in response to CS presentation. No data are currently available bearing on this point.

In summary, while there is some accord regarding the validity of results on habituation and classical conditioning, conclusions on the demonstration of instrumental learning in annelids vary. Ratner (1967) is reluctant to ascribe instrumental learning abilities to the worms, and instead states that "it is often not clear what aspects of the situation [are] essential for learning, nor is it clear whether learning [has been] demonstrated" (p. 394). However, on the basis of largely the same evidence, McConnell (1966), agreeing with Jacobson (1963), maintains that "there seems little doubt that annelids are capable of learning mazes" (p. 125). Much of the uncertainty might be removed if the animals were tested under more naturalistic circumstances. For an animal (like the earthworm) used to burrowing beneath the ground, mazes that require locomotor activity on a surface might well be expected to minimize whatever locomotor flexibility the animal might be capable of. Burrowing mazes making use of the organisms' natural locomotor tendences might present a far different picture of instrumental learning abilities in this group.

MOLLUSCS

The molluscs represent a diverse phylum of organisms whose most familiar members belong to three major classes: the *bivalves* (clams, mussels, and scallops), the *gastropods* (snails and slugs), and the *cephalopods* (octopus, cuttlefish, and squid). The extensive range of both structural and behavioral adaptations evident in the molluscs has recently become a focus of interest, especially in the area of learning. Because of the uniquely accessible nervous systems in some species, the possibility for correlating behavior change with observed neural change is more easily realized here than at any other point in the animal kingdom. These diverse organisms, moreover, include representation by those often regarded as the most "intelligent" invertebrates of all: the cephalopods. In these creatures learning abilities rival those normally considered the unique domain of the vertebrates. Their behavioral diversity and the unusual possibilities for neurophysiological analysis recommend molluscs as one of the most useful groups for exploring the biological basis of learning.

We will concentrate on the gastropods and the cephalopods, again largely because here is where the literature is most extensive. Each group will be instructive in a different way. The gastropods illustrate more clearly than any other creature what is known about the basic neurophysiological mechanisms underlying behavioral plasticity. The cephalopods apparently demonstrate the extremes of behavioral plasticity possible even at the invertebrate level. Here enhanced sensory-motor capacities allow the organism to meet the requirements of the natural environment in a manner described as intelligent.

Gastropods

It has not been our intent to this point to review the neurophysiology of learning. In assessing the behavioral plasticity of the gastropod molluscs, however, our treatment will briefly become uncharacteristically neurophysiological. This is because the neurophysiological bases of learning are to date nowhere more clearly demonstrated than in research on gastropods.[3] Here functional plasticity has been observed at the level of the individual neuron; these demonstrations have, moreover, been directly correlated with experientially induced changes in the organism's overt behavior. Specific cellular activity can be precisely related to molar behavior. These striking demonstrations are possible because of the unique nervous systems characteristic of some groups, notably *Aplysia* and *Tritonia*. Both are large marine slugs, apparently shell-less, though each has a vestigal internal shell. In both animals the primitive brain contains ganglia composed in part of giant neurons whose cell bodies have been measured at up to a millimeter in diameter.[4] The size and position of many of these cells are constant from animal to animal. These features enable investigators to identify individual neurons repeatedly across animals and therefore to analyze the altered functioning of an individual cell following different types of experience. Altered responding as a function of experience can actually be seen taking place simultaneously in behavior and in a single nerve cell.

Various neurophysiological constructs have been suggested as the possible biological mechanisms whereby the effects of previous experience bring about relatively permanent modifications in behavior. In the phenomenon of *post-tetanic potentiation*, for example, prolonged stimulation of a presynaptic neuron greatly increases the amplitude of the neural impulse subsequently produced by a single stimulus. This process, however, involves only monosynaptic pathways (those comprised of only one synapse), and most instances of behavior modification imply more complexity than that represented by a single synapse. That neural plasticity can also be heterosynaptic (involving two or more synapses), and therefore allow for much more behavioral complexity, has been shown by the

---

[3] For a more complete and detailed treatment of the cellular bases of learning and behavior in the gastropods, see E. Kandel, *The Cellular Basis of Behavior*, 1976.

[4] While the range in size is great, and no neuron can actually be considered typical, most neurons range in size from 5 to 100 microns. The "giants," by contrast, may actually be visible to the naked eye. Advantages for location and recording are obvious.

work of Eric Kandel and his associates on giant neurons located in the abdominal ganglion of *Aplysia* (Kandel and Tauc, 1965). As diagrammed in Figure 12.5, stimulus parameters in two different afferent nerves are arranged so that one, the test stimulus, produces a weak excitatory neural potential (below the threshold for an action potential) in the postsynaptic neuron. This impulse is termed an excitatory postsynaptic potential (EPSP). In the other afferent nerve, the priming stimulus produces a burst of spikes (action potentials) recorded in the same postsynaptic neuron. In input pairing of the two types of stimuli, the subthreshold (test) stimulus precedes the priming stimulus by 300 msec. As a result of a number of such pairings, subsequent neural responding to the test stimulus *alone* increased substantially in amplitude and even reached a level sufficient to generate an action potential. Some effect of pairing was observed for as long as 40 minutes following stimulation. Because this preparation involves facilitation (enhanced responding) following stimulation by two different neurons, the phenomenon is referred to as *heterosynaptic facilitation* (Kandel et al., 1970). Further investigation has suggested that these nonspecific facilitating effects most likely result from presynaptic alterations in the release of neural transmitter (Kandel, 1976).

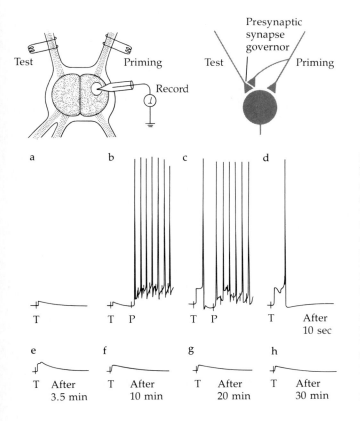

Figure 12.5
Heterosynaptic facilitation in the abdominal ganglion of the marine snail *Aplysia*. (a) Stimulation in a test pathway (T) produces a small neural response. (b) When a second "priming" pathway (P) is stimulated repeatedly, a much larger neural potential results. (c) Priming facilitates responding in the test pathway. (d–g) Even after priming stimulation has ceased, activity in the test pathway is elevated for some period of time. [From "Nerve Cells and Behavior" by E. R. Kandel. Copyright © 1970 by Scientific American, Inc. All rights reserved.]

Attempts to relate such examples of neural plasticity to overt behavior have led Kandel and his colleagues into an intensive study of the neural substrates of the modifiability of reflexive behavior in *Aplysia*. The animal is shown in locomotion in Figure 12.6. In response to tactile stimulation of the siphon or mantle shelf (see Figure 12.7), *Aplysia* engages in a defensive withdrawal reflex. This involves a contraction of the external organs of the mantle cavity surrounding the gill, including the gill, the siphon, and the mantle shelf. The animal's brain apparently plays no essential part in the production of this reflex. Only the abdominal ganglia need be intact, indicating that the responses comprising the withdrawal reflex are controlled by motorneurons located in these ganglia.

By individually stimulating the giant motorneurons in the abdominal ganglia and noting the movements of the organs of the mantle cavity, it

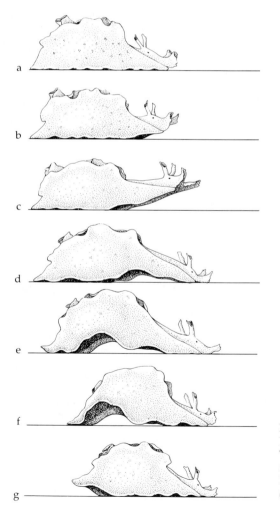

Figure 12.6
Locomotor response of the marine snail *Aplysia*. Taken together, stages a through g comprise one full "step." [From *Cellular basis of behavior* by E. R. Kandel. W. H. Freeman and Company. Copyright © 1976.]

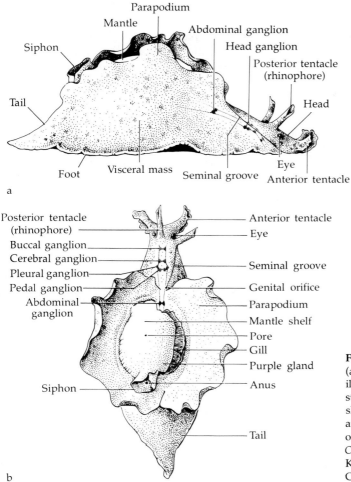

Parapodium
Mantle
Abdominal ganglion
Siphon
Head ganglion
Posterior tentacle
(rhinophore)

Tail
Head

Foot
Visceral mass
Seminal groove
Anterior tentacle
Eye

a

Posterior tentacle
(rhinophore)
Buccal ganglion
Cerebral ganglion
Pleural ganglion
Pedal ganglion
Abdominal
ganglion

Anterior tentacle
Eye

Seminal groove

Genital orifice
Parapodium
Mantle shelf
Pore
Gill
Purple gland
Anus

Siphon

Tail

b

Figure 12.7
(a) Side view of *Aplysia*,
illustrating external organs and
structures. (b) Dorsal view,
showing the exposed gill, siphon,
and mantle, as well as the location
of the various ganglia. [After
Cellular basis of behavior by E. R.
Kandel. W. H. Freeman and
Company. Copyright © 1976.]

has been possible to identify five cells that control the contraction of these organs. The cells constitute the motor component of the reflex; overt behavioral "twitches" are observed to occur in exact synchrony with single spike potentials recorded in one particular cell of the five mentioned. Following the identification of motorneurons involved in the execution of the response, mapping of the sensory receptive field was carried out by natural tactile stimulation of the body surface. This was done to determine which cells in the ganglion receive the sensory information produced by stimulation at the periphery. The same five motorneurons were found to respond vigorously to such stimulation. Moreover, the receptive fields of the neurons were coextensive with the group of cells controlling the overt withdrawal reflex.

Habituation   Extensive knowledge of the neural correlates of the withdrawal reflex now provides a basis for understanding behavior change. Investigations of the modifiability of the response have been undertaken in both semi-intact and isolated ganglion preparations (in which input–output parameters are simplified and a segment of the physiological system is exposed), as well as in exclusively behavioral preparations. Reasoning that the simplest learning process might be the most readily analyzed, researchers have focused on habituation. Behavioral habituation of the defensive withdrawal reflex has been shown to parallel the habituation processes described for vertebrates (Thompson and Spencer, 1966). The reflex habituates to within 30 percent of untrained control levels, with the "major part of habituation" occurring within 5 to 10 stimulus presentations. Response decrements are abolished by rest, with recovery apparently occurring in two distinct phases, which differ in recovery rate. Presentation of a novel stimulus (dishabituation) immediately reinstates the habituated response, and greater habituation occurs with weak rather than with strong stimuli. The amplitude of *spontaneously occurring* mantle contraction (mediated by the same set of motor units) does *not* change during either habituation or dishabituation of the elicited contraction response. This clearly indicates that the habituation of the elicited contractions is not due to muscular fatigue. Experimental distinction has also been made between habituation and sensory adaptation. Neurophysiological recordings of activity in single afferent units of the periphery indicated no changes in the neural activity of these cells in response to natural stimulation sufficient to produce behavioral habituation. Similarly, procedures in which stimulation was applied directly to the receptors indicated no change in the pattern of response habituation.

The neural analogue of behavioral habituation was also observed with repeated tactile stimulation. The amplitudes of excitatory neural potentials recorded from the motorneurons controlling the reflex *decreased* markedly with successive stimulus presentation. These and other manipulations suggest that behavioral habituation results from some change in synaptic efficacy.[5] *Increase* in the amplitudes of neural potentials was found to be associated with either rest or with the presentation of a dishabituating stimulus. If the afferent stimulation was chemically prevented from reaching the motorneurons, recovery continued even while stimulation of peripheral receptors was sustained. This manipulation renders the junction between sensory and motor cells ineffective, even though stimulation of the sensory cells continues. Because recovery proceeds (and no further habituation occurs) under these conditions, some aspect of the process by which cells communicate with one another at this junction is therefore an essential part of the habituation process.

---

[5]Broadly conceived, synaptic efficacy refers to how effective the chemical synapse is in transmitting its message. In learning, it is assumed that some synapses underlying the observed behavior change are more effective than they were prior to the training experience.

Finally, using isolated ganglion preparations in which the reflex is virtually isolated from the rest of the organism, monosynaptic EPSP decrements were recorded in a single motorneuron following the repeated stimulation of a single afferent fiber. Further research on monosynaptic habituation, that in which only one synapse is involved in the communication between two neurons, has revealed "the critical change accompanying habituation of the gill-withdrawal reflex is a decrease in the number of transmitter quanta released by the sensory neurons (Kandel, 1976, p. 575). This research need not suggest that similar mechanisms underlie all instances of habituation. In other response systems, as well as in other species, the available mechanisms for behavioral habituation may have been adapted to suit the existing attributes of the particular response or species at hand.

The behavior modifications thus far observed in *Aplysia* seem to last only as long as a few hours. Because such short-term modifcation is rather unrepresentative of changes typically occurring in higher organisms, it is important to demonstrate long-term habituation in *Aplysia*. Attempts to do so (Carew, Pinsker, and Kandel, 1972) indicate that long-term habituation of the siphon withdrawal reflex occurs following 4 days of habituation training consisting of a total of 10 trials per day. Retention of habituation was measured at 1, 7, and 21 days subsequent to training. Experimental animals exhibited significantly greater response decrement than controls that received only the retention tests. Comparison of response decrements evident at 21 days with those seen immediately following habituation training revealed only partial recovery of responding even after 3 weeks. Long-term habituation was specific to training with spaced as opposed to massed trials, and it also occurred with habituation of the gill withdrawal reflex. These findings enhance the conclusion that the cellular mechanisms described for habituation in these organisms may be very similar to those underlying long-term behavior change in more advanced organisms as well.

Again, the conveniently accessible nervous system of *Aplysia* has permitted more precise analysis of the long-term effects than would otherwise be possible. Carew and Kandel (1973) have reported that the long-term decrements in overt behavior just described are correlated with a long-term decreased synaptic efficacy in a single major motorneuron of the reflex. The decreased functioning of the neuron itself persists for up to 24 hours. One of two afferent nerves providing synaptic input to the motorneuron was repeatedly stimulated in one group of animals during 4 habituation sessions consisting of 10 trials each. This nerve was termed the "experimental" nerve. In the second group, the second nerve, designated the "control" nerve, received only a single 10-trial habituation session. Training was accomplished with the ganglion containing the motorneuron suspended outside, but still attached to the animal. Twenty-four hours later, with both ganglion and animal apparently quite responsive, the retention of the cell was assessed by presenting a single 10-trial block of stimuli to the appropriate nerve in all subjects. Presumably as a function of the more extensive experience on the previous day, stimuli presented to the experimental nerve evoked significantly less responding than those presented to the control nerve. Twenty-four hour retention of habituation is therefore evident within a single neuron in *Aplysia.*

Similar long-term effects, assessed to date only at the behavioral level, are also evident in the presistent three-week retention of sensitization (see Chapter 3) in the defensive withdrawal reflex in *Aplysia* (Pinsker, Hening, Carew, and Kandel, 1973). This enhanced responding persisted, however, only if the abdominal ganglion was intact. Animals from which the ganglion was removed showed no evidence of prolonged sensitization.

The provocative work on *Aplysia* has perhaps been instrumental in reviving interest in the learning capacities of other gastropod molluscs. Recent work has focused on freshwater snails with well-developed shells, animals rather closely related to *Aplysia.* Cook (1971) has investigated habituation of the withdrawal response in the freshwater snail *Limnaea stagnalis* using four different habituating stimuli: light offset, mechanical shock, vibration, and a moving shadow. These stimuli were individually applied in series with interstimulus intervals of 10 seconds. Decreases in the frequency of responding were observed over repeated trials. Moreover, the rates and patterns of the obtained decrements were found to be dependent on the nature of the habituating stimulus, as well as on the frequency with which that stimulus was presented. Habituation occurred at a more rapid rate for both vibratory stimuli and mechanical shock as compared with either the light offset or shadow stimuli. Cook went on to test the sensitivity of the snails to changes in the temporal patterning of the stimulus series. Work with mammals has indicated that even though habituation has occurred to a given stimulus presented at a particular intertrial interval, subsequent increases or decreases in that interval, accompanied by no other change in the stimulus, can produce responding once again. Cook therefore first habituated the snails to one temporal pattern of stimulation. When that pattern was then changed, for example from + − + + − − to + − + − + −, no responding occurred. A similar lack of sensitivity to the temporal dimension was evidenced by an absence of changes in responding following sizable changes in the duration of stimulation. The author concludes that there is no evidence suggestive of a sensitivity to the temporal patterning of stimuli in *Limnaea.*

These experiments also present some interesting data on interactions between habituating stimuli. The basic paradigm was as follows: Stimulus I was presented alone repeatedly for 20 trials; stimulus II was then presented alone repeatedly for 15 trials; finally, stimulus I was presented again, alone, for 10 trials. Two major results of these manipulations are reported. They are the "habituation effect" and the "retention effect." Both effects are decremental, and both are dependent on the groupings of stimuli employed in the paradigm. In the habituation effect, habituation to stimulus I resulted in less responding to stimulus II as compared with that seen in controls receiving only a stimulus II series. In the retention effect, retention of habituation to stimulus I was maintained by the interpolated habituation to stimulus II. That is, on retention tests no recovery of responding was evident when the second series of stimulus I events was presented. The initial level of responding observed during this sequence was lower than that obtained in animals receiving only two separate series of stimulus I events with no interpolated stimulus II series. Both the habituation and the retention effects occurred, however, only *within particular stimulus groups.* If stimulus I and stimulus II were *both* visual stimuli or *both* mechanical stimuli, the decremental effects occurred. If, however, the stimulus groups were mixed, so that stimulus I was visual and stimulus II was mechanical (or vice versa) no interactions were observed between habituating stimuli. Interactions between stimuli were seen to produce *incremental* effects when the two stimuli were either presented simultaneously or were paired on each trial. Moreover, the incremental interactions did occur with pairings of stimuli from different groups. The decremental effects may represent the *generalization of habituation* occurring within a stimulus modality, while the incremental effects may represent a more nonspecific sensitization process.

Several lines of evidence suggest that habituation in the gastropods is not limited to simple reflexive responses such as the defensive withdrawal responses described up to this point. Willows (1973) cites an early report by Buytendijk (1921) of habituation in the complex righting response of the land snail *Lymnaea*. If detached and replaced upside down on its substrate, this animal will quickly withdraw inside its upturned shell. Eventually, however, the snail will leave its shell, reattach its foot to the substrate, and pull the shell back over its exposed body. With repeated detachments the duration of the withdrawal, and hence of the latency to successful reorientation of the shell, decreases substantially.

The work of Abraham and Willows (1971) on the escape response of the marine slug *Tritonia* further illustrates plasticity in the more complex behavior of the gastropods. This particular response sequence is of additional interest because neurophysiological study indicates that it represents a true fixed action pattern. That is, the response represents a characteristically species-specific behavioral sequence (see Chapter 9) that, once evoked, continues to completion in the absence of any further environmental input. In the absence of environmental feedback, how then is the behavior modified, and what are the characteristics of the behavior change? Do they differ from the types of behavior modification evident in traditionally more flexible response sequences? Abraham and Willows have attempted to answer these questions by assessing changes in the slug's escape response under a number of different conditions. Recall that the response sequence consists of an elongation of the body coupled with a flattening of the anterior and posterior ends of the organism. This is followed by a series of dorsal and ventral flexions of the body, which effectively propel the animal away from the clutches of potential predators. Abraham and Willows measured changes in the response under four conditions representing different learning situations. The forward conditioning group received a stream of fresh water (the CS) followed in 10 seconds by the delivery of a strong salt solution (the UCS). The remaining three groups, a CS-only group, a UCS-only group, and a random stimulus group, each received the indicated treatment. Results demonstrated that while responding to the CS was greater in both the conditioning and random groups, the two did not differ significantly from one another. This was the case even after as many as 200 conditioning trials. The authors conclude that while no conditioning had taken place, the enhanced responsiveness of both dual-stimulus groups was evidence of the sensitization of the response sequence. Similarly, plasticity, again nonassociative, was evident in the decreased responsiveness of the UCS-only group. The duration of the complete swim was substantially decreased in a second series of 30 trials presented to this group, indicating that some habituation had taken place. Responding was shown to recover with rest (spontaneous recovery), and the presentation of a novel stimulus (manual removal from the tank) produced dishabituation. When stimulus intensity was increased to either moderate or strong levels, however, no habituatory decrement was in evidence. Apparently, under conditions of even moderately intense stimulation, plasticity in this response sequence becomes maladaptive. Because of the extensive knowledge that has been gained about the neurophysiological mechanisms underlying this response sequence, there is now a real possibility for understanding how plasticity might be superimposed upon stereotypy.

Classical Conditioning   Recent findings suggest that some gastropods may be capable of some forms of associative learning to response to complex stimulus manipulations. Lickey (1968) trained *Aplysia vaccaria* on three types of conditioning trials. On "food trials" the animal's lip was touched with a small piece of seaweed held in blunt forceps. The slug would seize the food, which was then released from the forceps to allow for ingestion. On "test trials" a similar procedure was followed except that the food was omitted and the lip was touched with the tip of the empty closed forceps. On "ambiguous trials" the lip was touched with the forceps and seaweed simultaneously. Ambiguous sessions consisted of 30 ambiguous trials, while test sessions consisted of 30 food trials alternated with 30 test trials. Subjects received 3 successive sessions (1 test and 1 ambiguous session) separated by an intersession interval of 4 days. Responses were categorized as either *ingestion* or *rejection*. Rejection responses initially occurred with a mean of about 25 times per 30-trial session during the test trials (forceps alone). However, the number of rejections of the forceps alone analyzed over blocks of 10 trials increased significantly within a session. For a given session, therefore, far more rejections were made in the last block as compared with the first block of 10 trials. By contrast, no significant differences were evident across trials during the ambiguous sessions. Moreover, the increased likelihood of rejections within test sessions was retained over the 4-day intersession interval. Lickey suggests that this increased frequency of rejections constitutes an "example of simple learning . . . analogous to the acquisition of a passive or inhibitory avoidance behavior in more complex animals" (Lickey, 1968, p. 716).

Many of the reports on classical conditioning in the gastropods are, however, equivocal. Appropriate procedural controls are often overlooked, and several failures to replicate have been reported (Willows, 1973). The most successful studies to date have involved aversion learning in food-related contexts. Mpitsos and Collins (1975), for example, investigated experimentally induced changes in the bite-strike response of the marine gastropod *Pleurobranchaea*. This response is normally a part of the feeding behavior of this carnivorous slug, and it is easily elicited by the presentation of a squid solution. The training sequence employed is illustrated in Figure 12.8. A group of experimental animals were first presented with the food stimulus (CS) as indicated in panel (b). Shocks (UCS) were then presented in 180 seconds, independently of whether or not the animal engaged in the feeding response. The shock stimulus elicits a rapid contraction of the body and head accompanied by head movement away from the stimulus (c). Control animals received alternate presentations of food and shock every half hour. As indicated in panel (f), within as few as 10 trials separated by as much as an hour each, presentation of the food stimulus by itself was sufficient to elicit contraction and withdrawal in the experimental animals. Interestingly, as training proceeded the CS began to evoke a combined approach-withdrawal response in both experimental and control groups (Figure 12.8e). However, by the end of the session these combined responses were superseded by complete withdrawal in the experimental animals alone. Postconditioning tests conducted 12 hours following training and at every succeeding 24-hour interval revealed substantial persistent differences between experimental and control animals. Percentage of withdrawal responses evoked by presentation of CS alone actually increased above training levels in the experimental group, while the control group reverted to near pretraining levels. Threshold and latency of the food-related bite-strike response were also much greater for the experimental animals. Moreover, extinction of the altered responding did not occur until as much as 132 hours following initial training. The authors conclude that the long-lasting behavior change is the result of the association of the two stimuli, and that the most pronounced behavior changes occur during a period of *consolidation* that *follows* training. The adaptive value of this type of conditioning

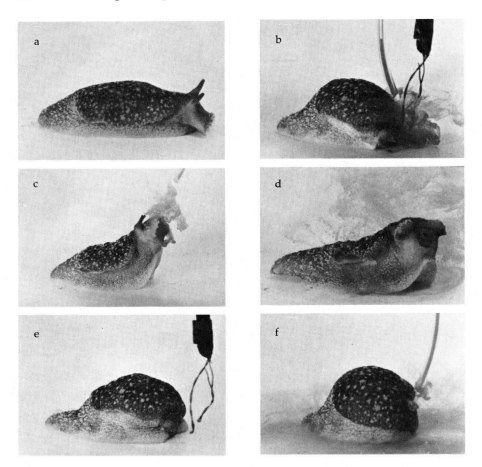

Figure 12.8
Development of a conditioned aversion to food in a marine gastropod. In (a) the animal is shown in normal locomotion prior to any conditioning. The pointed tentacle-like objects are located on the animal's head. [From G. Mpitsos and S. Collins, Learning: Rapid aversive conditioning in the gastropod mollusk *Pleurobranchaea, Science, 188,* 954–957. Copyright © 1975 by the American Association for the Advancement of Science.]

for the slug is readily apparent. For a predator, one of the most efficient responses available may be to learn not to pursue (to withdraw) when your prey retaliates.

The importance of considering the adaptive character of a particular instance of learning is clearly illustrated by Gelperin's (1975) work on rapid aversion learning in the land slug. Here we can easily see quick, reliable, biologically efficient learning occurring in what we might otherwise regard as an "intelligent" fashion. In fact, the land slug *(Limax maximus)* is not popularly regarded as an adept learner. Nonetheless, individual slugs in this situation learned quite easily. Gelperin fed his slugs a potato meal once daily for 8 days. Consistent eaters were then randomly assigned to experimental and control groups. Both groups were offered a novel food (mushrooms) following their daily potato rations. Experimental animals, however, also received 5-minute exposures to noxious CO_2 each time they ate a mushroom meal. Results indicated that mushroom intake was greatly reduced in these animals by only the second day of training. In fact, as many as 50 percent of the subjects receiving the CO_2 treatment immediately following ingestion were classified as rapid learners. That is, they consistently refused mushrooms after as few as one or two training trials. These animals were even observed to avoid noxious food when the application of CO_2 was delayed by as much as one hour following ingestion. However, much less rapid learning occurred with the long delay.

Operant Conditioning   Finally, again testing under seminatural conditions, Lee (1969, 1971) has reported that *Aplysia* may be capable of operant conditioning. Lee arranged the animal's tank with photocells such that the slug's location in any one of 10 positions could be recorded. One of these locations (position 9) was designated as the response to be reinforced. Any time the animal was found in position 9, the water level in the chamber was raised from one inch (animal one-half covered) to approximately 3.5 inches (animal completely submerged), and lowered again after up to 3 minutes. Because *Aplysia* can live for only a very short period of time out of water, it was assumed that complete submersion would be reinforcing for the animal. The experimental situation is diagramed in Figure 12.9. One subject spent only 4 percent of the first 2

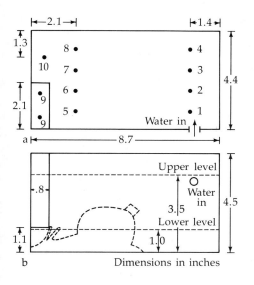

Figure 12.9
Experimental apparatus used to measure operant conditioning in *Aplysia*. (a) Top view. (b) Side view. The numbered dots (in part a) indicate the various positions in which the animal's presence was measured. The reinforcing increase in water level (in part b) was made contingent upon the animal being in position 9. [After Lee, 1969.]

hours of training in position 9. After 10–17 hours, however, 80 percent of the animal's time was spent in the reinforced position. Similar results were obtained for four of the remaining five animals tested. Lee further demonstrated that even through as many as 16 reversals in which position 9 and position 1 alternated as the "correct response," behavior was maintained by the contingency. In an additional experiment in which yoked controls received noncontingent water level variation, experimental animals were required to pass into position 3. If the animal was in position 3 already, it would have to leave and return in order to obtain complete submersion. Merely spending time in a position may reflect only inactivity; once there, the animal stays there. Requiring that an animal move into an area, however, necessitates active responding. Results support an operant conditioning interpretation. The number of half-hour intervals in which no response occurred was much greater for the controls. Additional probe trials in which the animal was taken out of the chamber and replaced 20 seconds later indicated that the latency to respond (that is, to move into position 3) was much shorter for the experimental animals.

Cephalopods

Among the invertebrates, the ways of the *cephalopods* (squid, octopus, and cuttlefish) are perhaps the most familiar. These largely predatory marine-dwellers, like vertebrates sexually dimorphic, possess extensive, complexly organized brains (typically sized between those of most fish and those of most birds). Like many vertebrates, they possess highly developed tactile and visual senses. The combined effect of these abilities renders their behavior among the most complex of the invertebrate realm. Moreover, their learning abilities appear equally complex. In fact, here we see the most obvious violation of the erroneous assumption that "intelligence increases as we ascend the phylogenetic scale" (see Hodos and Campbell, 1969, for the nature of proper inferences to be drawn from the structure of the phylogenetic scale). One of the most thoroughly studied of the cephalopods, the common octopus *(Octopus vulgaris)*, pictured in Figure 12.10, could put any number of vertebrates to shame in a contest of wits.

Because the octopus is both oceanic and bottom-dwelling, naturalistic studies of this organism are very difficult to perform. We can, however, tentatively assume that the similarity of the octopus' learning abilities to vertebrate learning reflects evolutionary convergence. Structures descended from the molluscan line have been phylogenetically modified to perform functions similar to those performed by many vertebrate species. Independent but similar environmental demands placed on these disparate groups have resulted in very similar solutions to very similar problems. Again, the environment directs evolution, and we find something

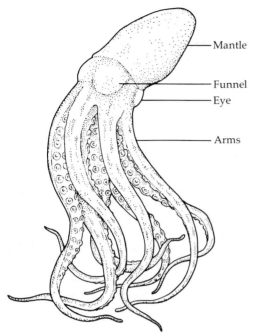

Mantle

Funnel

Eye

Arms

Figure 12.10
The common octopus. [Redrawn with permission of Macmillan Publishing Co., Inc., from *Invertebrate zoology*, 2nd ed., by R. W. Hegner and J. G. Engemann. Copyright © 1968 by Macmillan Publishing Co., Inc.]

close to advanced intelligence in what is otherwise regarded as a rather lowly creature.

The literature on the behavioral abilities of these cephalopods is quite extensive; we will not, therefore, attempt an exhaustive review (for more detail see Sanders, 1975; Young, 1971). Rather, we will try to illustrate representative abilities of the cephalopods, highlighting their uniqueness as invertebrates.

Very little systematic investigation of cephalopod learning has actually focused on the simpler learning paradigms of habituation and classical conditioning. In fact, the bulk of the recent literature (especially on *Octopus*) has been concerned with the elucidation of more complex forms of learning. Earlier studies suggest, however, that both of the simpler paradigms readily produce behavior change. Habituation has been demonstrated in the modification of both ingestion and escape responses, and, though perhaps less conclusive due to the lack of adequate controls, evidence for classical conditioning is also quite suggestive. The neglect of these simpler learning paradigms in cephalopods reflects the group's strikingly unique complex learning facility. Habituation and classical conditioning have assumed less importance with the recognition that in the cephalopods the vertebrate-like abilities so atypical of the bulk of the invertebrate realm are here the rule. The possibility of approaching the evolution of learning by assessing such vertebrate-like processes in a vastly different group has turned the attention of most investigators to an analysis of the basis and extent of this complexity.

Discrimination Learning   The most frequently used tests of complex learning in the cephalopods center on discrimination learning, and the bulk of the literature has addressed the octopus. In tests for discrimination learning the animal is presented with two discriminable stimuli, neither of which initially elicits the response of interest, usually predatory attack. Attack can, however, be induced by the presentation of food (crab or fish) in the presence of one of the two discriminative stimuli. Thereafter, this stimulus is regarded as the S^+, and attacks in its presence are always reinforced by the receipt of food. Attacks directed toward the second stimulus, now the S^-, are followed by the presentation of an electric shock. When such a procedure is used, the frequency of attacks directed to the S^+ increases well above chance levels. Similarly, attacks to the S^- decrease. Both food and shock by themselves produce transient changes in responding in the directions associated with training; however, these cannot account for the long-lasting effects that result from the establishment of a contingency. Young (1970), for example, produced quite persistent changes in behavior by shocking octopuses contingent upon crab-induced attack. Attacks fell to well below 30 percent of their initial level, and testing on the following day indicated very few attacks directed toward the crab as much as 24 hours later. Young's animals did, however, attack a verticle rectangle placed in the tank. Young therefore concludes that the observed behavior change cannot be attributed either to fatigue or to a generalized effect of shock. Rather, the effects appear to be specific to the stimuli used in training.

The signaling stimuli typically used in discrimination training with these animals are either visual or tactile, and both successive and simultaneous discrimination have been studied. Comparison of these two methods indicate that they are interchangeable with simple discriminations. With more difficult discriminations, however, the simultaneous procedure produces better performance (see Chapter 5). Visual discriminations frequently involve brightness, spatial orientation, or form of an object, and, as you might expect, all shapes and orientations are not equally discriminable. Moreover, experiments performed by Messenger and Sanders (1972) have demonstrated that the highest levels of performance are obtained with the use of multiple cues. Naive octopuses were trained using stimuli that were either rectangular or circular in shape, and either black or white. During training, on trials with white horizontal rectangles (S^+) responding was reinforced with food; responding to black vertical rectangles (S^-) was punished with electric shock. By the third training session animals were discriminating correctly on 85 percent of the trials. Transfer test trials employing grey vertical or horizontal rectangles, and either black or white circles were interspersed throughout training to assess the strength of the compound cue and the importance of each of the component stimuli. Orientation alone can be assessed with the grey rectangles (grey should be irrelevant), and brightness alone can be tested with black and white circles (circularity should be irrelevant). Results of the transfer tests indicated that the octopuses had employed both stimulus dimensions in forming the discrimination; responding was maintained significantly above chance levels by either stimulus alone. In most animals, however, the brightness cue by itself maintained more responding than did the orientation cue by itself.

Further tests were conducted comparing the behavior of three additional groups of animals to determine if the number of correct responses increased with increases in the number of relevant cues in the stimulus. That is, would the subjects receiving two relevant cues discriminate more accurately than the subjects receiving only one relevant cue? One group of octopuses was trained with cues that differed only on the brightness dimension (one vertical white rectangle and one vertical black rectangle); a second group was trained with orientation as the only relevant cue (one black vertical rectangle and one black horizontal rectangle); a third group was presented stimuli in which both brightness and orientation were relevant cues (one *black vertical* rectangle and one *white horizontal* rectangle). Animals in the two-cue condition performed significantly better than either of the two other groups.

These experiments indicate that the octopus can attend differentially to different sensory dimensions. Brightness by itself was found to be "more important" than orientation by itself. The animals do, however, form complex discriminations. With the double cue some behavior was maintained by each cue independently. Even after training with the double cue, therefore, each component presented alone sustained some responding. Moreover, the effectiveness of the complex discrimination is greater than that of either of the simple discriminations. These data are in striking accord with the discrimination learning results obtained with vastly different organisms. (Compare them, for example, with the results of research on attention in the pigeon presented in Chapter 5.) Like many advanced vertebrate species, octopuses appear to be capable both of selective attention and of the complex integration of several sensory dimensions.

Complex Learning Functions   A number of other phenomena reminiscent of vertebrate learning have also been demonstrated in the cephalopods. Among these are generalization, the long-term retention of complex learning, and learning in a number of more complex situations such as those involving long delays of reinforcement and the solution of detour problems.

Wells and Young (1970b) measured generalization gradients following training with tactile stimulation in octopuses. As mentioned earli·r, the cephalopod's tactile sense is very highly developed. The octopus's eight arms are arranged with dual rows of suckers. The suckers contain large numbers of chemical as well as mechanical receptors, and even blind animals can easily discriminate objects on the basis of both form and texture using information obtained via the suckers. Using differential reinforcement these researchers produced tactile discriminations based on the number of 1-mm wide ring-like grooves imprinted on a 3-cm diameter plastic sphere. The set of spheres used in testing ranged from those with no grooves to those with as many as 13. Following discrimination training with a pair of stimuli (one the S^+ and one the S^-) generalization was tested over the range of values represented by the different spheres. Training with extreme values resulted in both positive and negative generalization to related intermediate values. Moreover, training on intermediate values produced peak shift. That is, the strongest generalization around the positive stimulus value was shifted to the non-negative side of the positive stimulus (see Chapter 5). Comparable generalization effects have been demonstrated in the visual modality as well.

Retention data, obtained again largely on octopuses, attest to the permanence of the behavior changes produced in these individuals. Several authors (see Wells and Wells, 1958; Wells and Young, 1970a) report strong retention at from 2 to 5 days following training in S^+–S^- discrimination learning situations with both visual and tactile stimuli. Sanders (1970) has reported 50 percent retention as many as 24 days following tactile discrimination training. Of particular interest are the more recently collected data on *multiphasic retention* (Messenger, 1973a; Sanders and Barlow, 1971). Multiphasic retention refers to a phenomenon in which retention is actually seen to improve at various periods following the end of training. Messenger (1973a), for example, trained cuttlefish to cease attacking prawns (a shrimp-like prey) presented in enclosed transparent tubes. The three distinct components of the attack response — attention, positioning, and seizure — were found to decrease at quite different rates. The most rapid decrement was observed in the seizure component, which, under conditions of continuous stimulus presentation, decreased to a level of approximately 30 percent within the first 5 minutes of training. Messenger tested retention of the decrement in seizure at intervals of from 2 minutes to 2 days following training. Results, pictured in Figure 12.11, indicated that retention dropped off rapidly up to 22 minutes following training. Retention scores then *increased*, with far greater savings (97 percent) occurring at 60 minutes post training. Thereafter, responding increased (less retention) gradually up to 2 days, at which time testing ceased. The author speculates that the biphasic retention data may be indicative of two distinct memory systems in cephalopods, comparable to short-term memory (STM) and long-term memory (LTM) processes in vertebrates. According to this interpretation, STM peaks quickly and decays rapidly, producing the recovery of responding evident within the

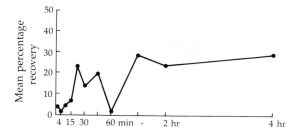

Figure 12.11
Multiphasic retention of habituation in the predatory seizure response of the cuttlefish. Note the increase in retention measured at the 60-min interval. [After Messenger, 1973a.]

first 22 minutes; LTM develops more gradually, peaking at 60 minutes, actually after STM has substantially decayed. Similar experiments in which octopuses were presented shock contingent upon attack tested retention at up to 30 hours following training (Sanders and Barlow, 1971). Phasic retention "peaks" were again observed, here occurring at 2 and 20 hours post training. These authors, too, invoke multi-process memory as an explanation consistent with the observed effects.

Still more complex behavior may be required when the cephalopods are faced with tasks involving the *delay of reinforcement* and the solution of *detour problems*. In the former, an interval of time separates the initiation of the response and the receipt of reinforcement. Dilly (1963) has shown that the octopus can correctly identify that stimulus which on prior trials was presented with a crab, even though delays of up to 20 seconds follow stimulus presentation. The detour problem involves delay of reinforcement plus a situation in which the subject must select an apparently circuitous route to reinforcement during that delay. Wells (1964; 1967) placed octopuses in a chamber similar to that pictured in Figure 12.12. Three corridors were visible from the animal's home point, itself located directly across from the entrance to the central corridor. Windows covered the entrances to the external corridors, and passage down the central corridor could lead to rear entry into the outer corridors. Through the windows the subject could see a crab placed in one of the two external corridors. The octopus initially attempted to attack the crab through the window, but the animal gradually learned to delay responding to the immediately

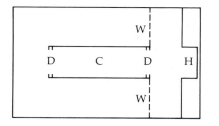

Figure 12.12
Detour apparatus used to measure modification in the behavior of octopuses exposed to complex learning paradigms. The prey object is visible to the octopus (positioned at H) through windows (W). The subject must detour beyond the prey and travel down the corridor (DCD) to reach the prey. [After Sanders, 1975.]

visible stimulus and take a detour through the central corridor to approach the crab. On reaching the end of the alley, the octopus then
turned toward the side on which the crab had been seen earlier, to approach and attack from behind. Even when the animal was detained for
two additional minutes within the central corridor, successful detours
were completed with up to 70 percent accuracy.

A great deal of research has been conducted on the cephalopod nervous system to explain the basis of these learning abilities. The cephalopod's brain consists of a collection of highly organized lobes, diagramed in Figure 12.13. Among these structures, the vertical lobe has
been shown in numerous studies (see Young, 1971) to be intimately related to the cephalopod's learning abilities. Lesioning or removal of the
vertical lobe appears to affect only those behaviors involved in learning
and memory. Interestingly, developmental studies of the posthatching
behavior of immature cuttlefish (Messenger, 1973b) indicate that the development of learning abilities (which emerge only after about one month
of life) is directly correlated with the rapid postnatal development of the
vertical lobes. While habituation appears largely unaffected by vertical
lobe removal, deficits are evident in numerous aspects of discrimination
learning. Both the learning and retention deficits that result are propor-
tional to the size of the lesion. Some of these deficits are, however, temporary and disappear a few months following surgery. Many suggestions
have been made concerning the specific functions of the vertical lobe system (see Sanders, 1975). While no firm conclusions have emerged from
the mass of data collected on the cephalopod nervous system, it is clear
that some aspect of the cephalopod's natural environment has rendered
the evolution of an extremely adaptive structure capable of complex learn-

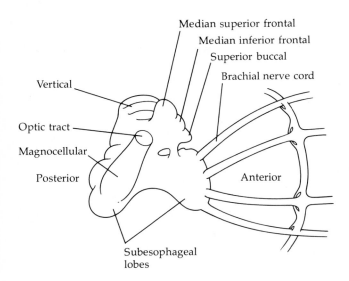

Figure 12.13
The brain of the common octopus,
showing the positions of the
vertical and subesophageal lobes.
Radial projections represent nerve
cords innervating the animal's
arms. [After Young, 1971.]

ing. Identification of these factors may elucidate the evolution of learning processes in many organisms, including, perhaps, the vertebrates.

In summary, there can be no doubt that learning processes comparable to those described in vertebrates are evident in the phylum Mollusca. The character of those processes, however, varies greatly among the various groups studied. Cephalopods clearly exhibit far more complex kinds of behavior change than do gastropods. In gastropods, however, associative learning, including operant conditioning, is apparent. These differences among major groups are instructive in that they permit analyses of the types of organismic and environmental factors that may sustain the evolution of complex learning processes.

ARTHROPODS

If you were to pick an organism at random from a giant vat containing all living animals, you would be more likely to pick an arthropod than any other living animal form. This is because most of the organisms on earth are arthropods. They in fact outnumber all other species combined. Their extensive numbers are, moreover, coupled with an almost bewildering behavioral diversity, and they are apparently well endowed with mechanisms for behavioral plasticity.

More than ten major classes of organisms comprise the phylum Arthropoda. Among these are creatures as familiar as crabs, spiders, insects, and scorpions, and as unfamiliar as the tiny water bear shown in Figure 12.14. All are characterized by bilateral symmetry, a chitinous exoskeleton offering protection from many different kinds of environmental onslaught, and a relatively complex nervous system consisting of several interconnected segmental ganglia regulated by the action of a primitive brain. Arthropods can be found in virtually any habitat on earth. They

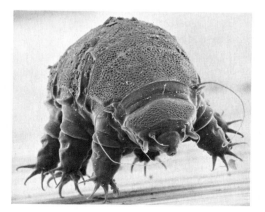

Figure 12.14
Electron micrograph of a tiny arthropod, the water bear. [Courtesy of Robert O. Schuster.]

therefore offer unusual promise for developing our understanding of the relationships between diversity and plasticity in behavior, and specific ecological circumstances.

Because they are so numerous, an even representatively comprehensive treatment of their learning abilities is well beyond the scope of this book. We shall therefore very briefly summarize the most generally held conclusions on the major groups and then concentrate on more specific accounts of learning in the class Insecta.

The bulk of the literature describing learning in arthropods other than insects has focused on two major groups: the crustacea and the chelicerates. Included in the former are crabs, crayfish, lobster, shrimp, barnacles, and so forth; the latter comprises the horseshoe crabs, spiders, and scorpions. Laboratory work has provided numerous demonstrations of habituation and classical conditioning in many representatives of these groups. Even the extremely primitive horseshoe crab, often considered to be among the phylogenetically oldest of the existing species, has been shown to be capable of habituation and, possibly, classical conditioning. Failures to replicate classical conditioning effects, however, render them far more questionable. Instrumental conditioning studies have been most successful at demonstrating learning in the decapod crustacea: crabs, lobsters, and crayfish. Here maze learning and avoidance learning as well as several types of discrimination learning are in evidence. Research on learning in each of these groups has been extensively reviewed by Krasne (1973) and by Lahue (1973).

As we shall see to be the case with the insects, these groups, too, offer an excellent opportunity to analyze how learning and behavioral plasticity are integrated within the very specific, often highly stereotyped behavioral requirements defined by the natural environment. Studies investigating the spider's retreat to the web after capturing prey, for example, illustrate this phenomenon. Numerous environmental factors provide the context for retreat, and this context is then superimposed upon a sequence of relatively "reflexive" responses by which retreat is accomplished. Optical orientation to the retreat site is apparently established through experience. If optical cues are reversed following a spider's departure from the retreat, the spider must learn a new pattern of (reversed) cues in order to reorient properly. Alteration in optical cues just prior to the spider's departure (preceding departure by as little as 30 seconds) is immediately incorporated, and the animal thereafter will maintain correct retreat following prey capture. To attempt a more complete analysis of this approach in which both innate and learned responses are treated, we will now turn to the insects.

Insects

Our treatment of arthropod learning abilities will focus on the insects. Perhaps because a great deal is known about their behavior under natural circumstances (Wilson, 1971), and because they represent the bulk of the arthropod numbers, insects offer the greatest potential for understanding the relationships between behavioral plasticity and ecological necessity. Also, in the insect, investigations of behavioral plasticity have been conducted both under controlled laboratory conditions and in more naturalistic circumstances. Frequently, however, these two approaches have proceeded independently. We will therefore present representative data first for the laboratory work and then for the field work. Where possible, the two will be brought together, and the chapter will conclude with a review of the learning abilities of the honeybee. Here laboratory and field techniques have been combined to illustrate, once again, how the capacity to learn has developed to facilitate the organism's solution to ecological problems. The results of this combination of techniques have illustrated the amazingly sophisticated learning abilities of the honeybee.

A final justification for focusing more intently on the insects derives, interestingly, from the stereotypy of their behavior. Many of the behavior sequences of insects probably involve little if any learning. Responses many occur in virtually the same, invariable order in different individuals of a given species; concentrated efforts to modify these sequences frequently fail. Insects should not be regarded as a generally plastic group. For this reason, they offer the possibility of valuable comparison with organisms whose behavior is more predominantly flexible — those for whom learning is the rule rather than the exception. These are the organisms that the psychology of learning has traditionally addressed more thoroughly. Comparisons with groups in which learning mechanisms are far less generally represented may yield valuable insight into the evolution of learning.

Laboratory Research

Little research has been done on habituation in insects — perhaps because their behavioral complexity has focused interest on more complex learning paradigms. Behavioral habituation has, however, been demonstrated in a number of species, including the cockroach. Interestingly, habituation is the only published demonstration of behavioral plasticity occurring in the pupal stage (the third stage) of complete metamorphosis. The pupa of the grain beetle, pictured along with the adult and larval forms in Figure 12.15, is almost completely lacking in behavior. While it is a free-living form (not encased in a cocoon or cell), the animal is virtually immobile, has no developed appendages, and no developed sensory systems. It does, however, engage in a few reflexes, including the *abdominal reflex*. This response consists of a back and forth twisting of the entire abdominal section of the animal; it can be elicited by shock, intense light, or strong tactile stimulation. Hollis (1963) has shown that with repeated elicitation by electric shock, the response habituates after about 40 trials.

Figure 12.15
Larva (bottom), pupa (middle), and adult (top) forms of the grain beetle. [Courtesy of Thomas M. Alloway.]

Interpolated stimulation by touch partially dishabituates the response to shock.

As is the case with the gastropod molluscs, habituation in insects, too, may take place in drastically simplified neural systems. The giant neurons that mediate escape responding in the cockroach exhibit radically decreased output following repeated stimulation. These changes are accompanied by no modification in the output of the sensory neurons stimulating the giant fibers (Niklaus, 1965 reviewed in Alloway, 1973). Here, too, therefore, habituation can be characterized as a synaptic phenomenon distinct from sensory adaptation.

By far the majority of the work investigating insect behavior change in standard associative learning paradigms has centered on response-contingent procedures. Again, the simpler paradigms have been neglected. Margaret Nelson's (1971) work on classical conditioning in the blowfly, however, elegantly illustrates the feasibility of classical conditioning in flies. These studies also indicate the kinds of problems encountered in conclusively designating an instance of behavior change in insects as a case of true associative conditioning. Nelson focused her efforts on the modification of flies' feeding behavior. Feeding in the blowfly (a close relative of the common housefly) consists of an extension of the proboscis, the animal's retractable "snout," upon receipt of a chemical stimulus such as sugar, salt, or acid. Chemoreceptive hairs on the fly's legs contain chemically sensitive cells that elicit neural impulses following stimulation. Presentation of an unusually strong sugar stimulus produces what Dethier (1969) has termed a *central excitatory state* (CES). That is, following intense sugar stimulation, the fly becomes generally more sensitive to stimuli that would not have elicited proboscis extension in the absence of the initial sugar stimulation. With such stimulation, however, a water-satiated fly will extend the proboscis in response to the presentation of water. This unexpected response to water seen in satiated flies presumably results from the generally sensitized state of the nervous system produced by the intense sugar stimulation. The CES has been observed to persist for up to two minutes following initial stimulation, and can apparently be completely "discharged" in response to a single water stimulus.

The central excitatory state manifests itself as an increased likelihood that a stimulus will elicit a response. Nelson's efforts to condition proboscis extension in the fly were therefore structured to allow for a distinction between modifications in behavior resulting from a CES and those representative of true classical conditioning. To accomplish this she employed a *compound conditional stimulus* procedure. Prior to training, the flies were water-satiated such that proboscis extension was no longer elicited by water. Thereafter, distilled water was used as one CS; the second CS was provided by a weak salt solution. The two conditional stimuli were presented successively for four seconds each, after which the fly received a sucrose solution (UCS) normally effective in eliciting proboscis extention. The UCS overlapped the second of the two CS's by one second. Using such a procedure two successive UCS's (each providing reinforcement on successive trials during conditioning) will be separated by two CS's. Each UCS will produce a central excitatory state, which should then gradually decay as the compound CS is presented during the interval between reinforcers. Nelson reasoned that if changes in responding were due to CES alone, the greatest increase in response frequency should be associated with the first of the two conditional stimuli. Because of its greater proximity to the UCS of the previous trial, the first CS occurs when the CES has undergone relatively less decay, and CES-induced increments should therefore be most evident during presentation of the first CS. The second CS actually overlaps with the reinforcing UCS on that trial, and conditioning effects should therefore be most evident during the presentation of the second CS. Results indicated that irrespective of which CS it was, the second stimulus always came to elicit significantly more proboscis extension than the first. Control flies that received compound CS's only (no sugar) exhibited far less responding than did any of the experimental groups. Comparison of experimental and control groups does not, however, rule out the occurrence of increments in response frequency produced by central excitatory states. Modified random presentation of the two conditional stimuli produced more responding when CS occurred after UCS than when CS occurred before UCS. With this procedure no conditioning can occur, and only CES can alter responding. As reported, greater increments in responding should therefore be evident only immediately after UCS presentation. The occurrence of a CES may facilitate the formation of a true association. However, because the greater increase in response frequency was associated with the second of the two conditional stimuli, Nelson concluded that the changes in responding were in part due to associative conditioning. While the two processes (CES and classical conditioning) do appear to be distinct, they may interact in ways that require their separate consideration in all insect learning studies.

Classical conditioning has also been demonstrated among the highly social insects in several social castes of honeybees, with a variety of olfactory CS's (Wells, 1973). Conditioned extension of the proboscis in queens and drones as well as in workers was established in a sizable portion of the subjects with only a single conditioning trial. Protrusion of the sting and fanning to ventilate the hive have also been conditioned in honeybees.

The bulk of the laboratory literature on insect learning deals primarily with instrumental learning paradigms such as maze learning and avoidance learning. The maze-learning abilities of ants were explored in a classic series of experiments by T. C. Schneirla (1943). Schneirla took the maze to be representative of the ants' natural foraging situation. In the wild, the ant's foraging behavior consists of repeated orientations from nest to food in which "the ant's route changes in the course of successive journeys from a highly involved and circuitous path to a fairly direct one with few detours" (Schneirla, 1972, p. 558). In the maze, the ant faces the same problem. Schneirla's mazes were constructed as a series of complex passages interposed between nest and food. Some mazes, such as that pictured in Figure 12.16, were doubled (nest to food on one side—food to nest on the other) so that the nature of the return route could be studied as well. Individual ants were given access to the maze repeatedly, and records were kept of the number of entrances into blind alleys, retracings of the same path, and the amount of time the ant remained in the maze. The number of errors (retracings and blind alleys) was observed to decrease in negatively accelerated fashion across successive runs. While groups with unstable intramaze cues and stable intramaze cues both exhibited improved performance, the decrease in number of errors was greater for the second group. These ants appeared to be relying on the specific recognition of local landmarks. Schneirla assumed that in the former group a more generalized type of habituation learning was occurring. Interestingly, when the maze patterns were reversed and the ants were required to retrace their paths, the insects appeared quite disoriented. Even after numerous attempts little if any learning was apparent. Not only, therefore, did the ants fail to transfer, but the reversal problem was far more difficult than the original maze task.

This *inability to transfer* or generalize may be characteristic of insect learning. Like Schneirla's ants, most insects tested under generalization conditions exhibit very little capacity to transfer learned information from

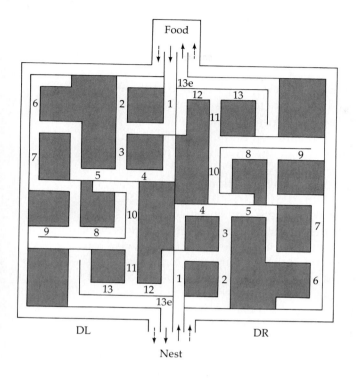

Figure 12.16
Apparatus used to measure maze learning in ants. The insect can be required to move either from the nest to the food (DR) or from the food to the nest (DL). [After Schneirla, 1946.]

one situation to another. By contrast, generalization and transfer are predominant characteristics of the learning abilities of the mammals and birds so extensively studied in psychology. These, however, are organisms in which extremely widespread involvement by learning mechanisms is presumably highly adaptive. In organisms like insects, in which learning is more the exception to a general scheme of stereotypy in behavior, mechanisms of generalization may be much less adaptive. In fact it might be damagingly maladaptive for an insect to transfer learned information to a situation for which the organism already exhibits a highly stereotyped and very adaptive behavior sequence. The single known exception to the insects' inabilities to transfer has been described in one of the most highly evolved groups (whose behavior is often considered amazingly plastic, for an insect): the honeybee. Russian researchers (reviewed in Wilson, 1971) trained bees to take food in the presence of a large square divided into quadrants. When the bees' feeding behavior was reinforced in the presence of a square in which the diagonal quadrants were the same color, the response generalized to other squares with the same patterned arrangement (same colors on the diagonal), even though the exact hue of the colors making up the pattern was different. The animals appeared to be making a same–different discrimination generalized across different sets of colors.

Instrumental avoidance learning has been studied extensively in the cockroach in a number of situations. In the earlier work the cockroach was placed in a closed box: half the box was darkened (cockroaches respond positively to darkness) and half was illuminated. Shock was administered to the animal through an electric grid positioned in the floor of the darkened side. With repeated exposure to shock in darkness the cockroaches learned to remain on the lighted side of the box. Similarly successful avoidance learning has been demonstrated in cockroaches in more complex maze situations. A more complete review of the older literature can be found in Alloway (1973).

Among the most revealing lines of investigation in insect avoidance learning are the studies conducted on the leg flexion response of the cockroach. In the typical experimental paradigm, the roach can avoid shocks by flexing its leg. The leg is suspended above an electrified saline bath. Extension of the leg below a preset level immerses an attached wire into the saline and generates an electric shock. Flexing prevents the shock. Numerous studies have indicated that animals that have undergone 30 to 45 minutes of training receive significantly fewer shocks during testing than yoked controls receiving an equal number of shocks uncorrelated with leg position (for example, Pritchatt, 1968). Of particular interest is the observation that learning proceeds similarly in headless animals and in "animals" whose leg is neurophysiologically connected to only its associated segmental ganglion, virtually isolated from the rest of the nervous system. The leg flexion avoidance response apparently can be mediated by a single isolated ganglion. Moreover, neurophysiological as well as biochemical changes have been described to occur in a systematic fashion correlated with both the acquisition and retention of the leg flexion response (Aranda and Luco, 1969; Kerkut, Oliver, Rick, and Walker, 1970).

Chen, Aranda, and Luco (1970) have attempted to analyze what the role of the head may be, given that it appears to be inessential for the acquisition of avoidance. In their experiment mild shock (eliciting only a slight jerk of the leg) served as a conditional stimulus signaling the onset of more severe shock 900 milliseconds later. Training was conducted over a number of 10-trial sessions across several days. Following training, avoidance learning was tested during 10 presentations of CS alone presented every 24 hours until the insect died. Data were collected in this fashion for intact and headless insects as well as for isolated segments of leg and ganglion. Results indicated that all subjects exhibited some degree of learning. Avoidance responses were, however, acquired much more slowly in headless animals and in isolated segments. Equally striking differences were evident in the retention data. In successive 24-hour tests intact animals retained the response for the duration of their lives in the experimental situation (in some animals up to as much as 12 days). Headless insects evidenced retention for only 2 to 3 days following training, while isolated segments failed to retain after as little as 24 hours. The authors conclude that the head is involved in long-term memory processing. That the remainder of the nervous system has some long-term memory capacity, however, is demonstrated by the surprising result that animals trained intact will retain over long periods even after decapitation or surgical isolation of the tested ganglion.

Field-Oriented Research

As indicated earlier, numerous cases of behavioral plasticity in insects have been observed under naturalistic conditions. Frequently, the behavior changes that occur cannot be readily described using the standard conditioning terminology of psychology. They do, however, almost universally represent sustained alterations in the organism's behavior produced by information or feedback from environmental events. For this reason, they require our attention. Much of the work we will describe involves naturalistic observation as well as the use of experimental techniques modifying or modeling the natural setting. These techniques are here collectively referred to as field research. The remainder of this chapter will review some representative examples. In the final chapter we will discuss what these two different realms of inquiry—the field and the laboratory—may have to offer one another.

Digger Wasps   Digger wasps are solitary wasps that exhibit no social behavior. Following copulation, the male and female resume their solitary ways, and the task of providing for the developing young falls entirely to the female. The female initiates her parental duties by digging a narrow hole in the ground, which serves as a nest for her developing larvae. After the nest is completed, she will capture a caterpillar, deposit it in her nest, then lay her egg on the caterpillar, and close the nest. Thereafter, she feeds the larva by capturing additional caterpillars, returning to the nest, reopening it, and depositing her larva's food inside. This *provisioning behavior* occurs on a daily basis over a period of several days, during which the wasp may maintain several nests simultaneously. Each houses a single developing wasp. The female's daily hunting trips take her far afield of her nests. Somehow she must find her way back. Field experiments have revealed that some species find their way back to the nest by learning the characteristics of the landmarks that surround the nest (Tinbergen, 1951). The wasp accomplishes this during an *orientation flight*, which consists of repeatedly circling the sealed nest, apparently to learn its location. When a circle of pinecones is placed around the nest, the wasp circles the nest area and observes the pinecone landmarks. If, after the wasp has gone to hunt, the pinecones are relocated, as diagrammed in Figure 12.17, in a new position away from the nest entrance, the returning wasp will fly to the pinecones even though they now guide her away

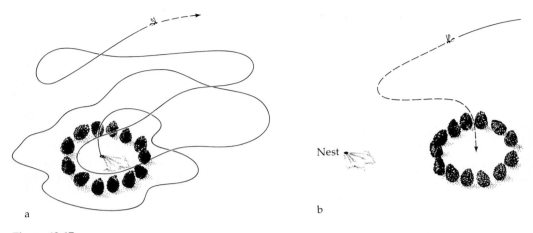

a   b

Figure 12.17
(a) The digger wasp learns the location of her nest using the pinecone landmarks as cues.
(b) When the pinecones are repositioned, the wasp incorrectly returns to the pinecones
and not to the nest. [After Tinbergen, 1951.]

from the nest. The wasp apparently relies on acquired cues to locate the
unique position of each of the individual nests that she provisions.

Her task also requires that she remember which caterpillars go with
which nests. The larvae are developing at different rates (because the
eggs were layed at slightly different times), and each nest therefore has a
unique food requirement. The female gauges the number and size of the
caterpillars needed on the basis of the size of her larvae. She must, however, be able to recall which nest requires a few small caterpillars and
which requires many large ones. How the wasp assesses the food requirements of her larvae reveals another puzzling aspect of her ability to
modify her behavior in response to environmental demands. Research on
members of the genus *Ammophila* has indicated that after each nest has
been constructed and the wasp's offspring housed inside, the female
makes a daily *inspection visit* to each nest. The visit always occurs in the
morning, and the wasp brings no food to the nest at that time. It has been
suggested that during the inspection visit the wasp determines how many
caterpillars are required for each of her larvae that day. Her behavior (the
amount of food she will deposit) is flexible, and depends on the environmental information (how large the larva has become) obtained during the
visit. Interestingly, however, the wasp can only avail herself of environmental input during the inspection visit. If, following her visit, the nests
are opened by experimenters and their contents modified, the wasp will
fail to take this information into account when she returns with the food.
If, for example, a very small larva is replaced by a very large one, the
wasp's behavior will conform to the situation she encountered during the

inspection visit (small larva) and not that immediately before her (large larva). She will place in the nest only enough food to sustain the smaller offspring. Even if the larva is completely removed (or if a large larva is replaced by a small one) the wasp will provision according to the conditions that prevailed during the inspection visit. However, if the larvae are switched or removed *prior to* the daily inspection visit, no matter what had transpired on the previous day, the female will adjust the day's provisioning accordingly. After the visit, she will again be incapable (for that day) of altering her behavior in keeping with environmental change. The wasp is, therefore, capable of a kind of learning, but the nature and timing of that behavior change is rigidly governed by other factors. In a sense, the nature of the wasp's behavior is similar to the imprinting-like, time-dependent perceptual learning described in Chapter 10.

Host Selection by Parasites   Many insects are *parasitic*. The energy (usually in the form of nutrition) for all or some portion of their development is provided at the expense of a *host organism* on which the insect lives for some period of time. Species of wasp of the family Ichneumonidae are typical parasitic insects. The adult female locates a suitable host species (often another insect) and deposits her own eggs within the larva of the host. The egg-laying process is called *oviposition*, and all the nutrients required for the development of the wasp egg, larva, and pupa are provided by the tissues of the host's body. In effect, the organism ultimately produced emerges in adult form as a wasp, having effectively "eaten" its host. When the parasite emerges as a reproductively mature adult, it then itself proceeds to locate a member of the host species within which to oviposit its own eggs. Among the prerequisites for successful parasitism are the location of the host's habitat and the identification of an individual host with that habitat. The early work of Thorpe and Jones (1937) is suggestive of the importance of learning mechanisms in *host selection* mediated by olfactory stimulation. If the parasite is reared on a host with a particular odor, the parasite will respond positively to the odor of that host even if the host is an unnatural one (one on which the parasite is not normally found). For the parasite, an initially neutral odor has become a very significant one as the result of experience.

More recently, Taylor (1974) has postulated that in some parasitic wasps the orienting stages during which the parasite locates a host involve learning. The bulk of the evidence suggests that many insect parasites locate their hosts by odor; host selection may therefore represent a process akin to olfactory conditioning. In more heterogeneous environments (where a small host may be difficult to find) the parasite may identify the presence of some relevant cues, such as the occurrence of a particular kind of food, as indicative of the type of microhabitat the host is likely to inhabit.

A particular adult wasp may oviposit numerous eggs during her life.

Taylor has assumed that the probability of oviposition occurring under certain conditions increases with the number of previously successful ovipositions. During such experiences the wasp gradually learns to associate particular environmental cues and particular odors with the presence of the host—that is, with successful oviposition. In Taylor's laboratory analogue of the natural setting, the host larvae were placed separately in plastic petri dishes covered with silk cloth. The larvae were positioned in the dish beneath the cloth, but within reach of the wasp's extended ovipositor. Several dishes were placed together in transparent plexiglass boxes (representative of the larvae's microhabitat); only some dishes actually contained larvae. The wasp's task, therefore, was to locate the dish containing the larva, and then, upon finding the larva, to probe through the cloth with her ovipositor and deposit her eggs in the host. Several aspects of the parasite's behavior in this situation were suggestive of learning. Typically, the wasps would engage in an extended period of "casual" hunting, with little time spent on the petri dishes and very few probings of the cloth. Suddenly, the wasp would shift quite rapidly to a period of more intense hunting during which most of the animal's time was spent searching and probing the silk cloth. "The end of the early casual period of hunting and the beginning of the intense period were marked by the first time the wasp pierced a larva with its ovipositor" (Taylor, 1974, p. 98). Taylor has assumed that following the first successful oviposition the parasite was able to respond selectively to the odor of the larva.

To demonstrate conclusively the importance of the association between successful oviposition and the establishment of the host odor as a reliable cue for the parasitic response, Taylor conducted a series of experiments in which two different groups of wasps were exposed to larvae positioned in the petri dishes so as to be either within reach or out of reach of the wasp's ovipositor. In both situations, of course, the larva is out of sight (beneath the cloth), but its odor easily reaches the surface of the cloth. If simple olfactory reception of the appropriate odor were sufficient to elicit oviposition repeatedly, without benefit of an association between successful oviposition and odor, then both groups should attempt to oviposit equally often. However, if an increase in the rate of attempted ovipositions is dependent upon successful piercing of the larva, then only those for whom the larva is within reach should exhibit frequent oviposition. In fact, this result was observed. Wasps given the opportunity to penetrate larvae (and therefore to associate odor cues with the act of successful oviposition) spent significantly more time on the silk cloth and probed through the cloth significantly more frequently. Continued successful host selection in parasitic insects appears, therefore, in this species to depend on prior associative experience. Other interpretations of the data are, however, possible. A single penetration of the host larva might, for example, release the occurrence of several subsequent ovipositions with no involvement by olfactory cues. To eliminate this alternative explanation, the olfactory mechanisms of the wasp might be modified such that no odor cues could be received. Under these conditions if learning were involved a single penetration of the host should fail to produce the "intense hunting" described by Taylor. However, if one penetration were to initiate a sequence of subsequent penetrations independently of olfactory experience, we would have to conclude that association of successful oviposition with olfactory cues plays no part in host selection. The results of such an experiment would permit firmer conclusions regarding the importance of learning mechanisms in host selection.

Honeybee Foraging   Among the most complete investigations of insect learning under natural circumstances are the studies of the foraging behavior of honeybees. The three castes of the complex honeybee social organization are pictured in Figure 12.18. The bees' use of a dance language as the means by which the location of a distant food source is communicated to other members of the hive, is well known (von Frisch, 1967). Foraging "scout" bees (workers) return to the hive from a foraging trip and perform a sophisticated dance inside the dark hive on the vertical surface of the comb. Tactile, olfactory, and auditory signals are there communicated to "recruits" who gain information regarding the distance and direction of the food with respect to the hive. With this combination of information, recruits locate the food and return to the hive to dance the news of their successful foraging venture to still more recruits. Because of this communicative process the number of bees arriving at a food source per unit time becomes much greater than would be expected if the bees were locating the food independently of one another. Recent investigations have revealed that honeybee foraging involves extremely well-developed sensory abilities, especially in the visual, olfactory, and temporal modalities (honeybees are even sensitive to the force of earth's magnetic field), as well as unusually sophisticated learning mechanisms.

Of the wonders of the dance, E. O. Wilson (1971) writes: "In one feature alone, the waggle dance, the species comes closest to standing truly apart from all other insects. The dance is a ritualized reenactment of the

  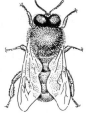

Figure 12.18
Members of the worker (a), queen (b), and drone (c) castes of honeybee society. [Redrawn with permission of Macmillan Publishing Co., Inc., from *Invertebrate zoology*, 2nd ed., by R. W. Hegner and J. G. Engemann. Copyright © 1968 by Macmillan Publishing Co., Inc.]

a   b   c

outward flight to food or new nest sites; it is performed within the nest and somehow understood by other workers in the colony, which are then, and this must be counted as the remarkable part, able to translate it back into an actual unrehearsed flight of their own" (p. 94). After describing the dance, we will restrict ourselves to an analysis of the involvement of learning in the honeybee's foraging behavior.

The form of the dance differs according to the distance of the food from the hive. If the food is near the hive, the scout performs the *round dance*, diagramed in Figure 12.19a. Only distance, no directional information, is conveyed by the round dance. If the food source is farther than about 100 meters from the hive, the returning scout performs the more complex *waggle dance*, seen in Figure 12.19b. The waggle dance is composed of the straight *waggle run* and the circular *return*. During the waggle run the recruits' antennae are in direct tactile contact with the body of the dancer, who is known to emit repeated bursts of sound. All forms of the dance are, of course, performed in the dark, on the vertical surface of the comb.

Unlike the round dance, the waggle dance conveys directional information as well as information about distance. While foraging, the scout somehow assesses the angle between the food source and the sun as measured at the hive. This angle conveys the direction of the food with respect to the sun. Inside the dark hive an equivalent angle (and, therefore, the direction of the food) is represented in the dance by the angle between the straight waggle run and the upward vertical. The means by which the dance communicates direction is diagramed in Figure 12.20. Distance is conveyed in part by the character of the waggle. The slower the waggle, the more distant the food source. With this information, the recruits emerge from the hive and eventually fly toward the food source,

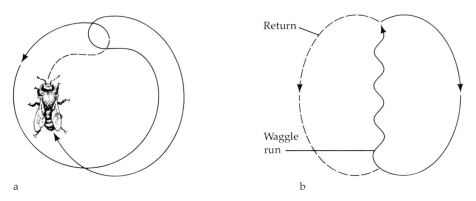

a   b

Figure 12.19
Dance patterns of the honeybee. (a) Round dance. (b) Waggle dance. [After K. von Frisch, *Biology,* translated by J. Oppenheimer. Copyright © 1964 by Bayerischer Schulbuch-Verlag. Redrawn by permission of Harper & Row, Publishers, Inc.]

presumably having "translated" the message from the original tactile and auditory modalities into the visual world outside.

The foraging range of the honeybee may be rather large. Moreover, scout bees may engage in foraging throughout much of the day, going back and forth to the hive several times over extended periods. The position of the sun—the bee's directional referent—is, however changing with time. In order to maintain a constant direction, the bee must have some kind of time-keeping mechanism that allows it to account for the changing position of the sun. In fact, the bee's sense of time is known to be exceptionally acute, and laboratory research has indicated that scouts learn to go to a particular food source at a particular time of day. They then remember on subsequent days at what time a visit to that food source will yield the greatest benefit. Experimental training consists of

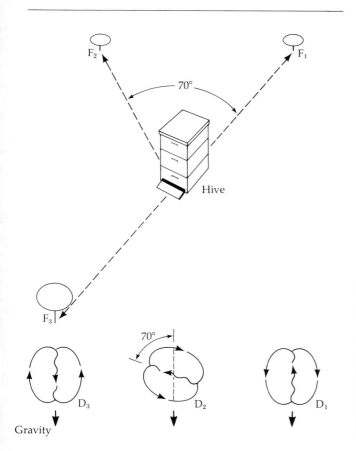

Figure 12.20
The information contained in the waggle dance. The angle between the direction of the sun and the food (F) is represented in the dance (D) by the angle between gravity and the waggle run. Food located at a 70-degree angle from the sun (F_2) is indicated by a 70-degree angle between gravity and the waggle run (D_2). [Illustration is reproduced from *The Evolution of Behavior* by Jerram L. Brown, with the permission of W. W. Norton & Company, Inc. Copyright © 1975 by W. W. Norton & Company, Inc.]

simply presenting food (sugar water) repeatedly at the same time each day; thereafter, even with the food dish continuously available, the bees habitually visit the food source predominantly at the training time. Most errors occur in the direction of anticipating the training time by as little as one hour. This ability appears to be based on the bee's internally regulated 24-hour timing cycle. Attempts to train temporal cycles other than 24 hours (for example, 19 or 48 hours) are usually unsuccessful. Flowers themselves exhibit regular daily rhythms of nectar secretion (the bee's natural food). Moreover, different flowers secrete at different times of the day. It would therefore be extremely efficient for the bees to incorporate their experience with this periodicity into their foraging habits; they only take the time and energy to visit an area at that time when the flowers are producing the most food. In fact, research indicates that honeybees are capable of maintaining as many as five different learned foraging rhythms simultaneously, each associated with a different food source. Even after food is no longer presented, the bees will continue to visit the appropriate location at the appropriate time for as long as six days. More recent experiments (reviewed in Koltermann, 1974) have found that if the light–dark schedule of trained bees is shifted and the bees are therefore set forward or backward in time, the bees' site-specific learned foraging rhythms will adjust to the new time within three days.

The bee's visual learning abilities are equally well suited to the foraging task. In experiments demonstrating these abilities, freely flying bees are fed sugar water on one of three glass disks, which can be illuminated from below with colored lights. During training the honeybees' feeding responses are reinforced with sugar water at the center disk, which is illuminated with a particular color. During testing the center disk is dark and no food is presented. Side dishes are, however, illuminated by two different colors, one of which is similar to or the same as the training color. Under these conditions, after as few as four or five reinforcements during training (the bees return to the hive after each ingestion episode and then come back for another), the bees direct over 80 percent of their foraging responses during testing to the color reinforced during training. Interestingly, learning proceeds more rapidly when certain colors are associated with reward. After only one reinforced trial, for example, bees choose the color violet on over 85 percent of the test trials. Bluish-green was at the same time very difficult to learn, while blue was learned readily (though not as rapidly as violet). Menzel, Erber, and Mashur (1974) point out that those colors which are most easily learned parallel nicely the bees' foraging habits. "The largest number of insect-visited flowers are violet, blue, or 'bee-purple.'[6] . . . [T]he learning system has phylogenetically adapted to the colouration of the nectar-bearing blos-

---

[6]Bee-purple is a color that bees respond to but that we do not see.

soms. This 'phylogenetic pre-learning' enables the bee to learn more quickly those colours which are more likely to be good signals" (p. 201). The bee's memory for such visual cues is outstanding. Bees tested after only three rewards still retain the experiences after two weeks. Moreover, colors that sustain more rapid learning, for example, violet, are retained longer than others.

Considerable controversy has raged in the recent literature regarding the relative importance of the dance versus acquired olfactory cues in the communication of foraging sites within the hive. Traditional accounts maintain that the dance itself (as described above) transmits precise information about the direction and distance of food (von Frisch, 1967). More recently, experiments by Wenner and Johnson (1967, 1969) have suggested that recruits are guided to the source of food by scents associated with the receipt of food in the hive. Scouts returning to the hive bring with them both the odor of the food itself (nectar scent) and the odor of the location (flower scent) where the food was obtained. These odor complexes, which may include the attracting smell of bees of the same hive, then serve as cues by which the recruits first search for and then locate the specific food source. Wenner and Johnson have formulated an *olfactory hypothesis* that maintains that recruitment is entirely determined by the acquisition of olfactory discriminations. These suggestions are supported by observational data (Wenner and Johnson, 1967) indicating that the search time that precedes arrival at the food source can be as long as 10 minutes, even though the direct flight time may be as little as 30 seconds. If no search were required (as would be the cast with dance communication), latency to arrival should more closely approximate the direct flight time. Similar observations indicate that, on leaving the hive, recruits fly a considerable distance downwind prior to the initiation of a search. This maneuver presumably allows the workers to sample the "odor landscape" and hence more efficiently locate that odor complex which serves as a cue for food.

Experimental work, too, suggests that the olfactory hypothesis may have some validity. When bees are placed in a situation in which unscented sucrose is available at an unscented site, recruitment rates (the number of new bees arriving per unit time) are very low. Under such conditions 10 foragers have been observed to recruit only 5 bees from a colony of 60,000 individuals. Much higher recruitment rates would be expected if the dance were sufficient to indicate the precise location of food.

Data collected on recruitment rates on successive days indicate that odor may accumulate in the hive across days. Odors introduced into the hive on one day might therefore affect foraging patterns on successive days. Working on the assumption of odor accumulation across days, Wenner, Wells, and Johnson (1969) designed an experiment to directly compare predictions generated by the dance language versus the olfactory hypotheses. A standard commercial bee hive was positioned in the field 280 meters distant from each of two experimental feeding sites. A third site, the control site, was located between the two experimental sites at a distance of about 200 meters from the hive. The presence of food at each of the three sites varied across days. Typically, on days in which both experimental feeding sites were stocked with a clover-scented sucrose solution, the control site was empty. On days when the control site was stocked with clover-scented sucrose, both experimental sites were unstocked. No foragers or recruits were ever allowed to return to the hive from the control site. The experimenters reasoned that odor would accumulate in the hive on days when scented food was available at experimental sites. Returning foragers would bring odor cues to the hives; odor cues would then guide scouts to one of the two sites. No foragers had ever returned from the unscented control site, and no dance information was, therefore, available for that site. If recruits were able to locate the control site, it must be on the basis of the accumulation of the previous day's olfactory cues, and not on the basis of the distance and directional information contained in the dance. Results indicated that on days during which the control site alone was stocked substantial numbers of recruits were collected at this site. These data suggest that the bees are capable of making a complex olfactory association, which aids them in the location of a rich food source. The authors concluded that even though the returning foragers continued to dance in the hive, "the presence of this information in the hive does not appear to contribute to the ecology of foraging or recruitment" (Wenner, Wells, and Johnson, 1969, p. 85).

The literature contains numerous conflicting reports on the relative importance of the dance. Gould (1975), for example, reports results of experiments in which dance information provided inaccurate accounts of food locale. Foraging sites were, however, scented so that odor cues provided accurate information with which to locate a prime food source. In this situation bees in fact behaved in accord with the inaccurate information contained in the dance. While no definite conclusion has been reached regarding the primary mode of foraging communication in honeybees, many investigators have concluded that both systems can be used. Factors governing the use of one system or another are defined by the ecological parameters prevailing in a given situation (an excellent attempt at resolving the controversy can be found in Gould, 1975). For our purposes, however, one result of the comparison of these two hypotheses has been the clear documentation of the learning abilities of the honeybees. Whether or not olfactory cues are of predominant importance in foraging, it is clear that the bees are capable of the formation of complex olfactory associations, which produce significant sustained alterations in behavior. We can further assume that visual and temporal cues are also employed in the regulation of foraging, making the amount of information on which the behavior change may be based very large indeed—perhaps sufficiently large for the bee's performance to be regarded as indicative of complex learning.

IV Integration

13 Toward an Integrated Approach to Behavior

In the foregoing chapters we have presented two distinct approaches to the phenomena of learning: the ontogenetic and the phylogenetic. Behavioral flexibility develops within the lifetime of each individual; yet its functional bases—and hence its limits—are determined by the phylogenetic history of the species. An understanding of behavior change therefore requires a combination of both approaches. Nonetheless, experimental and theoretical analyses within each realm have proceeded largely independently of work in the other. While some exchange of techniques has occurred, the two approaches have remained conceptually distinct. This separation of behavioral realms parallels, and to some extent results from, the long-standing rift between behavioral psychology and traditional behavioral biology (ethology). In their early years the two disciplines took opposite positions both in identifying the relevant questions to ask of behavior and in designating the procedures best suited to studying those questions. The ethologists from the start viewed behavior as a biological process and focused largely on the category of behavior for which this emphasis seemed most warranted: species-specific behavior sequences. (See Chapter 9.) Psychologists mistrusted the ethologists' reliance on what at the time were vague hereditary explanations, as well as their predominant use of observational techniques. Psychologists, by contrast, focused primarily on the laboratory-based analysis of behavior change. The ethologists, in turn, mistrusted the psychologists' neglect of molar biological concepts, their predominant focus on learning as the key to all behavior, and their almost exclusive use of laboratory techniques. As Alexander (1975) points out, neither group apparently understood how theoretical evolutionary biology could be brought to bear on an understanding of behavior.[1] Perhaps a more serious criticism concerns the inability of most members of either group to fully appreciate the importance of both approaches to behavior.

More recently, communication between the two disciplines has become more congenial, new schools of research have emerged that base their investigations of behavior on a complementary approach, and the opportunity for integration has become greater than ever before. The thesis presented here assumes that a complete understanding of the phenomena of behavior must be predicated upon the substantive and methodological integration of the ontogenetic and phylogenetic views. The conceptualizations of one approach must be consistent with and complement those of the other. Note that we are *not* advocating the conceptual reduction of one approach to the other; rather, what is needed is an integration in which the development of concepts in each area takes into account relevant principles of the other. Such efforts may result in the statement of general laws of learning that treat behavior change as a biological process, governed, as any other, by the principles of organic evolution. Learning must, however, be seen as a process whose function may represent a degree of flexibility unparalleled in any other biological process. Learning, in fact, functions to generate individual variability in behavior. Behavioral flexibility therefore defines a distinct level of analysis —analysis that focuses on mechanisms subject to systematic ontogenetic rules. These rules may take the form of functional relationships in which specific parameters are defined by the immediate situation; they represent the factors (such as schedules of reinforcement) responsible for the development and maintenance of behavior within the organism's lifetime.

In the remainder of this chapter we shall discuss the steps necessary to bring about an integration of the two approaches in both the conceptual and methodological realms. We shall then review representative areas in which an attempt at integration is in progress and close with a discussion of the role of general laws of learning. Because even partial integration is far from complete and certainly rests with the future, much of what we present must be regarded not as a product but as a promise. The first step in the realization of this promise, however, requires a reconsideration of an issue that has traditionally been central to the division between ethology and psychology: the nature–nurture question.

---

[1] In fairness, it should be pointed out that both movements were conceived at a time when evolutionary biology was in its infancy: a time when any extension to the complex questions of behavior would likely have been premature.

THE NATURE–NURTURE QUESTION

Peter Marler has asserted that the "most urgent" need facing students of behavior remains an understanding of how genetic and environmental factors interact in learning. He states that "no organism can properly be thought of as a *tabula rasa*, approaching learning tasks as a totally free agent, without constraints. As a first consideration, learning cannot take place without a certain kind of machinery, and that machinery cannot develop without genetic guidance" (1975, p. 254). Marler points out, however, that the impact of genetic factors on learning goes well beyond the simple "provision of the basic machinery." To paraphrase the oft-stated ethological position on learning, "species seem to possess more or less strictly localized dispositions to learn." That is, the character of the learning process will be defined by the particular response sequence in which flexibility is required. Further, the need for flexibility will depend on the function of the behavior in question. Hence localized dispositions to learn are defined by and imposed through environmental demands for behavioral flexibility.

The position represented here essentially requires that we again address the ancient *nature–nurture* question. The development of a complementary relationship between ontogeny and phylogeny in the analysis of behavior must be based on an enlightened statement of this age-old issue. The traditional approach to the question of the relative importance of learned versus innate factors in behavior asks whether a given behavior should be classed as learned *or* innate. Increased understanding of molecular genetics and embryology has made it clear that, phrased in this way—in terms of heredity *versus* environment—the question is inappropriate, even meaningless. Appropriately phrased, the question becomes a *developmental* one. Genes are said to provide a "blueprint" for development, organizing the complex of processes that will ultimately enable the organism to engage in a specific response. The genetic blueprint, however, must be realized in an actual environment. The development of behavior, including learned behavior, requires the interaction of environmental and genetic inputs at every stage of the developmental process. How then can we rephrase the nature–nurture question to emphasize the necessity of both types of input? Clearly, the either–or approach is futile. It is tempting to speculate, instead, that the differences between those behaviors traditionally termed innate and those traditionally termed learned are developmental ones centering on how much *flexibility* is possible during development. Behavior sequences differ in the extent of the *range of environmental inputs* consistent with normal development. All behaviors may be located on a continuum of developmental flexibility according to the extent of the range of acceptable environmental inputs. Those behaviors traditionally referred to as innate represent one extreme on this continuum (the inflexible end); those behaviors traditionally referred to as learned occur at the other extreme (the flexible end). Neither extreme may be representative of the bulk of behavior. The behaviors of most organisms very likely occupy intermediate positions on the continuum of developmental flexibility.

In those developmental programs termed "open" (Mayr, 1974), any one of a number of environmental inputs is acceptable at each developmental stage. Development thus allows a degree of flexibility that may continue throughout the organism's life, as in learning. The developed behavior will appear variable and flexible to the extent that different specific inputs have occurred for different individuals. In "closed" developmental programs (Mayr, 1974), only one or a few environmental inputs are consistent with the completion of normal development. Flexibility in development is minimal, and the behavior will therefore appear quite stereotyped; development will by necessity have occurred in very similar ways across individuals.

The nature–nurture question can now be rephrased in terms of *developmental flexibility*. How great is the range of environmental inputs consistent with normal development? If that range is great, if any one of a number of environmental inputs will result in a functional final product, then we must look to nurture to explain differences in behavior. If the range of acceptable environmental inputs is very small, phenotype will be highly correlated with genotype, and a focus on differences in nature (the genes themselves) is required to explain differences in behavior. Viewed in this way, the nature–nurture question refers to a continuum of differing developmental programs, the critical dimension being the range of acceptable environmental inputs. For *any* behavior, both genetic and environmental inputs are essential. Given this view, learned behaviors represent substantial developmental flexibility. Any of a number of acceptable environmental inputs are possible, and the period of flexibility *may* extend throughout the organism's life.

LABORATORY AND FIELD

Much of the literature described in the earlier chapters of this book has been generated by one of two rather distinct methodological strategies. One, the *experimental method*, has typically been emphasized by researchers in psychology. This method involves the rigorous regulation and control by the experimenter of the factors assumed to be most relevant to behavior change. *Control* is the key to the experimental method. By controlling several relevant variables while manipulating others, the experimenter can determine precisely the impact of each on the behavior in question. This type of explicit reliance on manipulation and control can often be achieved only in the laboratory, and this approach therefore frequently necessitates a drastic simplification of the animal's natural situation. It is very difficult to duplicate nature in the lab. Relevant features of the natural habitat may, for example, not be present at all; similarly, other members of the species, normally a part of the social community in which the behavior occurs, are typically absent, as are the members of other species (for example, predators, prey, and competitors), which may constitute a behaviorally important part of the biological community. It is, however, often only at the expense of simplification that the benefits of precise experimental control can be achieved. Simplification is to some degree inherent in the experimental method. Moreover, we can assume that the more complex the phenomenon under investigation, the greater the level of simplification implied in laboratory testing.

The second methodological strategy, more frequently employed by researchers in behavioral biology, minimizes, and in the extreme eliminates, manipulation and control. This is done in an effort to observe as precisely as possible how and when the behavior of interest occurs under natural circumstances. No attempt is made to control the situation, and it is assumed that a complete account of the behavior as it naturally occurs is required *before* the investigator can judge which of the many factors at work warrants more controlled investigation in the laboratory. If the situation is so complex that numerous factors interact in a manner that cannot be represented in the laboratory, such *field research* may be the investigator's only recourse. For example, the "cultural," that is, learned, factors important in determining the idiosyncratic social organization of many species of baboons would be almost impossible to duplicate in the laboratory. These animals range over great distances and may spend prolonged periods of time on terrain such as cliffs that cannot be represented in a circumscribed area. Capturing and confining only one or a few animals may (by virtue of the reduced number of individuals) destroy the very social situation in which the flexibility of interest is manifest. Beyond such practical considerations, if an evolutionary perspective is assumed to be appropriate for an understanding of behavior, field observations describe the circumstances that determine the phylogenetic development of behavior. These circumstances are the forces of natural selection. To deny or underestimate the importance of field research "would mean that the behavioral sciences would forever forsake any hope of knowing whether their most powerful theories have any relevance to the world of behavior outside the laboratory" (Altmann, 1974, p. 229).

As our earlier statements suggest, in the behavioral sciences these two approaches have traditionally been at odds with one another. Psychologists, for example, justly point out that analyses of observational samples of animal behavior in the field may involve important methodological deficiencies. The sample is inevitably an incomplete or partial record of the total behavioral stream, and the observer has no means for conclusively identifying the most definitive aspects of the situation. The control inherent in the experimental method is lacking in observational sampling. Proponents of field research methods, on the other hand, point out the dangers of simplification often associated with an exclusively experimental approach. In fact, both criticisms are valid, and neither approach *by itself* can provide a complete understanding of behavioral flexibility. Rather than being adversaries, therefore, these two approaches *must complement one another* if the behavioral sciences are ever to arrive at complete explanations of behavior. Fortunately, the weaknesses of one method are the strengths of the other; the problems of each become less critical through systematic integration with the other. For the psychologist, usually trained in the use of the experimental method, the important question becomes, "If conclusive demonstration of the operation of critical factors and reliable identification of controlling variables require explicit manipulation, what is the value of observational analyses?"

The Problem of Validity

Jeanne Altmann (1974) has assessed the relative strengths and weaknesses of *manipulative* versus *nonmanipulative* research. Note her choice of the terms "manipulative" and "nonmanipulative" rather than the more familiar usages "controlled" and "observational." The newer usage conveys the understanding that control is not lacking in the nonmanipulative (observational) situation. Rather, naturally occurring controlling variables, not artificially manipulated factors, determine the course of behavior. In either case, control is inherent in the situation; manipulative procedures simply facilitate the task of *identifying* the controlling variables. Altmann's comparison of the relative virtues of manipulative versus nonmanipulative methods centers on the degree of internal versus external *validity* associated with each. "The primary function of research design is to maximize the validity of the conclusions, that is, to minimize the number of plausible alternative hypotheses that are consistent with the data" (p. 229). *Internal validity* refers to the validity of conclusions drawn about changes in the behavior of the sample of organisms on which the investigation was conducted. *External validity,* on the other hand, refers to the validity of generalizations from these internally valid conclusions (drawn on the basis of sample results) to some other population or situation. Both types of validity are essential to the overall validity of any conclusion. If the investigator cannot eliminate alternative explanations of the behavior manifest in the sample under study (low internal validity), generalization to other situations will be irrelevant. If, however, a conclusion with high internal validity does not extend to the behavior of individuals beyond the immediate sample (low external validity), the result will not aid in the explanation of any naturally occurring behavioral phenomenon.

Because of the rigorous control exercised in manipulative research, this methodology can generate conclusions high in internal validity. When this is done at the cost of the extreme simplification of a very complex phenomenon, however, a substantial degree of external validity may be sacrificed even though internal validity may be high. Natural selection is maintained by the natural environment. For purposes of phylogenetic analysis, therefore, external validity is defined by the naturally occurring conditions. Because nonmanipulative research is conducted in the natural setting that governs the development of the behavior in question, this type of research may yield conclusions potentially high in external validity. The frequent inability to eliminate alternative hypotheses, however, may render the internal validity of field research quite low. Clearly, both methods have strengths and weaknesses; and in each case the method's weaknesses are unavoidably imposed by its strengths. The strengths and weaknesses of each are, moreover, magnified by the complexity of behavioral phenomena. Especially when viewed as an important component of a biological system, molar behavior is amazingly complex. In the face of such complexity the risk of oversimplification in the laboratory is a very real one. Many behavioral problems—for example, the social organization of whales—obviously cannot be modeled in the lab. Even where representation is possible, however, because the behavioral phenomena are so complex laboratory analogues of the natural situation will necessarily fall short. Similarly, in the field, enhanced complexity greatly increases the plausibility of alternative hypotheses. The task of eliminating alternative hypotheses becomes correspondingly more difficult. A generally valid explanation of behavior requires that the internal validity of the laboratory be complemented by the external validity of the field.

Methods for Increasing Validity

Recent recognition of the need for a complementary approach has resulted in attempts to minimize the loss of internal validity in the field and to maximize the external validity of the lab. These efforts have involved the construction of more realistic laboratory settings in which the experimenter develops a clear analogue of the natural setting, the use of field experiments in which experimental manipulations are actually performed in the field setting, and the development of observational sampling procedures containing "nonmanipulative controls" (Altmann, 1974) designed to maximize the internal validity of field observation. Among the most promising methods useful in extending greater control to the observation of naturally occurring behavioral phenomena are those that involve the application of *quasi-experimental design* (Campbell and Stanley, 1963; Hills, 1974). Here control is generated by the logic and timing of the comparisons made across naturally occurring groups. Such designs attempt to identify critical variables through the comparison of two or more naturally occurring groups that are similar in most respects but differ substantially along some dimension. Imagine a situation in which a given behavior occurs with very different frequencies or is perhaps absent altogether in one of two or more distinct populations of organisms. Observations suggest a hypothesis about which factors are responsible for the differences between groups. The experimenter then selects groups for comparison on the basis of the presence or absence of the relevant factor. If the behavior of interest is positively correlated with the presence of this factor, but fails to occur in the situation characterized by its absence, the hypothesized importance of this variable achieves a degree of internal validity. The following example should clarify the logic of this technique.

The evolutionary analysis of social organization (sociobiology) assumes that the diversity of societies observed in different species results from differences in the natural environments in which these groups have evolved. Certain conditions should foster the evolution of highly integrated, cohesive societies, while others dictate little or no social interaction among nearby individuals. How might one use observational comparisons to validate the hypothesis that complex social systems have evolved in some species as a function of the impact of particular environmental parameters? David Barash (1974) has selectively observed the social habits of various species of marmots under varying environmental conditions to determine if a relationship exists between specific features of the environment and the type of social organization.

Marmots are a group of medium-sized, coarse-furred rodents classified into several distinct species. By virtue of their close phylogenetic relatedness, the species are quite similar on a number of both behavioral and morphological dimensions. However, one species of the group, the *woodchucks*, exhibit a large amount of *social intolerance*. They are highly aggressive, adults interact socially only to mate, and the young leave the burrow quickly, as soon as they are able to fend for themselves. Beyond the mother–offspring bond, no social organization exists. By contrast, a second species of the group, the *Olympic marmot*, lives a highly social existence. These animals are rarely aggressive, dominance encounters between individuals are rare, and the animals live in organized colonies that allow for a great deal of social interaction among adults. This species is therefore quite socially tolerant. The differences in social organization between these two species are correlated with the type of environment inhabited by each. Olympic marmots live at high elevations where little food is available to rear the young; the young, moreover, must be fed over a prolonged period of time. Woodchucks inhabit lower elevations where food is much more bountiful and more evenly distributed. Barash has suggested that the social tolerance and the complex social organization of the Olympic marmots is necessary to provide sufficient food for the developing young. With less food available, development, and therefore the period of dependency, is prolonged. If the Olympic marmots were aggressively driven from the burrow (as are the woodchucks), they would very likely suffer starvation. Social cohesion allows the young to stay with the maternal group long enough to develop to independence. Any asocial tendencies have succumbed to the need to stay together. The woodchucks need no such social check on aggression (no tolerance) because the abundance of food enables the young to develop quickly. They are, in fact, aggressively driven from the nest far sooner than the Olympic marmots leave of their own accord.

If the negative correlation between social tolerance and the abundance of food is a valid one, marmots living at intermediate elevations, and therefore under conditions of intermediate food abundance, should enjoy intermediate levels of social tolerance. Barash reports that such conditions exist for yet a third species of marmot observed, the moderately social *yellow-bellied marmot*. An even more convincing case could be built if a fourth group were observed living at low elevations but under conditions that (for reasons independent of elevation) make their food scarce. Would their social tolerance approximate that of the nearby woodchuck (also living at low elevations but with abundant food) or that of the similarly impoverished Olympic marmot (living at high elevations)? Barash would predict the latter, and such a demonstration would eliminate the importance of high elevation *per se* as a plausible determinant of the differences in social organization. Observational sampling of the social behavior of such a group would therefore substantially strengthen the internal validity of Barash's hypothesis. With each observation, in the absence of experimental manipulation and on the basis of *observation-selective controls*, internal validity is increased. Manipulative control has been maintained by the natural situation, and the task of the scientist becomes the selection of the appropriate comparisons—those that allow him to extract control in the absence of manipulation.

In the following discussions we will see how various combinations of the field and laboratory procedures discussed here have been applied to the ontogeny of behavioral change. While these efforts are still very much in progress and remain somewhat incomplete, their preliminary results reveal the potential explanatory value of the combined field–laboratory methodology.

LABORATORY ANALOGUES TO NATURAL PHENOMENA

In order to increase the external validity of laboratory studies, one may perform the study in as natural a context as possible, either by bringing the laboratory into the field or by making the laboratory setting sufficiently complex that it mimics the field in certain important ways. In a study that may serve as an example of the first type of strategy, Baum (1974) placed an experimental chamber on the roof of an apartment building. Wild (urban) pigeons could enter the chamber and respond on either of two keys on VI schedules of food reinforcement, much as a trained experimental pigeon does in the laboratory. Baum's data show that birds did enter the chamber and responded in much the same way as the laboratory birds; that is, they matched their rates of responding on the two keys to the rates of reinforcement available on them (a finding replicating research on choice behavior, discussed in Chapter 7).

Multiple Response Environments

The second type of study involves changing the laboratory so that it represents a number of important aspects of the field. How might this be done? Consider, first, that in its natural environment the organism is repeatedly faced with several response alternatives. Activities are distributed among responses required for protection, food acquisition, parental behavior, reproduction, and many others. Time and energy are at a premium, and the organism is often faced with a choice between mutually exclusive responses. Such situations frequently dictate an economy of action in which only the requisite amount of time and energy is devoted to each activity. A male bird actively defending his territory, for example, has less time to devote to feeding his young. Complete neglect of the young might result in either retarded development or starvation. On the other hand, the complete neglect of territorial defense risks a loss of territory and ultimately perhaps vital resources essential for the young. The bird must strike a balance between time spent defending and time spent feeding, such that neither the territory nor the health of the young is placed in jeopardy. The organism must distribute its activities in accord with this balance. Laboratory studies of learning have usually attended to only one type of response at a time. Even studies of choice (Chapter 7) typically utilize equivalent response alternatives and reinforcers. More recently, however, another type of laboratory study, which may have particularly high external validity, has focused on behavior maintained in *multiple response environments*. Such studies utilize experimental chambers far more complex than those described in Chapter 4 and, therefore, presumably more representative of the natural environment. More responses are explicitly available and recorded than is typically the case, and interactions among response categories are accessible to study. Such techniques may reveal principles by which the organism distributes its time and energy among the several activities continuously required of it in the wild.

Kjos (1977), for example, utilizing an apparatus similar to that designed by Kavanau (1969), monitored the following behaviors in each of several mice: running in a running wheel, drinking, eating, nesting, wood-chewing, general activity, and "quiescent behavior." The apparatus was roughly similar in type to that shown in Figure 13.2 in that different activites were available in different areas of the chamber. Several aspects of each response were recorded; thus, for drinking, Kjos monitored the proportion of time spent drinking, the proportion of time spent in the drinking device, the number of discrete drink bursts, and the number of entries into the drinking device. The provision for a variety of responses in extended experimental sessions, including "24-hour sessions" in which the mouse essentially "lives" in the chamber on a daily basis, results in an environment that has much in common with naturally occurring ones. Many possibilities for specific research are evident, including investigation of the temporal distribution of the organism's activities and interactions between activities. Moreover, hypothetical mechanisms governing the maintenance of any one activity will very likely have greater external validity as a result of being assessed in a more natural context.

Kjos was particularly interested in assessing Premack's contention that running could reinforce drinking and eating under certain conditions — that is, when running was more probable. This prediction is a specific case of Premack's principle of reinforcement "reversibility" discussed in Chapter 4: While behaviors that are normally less probable will not reinforce more probable behaviors, if these relative probabilities are altered, for example by deprivation, a reinforcement effect should be obtained. The reversibility principle is plausible from a biological standpoint: If the opportunity to engage in a particular activity is restricted below its naturally occurring rate, and if the activity has biological significance for the organism, then its reinforcing potency should be temporarily enhanced. Kjos found that running reinforced eating or drinking only with difficulty, but that running readily reinforced wood-chewing. In his study the opportunity to run in a running wheel was made contingent on performing the instrumental activity (eating, drinking, or wood-chewing, depending on the condition) until a criterion was satisfied. These results raised two interesting possibilities: (1) that Premack's theory (see Chapter 4) is not generally valid in that reversibility is relative to the particular response sequence in question, and (2) that "unnatural" contingencies such as eating or drinking to run are less susceptible to reinforcement effects than a relatively more natural contingency such as wood-chewing to run. While neither conclusion is strongly supported by Kjos' data,[2] his study

---

[2]The eating and drinking contingencies that had to be satisfied in order to release the running wheel were specified in terms of *time* spent engaged in eating (or drinking), whereas the wood-chewing contingency was specified in terms of *number* of wood-chews. While this would appear to be a minor difference, internal evidence in Kjos' study — available because of the prodigious job of data collection — shows that number was far more sensitive than time to the imposed contingency, even for the eating and drinking conditions in which the contingency was defined in terms of time! Thus the conclusion that wood-chewing was more readily reinforced (than eating or drinking) by running may have been an artifact of the difference in how the various contingencies were specified. Similarly, Premack and his many adherents could argue that his theory was inadequately tested given the insensitivity of the temporal contingency. At the very least, however, Kjos' results set constraints on the generality of Premack's theory.

demonstrates that the multiple response repertoire environment offers a potential bonanza for the study of behavioral principles high in internal and external validity.

It should be clear that any environment is in fact a multiple response environment. Even when the experimenter provides only one explicit response, it is possible to measure additional responses made by the organism. Careful observation and measurement of what the organism does beyond what the experimental situation requires may contribute greatly to our appreciation of the control and organization of behavior. Excellent examples of work focusing on the organism's complete behavioral stream can be found in the research conducted in John Staddon's laboratory at Duke University (for example, Staddon and Simmelhag, 1971; Staddon and Ayres, 1975) and that conducted in Sara Shettleworth's laboratory at the University of Toronto (for example, Shettleworth, 1975, 1978a, 1978b; Anderson and Shettleworth, 1977).

Studies measuring a single activity have repeatedly shown that food delivered periodically on FI schedules results in the typical FI "scallop" (see Chapter 4) of response acceleration prior to reinforcement. Staddon and Simmelhag (1971) extended this finding by showing that a variety of other activities, which they labeled *interim activities*, occur during the early portion of the interfood interval on both response-dependent and response-independent food schedules (FI 12-sec and FT 12-sec schedules) in hungry pigeons. In addition, the response-independent schedule of food delivery (FT 12-sec) generated stereotyped *terminal activities* toward the end of the interfood interval. The activities observed and measured by these authors are shown in Table 13.1. Staddon and Simmelhag were interested in observing complex behavior patterns that might be induced in a context of periodic food deliveries. Figure 13.1 shows the results for a typical pigeon. Note that early in the interval responses R_5 and R_6 occur frequently (these are wing flapping and an orientation toward the wall of the chamber containing the observation window, respectively), whereas R_1 and R_7 (orienting toward the wall containing the food hopper and key-pecking, respectively) become more common later in the interval. Whereas all birds emitted these terminal activities (R_1 and R_7) on the FT 12-sec schedule, the nature of the interim activities varied from bird to bird. One factor was invariant, however: whereas the frequency of some behaviors (the interim activities) peaked early in the interfood interval, R_1 and R_7 (the terminal activities) reached their maximum rate of occurrence just prior to food delivery.

Anderson and Shettleworth (1977) studied the organization of behavior in food-deprived golden hamsters that received food every thirty seconds in both response-dependent and response-independent conditions. The experimenters monitored the hamsters' behavior continuously and recorded each of seventeen behavioral categories. They, too, found that behavior became organized into a class of terminal activities, which in-

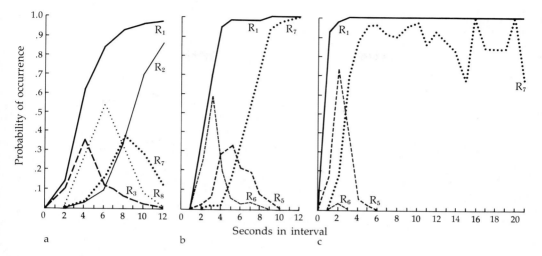

Figure 13.1
Probability of each behavior as a function of postfood time for one bird for all three experimental conditions, averaged over three sessions of stable responding under each condition. Each point gives the probability that a given behavior occurred in that second of postfood time. Data for the response-dependent condition are averaged across 2-sec blocks. Behaviors (R_1) are identified in Table 13.1. (a) Response-dependent FI. (b) Response-independent FI. (c) Response-independent VI. [After J. E. R. Staddon and V. L. Simmelhag, The "superstition" experiment: A re-examination of its implications for the principles of adaptive behavior. *Psychological Review, 78,* 3–43. Copyright © 1971 by the American Psychological Association. Redrawn by permission.]

creased in probability throughout the interfood interval, and a class of interim activities, which were most frequent earlier in the interfood interval. Moreover, the same activities belonged to the same class (terminal or interim) whether food was response-independent or whether it was contingent upon lever-pressing.

These studies show that the periodic delivery of food (whether response-independent or response-dependent) generates a high degree of patterned behavior. The nature of both the terminal and interim activities actually observed depends upon the organism being studied and the response opportunities afforded. For example, the typical terminal response on response-independent schedules includes pecking, for pigeons, gnawing or waiting by the feeder, for rats, and digging and gnawing in the feeder area, for golden hamsters (in response-dependent schedules, of course, the terminal response typically is the one specified by the contingency). These results raise the possibility that interim activities occur when the likelihood of food is low and the animal's behavior may be controlled by other, weaker, reinforcers in the chamber. If explicit alternative reinforcers were indeed available, we might expect their avail-

Table 13.1
Description of Observed Activities [From Staddon and Simmelhag, 1971.]

Response number	Name	Description
R_1	Magazine wall	An orientation response in which the bird's head and body are directed toward the wall containing the magazine.
R_2	Pecking key	Pecking movements directed at the key.
R_3	Pecking floor	Pecking movements directed at the floor.
R_4	Quarter circle	A response in which a count of one quarter circle would be given for turning 90° away from facing the magazine wall, a count of two for turning 180° away, three for 270°, and four for 360°.
R_5	Flapping wings	A vigorous up and down movement of the bird's wings.
R_6	Window wall	An orientation response in which the bird's head and body are directed toward the door of the experimental chamber containing the observation window.
R_7	Pecking	Pecking movements directed toward some point on the magazine wall. This point generally varied between birds and sometimes within the same bird at different times.
R_8	Moving along magazine wall	A side-stepping motion with the breastbone close to the magazine wall, a few steps to the left followed by a few steps to the right, etc. Sometimes accompanied by (a) beak pointed up to ceiling, (b) hopping, (c) flapping wings.
R_9	Preening	Any movement in which the beak comes into contact with the feathers on the bird's body.
R_{10}	Beak to ceiling	The bird moves around the chamber in no particular direction with its beak directed upward touching the ceiling.
R_{11}	Head in magazine	A response in which at least the beak or more of the bird's head is inserted into the magazine opening.
R_{12}	Head movements along magazine wall	The bird faces the magazine wall and moves its head from left to right and/or up and down.

Table 13.1 *(continued)*

Response number	Name	Description
R_{13}	Dizzy motion	A response peculiar to Bird 49 in which the head vibrates rapidly from side to side. It was apparently related to, and alternated with, Pecking (R_7).
R_{14}	Pecking window wall	Pecking movements directed at the door with the observation window in it.
R_{15}	Head to magazine	The bird turns its head toward the magazine.
R_{16}	Locomotion	The bird walks about in no particular direction.

ability to influence the interim activities accordingly. In fact, the large literature on *adjunctive behavior* shows that certain behaviors are highly probable after food is delivered on periodic schedules. Examples of such interim (or adjunctive) behaviors include aggression (Azrin, Hutchinson, and Hake, 1966), if a target pigeon is available, and drinking, if water is available, in a variety of species (see Falk, 1971; Segal and Holloway, 1963).

Staddon and Ayres (1975) provided female rats with response-independent periodic food deliveries in an environment that also contained several competing reinforcers. Specifically, they allowed female rats to locate themselves in any of six areas (a center area and five areas around it, each associated with one of the following: a feeder, a tunnel, observation of another rat, a water bottle, or a running wheel). Animals could engage in three measured behaviors: drinking, being in the running wheel, and being in the tunnel. The apparatus used is illustrated in Figure 13.2. Staddon and Ayres recorded the location of the rats and the behaviors they emitted. Food was delivered on a fixed-time 30-sec (FT 30-sec) schedule. Each of five rats developed a stable pattern of responding after about ten hours. The most typical pattern was excessive drinking early in the interfood interval, an activity known as schedule-induced polydipsia (Segal, 1965), running in the middle of the interval, and loitering by the feeder toward the end of the interval.[3] It will be interesting to determine to what extent these results regarding the sequential and temporal patterning of behavior on schedules of periodic food delivery prove

---

[3]As Anderson and Shettleworth (1977) have noted, the sequential nature of some of Staddon and Ayres' findings (for example, drinking followed by running) may have been enhanced since the activities were performed in different areas (for example, in the water-bottle area and in the running wheel area). In Anderson and Shettleworth, most of the different activities recorded could be performed anywhere. Hence less sequencing and more intermingling of activities tended to occur.

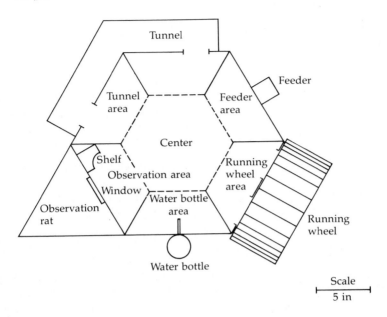

Figure 13.2
Plan view of the apparatus used to study multiple responses in female rats. Dashed lines show area boundaries. [After Staddon and Ayres, 1975.]

to have appreciable external validity. It is our expectation that the use of a multiple-response environment enhances this likelihood, since it simulates field conditions in important ways. Certainly in our own lives many significant events occur periodically and do so while a substantial array of additional activities are available.

With multiple responses available in relatively larger enclosures, the organism's environment more closely resembles the natural environment of the species. By studying the effects of reinforcement and punishment in such an environment the experimenter enhances the likelihood that his findings will have external validity without sacrificing internal validity. In addition, the study of multiple responses permits analysis of how an organism's total behavioral repertoire is organized. Shettleworth (1975) has noted that:

> when hungry hamsters are reinforced with food for engaging in various responses, some activities (digging, rearing, scrabbling, bar pressing) soon increase to high levels, while others (face washing, scratching with a hind leg, scent marking) are affected little if at all. Does this group of activities parallel anything in the normal organization of a hamster's behavior? For example, are the readily conditionable activities exploratory behaviors or the things a hamster does when hungry or expecting food? Further, if readily conditionable responses do belong to a definite system of behavior, does

this fact help us to understand why these activities are readily modified by reinforcement while those in another system are not? [Shettleworth, 1975, p. 57]

Shettleworth (1975, 1978a) has used the multiple-response environment to assess how the frequency of various activities is influenced by the effects of reinforcement and punishment. In these studies she examined the effects of reinforcing each of several activities ("action patterns" in her terminology) with food and punishing three of the same activities with mild electric shock. One activity, *scrabbling*, consisted of scraping against a wall with fore paws while standing erect. Scrabbling proved to be readily susceptible to the effect of reinforcement and punishment. However, a second activity, *open rearing* (standing on hind legs with fore paws off walls and floors), was successfully reinforced with food but was less readily suppressed with electric shock. Finally, the third activity, *face washing*, was readily suppressed with punishment but only modestly enhanced with reinforcement. Shettleworth's work suggests that the responses most readily reinforced by food are not necessarily those that are most readily punished by electric shock. These findings support the more general conclusion that different activities may be differentially sensitive to the effects of different reinforcers and punishers. With respect to aversive stimuli, of course, we noted in Chapters 8 and 10, and elsewhere, that different punishers will be differentially effective with different responses (see also Walters and Herring, 1978).

Shettleworth's research also raises the possibility that Pavlovian conditioning may help account for the differential effects of food reinforcement and electric shock on the activities of golden hamsters. Specifically, it may be possible to predict which activity will be readily reinforced with food and which readily punished with electric shock by first ascertaining the effects of Pavlovian conditional stimuli (CS) for food or shock on these activities. More generally, activities that are facilitated by a CS for food should be readily reinforced with food and vice versa. Similarly, an activity readily suppressed by electric shock should be inhibited by a CS for shock and vice versa. For example, on the basis of the results just described, scrabbling and open rearing, which were readily reinforced with food, should also be facilitated by a food CS (that is, a stimulus previously paired with food). Shettleworth (1978b), however, found only a partial correspondence between the results of contingent reinforcement and Pavlovian conditioning tests. Whereas open rearing was facilitated by a food CS, scrabbling actually decreased. Thus, as Shettleworth concludes, "The results of Pavlovian conditioning procedures may not unambiguously predict what . . . behaviors will be most readily modified by instrumental training with a given reinforcer" (p. 152).

This demonstration of an incomplete correspondence between the results of the instrumental and classical conditioning tests points to the care that must be taken (and was taken by Shettleworth) before generalizing the implications of research across different behavioral contexts. Recall that we made a similar point in Chapter 8 when discussing the role of species-specific defense reactions (SSDR's) in avoidance conditioning. Responses that are highly probable in the presence of a particular UCS (such as shock) may be more rapidly acquired than those that are less probable. In order to assess this, however, it is necessary to conduct careful parametric work in which the probabilities of various responses to a given UCS are determined independently of testing for the trainability of these responses in avoidance conditioning. The results from Shettleworth's laboratory underscore this cautionary note.

Foraging

The economy of action referred to earlier has implications for the distribution of responses within a behavioral category as well. Those responses of a given type that are most efficient will tend to be the most frequent. When discussing foraging behavior, we pointed out that one model of learned predation has stipulated that predators learn to concentrate their hunting activities in the most profitable areas—that is, those where prey density is highest or where preferred prey are most abundant and accessible. According to this model (Chapter 10) the predator samples various areas and learns to hunt in the area yielding the greatest gustatory gain, thereby maximizing efficiency. As we pointed out, this behavior may be viewed as a natural analogue to time and response matching found in laboratory studies of choice (Chapter 7). The analogy may be carried further by considering recent work by Krebs, Erichsen, Webber, and Charnov (1977) on prey selection in the great titbird.

   Krebs et al. (1977) investigated the great tit's preference for two prey types, which they designated profitable and unprofitable prey (the profitable prey consisted of mealworm segments twice as large as the unprofitable ones). The obvious analogue in the operant conditioning laboratory is the study of reinforcer amount. Here, a subject's choice of either of two reinforcer amounts has been studied typically with concurrent VI schedules, which provide equal rates of reinforcement but different reinforcer durations (Chapter 7). We would expect the subject to choose the larger amount, distributing its choice responses so that the ratio of choice responses is something less than the ratio of amounts. The choice proportion obtained might also be a function of reinforcement density: with short VI's (high density of reinforcement) the choice proportions might exceed matching and even become exclusive for the larger reinforcer (with sufficiently short VI's the subject can maximize its amount of reinforcement per unit time by responding only on the VI leading to the larger reinforcer); with long VI's (low density of reinforcement) the organism might become relatively indifferent to the two reinforcers (since with long VI's the organism is at a great temporal distance from reinforcement, receipt of either amount should be highly reinforcing; moreover, the subject now maximizes its amount of reinforcement per unit time by responding on both VI's). Similar predictions are generated by Charnov's (1976) optimal foraging model, which was tested by Krebs et al. (1977).

The actual procedure employed by Krebs et al. did not involve concurrent VI schedules but instead presented the subjects with the two prey types sequentially on a moving belt. The density of prey on the moving belt was varied across conditions. Thus in one condition the encounter rate with each prey was 0.025 prey per second; in another condition the encounter rate was 0.15 prey per second for each reinforcer. When the encounter rate with both prey types was low (equivalent to a low density of reinforcement in the choice analogue) the great tits were not selective. With higher encounter rates, however, overmatching was found—that is, the birds became highly selective. These results were thus consistent with the predictions generated by both the optimal foraging model and by operant work on choice. The findings of Krebs et al. (1977) have also been confirmed in a field study undertaken by Davies (1977). He found that the spotted flycatcher would feed much more on large prey when prey was abundant than when prey was relatively scarce.

A related question critical to an understanding of foraging concerns, not which prey are selected (as a function of different conditions, such as abundance of prey), but how the organism chooses *where* to forage. This problem of "optimal patch choice" has been studied in two elegant experiments by Smith and Sweatman (1974) and by Krebs, Kalcenik, and Taylor (1978). Smith and Sweatman varied the abundance of food in six areas and measured the number of prey their birds (titmice) took from each area. They found that the birds took more than half of their prey from the area with the highest abundance of food and that when the relative abundance of food was altered, so was the birds' food-searching behavior. Krebs et al. (1978) utilized concurrent variable-ratio schedules (*conc* VR VR) to assess how birds make patch choice decisions. They shaped nine captured wild grey tits to perform an operant task in an indoor aviary. Two feeding patches were represented by two identical feeding places at opposite ends of the aviary, each consisting of a disk enclosed in a shallow metal box. The disk contained 72 holes, each of which housed a piece of mealworm. The bird had access to only one hole at a time through a small window at the top of the box. In order to obtain the next piece of food the bird had to hop on a perch next to the disk. The hops brought the next piece of mealworm in line with the window on a VR schedule. After shaping, the birds were given a series of treatments in which the values of the VR schedules were varied. A given treatment was continued until the birds came to hop more than 90 percent of the time on a particular perch.

Krebs et al. found that the birds sampled both disks for an "initial sampling period" after which they devoted virtually all of their time to the more profitable perch. Their choice behavior in this latter phase is illustrated in Figure 13.3. The step function described by the data supports the view that the subjects are maximizing (the dotted step function) rather than matching (the diagonal), as would be expected on the basis of choice for ratio schedules of reinforcement (Chapter 7). Note, too, that the period of "initial sampling" is consistent with the general notion that all alternatives are sampled for some time. The work of Krebs and his colleagues, as well as other work reviewed here, demonstrates that the technology developed in the operant laboratory may be fruitfully applied to studying the variables controlling foraging behavior.

As Collier (1977) has also suggested, laboratory work may simulate important aspects of the field. Recent work from his laboratory at Rutgers University represents an experimental analysis of the entire behavior chain involved in feeding. This chain is illustrated in Figure 13.4. Collier notes that the typical laboratory study emphasizes only the last element in the chain, consumption.[4] The subject is in effect in a "welfare state" in which the obliging experimenter conveniently does the searching, identifying, procuring and handling of food that normally precedes consumption. Collier's group has studied several parts of the feeding chain (Collier and Kaufman, 1976; Collier, 1977), including the effect of different schedule requirements on the search and procurement stages. For example, in Collier and Kaufman (1976) the rat subject, which lived in the apparatus continuously, obtaining all its food there, was shaped to respond on two levers. When an FR schedule was satisfied on the first ("search") lever, the light below the lever went out and one of two lights under the second ("procurement") lever came on. Each of these lights under the procurement lever was associated with a different FR requirement for food—for example, FR 5 and FR 200 in one portion of the study. If the rat made a single response on the procurement lever within 7.5 sec of light onset, it was committed to completing the ratio. If the rat made no response for 7.5 sec, however, the procurement light went out and the search light was reinstated. In one study the search ratio was FR 5 and the procurement ratios were FR 5 and FR 50. The rats quickly came to discriminate between the two procurement schedules, taking close to 100 percent of the opportunities to procure food on FR 5, while rejecting most of the opportunities to obtain food on FR 50. In the next study the high procurement ratio was varied between 50 and 200. As expected, fewer opportunities to obtain food on the larger ratio were taken, the larger that ratio.

In a later study, the procurement ratios were held at 5 and 200 and the search ratios assumed the following values in different conditions: 5, 25,

---

[4] We should qualify Collier's statement by noting that research on simple concurrents, reviewed in Chapter 7, clearly implicates the procurement stage as well as the consumption stage.

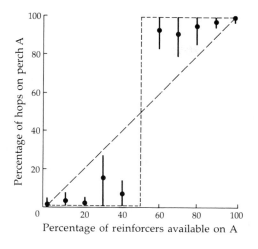

Figure 13.3
The proportion of hops on perch A plotted against the proportion of reinforcements available on A. The data do not describe a 45-degree line (the dashed diagonal), but approximate a step function, indicating maximizing behavior, rather than matching. [After Krebs, 1978.]

50, 100, and 200. As the search cost increases, will the rat be more likely to accept opportunities on the larger procurement ratio? Figure 13.5 shows that this was the case. Indeed, when the search ratio was 200, virtually all opportunities to obtain food were accepted on both procurement ratios. This result makes good sense if the rat is to maximize its food intake per unit time. When the search cost is low, higher rates of food intake may be obtained by passing up the high procurement ratio and waiting for the low ratio. When the search cost is sufficiently high, however, it is better to seize every opportunity. Thus when the search ratio is 200 and the procurement light is obtained, the rat is really faced with a choice between responding 200 times for food on the procurement lever or responding 200 times on the search lever for either the same or different procurement light. In the language of choice behavior (Chapter 7) either procurement light is correlated with a reduction in time to reinforcement as long as the search time is sufficiently great. With sufficiently shorter search times, only the FR 5 procurement schedule brings the subject closer to reinforcement, however. The reader may recognize that the search phase is somewhat analogous to the initial links of concurrent-

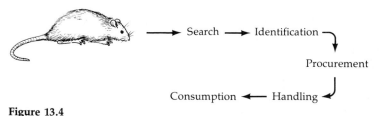

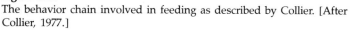

Figure 13.4
The behavior chain involved in feeding as described by Collier. [After Collier, 1977.]

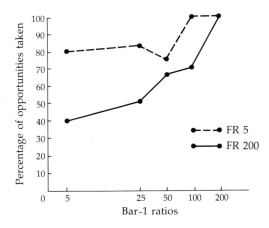

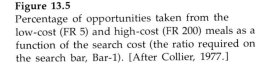

Figure 13.5
Percentage of opportunities taken from the low-cost (FR 5) and high-cost (FR 200) meals as a function of the search cost (the ratio required on the search bar, Bar-1). [After Collier, 1977.]

chains schedules studied extensively with pigeons, and that the procurement lever is analogous to the terminal links. Collier's results are therefore consistent with, and extend, the delay-reduction hypothesis developed in Chapters 6 and 7.

In the literature on behavior change in multiple response environments and in the experimental analysis of foraging we have seen the initial fruits of attempts to combine both the assumptions and methodologies of the laboratory and the field. The analysis of foraging strategies in several species of birds clearly illustrates the external validity of concepts such as matching and maximizing initially developed through the rigorous internal validity of the laboratory. The work of Krebs and others indicates that these concepts extend in a straightforward manner to the natural conditions under which birds learn to select foods. Similarly, in the multiple response environment the internal validity of the laboratory can be brought to bear on the analysis of how organisms distribute their responses in time when, as in nature, they are faced with numerous response alternatives.

THE CHALLENGE TO REINFORCEMENT THEORY

Much of the recent interaction between the psychological and biological approaches to learning has centered on controversies regarding findings collectively referred to as "constraints on learning" (Hinde and Stevenson-Hinde, 1973; Seligman and Hager, 1972). These findings in general represent situations in which learning has been shown to be "closely adapted to the species' way of life" (Hinde and Stevenson-Hinde, 1973, p. 3), such that (1) specific responses cannot be altered in an otherwise "flexible" organism, (2) some responses are much more readily altered than others, and (3) species can be seen to differ drastically both in what is learned and in how it is learned. Advocates of the constraints position have assumed that biological factors can severely limit behavioral plasticity in ways unique to a given species. It is held, therefore, that general laws of behavior change, including those of reinforcement theory, are inappropriate, in that general statements cannot encompass the vast array of diversity potentially evident in learning strategies. The validity of any position emphasizing the importance of reinforcement for behavior rests with the recognition that, while constraints indeed exist, general principles of behavior change remain useful.

The emphasis on constraints on learning has leveled two general criticisms against traditional reinforcement theory: (1) laboratory work on reinforcement theory is "artificial" and results in principles of the acquisition and maintenance of behavior that lack generality for any natural setting (that is, lack external validity), and (2) traditional reinforcement theorists incorrectly assume that "any emitted response and any reinforcer can be associated with approximately equal facility" (Seligman, 1970). This assumption has been termed the principle of equipotentiality (see Chapter 10). We shall discuss each of these criticisms in turn.

The first criticism in no way negates the value of laboratory research on principles of reinforcement and behavior change. Consider the issue of schedules of reinforcement. Here two questions are relevant: (1) Why is research on schedules of reinforcement important? (2) Can such research be done adequately under the artificial conditions imposed in the laboratory? As we have seen throughout this book, schedules of reinforcement are powerful determinants of behavior for many species. They tap an important dimension of any organism's environment: time. As we have seen before, the natural environment meticulously partitions accessibility to vital resources. Schedules of reinforcement essentially represent a laboratory analogue of the natural scheduling. The analysis of schedules of reinforcement would seem to have general validity for any organism exhibiting behavioral plasticity, because any natural environment requires the partitioning of both responses and time.

The fixed-interval scallop has, for example, been found with organisms studied with numerous different stimuli, responses, and reinforcers. One could, moreover, demonstrate the external validity of this procedure in cases where reinforcers are naturally programmed on FI schedules—for example, where prey or other food sources are prevalent only at certain times and places, such as water holes at dusk or flowers that secrete nectar at dawn. Under these circumstances the organism's investigation of these food locations may show a fixed-interval pattern quite comparable to that observed in the lab. Similarly, the pecking behavior of woodpeckers appears to be emitted at a high constant rate comparable to that generated by a variable-ratio schedule of reinforcement. This is perhaps due to the fact that insects are available on a VR schedule in the organism's natural environment. If the insects were available on a different schedule, would the woodpecker's pattern of pecking change? Presumably, it would be possible to show FI and other appropriate schedule behavior exhibited by woodpeckers tested in the laboratory. What is not certain is whether the woodpecker's VR behavior develops in the field in response to naturally occurring VR schedules of reinforcement, whether the woodpecker imitates parental pecking rates, or whether variable-ratio rates are relatively organized from the outset. In each of these cases, however, the natural environment has imposed a temporal regime on accessibility to resources. The study of schedules of reinforcement under rigidly defined conditions can help determine how natural restrictions result in behavior change.

The recent emphasis on constraints is well taken and suggests that different patterns of responding may emerge depending on what species we are studying and on how we select stimuli, responses, and reinforcers. Scheduling considerations nonetheless remain an important element of these interactions. If we are to understand how the effects of response and temporal partitioning—that is, schedules of reinforcement—*per se* are altered by constraints on learning, we must also understand how they operate in the absence of such constraints. Because the biological factors are demonstrably powerful, an arbitrary situation in which these factors are minimized becomes the most definitive way to analyze the isolated effects of timing. The principles that emerge must, however, at some point be integrated with principles of constraints presumed to operate in the wild. From this viewpoint the laboratory study of schedules of reinforcement is important because (1) schedules may reveal fundamental means by which behavior can be changed by limiting access to essential resources, and (2) these effects can be most clearly assessed under conditions in which the effects of biological factors are minimized.

The second criticism states that reinforcement theorists incorrectly assume that any responses and reinforcers may be associated with equal facility. This point is partially valid. Indeed, in practice, many (if not most) experimenters have seemed to assume that the particular selection of stimulus, response, reinforcer, and organism is relatively unimportant. Often this working assumption has proved manifestly untenable, as indicated in the 1950s and 1960s by research on avoidance learning (see Chapter 8). The assumption of equal associability has seldom been made explicit. In fact, Thorndike, Tolman, and Skinner explicitly acknowledged that it was invalid. Nonetheless, it may well be true that until the 1970s few investigators fully appreciated how commonplace differences in associability (between different response-reinforcer pairs, for example) were. Recent laboratory work makes it evident that it is quite difficult to select arbitrary or representative stimuli, responses, and reinforcers. For example, the pigeon's key-peck when reinforced with food is a nonarbitrary pairing, since pigeons normally peck at their food. Indeed, Jenkins and

Moore (1973) photographed pigeons' autopecks (in an autoshaping procedure; see Chapter 4) and showed that when the beak makes contact with the response key it is positioned as if seizing food, when food is the reinforcer, but *not* when water is the reinforcer. This suggests that, under certain conditions, the topography of the key-peck is influenced by the particular reinforcer with which it is paired. In any case, the test of whether or not particular selections of stimuli, responses, and reinforcers produce orderly results capable of generalization to other situations both within and across species (for example, with other selections of reinforcers and responses in the same subject or the same or different selection with organisms from a different species) remains an empirical one. Indeed, well before the issue of constraints on learning gained prominence Skinner (1938, 1969) acknowledged that complete prediction of behavior could not be generated by simply studying representative stimuli, responses, and reinforcers (see Skinner, 1938, pp. 10–11). Recognition of this fact prompted Skinner to select stimuli, responses, and reinforcers that would, he hoped, minimize intrusion by complicating biological factors. His hope was that the resulting behavior would be orderly and that its form would also describe and predict behavior maintained by other stimuli, responses, reinforcers, and organisms.

Although there is no reason to reject the validity of reinforcement principles established in the laboratory over the past several decades, as the constraints position indicates, the application of these principles involves heretofore underestimated complexity. The presentation of a reinforcer is a complex event, having not only reinforcing effects but also discriminative stimulus functions and sometimes response-eliciting and inhibitory functions.[5] Interactions among stimuli, responses, and reinforcers may, moreover, be quite specific to a given situation. For example, the rate of acquisition and the level of maintained performance found with one set of stimuli, responses, and reinforcers may be very different from that observed with a different set. With any set, however, many of the basic principles of reinforcement—scheduling effects, experimental extinction, stimulus control, conditioned reinforcement, and so on—should apply. Nevertheless, as we have seen, they need not exhaust the strategies of learning that natural environments may support. The principles appear quite valid. What is required is a detailed specification of exactly how they apply in any given situation, inevitably involving complex interactions with other types of factors. Behavior in any situation is a function of genetic programming, experience, and the particular situation in which

---

[5] As Lowe and Harzem (1977) have commented recently, after demonstrating differences between rats and pigeons in the temporal control of their behavior on fixed-interval and fixed-time schedules of reinforcement: "None of these properties of reinforcing stimuli indicate a failure of the principles of learning; rather, the present study suggests that it is only through a full understanding of such principles, in all their complexity, that species differences in behavior may be adequately comprehended" (p. 199).

the behavior is taking place. In relatively "arbitrary" situations genetic and historical determinants may be minimal; in nonarbitrary situations the effects of species-specific behavior patterns and/or past learning are bound to affect the behavior occurring. But as Schwartz (1974) has argued persuasively, "the mere fact that a situation is nonarbitrary does not imply that the principles it yields will not generalize to other situations . . . the central problem lies in understanding just which features of the phenomenon are attributable to general principles and which are attributable to situation-specific ones" (p. 195). Both the complexity and the diversity of behavior require that numerous principles, both ontogenetic and phylogenetic, become part of its explanation. Moreover, certain sets of principles may be more relevant to some species or situations than others. Insect behavior appears highly species-specific; phylogenetic factors may therefore assume far greater relevance here than in the explanation of the highly flexible behavior of humans. In humans, by contrast, the effects of response-dependent consequences and the occurrence of observational learning may far outweigh the phylogenetic factors that remain a part of our human heritage. The challenge is to achieve the balance of ontogenetic and phylogenetic principles that best explains the behavior of an individual member of a distinct species in a given situation.

EPILOG

E. O. Wilson (1977) has recently described the nature of the interdisciplinary interaction through which the social sciences, including the psychology of learning, may be influenced by theoretical biology. All behavior—the complex cultural behavior of humans and the relatively plastic behavior of other mammals and birds, as well as the highly stereotyped behaviors of so many invertebrates—must conform to the laws of evolution by natural selection. The learning strategies characteristic of various species in various situations constitute "idiosyncratic evolutionary adaptations" as unique to those species and as much a function of ecological demands as are patterns of external coloration or species-specific sequences. In Wilson's words, "The full range of learning potential of each species appears to be separately programmed" (1977, p. 135). The general laws that describe the genetically based propensities to learn characteristic of various species will be the laws of evolution and ecology. Wilson maintains that in this sense theoretical biology must be regarded as psychology's *antidiscipline:* that discipline which provides laws fundamental to the understanding of phenomena at a different level of analysis. The laws of biology (the antidiscipline) necessary for a complete understanding of psychological phenomena are, however, by no means sufficient. To the necessary phylogenetic base, psychology must add laws that describe how information acquired within the organism's lifetime is organized to produce new patterns of behavior historically unique to the individual (and not the species). These laws are essential for understanding how the individual influences the culture and the community in nongenetic ways—ways that themselves may actually alter the nature of future genetic change. Especially in the more highly flexible species, only through psychological laws that complement the base of theoretical biology can a complete understanding of behavior be attained.

> The laws of [the antidiscipline] are necessary to the discipline above, they challenge and force a mentally more efficient restructuring; but they are not sufficient for its purposes. Biology is the key to human nature; . . . But the social sciences are potentially far richer in content. Eventually they will absorb the relevant ideas of biology and go on to beggar them by comparison" [Wilson, 1977, p. 138].

References

Chapter 1

Koltermann, R. 1973. Rassen- bzw. artspezifische Duftbewertung bei der Honig-biene und ökologische Adaptation. *Journal of Comparative Physiology, 85,* 327–360.

Lorenz, K. 1965. *Evolution and modification of behavior.* Chicago: University of Chicago Press.

Menzel, R., and Erber, J. 1978. Learning and memory in bees. *Scientific American, 239,* 102–110.

Chapter 2

Boring, E. G. 1950. *A history of experimental psychology.* New York: Appleton-Century-Crofts.

Chaplin, J. D., and Krawiec, T. S. 1974. *Systems and theories of psychology,* 3rd ed. New York: Holt, Rinehart and Winston.

Guthrie, E. R. 1935. *The psychology of learning.* New York: Harper & Row.

Hartley, D. 1749. *Observations on man: His frame, his duty, and his expectations.* London.

Herrnstein, R. 1966. Superstition: A corollary of the principles of operant condi-tioning. In W. Honig (Ed.), *Operant behavior: Areas of research and application.* New York: Appleton-Century-Crofts.

Hilgard, E. R. 1956. *Theories of learning.* New York: Appleton-Century-Crofts.

Hull, C. L. 1943. *Principles of behavior.* New York: Appleton-Century-Crofts.

Hull, C. L. 1952. *A behavior system.* New Haven: Yale University Press.

Jennings, H. S. 1906. *Behavior of the lower organisms.* New York: Columbia University Press.

Löeb, J. 1918. *Forced movements, tropisms, and animal conduct.* Philadelphia: Lippincott.

Lowry, R. 1971. *The evolution of psychological theory.* New York: Aldine.

Maier, N. R. F., and Schneirla, T. C. 1964. *Principles of animal psychology.* New York: Dover. (Original edition 1935)

Pavlov, I. 1928. *Lectures on conditioned reflexes.* New York: International.

Romanes, G. 1882. *Animal intelligence.* London: Routledge and Kegan Paul.

Skinner, B. F. 1938. *The behavior of organisms: An experimental analysis.* New York: Appleton-Century-Crofts.

Skinner, B. F. 1953. *Science and human behavior.* New York: Free Press.

Thorndike, E. 1898. Animal intelligence. *Psychological Review Monograph Supplement,* No. 8.

Thorndike, E. L. 1913. *The psychology of learning.* New York: Teachers College.

Tolman, E. C., and Honzik, C. H. 1930. Introduction and removal of reward, and maze performance in rats. *University of California Publications in Psychology, 4,* 257–275.

Tolman, E. C. 1938. The determiners of behavior at a choice point. *Psychological Review, 45,* 1–41.

Tolman, E. C. 1967. *Purposive behavior in animals and man.* New York: Appleton-Century-Crofts.

Voeks, V. 1950. Formalization and clarification of a theory of learning. *Journal of Psychology, 30,* 341–362.

Voeks, V. 1955. Gradual strengthening of S–R connections or increasing number of S–R connections. *Journal of Psychology, 39,* 289–299.

Chapter 3

Balderrama, N., and Maldonado, H. 1971. Habituation of the deimatic response in the mantid *(Stagmatoptera biocellata). Journal of Comparative and Physiological Psychology, 75,* 98–106.

Barrass, R. 1961. A quantitative study of the behavior of the *Mormoniella vitripennis* (walker) *(Hymenoptera, Pteromalidae)* towards two constant stimulus situations. *Behaviour, 18,* 288–312.

Black, A. H., and de Toledo, L. 1972. The relationship among classically conditioned responses: Heart rate and skeletal behavior. In A. Black and W. Prokasy (Eds.), *Classical conditioning II: Current research and theory.* New York: Appleton-Century-Crofts.

Black, A. H., and Prokasy, W. F. (eds.) 1972. *Classical conditioning II: Current research and theory.* New York: Appleton-Century-Crofts.

Davis, M. 1970. Effects of interstimulus interval length and variability on startle response habituation in the rat. *Journal of Comparative and Physiological Psychology, 72,* 177–192.

Davis, M. 1972. Differential retention of sensitization and habituation of the startle response in the rat. *Journal of Comparative and Physiological Psychology, 78,* 260–267.

Davis, M. 1974a. Signal-to-noise ratio as a predictor of startle amplitude and habituation in the rat. *Journal of Comparative and Physiological Psychology, 86,* 812–825.

Davis, M. 1974b. Sensitization of the rat startle response by noise. *Journal of Comparative and Physiological Psychology, 87,* 571–581.

Dethier, V. 1969. Feeding behavior in the blowfly. In D. Lehrman, R. Hinde, and E. Shaw (Eds.), *Advances in the study of behavior,* Vol. 2. New York: Academic Press.

de Toledo, L., and Black, A. 1966. Heart rate: Changes during conditioned suppression in rats. *Science, 152,* 1404–1406.

Egger, D. M., and Miller, N. E. 1962. Secondary reinforcement in rats as a function of informational value and reliability of the stimulus. *Journal of Experimental Psychology, 64,* 97–104.

Franzisket, L. 1963. Characteristics of instinctive behavior and learning in reflex activity of the frog. *Animal Behaviour, 11,* 318–324.

Grant, D. A., and Norris, E. B. 1947. Eyelid conditioning as influenced by the presence of sensitized beta responses. *Journal of Experimental Psychology, 37,* 423–433.

Groves, P. and Thompson, R. 1970. Habituation: A dual-process theory. *Psychological Review, 77,* 419–450.

Hinde, R. A. 1960. Factors governing the changes in strength of a partially inborn response, as shown by the mobbing behavior of the chaffinch *(Fringilla coelebs).* III. The interaction of short-term and long-term incremental and decremental effects. *Proceedings of the Royal Society of London. B. 153,* 398–420.

Hinde, R. A. 1970a. *Animal behaviour.* New York: McGraw-Hill.

Hinde, R. A. 1970b. Behavioural habituation. In G. Horn and R. Hinde (Eds.), *Short-term changes in neural activity and behaviour.* Cambridge: Cambridge University Press.

James, W. 1890. *Principles of psychology.* New York: Henry Holt and Company.

Jennings, H. S. 1906. *Behavior of the lower organisms.* New York: Columbia University Press.

Keith-Lucas, T., and Guttman, N. 1975. Robust single-trial delayed backward conditioning. *Journal of Comparative and Physiological Psychology, 88,* 468–476.

Kimble, D., and Ray, R. 1965. Reflex habituation and potentiation in *Rana pipiens. Animal Behaviour, 13,* 530–533.

Kimble, G. A. 1961. *Hilgard and Marquis' conditioning and learning,* 2nd ed. New York: Appleton-Century-Crofts.

Kimmel, H. D. 1967. Instrumental conditioning of autonomically mediated behavior. *Psychological Bulletin, 67,* 337–345.

Kimmel, H. D., and Baxter, R. 1964. Avoidance conditioning of the GSR. *Journal of Experimental Psychology, 68,* 482–485.

Kimmel, H. D. and Kimmel, E. 1963. A replication of operant conditioning of the GSR. *Journal of Experimental Psychology, 65,* 212–213.

King, H., and Landis, C. 1943. A comparison of eyelid responses conditioned with reflex and voluntary reinforcement in normal individuals and psychiatric patients. *Journal of Experimental Psychology, 33,* 210–220.

Klopfer, P. 1973. *Behavioral aspects of ecology.* 2nd ed. Englewood Cliffs, NJ: Prentice-Hall.

Konorski, J. 1967. *Integrative activity of the brain.* Chicago: University of Chicago Press.

Kuenzer, P. 1958. Verhalten Physiologische Untersuchungen über das Zucken des Regenwurms. *Zeitschrift für Tierpsychologie, 15,* 31–49.

Mackintosh, N. 1974. *The psychology of animal learning.* New York: Academic Press.

Mahoney, W., and Ayers, J. 1976. One-trial simultaneous and backward fear conditioning as reflected in conditioned suppression of licking in rats. *Animal Learning and Behavior, 4*, 357–362.

Newton, J., and Gantt, W. 1966. One-trial cardiac conditioning in dogs. *Conditional Reflex, 1*, 251–265.

Pavlov, I. P. 1927. *Conditioned reflexes.* Translated by G. V. Anrep. Oxford: Clarendon Press.

Peeke, H., and Herz, M. 1973. *Habituation I: Behavioral studies.* New York: Academic Press.

Peeke, H. V. S., Herz, M., and Gallagher, J. 1971. Changes in aggressive behavior in adjacently territorial convict cichlids *(Cichlasoma nigrofasciatum):* The role of habituation. *Behaviour, 40*, 43–54.

Peeke, H. V. S., and Peeke, S. C. 1970. Habituation of aggressive responses in the Siamese fighting fish *(Betta splendens). Behaviour, 36*, 232–245.

Peeke, H. V. S., and Peeke, S. C. 1972. Habituation, reinforcement and recovery of predatory responses in two species of fish *(Carassius auratus* and *Macropodus opercularis). Animal Behaviour, 20*, 268–273.

Peeke, H. V. S., and Peeke, S. C. 1973. Habituation in fish with special reference to intraspecific aggressive behavior. In H. Peeke and M. Herz (Eds.), *Habituation I.* New York: Academic Press.

Peeke, H. V. S., and Veno, A. 1973. Stimulus specificity of habituated aggression in three-spined sticklebacks *(Gasterosteus aculeatus). Behavioral Biology, 8*, 427–432.

Pinsker, H., Hening, W., Carew, T., and Kandel, E. 1973. Long-term sensitization of a defensive withdrawal reflex in *Aplysia. Science, 182*, 1039–1042.

Razran, G. 1971. *Mind in evolution: An east/west synthesis of learned behavior and cognition.* Boston: Houghton Mifflin.

Rescorla, R. A. 1970. Informational variables in Pavlovian conditioning. In J. H. Reynierse (Ed.), *Current issues in animal learning.* Lincoln: University of Nebraska Press.

Rescorla, R. A. 1967. Pavlovian conditioning and its proper control procedures. *Psychological Review, 74*, 71–80.

Rescorla, R. A. 1968. Probability of shock in the presence and absence of CS in fear conditioning. *Journal of Comparative and Physiological Psychology, 66*, 1–5.

Rescorla, R. A., and Wagner, A. R. 1972. A theory of Pavlovian conditioning: Variations in the effectiveness of reinforcement and nonreinforcement. In A. H. Black and W. F. Prokasy (Eds.), *Classical conditioning II: Current research and theory.* New York: Appleton-Century-Crofts.

Russell, E. M. 1967. The effects of experience of surroundings on the response of *Lebistes reticulatus* to a strange object. *Animal Behaviour, 15*, 586–594.

Sherrington, C. S. 1906. *Integrative action of the nervous system.* Cambridge: Cambridge University Press.

Szlep, R. 1964. Change in the response of spiders to repeated web variations. *Behaviour, 23*, 203–238.

Terrace, H. S. 1973. Classical conditioning. In J. Nevin (Ed), *The study of behavior.* Glenview, IL: Scott, Foresman.

Thompson, R., Groves, P., Teyler, T., and Roemer, R. 1973. A dual-process theory of habituation. In H. Peeke and M. Herz (Eds.), *Habituation I: behavioral studies.* New York: Academic Press.

Thompson, R., and Spencer, W. A. 1966. Habituation: A model phenomenon for the study of neuronal substrates of behavior. *Psychological Review, 173*, 16–43.

Wagner, A. R. 1969. Stimulus-selection and a "modified continuity theory." In G. Bower and J. Spence (Eds.), *The psychology of learning and motivation,* Vol. III. New York: Academic Press.

Williams, J., Hamilton, L., and Carlton, P. 1974. Pharmacological and anatomical dissociation of two types of habituation. *Journal of Comparative and Physiological Psychology, 87,* 724–732.

Williams, J., Hamilton, L., and Carlton, P. 1975. Ontogenetic dissociation of two classes of habituation. *Journal of Comparative and Physiological Psychology, 89,* 733–737.

Chapter 4

Alferink, L. A., Crossman, E. K., and Cheney, C. D. 1973. Control of responding by a conditioned reinforcer in the presence of free food. *Animal Learning and Behavior, 1,* 38–40.

Atnip, G. W. 1977. Stimulus– and response–reinforcer contingencies in autoshaping, operant, classical, and omission training procedures in rats. *Journal of the Experimental Analysis of Behavior, 28,* 59–69.

Ayllon, T., and Michael, J. 1959. The psychiatric nurse as a behavioral engineer. *Journal of the Experimental Analysis of Behavior, 2,* 323–334.

Bachrach, A. J., Erwin, W. J., and Mohr, J. P. 1965. The control of eating behavior in an anorexic by operant conditioning techniques. In L. P. Ullman and L. Krasner (Eds.), *Case studies in behavior modification.* New York: Holt, Rinehart and Winston.

Baer, D. M., Peterson, R. F., and Sherman, J. A. 1967. The development of imitation by reinforcing behavioral similarity to a model. *Journal of the Experimental Analysis of Behavior, 10,* 405–416.

Bandura, A. 1969. *Principles of behavior modification.* New York: Holt, Rinehart and Winston.

Bernstein, D. J. 1973. Structure and function in response repertoires of humans. Unpublished doctoral dissertation, University of California, San Diego.

Brown, P. L., and Jenkins, H. M. 1968. Auto-shaping of the pigeon's key-peck. *Journal of the Experimental Analysis of Behavior, 11,* 1–8.

Eisenberger, R., Karpman, M., and Trattner, J. 1967. What is the necessary and sufficient condition for reinforcement in the contingency situation? *Journal of Experimental Psychology, 74,* 342–350.

Ellis, A. 1962. *Reason and emotion in psychotherapy.* New York: Lyle Stuart.

Fantino, E. 1977. Conditioned reinforcement: Choice and information. In W. H. Honig, and J. E. R. Staddon (Eds.), *Handbook of operant behavior.* Englewood Cliffs, NJ: Prentice-Hall.

Ferster, C. B., and Skinner, B. F. 1957. *Schedules of reinforcement.* New York: Appleton-Century-Crofts.

Gamzu, E., and Schwartz, B. 1973. The maintenance of key pecking by stimulus-contingent and response-independent food presentation. *Journal of the Experimental Analysis of Behavior, 19,* 65–72.

Gibbon, J., Baldock, M. D., Locurto, C., Gold, L., and Terrace, H. S. 1977. Trial and intertrial durations in autoshaping. *Journal of Experimental Psychology: Animal Behavior Processes, 3,* 264–284.

Gillan, P., and Rachman, S. 1974. An experimental investigation of desensitization in phobic patients. *British Journal of Psychiatry, 124,* 392–401.

Goldfried, M. R. 1971. Systematic desensitization as training in self-control. *Journal of Consulting and Clinical Psychology, 37,* 228–234.

Herrnstein, R. J. 1970. On the law of effect. *Journal of the Experimental Analysis of Behavior, 13,* 243–266.

Homme, L. E., deBaca, P. C., Devine J. V., Steinhorst, R., and Rickert, E. J. 1963. Use of the Premack principle in controlling the behavior of nursery school children. *Journal of the Experimental Analysis of Behavior, 6,* 544.

Humphreys, L. G. 1939. The effect of random alternation of reinforcement on the acquisition and extinction of conditioned eyelid reactions. *Journal of Experimental Psychology, 25,* 141–158.

Hursh, S. R., Navarick, D. J., and Fantino, E. 1974. "Automaintenance": The role of reinforcement. *Journal of the Experimental Analysis of Behavior, 21,* 117–124.

Krapfl, J. E. 1967. Differential ordering of stimulus presentation and semi-automated versus live treatment in the systematic desensitization of snake phobia. Unpublished doctoral dissertation, University of Missouri.

Lichtenstein, E., Harris, D. E., Birchler, G. R., Wahl, J. M., and Schmahl, D. P. 1973. Comparison of rapid smoking, warm, smoky air, and attention placebo in the modification of smoking behavior. *Journal of Consulting and Clinical Psychology, 40,* 92–98.

Locurto, C. 1977. Autoshaping in the rat: Effects of interposing delays between response and food. Paper read at meetings of the Eastern Psychological Association, Boston.

Locurto, C., Terrace, H. S., and Gibbon, J. 1976. Autoshaping, random control, and omission training in the rat. *Journal of the Experimental Analysis of Behavior, 26,* 451–462.

London, P. 1964. *The modes and morals of psychotherapy.* New York: Holt, Rinehart and Winston.

Lovaas, O. I., Berberich, J. P., Perloff, B. F., and Schaeffer, B. 1966. Acquisition of imitative speech in schizophrenic children. *Science, 151,* 705–707.

Lovaas, O. I., Koegel, R., Simmons, J. Q., and Long, J. S. 1973. Some generalization and follow-up measures on autistic children in behavioral therapy. *Journal of Applied Behavior Analysis, 6,* 131–166.

Lovaas, O. I., and Simmons, J. Q. 1969. Manipulation of self-destruction in three retarded children. *Journal of Applied Behavior Analysis, 2,* 143–157.

Miller, H. R., and Nawas, M. M. 1970. Control of aversive stimulus termination in systematic desensitization. *Behaviour Research and Therapy, 8,* 57–61.

Nawas, M. M., Fishman, S. T., and Pucel, J. C. 1970. A standardized desensitization program applicable to group and individual treatment. *Behaviour Research and Therapy, 8,* 49–56.

Nawas, M. M., Welsh, W. V., and Fishman, S. T. 1970. The comparative effectiveness of pairing aversive imagery with relaxation, neutral tasks and muscular tension in reducing snake phobia. *Behaviour Research and Therapy, 8,* 63–68.

Neuringer, A. J. 1969. Animals respond for food in the presence of free food. *Science, 166,* 399–401.

Osborne, S. R. 1977. The free food (contrafreeloading) phenomenon: A review and analysis. *Animal Learning and Behavior, 5,* 221–235.

Osborne, S. R., and Shelby, M. 1975. Stimulus change as a factor in response maintenance with free food available. *Journal of the Experimental Analysis of Behavior, 24,* 17–21.

Peterson, G. B., Ackil, J. E., Frommer, G. P., and Hearst, E. 1972. Conditioned approach and contact behavior for food or brain stimulation reinforcement. *Science, 177,* 1009–1011.

Premack, D. 1959. Toward empirical behavior laws: I. Positive reinforcement. *Psychological Review, 66,* 219–233.

Premack, D. 1962. Reversibility of the reinforcement relation. *Science, 136,* 255–257.

Rachlin, H., and Burkhard, B. 1978. The temporal triangle: Response substitution in instrumental conditioning. *Psychological Review, 85,* 22–47.

Rachman, S. 1968. The role of muscular relaxation in desensitization therapy. *Behaviour Research and Therapy, 6,* 159–166.

Rimm, D. C., and Medeiros, D. C. 1970. The role of muscle relaxation in participant modeling. *Behaviour Research and Therapy, 8,* 127–132.

Schneider, B. A. 1969. A two-state analysis of fixed-interval responding in the pigeon. *Journal of the Experimental Analysis of Behavior, 12,* 677–687.

Schubot, E. D. 1966. The influence of hypnotic and muscular relaxation in systematic desensitization of phobic behavior. Unpublished doctoral dissertation, Stanford University.

Schwartz, B., and Gamzu, E. 1977. Pavlovian control of operant behavior. In W. K. Honig, and J. E. R. Staddon, (Eds.), *Handbook of operant behavior.* Englewood Cliffs, NJ: Prentice-Hall.

Shull, R. L., and Brownstein, A. J. 1970. Interresponse time duration in fixed-interval schedules of reinforcement: Control by ordinal position and time since reinforcement. *Journal of the Experimental Analysis of Behavior, 14,* 49–53.

Silverstone, J. T., and Salkind, M. R. 1973. Controlled evaluation of intravenous drugs in the specific desensitization of phobias. *Canadian Psychiatric Association Journal, 18,* 47–52.

Skinner, B. F. 1938. *The behavior of organisms: An experimental analysis.* New York: Appleton-Century-Crofts.

Staddon, J. E. R. In press. Operant behavior as adaptation to constraint. *Journal of Experimental Psychology: General.*

Stampfl, T. G., and Levis, D. J. 1967. Essentials of implosive therapy: A learning-theory-based psychodynamic behavioral therapy. *Journal of Abnormal Psychology, 72,* 496–503.

Stiers, M., and Silberberg, A. 1974. Lever-contact responses in rats: Automaintenance with and without a negative response–reinforcer dependency. *Journal of the Experimental Analysis of Behavior, 22,* 497–506.

Sue, D. 1972. The role of relaxation in systematic desensitization. *Behaviour Research and Therapy, 10,* 153–158.

Terrace, H. S., Gibbon, J., Farrell, L., and Baldock, M. D. 1975. Temporal factors influencing the acquisition and maintenance of an autoshaped keypeck. *Animal Learning and Behavior, 3,* 53–62.

Timberlake, W. 1977. Licking one saccharin solution for access to another: Substitution or reinforcement? Paper presented at meetings of Psychonomic Society, Washington, DC.

Timberlake, W., and Allison, J. 1974. Response deprivation: An empirical approach to instrumental performance. *Psychological Review, 81,* 146–164.

Ulrich, R., Stachnik, T., and Mabry, J. 1966, 1970, 1974. *Control of human behavior,* Vol. I, II, III. Glenview, IL: Scott, Foresman.

Valins, S., and Ray, A. A. 1967. Effects of cognitive desensitization on avoidance behavior. *Journal of Personality and Social Psychology, 7,* 345–350.

Wallace, R. F., Osborne, S., Norborg, J., and Fantino, E. 1973. Stimulus change contemporaneous with food presentation maintains responding in the presence of free food. *Science, 12,* 1038–1039.

Wasserman, E. A., Hunter, N. B., Gutowski, K. A., and Bader, S. A. 1975. Autoshaping chicks with heat reinforcement: The role of stimulus–reinforcer and response–reinforcer relations. *Journal of Experimental Psychology: Animal Behavior Processes, 104,* 158–169.

Wilkins, W. 1971. Desensitization: Social and cognitive factors underlying the effectiveness of Wolpe's procedure. *Psychological Bulletin, 76,* 311–317.

Williams, D. R., and Williams, H. 1969. Auto-maintenance in the pigeon: Sustained pecking despite contingent non-reinforcement. *Journal of the Experimental Analysis of Behavior, 12,* 511–520.

Wolpe, J. 1958. *Psychotherapy by reciprocal inhibition.* Stanford, CA: Stanford University Press.

Wolpin, M., and Raines, J. 1966. Visual imagery, expected roles and extinction as possible factors in reducing fear and avoidance behavior. *Behaviour Research and Therapy, 4,* 25–37.

Zeiler, M. 1977. Schedules of reinforcement: The controlling variables. In W. K. Honig and J. E. R. Staddon (Eds.), *Handbook of operant behavior.* Englewood Cliffs, NJ: Prentice-Hall.

Chapter 5

Barlow, D. H., and Agras, W. S. 1973. Fading to increase heterosexual responsiveness in homosexuals. *Journal of Applied Behavior Analysis, 6,* 355–366.

Beninger, R. J., and Kendall, S. B. 1975. Behavioral contrast in rats with different reinforcers and different response topographies. *Journal of the Experimental Analysis of Behavior, 24,* 267–280.

Bernheim, J. W., and Williams, D. R. 1967. Time-dependent contrast effects in a multiple schedule of food reinforcement. *Journal of the Experimental Analysis of Behavior, 10,* 243–249.

Bloomfield, T. M. 1967. Behavioral contrast and relative reinforcement frequency in two multiple schedules. *Journal of the Experimental Analysis of Behavior, 10,* 151–158.

Bloomfield, T. M. 1969. Behavioural contrast and the peak shift. In R. M. Gilbert and N. S. Sutherland (Eds.), *Animal discrimination learning.* London: Academic Press.

Blough, D. S. 1966. The reinforcement of least-frequent interresponse times. *Journal of the Experimental Analysis of Behavior, 9,* 581–591.

Blough, D. S. 1967. Stimulus generalization as signal detection in pigeons. *Science, 158,* 940–941.

Blough, D. S. 1975. Steady state data and a quantitative model of operant generalization and discrimination. *Journal of Experimental Psychology: Animal Behavior Processes, 104,* 3–21.

Blough, D., and Blough, P. 1977. Animal psychophysics. In W. K. Honig and J. E. R. Staddon (Eds.), *Handbook of operant behavior.* Englewood Cliffs, NJ: Prentice-Hall.

Blough, P. M. 1972. Wavelength generalization and discrimination in the pigeon. *Perception and Psychophysics, 12,* 342–348.

Boneau, C. A., and Axelrod, S. 1962. Work decrement and reminiscence in pigeon operant responding. *Journal of Experimental Psychology, 64,* 352–354.

Brethower, D. M., and Reynolds, G. S. 1962. A facilitative effect of punishment on unpunished behavior. *Journal of the Experimental Analysis of Behavior, 5,* 191–199.

Buck, S. L., Rothstein, B., and Williams, B. A. 1975. A re-examination of local contrast in multiple schedules. *Journal of the Experimental Analysis of Behavior, 24,* 291–301.

Butter, C. M. 1963. Stimulus generalization along one and two dimensions in pigeons. *Journal of Experimental Psychology, 65,* 339–346.

Carr, E. G., Newsom, C. O., and Binkoff, J. A. 1976. Stimulus control of self-destructive behavior in a psychotic child. *Journal of Abnormal Psychology, 4,* 139–153.

Catania, A. C. 1963. Concurrent performances: Reinforcement interaction and response independence. *Journal of the Experimental Analysis of Behavior, 6,* 253–263.

Catania, A. C. 1966. Concurrent operants. In W. K. Honig (Ed.), *Operant behavior: Areas of research and application.* Englewood Cliffs, NJ: Prentice-Hall.

D'Amato, M. R., and Fazzaro, J. 1966. Attention and cue-producing behavior in the monkey. *Journal of the Experimental Analysis of Behavior, 9,* 469–473.

Desiderato, O. 1969. Generalization of excitation and inhibition in control of avoidance responding by Pavlovian CS's in dogs. *Journal of Comparative and Physiological Psychology, 68,* 611–616.

de Villiers, P. 1977. Choice in concurrent schedules and a quantitative formulation of the law of effect. In W. K. Honig and J. E. R. Staddon (Eds.), *Handbook of operant behavior.* Englewood Cliffs, NJ: Prentice-Hall.

Dukhayyil, A., and Lyons, J. E. 1973. The effect of overtraining on behavioral contrast and the peak shift. *Journal of the Experimental Analysis of Behavior, 20,* 253–263.

Ehrenfreund, D. 1952. A study of the transposition gradient. *Journal of Experimental Psychology, 43,* 81–87.

Ellis, W. R. 1970. Role of stimulus sequences in stimulus discrimination and stimulus generalization. *Journal of Experimental Psychology, 83,* 155–163.

Ernst, A. J., Engberg, L., and Thomas, D. R. 1971. On the form of stimulus generalization curves for visual intensity. *Journal of the Experimental Analysis of Behavior, 16,* 177–180.

Fantino, E. 1968. Effects of required rates of responding upon choice. *Journal of the Experimental Analysis of Behavior, 11,* 15–22.

Farley, J., and Fantino, E. 1976. Negative induction, behavioral contrast, and differential punishment. Paper presented at meetings of the Psychonomic Society, St. Louis.

Farthing, G. W. 1974. Behavioral contrast with multiple positive and negative stimuli on a continuum. *Journal of the Experimental Analysis of Behavior, 22,* 419–425.

Fink, J. B., and Patton, R. M. 1953. Decrement of a learned drinking response accompanying changes in several stimulus characteristics. *Journal of Comparative and Physiological Psychology, 46,* 23–27.

Gamzu, E., and Schwartz, B. 1973. The maintenance of key pecking by stimulus-contingent and response-independent food presentation. *Journal of the Experimental Analysis of Behavior, 19,* 65–72.

Ganz, L., and Riesen, A. H. 1962. Stimulus generalization to hue in the dark-reared macaque. *Journal of Comparative and Physiological Psychology, 55,* 92–99.

Grusec, T. 1968. The peak shift in stimulus generalization: Equivalent effects of errors and non-contingent shock. *Journal of the Experimental Analysis of Behavior, 11,* 239–249.

Gutman, A., Sutterer, J. R., and Brush, F. R. 1975. Positive and negative behavioral contrast in the rat. *Journal of the Experimental Analysis of Behavior, 23,* 377–383.

Guttman, N. 1959. Generalization gradients around stimuli associated with different reinforcement schedules. *Journal of Experimental Psychology, 58,* 335–340.

Guttman, N., and Kalish, H. I. 1956. Discriminability and stimulus generalization. *Journal of Experimental Psychology, 51,* 79–88.

Hailman, J. P. 1969. Spectral pecking preference in gull chicks. *Journal of Comparative and Physiological Psychology, 67,* 465–467.

Hamilton, B. E., and Silberberg, A. 1978. Contrast and autoshaping in multiple schedules varying reinforcer rate and duration. *Journal of the Experimental Analysis of Behavior, 30,* 107–122.

Hanson, H. M. 1959. Effects of discrimination training on stimulus generalization. *Journal of Experimental Psychology, 58,* 321–334.

Hearst, E. 1969a. Aversive conditioning and external stimulus control. In B. A. Campbell and R. M. Church (Eds.), *Punishment and aversive behavior.* New York: Appleton-Century-Crofts.

Hearst, E. 1969b. Excitation, inhibition and discrimination learning. In N. J. Mackintosh and W. K. Honig (Eds.), *Fundamental issues in associative learning.* Halifax, NS: Dalhousie University Press.

Heinemann, E. G., and Chase, S. 1970. On the form of stimulus generalization curves for auditory intensity. *Journal of Experimental Psychology, 84,* 483–486.

Heinemann, E. G., and Rudolph, R. L. 1963. The effect of discriminative training on the gradient of stimulus generalization. *American Journal of Psychology, 76,* 653–658.

Hemmes, N. S. 1973. Behavioral contrast in pigeons depends upon the operant. *Journal of Comparative and Physiological Psychology, 85,* 171–178.

Hemmes, N. S., and Eckerman, D. A. 1972. Positive interaction (induction) in multiple variable-interval, differential-reinforcement-of-high-rate schedules. *Journal of the Experimental Analysis of Behavior, 17,* 51–57.

Herrnstein, R. J., and Loveland, D. H. 1964. Complex visual concept in the pigeon. *Science, 146,* 549–551.

Herrnstein, R. J., Loveland, D. H., and Cable, C. 1976. Natural concepts in pigeons. *Journal of Experimental Psychology: Animal Behavior Processes, 2,* 285–302.

Honig, W. K. 1962. Prediction of preference, transposition, and transposition-reversal from the generalization gradient. *Journal of Experimental Psychology, 64,* 239–248.

Honig, W. K. 1965. Discrimination, generalization, and transfer on the basis of stimulus difference. In D. I. Mostofsky (Ed.), *Stimulus generalization.* Stanford, CA: Stanford University Press.

Honig, W. K. 1969. Attentional factors governing the slope of the generalization gradient. In R. M. Gilbert and N. S. Sutherland (Eds.), *Animal discrimination learning.* London: Academic Press.

Honig, W. K., Boneau, C. A., Burstein, K. R., and Pennypacker, H. S. 1963. Positive and negative generalization gradients obtained after equivalent training conditions. *Journal of Comparative and Physiological Psychology, 56,* 111–116.

Hull, C. L. 1943. *Principles of behavior.* New York: Appleton-Century-Crofts.

Jenkins, H. M., and Harrison, R. H. 1960. Effect of discrimination training on auditory generalization. *Journal of Experimental Psychology, 59,* 246–253.

Jenkins, H. M., and Harrison, R. H. 1962. Generalization gradients of inhibition following auditory discrimination learning. *Journal of the Experimental Analysis of Behavior, 5,* 435–441.

Jenkins, H. M., and Sainsbury, R. S. 1969. The development of stimulus control through differential reinforcement. In N. J. Mackintosh and W. K. Honig (Eds.), *Fundamental issues in associative learning.* Halifax, NS: Dalhousie University Press.

Jenkins, H. M., and Sainsbury, R. S. 1970. Discrimination learning with the distinctive feature on positive or negative trials. In D. Mostofsky (Ed.), *Attention: Contemporary theory and analysis.* New York: Appleton-Century-Crofts.

Johnson, D. F., and Cumming, W. W. 1968. Some determiners of attention. *Journal of the Experimental Analysis of Behavior, 11,* 157–166.

Kamin, L. J. 1969. Predictability, surprise, attention, and conditioning. In B. Campbell and R. Church (Eds.), *Punishment and aversive behavior.* Englewood Cliffs, NJ: Prentice-Hall.

Keller, K. 1974. The role of elicited responding in behavioral contrast. *Journal of the Experimental Analysis of Behavior, 21,* 249–257.

Klein, M., and Rilling, M. 1974. Generalization of free-operant avoidance behavior in pigeons. *Journal of the Experimental Analysis of Behavior, 21,* 75–88.

Kodera, T., and Rilling, M. 1976. Procedural antecedents of behavioral contrast: A re-examination of errorless learning. *Journal of the Experimental Analysis of Behavior, 25,* 27–42.

Lashley, K. S., and Wade, M. 1946. The Pavlovian theory of generalization. *Psychological Review, 53,* 72–87.

Lawrence, D. H. 1949. Acquired distinctiveness of cues: I. Transfer between discriminations on the basis of familiarity with the stimulus. *Journal of Experimental Psychology, 39,* 770–784.

Lawrence, D. H. 1950. Acquired distinctiveness of cues: II. Selective association in a constant stimulus situation. *Journal of Experimental Psychology, 40,* 175–188.

Lawrence, D. H., and DeRivera, J. 1954. Evidence for relational transposition. *Journal of Comparative and Physiological Psychology, 47,* 465–471.

Lovaas, O. I., and Simmons, J. Q. 1969. Manipulation of self-destruction in three retarded children. *Journal of Applied Behavior Analysis, 2,* 143–157.

Mackintosh, N. J. 1974. *The psychology of animal learning.* London: Academic Press.

Mackintosh, N. J. 1977. Stimulus control: Attentional factors. In W. K. Honig and J. E. R. Staddon (Eds.), *Handbook of operant behavior.* Englewood Cliffs, NJ: Prentice-Hall.

Mackintosh, N. J., Little, L., and Lord, J. 1972. Some determinants of behavioral contrast in pigeons and rats. *Learning and Motivation, 3,* 148–161.

Malone, J. C., Jr., and Staddon, J. E. R. 1973. Contrast effects in maintained generalization gradients. *Journal of the Experimental Analysis of Behavior, 19,* 167–179.

Marsh, G. 1967. Relational learning in the pigeon. *Journal of Comparative and Physiological Psychology, 64,* 519–521.

Miles, C. G. 1970. Blocking the acquisition of control by an auditory stimulus with pretraining on brightness. *Psychonomic Science, 19,* 133–134.

Miles, C. G., and Jenkins, H. M. 1973. Overshadowing in operant conditioning as a function of discriminability. *Learning and Motivation, 4,* 11–27.

Moore, J., and Fantino, E. 1975. Choice and response contingencies. *Journal of the Experimental Analysis of Behavior, 23,* 339–347.

Nevin, J. A. 1968. Differential reinforcement and stimulus control of not respond-ing. *Journal of the Experimental Analysis of Behavior, 11*, 715–726.

Nevin, J. A. 1973. Stimulus control. In J. A. Nevin and G. S. Reynolds (Eds.), *The study of behavior.* Glenview, IL: Scott, Foresman.

Nevin, J. A., and Shettleworth, S. J. 1966. An analysis of contrast effects in multiple schedules. *Journal of the Experimental Analysis of Behavior, 9*, 305–315.

O'Brien, F. 1968. Sequential contrast effects with human subjects. *Journal of the Experimental Analysis of Behavior, 11*, 537–542.

Pavlov, I. P. 1927. *Conditioned reflexes.* Oxford: Oxford University Press.

Pear, J. J., and Wilkie, D. M. 1971. Contrast and induction in rats on multiple schedules. *Journal of the Experimental Analysis of Behavior, 15*, 289–296.

Peterson, N. 1962. Effect of monochromatic rearing on the control of responding by wavelength. *Science, 136*, 774–775.

Pierrel, R. 1958. A generalization gradient for auditory intensity in the rat. *Journal of the Experimental Analysis of Behavior, 1*, 303–313.

Pierrel, R., and Sherman, J. G. 1960. Generalization of auditory intensity follow-ing discrimination training. *Journal of the Experimental Analysis of Behavior, 3*, 313–322.

Premack, D. 1969. On some boundary conditions of contrast. In J. Tapp (Ed.), *Reinforcement and behavior.* New York: Academic Press.

Purtle, R. B. 1973. Peak shift: A review. *Psychological Bulletin, 80*, 408–421.

Rachlin, H. 1973. Contrast and matching. *Psychological Review, 80*, 217–234.

Razran, G. 1949. Stimulus generalization of conditioned responses. *Psychological Bulletin, 46*, 337–365.

Redford, N. E., and Perkins, C. C., Jr. 1974. The role of autopecking in behavioral contrast. *Journal of the Experimental Analysis of Behavior, 21*, 145–150.

Reinhold, D. B., and Perkins, C. C., Jr. 1955. Stimulus generalization following different methods of training. *Journal of Experimental Psychology, 49*, 423–427.

Rescorla, R. A., and Wagner, A. R. 1972. A theory of Pavlovian conditioning: Variations in the effectiveness of reinforcement and non-reinforcement. In A. H. Black and W. F. Prokasy (Eds.), *Classical conditioning II: Current research and theory.* New York: Appleton-Century-Crofts.

Revusky, S. H., and Garcia, J. 1970. Learned associations over long delays. In G. H. Bower and J. T. Spence (Eds.), *The psychology of learning and motivation*, Vol. 4. New York: Academic Press.

Reynolds, G. S. Behavioral contrast. 1961a. *Journal of the Experimental Analysis of Behavior, 4*, 57–71.

Reynolds, G. S. 1961b. An analysis of interactions in a multiple schedule. *Journal of the Experimental Analysis of Behavior, 4*, 107–117.

Reynolds, G. S. 1961c. Relativity of response rate and reinforcement frequency in a multiple schedule. *Journal of the Experimental Analysis of Behavior, 4*, 179–184.

Reynolds, G. S. 1961d. Attention in the pigeon. *Journal of the Experimental Analysis of Behavior, 4*, 203–208.

Reynolds, G. S., and Catania, A. C. 1961. Behavioral contrast with fixed-interval and low-rate reinforcement. *Journal of the Experimental Analysis of Behavior, 4*, 387–391.

Reynolds, G. S., and Limpo, A. J. 1968. On some causes of behavioral contrast. *Journal of the Experimental Analysis of Behavior, 11*, 543–547.

Reynolds, G. S., and Limpo, A. J. 1969. Attention and generalization during a conditional discrimination. *Journal of the Experimental Analysis of Behavior, 12,* 911–916.

Riley, D. A. 1958. The nature of the effective stimulus in animal discrimination learning: Transposition reconsidered. *Psychological Review, 65,* 1–7.

Riley, D. A. 1968. *Discrimination learning.* Boston: Allyn and Bacon.

Riley, D. A., Ring, K., and Thomas, J. 1960. The effect of stimulus comparison on discrimination learning and transposition. *Journal of Comparative and Physiological Psychology, 53,* 415–421.

Rilling, M. 1977. Stimulus control and inhibiting processes. In W. K. Honig and J. E. R. Staddon (Eds.), *Handbook of operant behavior.* Englewood Cliffs, NJ: Prentice-Hall.

Robinson, J. S. 1955. The sameness-difference discrimination problem in chimpanzees. *Journal of Comparative and Physiological Psychology, 48,* 195–197.

Rosen, A. P., and Terrace, H. S. 1975. On the minimal conditions for the development of a peak shift and inhibitory stimulus control. *Journal of the Experimental Analysis of Behavior, 23,* 385–414.

Rudolph, R. L. 1967. Transposition and the post-discrimination gradient: Absolute and relational learning during hue discrimination. Paper presented at meetings of the Eastern Psychological Association, Boston.

Rudolph, R. L., and Honig, W. K. 1972. Effects of monochromatic rearing on spectral discrimination learning and the peak shift in chicks. *Journal of the Experimental Analysis of Behavior, 17,* 107–111.

Rudolph, R. L., Honig, W. K., and Gerry, J. E. 1969. Effects of monochromatic rearing on the acquisition of stimulus control. *Journal of Comparative and Physiological Psychology, 67,* 50–57.

Sainsbury, R. S. 1971. Effect of proximity of elements on the feature-positive effect. *Journal of the Experimental Analysis of Behavior, 16,* 315–325.

Sainsbury, R. 1973. Discrimination learning utilizing positive or negative cues. *Canadian Journal of Psychology, 27,* 46–57.

Schwartz, B., and Gamzu, E. 1977. Pavlovian control of operant behavior: An analysis of autoshaping and its implications for operant conditioning. In W. K. Honig and J. E. R. Staddon (Eds.), *Handbook of operant behavior.* Englewood Cliffs, NJ: Prentice-Hall.

Schwartz, B., Hamilton, B., and Silberberg, A. 1975. Behavioral contrast in the pigeon: A study of the duration of key pecking maintained on multiple schedules of reinforcement. *Journal of the Experimental Analysis of Behavior, 24,* 199–206.

Schwartz, B., and Williams, D. R. 1972. Two different kinds of key peck in the pigeon: Some properties of responses maintained by negative and positive response–reinforcer contingencies. *Journal of the Experimental Analysis of Behavior, 18,* 201–216.

Spence, K. W. 1937. The differential response in animals to stimuli varying within a single dimension. *Psychological Review, 44,* 430–444.

Stebbins, W. C. 1970. *Animal psychophysics.* Englewood Cliffs, NJ: Prentice-Hall.

Steinhauer, G. D., Davol, G. H., and Lee, A. 1977. A procedure for autoshaping the pigeon's key peck to an auditory stimulus. *Journal of the Experimental Analysis of Behavior, 28,* 97–98.

Terrace, H. S. 1963a. Discrimination learning with and without errors. *Journal of the Experimental Analysis of Behavior, 6,* 1–27.

Terrace, H. S. 1963b. Errorless transfer of a discrimination across two continua. *Journal of the Experimental Analysis of Behavior, 6,* 223–232.

Terrace, H. S. 1964. Wavelength generalization after discrimination learning with and without errors. *Science, 144,* 78–80.

Terrace, H. S. 1966a. Stimulus control. In W. K. Honig (Ed.), *Operant behavior: Areas of research and application.* New York: Appleton-Century-Crofts.

Terrace, H. S. 1966b. Behavioral contrast and the peak shift: Effects of extended discrimination training. *Journal of the Experimental Analysis of Behavior, 9,* 613–617.

Terrace, H. S. 1968. Discrimination learning, the peak shift, and behavioral contrast. *Journal of the Experimental Analysis of Behavior, 11,* 727–741.

Thomas, D. R., and Setzer, J. 1972. Stimulus generalization gradients for auditory intensity in rats and guinea pigs. *Psychonomic Science, 28,* 22–24.

Tracy, W. K. 1970. Wavelength generalization and preference in monochromatically reared ducklings. *Journal of the Experimental Analysis of Behavior, 13,* 163–178.

Urcuioli, P. J., and Nevin, J. A. 1975. Transfer of hue matching in pigeons. *Journal of the Experimental Analysis of Behavior, 24,* 149–155.

Van Houten, R., and Rudolph, R. 1972. The development of stimulus control with and without a lighted key. *Journal of the Experimental Analysis of Behavior, 18,* 217–222.

Wagner, A. R., Logan, F. A., Haberlandt, K., and Price, T. 1968. Stimulus selection in animal discrimination learning. *Journal of Experimental Psychology, 76,* 171–180.

Waite, W. W., and Osborne, J. G. 1972. Sustained behavioral contrast in children. *Journal of the Experimental Analysis of Behavior, 18,* 113–117.

Weisman, R. G. 1969. Some determinants of inhibitory stimulus control. *Journal of the Experimental Analysis of Behavior, 12,* 443–450.

Weisman, R. G. 1970. Factors influencing inhibitory stimulus control: Differential reinforcement of other behavior during discrimination training. *Journal of the Experimental Analysis of Behavior, 14,* 87–91.

Westbrook, R. F. 1973. Failure to obtain positive contrast when pigeons press a bar. *Journal of the Experimental Analysis of Behavior, 20,* 499–510.

Wilkie, D. M. 1973. Signalled reinforcement in multiple and concurrent schedules. *Journal of the Experimental Analysis of Behavior, 20,* 29–36.

Williams, B. A. 1975. The blocking of reinforcement control. *Journal of the Experimental Analysis of Behavior, 24,* 215–225.

Williams, B. A. 1976. Behavioral contrast as a function of the temporal location of reinforcement. *Journal of the Experimental Analysis of Behavior, 26,* 57–64.

Wilton, R. N., and Clements, R. O. 1972. A failure to demonstrate behavioral contrast when the S$^+$ and S$^-$ components of a discrimination schedule are separated by about 23 hours. *Psychonomic Science, 28,* 137–139.

Ziriax, J. M., and Silberberg, A. 1978. Discrimination and emission of different key-peck durations in the pigeon. *Journal of Experimental Psychology: Animal Behavior Processes, 4,* 1–21.

Chapter 6

Amsel, A., and Roussel, J. 1952. Motivational properties of frustration: I. Effect on a running response of the addition of frustration to the motivational complex. *Journal of Experimental Psychology, 43,* 363–368.

Armus, H. L., and Garlich, M. M. 1961. Secondary reinforcement strength as a function of schedule of primary reinforcement. *Journal of Comparative and Physiological Psychology, 54,* 56–58.

Atthowe, J. M., and Krasner, L. 1968. Preliminary report on the application of contingent reinforcement procedures (token economy) on a "chronic" psychiatric ward. *Journal of Abnormal Psychology, 73,* 37–43.

Auge, R. J. 1973. Effects of stimulus duration on observing behavior maintained by differential reinforcement magnitude. *Journal of the Experimental Analysis of Behavior, 20,* 429–438.

Auge, R. J. 1974. Context, observing behavior, and conditioned reinforcement. *Journal of the Experimental Analysis of Behavior, 22,* 525–533.

Ayllon, T., and Azrin, N. H. 1965. The measurement and reinforcement of behavior of psychotics. *Journal of the Experimental Analysis of Behavior, 8,* 357–383.

Ayllon, T., and Azrin, N. H. 1968. *The token economy: A motivational system for therapy and rehabilitation.* New York: Appleton-Century-Crofts.

Badia, P., Coker, C. C., and Harsh, J. 1973. Choice of higher density signalled shock over lower density unsignalled shock. *Journal of the Experimental Analysis of Behavior, 20,* 47–55.

Badia, P., and Culbertson, S. 1972. The relative aversiveness of signalled *vs.* unsignalled escapable and inescapable shock. *Journal of the Experimental Analysis of Behavior, 17,* 463–471.

Badia, P., Culbertson, S., and Harsh, J. 1973. Choice of longer or stronger signalled shock over shorter or weaker unsignalled shock. *Journal of the Experimental Analysis of Behavior, 19,* 25–32.

Badia, P., Culbertson, S. A., and Harsh, J. 1974. Relative aversiveness of signalled *vs.* unsignalled avoidable and escapable shock situations in humans. *Journal of Comparative and Physiological Psychology, 87,* 338–346.

Badia, P., Culbertson, S., and Lewis, P. 1971. The relative aversiveness of signalled *vs.* unsignalled avoidance. *Journal of the Experimental Analysis of Behavior, 16,* 113–121.

Badia, P., Harsh, J., and Coker, C. C. 1975. Choosing between fixed time and variable time shock. *Learning and Motivation, 6,* 264–278.

Badia, P., Harsh, J., Coker, C. C., and Abbott, B. 1976. Choice and the dependability of stimuli that predict shock and safety. *Journal of the Experimental Analysis of Behavior, 26,* 95–111.

Berlyne, D. E. 1960. *Conflict, Arousal, and Curiosity.* New York: McGraw-Hill.

Bersh, P. J. 1951. The influence of two variables upon the establishment of a secondary reinforcer for operant responses. *Journal of Experimental Psychology, 41,* 62–73.

Bijou, S. W., Peterson, R. F., Harris, F. R., Allen, K. E., and Johnston, M. S. 1969. Methodology for experimental studies of young children in natural settings. *Psychological Record, 19,* 177–210.

Blanchard, R. J. 1975. The effect of S⁻ on observing behavior. *Learning and Motivation, 6,* 1–10.

Bloomfield, T. M. 1972. Reinforcement schedules: Contingency or contiguity. In R. M. Gilbert and J. R. Millenson (Eds.), *Reinforcement: Behavioral analyses.* New York: Academic Press.

Bugelski, B. R. 1938. Extinction with and without sub-goal reinforcement. *Journal of Comparative Psychology, 26,* 121–134.

Bushell, D., Wrobel, P., and Michaelis, M. 1968. Applying "group" contingencies to the classroom study behavior of preschool children. *Journal of Applied Behavior Analysis, 1,* 55–62.

Butter, C. M., and Thomas, D. R. 1958. Secondary reinforcement as a function of the amount of primary reinforcement. *Journal of Comparative and Physiological Psychology, 51,* 346–348.

Cohen, H. L., and Filipczak, J. 1971. *A new learning environment.* San Francisco: Jossey-Bass.

Cowles, J. T. 1937. Food-tokens as incentive for learning by chimpanzees. *Comparative Psychology Monographs, 14,* 1–96.

D'Amato, M. R. 1955. Secondary reinforcement and magnitude of primary reinforcement. *Journal of Comparative and Physiological Psychology, 48,* 378–380.

D'Amato, M. R., Lachman, R., and Kivy, P. 1958. Secondary reinforcement as affected by reward schedule and the testing situation. *Journal of Comparative and Physiological Psychology, 51,* 737–741.

Davison, M. C. 1969. Preference for mixed-interval versus fixed-interval schedules. *Journal of the Experimental Analysis of Behavior, 12,* 247–252.

Davison, M. C. 1972. Preference for mixed-interval versus fixed-interval schedules: Number of component intervals. *Journal of the Experimental Analysis of Behavior, 17,* 169–176.

DeFran, R. H. 1972. Reinforcing effects of stimuli paired with schedules of aversive control. Doctoral dissertation, Bowling Green State University, 1972. *Dissertation Abstracts International, 33,* 1865B–2419B. (University Microfilms No. 72-27, 218).

deLorge, J. 1971. The effects of brief stimuli presented under a multiple schedule of second-order schedules. *Journal of the Experimental Analysis of Behavior, 15,* 19–25.

Dinsmoor, J. A. 1950. A quantitative comparison of the discriminative and reinforcing functions of a stimulus. *Journal of Experimental Psychology, 40,* 458–472.

Dinsmoor, J. A., Browne, M. P., and Lawrence, C. E. 1972. A test of the negative discriminative stimulus as a reinforcer of observing. *Journal of the Experimental Analysis of Behavior, 18,* 79–85.

Dinsmoor, J. A., Flint, G. A., Smith, R. F., and Viemeister, N. F. 1969. Differential reinforcing effects of stimuli associated with the presence or absence of a schedule of punishment. In D. P. Hendry (Ed.), *Conditioned reinforcement.* Homewood, IL: Dorsey Press.

Duncan, B., and Fantino, E. 1970. Choice for periodic schedules of reinforcement. *Journal of the Experimental Analysis of Behavior, 14,* 73–86.

Fantino, E. 1965. Some data on the discriminative stimulus hypothesis of secondary reinforcement. *Psychological Record, 15,* 409–415.

Fantino, E. 1967. Preference for mixed- *versus* fixed-ratio schedules. *Journal of the Experimental Analysis of Behavior, 10,* 35–43.

Fantino, E. 1968. Effects of required rates of responding upon choice. *Journal of the Experimental Analysis of Behavior, 11,* 15–22.

Fantino, E. 1969a. Choice and rate of reinforcement. *Journal of the Experimental Analysis of Behavior, 12,* 723–730.

Fantino, E. 1969b. Conditioned reinforcement, choice, and the psychological distance to reward. In D. P. Hendry (Ed.), *Conditioned reinforcement.* Homewood, IL: Dorsey Press.

Fantino, E. 1977. Conditioned reinforcement: Choice and information. In W. K. Honig and J. E. R. Staddon (Eds.), *Handbook of operant behavior.* Englewood Cliffs, NJ: Prentice-Hall.

Fantino, E., and Herrnstein, R. J. 1968. Secondary reinforcement and number of primary reinforcements. *Journal of the Experimental Analysis of Behavior, 11,* 9–14.

Ferster, C. B. 1953. The use of the free operant in the analysis of behavior. *Psychological Bulletin, 50,* 263–274.

Ferster, C. B., and Skinner, B. F. 1957. *Schedules of reinforcement.* New York: Appleton-Century-Crofts.

Ferster, C. B., and DeMyer, M. K. 1962. A method for the experimental analysis of the behavior of autistic children. *American Journal of Orthopsychiatry, 32,* 89–98.

Fischer, K., and Fantino, E. 1968. The dissociation of discriminative and conditioned reinforcing functions of stimuli with changes in deprivation. *Journal of the Experimental Analysis of Behavior, 11,* 703–710.

Gollub, L. R. 1958. The chaining of fixed-interval schedules. Unpublished doctoral dissertation, Harvard University.

Gollub, L. R. 1977. Conditioned reinforcement: Schedule effects. In W. K. Honig and J. E. R. Staddon (Eds.), *Handbook of operant behavior.* Englewood Cliffs, NJ: Prentice-Hall.

Harsh, J., and Badia, P. 1975. Choice for signalled over unsignalled shock as a function of shock intensity. *Journal of the Experimental Analysis of Behavior, 63,* 349–355.

Herrnstein, R. J. 1964a. Secondary reinforcement and the rate of primary reinforcement. *Journal of the Experimental Analysis of Behavior, 7,* 27–36.

Herrnstein, R. J. 1964b. Aperiodicity as a factor in choice. *Journal of the Experimental Analysis of Behavior, 7,* 179–182.

Hull, C. L. 1943. *Principles of behavior.* New York: Appleton-Century-Crofts.

Hursh, S. R., and Fantino, E. 1973. Relative delay of reinforcement and choice. *Journal of the Experimental Analysis of Behavior, 19,* 437–450.

Jenkins, H. M., and Boakes, R. A. 1973. Observing stimulus sources that signal food or no food. *Journal of the Experimental Analysis of Behavior, 20,* 197–207.

Jenkins, W. O. 1950. A temporal gradient of derived reinforcement. *American Journal of Psychology, 63,* 237–243.

Jwaideh, A. R., and Mulvaney, D. E. 1976. Punishment of observing by a stimulus associated with the lower of two reinforcement frequencies. *Learning and Motivation, 7,* 211–222.

Katz, H. N. 1976. A test of the reinforcing properties of stimuli correlated with nonreinforcement. *Journal of the Experimental Analysis of Behavior, 26,* 45–56.

Kazdin, A. E., and Bootzin, R. R. 1972. The token economy: An evaluative review. *Journal of Applied Behavior Analysis, 5,* 343–372.

Kelleher, R. T. 1957. Conditioned reinforcement in chimpanzees. *Journal of Comparative and Physiological Psychology, 50,* 571–575.

Kelleher, R. T. 1958. Fixed-ratio schedules of conditioned reinforcement with chimpanzees. *Journal of the Experimental Analysis of Behavior, 1,* 281–289.

Kelleher, R. T. 1966. Conditioned reinforcement in second-order schedules. *Journal of the Experimental Analysis of Behavior, 9,* 475–486.

Kelleher, R. T., and Gollub, L. R. 1962. A review of positive conditioned reinforcement. *Journal of the Experimental Analysis of Behavior, 5,* 543–597.

Keller, F. S., and Schoenfeld, W. N. 1950. *Principles of psychology.* New York: Appleton-Century-Crofts.

Kendall, S. B. 1973a. Redundant information in an observing-response procedure. *Journal of the Experimental Analysis of Behavior, 19,* 81–92.

Kendall, S. B. 1973b. Effects of two procedures for varying information transmission on observing responses. *Journal of the Experimental Analysis of Behavior, 20,* 73–83.

Kendall, S. B. 1974. Preference for intermittent reinforcement. *Journal of the Experimental Analysis of Behavior, 21,* 463–473.

Killeen, P. 1968. On the measurement of reinforcement frequency in the study of preference. *Journal of the Experimental Analysis of Behavior, 11,* 263–269.

Klein, R. M. 1959. Intermittent primary reinforcement as a parameter of secondary reinforcement. *Journal of Experimental Psychology, 58,* 423–427.

Lieberman, D. A. 1972. Secondary reinforcement and information as determinants of observing behavior in monkeys *(Macaca mulatta). Learning and Motivation, 3,* 341–358.

Lieberman, R. 1968. A view of behavior modification projects in California. *Behaviour Research and Therapy, 6,* 331–341.

Mason, D. J. 1957. The relation of secondary reinforcement to partial reinforcement. *Journal of Comparative and Physiological Psychology, 50,* 264–268.

Melching, W. H. 1954. The acquired reward value of an intermittently presented neutral stimulus. *Journal of Comparative and Physiological Psychology, 47,* 370–374.

Milan, M. A., and McKee, J. M. 1976. The cellblock token economy: Token reinforcement procedures in a maximum security correctional institution for adult male felons. *Journal of Applied Behavior Analysis, 9,* 253–275.

Moore, J., and Fantino, E. 1975. Choice and response contingencies. *Journal of the Experimental Analysis of Behavior, 23,* 339–347.

Mulvaney, D. E., Dinsmoor, J. A., Jwaideh, A. R., and Hughes, L. H. 1974. Punishment of observing by the negative discriminative stimulus. *Journal of the Experimental Analysis of Behavior, 21,* 37–44.

Nevin, J. A. 1973. Conditioned reinforcement. In J. A. Nevin and G. S. Reynolds (Eds.), *The study of behavior.* Glenview, IL: Scott, Foresman.

Nevin, J. A., and Mandell, C. 1978. Conditioned reinforcement and choice. *Journal of the Experimental Analysis of Behavior, 29,* 135–148.

Neuringer, A. J. 1967. Effects of reinforcement magnitude on choice and rate of responding. *Journal of the Experimental Analysis of Behavior, 10,* 417–424.

O'Leary, K. D., and Becker, W. C. 1967. Behavior modification of an adjustment class: A token reinforcement program. *Exceptional Children, 33,* 637–642.

O'Leary, K. D., Becker, W. C., Evans, M. B., and Saudargas, R. A. 1969. A token reinforcement program in a public school: A replication and systematic analysis. *Journal of Applied Behavioral Analysis, 2,* 3–13.

O'Leary, K. D., and Drabman, R. 1971. Token reinforcement programs in the classroom: A review. *Psychological Bulletin, 75,* 379–398.

Perkins, C. C. 1955. The stimulus conditions which follow learned responses. *Psychological Review, 62,* 341–348.

Prokasy, W. F. 1956. The acquisition of observing responses in the absence of differential external reinforcement. *Journal of Comparative and Physiological Psychology, 49,* 131–134.

Rachlin, H. 1976. *Behavior and learning.* San Francisco: W. H. Freeman and Company.

Rescorla, R. A. 1968. Probability of shock in the presence and absence of CS in fear conditioning. *Journal of Comparative and Physiological Psychology, 66,* 1–5.

Rescorla, R. A. 1972. Informational variables in Pavlovian conditioning. In G. Bower (Ed.), *The psychology of learning and motivation,* Vol. 6. New York: Academic Press.

Rose, J. E., and Fantino, E. 1978. Conditioned reinforcement and discrimination in second-order schedules. *Journal of the Experimental Analysis of Behavior, 29,* 393–418.

Ruch, F. L., and Zimbardo, P. G. 1971. *Psychology and life.* 8th ed. Glenview, IL: Scott, Foreman.

Saltzman, I. J. 1949. Maze learning in the absence of primary reinforcement: A study of secondary reinforcement. *Journal of Comparative and Physiological Psychology, 42,* 161–173.

Schaefer, H. H., and Martin, P. L. 1966. Behavior therapy for "apathy" of hospitalized schizophrenics. *Psychological Reports, 19,* 1147–1158.

Schaefer, H. H., and Martin, P. L. 1969. *Behavioral therapy.* New York: McGraw-Hill.

Schaub, R. E. 1969. Response–cue contingency and cue effectiveness. In D. P. Hendry (Ed.), *Conditioned reinforcement.* Homewood, IL: Dorsey Press.

Schaub, R. E., and Honig, W. K. 1967. Reinforcement of behavior with cues correlated with extinction. *Psychonomic Science, 1,* 15–16.

Schoenfeld, W. N., Antonitis, J. J., and Bersh, P. J. 1950. A preliminary study of training conditions necessary for secondary reinforcement. *Journal of Experimental Psychology, 40,* 40–45.

Seligman, M. E. P., Maier, S. F., and Solomon, R. L. 1971. Unpredictable and uncontrollable aversive events. In F. R. Brush (Ed.), *Aversive conditioning and learning.* New York: Academic Press.

Skinner, B. F. 1938. *The behavior of organisms.* New York: Appleton-Century-Crofts.

Skinner, B. F. 1953. *Science and human behavior.* New York: Macmillan.

Squires, N., Norborg, J., and Fantino, E. 1975. Second-order schedules: Discrimination of components. *Journal of the Experimental Analysis of Behavior, 24,* 157–171.

Steffy, R. A., Hart, J., Craw, M., Torney, D., and Marlett, N. 1969. Operant behaviour modification techniques applied to severely regressed and aggressive patients. *Canadian Psychiatric Association Journal, 14,* 59–67.

Stubbs, D. A. 1971. Second-order schedules and the problem of conditioned reinforcement. *Journal of the Experimental Analysis of Behavior, 16,* 289–313.

Waddell, T. R., Leander, J. D., Webbe, F. M., and Malagodi, E. F. 1972. Schedule interactions in second-order fixed-interval (fixed-ratio) schedules of token reinforcement. *Learning and Motivation, 3,* 91–100.

Wallace, R. F. 1973. Conditioned reinforcement and choice. Unpublished doctoral dissertation, University of California, San Diego.

Weisman, R. G., and Litner, J. S. 1971. Role of the intertrial interval in Pavlovian differential conditioning of fear in rats. *Journal of Comparative and Physiological Psychology, 74,* 211–218.

Wolf, M. M., Giles, D. K., and Hall, R. V. 1968. Experiments with token reinforcement in a remedial classroom. *Behaviour Research and Therapy, 6,* 51–64.

Wolfe, J. B. 1936. Effectiveness of token rewards for chimpanzees. *Comparative Psychology Monographs, 12,* 1–72.

Wyckoff, L. B., Jr. 1952. The role of observing responses in discrimination learning, Part I. *Psychological Review, 59,* 431–442.

Wyckoff, L. B., Jr. 1959. Toward a quantitative theory of secondary reinforcement. *Psychological Review, 66,* 68–78.

Wyckoff, L. B., Jr. 1969. The role of observing responses in discrimination learning. In D. P. Hendry (Ed.), *Conditioned reinforcement*. Homewood, IL: Dorsey Press.

Chapter 7

Ainslie, G. W. 1974. Impulse control in pigeons. *Journal of the Experimental Analysis of Behavior, 21,* 485–489.

Autor, S. M. 1960. The strength of conditioned reinforcers as a function of frequency and probability of reinforcement. Unpublished doctoral dissertation, Harvard University.

Autor, S. M. 1969. The strength of conditioned reinforcers as a function of frequency and probability of reinforcement. In D. P. Hendry (Ed.), *Conditioned reinforcement*. Homewood, IL: Dorsey Press.

Bacotti, A. V. 1977. Matching under concurrent fixed-ratio variable-interval schedules of food presentation. *Journal of the Experimental Analysis of Behavior, 25,* 171–182.

Baum, W. M. 1974. On two types of deviation from the matching law: Bias and undermatching. *Journal of the Experimental Analysis of Behavior, 22,* 231–242.

Baum, W. M. 1975. Time allocation in human vigilance. *Journal of the Experimental Analysis of Behavior, 23,* 45–53.

Baum, W. M., and Rachlin, H. C. 1969. Choice as time allocation. *Journal of the Experimental Analysis of Behavior, 12,* 861–874.

Bower, G., McLean, J., and Meacham, J. 1966. Value of knowing when reinforcement is due. *Journal of Comparative and Physiological Psychology, 62,* 184–192.

Brownstein, A. J., and Pliskoff, S. S. 1968. Some effects of relative reinforcement rate and changeover delay in response-independent concurrent schedules of reinforcement. *Journal of the Experimental Analysis of Behavior, 11,* 683–688.

Catania, A. C. 1963a. Concurrent performances: A baseline for the study of reinforcement magnitude. *Journal of the Experimental Analysis of Behavior, 6,* 299–300.

Catania, A. C. 1963b. Concurrent performances: Reinforcement interaction and response independence. *Journal of the Experimental Analysis of Behavior, 6,* 253–263.

Catania, A. C. 1972. Concurrent performances: Synthesizing rate constancies by manipulating contingencies for a single response. *Journal of the Experimental Analysis of Behavior, 17,* 139–145.

Catania, A. C. 1973. Self-inhibiting effects of reinforcement. *Journal of the Experimental Analysis of Behavior, 19,* 517–526.

Catania, A. C., and Cutts, D. 1963. Experimental control of superstitious responding in humans. *Journal of the Experimental Analysis of Behavior, 6,* 203–208.

Davison, M. C. 1969. Preference for mixed-interval *versus* fixed-interval schedules. *Journal of the Experimental Analysis of Behavior, 12,* 247–252.

Davison, M. C. 1972. Preference for mixed-interval *versus* fixed-interval schedules: Number of component intervals. *Journal of the Experimental Analysis of Behavior, 17,* 169–176.

de Villiers, P. 1977. Choice in concurrent schedules and a quantitative formulation of the law of effect. In W. K. Honig and J. E. R. Staddon (Eds.), *Handbook of operant behavior*. Englewood Cliffs, NJ: Prentice-Hall.

de Villiers, P. A., and Herrnstein, R. J. 1976. Toward a law of response strength. *Psychological Bulletin, 83,* 1131–1153.

Duncan, B., and Fantino, E. 1972. The psychological distance to reward. *Journal of the Experimental Analysis of Behavior, 18,* 23–24.

Fantino, E. 1966. Immediate reward followed by extinction *vs* later reward without extinction. *Psychonomic Science, 6,* 233–234.

Fantino, E. 1967. Preference for mixed- *versus* fixed-ratio schedules. *Journal of the Experimental Analysis of Behavior, 10,* 35–43.

Fantino, E. 1969. Choice and rate of reinforcement. *Journal of the Experimental Analysis of Behavior, 12,* 723–730.

Fantino, E. 1977. Conditioned reinforcement: Choice and information. In W. K. Honig and J. E. R. Staddon (Eds.), *Handbook of operant behavior.* Englewood Cliffs, NJ: Prentice-Hall.

Fantino, E., and Duncan, B. 1972. Some effects of interreinforcement time upon choice. *Journal of the Experimental Analysis of Behavior, 17,* 3–14.

Fantino, E., and Navarick, D. 1974. Recent developments in choice. In G. H. Bower (Ed.), *The psychology of learning and motivation,* Vol. 8. New York: Academic Press.

Fantino, E., and Reynolds, G. S. 1975. *Introduction to contemporary psychology.* San Francisco: W. H. Freeman and Company.

Fantino, E., Squires, N., Delbrück, N., and Peterson, C. 1972. Choice behavior and the accessibility of the reinforcer. *Journal of the Experimental Analysis of Behavior, 18,* 35–43.

Findley, J. D. 1958. Preference and switching under concurrent scheduling. *Journal of the Experimental Analysis of Behavior, 1,* 123–144.

Gollub, L. R. 1958. The chaining of fixed-interval schedules. Unpublished doctoral dissertation, Harvard University.

Graft, D. A., Lea, S. E. G., and Whitworth, T. L. 1977. The matching law in and within groups of rats. *Journal of the Experimental Analysis of Behavior, 25,* 183–194.

Guilkey, M., Shull, R. L., and Brownstein, A. J. 1975. Response-rate invariance in concurrent schedules: Effects of different changeover contingencies. *Journal of the Experimental Analysis of Behavior, 24,* 43–52.

Herrnstein, R. J. 1961. Relative and absolute strength of response as a function of frequency of reinforcement. *Journal of the Experimental Analysis of Behavior, 4,* 267–272.

Herrnstein, R. J. 1964a. Secondary reinforcement and rate of primary reinforcement. *Journal of the Experimental Analysis of Behavior, 7,* 27–36.

Herrnstein, R. J. 1964b. Aperiodicity as a factor in choice. *Journal of the Experimental Analysis of Behavior, 7,* 179–182.

Herrnstein, R. J. 1970. On the law of effect. *Journal of the Experimental Analysis of Behavior, 13,* 243–266.

Herrnstein, R. J. 1974. Formal properties of the matching law. *Journal of the Experimental Analysis of Behavior, 21,* 159–164.

Herrnstein, R. J., and Loveland, D. H. 1974. Hunger and contrast in a multiple schedule. *Journal of the Experimental Analysis of Behavior, 21,* 511–517.

Herrnstein, R. J., and Loveland, D. H. 1975. Maximizing and matching on concurrent ratio schedules. *Journal of the Experimental Analysis of Behavior, 24,* 107–116.

Heyman, G. M. 1979. A Markov model description of changeover probabilities on concurrent variable-interval schedules. *Journal of the Experimental Analysis of Behavior, 31,* 41–51.

Killeen, P. 1968. On the measurement of reinforcement frequency in the study of preference. *Journal of the Experimental Analysis of Behavior, 11,* 263–269.

Killeen, P. 1972. The matching law. *Journal of the Experimental Analysis of Behavior, 17,* 489–495.

Lander, D. G., and Irwin, R. J. 1968. Multiple schedules: Effects of the distributions of reinforcements between components on the distribution of responses between components. *Journal of the Experimental Analysis of Behavior, 11,* 517–524.

Logan, F. A. 1965. Decision making by rats: Delay versus amount of reward. *Journal of Comparative and Physiological Psychology, 59,* 1–12.

MacEwen, D. 1972. The effects of terminal-link fixed-interval and variable-interval schedules on responding under concurrent chained schedules. *Journal of the Experimental Analysis of Behavior, 18,* 253–261.

McSweeney, F. K. 1975. Matching and contrast on several concurrent treadle-press schedules. *Journal of the Experimental Analysis of Behavior, 23,* 193–198.

Moore, J., and Fantino, E. 1975. Choice and response contingencies. *Journal of the Experimental Analysis of Behavior, 23,* 339–347.

Myers, D. L. 1973. A quantitative description of performance on concurrent interval schedules, and concurrent ratio-interval schedules of reinforcement. Doctoral dissertation, University of California, San Diego, 1972. *Dissertation Abstracts International, 33,* 3989B. (University Microfilms No. 73-4423, 156.)

Myers, D. L., and Myers, L. E. 1977. Undermatching: A reappraisal of performance on concurrent variable-interval schedules of reinforcement. *Journal of the Experimental Analysis of Behavior, 27,* 203–214.

Navarick, D. J., and Fantino, E. 1974. Stochastic transitivity and unidimensional behavior theories. *Psychological Review, 81,* 426–441.

Navarick, D. J., and Fantino, E. 1975. Stochastic transitivity and the unidimensional control of choice. *Learning and Motivation, 6,* 179–201.

Navarick, D. J., and Fantino, E. 1976. Self-control and general models of choice. *Journal of Experimental Psychology: Animal Behavior Processes, 2,* 75–87.

Nevin, J. A. 1968. Differential reinforcement and stimulus control of not responding. *Journal of the Experimental Analysis of Behavior, 11,* 715–726.

Nevin, J. A. 1969. Interval reinforcement of choice behavior in discrete trials. *Journal of the Experimental Analysis of Behavior, 12,* 875–885.

Pliskoff, S. S. 1971. Effects of symmetrical and asymmetrical changeover delays on concurrent performances. *Journal of the Experimental Analysis of Behavior, 16,* 249–256.

Pliskoff, S. S., and Green, D. 1972. Effects on concurrent performances of a stimulus correlated with reinforcer availability. *Journal of the Experimental Analysis of Behavior, 17,* 221–227.

Premack, D. 1969. On boundary conditions of contrast. In J. T. Tapp (Ed.), *Reinforcement and behavior.* New York: Academic Press.

Rachlin, H., and Baum, W. M. 1972. Effects of alternative reinforcement: Does the source matter? *Journal of the Experimental Analysis of Behavior, 18,* 231–241.

Rachlin, H., and Green, L. 1972. Commitment, choice and self-control. *Journal of the Experimental Analysis of Behavior, 17,* 15–22.

Reynolds, G. S. 1963. Some limitations on behavioral contrast and induction during successive discrimination. *Journal of the Experimental Analysis of Behavior, 6,* 131–139.

Schneider, J. W. 1973. Reinforcer effectiveness as a function of reinforcer rate and magnitude: A comparison of concurrent performances. *Journal of the Experimental Analysis of Behavior, 20,* 461–471.

Shimp, C. P. 1966. Probabilistically reinforced choice behavior in pigeons. *Journal of the Experimental Analysis of Behavior, 9,* 443–455.

Shimp, C. P. 1969. Optimum behavior in free-operant experiments. *Psychological Review, 76,* 97–112.

Shimp, C. P. 1974. Time allocation and response rates. *Journal of the Experimental Analysis of Behavior, 21,* 491–499.

Shull, R. L., and Pliskoff, S. S. 1967. Changeover delay and concurrent schedules: Some effects on relative performance measures. *Journal of the Experimental Analysis of Behavior, 10,* 517–527.

Silberberg, A., and Fantino, E. 1970. Choice, rate of reinforcement, and the changeover delay. *Journal of the Experimental Analysis of Behavior, 13,* 187–197.

Spealman, R. D., and Gollub, L. R. 1974. Behavioral interactions in multiple variable-interval schedules. *Journal of the Experimental Analysis of Behavior, 22,* 471–481.

Squires, N., and Fantino, E. 1971. A model for choice in simple concurrent and concurrent-chains schedules. *Journal of the Experimental Analysis of Behavior, 15,* 27–38.

Staddon, J. E. R. 1972. Temporal control and the theory of reinforcement schedules. In R. M. Gilbert and J. R. Millenson (Eds.), *Reinforcement: Behavioral analyses.* New York: Academic Press.

Terrace, H. S. 1972. By-products of discrimination learning. In G. H. Bower (Ed.), *The psychology of learning and motivation,* Vol. 5. New York: Academic Press.

Wallace, R. F. 1973. Conditioned reinforcement and choice. Unpublished doctoral dissertation, University of California, San Diego.

Williams, B. A. 1972. Probability learning as a function of momentary reinforcement probability. *Journal of the Experimental Analysis of Behavior, 17,* 363–368.

Williams, B. A. 1976. Behavioral contrast as a function of the temporal location of reinforcement. *Journal of the Experimental Analysis of Behavior, 26,* 57–64.

Williams, B. A., and Fantino, E. 1978. Effects on choice of reinforcement delay and conditioned reinforcement. *Journal of the Experimental Analysis of Behavior, 29,* 77–86.

Chapter 8

Altenor, A., Kay, E., and Richter, M. 1977. The generality of learned helplessness in the rat. *Learning and Motivation, 8,* 54–61.

Anderson, N. H. 1969. Variation of CS–US interval in long-term avoidance conditioning in the rat with wheel turn and with shuttle tasks. *Journal of Comparative and Physiological Psychology, 68,* 100–106.

Appel, J. B. 1961. Punishment in the squirrel monkey *Saimiri sciurea. Science, 133,* 36–37.

Appel, J. B., and Peterson, N. J. 1965. Punishment: Effects of shock intensity on response suppression. *Psychological Reports, 16,* 721–230.

Ayllon, T., and Azrin, N. H. 1968. *The token economy: A motivational system for therapy and rehabilitation.* New York: Appleton-Century-Crofts.

Azrin, N. H. 1956. Some effects of two intermittent schedules of immediate and non-immediate punishment. *Journal of Psychology, 42*, 3–21.

Azrin, N. H. 1959. Punishment and recovery during fixed-ratio performance. *Journal of the Experimental Analysis of Behavior, 2*, 301–305.

Azrin, N. H. 1960. Effects of punishment intensity during variable-interval reinforcement. *Journal of the Experimental Analysis of Behavior, 3*, 123–142.

Azrin, N. H., and Hake, D. F. 1969. Positive conditioned suppression: Conditioned suppression using positive reinforcers as the unconditioned stimuli. *Journal of the Experimental Analysis of Behavior, 12*, 167–173.

Azrin, N. H., and Holz, W. C. 1966. Punishment. In W. K. Honig (Ed.), *Operant behavior: Areas of research and application.* New York: Appleton-Century-Crofts.

Azrin, N. H., Holz, W. C., and Hake, D. F. 1963. Fixed-ratio punishment. *Journal of the Experimental Analysis of Behavior, 6*, 141–148.

Azrin, N. H., Holz, W. C., Hake, D. F., and Ayllon, T. 1963. Fixed-ratio escape reinforcement. *Journal of the Experimental Analysis of Behavior, 6*, 449–456.

Baker, A. G. 1976. Learned irrelevance and learned helplessness: Rats learn that stimuli, reinforcers, and responses are uncorrelated. *Journal of Experimental Psychology: Animal Behavior Processes, 2*, 130–141.

Baron, A., DeWaard, R. J., and Lipson, J. 1977. Increased reinforcement when time out from avoidance includes access to a safe place. *Journal of the Experimental Analysis of Behavior, 27*, 479–494.

Baum, M. 1965. An automated apparatus for the avoidance training of rats. *Psychological Reports, 16*, 1205–1211.

Baum, M. 1969. Paradoxical effect of alcohol on the resistance to extinction of an avoidance response in rats. *Journal of Comparative and Physiological Psychology, 69*, 238–240.

Bitterman, M. E. 1965. The CS–US interval in classical and avoidance conditioning. In W. F. Prokasy (Ed.), *Classical conditioning.* New York: Appleton-Century-Crofts.

Blackman, D. 1977. Conditioned suppression and the effects of classical conditioning on operant behavior. In W. K. Honig and J. E. R. Staddon (Eds.), *Handbook of operant behavior.* Englewood Cliffs, NJ: Prentice-Hall.

Bolles, R. C. 1967. *Theory of motivation.* New York: Harper & Row.

Bolles, R. C. 1970. Species-specific defense reactions and avoidance learning. *Psychological Review, 77*, 32–48.

Bolles, R. C., and Grossen, N. E. 1969. Effects of an informational stimulus on the acquisition of avoidance behavior in rats. *Journal of Comparative and Physiological Psychology, 68*, 90–99.

Bolles, R. C., Stokes, L. W., and Younger, M. S. 1966. Does CS termination reinforce avoidance behavior? *Journal of Comparative and Physiological Psychology, 62*, 201–207.

Bolles, R. C., and Warren, J. A. 1965. The acquisition of bar-press avoidance as a function of shock intensity. *Psychonomic Science, 3*, 297–298.

Brady, J., and Harris, A. 1977. The experimental production of altered physiological states: Concurrent and contingent behavioral models. In W. K. Honig and J. E. R. Staddon (Eds.), *Handbook of operant behavior,* Englewood Cliffs, NJ: Prentice-Hall.

Brady, J. V., Kelly, D., and Plumlee, L. 1969. Autonomic and behavioral responses of the rhesus monkey to emotional conditioning. *Annals of the New York Academy of Science, 159*, 959–975.

Brown, J. S. 1969. Factors affecting self-punitive locomotor behavior. In B. A. Campbell and R. M. Church (Eds.), *Punishment and aversive behavior.* New York: Appleton-Century-Crofts.

Byrd, L. D. 1969. Responding in the cat maintained under response-independent electric shock and response-produced electric shock. *Journal of the Experimental Analysis of Behavior, 12,* 1–10.

Byrd, L. D. 1972. Responding in the squirrel monkey under second-order schedules of shock delivery. *Journal of the Experimental Analysis of Behavior, 18,* 155–167.

Campbell, B. A., Smith, N. F., and Misanin, J. R. 1966. Effects of punishment on extinction of avoidance behavior: Avoidance-avoidance conflict or vicious circle behavior? *Journal of Comparative and Physiological Psychology, 62,* 495–498.

Church, R. M. 1963. The varied effects of punishment on behavior. *Psychological Review, 70,* 369–402.

Church, R. M. 1969. Response suppression. In B. A. Campbell and R. M. Church (Eds.), *Punishment and aversive behavior.* New York: Appleton-Century-Crofts.

Clark, F. C., and Hull, L. D. 1966. Free operant avoidance as a function of the response–shock = shock–shock interval. *Journal of the Experimental Analysis of Behavior, 9,* 641–647.

Cohen, P. S. 1968. Punishment: The interactive effects of delay and intensity of shock. *Journal of the Experimental Analysis of Behavior, 11,* 789–799.

Cole, M., and Fantino, E. 1966. Temporal variables and trial discreteness in lever-press avoidance. *Psychonomic Science, 6,* 217–218.

Coulson, G., Coulson, V., and Gardner, L. 1970. The effect of two extinction procedures after acquisition on a Sidman avoidance contingency. *Psychonomic Science, 18,* 309–310.

D'Amato, M. R., and Fazzaro, J. 1966. Discriminated lever-press avoidance learning as a function of type and intensity of shock. *Journal of Comparative and Physiological Psychology, 61,* 313–315.

D'Amato, M. R., Fazzaro, J., and Etkin, M. 1967. Discriminated bar-press avoidance maintenance and extinction in rats as a function of shock intensity. *Journal of Comparative and Physiological Psychology, 63,* 351–354.

D'Amato, M. R., Fazzaro, J., and Etkin, M. 1968. Anticipatory responding and avoidance discrimination as factors in avoidance conditioning. *Journal of Experimental Psychology, 77,* 41–47.

D'Amato, M. R., Keller, D., and DiCara, L. 1964. Facilitation of discriminated avoidance learning by discontinuous shock. *Journal of Comparative and Physiological Psychology, 58,* 344–349.

Denny, M. R. 1971. Relaxation therapy and experiments. In F. R. Brush (Ed.), *Aversive conditioning and learning.* New York: Academic Press.

Denny, M. R., and Weisman, R. G. 1964. Long-term discriminated avoidance performance in the rat. *Journal of Comparative and Physiological Psychology, 57,* 123–126.

Dericco, D. A., Brigham, T. A., and Garlington, W. K. 1977. Development and evaluation of treatment paradigms for the suppression of smoking behavior. *Journal of Applied Behavior Analysis, 10,* 173–181.

de Toledo, L. E., and Black, A. H. 1966. Heart rate: Changes during conditioned suppression in rats. *Science, 152,* 1404–1406.

de Villiers, P. A. 1972. Reinforcement and response rate interaction in multiple random-interval avoidance schedules. *Journal of the Experimental Analysis of Behavior, 18,* 499–507.

de Villiers, P. A. 1974. The law of effect and avoidance: A quantitative relationship between response rate and shock-frequency reduction. *Journal of the Experimental Analysis of Behavior, 21,* 223–235.

de Villiers, P. A. 1977. Choice in concurrent schedules and a quantitative formulation of the law of effect. In W. K. Honig and J. E. R. Staddon (Eds.), *Handbook of operant behavior.* Englewood Cliffs, NJ: Prentice-Hall.

Dinsmoor, J. A. 1954. Punishment: I. The avoidance hypothesis. *Psychological Review, 61,* 34–46.

Dinsmoor, J. A. 1977. Escape, avoidance, punishment: Where do we stand? *Journal of the Experimental Analysis of Behavior, 28,* 83–95.

Dinsmoor, J. A., and Sears, G. W. 1973. Control of avoidance by a response-produced stimulus. *Learning and Motivation, 4,* 284–293.

Dinsmoor, J. A., and Winograd, E. 1958. Shock intensity in variable-interval escape schedules. *Journal of the Experimental Analysis of Behavior, 1,* 145–148.

Estes, W. K. 1944. An experimental study of punishment. *Psychological Monographs, 57,* No. 3.

Estes, W. K. 1969. Outline of a theory of punishment. In B. A. Campbell and R. M. Church (Eds.), *Punishment and aversive behavior.* Englewood Cliffs, NJ: Prentice-Hall.

Estes, W. K., and Skinner, B. F. 1941. Some quantitative properties of anxiety. *Journal of Experimental Psychology, 29,* 390–400.

Fantino, E. 1967. Preference for mixed- versus fixed-ratio schedules. *Journal of the Experimental Analysis of Behavior, 10,* 35–43.

Fantino, E. 1973. Aversive control. In J. A. Nevin and G. S. Reynolds (Eds.), *The study of behavior: Learning, motivation, emotion, and instinct.* Glenview, IL: Scott, Foresman.

Fantino, E., Sharp, D., and Cole, M. 1966. Factors facilitating lever-press avoidance. *Journal of Comparative and Physiological Psychology, 62,* 214–217.

Farley, J., and Fantino, E. 1978. The symmetrical law of effect and the matching relation in choice behavior. *Journal of the Experimental Analysis of Behavior, 29,* 37–60.

Ferster, C. B., and Skinner, B. F. 1957. *Schedules of reinforcement.* New York: Appleton-Century-Crofts.

Field, G. E., and Boren, J. J. 1963. An adjusting avoidance procedure with multiple auditory and visual warning stimuli. *Journal of the Experimental Analysis of Behavior, 6,* 537–543.

Fowler, H. 1971. Suppression and facilitation by response contingent shock. In F. R. Brush (Ed.), *Aversive conditioning and learning.* New York: Academic Press.

Fowler, H., and Miller, N. E. 1963. Facilitation and inhibition of runway performance by hind- and forepaw shock of various intensities. *Journal of Comparative and Physiological Psychology, 56,* 801–805.

Gibbon, J., Berryman, R., and Thompson, R. L. 1974. Contingency spaces and measures in classical and instrumental conditioning. *Journal of the Experimental Analysis of Behavior, 21,* 585–605.

Glazer, H. I., and Weiss, J. M. 1976a. Long-term and transitory interference effects. *Journal of Experimental Psychology: Animal Behavior Processes, 2,* 191–201.

Glazer, H. I., and Weiss, J. M. 1976b. Long-term interference effect: An alternative to "learned helplessness." *Journal of Experimental Psychology: Animal Behavior Processes, 2,* 202–213.

Grabowski, J., and Thompson, T. 1972. Response patterning on an avoidance schedule as a function of time-correlated stimuli. *Journal of the Experimental Analysis of Behavior, 18,* 525–534.

Grice, G. R. 1948. The relation of secondary reinforcement to delayed reward in visual discrimination learning. *Journal of Experimental Psychology, 38,* 1–16.

Hendry, D. P., and Hendry, L. S. 1963. Partial negative reinforcement: Fixed-ratio escape. *Journal of the Experimental Analysis of Behavior, 6,* 519–523.

Herrnstein, R. J., and Hineline, P. N. 1966. Negative reinforcement as shock-frequency reduction. *Journal of the Experimental Analysis of Behavior, 9,* 421–430.

Herrnstein, R. J., and Morse, W. H. 1957. Some effects of response-independent positive reinforcement on maintained operant behavior. *Journal of Comparative and Physiological Psychology, 50,* 461–467.

Hineline, P. N. 1977. Negative reinforcement and avoidance. In W. K. Honig and J. E. R. Staddon (Eds.), *Handbook of operant behavior.* Englewood Cliffs, NJ: Prentice-Hall.

Hineline, P. N., and Rachlin, H. 1969. Notes on fixed-ratio and fixed-interval escape responding in the pigeon. *Journal of the Experimental Analysis of Behavior, 12,* 397–401.

Hoffman, H. S. and Fleshler, M. 1962. A relay sequencing device for scrambling grid shock. *Journal of the Experimental Analysis of Behavior, 5,* 329–330.

Holz, W. C., and Azrin, N. H. 1961. Discriminative properties of punishment. *Journal of the Experimental Analysis of Behavior, 4,* 225–232.

Hurwitz, H. M. B. 1964. Method for discriminative avoidance training. *Science, 145,* 1070–1071.

Hutchinson, R. R. 1977. By-products of aversive control. In W. K. Honig and J. E. R. Staddon (Eds.), *Handbook of operant behavior.* Englewood Cliffs, NJ: Prentice-Hall.

Hutton, L., and Lewis, P. In press. Effects of response-independent negative reinforcers on negatively reinforced keypecking. *Journal of the Experimental Analysis of Behavior.*

Jackson, R. L., Maier, S. F., and Rapaport, P. M. 1978. Exposure to inescapable shock produces both activity and associative deficits in the rat. *Learning and Motivation, 9,* 69–98.

Kamin, L. J. 1956. The effects of termination of the CS and avoidance of the US on avoidance learning. *Journal of Comparative and Physiological Psychology, 49,* 420–424.

Kamin, L. J. 1957. The effects of termination of the CS and avoidance of the US on avoidance learning: An extension. *Canadian Journal of Psychology, 11,* 48–56.

Keehn, J. D. 1966. Avoidance responses as discriminated operants. *British Journal of Psychology, 57,* 375–380.

Keehn, J. D. 1967. Running and bar pressing as avoidance responses. *Psychological Reports, 20,* 591–602.

Keehn, J. D., and Walsh, M. 1970. Bar-holding with negative reinforcement as a function of press– and release–shock intervals. *Learning and Motivation, 1,* 36–43.

Kelly, D. D. 1973. Long-term prereward suppression in monkeys unaccompanied by cardiovascular conditioning. *Journal of the Experimental Analysis of Behavior, 20,* 93–104.

Killeen, P. 1968. Response rate as a factor in choice. *Psychonomic Science, 12,* 34.

Kintz, B. L., and Bruning, J. L. 1967. Punishment and compulsive avoidance behavior. *Journal of Comparative and Physiological Psychology, 63,* 323–326.

Krieckhaus, E. F., Miller, N. E., and Zimmerman, P. 1965. Reduction of freezing behavior and improvement of shock avoidance by d-amphetamine. *Journal of Comparative and Physiological Psychology, 60,* 36–49.

Kushner, M. 1965. Desensitization of a post-traumatic phobia. In L. P. Ullman and L. Krasner (Eds.), *Case studies in behavior modification.* New York: Holt, Rinehart and Winston.

Lambert, J. V., Bersh, P. J., Hineline, P. N., and Smith, G. D. 1973. Avoidance conditioning with shock contingent upon the avoidance response. *Journal of the Experimental Analysis of Behavior, 19,* 361–367.

Leaf, R. C. 1965. Acquisition of Sidman avoidance responding as a function of S–S interval. *Journal of Comparative and Physiological Psychology, 59,* 298–300.

LoLordo, V. M. 1971. Facilitation of food-reinforced responding by a signal for response-independent food. *Journal of the Experimental Analysis of Behavior, 15,* 49–56.

LoLordo, V. M., McMillan, J. C., and Riley, A. C. 1974. The effects upon food-reinforced pecking and treadle-pressing of auditory and visual signals for response-independent food. *Learning and Motivation, 5,* 24–41.

Mackintosh, N. J. 1974. *The psychology of animal learning.* London: Academic Press.

Macphail, E. M. 1968. Avoidance responding in pigeons. *Journal of the Experimental Analysis of Behavior, 11,* 629–632.

Maier, S. F. 1970. Failure to escape traumatic electric shock: Incompatible skeletal-motor responses or learned helplessness? *Learning and Motivation, 1,* 157–169.

Maier, S. F., Albin, R. W., and Testa, T. J. 1973. Failure to learn to escape in rats previously exposed to inescapable shock depends on nature of the escape response. *Journal of Comparative and Physiological Psychology, 85,* 581–592.

Maier, S. F., and Seligman, M. E. P. 1976. Learned helplessness: Theory and evidence. *Journal of Experimental Psychology: General, 105,* 3–46.

Maier, S. F., Seligman, M. E. P., and Solomon, R. L. 1969. Pavlovian fear conditioning and learned helplessness. In B. A. Campbell and R. M. Church (Eds.), *Punishment and aversive behavior.* New York: Appleton-Century-Crofts.

Marks, I. M. 1976. Management of sexual disorders. In H. Leitenberg (Ed.), *Handbook of behavior modification and behavior therapy.* Englewood Cliffs, NJ: Prentice-Hall.

McKearney, J. W. 1968. Maintenance of responding under a fixed-interval schedule of electric shock presentation. *Science, 160,* 1249–1251.

McKearney, J. W. 1970. Responding under fixed-ratio and multiple fixed-interval fixed-ratio schedules of electric shock presentation. *Journal of Experimental Analysis of Behavior, 14,* 1–6.

Meltzer, D., and Brahlek, J. A. 1970. Conditioned suppression and conditioned enhancement with the same positive UCS: An effect of CS duration. *Journal of the Experimental Analysis of Behavior, 13,* 67–73.

Meyer, D. R., Cho, C., and Wesemann, A. F. 1960. On problems of conditioning discriminated lever-press avoidance responses. *Psychological Review, 67,* 224–228.

Morse, W. H., and Kelleher, R. T. 1970. Schedules as fundamental determinants of behavior. In W. N. Schoenfeld (Ed.), *The theory of reinforcement schedules.* New York: Appleton-Century-Crofts.

Mowrer, O. H. 1947. On the dual nature of learning: A re-interpretation of "conditioning" and "problem solving." *Harvard Educational Review, 17,* 102–148.

Mowrer, O. H., and Lamoreaux, R. R. 1946. Fear as an intervening variable in avoidance conditioning. *Journal of Comparative and Physiological Psychology, 39,* 29–50.

Nathan, P. E. 1976. Alcoholism. In H. Leitenberg (Ed.), *Handbook of behavior modification and behavior therapy.* Englewood Cliffs, NJ: Prentice-Hall.

Navarick, D. J., and Fantino, E. 1974. Stochastic transitivity and unidimensional behavior theories. *Psychological Review, 81,* 426–441.

Neuringer, A. J. 1969. Delayed reinforcement *versus* reinforcement after a fixed interval. *Journal of the Experimental Analysis of Behavior, 12,* 375–383.

Overmier, J. B., and Seligman, M. E. P. 1967. Effects of inescapable shock upon subsequent escape and avoidance responding. *Journal of Comparative and Physiological Psychology, 63,* 28–33.

Pearl, J. 1963. Effects of preshock and additional punishment on general activity. *Psychological Reports, 12,* 155–161.

Pomerleau, O. F. 1970. The effects of stimuli followed by response-independent shock on shock-avoidance behavior. *Journal of the Experimental Analysis of Behavior, 14,* 11–21.

Rachlin, H. 1976. *Behavior and learning.* San Francisco: W. H. Freeman and Company.

Rachlin, H., and Herrnstein, R. J. 1969. Hedonism revisited: On the negative law of effect. In B. A. Campbell and R. M. Church (Eds.), *Punishment and aversive behavior.* Englewood Cliffs, NJ: Prentice-Hall.

Rands, B. A., and Dean, S. J. 1977. Vicious-circle behavior in the Y maze. *Learning and Motivation, 8,* 62–68.

Rescorla, R. A. 1966. Predictability and number of pairings in Pavlovian fear conditioning. *Psychonomic Science, 4,* 383–384.

Rescorla, R. A., and Skucy, J. C. 1969. Effect of response-independent reinforcers during extinction. *Journal of Comparative and Physiological Psychology, 67,* 381–389.

Rescorla, R. A., and Solomon, R. L. 1967. Two-process learning theory: Relationships between Pavlovian conditioning and instrumental learning. *Psychological Review, 74,* 151–182.

Riess, D. 1970. Sidman avoidance in rats as a function of shock intensity and duration. *Journal of Comparative and Physiological Psychology, 73,* 481–485.

Rose, J. E., and Fantino, E. 1977. Self-punitive behavior in humans: Effects of a self-fulfilling prophecy. Paper presented at the meetings of the Psychonomic Society, Washington, DC.

Schuster, R., and Rachlin, H. 1968. Indifference between punishment and free shock: Evidence for the negative law of effect. *Journal of the Experimental Analysis of Behavior, 11,* 777–786.

Seligman, M. E. P., and Beagley, G. 1975. Learned helplessness in the rat. *Journal of Comparative and Physiological Psychology, 88,* 534–541.

Seligman, M. E. P., and Maier, S. F. 1967. Failure to escape traumatic shock. *Journal of Experimental Psychology, 74,* 1–9.

Seligman, M. E. P., Rosellini, R. A., and Kozak, M. J. 1975. Learned helplessness in the rat: Time course, immunization, and reversibility. *Journal of Comparative and Physiological Psychology, 88,* 542–547.

Sidman, M. 1953. Two temporal parameters in the maintenance of avoidance behavior of the white rat. *Journal of Comparative and Physiological Psychology, 46,* 253–261.

Sidman, M. 1955. Some properties of the warning stimulus in avoidance behavior. *Journal of Comparative and Physiological Psychology, 48,* 444–450.

Sidman, M. 1957. Conditioned reinforcing and aversive stimuli in an avoidance situation. *Transactions of the New York Academy of Science, 19,* 534–544.

Sidman, M. 1962. Reduction of shock frequency as reinforcement for avoidance behavior. *Journal of the Experimental Analysis of Behavior, 5,* 247–257.

Sidman, M., and Boren, J. J. 1957a. A comparison of two types of warning stimulus in an avoidance situation. *Journal of Comparative and Physiological Psychology, 50,* 282–287.

Sidman, M., and Boren, J. J. 1957b. The relative aversiveness of warning signal and shock in an avoidance situation. *Journal of Abnormal and Social Psychology, 55,* 339–344.

Skinner, B. F. 1938. *The behavior of organisms.* New York: Appleton-Century-Crofts.

Skinner, B. F. 1953. *Science and human behavior.* New York: Macmillan.

Smith, K. 1974. The continuum of reinforcement and attenuation. *Behaviorism, 2,* 124–145.

Solomon, R. L., and Brush, E. S. 1956. Experimentally derived conceptions of anxiety and aversion. In M. R. Jones (Ed.), *Nebraska symposium on motivation, 1956.* Lincoln: University of Nebraska Press.

Solomon, R. L., Kamin, L. J., and Wynne, L. C. 1953. Traumatic avoidance learning: The outcome of several extinction procedures with dogs. *Journal of Abnormal and Social Psychology, 48,* 291–302.

Storms, L. H., Boroczi, G., and Broen, W. E., Jr. 1962. Punishment inhibits an instrumental response in hooded rats. *Science, 135,* 1133–1134.

Stretch, R., Orloff, E. R., and Dalrymple, S. D. 1968. Maintenance of responding by fixed-interval schedule of electric shock presentation in squirrel monkeys. *Science, 162,* 583–586.

Taub, E., and Berman, A. J. 1963. Avoidance conditioning in the absence of relevant proprioceptive and exteroceptive feedback. *Journal of Comparative and Physiological Psychology, 56,* 1012–1016.

Taub, E., and Berman, A. J. 1968. Movement and learning in the absence of sensory feedback. In S. J. Freedman (Ed.), *The neuropsychology of spatially oriented behavior.* Homewood, IL: Dorsey Press.

Tinsley, J. B., and Renner, K. E. 1975. Self-punitive behavior with changing percentages of reinforcement: The proper role of discrimination. *Learning and Motivation, 6,* 448–458.

Ulrich, R. E., Holz, W. C., and Azrin, N. H. 1964. Stimulus control of avoidance behavior. *Journal of the Experimental Analysis of Behavior, 7,* 129–133.

Wahlsten, D., Cole, M., Sharp, D., and Fantino, E. 1968. Facilitation of bar-press avoidance by handling during the intertrial interval. *Journal of Comparative and Physiological Psychology, 65,* 170–175.

Wallace, J., and Scobie, S. S. 1977. Avoidance extinction in goldfish. *Learning and Motivation, 8,* 18–38.

Watson, J. B., and Rayner, R. 1920. Conditioned emotional reactions. *Journal of Experimental Psychology, 3,* 1–14.

Weiner, H. 1962. Some effects of response cost upon human operant behavior. *Journal of the Experimental Analysis of Behavior, 5,* 201–208.

Weisman, R. G., and Litner, J. S. 1969. The course of Pavlovian excitation and inhibition of fear in rats. *Journal of Comparative and Physiological Psychology, 69,* 667–672.

Weiss, J. M., and Glazer, H. I. 1975. The effects of acute exposure to stressors on subsequent avoidance–escape behavior. *Psychosomatic Medicine, 37,* 499–521.

Winograd, E. 1965. Escape behavior under fixed ratios and shock intensities. *Journal of the Experimental Analysis of Behavior, 8,* 117–124.

Wolf, M. M., Risley, T., and Mees, H. 1964. Application of operant conditioning procedures to the behaviour problems of an autistic child. *Behaviour Research and Therapy, 1,* 305–312.

Chapter 9

Adler, N., and Hogan, J. A. 1963. Classical conditioning and punishment of an instinctive response in *Betta splendens. Animal Behaviour, 11,* 351–354.

Alcock, J. 1975. *Animal behavior: An evolutionary approach.* Sunderland, MA: Sinauer Associates.

Andrew, R. J. 1956. Some remarks on behaviour in conflict situations, with special reference to *Emberiza* spp. *British Journal of Animal Behaviour, 4,* 41–45.

Bentley, D. R., and Hoy, R. R. 1970. Postembryonic development of adult motor patterns in crickets: A neural analysis. *Science, 170,* 1409–1411.

Bentley, D. R., and Hoy, R. R. 1972. Genetic control of the neuronal network generating cricket *(Teleogryllus gryllus)* song patterns. *Animal Behaviour, 20,* 478–492.

Bentley, D. R., and Hoy, R. R. 1974. The neurobiology of cricket song. *Scientific American, 231,* 34–44.

Blest, A. D. 1957. The evolution of protective displays in the *Saturnoidea* and *Sphingidae (Lepidoptera). Behaviour, 11,* 257–309.

Darwin, C. 1859. *On the origin of species by means of natural selection, or the preservation of the favored races in the struggle for life.* Facsimile ed. Cambridge, MA: Harvard University Press, 1964.

Darwin, C. 1872. *Expression of the emotions in man and animals.* London: Murray.

Davis, D. M. 1928. Self-selection of diet by newly weaned infants. *American Journal of Diseases of Children, 36,* 651–679.

Dethier, V. G., and Bodenstein, D. 1958. Hunger in the blowfly. *Zeitschrift für Tierpsychologie, 15,* 129–140.

Dobzhansky, T., Ayala, F., Stebbins, G., and Valentine, J. 1977. *Evolution.* San Francisco: W. H. Freeman and Company.

Eibl-Eibesfeldt, I. 1970. *Ethology: The biology of behavior.* New York: Holt, Rinehart and Winston.

Emlen, J. M. 1973. *Ecology: An evolutionary approach.* Reading, MA: Addison-Wesley.

Fantino, E. Weigele, S., and Lancy, D. 1972. Aggressive display in the Siamese fighting fish *(Betta splendens). Learning and Motivation, 3,* 457–468.

Galef, B. G., Jr. 1976. Social transmission of acquired behavior: A discussion of tradition and social learning in vertebrates. In J. S. Rosenblatt, R. A. Hinde, E. Shaw, and C. Beer (Eds.), *Advances in the study of behavior,* Vol. 6. New York: Academic Press.

Galef, B. G., Jr. 1977. Social transmission of food preferences: An adaption for weaning rats. *Journal of Comparative and Physiological Psychology, 91,* 1136–1140.

Galef, B. G., Jr., and Clark, M. M. 1971a. Parent–offspring interactions determine the time and place of first ingestion of solid food by wild rat pups. *Psychonomic Science*, 25, 15–16.

Galef, B. G., Jr., and Clark, M. M. 1971b. Social factors in the poison avoidance and feeding behavior of wild and domesticated rat pups. *Journal of Comparative and Physiological Psychology*, 75, 341–357.

Galef, B. G., Jr., and Clark, M. M. 1972. Mother's milk and adult presence: Two factors determining initial dietary selection by weanling rats. *Journal of Comparative and Physiological Psychology*, 78, 220–225.

Galef, B. G., Jr., and Heiber, L. 1976. Role of residual olfactory cues in the determination of feeding site selection and exploration patterns of domestic rats. *Journal of Comparative and Physiological Psychology*, 90, 727–739.

Galef, B. G., Jr., and Sherry, D. F. 1973. Mother's milk: A medium for transmission of cues reflecting the flavor of mother's diet. *Journal of Comparative and Physiological Psychology*, 83, 374–378.

Hinde, R. A. 1958. The nest-building behaviour of domesticated canaries. *Proceedings of the Zoological Society of London*, 131, 1–48.

Hinde, R. A. 1970. *Animal behaviour*. 2nd ed. New York: McGraw-Hill.

Hoy, R. R., Hahn, J., and Paul, R. 1977. Hybrid cricket auditory behavior: Evidence for genetic coupling in animal communication. *Science*, 195, 82–83.

Kuo, Z.-Y. 1931. The genesis of cat's responses to the rat. *Journal of Comparative Psychology*, 11, 1–35.

Lehrman, D. S. 1964. The reproductive behavior of ring doves. *Scientific American*, 211, 47–53.

Leon, M., and Moltz, H. 1972. The development of the pheromonal bond in the albino rat. *Physiology and Behavior, 8*, 683–686.

Lorenz, K. 1935. Der Kumpan in der Umwelt des Vögels. *Journal für Ornithologie, 83*, 137–213. Translated in K. Lorenz, *Studies in animal and human behaviour*, Vol. 1. Cambridge, MA: Harvard University Press, 1970.

Lorenz, K. 1950. The comparative method in studying innate behaviour patterns. *Symposium of the Society for Experimental Biology, 4*, 221–268.

Lorenz, K. 1965. *Evolution and modification of behavior*. Chicago: University of Chicago Press.

Lorenz, K. 1966. *On aggression*. New York: Harcourt Brace Jovanovich.

Lorenz, K., and Tinbergen, N. 1938. Taxis und Instinkthandlung in der Eirollbewegung der Graugans I. *Zeitschrift für Tierpsychologie, 2*, 1–29.

Manning, A. 1972. *An introduction to animal behavior*. 2nd ed. Reading, MA: Addison-Wesley.

Mayr, E. 1970. Evolution at the species level. In J. A. Moore (Ed.), *Ideas in evolution and behavior*. New York: Natural History Press (Doubleday).

Pfaffman, C., and Bare, J. K. 1950. Gustatory nerve discharges in normal and adrenalectomized rats. *Journal of Comparative and Physiological Psychology, 43*, 320–324.

Richter, C. P., Holt, L. E., and Barelare, B. 1938. Nutritional requirements for normal growth and reproduction in rats studied by the self-selection method. *American Journal of Physiology, 122*, 734–744.

Rothenbuhler, W. C. 1967. Genetic and evolutionary considerations of social behavior of honeybees and some related insects. In J. Hirsch (Ed.), *Behavior-genetic analysis*. New York: McGraw-Hill.

Rowell, C. H. F. 1961. Displacement grooming in the chaffinch. *Animal Behaviour, 9*, 38–63.

Rozin, P. 1976. The selection of foods by rats, humans, and other animals. In J. S. Rosenblatt, R. A. Hinde, E. Shaw, and C. Beer (Eds.), *Advances in the study of behavior*, Vol. 6. New York: Academic Press.

Rozin, P., and Kalat, J. W. 1971. Specific hungers and poison avoidance as adaptive specializations in learning. *Psychological Review, 78,* 459–486.

Savage, J. M. 1977. *Evolution.* 3rd ed. New York: Holt, Rinehart and Winston.

Schleidt, W. 1961. Reaktionen von Truthühnern auf fliegende Raubvögel und Versuche zür Analyse ihrer AAM's. *Zeitschrift für Tierpsychologie, 18,* 534–560.

Thorpe, W. H. 1948. The modern concept of instinctive behavior. *Bulletin of Animal Behavior, 1,* 1–12.

Tinbergen, N. 1948. Social releasers and the experimental method required for their study. *Wilson Bulletin, 60,* 6–51.

Tinbergen, N. 1951. *The study of instinct.* New York: Oxford University Press.

Tinbergen, N., and Perdeck, A. C. 1950. On the stimulus situation releasing the begging response in the newly hatched herring gull chick (*Larus a. argentatus* Pont.), *Behaviour, 3,* 1–39.

Whalen, R. E. 1971. The concept of instinct. In J. L. McGaugh (Ed.), *Psychobiology: Behavior from a biological perspective.* New York: Academic Press.

Willows, A. O. D. 1971. Giant brain cells in mollusks. *Scientific American, 224,* 68–75.

Willows, A. O. D., and Hoyle, G. 1969. Neuronal network triggering a fixed-action pattern. *Science, 166,* 1549–1551.

Young, P. T., and Chaplin, J. P. 1945. Studies of food preference, appetite and dietary habit: III. Palatability and appetite in relation to bodily need. *Comparative Psychology Monographs, 18,* No. 3, 1–45.

Chapter 10

Alcock, J. 1975. *Animal behavior: An evolutionary approach.* Sunderland, MA: Sinauer Associates.

Bateson, P. P. G. 1966. The characteristics and context of imprinting. *Biological Reviews of the Cambridge Philosophical Society, 41,* 177–220.

Benvenuti, S., Fiaschi, V., Fiore, L., and Papi, F. 1973. Homing performances of inexperienced and directionally trained pigeons subjected to olfactory nerve section. *Journal of Comparative Physiology, 83,* 81–92.

Brower, L. P. 1971. Prey coloration and predator behavior. In V. Dethier (Ed.), *Topics in animal behavior, topics in the study of life:* The BIO source book, Part 6. New York: Harper & Row.

Brown, J. 1975. *The evolution of behavior.* New York: Norton.

Croze, H. 1970. Searching images in carrion crows. *Zeitschrift für Tierpsychologie, Beiheft, 5,* 85–92.

Dawkins, M. 1971. Perceptual changes in chicks: Another look at the "search image" concept. *Animal Behaviour, 19,* 566–574.

Garcia, J., Clarke, J., and Hankins, W. 1973. Natural responses to scheduled rewards. In P. Bateson and P. Klopfer (Eds.), *Perspectives in ethology.* Vol. 1. New York: Plenum.

Garcia, J., and Ervin, F. 1968. Appetites, aversions and addictions: A model for visceral memory. In J. Wortis (Ed.), *Advances in biological psychiatry.* New York: Plenum.

Garcia, J., and Koelling, R. 1966. Relation of cue to consequence in avoidance learning. *Psychonomic Science, 4,* 123–124.

Garcia, J., McGowen, B., and Green, K. 1972. Biological constraints on conditioning. In A. Black and W. Prokasy (Eds.), *Classical conditioning II: Current research and theory.* New York: Appleton-Century-Crofts.

Gottlieb, G. 1968. Prenatal behavior of birds. *Quarterly Review of Biology, 43,* 148–174.

Gottlieb, G. 1971. Ontogenesis of sensory function in birds and mammals. In E. Tobach, L. Aronson, and E. Shaw (Eds.), *The biopsychology of development.* New York: Academic Press.

Green, L., Bouzas, A., and Rachlin, H. 1972. Test of an electric shock analogue to illness-induced aversion. *Behavioral Biology, 7,* 513–518.

Hartwick, R. F., Foa, A., and Papi, F. 1977. The effect of olfactory deprivation by nasal tubes upon homing behavior in pigeons. *Behavioral Ecology and Sociobiology, 2,* 81–89.

Hess, E. H. 1958. Imprinting in animals. *Scientific American, 198,* 81–89.

Hess, E. H. 1972. "Imprinting" in a natural laboratory. *Scientific American, 227,* 24–31.

Hess, E. H. 1973. *Imprinting.* New York: Van Nostrand Reinhold.

Hinde, R. A. 1970. *Animal behavior: A synthesis of ethology and comparative psychology.* New York: McGraw-Hill.

Hoffman, H., and Ratner, A. 1973. A reinforcement model of imprinting: Implication for socialization in monkeys and men. *Psychological Review, 80,* 527–544.

Hooker, T., and Hooker, B. 1969. Duetting. In R. A. Hinde (Ed.), *Bird vocalizations.* London: Cambridge University Press.

Immelmann, K. 1969. Song development in the zebra finch and other estrildid finches. In R. A. Hinde (Ed.), *Bird vocalizations.* London: Cambridge University Press.

Immelmann, K. 1972. Sexual and other long term aspects of imprinting in birds and other species. In D. Lehrman, R. Hinde, and E. Shaw (Eds.), *Advances in the study of behavior,* Vol. 4. New York: Academic Press.

Keeton, W. T. 1969. Orientation by pigeons: Is the sun necessary? *Science, 165,* 922–928.

Keeton, W. T. 1973. Release-site bias as a possible guide to the "map" component in pigeon homing. *Journal of Comparative Physiology, 86,* 1–16.

Keeton, W. T. 1974a. The orientational and navigational basis of homing in birds. In D. Lehrman, R. Hinde, and E. Shaw (Eds.), *Advances in the study of behavior,* Vol. 5. New York: Academic Press.

Keeton, W. T. 1974b. The mystery of pigeon homing. *Scientific American, 231,* 96–107.

King, A., and West, M. 1977. Species identification in the North American cowbird: Appropriate responses to abnormal song. *Science, 195,* 1002–1004.

Krebs, J. 1973. Behavioral aspects of predation. In P. Bateson and P. Klopfer (Eds.), *Perspectives in ethology.* Vol. 1. New York: Plenum.

Kroodsma, D. 1977. A re-evaluation of song development in song sparrows. *Animal Behaviour, 25,* 390–399.

Lorenz, K. 1965. *Evolution and modification of behavior.* Chicago: University of Chicago Press.

Marler, P. 1970a. A comparative approach to vocal learning: Song development in white-crowned sparrows. *Journal of Comparative and Physiological Psychology, Monograph Supplement, 71,* 1–25.

Marler, P. 1970b. Birdsong and speech development: Could there be parallels? *American Scientist, 58,* 669–673.

Marler, P. 1975. On the origins of speech from animal sounds. In J. Kavanagh and J. Cutting (Eds.), *The role of speech in language.* Cambridge, MA: MIT Press.

Marler, P., and Waser, M. S. 1977. Role of auditory feedback in canary song development. *Journal of Comparative and Physiological Psychology, 91,* 8–16.

Nottebohm, F. 1972. The origins of vocal learning. *The American Naturalist, 106,* 116–140.

Revusky, S., and Garcia, J. 1970. Learned associations over long delays. In G. H. Bower (Ed.), *The psychology of learning and motivation,* Vol. 4. New York: Academic Press.

Rozin, P. 1976. The selection of foods by rats, humans, and other animals. In D. Lehrman, R. Hinde, and E. Shaw (Eds.), *Advances in the study of behavior,* Vol. 4. New York: Academic Press.

Rudy, J. W., Iwens, J., and Best, P. J. 1977. Pairing novel exteroceptive cues and illness reduces illness-induced taste aversions. *Journal of Experimental Psychology: Animal Behavior Processes, 3,* 14–25.

Rudy, J. W., Rosenberg, L., and Sandell, J. H. 1977. Disruption of a taste familiarity effect by novel exteroceptive stimulation. *Journal of Experimental Psychology: Animal Behavior Processes, 3,* 26–36.

Salinger, W., Schwartz, M., and Wilkerson, P. 1977a. Selective loss of lateral geniculate cells in the adult cat after chronic monocular paralysis. *Brain Research, 125,* 257–263.

Salinger, W., Schwartz, M., and Wilkerson, P. 1977b. Selective cell loss in the lateral geniculate nucleus of adult cats following binocular lid suture. *Brain Research, 130,* 81–88.

Salzen, E. 1970. Imprinting and environmental learning. In L. Aronson, E. Tobach, D. Lehrman, and J. Rosenblatt (Eds.), *Development and the evolution of behavior.* San Francisco: W. H. Freeman and Company.

Schutz, F. 1971. Prägung des sexual Verhaltens von Enten und Gansen durch Sozialeindrücke während der Jugendphase. *Journal of Neurovisceral Relations, Supplementum, 10,* 399–357.

Seligman, M., and Hager, J. 1972. *Biological boundaries of learning.* New York: Appleton-Century-Crofts.

Teitelbaum, P. 1966. The use of operant methods in the assessment and control of motivational states. In W. Honig (Ed.), *Operant behavior: Areas of research and application.* New York: Appleton-Century-Crofts.

Tinbergen, L. 1960. The natural control of insects in pine woods. I. Factors influencing the intensity of predation by songbirds. *Archieves Neerlandaises de Zoologie, 13,* 265–343.

Turner, J. R. G. 1975. A tale of two butterflies. *Natural History, 84,* 28–37.

Walcott, C., and Green, R. 1974. Orientation of homing pigeons altered by a change in the direction of an applied magnetic field. *Science, 184,* 180–182.

Wilcoxon, H., Dragoin, W., and Kral, P. 1971. Illness-indiced aversions in rat and quail: Relative salience of visual and gustatory cues. *Science, 171,* 826–828.

Wiltschko, W., Wiltschko, R., and Keeton, W. 1976. Effects of a "permanent" clock-shift on the orientation of young homing pigeons. *Behavioral Ecology and Sociobiology, 1,* 229–243.

Chapter 11

Aderman, M., and Dawson, J. N. 1970. Comparison of forced-choice alternation in goldfish and planaria. *Journal of Comparative and Physiological Psychology, 71*, 29–33.

Applewhite, P. 1968. Non-local nature of habituation in a rotifer and protozoan. *Nature, 217*, 287–288.

Applewhite, P., and Gardner, F. 1971. A theory of protozoan habituation. *Nature, 230*, 285–287.

Applewhite, P., and Morowitz, H. 1967. Memory and the microinvertebrates. In W. Corning and S. Ratner (Eds.), *The chemistry of learning: Invertebrate research*. New York: Plenum.

Beck, H. 1976. Dishabituation in the protozoan *Spirostomum ambiguum*. Paper presented at Southeastern Animal Behavior Society.

Bergström, S. 1968. Acquisition of an avoidance reaction to light in the protozoa *Tetrahymena*. *Scandinavian Journal of Psychology, 9*, 220–224.

Bergström, S. 1969. Avoidance behaviour to light in the protozoa *Tetrahymena*. *Scandinavian Journal of Psychology, 10*, 81–88.

Best, J. 1965. Behavior of planaria in instrumental learning paradigms. *Animal Behaviour, 13* (Suppl. 1), 69–75.

Brown, H. M. 1967. Effects of ultraviolet and photorestorative light on the phototaxic behavior of planaria. In W. Corning and S. Ratner (Eds.), *Chemistry of learning: Invertebrate research*. New York: Plenum.

Brown, J. 1975. *The evolution of behavior*. New York: Norton.

Bullock, T., and Horridge, G. 1965. *Structure and function of the nervous systems of invertebrates*. San Francisco: W. H. Freeman and Company.

Corning, W., Dyal, J., and Willows, A. O. D. (Eds.) 1973. *Invertebrate learning*, Vol. 1. New York: Plenum.

Corning, W., and Freed, S. 1968. Planarian behavior and biochemistry. *Nature, 219*, 1227–1230.

Corning, W., and Kelly, S. 1973. Platyhelminthes: The turbellarians. In W. Corning, J. Dyal, and A. O. D. Willows (Eds.), *Invertebrate learning*, Vol. 1. New York: Plenum.

Corning, W., and Lahue, R. 1972. Invertebrate strategies in comparative learning studies. *American Zoologist, 12*, 455–469.

Corning, W., and Ratner, S. 1967. *Chemistry of learning: Invertebrate research*. New York: Plenum.

Corning, W., and Riccio, D. 1970. The planarian controversy. In W. Byrne (Ed.), *Molecular approaches to learning and memory*. New York: Academic Press.

Corning, W., and Von Burg, R. 1973. Protozoa. In W. Corning, J. Dyal, and A. O. D. Willows (Eds.), *Invertebrate learning*, Vol. 1. New York: Plenum.

Crawford, T. 1967. Behavioral modification of planarians. In W. Corning and S. Ratner (Eds.), *Chemistry of learning: Invertebrate research*. New York: Plenum.

Crawford, T., and Skeen, L. 1967. Operant responding in the planarian: A replication study. *Psychological Reports, 20*, 1023–1027.

Dyal, J., and Corning, W. 1973. Invertebrate learning and behavior taxonomies. In W. Corning, J. Dyal, and A. O. D. Willows (Eds.), *Invertebrate learning*, Vol. 1. New York: Plenum.

Eisenstein, E., and Peretz, B. 1973. Comparative aspects of habituation in invertebrates. In H. Peeke and M. Herz (Eds.), *Habituation II*. New York: Academic Press.

Gee, W. 1913. Modifiability in the behavior of the California shore-anemone *Cribrina xanthogrammic* Brandt. *Animal Behaviour, 3,* 305–328.

Gelber, B. 1952. Investigations of the behavior of *Paramecium aurelia:* I. Modification of behavior after training with reinforcement. *Journal of Comparative and Physiological Psychology, 45,* 58–65.

Gelber, B. 1957. Food or training in paramecium? *Science, 126,* 1341–1350.

Hailman, J. P. 1969. How an instinct is learned. *Scientific American, 221*(6), 98–106.

Hamilton, T., Thompson, J., and Eisenstein, E. 1974. Quantitative analysis of ciliary and contractile responses during habituation training in *Spirostomum ambiguum. Behavioral Biology, 12,* 393–407.

Haynes, S., Jennings, L., and Wells, P. 1965. Planaria learning: Non-transfer and non-facilitation in a Van Oye maze. *American Zoologist, 4,* 424.

Hodos, W., and Campbell, C. 1969. *Scala Naturae:* Why there is no theory in comparative psychology. *Psychological Review, 76,* 337–350.

Jacobson, A., Horowitz, S., and Fried, C. 1967. Classical conditioning, pseudoconditioning, or sensitization in the planarian. *Journal of Comparative and Physiological Psychology, 64,* 73–79.

James, R., and Halas, E. 1964. No difference in extinction behavior in planaria following various types and amounts of training. *Psychological Record, 14,* 1–11.

Jennings, H. S. 1906. *Behavior of the lower organisms.* New York: Columbia University Press.

Jensen, D. 1957. Experiments on "learning" in paramecia. *Science, 125,* 191–192.

Jensen, D. 1965. Paramecium, planaria, and pseudo-learning. *Animal Behaviour, 13* (Suppl. 1), 9–20.

Katz, M., and Deterline, W. 1958. Apparent learning in the paramecium. *Journal of Comparative and Physiological Psychology, 51,* 243–247.

Klopfer, P. 1973. *Behavioral aspects of ecology.* Englewood Cliffs, NJ: Prentice-Hall.

Lee, R. M. 1963. Conditioning of a free operant response in planaria. *Science, 139,* 1048–1049.

Logan, C. 1975. Topographic changes in responding during habituation to waterstream stimulation in sea anemones *(Anthopleura elegantissima). Journal of Comparative and Physiological Psychology, 89,* 105–117.

Logan, C., and Beck, H. 1978. Long term retention of habituation in the absence of a central nervous system. *Journal of Comparative and Physiological Psychology, 92,* 928–934.

Lorenz, K. 1965. *Evolution and modification of behavior.* Chicago: University of Chicago Press.

McConnell, J. V. 1962. Memory transfer through cannibalism in planarians. *Journal of Neuropsychiatry, 3* (Suppl. 1), s42.

McConnell, J. V. 1966. Comparative physiology: Learning in invertebrates. *Annual Review of Physiology, 28,* 107–136.

McConnell, J. 1967. Specific factors influencing planarian behavior. In W. Corning and S. Ratner (Eds.), *Chemistry of learning: Invertebrate research.* New York: Plenum.

McConnell, J., and Jacobson, A. 1970. Invertebrate learning. In D. Dewsbury and D. Rethlingshafer (Eds.), *Comparative psychology.* New York: McGraw-Hill.

Riccio, D., and Corning, W. 1969. Slime and planarian behavior. *Psychological Record, 19,* 507–513.

Ross, D. M. 1965a. The behavior of sessile coelenterates in relation to some conditioning experiments. *Animal Behaviour, 13* (Suppl. 1), 43–55.

Ross, D. M. 1965b. Complex and modifiable patterns in *Calliactis* and *Stomphia*. *American Zoologist, 5*, 573–580.

Rushforth, N. 1965. Behavioral studies of the coelenterate *Hydra pirardi* Brien. *Animal Behaviour, 13* (Suppl. 1), 30–42.

Rushforth, N. B. 1967. Chemical and physical factors affecting behavior in *Hydra:* Interactions among factors affecting behavior in *Hydra*. In W. Corning and S. Ratner (Eds.), *Chemistry of learning*. New York: Plenum.

Rushforth, N. B. 1971. Behavioral and electrophysiological studies of *Hydra*. I. An analysis of contraction pulse patterns. *Biological Bulletin, 140*, 502–519.

Rushforth, N. B. 1973. Behavioral modifications in coelenterates. In W. Corning, J. Dyal, and A. O. D. Willows (Eds.), *Invertebrate learning*, Vol. 1. New York: Plenum.

Rushforth, N., Burnett, A., and Maynard, R. 1963. Behavior in *Hydra*. Contraction responses of *Hydra pirardi* to mechanical and light stimuli. *Science, 139*, 760–761.

Sund, P. 1958. A study of the muscular anatomy and swimming behavior of the sea anemone, *Stomphia coccinea*. *Quarterly Journal of Microscopical Science, 99*, 401–420.

Van Oye, P. 1920. Over het geheugen bij fr flatwormen en andere biologische waarnemingen bji deze dieren. *Natuurwet. Tijdschr., 2*, 1.

Vattano, F., and Hullett, J. 1964. Learning in planarians as a function of interstimulus interval. *Psychonomic Science, 1*, 331–332.

Wells, P. 1967. Training flatworms in a Van Oye maze. In W. Corning and S. Ratner (Eds.), *Chemistry of learning: Invertebrate research*. New York: Plenum.

Wells, P., Jennings, L., and Davis, M. 1966. Conditioning planarian worms in a Van Oye type maze. *American Zoologist, 6*, 295.

Westerman, R. A. 1963. A study of the habituation responses to light in the planarian *Dugesia dorotocephala*. *Worm Runner's Digest, 5*, 6–11.

Wood, D. C. 1970a. Parametric studies of the response decrement produced by mechanical stimuli in the protozoan *Stentor coeruleus*. *Journal of Neurobiology, 1*, 345–360.

Wood, D. C. 1970b. Electrophysiological studies of the protozoan *Stentor coeruleus*. *Journal of Neurobiology, 1*, 363–377.

Wood, D. C. 1970c. Electrophysiological correlates of the response decrement produced by mechanical stimuli in the protozoan *Stentor coeruleus*. *Journal of Neurobiology, 2*, 1–11.

Wood, D. C. 1973. Stimulus specific habituation in a protozoan. *Physiology and Behavior, 11*, 349–354.

Yerkes, R. M. 1912. The intelligence of earthworms. *Journal of Animal Behavior, 2*, 332–352.

Chapter 12

Abraham, F. D., and Willows, A. O. D. 1971. Plasticity of a fixed action pattern of behavior in the sea slug *Tritonia diomedia*. *Communications in Behavioral Biology, A6*, 271–280.

Alloway, T. M. 1972. Learning and memory in insects. *Annual Review of Entomology, 17*, 43–56.

Alloway, T. M. 1973. Learning in insects except Apoidea. In W. Corning, J. Dyal, and A. O. D. Willows (Eds.), *Invertebrate learning*, Vol. 2. New York: Plenum.

Aranda, L., and Luco, J. 1969. Further studies of an electric correlate to learning: Experiments in an isolated insect ganglion. *Physiology and Behavior, 4*, 133–137.

Biology Today, 1972. CRM.

Brown, J. 1975. *The evolution of behavior.* New York: Norton.

Buytendijk, F. 1921. Une formation d'habitude simple chez le limacon d'eau douce (*Limnaea*). *Archives Néerlandaises de Physiologie de l'homme et des animaux, 5*, 458–466.

Carew, T. J., and Kandel, E. 1973. Acquisition and retention of long-term habituation in *Aplysia:* Correlation of behavioral and cellular processes. *Science, 182*, 1158–1160.

Carew, T. J., Pinsker, H. M., and Kandel, E. 1972. Long-term habituation of a defensive withdrawal reflex in *Aplysia. Science, 175*, 451–454.

Castellucci, V., Pinsker, H., Kupfermann, I., and Kandel, E. 1970. Neuronal correlates of habituation and dishabituation of the gill-withdrawal reflex in *Aplysia. Science, 167*, 1743–1748.

Chen, W. Y., Aranda, L. C., and Luco, J. V. 1970. Learning and long-term and short-term memory in cockroaches. *Animal Behaviour, 18*, 725–732.

Clark, R. 1965. The learning abilities of nereid polychaetes and the role of the supraesophageal ganglion. *Animal Behaviour, 13* (Suppl. 1), 89–100.

Cook, A. 1971. Habituation in a fresh water snail (*Limnaea stagnalis*). *Animal Behaviour, 19*, 463–474.

Corning, W., Dyal, J., and Willows, A. O. D. (Eds.) 1973a. *Invertebrate learning*, Vol. I. New York: Plenum.

Corning, W., Dyal, J., and Willows, A. O. D. (Eds.) 1973b. *Invertebrate learning*, Vol. II. New York: Plenum.

Corning, W., Dyal, J., and Willows, A. O. D. (Eds.) 1975. *Invertebrate learning*, Vol. III. New York: Plenum.

Dethier, V. G. 1969. Feeding behavior in the blowfly. In D. Lehrman, R. Hinde, and E. Shaw (Eds.), *Advances in the study of behavior*, Vol. 2. New York: Academic Press.

Dilly, P. N. 1963. Delayed responses in *Octopus. Journal of Experimental Biology, 40*, 393–401.

Disterhoft, J. F. 1972. Learning in the intact cockroach (*Periplaneta americana*) when placed in a punishment situation. *Journal of Comparative and Physiological Psychology, 79*, 1–7.

Evans, S. M. 1963. Behaviour of the polychaete *Nereis* in T-mazes. *Animal Behaviour, 11*, 379–392.

Evans, S. M. 1965. Learning in the polychaete, *Nereis. Nature, 207*, 1420.

Evans, S. M. 1966a. Non-associative avoidance learning in nereid polychaetes. *Animal Behaviour, 14*, 102–106.

Evans, S. M. 1966b. Non-associative behavioural modifications in the polychaete *Nereis diversicolor. Animal Behaviour, 14*, 107–119.

Gardner, L. E. 1968. Retention and overhabituation of a dual-component response in *Lumbricus terrestris sp. Journal of Comparative and Physiological Psychology, 66*, 315–318.

Gee, W. 1912. The behavior of leeches with special reference to its modifiability. *University of California Publications in Zoology, 11*, 197–305.

Gelperin, A. 1975. Rapid food-aversion learning by a terrestrial mollusk. *Science*, *189*, 567–570.

Gould, J. L. 1975. Honey bee recruitment: The dance-language controversy. *Science*, *189*, 685–693.

Hegner, R. W., and Engemann, J. B. 1968. *Invertebrate zoology*. 2nd ed. New York: Macmillan.

Henderson, T. B., and Strong, P. 1972. Classical conditioning in the leech *Macrobdella ditetra* as a function of CS and UCS intensity. *Conditioned Reflex, 7*, 210–215.

Herz, M. J., Peeke, H. V. S., and Wyers, E. J. 1964. Temperature and conditioning in the earthworm *Lumbricus terrestris*. *Animal Behaviour, 12*, 502–507.

Hodos, W., and Campbell, C. 1969. *Scala Naturae:* Why there is no theory in comparative psychology. *Psychological Review, 76*, 337–350.

Hollis, J. H. 1963. Habituatory response decrement in pupae of *Tenebrio molitor*. *Animal Behaviour, 11*, 161–163.

Kandel, E. R. 1976. *The cellular basis of behavior*. San Francisco: W. H. Freeman and Company.

Kandel, E. R., Castellucci, V., Pinsker, H., and Kupfermann, I. 1970. The role of synaptic plasticity in the short-term modification of behaviour. In G. Horn and R. Hinde (Eds.), *Short-term changes in neural activity and behaviour*. London: Cambridge University Press.

Kandel, E. R., and Tauc, L. 1965. Heterosynaptic facilitation in neurons of the abdominal ganglion of *Aplysia depilans*. *Journal of Physiology* (London), 181, 1–27.

Kerkut, G., Oliver, G., Rick, J., and Walker, R. 1970. Biochemical changes during learning in an insect ganglion. *Nature* (London), *227*, 722–723.

Kirk, W. E., and Thompson, R. 1967. Effects of light, shock, and goal box conditions on runway performance of the earthworm. *Psychological Record, 17*, 49–54.

Koltermann, R. 1974. Periodicity in the activity and learning performance of the honeybee. In L. B. Browne (Ed.), *Experimental analysis of insect behaviour*. New York: Springer-Verlag.

Jacobson, A. L. 1963. Learning in flatworms and annelids. *Psychological Bulletin, 60*, 74–94.

Krasne, F. B. 1973. Learning in crustacea. In W. Corning, J. Dyal, and A. O. D. Willows (Eds.), *Invertebrate learning*, Vol. II. New York: Plenum.

Lahue, R. 1973. The chelicerates. In W. Corning, J. Dyal, and A. O. D. Willows (Eds.), *Invertebrate learning*, Vol. II. New York: Plenum.

Lee, R. M. 1969. *Aplysia* behavior: Effects of contingent water level variation. *Communications in Behavioral Biology, 3*, 157–164.

Lee, R. M. 1970. *Aplysia* behavior: Operant-response differentiation. *Proceedings of the American Psychological Association, 5*, 249–250.

Lickey, M. E. 1968. Learned behavior in *Aplysia vaccaria*. *Journal of Comparative and Physiological Psychology, 66*, 712–718.

Maier, N. R. F., and Schneirla, T. C. 1964. *Principles of animal psychology*. New York: Dover Publications.

Menzel, R., Erber, J., and Mashur, T. 1974. Learning and memory in the honeybee. In L. B. Browne (Ed.), *Experimental analysis of insect behaviour*. New York: Springer-Verlag.

Messenger, J. B. 1973a. Learning in the cuttlefish, *Sepia. Animal Behaviour, 21,* 801–826.

Messenger, J. B. 1973b. Learning performance and brain structure: A study in development. *Brain Research, 58,* 519–523.

Messenger, J. B., and Sanders, G. 1972. Visual preference and two cue discrimination learning in Octopus. *Animal Behaviour, 20,* 580–585.

Mpitsos, G., and Collins, S. 1975. Learning: Rapid aversive conditioning in the gastropod mollusk *Pleurobranchaea. Science, 188,* 954–957.

Nelson, M. C. 1971. Classical conditioning in the blowfly *(Phormia regina):* Associative and excitatory factors. *Journal of Comparative and Physiological Psychology, 77,* 353–368.

Pinsker, H., Hening, W., Carew, T., and Kandel, E. 1973. Long-term sensitization of a defensive withdrawal reflex in *Aplysia. Science, 182,* 1039–1042.

Pinsker, H., Kupfermann, I., Castellucci, V., and Kandel, E. 1970. Habituation and dishabituation of the gill-withdrawal reflex in *Aplysia. Science, 167,* 1740–1742.

Pritchatt, D. 1968. Avoidance of electric shock by the cockroach *Periplaneta americana. Animal Behaviour, 16,* 178–185.

Ratner, S. C. 1962. Conditioning of decerebrate worms, *Lumbricus terrestris. Journal of Comparative and Physiological Psychology, 55,* 174–177.

Ratner, S. C. 1964. Worms in a straight alley: Acquisition and extinction or phototaxis? *Psychological Record, 14,* 31.

Ratner, S. C. Annelids and learning: A critical review. In W. Corning and S. Ratner (Eds.), *Chemistry of learning.* New York: Plenum.

Ratner, S. C. 1970. Habituation: Research and theory. In J. Reynierse (Ed.), *Current issues in animal learning.* Lincoln: University of Nebraska Press.

Ratner, S. C. 1972. Habituation and retention of habituation in the leech *(Macrobdella decora). Journal of Comparative and Physiological Psychology, 81,* 115–121.

Ratner, S. C., and Miller, K. R. 1959. Classical conditioning in earthworms, *Lumbricus terrestris. Journal of Comparative and Physiological Psychology, 52,* 102–105.

Ratner, S. C., and Stein, D. G. 1965. Responses of worms to light as a function of an intertrial interval and ganglion removal. *Journal of Comparative and Physiological Psychology, 59,* 301–304.

Ray, A. J. 1968. Instrumental light avoidance by the earthworm. *Communications in Behavioral Biology, 1,* 205–208.

Ressler, R., Cialdini, R., Ghoca, M., and Kleist, S. 1968. Alarm pheromone in the earthworm *Lumbricus terrestris. Science, 161,* 597–599.

Reynierse, J. H. 1968. Effects of temperature and temperature change on earthworm locomotor behavior. *Animal Behaviour, 16,* 480–484.

Reynierse, J. H., Halliday, R. A., and Nelson, M. R. 1968. Non-associative factors inhibiting earthworm straight alley performance. *Journal of Comparative and Physiological Psychology, 65,* 160–163.

Reynierse, J. H., and Ratner, S. C. 1964. Acquisition and extinction in the earthworm, *Lumbricus terrestris. Psychological Record, 14,* 383–387.

Rosenkoetter, J. S., and Boice, R. 1975. Earthworm pheromones and T-maze performance. *Journal of Comparative and Physiological Psychology, 88,* 904–910.

Sanders, G. 1970. Long-term memory of a tactile discrimination in *Octopus vulgaris* and the effect of vertical lobe removal. *Brain Research,* 59–73.

Sanders, G. 1975. The cephalopods. In W. Corning, J. Dyal, and A. O. D. Willows (Eds.), *Invertebrate learning,* Vol. III. New York: Plenum.

Sanders, G., and Barlow, J. 1971. Variations in retention performance during long-term memory formation. *Nature, 232,* 203–204.

Schneirla, T. C. 1943. The nature of ant learning: II. The intermediate stage of segmental maze adjustment. *Journal of Comparative Psychology, 34,* 149–176.

Schneirla, T. C. 1946. Ant learning as a problem in comparative psychology. In P. L. Harriman (Ed.), *Twentieth-century psychology.* New York: Philosophical Library.

Taylor, R. J. 1974. Role of learning in insect parasitism. *Ecological Monographs, 44,* 89–104.

Thompson, R., and Spencer, W. A. 1966. Habituation: A model phenomenon for the study of neuronal substrates of behavior. *Psychological Review, 73,* 16–43.

Thorpe, W., and Jones, F. 1937. Olfactory conditioning in a parasitic insect and its relation to the problem of host selection. *Proceedings of the Royal Society of London, 124,* 56–81.

Tinbergen, N. 1951. *The study of instinct.* London: Oxford University Press.

von Frisch, K. 1964. *Biology.* Translated by J. Oppenheimer. Bayerischer Schulbuch-Verlag.

von Frisch, K. 1967. *The dance language and orientation of bees.* Cambridge, MA: Harvard University Press.

Wells, M. 1964. Detour experiments with octopus. *Journal of Experimental Biology, 41,* 621–642.

Wells, M. 1967. Short-term learning and interocular transfer in detour experiments with octopuses. *Journal of Experimental Biology, 47,* 383–408.

Wells, M., and Wells, J. 1958. The effect of vertical lobe removal on the performance of octopuses in retention tests. *Journal of Experimental Biology, 35,* 337–348.

Wells, M., and Young, J. Z. 1970a. Single session learning by octopuses. *Journal of Experimental Biology, 53,* 779–788.

Wells, M. J., and Young, J. Z. 1970b. Stimulus generalisation in the tactile system of *Octopus. Journal of Neurobiology, 2,* 31–46.

Wells, P. H. Honey bees. 1973. In W. Corning, J. Dyal, and A. O. D. Willows, (Eds.), *Invertebrate learning,* Vol. II. New York: Plenum.

Wenner, A. M., and Johnson, D. L. 1967. Honeybees: Do they use direction and distance information provided by the dance? *Science, 158,* 1076–1077.

Wenner, A. M., Wells, P. H., and Johnson, D. 1969. Honey bee recruitment to food sources: Olfaction or language? *Science, 164,* 84–86.

Willows, A. O. D. 1973. Learning in gastropod mollusks. In J. Dyal, W. Corning, and A. O. D. Willows (Eds.), *Invertebrate learning,* Vol. II. New York: Plenum.

Wilson, E. O. 1971. *The insect societies.* Cambridge, MA: Harvard-Belknap.

Wyers, E., Peeke, H., and Herz, M. 1964. Partial reinforcement and resistance to extinction in the earthworm. *Journal of Comparative and Physiological Psychology, 57,* 113–116.

Yerkes, R. M. 1912. The intelligence of earthworms. *Journal of Animal Behavior, 2,* 332–352.

Young, J. Z. 1970. Short and long memories in *Octopus* and the influence of the vertical lobe system. *Journal of Experimental Biology, 52,* 385–393.

Young, J. Z. 1971. *The anatomy of the nervous system of octopus vulgaris.* Oxford: Clarendon Press.

Chapter 13

Alexander, R. D. 1975. The search for a general theory of behavior. *Behavioural Science, 20,* 77–100.

Altmann, J. 1974. Observational study of behavior: Sampling methods. *Behaviour, 49,* 227–262.

Anderson, M. C., and Shettleworth, S. J. 1977. Behavioral adaptation to fixed-interval and fixed-time food delivery in golden hamsters. *Journal of the Experimental Analysis of Behavior, 27,* 33–49.

Azrin, N. H., Hutchinson, R. R., and Hake, D. F. 1966. Extinction-induced aggression. *Journal of the Experimental Analysis of Behavior, 9,* 191–204.

Barash, D. 1974. The evolution of marmot societies: A general theory. *Science, 185,* 415–420.

Baum, W. M. 1974. Choice in free-ranging wild pigeons. *Science, 185,* 78–79.

Campbell, D. T., and Stanley, J. C. 1963. *Experimental and quasi-experimental designs for research.* Chicago: Rand McNally.

Charnov, E. L. 1976. Optimal foraging: Attack strategy of a mantid. *American Naturalist, 110,* 141–151.

Collier, G. 1977. Optimal feeding strategies in animals: Laboratory simulation. Paper presented at the meetings of the Eastern Psychological Association, Boston.

Collier, G. H., and Kaufman, L. W. 1976. The patchy environment: A laboratory simulation. Paper presented at the meetings of the Psychonomic Society, St. Louis.

Davies, N. B. 1977. Prey selection and the search strategy of the spotted flycatcher *(Muscicapa striata):* A field study on optimal foraging. *Animal Behaviour, 25,* 1016–1033.

Falk, J. L. 1971. The nature and determinants of adjunctive behavior. *Physiology and Behavior, 6,* 577–588.

Hills, M. 1974. *Statistics for comparative studies.* New York: Walstead.

Hinde, R. A., and Stevenson-Hinde, J. (Eds.). 1973. *Constraints on learning.* New York: Academic Press.

Jenkins, H. M., and Moore, B. R. 1973. The form of the auto-shaped response with food or water reinforcers. *Journal of the Experimental Analysis of Behavior, 20,* 163–181.

Kavanau, J. L. 1969. Behavior of captive white-footed mice. In E. P. Williams and H. L. Raush (Eds.), *Naturalistic viewpoints in psychological research,* New York: Holt, Rinehart and Winston.

Kjos, G. L. 1977. Constraints on the reinforcement relation: Tests of instrumental response type in a multiple response repertoire environment. Unpublished doctoral dissertation, University of California, San Diego.

Krebs, J. R. 1978. Optimal foraging: Decision rules for predators. In J. R. Krebs and N. B. Davies (Eds.), *Behavioural ecology: An evolutionary approach.* Oxford: Blackwell Scientific Publications, Ltd.

Krebs, J. R., Erichsen, J. T., Webber, M. I., and Charnov. E. L. 1977. Optimal prey selection in the great tit *(Parsus major). Animal Behaviour, 25,* 30–38.

Krebs, J. R., Kalcenik, A., and Taylor, P. 1978. Test of optimal sampling by foraging great tits. *Nature, 275,* 27–31.

Lowe, F. C., and Harzem, P. 1977. Species differences in temporal control of behavior. *Journal of the Experimental Analysis of Behavior, 28,* 189–201.

Marler, P. 1975. On strategies of behavioural development. In G. Baerends, C. Beer, and A. Manning (Eds.), *Function and evolution in behaviour.* Oxford: Clarendon Press.

Mayr, E. 1974. Behavioral programs and evolutionary strategies. *American Scientist, 62,* 650–659.

Schwartz, B. 1974. On going back to nature: A review of Seligman and Hager's *Biological boundaries of learning. Journal of the Experimental Analysis of Behavior, 21,* 183–198.

Segal, E. F. 1965. The development of water drinking on a dry-food free-reinforcement schedule. *Psychonomic Science, 2,* 29–30.

Segal, E. F. 1969. The interaction of psychogenic polydipsia with wheel running in rats. *Psychonomic Science, 14,* 141–144.

Segal, E., and Holloway, S. M. 1963. Timing behavior in rats with water drinking as a mediator. *Science, 140,* 888–889.

Seligman, M. E. P. 1970. On the generality of the laws of learning. *Psychological Review, 77,* 406–418.

Seligman, M. E. P., and Hager, J. L. (Eds.). 1972. *Biological boundaries of learning.* New York: Appleton-Century-Crofts.

Shettleworth, S. J. 1975. Reinforcement and the organization of behavior in golden hamsters: Hunger, environment, and food reinforcement. *Journal of Experimental Psychology: Animal Behavior Processes, 1,* 56–87.

Shettleworth, S. J. 1978a. Reinforcement and the organization of behavior in golden hamsters: Punishment of three action patterns. *Learning and Motivation, 9,* 99–123.

Shettleworth, S. J. 1978b. Reinforcement and the organization of behavior in golden hamsters: Pavlovian conditioning with food and shock unconditioned stimuli. *Journal of Experimental Psychology: Animal Behavior Processes, 4,* 152–169.

Skinner, B. F. 1938. *The behavior of organisms.* New York: Appleton-Century-Crofts.

Skinner, B. F. 1969. The phylogeny and ontogeny of behavior. In B. F. Skinner (Ed.), *Contingencies of reinforcement: A theoretical analysis.* New York: Appleton-Century-Crofts.

Smith, J. N. M., and Sweatman, H. P. A. 1974. Food-searching behavior of titmice in patchy environments. *Ecology, 55,* 1216–1232.

Staddon, J. E. R., and Ayres, S. L. 1975. Sequential and temporal properties of behavior induced by a schedule of periodic food delivery. *Behaviour, 54,* 26–49.

Staddon, J. E. R., and Simmelhag, V. L. 1971. The "superstition" experiment: A re-examination of its implications for the principles of adaptive behavior. *Psychological Review, 78,* 3–43.

Walters, G. C., and Herring, B. 1978. Differential suppression by punishment of nonconsummatory licking and lever pressing. *Journal of Experimental Psychology: Animal Behavior Processes, 4,* 170–187.

Wilson, E. O. 1977. Biology and the social sciences. *Daedalus, 106,* 127–140.

Index of Names

Abbot, B., 205
Abraham, F., 441
Ackil, J. E., 95
Aderman, M., 419
Agras, W. S., 161–163
Ainslie, G. W., 239–241
Alcock, J., 241, 378
Alexander, R. D., 474
Alferink, L. A., 112
Allen, K. E., 193
Allison, J., 111, 114
Alloway, T., 456, 460
Altenor, A., 288, 291
Altmann, J., 477–479
Amsel, A., 175
Anderson, M. C., 487
Anderson, N. H., 264
Andrew, R., 324
Antonitis, J. J., 194
Apple, J. B., 246
Applewhite, P., 400, 420
Aranda, L., 460
Armus, H. L., 179
Atnip, G. W., 95
Atthowe, J. M., 189
Auge, R. J., 203
Autor, S. M., 228, 229
Axelrod, S., 126
Ayala, F., 306
Ayers, J., 68
Ayllon, T., 101, 186, 188, 189, 192, 193, 248, 261
Ayres, S. L., 484, 487, 488
Azrin, N. H., 186, 188, 189, 192, 193, 244–250, 252, 261, 275, 487

Bachrach, A. J., 101
Bacotti, A. V., 225
Bader, S. A., 95
Badia, P., 203–206
Baer, D. M., 92, 93, 266
Baker, A. G., 287
Balderrama, N., 47
Baldock, M. D., 95, 109
Bandura, A., 92
Barash, D., 480–481
Bare, J., 335
Barelare, B., 336
Barlow, D. H., 161–163
Barlow, J., 450–451
Baron, A., 272, 282
Barrass, R., 53
Bateson, P., 268, 368
Baum, M., 226, 264, 481, 482
Baum, W. M., 218, 222, 225, 226, 241
Baxter, R., 70
Beagley, G., 290
Beck, H., 401, 411
Becker, W. C., 190
Beninger, R. J., 128
Bentley, D., 302–303, 305
Benvenuti, S., 363
Berberich, J. P., 92
Bergström, S., 396
Berlyne, D. E., 197
Berman, A. J., 280
Bernstein, D. J., 114
Bersh, P. J., 178, 180–181, 194, 280
Best, J., 412, 317
Best, P., 247
Bijou, S. W., 193

Binkoff, J. A., 167
Bishop, J. A., 352
Bitterman, M. E., 264
Black, A. H., 62, 73, 251
Blackman, D., 251
Blanchard, R. J., 202
Blest, A., 315
Bloomfield, T. M., 127, 131, 135, 197, 201, 204
Blough, D., 120, 122, 123, 155
Blough, P., 120, 155
Boakes, R. A., 201, 202
Bodenstein, D., 457
Boice, R., 432
Bolles, R. C., 253, 263, 264, 266, 273, 275
Boneau, C. A., 126, 135, 136
Bootzin, R. R., 186, 187, 188, 192, 193
Boren, J. J., 275, 276, 277
Boring, E., 13
Boroczi, G., 246
Bouzas, A., 345
Bower, G., 234
Brady, J. V., 251, 252
Brahlek, J. A., 249
Brethower, D. M., 130
Brigham, T. A., 258
Broen, W. E., 246
Brower, L., 342–343, 348–350
Brown, H., 416
Brown, J., 283, 284, 377, 467
Brown, P. L., 93
Browne, M. P., 201, 202
Brownstein, A. J., 96, 210, 211, 218
Bruning, J. L., 285
Brush, E. S., 263
Brush, F. R., 128
Buck, S. L., 126, 127, 135
Bugelski, B. R., 173
Bullock, T., 404
Burkhard, B., 113, 115
Burnett, A., 408
Burstein, K. R., 135, 136
Bushell, D., 186, 190
Butter, C. M., 156, 177
Buytendijk, F., 441
Byrd, L. D., 283–285, 287

Cable, C., 165
Campbell, B. A., 285
Campbell, C., 390, 446
Campbell, D. T., 479
Carew, T., 59, 439, 440
Carlton, P. L., 51
Carr, E. G., 167
Catania, A. C., 128, 142, 212–214, 217–220, 222, 227
Chaplin, J., 335
Charnov, E. L., 490, 491
Chase, S., 137
Chen, W., 460
Cheney, C. D., 112
Cho, C., 265
Church, R. M., 252, 284
Cialdini, R., 432
Clark, F. C., 268, 279
Clark, M., 338
Clark, R., 424, 426
Clarke, F., 340

Cohen, H. L., 186, 190, 191
Cohen, P. S., 246
Coker, C. C., 204, 205
Cole, M., 263–265, 271
Collier, G., 492–494
Collins, S., 443, 444
Cook, A., 440–441
Cook, L. M., 352
Corning, W., 387, 394, 396–397, 413–418, 420, 423
Coulson, G., 285
Coulson, V., 285
Cowles, J. T., 169, 186
Craig, W., 310
Craw, M., 189
Crawford, T., 415–417
Crossman, E. K., 112
Croze, H., 254
Culbertson, S., 204–205
Cumming, W. W., 156, 158
Cutts, D., 219–220

Dalrymple, S. D., 282
D'Amato, M. R., 158–159, 177, 179, 263–264, 274
Darwin, C., 10, 12, 26, 297–298, 306
Davies, N. B., 491
Davis, D., 334
Davis, M., 45–46, 56–58, 418
Davison, M. C., 180, 234
Davol, G. H., 152
Dawkins, M., 253–355
Dawson, J., 419
Dean, S. J., 285
deBaca, P. C., 111
DeFran, R. H., 204
Delbrück, N., 214
deLorge, J., 172
DeMyer, M. K., 188
Denny, M. R., 275
Dericco, D. A., 258
DeRivera, J., 141
Descartes, R., 9–10
Desiderato, O., 136
Deterline, W., 395
Dethier, V., 60, 457
de Toledo, L. E., 73, 251
de Villiers, P. A., 128, 220, 222–223, 225, 227, 260, 279
Devine, J. V., 111
DeWaard, R. J., 272
DiCara, L., 263
Dilly, P., 451
Dinsmoor, J. A., 193–194, 201–202, 204, 260, 271, 275, 279
Dobzhansky, T., 306
Drabman, R., 186
Dragoin, W., 346
Dukhayyil, A., 142
Duncan, B., 194, 227, 235–236
Dyal, J., 423

Ebbinghaus, H., 13
Eckerman, D. A., 130
Egger, D. M., 78
Ehrenfreund, D., 140
Eibl-Eibesfeldt, I., 319–320
Eisenberger, R., 114

Eisenstein, E., 400, 401
Ellis, A., 107
Ellis, W. R., 135, 142
Emlen, J. M., 306
Engberg, L., 137–138
Engemann, J., 404, 412, 425, 447, 465
Erber, J., 4, 468–469
Erichsen, J. T., 460
Ernst, A. J., 137–138
Ervin, F., 344
Erwin, W. J., 101
Estes, W. K., 249, 252–254, 257
Etkin, M., 264, 274
Evans, M. B., 190
Evans, S. M., 424, 429–431

Falk, J. L., 487
Fantino, E., 89, 94–95, 97, 108, 111–112,
    123, 130, 133–134, 170, 172, 179–180,
    182–184, 194–197, 199, 201, 211–212,
    214, 220–222, 227, 228, 231–236,
    238–241, 247, 252, 257, 260, 263–265,
    271–272, 279, 283, 285, 317
Farley, J., 120, 130, 256
Farrell, L., 109
Farthing, G. W., 129
Fazzaro, J., 158–159, 263–264, 274
Fechner, G., 12
Ferster, C. B., 99, 175, 188, 196, 254
Fiaschi, V., 363
Field, G. E., 276–277
Filipczak, J., 186, 190–191
Findley, J. D., 210
Fink, J. B., 156
Fiore, L., 363
Fischer, K., 196
Fishman, S. T., 106, 107
Fleshler, M., 264
Flint, G. A., 204
Foa, A., 363
Fowler, H., 253, 285
Franzisket, L., 53
Freed, S., 414
Fried, C., 414–415
Freud, S., 257
Frommer, G. P., 95

Galef, B., 338
Gallagher, J. E., 45
Gamzu, E., 108, 109, 131, 133, 134
Gantt, W., 72
Ganz, L., 145–147
Garcia, J., 163, 338, 340, 344–347, 351
Gardner, F., 400
Gardner, L., 285, 426–427
Garlich, M. M., 179
Garlington, W. K., 258
Gee, W., 405, 430
Gelber, B., 394–395
Gelperin, A., 444–445
Gerry, J. E., 147
Ghoca, M., 432
Gibbon, J., 95, 109, 278
Giles, D. K., 190
Gillan, P., 107
Glazer, H. I., 287–291
Gold, L., 95
Goldfried, M. R., 107

Gollub, L. R., 175, 182–184, 226, 235
Gottlieb, G., 371–273
Gould, J., 470
Grabowski, J., 275, 276
Graft, D. A., 222
Grant, D. A., 71
Green, D., 218
Green, K., 351
Green, L., 240–241
Green, R., 359
Grice, G. R., 246
Grossen, N. E., 275
Groves, P., 55
Grusec, T., 136
Guilkey, M., 218, 221
Guthrie, E. R., 19–24, 87, 107
Gutowski, K. A., 95
Guttman, A., 128
Guttman, N., 66–68, 120, 136, 145, 150,
    152

Haberlandt, K., 153
Hager, J., 346
Hahn, J., 305
Hailman, J. P., 153
Hake, D. F., 245–247, 249–250, 261, 487
Halas, E., 414
Hall, R. V., 190
Halliday, R., 431
Hamilton, B. E., 131, 135
Hamilton, L. W., 51
Hamilton, T., 401–402
Hankins, W., 340
Hanson, H. M., 123, 135
Harden, C., 397
Harlow, H. F., 88
Harris, F. R., 193
Harrison, R. H., 135, 150–153
Harsh, J., 203–205
Hart, J., 189
Hartley, D., 10–11
Hartwick, R., 363
Harzem, P., 497
Haynes, S., 418
Hearst, E., 95, 120, 129, 142
Hegner, R., 404, 412, 425, 447, 465
Heiber, L., 338
Heinemann, E. G., 137, 148, 150, 152
Heinroth, O., 310
Hemmes, N. S., 128, 130, 135
Henderson, T., 430
Hendry, D. P., 260–261
Hendry, L. S., 260–261
Hening, W. A., 59, 440
Herring, B., 489
Herrnstein, R. J., 37, 108, 165, 179–180,
    196, 208, 212, 215, 217, 220–221,
    223–227, 229–230, 234, 250, 253, 269,
    271, 278–279, 286
Herz, M., 45, 429
Hess, E., 363–364, 368–369, 371, 373,
    376
Heyman, G. M., 227
Hilgard, E., 15, 17, 23, 29, 37
Hills, M., 479
Hinde, R. A., 494
Hineline, P. N., 259–260, 268–269, 271,
    277–280, 282, 286

Hodos, W., 390, 446
Hoffman, H. S., 264, 367
Hollis, J., 455
Holloway, S. M., 487
Holt, L., 336
Holz, W. C., 245, 246–248, 252, 261, 275
Homme, L. E., 111
Honig, W. K., 135–136, 141, 143, 146–147, 165–166, 201
Honzik, C., 32
Hooker, B., 384
Hooker, T., 384
Horowitz, S., 414–415
Horridge, G. A., 404
Hoy, R., 302–303, 305
Hoyle, G., 326
Hughes, L. H., 202
Hull, C. L., 19, 24–28, 100, 107, 136, 140, 144–146, 148–149, 152, 154, 155, 168, 196
Hull, L. D., 268, 279
Hullett, J., 413
Humphreys, L. G., 100
Hunter, N. B., 95
Hursh, S. R., 95, 180
Hurwitz, H. M. B., 263
Hutchinson, R. R., 284, 287, 487
Hutton, L., 256

Immelman, K., 371, 383
Irwin, R. J., 226
Iwens, J., 347

Jackson, R. L., 291
Jacobson, A., 395–396, 414–415, 433
James, R., 415
James, W., 61
Jenkins, H. M., 93, 135, 150–151, 153, 158–159, 201, 202, 291, 496
Jenkins, W. O., 180–181
Jennings, H. S., 38, 40, 388, 391–394, 396, 404
Jennings, L., 418
Jensen, D., 395
Johnson, D. F., 156, 158
Johnson, D. L., 469–470
Johnston, M. S., 193
Jones, F., 463
Jwaideh, A. R., 202–203

Kalat, J., 338
Kalcenik, A., 491
Kalish, H. I., 120, 145, 150, 152
Kamin, L. J., 158, 273–274, 283
Kandel, E. R., 59, 435–437, 439–440
Karpman, M., 114
Katz, H. N., 202
Katz, M., 395
Kaufman, L. W., 492
Kavanau, J. L., 482
Kay, E., 288
Kazdin, A. E., 186–188, 192, 193
Keehn, J. D., 263, 256
Keeton, W. T., 357–362
Keith-Lucas, T., 66–68
Kelleher, R. T., 182, 184–187, 283
Keller, D., 263
Keller, F. S., 194

Keller, K., 131, 194
Kelly, D. D., 250–252
Kelly, S., 413, 420
Kendall, S. B., 128, 189, 201–202
Kerkut, G., 460
Killeen, P., 180, 226, 234, 255
Kimble, D. P., 53
Kimble, G. A., 72
Kimmel, E., 70
Kimmel, H. D., 70
King, A., 383
King, H., 69
Kintz, B. L., 285
Kirk, W., 431
Kivy, P., 179
Kjos, G. L., 482, 483
Klein, M., 120
Klein, R. M., 179
Kleist, S., 432
Klopfer, P., 41
Kodera, T., 129
Koegel, R., 105
Koelling, R., 344
Koltermann, R., 4, 468
Konorski, J., 73
Kozak, M. J., 288
Kral, P., 346
Krapfl, J. E., 106
Krasne, F., 454
Krasner, L., 189
Krawiec, T. S., 335
Krebs, J. R., 351, 353–356, 490–491, 493
Krieckhaus, E. F., 265
Kroodsma, D., 384
Kuenzer, P., 50
Kuo, Z.-Y., 299–300, 312
Kushner, M., 257

Lachman, R., 179
Lahue, R., 387, 454
Lambert, J. V., 280
Lamoreaux, R. R., 263
Lancy, D., 317
Lander, D. G., 226
Landis, C., 69
Lashley, K. S., 144–149, 152–155, 164
Lawrence, C. E., 201–202
Lawrence, D. H., 141, 164
Lea, S. E. G., 222
Leaf, R. C., 268
Leander, J. D., 187
Lee, A., 152
Lee, R., 418, 445–446
Lehrman, D., 331–334
Leon, M., 363
Levis, D. J., 106
Lewis, P., 204, 256
Lickey, M., 442–443
Lieberman, D. A., 201
Lieberman, R., 192
Limpo, A. J., 127, 161
Lindauer, M., 4
Lipson, J., 272
Litner, J. S., 205, 281, 282
Little, L., 127
Locke, J., 9
Locurto, C., 95
Löeb, J., 38

Logan, C., 410, 411
Logan, F. A., 153, 215
LoLordo, V. M., 250
London, P., 107
Long, J. S., 105
Lord, J., 127
Lorenz, K., 301, 310, 316, 321, 322–323,
    334, 343, 363–365
Lovaas, O. I., 92, 103–105, 166
Loveland, D. H., 165, 215, 225
Lowe, F. C., 497
Lowry, R., 25
Luco, J., 460
Lyons, J. E., 142

MacEwen, D., 234
Mackintosh, N., 62, 72, 127, 128, 129, 137,
    149, 153–156, 285
Macphail, E. M., 264
Mahoney, W., 68
Maier, F., 205
Maier, N., 38, 425
Maier, S., 287, 288, 289, 291
Malagodi, E. F., 187
Maldonado, H., 47
Malone, J. C., 126
Mandell, C., 186
Manning, A., 315
Marks, I. M., 258
Marler, P., 376, 378–380, 382, 384–385,
    475
Marlett, N., 189
Marsh, G., 141
Martin, P. L., 190, 193
Mashur, T., 468–469
Mason, D. J., 179
Maynard, R., 408
Mayr, E., 306, 476
McConnell, J., 395, 396, 413, 416, 418, 433
McDougall, W., 298
McGowen, B., 351
McKearney, J. W., 283
McKee, J. M., 186
McLean, J., 234
McMillan, J. C., 250
McSweeney, F. K., 222, 225
Meacham, J., 234
Medeiros, D. S., 106
Mees, H., 257
Melching, W. H., 173–174
Meltzer, D., 249
Menzel, R., 4, 468–469
Messenger, J., 448, 450–452
Meyer, D. R., 265
Michael, J., 101
Michaelis, M., 186, 190
Milan, M. A., 186
Miles, C. G., 158
Miller, H. R., 106
Miller, K., 428, 429
Miller, N. E., 78, 253, 265
Misanin, J. R., 285
Mohr, J. P., 101
Moltz, H., 363
Moore, B. R., 497
Moore, J., 130, 196, 235
Morowitz, H., 400
Morse, W. H., 250, 283

Mowrer, O. H., 253, 263, 271, 284
Mpitsos, G., 443–444
Mulvaney, D. E., 202–203
Myers, D. L., 222
Myers, L. E., 222

Nathan, P. E., 258
Navarick, D. J., 95, 211, 212, 235, 239,
    240, 241, 253
Nawas, M. M., 106, 107
Nelson, M. A., 431
Nelson, M. C., 456–458
Neuringer, A. J., 111, 178, 255
Nevin, J. A., 126, 127, 141, 146–147,
    166, 186, 195–196, 226–227
Newsom, C. O., 167
Newton, I., 11, 24
Newton, J., 72
Nissen, H., 169
Norborg, J., 111, 112, 184
Norris, E. B., 71
Nottebohm, F., 377, 385

O'Brien, F., 128
Olds, J., 89
O'Leary, K. D., 186, 190
Oliver, G., 460
Orloff, E. R., 283
Osborne, J. G., 128
Osborne, S., 111, 112, 113
Overmier, J. B., 287, 288

Papi, F., 363
Patton, R. M., 156
Paul, R., 305
Pavlov, I. P., 18, 60–62, 158, 159
Pear, J. J., 128
Pearl, J., 263
Peeke, H., 43–45, 49, 429
Peeke, S. C., 45, 49
Pennypacker, H. S., 135, 136
Perdeck, A., 319
Peretz, B., 400–402
Perkins, C. C., 131, 165, 204
Perloff, B. F., 92
Peterson, C., 214
Peterson, G. B., 95
Peterson, N. J., 145–147, 246
Peterson, R. F., 92, 193
Pfaffman, C., 335
Pierrel, R., 120, 135
Pinsker, H., 59, 439–440
Pliskoff, S. S., 210–211, 218, 220–222
Plumlee, L., 251–252
Pomerleau, O. F., 282
Premack, D., 109–111, 113, 131, 226, 483
Price, T., 153
Pritchatt, D., 460
Prokasy, W. F., 62, 195
Pucel, J. C., 107
Purtle, R. B., 135

Rachlin, H., 113, 115, 134–135, 197,
    204–205, 218, 222, 225, 240–241,
    253–255, 260, 345
Rachman, S., 106–107
Raines, J., 106
Rands, B. A., 285

Rapaport, P. M., 291
Ratner, A., 367
Ratner, S., 413, 426–429, 431, 433
Ray, A. A., 107, 432
Ray, R. S., 53
Rayner, R., 249
Razran, G., 41, 53, 137
Redford, N. E., 131
Reinhold, D. B., 165
Renner, K. E., 284–285
Rescorla, R. A., 67, 74–76, 78–80, 124, 159, 197, 205, 253, 280–281, 286
Ressler, R., 432
Revusky, S. H., 163, 245
Reynierse, J., 429, 431
Reynolds, G. S., 89, 94, 97, 121, 124–125, 127–128, 130, 142, 155–157, 161, 170, 196, 226
Riccio, D., 413, 416, 418
Richter, C., 336
Richter, M., 288
Rick, J., 460
Rickert, E. J., 111
Riesen, A. H., 145–147
Riess, D., 264
Riley, A. C., 250
Riley, D. A., 140–141
Rilling, M., 120, 129
Rimm, D. C., 106
Ring, K., 141
Risley, T., 257
Robinson, J. S., 166
Roemer, R. A., 55
Romanes, G., 12
Rose, J. E., 172, 186, 197, 283, 285
Rosellini, R. A., 288
Rosen, A. P., 142
Rosenberg, L., 347
Rosenkoetter, J., 432
Ross, D., 404, 407–408
Rothenbuhler, W., 308–309
Rothstein, B., 126
Roussel, J., 175
Rowell, C., 325
Rozin, P., 336–338, 353
Ruch, F. L., 192
Rudolph, R. L., 141, 146–148, 150, 152–153
Rudy, J., 347
Rushforth, N., 404, 408–410
Russell, E. M., 45

Sainsbury, R., 159, 160
Salinger, W., 368
Salkind, M. R., 106
Saltzman, I. J., 175
Salzen, 364, 365
Sandell, J., 347
Sanders, G., 447, 448, 450–451, 452
Saudargas, R. A., 190
Savage, J., 306
Schaefer, H. H., 190, 193
Schaeffer, B., 92
Schaub, R. E., 201
Schleidt, W., 319
Schneider, B. A., 96
Schneider, J. W., 214
Schneirla, T. C., 38, 425, 458–459

Schoenfeld, W. N., 194
Schubot, E. D., 106
Schuster, R., 254, 255, 453
Schutz, F., 366
Schwartz, B., 108, 109, 131, 133, 134, 498
Schwartz, M., 368
Scobie, S. S., 285, 287
Sears, G. W., 275
Segal, E. F., 487
Seligman, M. E. P., 205, 287, 288, 289, 290, 291, 346, 494, 495
Setzer, J., 138–139
Sharp, D., 265, 271
Shelby, M., 112
Sherman, J. A., 92
Sherman, J. G., 135
Sherrington, C. S., 40
Sherry, D., 338
Shettleworth, S. J., 126–127, 484, 487–489, 490
Shimp, C. P., 226–227
Shull, R. L., 96, 218, 221, 222
Sidman, M., 262, 267–269, 271, 275–277
Silberberg, A., 95, 131, 134, 135, 220–222
Silverstone, J. T., 106
Simmelhag, V. L., 484–486
Simmons, J. Q., 103–105, 167
Skeen, L., 417
Skinner, B. F., 19, 33–37, 39, 90, 99–100, 107, 168, 173, 175, 246, 249, 253–254, 257, 291, 469, 497
Skucy, J. C., 286
Small, S. S., 85, 90
Smith, G. D., 280
Smith, J. N. M., 491
Smith, K., 253
Smith, N. F., 285
Smith, R. F., 204
Solomon, R. L., 205, 253, 263, 280, 283, 287
Spealman, R. D., 226
Spence, K. W., 139–141, 144–146, 148–149, 152, 154–155
Spencer, W. A., 50, 427, 438
Squires, N., 184, 185, 187, 197, 214, 233
Staddon, J. E. R., 113, 115, 126, 226, 484–488
Stampfl, T. G., 106
Stanley, J. C., 479
Stebbins, G., 306
Stebbins, W. C., 155
Steffy, R. A., 189
Stein, D., 426, 429
Steinhauer, G. D., 152
Steinhorst, R., 111
Stevenson-Hinde, J., 494
Stiers, M., 95
Stokes, L. W., 273
Storms, L. H., 246
Stretch, R., 283
Strong, P., 430
Stubbs, D. A., 184
Sue, D., 106
Sund, P., 406
Sutterer, J. R., 128
Sweatman, H. P. A., 491
Szlep, R., 54

Taub, E., 280
Tauc, L., 435
Taylor, P., 491
Taylor, R., 463–465
Teitelbaum, P., 346
Terrace, H. S., 61, 95, 109, 126–127, 136, 141–143, 146–148, 161–163, 226
Testa, T. J., 287
Teyler, T. J., 55
Thomas, D. R., 137–139, 177
Thomas, J., 141
Thompson, J., 401–402
Thompson, R. L., 50, 55, 278, 427, 431, 438
Thompson, T., 275, 276
Thorndike, E. L., 13–18, 87, 291, 496
Thorpe, W., 325, 384, 463
Timberlake, W., 111, 114
Tinbergen, L., 351, 354
Tinbergen, N., 310, 313–314, 316, 319, 321, 330, 461, 462
Tinsley, J. B., 284–285
Tolman, E. C., 18–19, 28–33, 107, 291, 496
Torney, D., 189
Tracy, W. K., 147
Trattner, J., 114
Turner, J. R. G., 349

Ulrich, R. E., 275
Urcuioli, P. J., 166

Valentine, J., 306
Valins, S., 107
Van Houten, R., 153
Van Oye, P., 417
Vattano, F., 413
Veno, A., 43–44
Viemeister, N. F., 204
Voeks, V., 21–22, 24
Von Burg, R., 394, 396–397
von Frisch, K., 465–466, 469

Waddell, T. R., 187
Wade, M., 144–149, 152–154
Wagner, A. R., 76, 78–80, 124, 153, 159
Wahlsten, D., 271
Waite, W. W., 128
Walcott, C., 359
Walker, R., 460
Wallace, J., 285, 287
Wallace, R. F., 111–112, 182, 235, 237
Walsh, M., 266
Walters, G. C., 489
Warren, J. A., 264

Waser, M., 382
Wasserman, E. A., 95
Watson, J. B., 19, 249
Webbe, F. M., 187
Webber, M. I., 490
Weigele, S., 317
Weiner, H., 245
Weisman, R. G., 136, 141, 205, 275, 281–282
Weiss, J. M., 287–291
Wells, J., 450
Wells, M., 449–451
Wells, P., 417–418, 458, 469–470
Welsch, W. V., 106
Wenner, A., 469–470
Wesemann, A. F., 265
West, M., 383
Westbrook, R. F., 128
Westerman, R., 420
Whalen, R., 301
Whipple, W., 133–134
Whitworth, T. L., 222
Wilcoxon, H., 346
Wilkerson, P., 368
Wilkie, D. M., 127–128
William of Ockham, 21
Williams, B. A., 126, 158, 227, 234
Williams, D. R., 94, 131
Williams, H., 94
Williams, J. M., 51
Willows, A. O. D., 326, 329, 423, 441, 443
Wilson, E. O., 455, 459, 465, 498–499
Wiltschko, R., 361–362
Wiltschko, W., 361–362
Winograd, E., 260
Wolf, M. M., 190, 257
Wolfe, J. B., 169, 186
Wolpe, J., 105
Wolpin, M., 106
Wood, D., 298–401
Wrobel, P., 186, 190
Wundt, W., 12
Wyckoff, L. B., 194, 195, 196, 198, 199, 200, 201
Wyers, E., 429
Wynne, L. C., 283

Yerkes, R., 430
Young, J., 447, 448, 449, 452
Young, P. T., 335
Younger, M. S., 273

Zeiler, M., 99
Zimbardo, P. G., 192
Zimmerman, P., 265
Ziriax, J. M., 134

Index of Topics

Absolute generalization gradient, 120
Absolute rate of responding, 209
Acquired distinctiveness of cues, 164
Acquisition, 91–92
Action-specific energy, 322
Additivity theory of contrast, 131–135
Adjunctive behavior, 487
Aggression, 487
Alarm calls, development of, 330–331
Alpha response, 71
Amount of primary reinforcement: *See*
   Magnitude of primary
   reinforcement
Annelids:
   classical conditioning in, 428–429
   habituation in, 424–428
   instrumental conditioning in, 430–433
Anthopleura elegantissima:
   dishabituation in, 411
   habituation in, 410–412
   retention in, 411
Ants, instrumental learning in, 458–460
Anxiety, 150–107, 249–251
Apis cerana, 4
Apis mellifera:
   dance langauge of, 466–468
   discrimination training in, 468–469
   foraging of, 3, 465–468
   generalization in, 459
   hygienic behavior, genetic analysis of,
      308–310
   olfactory discrimination of, 5,
      469–470
   species-specificity of learning in, 5
   temporal learning in, 467–468

Aplysia californica:
   defensive withdrawal reflex of, 436
   neural analysis of habituation in,
      438–440
   operant conditioning in, 445–446
   retention of habituation in, 439
   sensitization in, 59–60, 440–441
Aplysia vaccaria, classical conditioning in,
      442–443
Apparatus, in operant conditioning, 85–91
Apparatus-fear hypothesis, 271–273
Arthropods:
   learning abilities of, 454
   species diversity in, 453–454
Association:
   by contiguity, 20
   as defined by Hartley, 10
   philosophy of, 9
   principle of (Guthrie), 21
Associative shifting, 17
Associative strength, in classical
   conditioning, 77–80
Asymmetrical intensity gradients,
   136–138
Attention, 101–105, 149–150, 155–165
   acquired distinctiveness of cues in, 164
   blocking, 157–159
   conditioned attentiveness, 164–165
   conditioned stimulus control in, 161
   feature-value effect in, 159–161, 164
   overshadowing, 157–159, 163–164
   Rescorla–Wagner model, 159
   stimulus salience in, 157–159
   transferring stimulus control in, 161–163
Autistic children, 103, 257

Automimicry, 349
Autonomic responses, 69
Autoshaping, 93–96, 108–109, 131, 185, 250, 497
Aversion therapy, 103, 257–258
Aversive control, 242–291
    aversion therapy in, 257–258
    avoidance in, 262–283
    conditioned suppression in, 249–251
    escape in, 259–261
    learned helplessness in, 287–291
    negative reinforcement, overview of, 258–259
    punishment, empirical overview of, 243–251
    punishment, theory of, 251–256
    self-punitive behavior in, 283–287
    See also Avoidance; Escape
Aversive stimulus: *See* Punisher
Avoidance, 83, 259, 262–287, 496
    discrete-trial, 262–287
    extinction of, and self-punitive behavior, 283–287
    free-operant, 267–270
    Pavlovian processes in, 280–283
    reinforcer in, 270–277
    shock-frequency reduction theory of, 277–280
    two-factor theory of, 271–277

Backward conditioning, 65–68
Batesian mimicry, 349, 350
Behavioral contrast, 122–124, 141–143, 217, 226
Behavioral genetics, 308–310, 475–476
Behavioral tendency, 26
Behavior chains, 92–93, 168–173
Behaviorism, 19
Behavior modification: *See* Behavior therapy
Behavior therapy, 101–107, 186–193, 257–258
Belongingness, 17
Beta response, 71–72
Betta splendens, 45
    releaser of aggressive display in, 317
Between-subjects procedure, 177–179
Birdsong learning:
    in brood parasites, 382–383
    constraints on, 381–383
    critical periods in, 380
    crystallization in, 382
    and deafening, 380–381
    and dialects, 378
    as a general process, 382
    ontogeny of, 377–378
    theories of, 384–385
Bivalve mollusc, 433
Blocking, 157–159, 163–164
Blowfly, classical conditioning in, 456–458

Central excitatory state (CES), 457
Cephalopod molluscs:
    complex learning in, 451–452
    discrimination and generalization in, 448–450

and simple learning paradigms, 446–448
Chaffinch:
    courtship patterns in, 316
    displacement preening in, 325
    habituation in, 50
Chain schedules, 98–99, 109, 175–177, 182–186, 228–237
Changeover delay (COD), 218–221
Choice (behavior), 108, 154–155, 208–241, 482, 490–491, 493
    and electric shocks, 254–255
    methods for studying, 209–212
    molecular characteristics of, 234–237
    quantitative law of effect in, 221–227
    and rate of reinforcement, 217–218
    and reinforcer magnitude, 214–216
    for schedules of reinforcement, 227–234
    self-control in, 237–241
    superstition and the changeover delay in, 218–221
    as a technique, 212–214
Classical conditioning, 94–95, 108
    adaptive value of, 60
    in annelids, 428
    in arthropods, 454
    of autonomic responses, 68–69
    in autoshaping and negative automaintenance, 94–95
    in coelenterates, 405–408
    and compound stimuli, 76–79
    contingency vs. contiguity in, 74–76
    control procedures in, 74–75
    correlational view of, 75–76
    in gastropod molluscs, 442–445
    in insects, 456–458
    and instrumental conditioning, 19, 69
    parallels of, in avoidance, 278
    in planaria, 413–416
    in protozoa, 396
    reinforcement in, 63
    Rescorla–Wagner model of, 78–80
    response independence of, 64
    role of, in avoidance, 278, 280–283
    of skeletal responses, 69–70
    stimulus-stimulus contiguity in, 61
    as stimulus substitution, 71
Clever Hans, 165
Clockshifting:
    effects on magnetic compass, 359–360
    effects on sun compass, 358
Cockroach:
    avoidance learning in, 460–461
    neural analyses of learning in, 460–461
Coelenterates:
    associative conditioning in, 405–408
    habituation in, 408–412
Cognitive map, 29
Commitment (and self-control), 239–241
Competing-response theory of punishment (and of conditioned suppression), 250–256
Concurrent-chains schedule, 227–237, 254–255, 258, 492–494
Concurrent-interval and concurrent-ratio schedules, differing characteristics of, 215–216
Concurrent schedules, 98

Conditional response (CR):
  complexes of, 72–73
  definition of, 63
  preparatory vs. consummatory, 73
  vs. unconditional response, 71
Conditional stimulus (CS), 62, 76
  compound, 457
Conditional stimulus control, 161
Conditioned attentiveness, 164–165
Conditioned elation, 250
Conditioned emotional reactions,
    249–251
Conditioned inhibitor, 281
Conditioned reinforcement, 95, 108–109,
    168–207
  in avoidance, 222
  behavior chains in, 168–173
  chained schedules in, 182–186
  experimental technique in, 173–177
  observing responses in, 198–207
  strength of, 177–181
  theory of, 193–197
  token economy in, 186–193
Conditioned suppression, 249–251
Constraints, on learning, 494–498
Contingency, in classical conditioning, 74
Continuous avoidance: See Free-operant
    avoidance
Continuous reinforcement schedule
    (CRF), 96, 100
Contra-free-loading phenomenon,
    111–113
Cricket song:
  development of, 302–303
  female response to, 305
  as fixed action pattern, 302–305
  in hybrid species, 304–305
Critical period:
  in imprinting, 369
  in song learning, 380
Cue strength hypothesis of conditioned
    reinforcement, 194–196
Cuttlefish, retention of habituation in,
    450–451

D-amphetamine, effects of, on avoidance,
    265
Dance language controversy, 469–470
Delay, of reinforcement, 90, 215, 237
  in octopus, 451
Delayed conditioning, 65
Delay-reduction hypothesis, 197, 232–237,
    241, 494
Deprivation, 245–246
Derived reinforcers: See Conditioned
    reinforcement
Detour problem, in octopus, 451–452
Developmental flexibility, 475–476
Differential reinforcement, 92, 122–124
  of high rates schedule (DRH), 98–99,
    130–131, 281–282
  of low rates schedule (DRL), 98,
    281–282
Digger wasp:
  inspection visit in, 462
  learning to locate nest in, 461–462
  nest provisioning in, 461–462
  orientation flight in, 461

Discrete-trials avoidance, 262–267
Discrete-trials procedure 209
Discriminated avoidance: See
    Discrete-trials avoidance
Discrimination, 119
Discrimination hypothesis (of
    self-punitive behavior), 284–287
Discriminative conditioning, 74–75,
    448–449
Discriminative stimuli, 82, 169–172,
    193–195, 248–249, 280
  in avoidance conditioning, 270–283
Discriminative stimulus hypothesis of
    conditioned reinforcement, 194–201
Dishabituation:
  in coelenterates, 411
  definition of, 51–52
  in gastropod molluscs, 442
  in protozoa, 401
Displacement activity:
  and conflict, 324
  displacement fanning in, 323
  independence of external stimulus in,
    325
  in stickleback, 323
Drive reduction, 27
Dual-process theory, 54–56
Duetting, 384
Duration, 84
  of primary reinforcement: See
    Magnitude of primary
    reinforcement

Earthworm: See Lumbricus terrestris
Elicited responding, 81, 128, 131–135, 250
  in escape procedures, 260–261
Eliciting stimuli, 165
Emitted responding, 81
Empiricism, philosophy of, 9–10
Entrainment, 66
Epistemology, 9
Errorless discrimination learning,
    148–149
Escape, 83, 259–261
Ethogram, 311
Ethology:
  and the analysis of function in behavior,
    311
  classical theory of, 314–320
  definition of, 310
  techniques of, 311–313
Evolution:
  and genetic change, 306–307
  and natural selection, 306
  and variability, 307
Expectancy, 29
Experimental method and field research,
    476–494
  laboratory analogues to natural
    phenomena, 481–494
  overview of problem, 476–481
External validity, 478–481, 484, 488,
    494–495
Extinction, 99–101
  of avoidance, 283–287
  in classical conditioning, 64
  for Guthrie, 23
  for Hull, 28

Extinction technique:
  for assessing conditioned
    reinforcement, 173–175
  of generalization testing, 120–121
Eyeblink conditioning, 69, 71–72
Eyespots, as sign stimuli, 315

Fading technique, 92, 161
Fear, 249–251, 270–277, 280
Fear conditioning, 197, 205
Feature-value effect, 159–161, 164
Fetish, definition and treatment of, by
    aversion therapy, 257–258
Filial imprinting, 364–366
Field research and experimental method,
    476–494
  laboratory analogues to natural
    phenomena, 481–494
  overview of problem, 476–481
Findley procedure, 210–211
Fixed action pattern:
  characteristics of, 319
  interaction of, with taxes, 320
  in slugs' escape response, 327–328
  in snail courtship, 297
  in spiders' cocoon spinning, 319–320
Fixed-interval scallop, 96–97, 176–177,
    484, 495
Fixed-interval schedule (FI), 96–97
Foraging, 490–494
  and learning, 351–356
  and prey density, 351–353
Free-operant avoidance, 267–270
Free-operant choice procedures,
    defined, 210
Free will, 238
Frustration, 280
  effects of, 175
Functionalist movement, 12

Galvanic skin response, 70
Gasterosteus aculeatus:
  courtship dance in, 323
  displacement digging in, 323
  displacement fanning in, 324
  habituation in, 45
  territorial aggression in, 313
Gastropod molluscs:
  classical conditioning in, 442–444
  habituation in, 438–442
  operant conditioning in, 445–446
Generalist feeder, 352
Generalization, 119
  of habituation, 47–48, 441
  in insects, 458–459
  in octopus, 449–450
Generalization gradients, 119–124
  absolute, 120–121
  behavioral contrast, 122–135
  extinction technique, 120–121
  intensity, 136–138
  interactions of stimulus control,
    141–143
  maintained, 120
  measures of generalization, 121
  not-responding, 135–143
  peak shift, 122–124
  postdiscrimination, 122–124

relative, 121
  transposition, 138–141
Generalized reinforcers, 187
Gradients of not-responding, 135–143,
    148–149
Grain beetle, habituation in, 455

Habit, 24, 27
Habit strength, 27, 137
Habituation:
  adaptive value of, 41
  in annelids, 424–428
  in Aplysia, 438–440
  in arthropods, 454
  in cephalopod molluscs, 447
  in coelenterates, 408–412
  definition of, 42
  in gastropod molluscs, 438–442
  interactions of, with sensitization,
    56–59
  in planaria, 419–421
  in protozoa, 396–399
  rate of, 43–45
  and response topography, 427–428
  retention of, 50, 57
  vs. sensory adaptation and fatigue, 42
  in single neuron, 439–440
  stimulus-specificity of, 42–43
Hampton Court garden maze, 85, 90
Helix pomatia, courtship in, 295–296
Hermaphrodite, 295
Heterosynaptic facilitation, 435
Heterozygosity, 309
Homing:
  map and compass hypothesis of,
    357–358
  and olfaction, 363
  in pigeons, 357–363
Homozygosity, 309
Honeybee: See Apis mellifera
Hope, 280
Host selection, in insects, 463–465
Hull–Spence theory of discrimination
    learning, 144–155
Humphreys' paradox, 100
Hydra pirardi:
  habituation in, 408–409
  retention in, 409–410
Hydraulic model, 321–322
Hypothetico-deductive method, 24

Imitation, 92–93
Implosive therapy, 106
Imprinting:
  auditory, 371–376
  characteristics of, 365–369
  critical periods in, 367–369
  definition of, 364
  irreversibility of, 367
  in mallard ducks, 366–367
  olfactory, 371
  prenatal, 372–376
  and species recognition, 369–371
Incentive, 27
Incidental stimuli, 152
Information hypothesis of conditioned
    reinforcement, 197–207
Innate behavior, 301–302

Innate releasing mechanism, 322, 328–329
Insect learning:
    field research on, 461
    laboratory research on, 455–460
Instinct:
    anti-instinct revolt, 299
    history of, 297–298
    rat-killing, in cats, 299–300
Instrumental conditioning, 81
    in earthworms, 430–432
    In insects, 458–461
    in planaria, 416–418
Intensity generalization gradients, 136–138
Interdimensional discrimination training, 146, 150–152
Interim activities, 484
Internal validity, 478–479
Interreinforcement interval:
    and choice, 234–237
    and strength of conditioned reinforcement, 180–181
Interresponse time (IRT), 226–227
Interstimulus interval, in habituation, 45–46
Intracranial stimulation, 250
Intradimensional discrimination training, 146, 150–152
Isolation study, 146, 299, 312–313

Joy experiment, 250

Labotatory analogues to natural phenomena, 481–494
    in foraging, 490–494
    in multiple response environments, 482–490
Lashley jumping stand, 85, 86
Lashley–Wade theory of discrimination learning, 144–155
Latency, 84
Latent learning, 31
Law of effect:
    for Herrnstein, 221–227
    for Skinner, 35
    for Thorndike, 15–16
    truncated, 16
Law of exercise, 10
Law of readiness, 16
Learned helplessness, 267, 287–291
Learning:
    as a product of evolution, 341
    situation-specificity of, 342
Leech (Macrobdilla decora):
    classical conditioning in, 430
    habituation in, 426–428
Limax maximus, avoidance conditioning in, 444
Love dart, 295
Lumbricus terrestris:
    alarm pheromone in, 432
    avoidance learning in, 432–433
    classical conditioning in, 428–429
    habituation in, 426–427
    instrumental conditioning in, 431–432
    recovery of habituation in, 50

Magnetic compass, 359–360

Magnitude of primary reinforcement, 212–216
    and strength of conditioned reinforcement, 177–178
Maintained generalization procedure, 120
Manipulative research, 478–479
Map and compass hypothesis, 358
Matching, 482, 490–491
Matching relation (of choice and rate of reinforcement), 217–234
Measurement of operant behavior, 84–91
Mechanism, philosophy of, 11
Migration, 357
Mixed schedule, 98–99, 198, 199
Modeling, 92–93
Models:
    in birdsong, 380–383
    in classical ethology, 313
Molluscan learning, 433–453
Momentary reinforcement probabilities, 226–227
Monarch butterfly, mimicry in, 347–349
Multiphasic retention, in cephalopod molluscs, 450–451
Multiple response environments, 482–490
Multiple schedule, 98–99, 198–199
Mutation, 307
Müllerian mimicry, 347–348

Naturalistic approach, 341–342
Natural selection:
    and adaptation, 307
    definition of, 306–307
    and learning, 341
    and reproductive success, 307
    and variability, 307
Nature–nurture question, 475–476
Negative automaintenance, 94–95, 185
Negative contingency, in classical conditioning, 74–75
Negative punisher, 83, 103
Negative punishment, 84
Negative reinforcement, 83, 103, 242–243, 258–291
    avoidance in, 262–283
    escape in, 259–261
    learned helplessness in, 287–291
    self-punitive behavior and extinction of avoidance in, 283–287
Negative reinforcer, 82–83, 242
Neophobia, 337
Nerve net, 403–404
New-response technique (for assessing conditioned reinforcement), 175, 177
Nonassociative learning, 40
Nonmanipulative research, 478–479
Number of pairings with primary reinforcement (and strength of conditioned reinforcement), 178–179

Observation-selective controls, 481
Observing responses, 198–207
Octopus vulgaris:
    complex learning in, 451–452
    discrimination learning in, 448–449
    generalization in, 449–450
    neural bases of learning in, 452–453
Omission procedure, 83–84

Ontogeny, 5–6, 39
Operant behavior, 34
Operant conditioning:
  in *Aplysia*, 445–446
  applications of, in behavior therapy,
    101–107
  basic concepts of, 82–84
  basic phenomena of, 91–101
  definition of, 35
  measurement of, 84–91
  nature of reinforcement in, 107–115
Optimal period, 369
Orb-weaving spider, 54
Orientation flight, 461
Overhabituation, 427
Overshadowing, 157–159, 162–164
Oviposition, 463
Oyster catcher, incubation by, of
  supernormal egg, 318

Paired brief stimuli (in second-order
  schedules), 183–186
Pairing hypothesis of conditioned
  reinforcement, 182–186, 196–197
Paramecia, associative conditioning in,
  395–396
Partial-reinforcement effect, 100
Patellar reflex, 69
Pavlovian conditioning, 81, 128,
  131–135, 489
  interactions of, with operant
    conditioning, 93–96, 253–256,
    280–283
Peak shift, 122–124, 135–143
Perceptual learning, 254, 365
Phobias, 105–107, 165
Phylogeny, 5–6, 39, 297
  of learning, 387–389
Place vs. response learning, 30
Planarian controversy, 420–422
Planarians:
  and cannibalism, 413
  classical conditioning in, 413–416
  differential conditioning in, 414–415
  habituation in, 419–421
  instrumental conditioning in, 416–418
  pseudoconditioning in, 414
  reactive inhibition in, 418–419
Plastic song, 377
Pleurobranchaea, aversive conditioning in,
  443–444
Polychaetes:
  classical conditioning in, 429–430
  habituation in, 424
Polydipsia, 487
Positive conditioned suppression,
  250–251
Positive reinforcement, 83
Positive reinforcer, 83
Postdiscrimination gradient, 122–124,
  140–141, 143–144, 149
Post-tetanic potentiation, 434
Potentiation of habituation, 51
Praying mantis, 48
Preference after recovery, 335–337
Premack principle, 109–111, 188, 483
Preparatory-response theory, 205
Primary (full) song, 377

Principle:
  of confirmation, 30
  of dynamic situations, 21
  of equipotentiality, 346, 495
  of postremity, 21
  of primary reinforcement, 27
  of response probability, 21
Probability, of responding, 84
Problem boxes, 15
Protozoans:
  adaptive value of learning in, 391–394
  associative conditioning in, 394–396
  avoidance conditioning in, 396
  habituation in, 396–399
  stimulus-specificity of, 399
Provisioning behavior, 461
Pseudoconditioning:
  definition of, 53
  in planaria, 414
  in polychaetes, 430
Psychological empiricism, doctrine of,
  9–10
Psychophysical movement, 12
Punisher, 83, 242
Punishment, 83, 103–104, 130–131,
  242–258, 279
  in aversion therapy, 257–258
  as conditioned suppression, 249–251
  current theory of, 251–256
  as discriminative stimulus, 248–249
  empirical overview of, 243–251
  maintenance of punished behavior in,
    243–246
  parameters of, 246–247
  self-punitive behavior in, 283–287
Purpose, 37–39

Quantitative law of effect, 221–227
Quasi-experimental design, 479

Rate:
  of reinforcement (and choice), 217–234
  of responding, 84
Ratner–Miller conditioning ring, 428
Reaction potential, 26, 137
Reactive inhibition, 28
Reciprocal inhibition, 106
Reflexive behavior, 81
Reinforcement, 82
  in classical conditioning, 63
  for Guthrie, 23
  for Hull, 26
  for Skinner, 35–36
Reinforcement interaction (in concurrent
  schedules), 218
Reinforcer, 35
Relational learning, 138–141
Relative generalization gradients, 121
Relative rate of responding, 209
Releaser, 314–315
Release site bias, 362
Relevance of behavior rule, 193
Rescorla–Wagner model, of classical
  conditioning, 78–80, 124, 159
Respondent behavior, 34
Respondent conditioning, 35
Response deprivation, 113–115

Response independence (in concurrent schedules), 218–221
Ring dove:
  hormonal stimulation of reproductive cycle in, 333–334
  reproductive cycle of, 331–333

Safety signals (as conditioned reinforcers), 204–207
Sameness–difference discrimination task, 165
Satiation, 245–246
Schedule of primary reinforcement (and strength of conditioned reinforcement), 179–180
Schedules of reinforcement, 36, 96, 128–129, 496
  choice for, 227–237
Search image formation, 354–356
Secondary reinforcement: See Conditioned reinforcement
Second-order schedules, 184–186, 198
Self-control, 237–241, 279–280
Self-destructive behavior, 103–105, 166–167
Self-punitive behavior, 247, 267, 283–287
Sensitive period, 367–369
Sensitization:
  adaptive value of, 54
  in Aplysia, 59–60, 440, 441
  definition of, 52–53
  interactions of, with habituation, 56–59
  retention of, 53, 57, 59
Sexual dimorphism, 366
Sexual imprinting, 365–367
Shaping, 91–92
Shock-frequency reduction theory, 271–280, 282–283
Siamese fighting fish: See Betta Splendens
Sidman avoidance: See Free-operant avoidance
Sign stimuli, 153, 314–315
Simultaneous conditioning, 65
Simultaneous discrimination, 122
Single-process theory, of punishment, 253
Skeletal responses, 69
Skinner box, 85, 87, 90, 209
Social releaser, 316–317
Sociobiology, 480
Specialist feeder, 352
Species-specific behavior, 128, 297, 301, 473
  development of, 329–330
Species-specific defense reaction, 226–267, 272, 490
Specific hungers:
  in humans, 334
  as master instinct, 334
  mechanism of, 335–336
  in rats, 335
  as specific aversion, 337
  for thiamin, 337–338
Spider:
  fixed action pattern in, 319–320
  habituation in, 54
  predatory retreat in, 454
Spirostomum ambiguum:
  dishabituation in, 401

habituation in, 400
retention in, 400
Spontaneous recovery, 100–101
  of habituation, 48
Spread of effect, 17–18
Stentor coeruleus:
  habituation in, 397–399
  retention in, 398, 400
Stickleback: See Gasterosteus aculeatus
Stimulus control, 119–167
Stimulus intensity dynamism, 27, 136
Stimulus salience, 157–159, 163–164
Stomphia coccinea, conditioning in, 405–408
Structuralism, 12
Subsong, 377
Successive approximations, 92
Successive discrimination, 122
Sun compass:
  evidence for, 358
  ontogeny of, 361–362
Supernormal stimulus, 318, 383
Superstitious behavior, 218–211
Suppression ratio, 249
Supraordinate stimulus, 161
Symmetrical law of effect, 152, 251–256
Systematic desensitization, 101, 105–107, 258

Tandem schedule, 98–99, 175–177, 182–186
Taste aversion, 267
Taste aversion learning:
  in blue jay, 349–350
  generalization in, 351
  interactions between stimulus and consequence in, 345
  in quail, 345
  in rats, 344–345
Temporal conditioning, 65
Terminal activities, 484
Territorial aggression, habituation of, 45
Three-term contingency, 82, 85
Time-out procedures, 103
Time-out rooms, 257
T-maze, 85–86, 209, 215
Token economy, 186–193
Trace conditioning, 65
Transferring stimulus control, 161–163
Transitivity of choice, 235
Transposition, 136, 138–141
Traumatic avoidance learning, 283
Tritonia diomedia:
  escape sequence as fixed action pattern in, 326
  habituation in, 441–442
  neural analysis of escape response in, 327–328
Tropisms, 38
Two-factor theory, of avoidance, 271–281

Uncertainty-reduction hypothesis, 197–207
Unconditional response (UCR), 62
Unconditional stimulus (UCS), 62

Vacuum activity, 323, 325
Validity: See External validity; Internal validity

Value hypothesis, of contrast, 130–135
Van Oye maze, 417–418
Variable-interval schedule (VI), 96–98
Variable-interval timer, 215–216
Variable-ratio programmer, 216
Variable-ratio schedule (VR), 96–98
Variable-time schedule (VT), 108–109, 127
Vibratiuncle, 12
Vicious-circle effect, 283–287

Waggle dance, 466
Weak two-factor theory, 280
White-crowned sparrow: *See Zonotrichia leucophrys*
Within-subjects procedure, 177–179, 192–193

Zonotrichia leucophrys, song learning in, 378–380